Database Programming with Visual Basic .NET, Second Edition

CARSTEN THOMSEN

Database Programming with Visual Basic .NET, Second Edition
Copyright ©2003 by Carsten Thomsen

ISBN (pbk): 1-59059-032-5

Printed and bound in the United States of America 12345678910

Trademarked names may appear in this book. Rather than use a trademark symbol with every occurrence of a trademarked name, we use the names only in an editorial fashion and to the benefit of the trademark owner, with no intention of infringement of the trademark.

Technical Reviewer: John Mueller

Editorial Directors: Dan Appleman, Gary Cornell, Jason Gilmore, Simon Hayes, Karen Watterson, John Zukowski

Managing and Production Editor: Grace Wong

Copy Editor: Ami Knox

Compositor: Susan Glinert Stevens

Illustrators: Allan Rasmussen; Cara Brunk, Blue Mud Productions

Indexer: Lynn Armstrong, Shane-Armstrong Information Systems

Cover Designer: Kurt Krames

Manufacturing Manager: Tom Debolski

Marketing Manager: Stephanie Rodriguez

Distributed to the book trade in the United States by Springer-Verlag New York, Inc., 175 Fifth Avenue, New York, NY, 10010 and outside the United States by Springer-Verlag GmbH & Co. KG, Tiergartenstr. 17, 69112 Heidelberg, Germany.

In the United States, phone 1-800-SPRINGER, email orders@springer-ny.com, or visit http://www.springer-ny.com.

Outside the United States, fax +49 6221 345229, email orders@springer.de, or visit http://www.springer.de.

For information on translations, please contact Apress directly at 2560 Ninth Street, Suite 219, Berkeley, CA 94710. Phone 510-549-5930, fax: 510-549-5939, email info@apress.com, or visit http://www.apress.com.

The source code for this book is available to readers at http://www.apress.com in the Downloads section. You will need to answer questions pertaining to this book in order to successfully download the code.

Contents at a Glance

Contents

Part Three   ADO.NET Disconnected

Appendix C Connected Layer Properties, Methods, and Events 793

Appendix D Disconnected Layer Properties, Methods, and Events 881

Index 919

About the Author

CARSTEN THOMSEN is a Microsoft MVP, a recognition he received in August 1999. He lives in his native Denmark and currently holds the MCSE and MCSD certifications. Carsten has been programming in Visual Basic for almost 10 years, and he specializes in data access.

However, with the advent of Visual Studio .NET, he has shifted his focus from Visual Basic "classic" to two new programming languages, Visual Basic .NET and C#. Carsten is the author of the first edition of this book and also *Database Programming with C#*, both from Apress, and has almost completed two more: *Enterprise Development with Visual Studio .NET, UML, and MSF,* and *Building Web Services with Visual Basic .NET.*

Carsten and his girlfriend, Mia, live in Esbjerg, Denmark. They have a 3-year old daughter, Caroline, and 4-month old daughter, Cecilie. Nicole, 8, is Carsten's oldest daughter, and she lives with her mother in Dublin, Ireland. Carsten enjoys traveling to Dublin several times a year to spend time with Nicole.

Carsten has recently founded .NET Services (http://www.dotnetservices.biz) with a colleague of his, Michael Thomhav. The company is based on the .NET knowledge acquired by the two over the last 3 years, and deals exclusively with .NET projects and solutions. .NET Services implements solutions modeled, managed, and documented with the Unified Modeling Language (UML), and the Microsoft Solutions Framework (MSF). If you're looking for a partner to help you out with your .NET development, or simply want someone else to manage and implement your .NET projects, do check out the .NET Services Web site.

About the Technical Reviewer

JOHN MUELLER is a freelance author and technical editor. He has writing in his blood, having produced 56 books and over 200 articles to date. The topics range from networking to artificial intelligence and from database management to heads-down programming. Some of his current books include several C# developer guides, a small business and home office networking guide, a book on SOAP, and several Windows XP user guides. His technical editing skills have helped over 31 authors refine the content of their manuscripts. John has provided technical editing services to both *Data Based Advisor* and *Coast Compute* magazines. He has also contributed articles to magazines such as *SQL Server Professional, Visual C++ Developer,* and *Visual Basic Developer.* He is currently the editor of the .NET electronic newsletter for Pinnacle Publishing.

When John isn't working at the computer, he's in his workshop. He's an avid woodworker and candle maker. On any given afternoon you can find him working at a lathe or putting the finishing touches on a bookcase. One of his newest craft projects is glycerin soap making, which comes in pretty handy for gift baskets. John is also setting up a Web site at http://www.mwt.net/~jmueller/, and he invites readers to take a look and make suggestions on how he can improve it. One of his current projects is creating book-specific FAQ sheets that should help you find the book information you need much faster. You can reach John on the Internet at JMueller@mwt.net.

Acknowledgments

THIS BOOK IS BASED ON *Database Programming with VB .NET (First Edition)*, and *Database Programming with C#*, and even if this is a second edition, it's really a new book—not only because it's twice a big, but also because of the depth of the ADO.NET coverage.

I have had some great help from John Mueller, the official technical reviewer on this book, and I certainly couldn't have produced the kind of quality this book represents without his help.

Nothing's so bad that it isn't good for something. This old saying came true for me on this book when I managed to get Phil Pledger, Idoneous Technologies, to do an informal and unofficial technical review of the book. Phil was one the critics of the first edition of this book, and his assistance has been crucial in helping me make this book a lot more than "just" a second edition. Phil can be reached at this address: `ppledger@idoneous.com`.

John and Philip have helped me reorganize and improve on the content of the first edition of the book, and I hope you like the result.

Now, I've been appraising the TRs (tech reviewers) on this book, but there's so much more to creating a technical book than "just" the writing and technical reviewing. Ami Knox was the copy editor on this book, and she really has been a tremendous help in finding those awkwardly phrased sentences that the rest of us missed. She takes on the role of a typical novice reader and finds the things that elude the rest of us. However, she's also extremely competent when it comes to finding inaccurate technical information and references, and all this, coupled with the work done by yours truly and the two fantastic TRs, makes this a very good database book.

Carsten Thomsen, `carstent@dotnetservices.biz`
Esbjerg, Denmark
September 2002

Introduction

THIS BOOK IS ALL ABOUT accessing databases of various kinds—not just SQL Server, but also Active Directory, Exchange Server 2000, and the Message Queuing database. My intention with this book is to give you an in-depth insight into how ADO.NET works and how you can use its classes. Having said that, my goal was to make the book as easy to read as possible, and although there are technical sections that will require you to really concentrate and experiment, I think I've managed to accomplish what I set out to do.

Who This Book Is For

This book is targeted at intermediate users, meaning users who already know a little about Visual Studio .NET and/or previous versions of Visual Basic. Basic knowledge of Object Oriented Programming (OOP), ADO, and database design is also assumed. Still, no two readers are the same. Beginning-level material appears where I feel it is appropriate to make sure you really understand what is being explained. The many listings and the tables in Appendixes C and D make this a good reference book, but I really wrote the book to be read sequentially from cover to cover. It will take you through all the data access aspects of Visual Studio .NET with example code in VB .NET. This includes how to create the various database items, such as databases, tables, constraints, database projects, stored procedures, views, triggers, and so on. For the most part, I show you how to do this from within the VS .NET IDE as well as programmatically where possible. You'll build on the same example code from the beginning of the book until you wrap it up in the very last chapter. The book's major example application, UserMan, is a complete (Windows application) user management system based on SQL Server, Active Directory, and Message Queuing.

How This Book Is Organized

This book is organized in thirteen parts:

> *Part One* is a general introduction to Visual Studio .NET and the .NET Framework, and it takes a look at databases in general, including how you design a relational database using the normal forms.

Part Two is a general introduction to ADO.NET, and an in-depth look at the various classes in the ADO.NET connected layer. You'll learn what a .NET Data Provider is, and you'll see how you can use the Connection, Transaction, Command, Parameter, DataReader, DataAdapter, and CommandBuilder classes, and more importantly, how they work together in a disconnected application scenario.

Part Three is an in-depth look at the disconnected layer of ADO.NET, including how to build your own disconnected database, how to work with data relations, and how the various classes of the ADO.NET disconnected layer work together to form a database structure. You'll also see how the disconnected layer uses the connected layer to retrieve and update data at the data source.

Part Four teaches you how to work with databases from within the Visual Studio .NET IDE. This includes how you create, edit, and delete databases, tables, views, triggers, stored procedures, and message queues.

Part Five is all about exception handling in general and more specifically how you use it with database applications. You also get to see how the **Debug** and **Trace** classes can be used to profile and trace your applications.

Part Six shows you how you set up and use server-side processing, such as stored procedures, views, and triggers, from your application. This part also has a general discussion of server-side processing and application optimization.

Part Seven is about hierarchical databases in general and how you can access Active Directory and Exchange Server 2000.

Part Eight teaches you all the basics of implementing and working with message queuing in your application. You also see how MSMQ 3.0 works with triggers and exposes message queuing over HTTP.

Part Nine is about how you can use XML with SQL Server 2000 and more specifically how you can use the SQLXML 3.0 plug-in to work with data from SQL Server 2000 in XML format. This includes how to expose data over HTTP.

Part Ten discusses and teaches you how to wrap your data access in classes, thereby ensuring safe access and data manipulation.

Part Eleven is about working with data-bound controls from Windows and Web applications.

Part Twelve is where you finish the UserMan example application.

Appendixes includes the four appendixes, which cover cursors and locking/concurrency, classic ADO and COM Interop, and reference tables for the many classes and enums in ADO.NET.

Technology Requirements

From the example code, you can connect to SQL Server using any of these three .NET Data Providers: SQL Server .NET Data Provider, OLE DB .NET Data Provider, or ODBC .NET Data Provider. The example code also includes how to connect to and manipulate data in MySQL 3.23.51 or later, Oracle 8i or later, Microsoft Access 2000 or later, IBM DB2 7.2 EE or later, and SQL Server. For connecting to SQL Server 2000, you can find coverage of the SQLXML 3.0 plug-in for manipulating SQL Server data using XML from managed code or using HTTP. Exchange Server 2000 connection and data manipulation is also covered.

Since I'm using some of the Enterprise functionality of Visual Studio .NET, you'll need either of the two Enterprise editions to follow all the exercises. However, the Professional edition will do for most of the example code, and it will certainly do if you just want to see how everything is done while you learn ADO.NET. This means that the only thing extra you get from the Enterprise editions in terms of database access is an additional set of database tools to be used from within the IDE.

Example Code

All the example code for this book can be found on the Apress Web site (http://www.apress.com) in the Downloads section, or on the UserMan Web site (http://www.userman.dk).

Data Source

The data source for the example code in this book is shown running on SQL Server 2000. However, the example code also includes examples on how to connect to and manipulate data in MySQL 3.23.51 or later, Oracle 8i or later, IBM DB2 7.2 EE or later, Microsoft Access 2000 or later, and SQL Server.

Feedback

I can be reached at carstent@dotnetservices.biz and I'll gladly answer any e-mail concerning this book.

I have set up a Web site for the UserMan example application, where you can post and retrieve ideas on how to take it further. The Web site address is http://www.userman.dk. Please check it out.

Part One

Getting Started with .NET and Databases

CHAPTER 1

A Lightning-Quick Introduction to Visual Basic .NET

THE .NET FRAMEWORK is an environment for building, deploying, and running services and other applications. This environment is all about code reuse and specialization, multilanguage development, deployment, administration, and security. The .NET Framework will lead to a new generation of software that melds computing and communication in a way that allows the developer to create truly distributed applications that integrate and collaborate with other complementary services. In other words, you now have the opportunity to create Web services, such as search engines and mortgage calculators, that will help transform the Internet as we know it today. No longer will it be about individual Web sites or connected devices; it's now a question of computers and devices, such as handheld computers, tablet PCs, wristwatches, and mobile phones, collaborating with each other and thus creating rich services. As an example, imagine calling a search engine to run a search and then displaying and manipulating the results of the search in your own application.

There have been rumors that the .NET Framework is solely for building Web sites, but this is not true. You can just as easily create conventional desktop Windows applications with the .NET Framework. The .NET Framework is actually more or less what would have been called COM+ 2.0 if Microsoft had not changed its naming conventions. Granted, the .NET Framework is now a far cry from COM+, but initially the development did start from the basis of COM+. I guess not naming it COM+ 2.0 was the right move after all.

This book is based on the assumption that you already know about the .NET Framework. However, this chapter provides a quick run-through of .NET concepts and terms. Although the terms are not specific to Visual Basic .NET (VB .NET), but rather are relevant to all .NET programming languages, you'll need to know them if you're serious about using VB .NET for all your enterprise programming. Enterprise programming is fundamentally about getting several pieces of application logic to work together, generally across a network, be it LAN or WAN. This means encapsulating business logic into reusable components to avoid duplication, simplify change control, make it auditable, and minimize the chance of business rules being contradicted.

Reviewing Programming Concepts

The .NET environment introduces some programming concepts that will be new even to those who are familiar with a previous version of a Windows programming language, such as Visual Basic or Visual C++. In fact, these concepts will be new to most Windows developers because the .NET programming tools, such as VB .NET, are geared toward enterprise development in the context of Web-centric applications. This does not mean the days of Windows platform–only development is gone, but .NET requires you to change the way you think about Windows programming. If you're already familiar with object-oriented enterprise development, things should be easier for you though. The good old Registry is "gone"—that is, it's no longer used for registering your type libraries in the form of ActiveX/COM servers. Components of .NET Framework are self-describing; all information about referenced components, and so on, are part of the component in the form of metadata.

Visual Studio .NET is based on the Microsoft .NET Framework, which obviously means that the VB .NET programming language is as well. VB .NET is part of the Visual Studio .NET package, and it's just one of the programming languages that Microsoft ships for the .NET platform.

At first, some of these new terms and concepts seem a bit daunting, but they really aren't that difficult. If you need to refresh your memory regarding .NET programming concepts and the .NET Framework, simply keep reading, because this chapter is indeed a very brief review of these basics.

A Quick Look at Components of the .NET Framework

The .NET Framework adheres to the common type system (CTS) for data exchange and the Common Language Specification (CLS) for language interoperability. In short, three main parts make up the .NET Framework:

- Active Server Pages.NET (ASP.NET)

- Common language runtime (CLR)

- .NET Framework class library (the base classes)

The .NET Framework consists of these additional components:

- Assemblies

- Namespaces

- Managed components

- Common type system (CTS)

- Microsoft intermediate language (MSIL)

- Just-In-Time (JIT) compiler

I discuss all of these components in the following sections.

Active Server Pages.NET

Active Server Pages.NET is an evolution of Active Server Pages (ASP) into so-called managed space, or rather managed code execution (see the "Common Language Runtime" and "Managed Data" sections later in this chapter). ASP.NET is a framework for building server-based Web applications. ASP.NET pages generally separate the presentation (HTML) from the logic/code. This means that the HTML is placed in a text file with an .aspx extension, and the code is placed in a text file with a .vb extension (when you implement your application logic/code in VB .NET, that is).

ASP.NET is largely syntax compatible with ASP, which allows you to port most of your existing ASP code to the .NET Framework and then upgrade the ASP files one by one. ASP.NET has different programming models that you can mix in any way. The programming models are as follows:

- *Web Forms* allow you to build Web pages using a forms-based UI. These forms are quite similar to the forms used in previous versions of Visual Basic. This also means that you have proper event and exception handling, unlike in ASP, where event and especially exception handling is difficult to implement.

- *XML Web services* are a clever way of exposing and accessing functionality on remote servers. XML Web services are based on the Simple Object Access Protocol (SOAP), which is a firewall-friendly protocol based on XML. SOAP uses the HTTP protocol to work across the Internet. XML Web services can also be invoked using the HTTP GET method simply by browsing to the Web service and the HTTP POST method.

- *Standard HTML* allows you to create your pages as standard HTML version 3.2 or 4.0.

Common Type System

The .NET environment is based on the common type system (CTS), which means that all .NET languages share the same data types.[1] This truly makes it easy to exchange data between different programming languages. It doesn't matter if you exchange data directly in your source code (for example, inheriting classes created in a different programming language) or use Web services or COM+ components. CTS is built into the common language runtime (CLR). Have you ever had a problem exchanging dates with other applications? If so, I'm sure you know how valuable it is to have the CTS to establish the correct format. You don't have to worry about the format being, say, DD-MM-YYYY; you simply need to pass a **DateTime** data type. This also removes the need to write casting functions or include coercion statements in most circumstances.

Common Language Specification

The Common Language Specification (CLS) is a set of conventions used for promoting language interoperability. This means that the various programming languages developed for the .NET platform must conform to the CLS in order to make sure that objects developed in different programming languages can actually talk to each other. This includes exposing only those features and data types that are CLS compliant. Internally, your objects, data types, and features can be different from the ones in the CLS, as long as the exported methods, procedures, and data types are CLS compliant. In other words, the CLS is really nothing more than a standard for language interoperability used in the .NET Framework.

Common Language Runtime

The common language runtime (CLR) is the runtime environment provided by the .NET Framework. The CLR's job is to manage code execution, hence the term *managed code.* The compilers for Visual Basic .NET and C# both produce managed code, whereas the Visual C++ compiler produces both managed and unmanaged code, even in the same project. By *unmanaged code,* I mean code for the Windows platform like that produced by the compilers for the previous versions of Visual C++. You can, however, use the managed code extensions for Visual C++ for creating managed code from within Visual C++.

---

1. Actually, this is only part of the truth, because some languages support data types that aren't part of CTS, such as unsigned integers. This is, however, one data type that VB .NET doesn't support.

Implications for JScript

Do the appearance of .NET and the CLR mean the end of JScript? Well, not quite. If you're referring to server-side development in the new compiled JScript language, I guess it's up to the developer. JScript as it is known today (that is, client-side code execution) will continue to exist, largely because of its all-browser adoption. But if the CLR is ported to enough platforms and supported by enough software vendors, it might well stand a good chance of competing with the Virtual Machine for executing Java applets. Microsoft now also has a programming language called J#, which comes with upgrade tools for Visual J++ 6.0. J# can be an excellent choice as a programming language for you, if you've crossed over from the Java camp.

VBScript, VBA, and VSA

Okay, what about VBScript and Visual Basic for Applications (VBA)? This is obviously another issue that relates to the introduction of VB .NET. A new version of VBA, Visual Studio for Applications (VSA), is available for customizing and extending the functionality of your Web-based applications. VSA is built with a language-neutral architecture, but the first version only comes with support for one programming language, Visual Basic .NET. However, later versions will support other .NET languages such as C#.

Built-in CLR Tasks

The CLR performs the following built-in tasks:

- Managing data

- Performing automatic garbage collection

- Sharing a common base for source code

- Compiling code to the Microsoft intermediate language (MSIL)

I discuss these features in the next few sections.

Managed Data

The .NET Framework compilers mainly produce managed code, which is managed by the CLR. Managed code means managed data, which in turn means data with lifetimes managed by the CLR. This is also referred to as *garbage collection,* which you can read about in the next section. Managed data will definitely help eliminate memory leaks, but at the same time it also means you have less control over your data, because you no longer have deterministic finalization, which is arguably one of the strengths of COM(+).

Automatic Garbage Collection

When objects are managed (allocated and released) by the CLR, you don't have full control over them. The CLR handles the object layout and the references to the objects, disposing of the objects when they're no longer being used. This process, called *automatic garbage collection,* is very different from the one for handling objects in previous versions of Visual Basic or Visual C++, which is known as *deterministic finalization.* These programming languages used COM as their component model and, as such, they used the COM model for referencing and counting objects. As a result, whenever your application instantiated an object, a counter for this object reference was incremented by one, and when your application destroyed the object reference or when it went out of scope, the counter was decremented. When the counter hit zero, the object would be released automatically from memory. This is something you have to be very aware of now, because you no longer have full control over your object references. If you're a Java programmer, you probably already know about this.

Source Code Shares Common Base

Because all the CLR-compliant compilers produce managed code, the source code shares the same base—that is, the type system (CTS) and to some extent the language specification (CLS). This means you can inherit classes written in a language other than the one you're using, a concept known as *cross-language inheritance.* This is a great benefit to larger development teams, where the developers' skill sets are likely to be rather different. Another major benefit is when you need to debug— you can now safely debug within the same environment source code across various programming languages.

Intermediate Language Compilation

When you compile your code, it's compiled to what is called Microsoft intermediate language (MSIL) and stored in a portable executable (PE) file along with metadata that describes the types (classes, interfaces, and value types) used in the code. Because the compiled code is in an "intermediate state," the code is platform independent. This means the MSIL code can be executed on any platform that has the CLR installed. The metadata that exists in the PE file along with the MSIL enables your code to describe itself, which means there is no need for type libraries or Interface Definition Language (IDL) files. The CLR locates the metadata in the PE file and extracts it from there as necessary when the file is executed.

At runtime, the CLR's JIT compilers convert the MSIL code to machine code, which is then executed. This machine code is obviously appropriate for the platform on which the CLR is installed. The JIT compilers and the CLR are made by various vendors, and I suppose the most notable one is Microsoft's Windows CLR (surprise, eh?).

JIT: Another Word for Virtual Machine?

I believe we've all heard about the Virtual Machine used by Java applets. In short, the CLR's JIT compiler is the same as a Virtual Machine in the sense that it executes intermediate code and as such is platform independent. However, there is more to the way the CLR's JIT compiler handles the code execution than the way the so-called Virtual Machine does. The JIT compiler is dynamic, meaning that although it's made for a specific OS, it will detect and act upon the hardware layer at execution time.

The JIT compiler can optimize the code for the specific processor that's used on the system where the code is being executed. This means that once the JIT compiler detects the CPU, it can optimize the code for that particular CPU. For instance, instead of just optimizing code for the Pentium processor, the compiler can also optimize for a particular version of the Pentium processor, such as the Pentium IV. This is good, because legacy code can take advantage of later processor improvements without the need to recompile. Although the current execution of managed code is somewhat slower than unmanaged code, we're probably not far from the point in time when managed code will execute faster than unmanaged code.

Another major difference between the Java Virtual Machine and the CLR is that whereas the former is invoked for every new process/application, this is not true for the latter.

Assemblies and Namespaces

The .NET Framework uses assemblies and namespaces for grouping related functionality, and you have to know what an assembly and a namespace really are. You could certainly develop some simple .NET applications without really understanding assemblies and namespaces, but you won't get too far.

Assemblies

An *assembly* is the primary building block for a .NET Framework application, and it's a fundamental part of the runtime. All applications that use the CLR must consist of one or more assemblies. Each assembly provides the CLR with all the necessary information for an application to run. Please note that an application can be and often is made up of more than one assembly—that is, an assembly is not a unit of application deployment. You can think of an assembly in terms of classes in a DLL.

Although I refer to an assembly as a single entity, it might in fact be composed of several files. It is a logical collection of functionality that's deployed as a single unit (even if it's more than one file). This has to do with the way an assembly is put together. Think of an assembly in terms of a type library and the information you find in one. However, an assembly also contains information about everything else that makes up your application and is therefore said to be self-describing.

Because an assembly is self-describing by means of an assembly manifest, you won't have to deal anymore with shared DLLs in your application and the problems they have created over the years since Windows came of age. However, because you no longer use shared DLLs, your code will take up more memory and disk space, as the same functionality can now be easily duplicated on your hard disk and in memory. It is possible to share assemblies to get around this.

Actually, you can still use COM+ services (DLLs and EXEs) from within the .NET Framework, and you can even add .NET Framework components to a COM+ application. However, this book concentrates on using .NET Framework components.

As I touched upon previously, an assembly contains a *manifest,* which is little more than an index of all the files that make up the assembly. The assembly manifest is also called the assembly's metadata. (As mentioned earlier, *metadata* is data used to describe the main data.) Within the manifest, you have the components listed in Table 1-1.

Besides the assembly manifest components, a developer can also add custom assembly attributes. These information-only attributes can include the title and description of the assembly. The assembly manifest can be edited through the AssemblyInfo.vb file that is automatically created when you create a new project on the VS .NET IDE, as shown in Figure 1-1.

Table 1-1. Assembly Manifest Components

Item	Description
Identity	Name, version, shared name, and digital signature
Culture, processor, OS	The various cultures, processors, and OSs supported
File table	Hash and relative path of all other files that are part of the assembly
Referenced assemblies	A list of all external dependencies (that is, other assemblies statically referenced)
Type reference	Information on how to map a type reference to a file containing the declaration and implementation
Permissions	The permissions your assembly requests from the runtime environment in order to run effectively

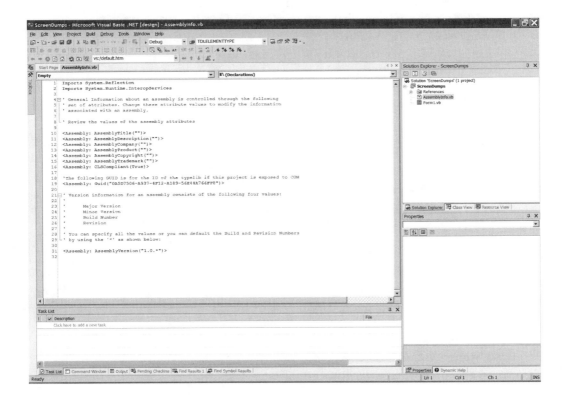

Figure 1-1. The AssemblyInfo.vb manifest file

In Figure 1-1, you can see the parts of the AssemblyInfo.vb manifest file that concern title, description, configuration, version information, and so on.

Namespaces

A *namespace* is a logical way to group or organize related types (classes, interfaces, or value types). A .NET namespace is a design-time convenience only, which is used for logical naming/grouping. At runtime, it's the assembly that establishes the name scope.

The various .NET Framework types are named according to a hierarchical naming scheme with a dot syntax. Because the naming scheme is hierarchical, there is also a root namespace. The .NET root namespace is called **System**. To illustrate the naming scheme, for the second-level namespace **Timers** in the **System** namespace, the full name is **System.Timers**. In code, you would include the following to use types within the **System.Timers** namespace:

```
Imports System.Timers
```

When you use the **Imports** statement to include a reference to a specific namespace, you get easy access to the types within that namespace. So to declare an object as an instance of the **Timer** class in the **System.Timers** namespace, you would enter the following:

```
Dim tmrTest As New Timer()
```

When the compiler encounters this declaration statement, it looks for the **Timer** class within your assembly, but when that fails, it appends **System.Timers.** to the **Timer** class to see if it can find the **Timer** class in that namespace. However, you can also directly prefix the class with the namespace, so that it is fully described, meaning you'd enter the following to declare an object as an instance of the **Timer** class in the **System.Timer** namespace:

```
Dim tmrTest As New System.Timers.Timer()
```

As you can see, using the **Imports** statement can save you a fair bit of typing. I believe it will also make your code easier to read and maintain if you have all your **Imports** statements at the top of your class or module file. One look and you know what namespaces are being used.

A namespace is created using the following syntax:

```
Namespace <NsName>
End Namespace
```

where *<NsName>* is the name, you want to give to your namespace. All types that are to be part of the namespace must be placed within the namespace block.

You need namespaces to help prevent ambiguity, which is also known as *namespace pollution.* This happens when two different libraries contain the same names, causing a conflict. Namespaces help you eliminate this problem.

If two namespaces actually do have the same class, and you reference this class, the compiler simply won't compile your code, because the class definition is ambiguous and the compiler won't know which one to choose. Say that you have two namespaces, Test1 and Test2, which both implement the class Show. You need to reference the Show class of the Test2 namespace and other classes within both the two namespaces, so you use the **Imports** statement:

```
Imports Test1
Imports Test2
```

Now, what happens when you create an object as an instance of the Show class within the same class or code file as the **Imports** statements, as follows:

```
Dim Test As New Show()
```

Well, as I stated before, the compiler simply won't compile your code, because the Show class is ambiguous. It's only a warning, and you can choose to continue to build your application, but any references to Show will be left out and will *not* be part of the compiled application. What you need to do in this case is this:

```
Dim Test As New Test2.Show()
```

Namespaces can span more than one assembly, making it possible for two or more developers to work on different assemblies but create classes within the same namespace. Namespaces within the current assembly are accessible at all times; you do not have to import them.

 NOTE Namespaces are explicitly public, and you cannot change that by using an access modifier such as **Private**. However, you have full control over the accessibility of the types within the namespace. As stated, the visibility of a namespace is public, but the assembly in which you place it determines the accessibility of a namespace. This means the namespace is publicly available to all projects that reference the assembly into which it's placed.

The runtime environment does not actually know anything about namespaces, so when you access a type, the CLR needs the full name of the type and the assembly that contains the type definition. With this information, the CLR can load the assembly and access the type.

The .NET Framework Class Library

The .NET Framework class library includes base classes and classes derived from the base classes. These classes have a lot of functionality, such as server controls, exception handling, and data access, of course, which is the subject of this book. The .NET Framework classes give you a head start when building your applications, because you don't have to design them from the ground up. The class library is actually a hierarchical set of unified, object-oriented, extensible class libraries, also called application programming interfaces (APIs). This differs from previous versions of various Windows programming languages, such as Visual Basic and Visual C++, in which a lot of system and OS functionality could only be accessed through Windows API calls.

Getting Cozy with the VS .NET Integrated Development Environment

The Integrated Development Environment (IDE) hosts an abundance of new, fantastic features, and I will discuss the following ones very briefly:

- All languages share the IDE

- Two interface modes

- Built-in Web browser functionality

- Command Window

- Built-in object browser

- Integrated debugger

- Integrated Help system

- Macros

- Upgraded deployment tools

- Text editors

- IDE and tools modification

- Server Explorer

- Data connections

- Toolbox

- Task List

All Languages Share the IDE

VS .NET provides an IDE for all .NET languages to share (see Figure 1-2), giving developers the benefit of the same tools across the various programming languages. Basically, by "share" I mean that whether you open a VB .NET or C# project, the VS .NET IDE generally looks and feels the same. This is true for whatever .NET language you are developing in.[2] However, you can use other IDEs, like the Antechinus C# Programming Editor (http://www.c-point.com/csharp.htm), which is available for C#, if you dislike the Microsoft IDE.

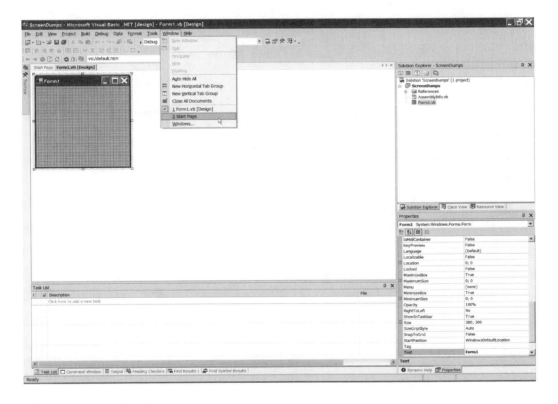

Figure 1-2. One shared IDE

---

2. Actually, it's up to the vendor of the .NET language to integrate it with the VS .NET IDE, and some languages come with their own IDE.

Two Interface Modes

The IDE supports two *interface modes,* which arrange windows and panes:

- *Multiple document interface (MDI) mode:* In this mode, the MDI parent window hosts a number of MDI children within the MDI parent window context. In Figure 1-3, you can see the two open windows, Start Page and Form1.vb [Design], overlap as MDI children windows.

- *Tabbed documents mode:* This is the default mode, and I personally prefer this mode, as it seems easier to arrange all your windows and panes than MDI mode. Either of the two open windows in Figure 1-2 can be displayed by clicking the appropriate tab, Start Page or Form1.vb [Design].

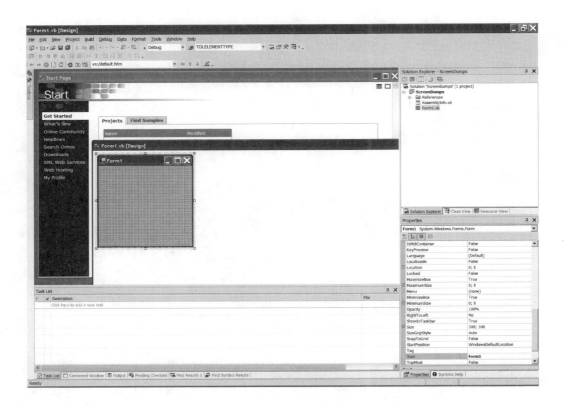

Figure 1-3. IDE in MDI mode

You can switch between the two interface modes using the Options dialog box. See the "IDE and Tools Modification" section later in this chapter.

Built-in Web Browser Functionality

The IDE has built-in Web browser capabilities, so you don't need to have a separate browser installed on your development machine. However, I do recommend installing at least one separate Web browser, for testing purposes, that runs outside the IDE. The built-in Web browser is great for viewing Web pages without having to compile and run the whole project. See the UserMan.dk window in Figure 1-4, which displays the home page for the UserMan.dk site within the built-in Web browser. If your IDE doesn't show the address bar, which you can see in Figure 1-4 where the mouse pointer is located, you can right-click any toolbar and select the Web command from the pop-up menu. You can also select the View ➤ Toolbars ➤ Web menu command to show the address bar.

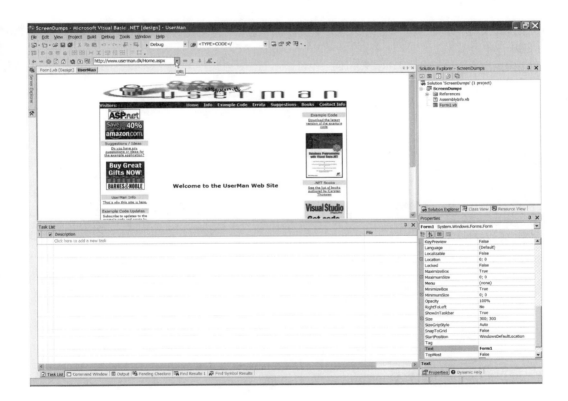

Figure 1-4. Built-in Web browser

In Figure 1-4, you see an HTML page from the UserMan.dk site, which is the site for the example application of this book. To browse to a specific URL, you can type in any URL (or filename, for that matter) to browse to a Web site or open a file. The built-in Web browser is just like your ordinary browser, which is in fact what it is.

Command Window

The Command Window has two modes:

- *Command mode,* which you can access by pressing Ctrl+Alt+A, allows you to type your IDE commands and create short name aliases for often-used commands (see Figure 1-5).

- *Immediate mode,* which you can access by pressing Ctrl+Alt+I, lets you evaluate expressions, set or read the value of variables, assign object references, and execute code statements (see Figure 1-6).

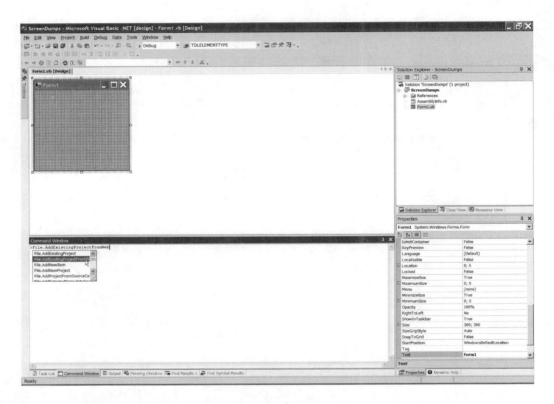

Figure 1-5. Command Window in Command mode

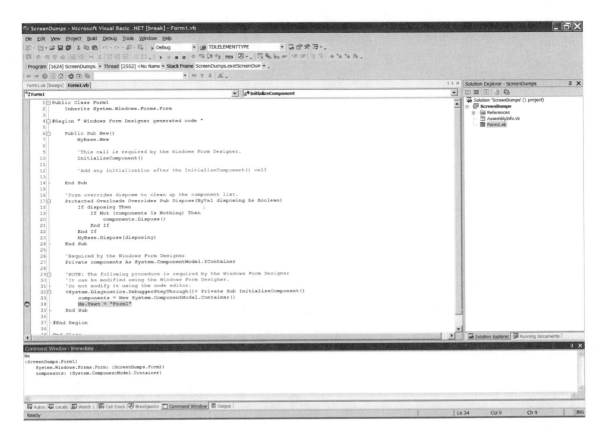

Figure 1-6. Command Window in Immediate mode

Built-in Object Browser

The built-in object browser, which you can open by pressing Ctrl+Alt+J, lets you examine objects and their methods and properties. The objects you can examine (also called the *object browser's browsing scope*) can be part of external or referenced components, or components in the form of projects in the current solution. The components in the browsing scope include COM components and .NET Framework components (obviously). Figure 1-7 shows the object browser.

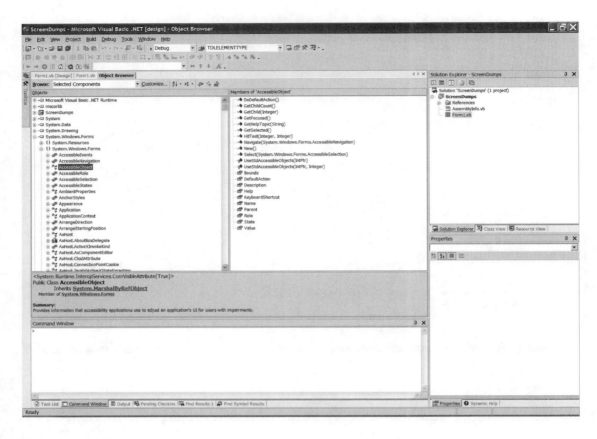

Figure 1-7. Object browser

Integrated Debugger

The integrated debugger now supports cross-language debugging from within the IDE. You can also debug multiple programs at the same time, either by launching the various programs from within the IDE or by attaching the debugger to already running programs or processes (see Figure 1-8). One thing you must notice, especially if you've worked with an earlier version of Visual Basic, is that it's no longer possible to edit your code when you've hit a breakpoint and then continue code execution with the modified code. Last I heard, Microsoft was working on this for the next release.

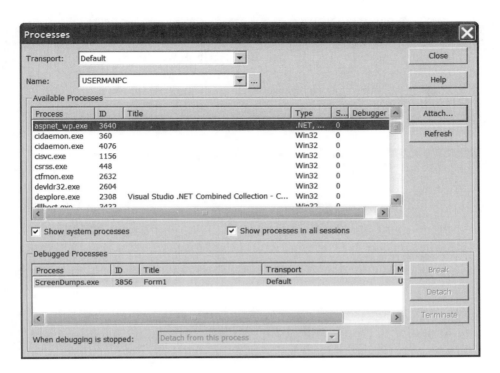

Figure 1-8. Debugger Processes window

Integrated Help System

The Help system in VS .NET is somewhat advanced and consists of the following:

- *Dynamic Help*: The Dynamic Help is great because the content of the Dynamic Help window is based on the current context and selection. This means that the Dynamic Help window, which is located in the lower-right corner of the IDE by default, changes its content to reflect the current selection when you move around in the code editor. This works not only when you are in the code editor, but also when you edit HTML code, use the XML Designer, design reports, edit Cascading Style Sheets (CSS), and so on.

  When you want to view one of the topics displayed in the Dynamic Help window, as shown in Figure 1-9, you simply click the topic and the help text pops up, either in the MSDN Library application or within the IDE as a document. This depends on whether your Help settings indicate external or internal display.

- *Microsoft Visual Studio .NET documentation:* The complete Help system for VS .NET is included, as is the Platform SDK and the .NET Framework SDK documentation. The Help browser has been improved from previous versions (as the one that comes with previous versions of Microsoft programming languages), and it's now a browser-style application with links to appropriate information on the various Microsoft Web sites.

Figure 1-9. Dynamic Help window

Macros

You know that you must do some tasks or series of tasks repeatedly when developing. The VS .NET IDE gives you the opportunity to automate these repetitive tasks using macros. Macros can be created and/or edited using either the Recorder or the Macros IDE. The Macros IDE is actually a rather familiar friend if you ever did any VBA programming, as it's quite similar. So too is the language, which looks like VBA. In fact, it's now called Visual Studio for Applications (VSA), as discussed earlier, and the macro language is based on Visual Basic .NET in this first version. However, newer versions will support other .NET languages as well, including C#. Figure 1-10 shows you the Macros IDE, which you can access from the VS .NET IDE by pressing Alt+F11 or by selecting the Macros IDE command in the Tools ➤ Macros submenu.

Figure 1-10. Visual Studio .NET Macros IDE

In Figure 1-10, you can see one of the accompanying sample macros, the VSDebugger macro, displayed in the Macros IDE. The source code is VB .NET, and I have inserted a breakpoint just to show you that the Macros IDE works pretty much the same as the VS .NET IDE.

Upgraded Deployment Tools

The deployment tools in VS .NET have been heavily upgraded since the previous version of VS. In VS .NET, you can perform the following tasks, among others:

- Deploy application tiers to different test servers for remote debugging.

- Deploy Web applications.

- Distribute applications using the Microsoft Windows Installer.

Text Editors

The various text editors in the IDE all have the same functionality that you've come to expect from a Windows editor. The shortcuts are the same, and most of the accelerator keys are well known.

However, something that may be new to you is the inclusion of line numbers, which are displayed at the left side of the editor. These optional line numbers are not part of the code or text, but are merely displayed for your convenience (see Figure 1-11). Actually, the default is not to show line numbers, but you can turn them on for one programming language or all of them using the Text Editor category from the Options dialog box, as discussed in the next section.

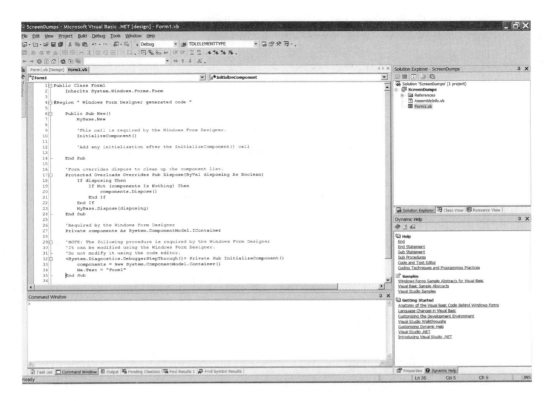

Figure 1-11. The text editor with line numbers

IDE and Tools Modification

By default, the IDE and all the tools within it have a certain look and feel, but you can modify most of the functionality from the Options dialog box, which you can access by selecting Tools ➤ Options (see Figure 1-12).

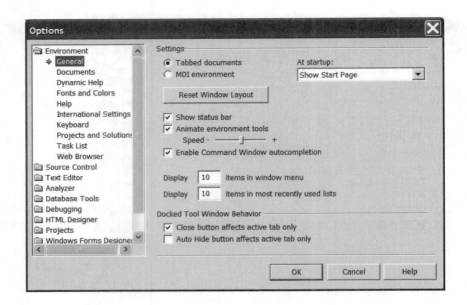

Figure 1-12. The IDE Options dialog box

In the Options dialog box, you can change the default behavior and look of the IDE and related tools. On the left you have the tree view with all the categories you can change options for. In Figure 1-12, the Environment category or node is selected, which means you can change options such as whether you want the status bar to be shown in the IDE, and choose if you want to use tabbed documents or the MDI mode within the IDE.

The various programming languages have slightly different settings, so if you need certain settings, such as tab size and font, to be the same in all the programming languages you use, you need to explicitly set these.

Server Explorer

You can use the Server Explorer window, which is located on the bar on the left side of the IDE by default, for manipulating resources on any server you can access. The resources you can manipulate include the following:

- Database objects

- Report services

- Performance counters*

- Message queues*

- Services*

- Event logs*

Most of these resources are new (denoted by an asterisk), and you can drag them onto a Web Form or Windows Form and then manipulate them from within your code (see Figure 1-13). Please note that the accessibility of these resources from Server Explorer depends on the version of Visual Studio .NET you buy.

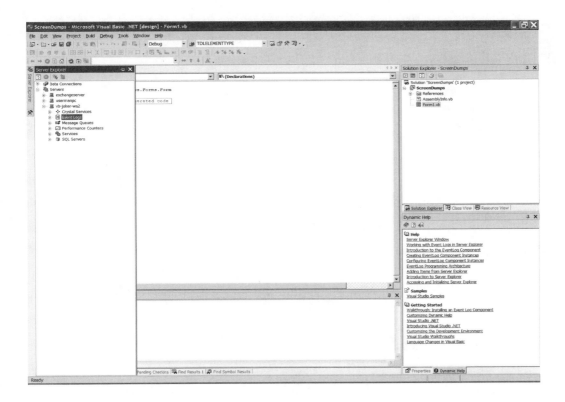

Figure 1-13. The Server Explorer window

Data Connections

You can set up connections to a database and manipulate the database objects in a number of ways. Hey, wait a minute—I go into greater detail on this subject from Chapter 3 on, so don't get me started here!

Toolbox

The Toolbox window, which is located on the bar on the left side of the IDE by default, contains all the intrinsic tools you can use in the various design and editor modes, such as HTML design, Windows Form design, Web Form design, Code Editor, and UML Diagram design. When you have a window open, the content of the Toolbox changes according to what is available to work with in the current window (see Figure 1-14).

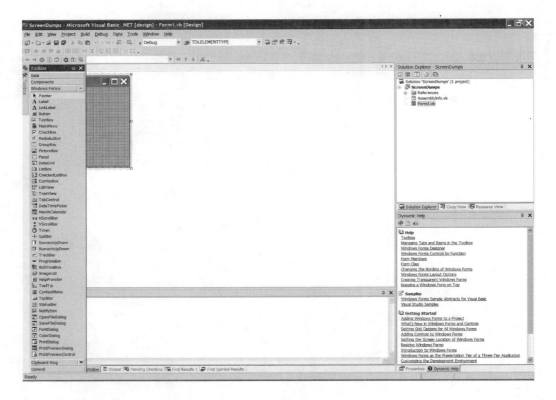

Figure 1-14. The Toolbox

Task List

The Task List window, which is docked at the bottom of the IDE by default, helps you organize and manage the various tasks you need to complete in order to build your solution. If the Task List window isn't shown, you can access it by pressing

Ctrl+Alt+K. The developer and the CLR both use the Task List. This means that the developer can add tasks manually, but the CLR also adds a task if an error occurs when compiling. When a task is added to the list, it can contain a filename and line number. This way, you can double-click the task name and go straight to the problem or unfinished task.

Once you finish a certain task, you can select the appropriate check box to indicate the task has been completed (see Figure 1-15).

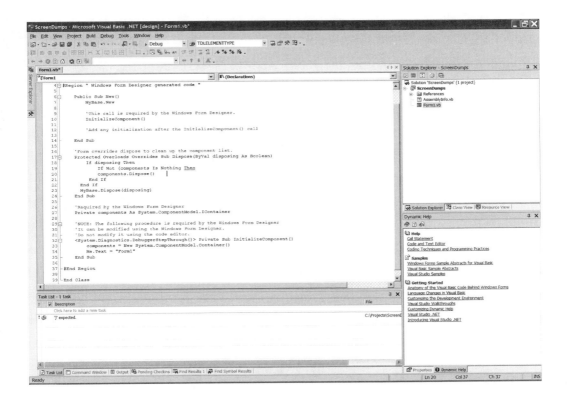

Figure 1-15. The Task List window

Summary

This chapter provided a quick rundown of the concepts and terms in VB .NET. I discussed assemblies and namespaces, and how they fit in the .NET Framework; the common language runtime (CLR), which unifies the .NET programming languages with a common base; the Common Language Specification (CLS), which is the standard all .NET languages must adhere to; the common type system (CTS), which dictates the base types used for data exchange; server-based Active Server Pages programming; and the .NET Framework class library. Finally, I presented a quick look at some of the new features of the shared IDE, such as line numbering in the text editors and the integrated debugger.

The next chapter is a short side trip from VB .NET. It's a general chapter on how to design and talk to databases. Amongst other concepts, it covers how to normalize a database.

CHAPTER 2

Using Databases

A Short Introduction to General Database Terms and Concepts

IN THIS CHAPTER I introduce you to the terms and concepts that I'll be using throughout the rest of the book. Consider this chapter a reference for the following chapters. I'll be looking at what a database really is, why you should use a database, and how to design a relational database. Although this chapter is not intended to teach you everything there is to know about designing a relational database, you'll get the basics. Please note that if you already know about database design, referential integrity, indexes, keys, and so on, this chapter will serve as a refresher. For additional information, you'll find a good article on database design and a link for database normalization at the following address on the Microsoft Product Services site: http://support.microsoft.com/support/kb/articles/Q234/2/08.ASP.

The hands-on exercise in the "UserMan Database Schema" section at the end of this chapter will reinforce the database concepts I present to you here.

What Is a Database?

I'm sure you know what a *database* is, but why not keep reading? You might just find something new or different to add to what you already know. Anyway, there are probably as many definitions of the term "database" as there are different software implementations of electronic databases. So for that reason, I'll try to keep it simple. A database is a collection of *data,* which can be information about anything really. A phone number is data, a name is data, a book contains data, and so on. What the data is about is not really important in the context of defining data.

A database is usually organized in some way. A phone book is a database, usually organized or sorted alphabetically by surname, or last name. The main objective of a phone book is for the reader to be able to locate a phone number. With any given phone number you generally associate a name, consisting of a first name and surname, an address, and perhaps the title of the person who "owns" the phone number. Here I'm actually in the process of taking the phone book apart, or perhaps I should call it figuring out how the phone book is organized.

As you can see, a database doesn't have to be an electronic collection of data (a phone book isn't), and it doesn't have to be organized in any particular way. However, this book deals with electronic databases exclusively.

Why Use a Database?

When thinking of reasons for using databases, some words immediately spring to mind: storage, accessibility, organization, and manipulation.

- *Storage:* For a database to exist elsewhere other than in your head, you need to store it in some form. You can store it electronically on a disk and bring it with you, if that's what you want to do, or hand it to someone else. Your database could be in the form of a Microsoft Excel spreadsheet or a Microsoft Access database.

- *Accessibility:* Well, if you can't access your data within the database, the database is of no use to anyone. When using an electronic database, such as one created in Microsoft Access, you generally have a lot of options for accessing it. You can access a Microsoft Access database using the Microsoft Access front-end, or indeed any application capable of communicating with a driver that can talk to the Microsoft Access database. Now, accessibility depends on the format the database is saved in, but for argument's sake let's just say that it's a standard format, such as dBase or Microsoft Access, which means it's easy to get hold of a driver and/or application that can access and read the data in the database.

- *Organization:* The most logical way to organize a phone book is alphabetically. However, the phone book has a lot of duplicated data, which can take up twice as much space as you would expect nonduplicated data to take. The data is duplicated to allow you to use more than one way to look up data. In most countries, you can look up a listing under the surname, you can look up a listing using the address, and so on. Duplication is not a problem when speaking of an electronic database, if it has been properly implemented. You can use indexes to give your clients a variety of ways to access the data without duplicating it. Keys serve as pointers to the data, which means they're valuable tools for avoiding duplicated data.

- *Manipulation:* Editing a phone book is certainly not an easy task. You can strike over the text in case a phone number no longer exists, but what about changing the owner of a phone number or adding a new phone number?

In how many places will you have to edit and/or add data? This just won't work, unless you're willing to redo the whole phone book! When it comes to your electronic database, if it has been properly implemented, it's simply a matter of locating the information you want to edit or delete, entering the data, and off you go. The data is now added and changed in all the right places.

Okay, so to quickly summarize, here are the benefits of using a database:

- Locating and manipulating the data is much easier when your data is in one place.

- Organization of the data is easier when it's in one place and it's stored electronically.

- You can access the data from a variety of applications and locations when your data is put in one place, your database.

From this point on, all references to databases are to electronic databases.

Relational vs. Hierarchical

Today there are two types of databases widely deployed, *relational* and *hierarchical*. The relational database is by far the most popular of these and it's probably the one you already know about. Mind you, you've probably been using a hierarchical database without knowing it! The Windows Registry and Active Directory in Windows 2000 are both hierarchical databases.

Hierarchical Databases

A *hierarchical database* has a treelike structure with a root element at the top (see Figure 2-1). The root element has one or more nodes, and the nodes themselves have nodes. It's just like a tree with branches and leaves. You've probably been using the Windows Explorer file manager, which relies on a treelike structure for representing your disk and files. Windows Explorer is more like a hierarchical DBMS (see the "What Is a Database Management System?" section later in this chapter) with multiple databases—that is, My Computer is a database, drive C on your local computer is a node of the root element My Computer, the folders on drive C are nodes of drive C, and so on.

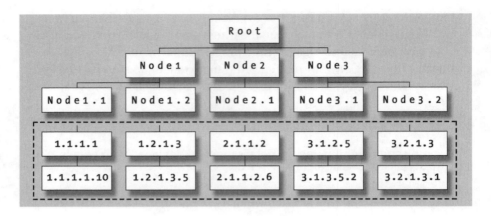

Figure 2-1. Hierarchical database

Hierarchical databases are usually very fast, because the data structures are directly linked, but they are not good for modeling complex relations such as the ones you have in a warehouse system with raw materials, products, boxed products, shelves, rows of shelves, and so on. All these items are somewhat interrelated, and it's difficult to represent these relations in a hierarchical database without duplicating data and loss of performance.

These are some good candidates for hierarchical databases:

- File and directory systems

- Management/organization rankings

I'm sure you can think of a few more yourself.

Hierarchical databases are generally hard to implement, set up, and maintain, because fewer tools are available, and they usually require a systems programmer to do so. However, IBM produces a hierarchical database system called the Information Management System (IMS), which you can find at http://www-4.ibm.com/software/data/ims/. IMS has tools similar to those in relational database systems (discussed next) for setting up and implementing your hierarchical database. I won't implement a hierarchical database in this book, but I'll show you how to access one, Active Directory. See Chapter 19 for more information on Active Directory and hierarchical databases in general.

NOTE   Keep in mind that XML is a form of hierarchical database, and it's commonly used to transport result sets.

Relational Databases

A *relational database* consists of tables (see the "What Are Tables?" section later in this chapter) that are related to each other in some way, either directly or indirectly. If you think in terms of objects, tables represent the objects, and these objects/tables are connected using relationships. One example might be an order system, where you have products, customers, orders, and so on. In a rather simple order system you'll have separate objects or tables for holding information pertaining to orders, customers, and products. A customer has zero or more orders, and an order consists of one or more products, which means you have relationships between the objects, or rather tables. Please see the "What Is Relational Database Design?" section later in this chapter for more information on how a relational database should be designed.

What VB .NET Programmers Need to Know about Relational Databases

In this section you'll be introduced to a number of Frequently Asked Questions (FAQs) and answers to these questions. All the FAQs are related to what you really need to know if you design your own databases as a VB .NET programmer. Although the rest of this chapter is in typical FAQ style, I recommend that you follow along from the beginning, because it might answer some of the questions raised by you in later chapters.

What Is a Database Management System?

The term *database management system* (DBMS) is used in variety of contexts, some more correct than others. A complete DBMS consists of hardware, software, data, and users. However, in the context of this book, a DBMS is a software package through which you can administer one or more databases, manipulate the data within a database, and export to/import from different data formats. A DBMS is not necessarily a database server system such as Microsoft SQL Server or

Oracle; it can also be a desktop database such as Microsoft Access or Lotus Approach. A desktop database doesn't require a server; it's simply a file (or a set of related files) that you can access using the right software driver from within your own application or using accompanying front-end software.

Throughout this book, I'll use the terms *database* and *DBMS* interchangeably, for the sake of discussing the connection to and manipulation of data in a database.

What Are Tables?

A (database) *table* is a structure for holding a collection of related data, such as a table of orders in an order system. The structure of a table is made up of columns and the content of a table is grouped in rows.

What Are Rows and Records?

Rows are entities in a table, which means that a single row contains information about a single instance of the object that the table holds, such as an order in an order system. *Rows* and *records* are the exact same thing. Remember that when you come across the two terms in the same context.

What Are Columns and Fields?

A *column* is the building block of the table structure, and each column in a table structure holds a specific piece of named data relating to the object that the table encapsulates, such as a column in an order table that holds the Order ID in an order system. Like rows and records, the terms *column* and *field* are synonymous.

What Are Null Values?

The special value *null* refers to an empty or nonassigned value. When I say empty value, that's not to be compared to an empty string, because an empty string is an actual value ("").

What Is the Relational Database Model?

The *Relational Database Model*, which was "created" by E. F. Codd,[1] has become the de facto standard for relational database design today. The idea behind this model is not very complex, although it can be hard to grasp at first. Please see the next FAQ, "What Is Relational Database Design," for more information.

What Is Relational Database Design?

Relational database design is the way in which you design your relational database. Okay, I know this is pretty obvious, but basically that's what it is. It's all about identifying the objects you need to store in your database and finding the relationships between these objects.

It's very important that you design your database as accurately as possible the first time around, because it's so much harder to make structural changes after you've deployed it. Other reasons for implementing a good database design are performance and maintainability. Sometimes after you've been working on your database for a while, you end up modifying the structure simply because you find out that the current design doesn't facilitate what you're trying to achieve. Design your database, go over the design, and change it according to your findings. You should keep doing this until you no longer find any problems with it.

There are many excellent tools for modeling a relational database, but even though these tools are good, you still need to know how to construct a relational database to fully exploit one of these tools. Here's a list of some of the tools available:

- ICT Database Designer Tool (`http://www.ict-computing.com/prod01.htm`)

- ER/Studio (`http://www.embarcadero.com/products/erstudio/index.asp`)

- ER*win* (`http://www.cai.com/products/alm/erwin.htm`)

- Visible Analyst DB Engineer (`http://www.visible.com/Products/Analyst/vadbengineer.html`)

---

1. You can find the collected works of E.F. Codd at this address:
   `http://www.informatik.uni-trier.de/~ley/db/about/codd.html`.

How Do You Identify Objects for Your Database?

When you set out to design your relational database, the first thing you need to do is to sit down and find out what objects your database should hold. By "objects," I mean the distinct items and attributes. In an order system, for instance, objects represent customers (Customer objects), orders (Order objects), and products (Product objects), which you would find in a typical order system. It can be difficult to identify these objects, especially if you're new to relational database design. If this is so, I'm quite sure that the first object you identify, and perhaps the only object you can identify, is the Order object. The important thing to remember here is that while the Order object is a perfectly legitimate object, there is more to it than that. You need to keep breaking the objects apart until you're at the very lowest level. In the example order system, an order is made up of one or more OrderItem objects, a Customer object, and so on. The OrderItem object itself can be broken into more objects. An order item consists of product type and the number of products. The Price object can be derived from the Product object. Here's a list of typical objects for this order system:

- Order

- Customer

- Product

- OrderItem

- Price

Something's wrong with this list, however. When you split your objects into smaller ones, the criterion for doing so should be whether the derived object actually has a life of its own. Take a look at the Price object. Should it be an object, or is it simply a property of the Product object? By "property," I mean something that describes the object, an attribute of it. The Price object will probably correspond to more than one Product object, and as such it will be duplicated. The price could be a separate object, but it would make more sense to have it be a property of the Product object. Consider the following questions and answers:

- **Q:** Does one price correspond to more than one product, or will the price be duplicated within the Product object?

- **A:** The price probably will correspond to more than one product, and as such it will be duplicated. You could treat the price as a separate object, but it would make more sense to have it be a property of the Product object. Although the price will be duplicated, you also have to think about maintainability. If you need to change the price of one product, what happens when you change the Price object and more than one product is linked to it? You change the price for all related products!

- **Q:** Does a price describe a product, or is it generic?

- **A:** The price relates to one product and one product only.

- **Q:** Is the price calculated (or will it be) when invoicing?

- **A:** The price is fixed so you'll have to store it somewhere.

It's necessary to identify these objects so you can start creating tables; the objects I have identified so far are indeed tables. The properties that I've come across, such as the price, are columns in a table.

What Are Relationships?

When you've identified objects for your database, you need to tell the DBMS how the various objects or tables are related by defining *relationships*. There are basically three kinds of relationships:

- One-to-one

- One-to-many

- Many-to-many

Relationships are established between a *parent table* and *child tables*. The parent table is the primary object and the child tables are the related objects, meaning that data in the child tables relates to data in the parent table in such a way that the data in the child tables can only exist if it has related data in the parent table.

What Is a One-to-One Relationship?

You use a *one-to-one relationship* when you want to create a direct relationship between two objects, a parent table and a child table. Basically, one-to-one relationships require that the related columns in the two tables are unique. Normally, information that makes up a one-to-one relationship would be put in one table, but sometimes it's necessary to keep some information in a separate table, effectively establishing a direct link or a one-to-one relationship between the two new tables. You can see reasons for such a relationship in Table 2-1.

Table 2-1. One-to-One Relationships

Split Reason	Description
Large table structure	If you have a large table structure (many columns), quite often only some of the columns are accessed and, in such cases, it can be advantageous to split the table into two, moving the least accessed columns into a new table.
Security concerns	Some columns are considered a security risk and are therefore moved to a new table, creating a one-to-one relationship. However, there are often other ways of getting around this, such as creating views. See Chapter 17 for more information about views.

Table 2-1 explains why you would split up an existing table into two tables, which is mostly the reason for having a one-to-one relationship, and provides a description of the reason you should split the table. In general, reference or lookup tables have a one-to-one relationship with a parent table.

What Is a One-to-Many Relationship?

A *one-to-many relationship* is the most common database relationship, and you will implement it many times over the years as a database designer. This type of relationship exists between a parent table and a child table in cases where the parent row can have zero or more child rows. Table 2-2 provides examples of such a relationship.

Table 2-2. One-to-Many Relationships

Parent Table	Child Table
Orders	OrderItems
Customers	Orders
Products	OrderItems

You interpret Table 2-2 as follows: One order can have one or more order items, one customer can have one or more orders, and one product may belong to one or more order items.

What Is a Many-to-Many Relationship?

A *many-to-many relationship* exists in cases where a row in the parent table has many related rows in the child table and vice versa. Table 2-3 displays one example of such a relationship.

Table 2-3. Many-to-Many Relationship

Parent Table	Link Table	Child Table
Products	ProductParts	Parts

Many-to-many relationships can't be modeled directly between a parent table and a child table. Instead, you define two one-to-many relationships using a third table, called a *link table*. This table holds a unique ID of the row in the parent row as well as a unique ID of the row in the child table as one row (see Figure 2-2). So, in order to find a particular row in the link table, you need the unique IDs of both the parent and child rows. The two IDs are very good candidates for a composite primary key (see the next FAQ, "What Are Keys?"). Figure 2-2 should be read like this:

- One product contains one or more parts.

- One part belongs to zero or more products.

- A product part belongs to one product only and consists of one part only. The ProductParts table is the link table in this case.

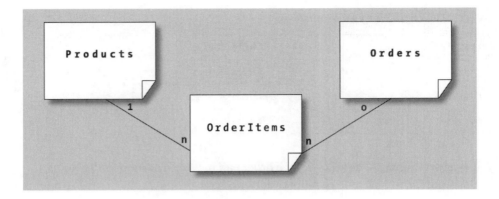

Figure 2-2. Many-to-many relationship

 ## What Are Keys?

 Keys are important in relational database design, because they're used as row identifiers and for sorting query output. There are two types of keys: primary keys and foreign keys.[2] Please note that any key is really just an index, meaning that a key is based on an index. See the "What Is an Index?" FAQ later in this chapter for more information on indexes.

What Is a Primary Key?

The *primary key* of a table is always unique; that is, no two rows in the table hold the same value in the column(s) that's designated as the primary key. This means the primary key uniquely identifies each row in the table. This also means that a column that makes up or is part of a primary key can't contain a null value. The primary key index also functions as a *lookup key,* which helps you locate a specific row when you search for a value in the primary key index. In terms of relationships, the primary key of the parent table is always used in combination with a foreign key (discussed next) in the child table. In Figure 2-3, the primary key in the (parent) Orders table is marked PK. One row in the Orders table relates to zero or more rows in the OrderItems table.

---

2. There are actually more types of keys than these two, but for understanding relational database design at the level presented in this chapter, these two types will suffice. In any case, the other types of keys generally refer back to the two mentioned types in one form or another.

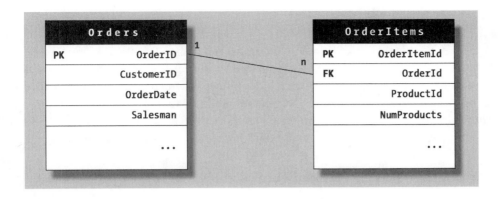

Figure 2-3. Primary and foreign keys

 ## What Is a Foreign Key?

A *foreign key* is used in relationships as the lookup value in the child table. This means it directly corresponds to the value of the primary key in the parent table, so that you can use the value of the primary key to look up a related row in the child table. In a one-to-one relationship, the foreign key must be unique. In Figure 2-3, the foreign key in the OrderItems table is marked FK. There can be many rows in the OrderItems table that relate to a row in the Orders table. Please note that the Salesman column in the Orders table is a foreign key candidate for looking up orders belonging to a certain salesman. This obviously requires a separate Salesman table with a unique Id column as the primary key.

 ## What Is a Composite Key?

A key consisting of more than one column is called a *composite key,* simply because it is made up of more than one column. So you either have a composite key (more than one column) or a single-column key.

What Is an Index?

You create an *index* to specify lookup columns. With many DBMSs you don't have to create an index for primary or foreign keys, because primary and foreign keys are automatically created as indexes to your tables. When you create an index, it's usually much faster to search for a value in the column(s) that makes up the index. There is some overhead when you create an index, but if you're careful when selecting the columns you want to use in indexes, the advantages outweigh the disadvantages.

The overhead results in extra disk space consumption and a slight performance penalty when adding or editing rows. Sometimes you need to try out an index and do some performance testing to see if you'll gain or lose performance by implementing it. One candidate for an index is the Name column in a Customer table. You can't use it as a primary key column, as it more than likely will be duplicated because many people have the same names. However, you'll probably need to look up a customer using his or her name, as he or she might not remember his or her customer ID (which could be the primary key) if the customer gives you a call.

What Is Data Integrity?

Data integrity ensures that the content of a database can be "trusted." A database should always be in a consistent state. In other words, data integrity means that no data is outdated or orphaned because of updates to related data. Data integrity can be ensured by checking for one or more of the following:

- Entity integrity

- Referential integrity

- Domain integrity

What Is Entity Integrity?

Entity integrity states that no value in a primary key can be null. This goes for composite primary keys as well as single-column primary keys. Since primary keys must be unique, they must not be allowed to contain null values, and hence you should apply entity integrity when designing your database. Mind you, most DBMSs won't allow you to create primary keys that allow null values.

What Is Referential Integrity?

Referential integrity has to do with relationships. Referential integrity ensures that no row in a child table has a foreign key that doesn't exist as a primary key in the parent table. This means that when you enforce referential integrity, you can't add a row to the child table with a foreign key that doesn't match a primary key in the parent table.

Depending on whether you specify restrictions or cascades when you set up referential integrity, the behavior in Table 2-4 is applied. A *cascade* refers to the process whereby related tables are updated when you update or delete a row in a parent table.

Table 2-4. Referential Integrity Behavior

Task	Cascade	Restriction
Delete a row in a parent table for which there are related rows in a child table.	The related rows in the child table are also deleted.	The deletion is disallowed.
Update/change the primary key of a row in a parent table for which there are related rows in a child table.	The related rows in the child table are also updated.	The update/change is disallowed.

Referential integrity ensures that no row in a child table is *orphaned,* that is, has no related record in the parent table. There are two kinds of referential integrity: declarative integrity and procedural integrity.

What Is Declarative Referential Integrity?

Declarative referential integrity (DRI) is the easiest to implement, because you simply define what action to take at the time of creating your relationships. This means that you tell the DBMS to either restrict or cascade an update or deletion to tables that have a relationship. SQL Server 2000 was the first version of Microsoft SQL Server to support cascading DRI.

What Is Procedural Referential Integrity?

Procedural referential integrity (PRI) is when you create procedures in your database, or even in components handling your database access, that manage your referential integrity. This is normally handled by triggers that are invoked either before or after an update to a table in your database. See Chapter 18 for more information about triggers.

Procedural referential integrity gives you more control over how updates and deletions to your tables are handled, because you can specify just about any action in your triggers. However, using procedural referential integrity also means more work for you, because you need to program these triggers yourself, whereas DRI is handled by the DBMS.

What Is Domain Integrity?

Domain integrity ensures that values in a particular column conform to the domain description in place, meaning that values in the column must match a particular format and/or data type. Domain integrity is ensured through physical and logical constraints applied to a specific column. When you try to add an invalid value to a column with domain constraints, the value will be disallowed. Such a domain constraint could be applied to a Phone Number column in the Customers table, as follows:

- Physical constraint: data type: string, length: 13

- Logical constraint: input format: (999) 9999999

What Is Normalization?

Normalization is a process that can be applied to relational database design. *Normalization* is a method of data analysis you can use when you're designing your database. The normalization process, which is a series of progressive sets of rules, can be referred to as *normal forms*. A "progressive set of rules" means that one rule builds upon the previous rule and adds new restrictions. Think of it like this: The first rule states that a value must be of type integer. The second rule enforces the first rule, but it also adds another restriction: The value must be 5 or higher. The third rule enforces first and second rules and adds the restriction that the maximum value is 1500, and so on. (I'm sure you get the idea.)

Anyway, the purpose of normalization is to define tables, which you can modify with predictable results, and thus ensure data integrity with minimal maintenance. A "predictable result" means that no data inconsistency and/or redundancy occur when you modify the data. Inconsistency is when, for example, you update a value in one place and that value isn't updated in another place where it's referenced. Redundancy is, generally speaking, when you have some data that's duplicated. The normal forms were defined in the 1970s to overcome problems with table relations. These problems are also called *anomalies*.

What Are the Normal Forms?

The *normal forms* are a progressive set of rules that should be applied to your database design beginning with the First Normal Form, then the Second Normal Form, and so on. (The various form levels are discussed later in this section.) Mind you, not all of the normal forms have to be applied to your database design. I would think that a lot of databases out there that have been normalized only adhere to the first three normal forms. I believe it's up to you as a database designer to pull the plug on the process, once you feel you've achieved your goal.

NOTE   I had a hard time understanding the normal forms when I first came across them some years ago. These days I hardly think about them when I design my databases. I just design them and they generally conform to the first three to four normal forms. Actually, if you're going to design a number of databases in your career, I can only suggest you get to know these normal forms by heart. The hard work will pay off, believe me. If you already know about normalization and generally apply it to your database design, your job for the rest of this book is to catch my mistakes!

How Do You Achieve the First Normal Form?

You can achieve the *First Normal Form* (1NF) by putting all repeating groups of data (duplicated data) into separate tables and connecting these tables using one-to-many relationships. One example of this might be if the Orders table had columns for four OrderItems, as shown in Figure 2-4.

Figure 2-4. 1NF violation

Don't tell me you never made the mistake displayed in Figure 2-4. Think back to when you were first designing databases that were effectively flat file databases—that is, databases where all data is placed in the same table or file. If you want to conform to 1NF, your table design should instead look like Figure 2-5.

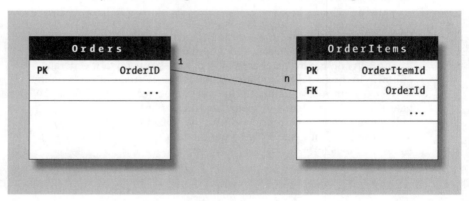

Figure 2-5. 1NF conformance

What Is the Second Normal Form?

To conform to the *Second Normal Form* (2NF), you must first conform to 1NF. Actually, 2NF only applies to tables in 1NF with composite primary keys (see the "What Is a Composite Key" FAQ earlier in this chapter). So if your database conforms to 1NF and your tables only have primary keys made up of a single column, your database automatically conforms to 2NF. However, if your table does have a composite primary key, you need to eliminate the functional dependencies on a partial key. You can achieve this by putting the violating columns into a separate table.

Functional dependencies, you say? Okay, try this: If you have an OrderItems table and it contains the columns shown in Figure 2-6, the ProductDescription column violates 2NF. 2NF is violated because the ProductDescription column only relates to the ProductId column and not the OrderId column. This means that to conform to 2NF, you will have to move the ProductDescription column to the Products table. You can use the ProductId as a lookup value to retrieve the product description.

Figure 2-6. 2NF violation

What Is the Third Normal Form?

You can achieve *Third Normal Form* (3NF) conformance by conforming to 2NF and by eliminating functional dependencies on nonkey columns. As is the case with 2NF, if you put the violating columns into a separate table, this condition is met.[3] This means all nonkey columns will then be dependent on the whole key and only the whole key.

---

3. Well, only if the same rules are applied to the new, separate table, of course.

In Figure 2-7, the Location column is not dependent on the ProductId column, which is the primary key, but instead on the Warehouse column, which is not a key. Therefore, 3NF is violated, and you should create a new Warehouse table with the Warehouse and Location columns to conform to 3NF. You can then use the Warehouse column as a lookup value to retrieve the Warehouse location.

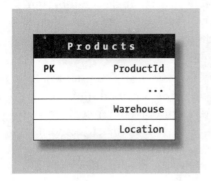

Figure 2-7. 3NF violation

 What Is the Fourth Normal Form?

If you want your database to conform to the *Fourth Normal Form* (4NF), the rows in your tables must conform to 3NF and they must have no multivalued dependencies. You can think of *multivalued dependencies* like this: A row may not contain two or more independent multivalued facts about an entity.

4NF only concerns relations that have three or more attributes, so if you don't have relations, or primary keys for that matter, with three or more attributes, your database automatically conforms to 4NF. If, however, your database does have relations with three or more attributes, you need to make sure that the primary key doesn't contain two or more independent multivalued facts about an entity. Confusing, eh? Okay, think about this:

- A customer can speak one or more languages.

- A customer can have one or more payment options.

In the example shown in Figure 2-8, you have the option of storing a payment option and a language for each customer. The only problem is that the language and the payment option are multivalued; that is, there is more than one language and more than one payment option, and the language and payment attributes are mutually independent attributes. This effectively means a single customer who speaks the languages English and Danish and has the payment options Cash On Delivery (COD) and Credit will require more than one customer row. Actually, this customer will require four rows if you need to hold all combinations (two languages × two payment options). Can you imagine the nightmare of updating all these rows once you change, say, a payment option? Another problem with this relation is that if only one row contains the value Danish in the Language column and you delete this row, what happens then? The Danish language would be lost from the database.

Figure 2-8. 4NF violation

To avoid violating 4NF as shown in Figure 2-8, you need to decompose the relation (Customers) into two separate relations (CustomerPayments and CustomerLanguages), as in Figure 2-9.

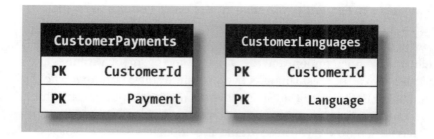

Figure 2-9. 4NF conformance

You need to conform to 4NF to make sure you don't have data redundancy and to make data updates easy.

What Is the Fifth Normal Form?

The first four normal forms all relate to functional dependence, but the *Fifth Normal Form* (5NF) relates to join dependence. *Join dependence* means that when a table has been decomposed into three or more smaller tables, these smaller tables can be joined to form the original table.

Rows in your tables conform to 5NF when the information contained in the rows can't be reconstructed from several smaller rows (each row has fewer columns than the original row). This means that the information in a table can't be decomposed into smaller tables without them having the same key.

5NF is not much different from 4NF, and many experts believe that tables that conform to 4NF also conform to 5NF in most cases.

Normalization Quick Round-Up

- *First Normal Form Test:* Can any attribute on a single table have multiple values? If so, flatten the table into further tables.

- *Second Normal Form Test:* Is any attribute dependent on only part of the key? If so, split the relationship.

- *Third Normal Form Test:* Is any attribute dependent on another attribute that isn't a key? If so, split the relationship until all attributes are dependent on the key only.

- *Forth and Fifth Normal Form Test:* Does the relation contain independent multivalued dependencies? If so, split the relation until no independent dependencies remain.

What Is Denormalization?

Denormalization is the process of reversing normalization, usually because of poor performance as a result of the normalization process. However, there are no hard-and-fast rules for when you need to start the denormalization process. Before you start doing any normalization, you can benchmark your current system and establish a baseline. When you're done with the normalization, you can again benchmark your system to see if any performance has been gained or lost. If the performance loss is too great, like when you have too many joins nested too deep, you start the denormalization process, where you reverse one or more of the changes you made in the normalization process, one at a time. It's very important that you only reverse one such change at a time in order to test for possible performance gains after every change.

Generally, you start with a properly normalized database model and realize that you need to join six tables to get the result set(s) you need! That can be and often is far too slow, which means you have to break the rules (denormalize). So, the point is that you break the rules to speed up performance and risk creating associated maintenance issues.

Denormalization is also an important aspect to keep in mind when your database matures, because performance is most often degraded when you start adding data to your database.

If you want to know more about normalization and denormalization, I can recommend reading this book:

> *Fundamentals of Database Systems, Third Edition,* by Ramez Elmasri and Shamkant Navathe. Addison-Wesley. ISBN: 0805317554.

It's a very theoretical book, but there's a lot to be learned from it, if you feel that's the way you want to go.

UserMan Database Schema

The UserMan example application that I build on throughout this book will feature a database, of course. The schema for this SQL Server database is shown in Figure 2-10.

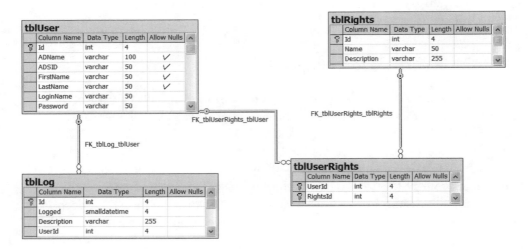

Figure 2-10. UserMan database schema

As you can see in Figure 2-10, the database includes four tables:

- *tblUser:* This is the main table that holds all standard information about a user, such as first name, last name, and so on.

- *tblUserRights:* This is a link table that resolves the many-to-many relationship between the tblUser and tblRights tables.

- *tblRights:* This table holds the various rights a user can be assigned in the system, which could allow a user to create a new user, delete an existing user, and so on.

- *tblLog:* The log table holds information on when a user did what. Let's keep those users under tight control!

Exercise

Examine the UserMan database schema and see if you can find a way to improve the design according to the various design tools I've covered in this chapter.

As stated before, I'll be working on this database throughout this book, and in the final chapter I'll give you ideas on how to extend the current schema and the sample application.

UserMan Database Conforms to 5NF

The UserMan database conforms to 5NF, but how can you tell? Figure 2-10 shows you the database schema with the four tables. Let's check the normal forms one by one and see if the UserMan database really does conform to 5NF.

- *1NF:* All repeating groups of data have been put into separate tables.
- *2NF:* Only the tblUserRights table has a composite primary key, but this table is a link table and therefore doesn't hold any "real" data. Basically, the absence of nonkey columns means that you don't have any functional dependencies on a partial key.
- *3NF:* All nonkey fields in the tables relate to the primary key.
- *4NF:* The UserMan database has doesn't have any relations or primary keys with three or more attributes; thus, no multivalued dependencies exist.
- *5NF:* None of tables can be further decomposed without using the same key—or can they?

Summary

This chapter explained databases, why you should use them, and how you should design them. I briefly outlined the differences between a relational database and a hierarchical database. Then I discussed designing a relational database, and I showed you most of the concepts involved in building a relational database, such as the normal forms, keys (primary and foreign), the various types of relationships between tables and how to implement them logically, and indexes. I also covered data integrity in the form of entity, referential, and domain integrity.

The last section of this chapter detailed the database schema for the UserMan sample application. I'll be working with this database throughout the book.

The following chapter takes you on a journey through most of the classes in ADO.NET and explains how to use them.

Part Two

ADO.NET Connected Layer Reference

CHAPTER 3

Understanding ADO.NET

THIS CHAPTER IS a lead-in to the coming chapters in Parts Two and Three of this book. Basically, this chapter will compare, in overview, the differences and similarities between Active Data Objects (ADO) and Active Data Objects.NET (ADO.NET), and tell you the differences between the two layers of ADO.NET:

- The connected layer

- The disconnected layer

The various classes in ADO.NET can be categorized into either of these two groups, where the connected layer is provider specific, meaning you need to use a .NET Data Provider that supports your database, whereas the disconnected layer can be used with all of the .NET Data Providers. See Chapter 4 for more information on data providers.

Simply put, you can use the disconnected layer if you don't need to access a data source and really just want to work with temporary data, or data that is being read and written to XML streams or files. If you need to retrieve data from, insert data into, update data in, or delete data from a data source, you need to use the connected layer. However, most often you'll be using classes from both layers, as you'll see from the chapters in Parts Two and Three of the book, and the corresponding example code.

The fact that ADO.NET is split into two layers makes it very different from previous versions of ADO, which are based on a connected architecture. For some years now, ADO has been the preferred interface for accessing various data sources, with ADO 2.7 being the latest version of this data access technology. This is especially true for Visual Basic programmers, who started out with Data Access Objects (DAO) in the mid-1990s, followed by Remote Data Objects (RDO), which was based on the Open Database Connectivity (ODBC) data access technology. Then in the late 1990s came ADO, which was and still is based on OLE DB. See Chapter 4 for more information on OLE DB.

With the advent of ADO.NET and VS .NET, this technology is no longer just for Visual Basic programmers.[1] Many other programmers using programming languages, like C#, can finally use ADO(.NET) as well. ADO.NET has been designed from the ground up to be a disconnected and distributed data access technology based on XML, and therefore has very little in common with ADO, which is COM based, but the common support of OLE DB. This fits very well into the new, Microsoft strategy of making it run on every platform that supports XML. It also means that you can easily pass ADO.NET data sets from one location to another over the Internet, because ADO.NET or rather the underlying protocols, XML and SOAP, can penetrate firewalls.

ADO vs. ADO.NET

This book refers to both of these data access technologies. Here is how you can distinguish one from the other:

- *ADO* will be used to describe the ADO technology that has been with us for some years now. This technology is COM-based and can only be used through COM Interop. This data access technology is also referred to as "classic" ADO.

- *ADO.NET* is a new version of ADO based entirely on the .NET Framework, and the underlying technology is very different from the COM-based ADO. Although the name ADO is still there, these are different technologies.

However, as you probably know, ADO is still here, although it requires COM Interop (interoperability) if you want to use it from within the .NET Framework. You will get a chance to look at COM Interop in Appendix B, but you can also try these books from Apress that cover COM Interop:

- *Moving to Visual Basic.NET: Strategies, Concepts, and Code* by Dan Appleman. Apress, June 2001. ISBN 1-893115-97-6.

- *COM and .NET Interoperability* by Andrew Troelsen. Apress, April 2002. ISBN 1-59059-011-2.

ADO.NET is what you will be using in most, if not all, of your .NET applications, because of its disconnected architecture. However, you should keep in mind that ADO.NET is firmly targeted at n-tier applications, or applications that are distributed

---

1. ADO has been available to programmers other than VB programmers, but it has never been as easy to use for them as it was for VB programmers.

over a number of different servers. This doesn't mean that you can't use it to build n-tier or client-server solutions for the Windows platform, but it does mean that you should still look into using good old ADO as well, before you make a decision on what data access technology you want to use. Please note that it's possible and perfectly legitimate to use both technologies in your applications, if you so desire or even need to; one technology doesn't rule out the other.

You will get a look at ADO as well as ADO.NET in Parts Two and Three of this book, but I will not be covering ADO in the same detail as ADO.NET. If you need more information on ADO, try these books from Apress:

- *Serious ADO: Universal Data Access with Visual Basic,* by Rob Macdonald. Apress, August 2000. ISBN 1-893115-19-4.

- *ADO.NET and ADO Examples and Best Practices for VB Programmers, Second Edition*, by William R. Vaughn. Apress, February 2002. ISBN 1-893115-68-2.

The overall object model looks the same for ADO and ADO.NET: In order to access a data source, you need a data provider. A *data provider* is really another word for driver, and it's simply a library that can access the data source in binary form. See Chapter 4 for more details. Once you have the data provider, you need to set up a connection from your application that uses the data provider to gain access to the data source. Chapter 5 explains the connection class. See Figure 3-1 for a simplified picture. Now that the connection is set up and opened, you can execute queries and retrieve, delete, manipulate, and update data from the data source.

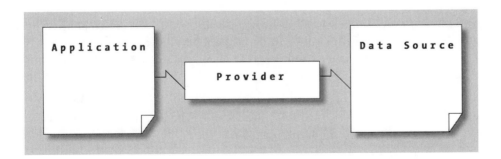

Figure 3-1. How a data provider works

You need data objects in order to manipulate data. These data objects will be explained in detail in the following chapters.

NOTE Most of the code listings in Parts Two and Three of this book are based on the SQL Server .NET Data Provider. However, the example code that can be downloaded from Apress (http://www.apress.com) or from the UserMan site (http://www.userman.dk) also shows you how to do it using the OLE DB .NET Data Provider and the ODBC .NET Data Provider. Basically, this means that you can use the example code to access the following data sources and more: SQL Server, MS Access, Oracle 8i and later, MySQL 3.23.51 and later, plus many more. Examples for the mentioned DBMSs can be found in the example code.

Data-Related Namespaces

There are a number of namespaces in the .NET Framework that are of interest when dealing with data (see Table 3-1). These namespaces hold the various data classes that you must import into your code in order to use the classes.

Table 3-1. Data-Related Namespaces

Namespace	Description
System.Data	Holds the disconnected ADO.NET classes, like the **DataSet** and **DataTable** classes, and other miscellaneous generic classes, or classes that are subclassed in the .NET data providers. These classes are explained in Part Three of this book.
System.Data.SqlClient	Holds the classes specific to MS SQL Server 7.0 or later. This is the SQL Server.NET Data Provider. This provider and related classes are explained in the following chapters.
System.Data.OleDb	Holds the collection of classes that are used for accessing an OLE DB data source. This is the OLE DB .NET Data Provider. This provider and related classes are explained in the following chapters.
Microsoft.Data.Odbc	Holds the collection of classes that are used for accessing an Open Database Connectivity (ODBC) data source. This is the ODBC .NET Data Provider.[a] This provider and related classes are explained in the following chapters.

a. The ODBC .NET Data Provider is a separate download and it's not included in the VS .NET package. Well, at least not at the time of writing this (September 2002). For the latest version of the download, please look here: http://www.microsoft.com/data.

CROSS-REFERENCE   If you are uncertain about what a namespace really is, see Chapter 1.

You can import namespaces into a class in your code with the **Imports** statement, like this:

```
Imports System.Data
```

Instead of importing the namespaces, you can prefix the classes when declaring and/or instantiating your objects, like this:

```
Dim cnnUserMan As System.Data.SqlClient.SqlConnection' Declare new connection
cnnUserMan = New System.Data.SqlClient.SqlConnection() " Instantiate connection
```

In the following chapters you can see exactly what classes the namespaces contain, what the classes do, and when and how you use them.

Summary

This chapter was a brief introduction to the two layers of ADO.NET:

- The connected layer

- The disconnected layer

Basically, this chapter is a lead-in to the chapters in Parts Two and Three of this book, which cover these two layers of ADO.NET. This chapter briefly discussed when you should one choose layer over the other, and why in most cases it's advisable to use classes from both layers.

You also saw how the various classes of ADO.NET are split into different namespaces; one for the disconnected layer, and several for the connected layer, with each namespace representing a .NET Data Provider.

The coming chapter explains what a data provider is and how it fits in with ADO.NET.

CHAPTER 4

Looking at
Data Providers

A *DATA PROVIDER* IS simply just another phrase for driver, meaning it's a binary library that exposes an API that can be called from within your application. The library is a DLL file, and sometimes this DLL is dependent on other DLLs, so in fact a data provider can be made up of several files. The data providers and drivers discussed here are called *OLE DB providers* and *ODBC drivers,* and they can be accessed directly. However, when you use VB .NET, you won't be accessing the OLE DB providers or ODBC drivers directly, but instead you'll be using the ADO.NET classes that wrap the API exposed by the provider or driver library. So, you don't have to worry about this low-level kind of programming. All you need to do is specify the name of the provider when you set up or open a connection.

OLE DB is really a specification that is used by OLE DB providers, and the primary purpose of an OLE DB provider is to translate OLE DB instructions into the language of the data source and vice versa. The same can be said about ODBC; it's a specification used by the native ODBC drivers for translating ODBC instructions into the language of the data source and vice versa.

There's one important distinction between ADO and ADO.NET: ADO calls the OLE DB provider using COM, whereas ADO.NET uses the DataAdapter class, which then calls the OLE DB provider or the ODBC driver through COM Interop; Figure 4-1 highlights the latter. Actually, sometimes the DataAdapter object directly accesses the API exposed by the DBMS, as can be the case with Microsoft SQL Server 7.0 or later (see Figure 4-2). The .NET Data Provider for SQL Server uses a private protocol named tabular data stream (TDS) to talk to SQL Server. This means that if you're using ADO.NET and the OLE DB .NET Data Provider, the connected layer is using COM to access the OLE DB provider. However, you should note that the disconnected layer, which is discussed in Part Three, doesn't use COM at all, even if COM Interop is used for talking to the OLE DB provider.

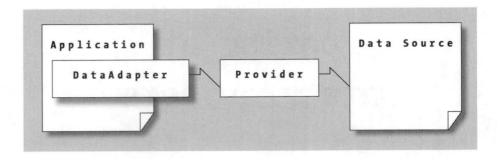

Figure 4-1. DataAdapter using an OLE DB provider to access the data source

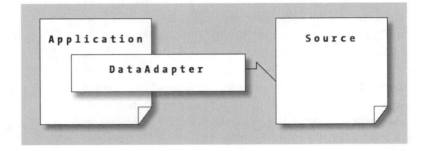

Figure 4-2. DataAdapter accessing the data source directly

 NOTE In ADO you can also access ODBC data sources, but this is done through the OLE DB ODBC provider, therefore you have to go through three layers (ADO, OLE DB, ODBC) in order to access your ODBC data.

If you know at compile time that you have a .NET Data Provider for one of the data sources you need to connect to, then use that provider, because it has been optimized for that specific data source. If on the other hand you are creating a generic data wrapper to be used when you don't know the data sources you will be connecting to at runtime, go with the generic OLE DB .NET Data Provider. The ODBC .NET Data Provider is for accessing ODBC data sources exclusively and can only be used in cases where you have the appropriate ODBC driver.

The OLE DB providers listed in Table 4-1 work with the OLE DB .NET Data Provider. See the ".NET Data Providers" section later in this chapter for details. This list is far from exhaustive, but it does show you which current Microsoft OLE DB providers are compatible with the OLE DB .NET Data Provider.

Table 4-1. OLE DB Providers Compatible with the OLE DB .NET Data Provider

Provider Name	Description
SQLOLEDB	Use with Microsoft SQL Server 6.5 or earlier
MSDAORA	Use with Oracle version 7 and later
Microsoft.Jet.OLEDB.4.0	Use with JET databases (MS Access)

In Table 4-1, the SQLOLEDB data provider is listed as good for connecting to Microsoft SQL Server 6.5 or earlier. However, it can also connect to SQL Server 7.0 or later, but because the SQL Server .NET Data Provider is an optimized data provider for these RDBMSs, I highly recommend you use that one instead.

The OLE DB .NET Data Provider doesn't support OLE DB version 2.5 interfaces or earlier, which also means that you need to install Microsoft Data Access Components (MDAC) 2.6 or later on your system. However, MDAC 2.7 is distributed and installed along with VS .NET.

NOTE   One thing you should note about MDAC 2.6 and later is that the Microsoft.Jet.OLEDB.4.0 provider is no longer distributed with MDAC. So, if you want to use the Microsoft.Jet.OLEDB.4.0 provider to access your Microsoft Access databases, you'll need to have installed MDAC 2.5 or earlier or otherwise install the provider yourself. Check out http://www.microsoft.com/data/download.htm for downloading MDAC.

Specifying a Provider or Driver When Connecting from Code

There are several ways to open or set up a connection from code, but here is one way of specifying what provider or driver you want to use:

```
cnnUserMan.ConnectionString = "Provider=SQLOLEDB;Data Source=USERMANPC;" & _
  "User ID=UserMan;Password=userman;Initial Catalog=UserMan;"
```

In the **ConnectionString** property of the connection cnnUserMan (declared and instantiated elsewhere, obviously), specify that you want to use the SQL Server provider (Provider=SQLOLEDB). See the "ConnectionString Property" section in Chapter 5. Here you can see how to set up an ODBC connection string:

```
cnnUserMan.ConnectionString = "DRIVER={SQL Server};SERVER=USERMANPC;" & _
  "UID=UserMan;PWD=userman;DATABASE=UserMan;"
```

The two connection strings are used for connecting to the same data source, the SQL Server by the name of USERMANPC, using the UserMan user credentials (userman as password) to the UserMan database.

.NET Data Providers

.NET Data Providers are a core part of the new ADO.NET programming model. Although a .NET Data Provider loosely maps to an OLE DB provider, it's in fact a lot closer to the ADO object model. This is because the OLE DB and ADO layers have been merged in the .NET Framework, giving the .NET Data Providers higher performance. The higher performance results from the fact that when using ADO.NET, you are effectively using only one layer as compared to using the ADO layer connected to the OLE DB layer. Nearly the same can be said about the ODBC .NET Data Provider, but this is even more of a "merger," because with ADO you also have the OLE DB provider and the ODBC driver to pass through when connecting to an ODBC data source.

Another way of looking at this is that previously you would tinker directly with the low-level OLE DB or ODBC API only if you really knew what you were doing. The reason for doing so was higher performance. No more, my friend! Now you have ADO.NET with its high-level programming interface, exposed by the ADO.NET object model, and yet you get the same performance as using OLE DB or ODBC directly. Isn't that great? Okay, before you start celebrating too much, let me make one final point: OLE DB and ODBC as specifications expose a data source in a rich way—that is, they expose all the functionality of all the various types of data sources out there, whereas .NET Data Providers expose minimal functionality. So OLE DB, or ODBC for that matter, isn't likely to disappear anytime soon, and as such will only be replaced by .NET Data Providers in the context of disconnected and distributed data access.

A .NET Data Provider actually consists of the following four data classes:

- Connection

- DataAdapter

- Command

- DataReader

These classes are discussed in detail in the following chapters. The .NET Data Provider is the first of two layers that compose the ADO.NET object model. This first layer is also called the *connected layer*, and the other layer is surprisingly called the *disconnected layer.* The disconnected layer is the **DataSet** class and related classes. See Chapter 9 for more information on the **DataSet** class.

Third-Party .NET Data Providers

It's only a matter of time before there is a .NET Data Provider for almost any recognized and commonly used data source. I've only had the privilege of trying out one of these, dbProvider, the.NET Data Provider for the MySQL Database. In this book, I cover the use of the ODBC .NET Data Provider to connect to a MySQL database, but minimal testing has convinced me that the dbProvider .NET Data Provider is more efficient than using ODBC, which it should be. Although I don't cover this .NET Data Provider in the book, I have created provider-specific procedures for all the listings in the book. Please see the example code.

In the following sidebar, you'll find the official description for the dbProvider .NET Data Provider.

---

dbProvider .NET Data Provider

dbProvider is the managed .NET Provider to the MySQL Database, serving a similar role as Microsoft's **SqlClient** and **OleDb** namespaces. Before dbProvider, developers accessing a MySQL database were forced to go through the ODBC drivers or OLEDB providers, which have had reliability and performance issues. With dbProvider, a direct, high-performance connection is created to MySQL. No more ODBC DSN hassles, no more OLEDB performance hits, no more buggy drivers or providers.

The dbProvider provider implements the full Microsoft ADO.NET Provider interface. To users accustomed to the SQL Server .NET Data Provider or the OLE DB .NET Data Provider, dbProvider will require very little learning time.

The following ADO.NET classes are implemented:

- *MySqlConnection:* The main connection to the MySQL database
- *MySqlCommand:* Enables the execution of any command against the database
- *MySqlDataReader:* Provides fast, forward-only read access to the database
- *MySqlDataAdapter:* Serves as an interface between the MySQL data classes and the Microsoft **DataSet** class
- *MySqlParameter:* Used to store dynamic parameters for a command
- *MySqlTransaction:* Used to represent a MySQL transaction

Samples are provided with the dbProvider release that show the proper way to interact with the classes, but almost any Microsoft example can be used by simply changing any **System.Data.SqlClient** objects to objects from the **eInfoDesigns.dbProvider** namespace.

dbProvider is developed and supported by eInfoDesigns, and can be found at `http://www.einfodesigns.com`.

In addition to the official description of the dbProvider .NET Data Provider, I'd like to add that converting the SQL Server .NET Data Provider–specific example code that accompanies this book only took me about 20 minutes, and it works like a charm. However, because of lack of time, I haven't been able to do some proper testing of the provider. This means that if you work with a MySQL database, I recommend you do try it out, because you won't regret it. However, I am not endorsing the product.

I've found the following problem: no support for nested transactions. Matt Culbreth of eInfoDesigns has told me that this will be supported at a later date. You can find specific information about this at the eInfoDesigns Web site.

Summary

This chapter was an introduction to data providers or drivers, in the form of OLE DB providers, ODBC drivers, and .NET Data Providers, and how they relate to each other.

The following chapter covers the Connection and Transaction classes in ADO.NET.

CHAPTER 5

Connections and Transactions

THIS CHAPTER INTRODUCES you to the Connection and Transaction classes of ADO.NET, and connections and transactions in general. I'll be making comparisons to classic ADO classes where appropriate, and you'll learn how to set up a connection using a connection string, and how to work with transactions to ensure data integrity. Tables with the properties, methods, and events of the classes discussed in this chapter can be found in Appendix C.

Connections

The Connection class is part of the .NET Data Provider. You need a connection when you want to access a data source, but if you just want to save some related data in a table, you don't actually need one. I'll cover this topic in the "Building Your Own DataTable" section in Chapter 10. I won't be discussing the ADO connection in this section, just the ADO.NET connection. From a source code point of view, the ADO connection has the same look and feel as the ADO.NET connection anyway. If you need specific information on the ADO Connection class, you may want to read one of the books mentioned at the beginning of Chapter 3.

Three of the managed connections that Microsoft provides with the .NET Framework are **OdbcConnection**, **OleDbConnection**, and **SqlConnection**. *Managed* means executed by and in the context of the common language runtime (CLR).

 CROSS-REFERENCE   See the "Common Language Runtime" section in Chapter 1 for details.

Although the **OdbcConnection** and **OleDbConnection** classes can be used with SQL Server data sources, you should use **SqlConnection** for SQL Server 7.0 or later, as it has been optimized for connecting to this specific data source. Use **OleDbConnection** or **OdbcConnection** for all other data sources, unless you can get ahold of a third-party .NET Data Provider (and thus the specific Connection class) for your specific data source.

NOTE The **OdbcConnection** class, which uses Platform Invoke, is roughly twice as fast for standard applications as the **OleDbConnection**. The latter uses COM, which is chatty, and hence has more server round-trips. So unless your application is shipping large amounts of data (hundreds of thousands of rows or more) per data request, you should at least consider using the **OdbcConnection** class. **SqlConnection** is roughly 20 percent faster than **OdbcConnection**. Please be aware that any performance comparison is subject to the bias of the person who does the comparison. The numbers stated here are based on my and my colleagues experience and testing, but it's by no means a scientific test.

OdbcConnection

You should use the managed **OdbcConnection** class to connect with all your .NET-enabled applications when you have an ODBC driver for your data source. **OleDbConnection** is useful for creating a generic data wrapper to use when you need to connect to various data sources.

OleDbConnection

Use the managed **OleDbConnection** class to connect with all your .NET-enabled applications. The **OleDbConnection** is useful for creating a generic data wrapper to use when you need to connect to various data sources. **OleDbConnection** is for establishing a connection through an OLE DB provider.

SqlConnection

The **SqlConnection** class is only for use with Microsoft SQL Server 7.0 or later. It has been specifically optimized for connecting to this particular data source, and unless you are building a generic data wrapper, I recommend always using this managed connection with your .NET-enabled applications. If you need to connect to Microsoft SQL Server 6.5 or earlier, you must use **OdbcConnection** or **OleDbConnection** instead. With SQL Server 6.5, you should also install Service Pack 5a for the ODBC drivers to work correctly. You can find the download for this service pack here: http://support.microsoft.com/default.aspx?scid=kb;EN-US;q197177.

ConnectionString Property

The **ConnectionString** property, which is similar to an OLE DB or ODBC connection string, is used for specifying the values for connecting to a data source. The connection string that is returned is the same as the user-supplied **ConnectionString**, but it doesn't hold any security information unless the **Persist Security Info** value is set to 'true'. This is also true for the password. Please note that the **Persist Security Info** value name can't be used with ODBC. This means that UID is always returned, whereas PWD is never returned in the connection string.

> **NOTE** You can set the **DSN** value in the connection string, if you need to keep the security information safe. See Table C-1 in Appendix C for more information on **DSN** values.

You can set and get this property, the default value of which is an empty string, only when the connection is closed. All values may be specified by enclosing them in single quotes or double quotes, but this is optional. All value pairs (*valuename=value*)[1] must be separated with a semicolon (;).

> **NOTE** The separator used in the **ConnectionString** property is the same at all times. Even if you are an international user who relies on different character sets, separators, and so on, you still need to use the semicolon (ANSI character 0059) as the list separator for this property!

The value names in a connection string are case insensitive, whereas some of the values, such as the value for the **Password** or **PWD** value name, may be case sensitive. Table C-1 in Appendix C lists all of the common **ConnectionString** property values. Note that only the most commonly used ODBC value names (all UPPERCASE) are listed, so please check the documentation for your specific ODBC driver.

Many of the **ConnectionString** property values have corresponding properties, such as the **ConnectionTimeout** property, that you can read separately (see the upcoming "Connection Class Properties" section for more details). The corresponding properties are set when you set the **ConnectionString** property.

When you set the connection string, it will be parsed immediately, which means that syntax errors will be caught straight away, and an exception will be

---

1. Value pairs are sometimes referred to as Named Value Pairs (NVP).

thrown. Only syntax errors are caught at this time, as other errors are found only when you try to open the connection.

Once you open the connection, the validated connection string is returned as part of the Connection object, with properties updated. Mind you, if you don't set the **Persist Security Info** value (which can't be used with ODBC) or if you set it to 'false', then sensitive information will *not* be returned in the **ConnectionString**. The same goes for value names with default values; they are not returned in the connection string. This is important to know, if you want to examine the **ConnectionString** property after it has been set.

If you set a value more than once in the **ConnectionString** property, only the last occurrence of the *valuename=value* pair counts. Actually, the exact opposite is true for ODBC connection strings, where it's the first occurrence that counts. In addition, if you use one of the synonyms, like **Pwd** instead of **Password**, the "official" value name will be returned (**Password** in this case).

Finally, white space is stripped from values and from between value names, unless you use single quotes or double quotes to delimit the values, in which case the white space counts!

Listing 5-1 shows you some examples of common connection strings that are grouped by the server they connect to, and the .NET Data Provider used (see Table C-1 in Appendix C for more information on the various value names).

Listing 5-1. Common Connection Strings

```
' ODBC .NET Data Provider connection strings, connecting to the USERMANPC
' SQL Server.
"DRIVER={SQL Server};SERVER=USERMANPC;" & _
    "User ID=UserMan;Password=userman;Initial Catalog=UserMan"
"DRIVER={SQL Server};SERVER=USERMANPC;" & _
    "UID=UserMan;PWD=userman;Initial Catalog=UserMan"
"DRIVER={SQL Server};SERVER=USERMANPC;" & _
    "UID=UserMan;PWD=userman;DATABASE=UserMan"


' ODBC .NET Data Provider connection strings, connecting to the UserMan.mdb
' MS Access database. No security has been implemented
"DRIVER={Microsoft Access Driver (*.mdb)};DBQ=C:\DBPWVBNET\UserMan.mdb;"
"DRIVER={Microsoft Access Driver (*.mdb)};DBQ=C:\DBPWVBNET\UserMan.mdb;" & _
    "FIL=MS Access;"
"DSN=UserMan;" ' You need to create a DSN pointing to the UserMan.mdb


' ODBC .NET Data Provider connection strings, connecting to the USERMANPC
' MySQL Server with IP Address 10.8.1.30
"DRIVER={MySQL};SERVER=10.8.1.30;UID=UserMan;PWD=userman;DATABASE=UserMan"
```

```
"DRIVER={MySQL};SERVER=10.8.1.30;UID=UserMan;PWD=userman;"
   "Initial Catalog=UserMan"
"DRIVER={MySQL};SERVER=USERMANPC;UID=UserMan;PWD=userman;DATABASE=UserMan"


' ODBC .NET Data Provider connection strings, connecting to the USERMANPC
' IBM DB2 Server with IP Address 10.8.1.30
"DRIVER={IBM DB2 ODBC DRIVER};PWD=userman;UID=USERMAN;DBALIAS=USERMAN;"


' ODBC .NET Data Provider connection strings, connecting to the USERMAN
' Oracle Server
"DRIVER={Microsoft ODBC for Oracle};PWD=userman;UID=USERMAN;SERVER=USERMAN;"


' OLE DB .NET Data Provider connection strings, connecting to the UserMan.mdb
' MS Access database. No security has been implemented,  hence the blank
' user id and password
"Provider=Microsoft.Jet.OLEDB.4.0;Data Source=C:\DBPWVBNET\UserMan.mdb;" & _
   "User Id=;Password=;Mode=Share Deny None;"
"Provider=Microsoft.Jet.OLEDB.4.0;Data Source=C:\DBPWVBNET\UserMan.mdb;" & _
   "Mode=Share Deny None;"


' OLE DB .NET Data Provider connection strings, connecting to the USERMAN
' Oracle database
"Provider=MSDAORA;Password=userman;User ID=USERMAN;Data Source=USERMAN;"


' OLE DB .NET Data Provider connection strings, connecting to the USERMAN
' DB2 database
"Provider=IBMDADB2;Password=userman;User ID=USERMAN;Data Source=USERMAN;"


' OLE DB .NET Data Provider connection strings, connecting to the USERMANPC
' SQL server. Except for the Provider value name, it's the same as using
' value names for the SQL Server .NET Data Provider
"Provider=SQLOLEDB;Data Source=USERMANPC;"User ID=UserMan;" & _
   "Password=userman;Initial Catalog=UserMan"


' SQL Server .NET Data Provider connection strings, connecting to the USERMANPC
' server with IP Address 10.1.1.1
"Data Source=USERMANPC;User ID=UserMan;Password=userman;Initial Catalog=UserMan"
"Server=USERMANPC;User ID=UserMan;Password=userman;Initial Catalog=UserMan"
"Addr=USERMANPC;User ID=UserMan;Password=userman;Initial Catalog=UserMan"
"Address=10.1.1.1;User ID=UserMan;Password=userman;Initial Catalog=UserMan"
"Network Address=10.1.1.1;User ID=UserMan;Password=userman;" & _
   "Initial Catalog=UserMan"
"Address=10.1.1.1;User ID=UserMan;Password=userman;Database=UserMan"
"Address=10.1.1.1;User ID=UserMan;Pwd=userman;Database=UserMan"
"Address=10.1.1.1;UID=UserMan;Pwd=userman;Database=UserMan"
```

The connection strings shown all connect to a UserMan database, using the UserMan user ID, and userman password, except for the Microsoft Access UserMan.mdb database that hasn't had security implemented.

The first group employs the ODBC .NET Data Provider that uses the SQL Server ODBC Driver ({SQL Server}), specified with the **DRIVER** value name, to connect to SQL Server.

The second group employs the ODBC .NET Data Provider that uses the Microsoft Access Driver ({Microsoft Access Driver (*.mdb)}), specified with the **DRIVER** value name, to connect to the Microsoft Access UserMan.mdb. If you want to use the last connection string, you must make sure there's an ODBC Data Source Name (DSN) on your system with the UserMan that connects to the UserMan.mdb. You can do this with the ODBC Data Source Administrator application. (See Figure 5-2 later in this chapter.)

The third group employs the ODBC .NET Data Provider that uses the MySQL ODBC 2.5 Driver ({MySQL}), specified with the **DRIVER** value name, to connect to the MySQL USERMAN database. You can download the driver from http://www.mysql.com.

The fourth group employs the ODBC .NET Data Provider that uses the IBM DB2 ODBC Driver ({IBM DB2 ODBC DRIVER}), specified with the **DRIVER** value name, to connect to the DB2 USERMAN database. Please note the use of the driver-specific **DBALIAS** value name, which is identical to the generic **DATABASE** and **SERVER** value names, or the **DSN** value name, used in other ODBC connection strings. Unless you specify a different alias for your database, the alias is the same as the database name.

The fifth group employs the ODBC .NET Data Provider that uses the Microsoft Oracle ODBC Driver ({Microsoft ODBC for Oracle}), specified with the **DRIVER** value name, to connect to the Oracle USERMAN database.

The sixth group employs the OLE DB .NET Data Provider that uses the Microsoft.Jet.OLEDB.4.0 OLE DB Provider, specified with the **Provider** value name, to connect to the Microsoft Access UserMan.mdb.

The seventh group employs the OLE DB .NET Data Provider that uses the MSDAORA Provider, specified with the **Provider** value name, to connect to the USERMAN Oracle database. You need to install and configure the Oracle client tools on the machine from which you want to connect to the Oracle server. Please check the Oracle documentation for information on how to do this.

The eighth group employs the OLE DB .NET Data Provider that uses the IBMDADB2 Provider, specified with the **Provider** value name, to connect to the USERMAN DB2 database. You need to install and configure the DB2 client tools on the machine from which you want to connect to the DB2 server. Please check the IBM DB2 documentation for information on how to do this.

The ninth group employs the OLE DB .NET Data Provider that uses the SQLOLEDB OLE DB Provider, specified with the **Provider** value name, to connect to SQL Server. Only one example is shown in this group, as the useable value names are the same as those for the SQL Server .NET Data Provider.

The last group uses the SQL Server .NET Data Provider, which means you don't have to, or rather can't, specify the **Provider** value name.

> **NOTE**   You can see from Listing 5-1 that SQL Server, or rather the Microsoft drivers and providers, recognizes most OLE DB and ODBC value names, even if they're not SQL Server specific.

Connection Class Properties

Instead of reading the **ConnectionString** property, you can actually get the various values individually by using their corresponding properties. Tables C-2, C-3, and C-4 in Appendix C list the public, noninherited Connection class properties in alphabetical order.

All of the properties, with the exception of the **ConnectionString** property, are read-only. You can see how the various properties are used in the various listings in this chapter.

Connection Class Methods

Tables C-5, C-6, and C-7 in Appendix C list the public methods of the Connection class. Methods inherited from classes other than the base classes, like **Object**, are not shown. These tables are only reference lists, so if you need information on how to use the methods, such as how to open a connection, then refer to the explanations in the coming sections. See the "Handling Connection and Transaction Exceptions" section later in this chapter for details on handling exceptions that can be thrown when working with the Connection class.

Connection Class Events

All three Connection classes covered in this chapter, **OdbcConnection**, **OleDbConnection**, and **SqlConnection**, expose the same events, and the noninherited events are shown in Table C-8 in Appendix C.

Opening a Connection

Once you have set the properties required to open a connection, it's time to actually open it. This is quite simple if you've set the connection properties correctly. See Listing 5-2 for an example.

Listing 5-2. Opening a Connection

```
1 Public Sub OpenConnection()
2    ' Declare connection object
3    Dim cnnUserMan As SqlConnection
4
5    ' Instantiate the connection object
6    cnnUserMan = New SqlConnection()
7
8    Try
9    ' Set up connection string
10   cnnUserMan.ConnectionString = PR_STR_CONNECTION_STRING
11      ' Open the connection
12      cnnUserMan.Open()
13   Catch objE As Exception
14      ' Deal with exception
15   End Try
16 End Sub
```

In Listing 5-2 you can see how simple it is to open a connection. The PR_STR_CONNECTION_STRING has been defined elsewhere; see Listing 5-1 for examples. Note that the **Open** method doesn't take any arguments, so you need to be sure that you've set the properties necessary to connect to your data source. If you haven't set all the required properties or the connection is already open, an exception is thrown, which is why the **Try . . . Catch . . . End Try** construct is there. It's generally a good idea to have the **Open** method of the Connection class in an exception handler, because any number of exceptions, such as connection time-outs, can be thrown. Any exception thrown should be dealt with in the **Catch** block (Line 14), but see the "ConnectionString Property Exceptions" section later in this chapter for more details on the possible exceptions, and Chapter 14 for more information on exception handling in general.

When you open a connection, the **StateChange** event is triggered. See the "Handling Connection State Changes" section later in this chapter for more information.

If you're using the OLE DB .NET Data Provider, you can use a Universal Data Link (UDL) file (with the extension .udl), instead of using a connection string in the form of a string defined in your code, like in Listing 5-3.

Listing 5-3. Opening a Connection Using a UDL File

```
1 Public Sub OpenConnectionUsingUDLFile()
2    ' Declare connection object
3    Dim cnnUserMan As OleDbConnection
4
5    ' Instantiate the connection object
6    cnnUserMan = New OleDbConnection()
7    ' Set up connection string
8    cnnUserMan.ConnectionString = _
9       "File Name=C:\DBPWVBNET\Chapter 05\USERMANPC.udl"
10
11   ' Open the connection
12   cnnUserMan.Open()
13 End Sub
```

In Listing 5-3, you can see how simple the connection string is, if you're using the OLE DB .NET Data Provider with a UDL file. All you need to specify in the connection string is the **File Name** value, as shown on Line 9. However, the file must exist and be valid, or an exception is thrown. UDL files are simple text files that hold the same information you normally specify in a connection string. The easiest way to create one is to create an empty text file with the .udl extension. Once created, you can double-click it and the Data Link Properties dialog box opens. This dialog box, which is shown in Figure 5-1, is the same as the one you use to specify a new data connection in the Server Explorer. You'll learn more about creating data connections in the Server Explorer in Chapter 13.

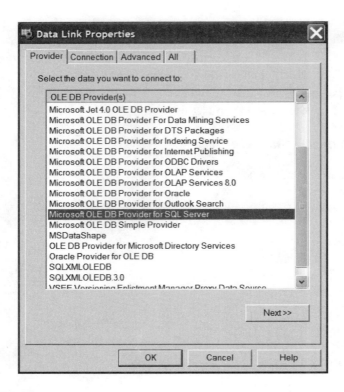

Figure 5-1. The Data Link Properties dialog box

The UDL file referenced in Listing 5-3 was created to specify a connection to SQL Server at the 10.8.1.12 IP address. The content of the file looks like this:

```
[oledb]
; Everything after this line is an OLE DB initstring
Provider=SQLOLEDB.1;Password=userman;User ID=UserMan;
   Initial Catalog=UserMan;Data Source=10.8.1.12
```

The content of the USERMANPC.udl file has been wrapped to make it look nice, but as you can see, it's really the same as an ordinary connection string.

Closing a Connection

Close a connection whenever you don't need to use it so it doesn't consume any more memory than needed. Closing a connection also returns it to the connection pool, which is the default behavior, if it belongs to one. You close a connection like this:

```
cnnUserMan.Close()
```

When you call the **Close** method, all pending transactions are rolled back. When you close a connection, the **StateChange** event is triggered. See the "Handling Connection State Changes" section later in this chapter for more information.

 NOTE No exceptions are thrown, if the connection is already closed when you try to close it.

Disposing of a Connection

You can dispose of your connection by calling the **Dispose** method, like this:

```
cnnUserMan.Dispose()
```

The **Dispose** method releases unmanaged resources used by the connection, if any, and destroys the reference to the connection, or rather indirectly tells the Garbage Collector that it can do its job and destroy the connection itself, assuming of course that this is the only reference to the connection. The **Dispose** method also closes the connection if it's open, so if you like the idea of having the minimum of code in your applications, you can call the **Dispose** method, instead of calling both the **Close** and **Dispose** methods. However, I personally think that calling both statements makes your code more readable.

Comparing Connection Objects

If you have been copying a Connection object, or setting one connection variable equal to another, it can be hard to know if two instances of a Connection class are in fact the same connection, or if they point to the same location in memory. Mind you, it isn't too difficult to find out programmatically. You can perform a comparison using the following:

- The **Is** operator

- The **Equals** method

- The **Shared ReferenceEquals** method of the **Object** class

Comparing Using the Is Operator

Using the **Is** operator is perhaps the easiest way of comparing two Connection objects:

```
blnEqual = cnnUserMan1 Is cnnUserMan2
```

The **Boolean** variable blnEqual will be set to **True** if cnnUserMan1 and cnnUserMan2 refer to the same location in memory; otherwise, it's set to **False**.

NOTE The problem with using the **Is** operator is that if both connections or objects are **Nothing**, the expression will return **True**. You should use one of the other ways of comparing your Connection objects, if that's a real possibility.

Comparing Using the Equals Method

The **Equals** method, which is inherited from the **Object** class, is actually intended to be used for comparing values and not references. When two connection variables hold a reference to the same location in memory, however, they actually hold the same "value." As such, you can use the **Equals** method for Connection object comparison. The **Equals** method comes in two flavors. One checks if the passed Connection object is equal to the Connection object that performs the method:

```
blnEqual = cnnUserMan1.Equals(cnnUserMan2)
```

The **Boolean** variable blnEqual will be set to **True** if cnnUserMan1 and cnnUserMan2 refer to the same connection; otherwise, it's set to **False**. The second, overloaded version of the method takes two Connection objects as arguments and checks if these are equal:

```
blnEqual = Object.Equals(cnnUserMan1, cnnUserMan2)
```

The **Boolean** variable blnEqual will be set to **True** if cnnUserMan1 and cnnUserMan2 refer to the same connection; otherwise, it's set to **False**. With this overloaded version of the method, you can actually compare two Connection objects separate from the Connection object performing the method. Please note that the second overloaded version of the **Equals** method is shared and as such, it must be called using the type identifier (**Object** in this case).

Comparing Using the ReferenceEquals Method

The **Shared ReferenceEquals** method of the **Object** class is for comparing references, and as such it should be preferred over the **Equals** method, which is for comparing values. Here is how you use the **ReferenceEquals** method:

```
blnEqual = Object.ReferenceEquals(cnnUserMan1, cnnUserMan2)
```

The **Boolean** variable blnEqual will be set to **True** if cnnUserMan1 and cnnUserMan2 refer to the same connection; otherwise, it's set to **False**.

 NOTE The **Equals** and the **ReferenceEquals** methods use arguments of data type **Object**. This means the comparison can be done using any data type inherited from the base type **Object**.

Manipulating the Connection State

When dealing with connections, it's often a good idea to check their state before attempting to get or set one of the properties or execute one of the methods. You can use the Connection class's **State** property to determine the current state. (See "Connection Class Properties" earlier in this chapter for details.) You check the **State** property against the **ConnectionState** enum.[2] See Table C-9 in Appendix C for a list of the members of the **ConnectionState** enum. Although Table C-9 shows you all the members of the **ConnectionState** enum, currently only the **Closed** and **Open** members are supported.

Comparing State to ConnectionState

You can compare the **State** property with the **ConnectionState** enum using the following statement:

```
If cnnUserMan.State = ConnectionState.Open Then
```

I use the = operator to perform a comparison between the two enum values. In this case I am checking if the connection is open. If you want to check if the connection is closed, you can do it like this:

```
If cnnUserMan.State = ConnectionState.Closed Then
```

---

2. It's common practice to call an enumeration in programming for an enum.

Handling Connection State Changes

If you want to handle changes to the connection state, you need to set up an event handler that can receive and process these changes. Listing 5-4 shows you how to do this.

Listing 5-4. Handling Connection State Changes

```
1 Public Class CGeneral
2    Private Const PR_STR_CONNECTION_STRING As String = _
3       "Data Source=10.8.1.12;User ID=UserMan;Password=userman;" & _
4       "Initial Catalog=UserMan"
5
6    ' Declare and instantiate connection
7    Private prcnnUserMan As SqlConnection = _
8       New SqlConnection(PR_STR_CONNECTION_STRING)
9
10   Public Sub New()
11      MyBase.New()
12      ' Set up StateChange event handler
13      AddHandler prcnnUserMan.StateChange, New _
14         StateChangeEventHandler(AddressOf OnStateChange)
15   End Sub
16
17   Private Shared Sub OnStateChange(ByVal sender As Object, _
18      ByVal args As StateChangeEventArgs)
19      ' Display the original and the current state
20      MessageBox.Show("The original connection state was: " & _
21         args.OriginalState.ToString() & vbCrLf & _
22         "The current connection state is: " & _
23         args.CurrentState.ToString())
24   End Sub
25
26   Public Sub TriggerStateChangeEvent()
27      ' Open the connection
28      prcnnUserMan.Open()
29      ' Close the connection
30      prcnnUserMan.Close()
31   End Sub
32 End Class
```

In Listing 5-4 you can see how you can capture connection state changes. On Lines 7 and 8, I declare and instantiate the connection and in the class constructor I set up the event handler (Lines 13 and 14). Lines 17 through 24 are the actual event handler procedure, which shows the two properties of the **StateChangeEventArgs** argument, **OriginalState** and **CurrentState**. Finally, Lines 26 through 31 define the procedure that triggers the state change event. The event is actually triggered twice—when you open the connection and when you close it again. You can find an example of declaring and instantiating the CGeneral class in the example code, available on the Apress Web site. The example calls the TriggerStateChangeEvent method to trigger the **StateChange** event. Listing 5-4 uses the SQL Server .NET Data Provider, but see the example code for examples using the ODBC .NET Data Provider and the OLE DB .NET Data Provider.

Pooling Connections

Connection pooling, or connection sharing and reuse between applications and components, is automatically applied to the OLE DB .NET Data Provider and the ODBC .NET Data Provider. This is important, because connection pooling will preserve resources, as the connections are being reused. Connection pooling provides a performance benefit, when the same connection is repetitively open and closed, as the last one created is still in memory. However, the SQL Server .NET Data Provider uses an implicit pooling model by default, and you can use the **ConnectionString** property to control the implicit pooling behavior of a **SqlConnection** object.

A connection pool is distinct on one count only, the **ConnectionString** property. This means that all connections in any given pool have the exact same connection string. You must also know that white space in the connection string will lead to two otherwise identical connections being added to different connection pools. White space is "extra" space characters in places where they're not needed. You can check this yourself, if you're using the SQL Server .NET Data Provider: The two instances of **SqlConnection** in Listing 5-5 will *not* be added to the same pool, because of the white space in the connection string for the cnnUserMan2 connection. There's an extra space character after the separator (semicolon) that separates the **Password** and **Data Source** value names.

*Listing 5-5. White Space in **ConnectionString** Property*

```
1 Public Sub CheckConnectionStringWhiteSpace()
2    Dim cnnUserMan1 As New SqlConnection()
3    Dim cnnUserMan2 As New SqlConnection()
4
5    Try
5       ' Set the connection string for the connections
6       cnnUserMan1.ConnectionString = "User Id=UserMan;Password=userman;" & _
7          "Data Source=USERMANPC;Initial Catalog=UserMan;" & _
8          "Max Pool Size=1;Connection Timeout=5"
9       cnnUserMan2.ConnectionString = "User Id=UserMan;Password=userman; " & _
10         "Data Source=USERMANPC;Initial Catalog=UserMan;" & _
11         "Max Pool Size=1;Connection Timeout=5"
12
13      ' cnnUserMan1 and cnnUserMan2 will NOT be added to the same connection
14      ' pool because cnnUserMan2 contains an extra space character right
15      ' after Password=userman;
16
17      ' Open the cnnUserMan1 connection
18      cnnUserMan1.Open()
19      ' Open the cnnUserMan2 connection
20      cnnUserMan2.Open()
21   Catch objE As Exception
22      ' This message will be be displayed if the two connection strings are
23      ' the same, because then the connection pool will have reached its
24      ' max size (1) If you don't see the message, the connections are
25      ' drawn from different pools
26      MsgBox(objE.Message)
27   End Try
28 End Sub
```

In Listing 5-5, the two **SqlConnection** objects (cnnUserMan1, cnnUserMan2) are not added to the same connection pool, which also means you won't see an error message, because no exception is thrown.

Pooling Connections of Data Type OdbcConnection

Although the ODBC .NET Data Provider supplies automatic pooling, you can still manually override or even disable it. Actually, the ODBC Driver Manager utility manages this, but as stated, it's applied automatically.

Disabling ODBC Connection Pooling

It's not possible to disable the automatic connection pooling from the connection string, and in fact, it's not possible by using methods or properties from the **Microsoft.Data.Odbc** namespace. However, you can manually disable it from the ODBC Data Source Administrator,[3] which is usually located under Programs ➤ Administrative Tools in the Start menu, but sometimes it can also be accessed from the Control Panel as well (see Figure 5-2).

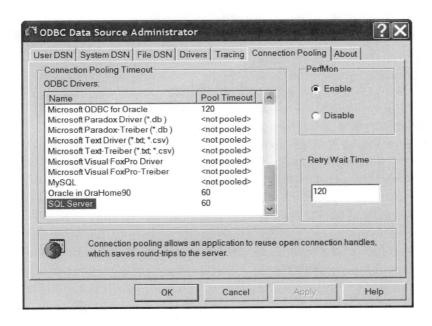

Figure 5-2. The ODBC Data Source Administrator application

In Figure 5-2, you can see the ODBC Data Source Administrator open on the Connection Pooling tab. You need to enable or disable connection pooling from this tab, and you do this on a per-driver basis: On the ODBC Drivers list, double-click the driver for which you want to change the connection pooling options. This brings up the Set Connection Pooling Attributes dialog box as shown in Figure 5-3.

---

3. The name of this utility seems to change with every version of Windows, but you can run it from the command prompt by entering its filename, which is ODBCAD32.EXE.

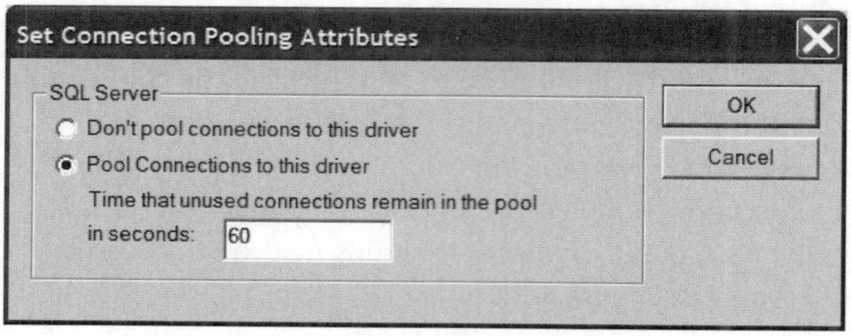

Figure 5-3. The Set Connection Pooling Attributes dialog box

In the Set Connection Pooling Attributes dialog box shown in Figure 5-3, you can disable or enable the connection pooling for the selected driver. If you enable connection pooling, you must also make sure you have set the connection lifetime, meaning how long the connection remains in the pool after being released from your application. The default is 60 seconds as shown.

You can learn more about ODBC by reading the document "ODBC Programmer's Reference" at this address: http://msdn.microsoft.com/library/default.asp?url=/ library/en-us/odbc/htm/odbcabout_this_manual.asp?frame=true.

Clearing ODBC Object Pooling

Because the connection pool is being cached when a driver is created, it's important to call the connection's **ReleaseObjectPool** method when you are done using your connection.

Using the ReleaseObjectPool Method

The **ReleaseObjectPool** method tells the connection pooler that the connection pool can be cleared when the last driver is released. You should call this method when you have closed your connection and you know you won't need the connection within the period the ODBC Driver Manager keeps pooled connections alive (see Listing 5-6).

*Listing 5-6. When to Call the **ReleaseObjectPool** Method*

```
1 ' Declare connection object
2 Dim cnnUserMan As OdbcConnection
3
4 ' Instantiate the connection object
5 cnnUserMan = New OdbcConnection(PR_STR_CONNECTION_STRING)
```

```
 6 ' Open the connection
 7 cnnUserMan.Open()
 8
 9 ' Do your stuff
10 ' ...
11
12 ' Close connection and release pool
13 cnnUserMan.Close()
14 cnnUserMan.ReleaseObjectPool()
```

Pooling Connections of Data Type OleDbConnection

Although the OLE DB .NET Data Provider supplies automatic pooling, you can still manually override or even disable it programmatically.

Disabling OLE DB Connection Pooling

It's possible to disable the automatic connection pooling if you specify the **OLE DB Services** value in your connection string. The connection in Listing 5-7 will *not* have automatic connection pooling.

Listing 5-7. Disabling Automatic OLE DB Connection Pooling

```
1 Dim cnnUserMan As OleDbConnection
2
3 ' Instantiate and open the connection
4 cnnUserMan = New OleDbConnection(PR_STR_CONNECTION_STRING & _
5    ";OLE DB Services=-4")
6 cnnUserMan.Open()
```

The example code in Listing 5-7 disables automatic connection as intended, but it also disables automatic transaction enlistment. See the "Transactions" section later in this chapter for more information on transactions. You can also disable automatic connection pooling by setting the **OLE DB Services** value to 0, or -8. You can learn more about the **OLE DB Services** value by reading the document "OLE DB Programmer's Reference" at this address: http://msdn.microsoft.com/library/ default.asp?url=/library/en-us/oledb/htm/oledbabout_the_ole_db_documentation.asp.

Clearing OLE DB Object Pooling

Because the connection pool is being cached when a provider is created, it's important to call the connection's **ReleaseObjectPool** method when you have finished using your connection.

Using the ReleaseObjectPool Method

The **ReleaseObjectPool** method tells the connection pooler that the connection pool can be cleared when the last provider is released. You should call this method when you have closed your connection and you know you won't need the connection again within the time frame the **OLE DB Services** normally keeps pooled connections alive (see Listing 5-8).

*Listing 5-8. When to Call the **ReleaseObjectPool** Method*

```
1 ' Declare connection object
2 Dim cnnUserMan As OleDbConnection
3
4 ' Instantiate the connection object
5 cnnUserMan = New OleDbConnection(PR_STR_CONNECTION_STRING)
6 ' Open the connection
7 cnnUserMan.Open()
8
9 ' Do your stuff
10 ' ...
11
12 ' Close connection and release pool
13 cnnUserMan.Close()
14 cnnUserMan.ReleaseObjectPool()
```

Pooling Connections of Data Type SqlConnection

When you set up the **SqlConnection** class's **ConnectionString** property, you must set the **Pooling** value name to the value 'true' or leave out the value pair, as 'true' is the default value for **Pooling**. Therefore, by default, a **SqlConnection** object is taken from a connection pool when the connection is opened, and if no pool exists, one is created to hold the connection being opened.

The **Min Pool Size** and **Max Pool Size** value names of the **ConnectionString** property determine how many connections a pool can hold. Connections will be added to a pool until the maximum pool size is reached. Requests will then be queued by the object pooler, and a time-out will occur if no connections are returned to the pool before the time-out period elapses. Connections are only returned to the pool when they are closed using the **Close** method or if you explicitly destroy your connections with a call to the **Dispose** method. This is also true even if the connections are broken. Once a broken or invalid connection is returned to the pool, the object pooler removes the connection from the pool. This is done at regular intervals, when the object pooler scans for broken connections.

Another way to remove connections from the pool automatically is to specify a value for the **Connection Lifetime** value name of the **ConnectionString** property. This value is 0 by default, which means that the connection will never automatically be removed from the pool. If you specify a different value (in seconds), this value will be compared to the connection's time of creation and the current time once the connection is returned to the pool. If the lifetime exceeds the value indicated in the **Connection Lifetime** value name, the connection will be removed from the pool.

Resetting Connections in the Connection Pool

The **Connection Reset** value name is used for determining if the connection should be reset when it's returned to the pool. The default value is 'true', indicating the connection is reset upon returning to the pool. This is quite meaningful, if you've tampered with the properties when the connection was open. If you know that your connections stay the same whenever open, you can set the value to 'false' and thus avoid the extra round-trip to the server, sparing network load and saving time.

Testing for the Same Pool with SqlConnection Objects

One way to test if your **SqlConnection** objects go in the same pool or not is to set up two connections with identical connection strings and make sure the **Max Pool Size** value is set to 1. When you open the first connection, a new pool will be created for this specific connection string, and the connection will be added. When you try to open the second connection, the object pooler will try and add it to the existing pool. Because the existing pool doesn't allow any more connections (the maximum pool size has been reached), the request is queued. If the first connection isn't returned to the pool (by closing the connection), a time-out will occur for the second connection, when the **ConnectionTimeout** period elapses. Once you have set up this scenario, you can change the connection strings, and if a time-out occurs at runtime, then your connections do go in the same pool. Listing 5-9 shows you how to set it up.

*Listing 5-9. Testing for the Same Pool with **SqlConnection** Objects*

```
1 Public Sub CheckConnectionPooling()
2    Dim cnnUserMan1 As SqlConnection
3    Dim cnnUserMan2 As SqlConnection
4
```

```
 5    Try
 6        ' Instantiate and open the first SQL connection
 7        cnnUserMan1 = New SqlConnection(PR_STR_CONNECTION_STRING & _
 8            ";Max Pool Size=1;Connection Timeout=5")
 9        cnnUserMan1.Open()
10        ' Instantiate and open the second SQL connection
11        cnnUserMan2 = New SqlConnection(PR_STR_CONNECTION_STRING & _
12            ";Max Pool Size=1;Connection Timeout=5")
13        cnnUserMan2.Open()
14    Catch objE As Exception
15        MsgBox(objE.Message)
16    End Try
17 End Sub
```

Handling Provider, Driver, and Data Source Messages

If you want to handle warnings and messages from the provider, driver, or data source, you need to set up an event handler that can receive and process these warnings and messages. In general, warnings are simply "insignificant" errors that don't constitute an exception being thrown, like when there's an invalid value name in the connection string, but the connection string is otherwise okay.

Listings 5-10, 5-11, and 5-12 show you how to handle these information messages for the ODBC .NET Data Provider, the OLE DB .NET Data Provider, and the SQL Server .NET Data Provider.

*Listing 5-10. Handling Info Messages for the **OdbcConnection***

```
 1 Public Class CGeneral
 2    Private Const PR_STR_CONNECTION_STRING As String = _
 3        "DRIVER={IBM DB2 ODBC DRIVER};PWD=userman;UID=USERMAN;DBALIAS=USERMAN;"
 4
 5    ' Declare and instantiate connection
 6    Private prcnnUserMan As OdbcConnection = _
 7        New OdbcConnection(PR_STR_CONNECTION_STRING)
 8
 9    Public Sub New()
10        MyBase.New()
11        ' Set up InfoMessage event handler
12        AddHandler prcnnUserMan.InfoMessage, New _
13            OdbcInfoMessageEventHandler(AddressOf OnInfoMessage)
14    End Sub
```

```
15
16    Private Shared Sub OnInfoMessage(ByVal sender As Object, _
17       ByVal args As OdbcInfoMessageEventArgs)
18       Dim objError As OdbcError
19
20       ' Loop through all the error messages
21       For Each objError In args.Errors
22          ' Display the error properties
23          MessageBox.Show("The " & objError.Source & _
24             " has raised a warning. These are the properties :" & _
25             vbCrLf & vbCrLf & "Native Error: " & objError.NativeError & _
26             vbCrLf & "SQL State: " & objError.SQLState & vbCrLf & _
27             "Message: " & objError.Message)
28       Next
29    End Sub
30
31    Public Sub TriggerInfoMessageEvent()
32       ' By adding the SERVER value name to the connection string, the
33       ' InfoMessage event is triggered, because this is an invalid value name
34       ' for the DB2 ODBC driver
35       prcnnUserMan.ConnectionString = "SERVER=10.8.1.30"
36       ' Open the connection
37       prcnnUserMan.Open()
38    End Sub
39 End Class
```

*Listing 5-11. Handling Info Messages for the **OleDbConnection***

```
 1 Public Class CGeneral
 2    Private Const PR_STR_CONNECTION_STRING As String = _
 3       "Provider=IBMDADB2;Password=userman;User ID=USERMAN;" & _
 4       "Data Source=USERMAN;"
 5
 6    ' Declare and instantiate connection
 7    Private prcnnUserMan As OleDbConnection = _
 8       New OleDbConnection(PR_STR_CONNECTION_STRING)
 9
10    Public Sub New()
11       MyBase.New()
12       ' Set up InfoMessage event handler
13       AddHandler prcnnUserMan.InfoMessage, New _
14          OleDbInfoMessageEventHandler(AddressOf OnInfoMessage)
15    End Sub
16
```

```
17    Private Shared Sub OnInfoMessage(ByVal sender As Object, _
18       ByVal args As OleDbInfoMessageEventArgs)
19       Dim objError As OleDbError
20
21       ' Loop through all the error messages
22       For Each objError In args.Errors
23          ' Display the error properties
24          MessageBox.Show("The " & objError.Source & _
25             " has raised a warning. These are the properties :" & _
26             vbCrLf & vbCrLf & "Native Error: " & _
27             objError.NativeError & vbCrLf & "SQL State: " & _
28             objError.SQLState & vbCrLf & "Message: " & objError.Message)
29       Next
30
31       ' Display the message and the source
32       MessageBox.Show("Info Message: " & args.Message & _
33          vbCrLf & "Info Source: " + args.Source)
34    End Sub
35
36    Public Sub TriggerInfoMessageEvent()
37       ' By adding the SERVER value name to the connection string,
38       ' the InfoMessage event is triggered, because this is an
39       ' invalid value name for the DB2 OLE DB provider
40       prcnnUserMan.ConnectionString = "SERVER=10.8.1.30"
41       ' Open the connection
42       prcnnUserMan.Open()
43    End Sub
44 End Class
```

*Listing 5-12. Handling Info Messages for the **SqlConnection***

```
1 Public Class CGeneral
2    Private Const PR_STR_CONNECTION_STRING As String = _
3       "Data Source=10.8.1.12;User ID=UserMan;Password=userman;" & _
4       "Initial Catalog=UserMan"
5
6    ' Declare and instantiate connection
7    Private prcnnUserMan As SqlConnection = _
8       New SqlConnection(PR_STR_CONNECTION_STRING)
9
```

```
10    Public Sub New()
11      MyBase.New()
12      ' Set up InfoMessage event handler
13      AddHandler prcnnUserMan.InfoMessage, New _
14          SqlInfoMessageEventHandler(AddressOf OnInfoMessage)
15    End Sub
16
17    Private Shared Sub OnInfoMessage(ByVal sender As Object, _
18        ByVal args As SqlInfoMessageEventArgs)
19        Dim objError As SqlError
20
21        ' Loop through all the error messages
22        For Each objError In args.Errors
23          ' Display the error properties
24          MessageBox.Show("The " & objError.Source & _
25              " has raised a warning on the " & _
26              objError.Server & " server. These are the properties :" & _
27              vbCrLf & vbCrLf & "Severity: " & objError.Class & vbCrLf & _
28              "Number: " & objError.Number & vbCrLf & "State: " & _
29              objError.State & vbCrLf & "Line: " & objError.LineNumber & _
30              vbCrLf & "Procedure: " & objError.Procedure & vbCrLf & _
31              "Message: " & objError.Message)
32        Next
33
34        ' Display the message and the source
35        MessageBox.Show("Info Message: " & args.Message & _
36            vbCrLf & "Info Source: " + args.Source)
37    End Sub
38
39    Public Sub TriggerInfoMessageEvent()
40        Dim cmmUserMan As SqlCommand = New _
41            SqlCommand("RAISERROR('This is an info message event.', 10, 1)", _
42            prcnnUserMan)
43        ' Open the connection
44        prcnnUserMan.Open()
45        ' Execute the T-SQL command
46        cmmUserMan.ExecuteNonQuery()
47    End Sub
48 End Class
```

In Listing 5-10, you can see how to capture warnings and messages from the ODBC .NET Data Provider, the {IBM DB2 ODBC DRIVER} driver, and the IBM DB2 data source. On Lines 6 and 7, I declare and instantiate the connection, and in the class constructor I set up the event handler (Lines 12 and 13). Lines 16 through 29 are the actual event handler procedure, which displays all properties of the Error objects in the **Errors** collection of the **OdbcInfoMessageEventArgs** argument. Finally, Lines 31 through 38 shows the procedure that triggers the info message event. This is done by adding an invalid value name (SERVER) to the connection string (Line 35), before the **OdbcConnection** object is opened on Line 37. You can find a description of the various properties of the **OdbcError** class in Table C-16 in Appendix C.

TIP As you can see from Listings 5-10 and 5-11, you can actually use the InfoMessage event to pick up non–exception throwing problems with the **ConnectionString** property. This is especially important with user-generated and/or dynamically created connection strings. However, each ODBC driver and OLE DB provider responds differently to invalid value names, so it's up to you to check these things.

In Listing 5-11, you can see how to capture warnings and messages from the OLE DB .NET Data Provider, the IBMDADB2 OLE DB provider, and the IBM DB2 data source. On Lines 7 and 8, I declare and instantiate the connection, and in the class constructor I set up the event handler (Lines 13 and 14). Lines 17 through 34 are the actual event handler procedure, which displays all properties of the Error objects in the **Errors** collection of the **OleDbInfoMessageEventArgs** argument. Then the two properties of the **OleDbInfoMessageEventArgs** argument, **Message** and **Source**, are displayed. Finally, Lines 36 through 43 show the procedure that triggers the info message event. This is done by adding an invalid value name (SERVER) to the connection string (Line 40), before the **OleDbConnection** object is opened on Line 42. You can find a description of the various properties of the **OleDbError** class in Table C-19 in Appendix C.

In Listing 5-12, you can see how to capture warnings and messages from the provider, driver, and data source. On Lines 7 and 8, I declare and instantiate the connection, and in the class constructor I set up the event handler (Lines 13 and 14). Lines 17 through 37 are the actual event handler procedure, which displays all properties of the Error objects in the **Errors** collection of the **SqlInfoMessageEventArgs** argument. Then the two properties of the **SqlInfoMessageEventArgs** argument, **Message** and **Source**, are displayed. Finally, Lines 39 through 47 shows the procedure that triggers the info message event. This is done by calling the T-SQL function RAISERROR through the cmmUserMan **SqlCommand** object with a severity of 10 and a state of 1. If you set the severity to a value between 11 and 19, an exception is thrown instead. A severity of 20 through 25 is considered fatal by SQL Server, which closes down the connection! Please check SQL Server Books Online for more information on the RAISERROR T-SQL function, such as who can use RAISERROR with a particular severity. You can find a description of the various properties of the **SqlError** class in Table C-22 in Appendix C.

NOTE   In Listings 5-10, 5-11, and 5-12, I've set up the `OnInfoMessage` procedure to receive InfoMessage events from my data source. Although there's also a specific triggering of this event for the sake of the example, I've found that these events can be quite important. Although the events are warnings or messages of an informational nature, I personally feel that it's worth setting up the event handler to receive the messages. I found a number of unsuspected "problems" with my connection strings when I changed them for the various .NET Data Providers. I guess "unsuspecting" is the keyword here; you can't always foresee what will happen!

Transactions

Transactions are a way of grouping a number of individual database[4] operations into a single atomic unit of work, so that if one fails, they all fail. Likewise, if they all succeed, the changes will be applied permanently to the data source. Therefore, transactions are a safety net, ensuring that your data stays consistent.

One classic example of a transaction is a banking system. Suppose you are moving money from your savings account to your current account. This is an operation that requires two updates: Credit the amount to the current account and debit the amount from the savings account. Let's assume that this operation is under way, and the amount has been credited to the current account. Now, for whatever reason, the system crashes, and the amount is never debited from the savings account. This is no good, and it will certainly make someone unhappy. If this operation had been performed within a single transaction, the amount credited to the current account would have been rolled back once the system was back up and running. Although I have simplified the whole process, it should be clear why and/or when you want to use transactions!

ADO.NET offers you two ways of handling transactions within your application: manual and automatic.

---

4. It's not just database operations that can be part of a transaction, but for the sake of discussion in this book, I'll keep the focus on these operations when covering transactions.

Defining Transaction Boundaries

All transactions have a *boundary,* which is the scope or the "surrounding border" for all the resources within a transaction. Resources within the boundary share the same transaction identifier. This means internally all the resources, such as a database server, are assigned this identifier, which is unique to the transaction boundary. A transaction boundary is an abstract concept, meaning that it's like an invisible frame. The boundary can also be extended and reduced. How this is done all depends on whether you are using automatic (implicit) or manual (explicit) transactions. See the "Manual Transactions" and "Automatic Transactions" sections later in this chapter for more information.

Manual Transactions

The .NET Data Providers that come with ADO.NET support manual transactions through methods of the Connection class. When dealing with manual transactions, it's a good idea to check the state of the connection before attempting to perform one of the transaction methods. See "Manipulating the Connection State" earlier in this chapter for details.

Starting a Manual Transaction

To start a transaction, you need to call the **BeginTransaction** method of the Connection class. You must call this method before performing any of the database operations that are to take part in the transaction. The call in its simplest form is performed as shown in Listing 5-13.

Listing 5-13. Begin Transaction with Default Values

```
traUserMan = cnnUserMan.BeginTransaction()
```

The Connection object cnnUserMan must be a valid and open connection, or the **InvalidOperationException** is thrown. See "BeginTransaction Method Exceptions" later in this chapter for more details. traUserMan now holds a reference to the Transaction object created by the **BeginTransaction** method. The **BeginTransaction** method is overloaded, and Tables C-10, C-11, and C-12 in Appendix C show you the various versions of the method.

All the overloaded versions of the **BeginTransaction** method return an instance of the Transaction class inherited from the **SqlTransaction**, **OleDbTransaction**, or **OdbcTransaction** class. The **IsolationLevel** enum, which belongs to the **System.Data** namespace, specifies the local transaction locking behavior for the connection. If the isolation level is changed during a transaction, the server is expected to apply the new locking level to all the remaining statements. See Table C-13 in Appendix C for an overview of the **IsolationLevel** enum.

In Listing 5-14, you can see how a transaction is started with the **BeginTransaction** method of the **SqlConnection** class. The transaction is using a nondefault isolation level, read committed. Please refer to the example code, available on the Apress Web site, for examples of using this overload of the **BeginTransaction** method with the **OdbcConnection** and **OleDbConnection** classes.

Listing 5-14. Beginning a Transaction with a Nondefault Isolation Level

```
1 Public Sub BeginNonDefaultIsolationLevelTransaction()
2    Dim cnnUserMan As SqlConnection
3    Dim traUserMan As SqlTransaction
4
5    ' Instantiate the connection
6    cnnUserMan = New SqlConnection(PR_STR_CONNECTION_STRING)
7    ' Open the connection
8    cnnUserMan.Open()
9    ' Begin transaction
10   traUserMan = cnnUserMan.BeginTransaction( _
11       IsolationLevel.ReadCommitted)
12 End Sub
```

In Listing 5-15, you can see how a named transaction is started with the **BeginTransaction** method of the **SqlConnection** class. This overload only works with the **SqlConnection** class.

Listing 5-15. Beginning a Named Transaction

```
1 Public Sub BeginNamedTransaction()
2    Const STR_MAIN_TRANSACTION_NAME As String = "MainTransaction"
3
4    Dim cnnUserMan As SqlConnection
5    Dim traUserMan As SqlTransaction
6
7    ' Instantiate the connection
8    cnnUserMan = New SqlConnection(PR_STR_CONNECTION_STRING)
9    ' Open the connection
10   cnnUserMan.Open()
11   ' Begin transaction
12   traUserMan = cnnUserMan.BeginTransaction(STR_MAIN_TRANSACTION_NAME)
13 End Sub
```

In Listing 5-16, you can see how a named transaction is started with the **BeginTransaction** method of the **SqlConnection** class. The transaction is using a nondefault isolation level, read committed. This overload only works with the **SqlConnection** class.

Listing 5-16. Beginning a Named Transaction with a Nondefault Isolation Level

```
 1 Public Sub BeginNamedNonDefaultIsolationLevelTransaction()
 2    Const STR_MAIN_TRANSACTION_NAME As String = "MainTransaction"
 3
 4    Dim cnnUserMan As SqlConnection
 5    Dim traUserMan As SqlTransaction
 6
 7    ' Instantiate the connection
 8    cnnUserMan = New SqlConnection(PR_STR_CONNECTION_STRING)
 9    ' Open the connection
10    cnnUserMan.Open()
11    ' Begin transaction
12    traUserMan = cnnUserMan.BeginTransaction(IsolationLevel.ReadCommitted, _
13       STR_MAIN_TRANSACTION_NAME)
14 End Sub
```

In Listings 5-15 and 5-16, the transaction is named using a constant, which obviously makes it easier later on to recognize the transaction you want to deal with. See the "Nesting Transactions and Using Transaction Save Points with SqlTransaction" section later in this chapter for details on using named transactions.

 NOTE It's actually not necessary to save the returned Transaction object, which means that you can leave out the traUserMan = bit in Listings 5-13 through 5-16. Mind you, there's no point in doing so, since you probably want to commit or roll back the pending changes at a later stage. This is only possible if you save the reference to the Transaction object. This differs from classic ADO, where the rollback and commit functionality were methods of the Connection class. In ADO.NET, this functionality is now part of the Transaction class.

Any operation you perform using the Connection object, after you start a transaction, can be either committed or rolled back at a later point, if the Connection object stays open and valid. This means that it doesn't matter if you use a Command object to execute action queries, the DataAdapter to update the data source based on changes to a **DataTable** and/or **DataSet**, or any other method of updating the data source—all changes made to the data source will be part of the transaction.

You can find more information about the Command class in Chapter 6, the DataAdapter class in Chapter 8, the **DataSet** class in Chapter 9, and finally the **DataTable** class in Chapter 10.

Examining the Isolation Level

The isolation level of a transaction dictates how the data source behaves with respect to the ability of other connections to change the data that is part of the transaction. Table C-13 in Appendix C shows the various members of the **IsolationLevel** enum, which is used for specifying the isolation level for a transaction. Depending on the scenario in which your application is deployed, you'll probably need to change the default isolation level when you use transactions.

A high isolation level means that data in the database stays correct at all times, but because of the locking applied at the data source, it can also result in deadlocked requests. Deadlocked requests happens when two or more transactions fight for the same sets of data, where one transaction has locked data set A, while waiting to gain access to data set B. The other transaction has currently placed a lock on data set B, while waiting to access data set A. Because the two transactions are locking each other out, with no automatic solution to the problem, the requests are deadlocked. Some DBMSs, like SQL Server, automatically detect deadlocks and terminate one of the transactions, meaning the transaction is aborted. Thus, the deadlock victim must try again, and the other transaction is successful.

Using a low isolation level generally avoids deadlocks, and thus increases concurrency. However, this happens at the expense of data correctness. Data correctness means that the data you read is not guaranteed to be the same when you reread it, or it might have changed or been deleted when you try to update it.

You can change the isolation level of a transaction as often as you want, and it's the data source's responsibility to make sure that a changed isolation level is applied to the remaining operations.

Determining the Isolation Level of a Running Transaction

If you are uncertain of the isolation level of a running transaction, you can use the **IsolationLevel** property of the Transaction class, as shown in Listing 5-17.

Listing 5-17. Determining the Isolation Level of a Running Transaction

```
1 Public Sub DetermineTransactionIsolationLevel()
2     Const STR_MAIN_TRANSACTION_NAME As String = "MainTransaction"
3
4     Dim cnnUserMan As SqlConnection
5     Dim traUserMan As SqlTransaction
6     Dim intIsolationLevel As Integer
```

```
 7
 8    ' Instantiate the connection
 9    cnnUserMan = New SqlConnection(PR_STR_CONNECTION_STRING)
10    ' Open the connection
11    cnnUserMan.Open()
12
13    ' Start named transaction with non-default isolation level
14    traUserMan = cnnUserMan.BeginTransaction(IsolationLevel.ReadCommitted, _
15      STR_MAIN_TRANSACTION_NAME)
16
17    ' Return the isolation level as text
18    MsgBox(traUserMan.IsolationLevel.ToString)
19    ' Return the isolation level as an integer value
20    intIsolationLevel = traUserMan.IsolationLevel
21 End Sub
```

Nesting Transactions

Sometimes a single transaction is not sufficient; you need other subtransactions within the main transaction. This is generally called *transaction nesting,* and you can apply it to your connection as discussed in the following sections.

The main reason for having nested transactions is that you can roll back smaller portions of your main transaction, and thus avoid having to roll back a whole series of operations, if an error occurs. It means that you can roll back to a specific point of the main transaction,[5] if an error occurs further down the line of operations performed on the data accessed using the connection associated with the main transaction.

Nesting Transactions with OdbcTransaction

Unlike the **OleDbTransaction** and **SqlTransaction** classes, the **OdbcTransaction** class doesn't support nested transactions, which means that you can have only one transaction per Connection object at any given time.

Nesting Transactions with OleDbTransaction

This topic is only valid for the **OleDbConnection** class. Unlike ADO, where you can start several transactions on a connection by calling the **BeginTransaction** method a number of times, you only have the one transaction, also starting with

---

5. "A specific point" in this case refers to when a nested transaction is started or a save point has been saved. It's up to you to begin a nested transaction or save a save point at stages of the main transaction where it's valid according to your business logic to commit or roll back to.

the **BeginTransaction** method. However, the Transaction object that is returned from the **BeginTransaction** method has a **Begin** method that can be used for nesting purposes. An example of using the **OleDbTransaction** class's **Begin** method is shown in Listing 5-18.

Listing 5-18. Beginning a Nested OLE DB Transaction

```
1 Public Sub NestTransactions()
2    Dim cnnUserMan As OleDbConnection
3    Dim traUser2 As OleDbTransaction
4    Dim traUser3 As OleDbTransaction
5    Dim traUser99 As OleDbTransaction
6    Dim cmmDelete As New OleDbCommand()
7
8    ' Instantiate the connection
9    cnnUserMan = New OleDbConnection(PR_STR_CONNECTION_STRING)
10   ' Open the connection
11   cnnUserMan.Open()
12   ' Initialize the command
13   cmmDelete.Connection = cnnUserMan
14
15   ' Start main transaction
16   traUser99 = cnnUserMan.BeginTransaction()
17   ' Delete User99
18   cmmDelete.CommandText = "DELETE FROM tblUser WHERE LoginName='User99'"
19   cmmDelete.Transaction = traUser99
20   cmmDelete.ExecuteNonQuery()
21   ' Begin nested transaction
22   traUser3 = traUser99.Begin()
23   ' Delete User3
24   cmmDelete.CommandText = "DELETE FROM tblUser WHERE LoginName='User3'"
25   cmmDelete.Transaction = traUser3
26   cmmDelete.ExecuteNonQuery()
27   ' Begin nested transaction
28   traUser2 = traUser3.Begin()
29   ' Delete User2
30   cmmDelete.CommandText = "DELETE FROM tblUser WHERE LoginName='User2'"
31   cmmDelete.Transaction = traUser2
32   cmmDelete.ExecuteNonQuery()
33   ' Roll back deletion of User2
34   traUser2.Rollback()
35   ' Commit all pending changes in main transaction
36   traUser99.Commit()
37 End Sub
```

In Listing 5-18, the connection is instantiated and opened (Lines 9 and 11), the Command object initialized on Line 13,[6] the main transaction (traUser99) started on Line 16, and User99 deleted from the tblUser table. After this, the nested traUser3 transaction is started on Line 22, User3 deleted from the tblUser table, and again a nested transaction started—the traUser2 transaction on Line 27. Then the changes applied to the database after User3 was deleted are rolled back and the main transaction committed. The outcome of running the example code in Listing 5-17 is that User99 and User3 are deleted from the tblUser table, whereas User2 isn't, because that change was rolled back. It should be clear that when you roll back or commit a transaction, any transactions nested within the transaction being rolled back or committed will also be rolled back or committed.

Please note that the SQLOLEDB OLE DB provider doesn't support nesting. Therefore, if you run Listing 5-18 using this provider, an **InvalidOperationException** exception is thrown. If you need to use transaction nesting with SQL Server 7.0 or later, then use the SQL Server .NET Data Provider instead. The IBMDADB2 OLE DB provider doesn't support nesting either, so an **OleDbException** exception is thrown if you run Listing 5-18 using this provider.

 NOTE The Microsoft.Jet.OLEDB.4.0 OLE DB provider doesn't support nesting of more than five levels. This is usually enough, but you need to be aware of this limitation. Please check the documentation of your data source and/or provider, to see what transaction nesting limitation it has, if any.

Nesting Transactions and Using Transaction Save Points with SqlTransaction

This topic is only valid for the **SqlConnection** and **SqlTransaction** classes. If you're nesting your transactions, it's good idea to give each transaction a name that is readily identifiable, making it easier for yourself later on to tell the transactions apart. Well, I say transactions, but in ADO.NET, you can't have more than one transaction on a single connection. Unlike ADO, where you can start several transactions on a connection by calling the **BeginTransaction** method a number of times and specifying a name for each transaction, you only have the one transaction, also starting with the **BeginTransaction** method. However, the Transaction object that is returned from the **BeginTransaction** method has a **Save** method that can be used for the very same purpose. Actually, I think it has become somewhat easier to nest transactions in ADO.NET, but you be the judge of that.

---

6. You can find a discussion of the Command class in Chapter 6.

So let's have a look at this new way of nesting transactions. It's actually not nesting as such, but a way of saving specific points in a transaction that you can roll back to. The **SqlTransaction** class's **Save** method is used for saving a reference point in the transaction, as shown in Listing 5-19.

Listing 5-19. Saving a Reference Point in a Transaction

```
1 Public Sub UseTransactionSavePoints()
2    Const STR_USER99_TRANSACTION_NAME As String = "User99"
3    Const STR_USER3_TRANSACTION_NAME As String = "User3"
4    Const STR_USER2_TRANSACTION_NAME As String = "User2"
5
6    Dim cnnUserMan As SqlConnection
7    Dim traUserMan As SqlTransaction
8    Dim cmmDelete As New SqlCommand()
9
10   ' Instantiate the connection
11   cnnUserMan = New SqlConnection(PR_STR_CONNECTION_STRING)
12   ' Open the connection
13   cnnUserMan.Open()
14
15   ' Start named main transaction
16   traUserMan = cnnUserMan.BeginTransaction(STR_USER99_TRANSACTION_NAME)
17   ' Initialize the command
18   cmmDelete.Connection = cnnUserMan
19   cmmDelete.Transaction = traUserMan
20   ' Delete User99
21   cmmDelete.CommandText = "DELETE FROM tblUser WHERE LoginName='User99'"
22   cmmDelete.ExecuteNonQuery()
23   ' Save transaction reference point
24   traUserMan.Save(STR_USER3_TRANSACTION_NAME)
25   ' Delete User3
26   cmmDelete.CommandText = "DELETE FROM tblUser WHERE LoginName='User3'"
27   cmmDelete.ExecuteNonQuery()
28   ' Save transaction reference point
29   traUserMan.Save(STR_USER2_TRANSACTION_NAME)
30   ' Delete User2
31   cmmDelete.CommandText = "DELETE FROM tblUser WHERE LoginName='User2'"
32   cmmDelete.ExecuteNonQuery()
33   ' Roll back deletion of User2
34   traUserMan.Rollback(STR_USER2_TRANSACTION_NAME)
35   ' Commit all pending changes in main transaction
36   traUserMan.Commit()
37 End Sub
```

In Listing 5-19 the connection is opened on Line 13, the main transaction started on Line 16, and User99 deleted from the tblUser table. After this a reference point is saved (Line 24) before another update of the database. This time User3 is deleted and again a reference point is saved (Line 29). User2 is then deleted, and a roll back to a named reference (save point) in the transaction occurs (Line 34), namely to the point after User3 was deleted. Finally, the main transaction is committed. The outcome of running the example code in Listing 5-19 is that User99 and User3 are deleted from the tblUser table, whereas User2 isn't, because that change was rolled back. It should be clear that when you roll back or commit a transaction, any transaction save points within the transaction being rolled back or committed will be ignored.

For more information on the **Rollback** method of the Transaction class, please see the next section, "Aborting a Manual Transaction."

Always Use Named Transactions

Although you can call the **Rollback** method without passing the name of a transaction, it's advisable that you do include a transaction name if you are using the **SqlTransaction** class (the **OleDbTransaction** and **OdbcConnection** classes don't have this feature). When you start the transaction, use one of the overloaded **BeginTransaction** methods that let you pass the name of a transaction as an argument as demonstrated in Listings 5-15, 5-16, and 5-18. This way you can always use the overloaded **Rollback** method of the Transaction class and pass the name of the transaction. When you use the standard version of the **Rollback** method, all pending changes will be rolled back. Personally, I think it makes the code more readable if you always supply the transaction name when you begin the transaction, save a reference point, and roll back a transaction.

Aborting a Manual Transaction

If for some reason you want to abort the transaction—that is, roll back all the changes since you started the transaction (whether it's a nested transaction and/or has nested transactions makes no difference)—you need to call the Transaction class's **Rollback** method. This will ensure that no changes are applied to the data source; or rather, the data source is rolled back to its original state. The call is performed like this:

```
traUserMan.Rollback()
```

You can also use the overloaded version of the **Rollback** method with which you specify the name of the transaction, as was done in Listing 5-19. The **Rollback** method can't be used before the **BeginTransaction** method of the Connection class has been called, and it must be called before the Transaction class's **Commit** method is called. An **InvalidOperationException** exception is thrown if you don't do as prescribed.

Committing a Manual Transaction

When you have finished manipulating your data, it's time to commit the changes to the data source. Calling the Transaction class's **Commit** method does this. All the changes you have made to the data since you started the transaction will be applied to the data source. Actually, this is only fully true for the **OdbcTransaction** class. If you are using the **SqlTransaction** class, you might have saved some reference points and used the **Rollback** method to roll back to one or more of these reference points. In such a case, the operations that have been rolled back obviously won't be committed. The same is true for the **OleDbTransaction** class, when you roll back nested transactions within the transaction you commit; the rolled back changes will not be committed to the data source. The call is performed like this:

```
traUserMan.Commit()
```

Examining the Transaction Class

The Transaction class, which can only be instantiated by the Connection class's **BeginTransaction** method, or the **OleDbTransaction** class's **Begin** method (for nested transactions), can't be inherited. Once a transaction has been started, all further transaction operations are performed on the Transaction object returned by the **BeginTransaction** or **Begin** methods. In Table C-14 in Appendix C, you can see the public properties of the Transaction classes, and in Table C-15, you can see the public methods of the Transaction classes. Inherited and overridden methods are not shown.

All the properties and methods shown in the two mentioned tables are used in the previous listings in the "Transactions" section.

Manual Transaction Summary

Handling manual transactions isn't that big a deal. Here are the few steps you need to remember:

- Start a transaction by using the **BeginTransaction** method of the Connection class. You can only execute **BeginTransaction** once per connection; or rather, you can't have parallel transactions. You need to commit a running transaction before you can use the **BeginTransaction** method again on the same connection. The **BeginTransaction** returns the Transaction object needed for rolling back or committing the changes to the data source.

- Nested transactions can be started using the **Begin** method of the **OleDbTransaction** class, or you can use transaction save points with the **SqlTransaction** class.

- Roll back a transaction by using the **Rollback** method of the Transaction class.

- Commit a transaction by using the **Commit** method of the Transaction class.

Automatic Transactions

Automatic transactions are a little different from manual transactions in the sense that they aren't necessarily applied. When I say not necessarily, I mean the following: If the object in which you are using the .NET Data Provider data classes isn't enlisted in a transaction, your data source won't be either. Therefore, to cut it short, if you're using transactions for your application, then the data source will be enlisted automatically.

The .NET Data Providers OLE DB .NET Data Provider, ODBC .NET Data Provider, and SQL Server .NET Data Provider all automatically enlist in a transaction and obtain the details of the transaction from the Windows Component Services context (also known as COM+).

ASP.NET has its own way of handling automatic transactions; it's outside the scope of this book to cover this, but I'll briefly outline how you can make your .NET Framework classes transactional:

- Make sure your class inherits from the **ServicedComponent** class.

- Mark your class transactional using attributes.

- Sign the assembly that hosts your class with a strong name.

In the example code, you'll find the CTransactional class (CTransactional.vb), which is transactional. It's part of the Automatic Transaction Assembly project.

Inherit from the ServicedComponent Class

Your class must inherit from the **ServicedComponent** class, which is located in the **System.EnterpriseServices** namespace. This namespace isn't automatically referenced from a new project, so you'll have to add this reference to the project yourself. This is what your class declaration should look like:

```
Imports System.EnterpriseServices

Public Class CTransactional
    Inherits ServicedComponent

End Class
```

This is just the empty class, which is inherited from the **ServicedComponent** class.

Mark Your Class Transactional

You need to mark your class as transactional using the **Transaction** attribute, and optionally one of the **TransactionOption** enum members. You do this by applying the attribute to the class declaration, like this:

```
<Transaction(TransactionOption.Supported)> _
Public Class CTransactional
```

Please note that the example code could be put on one line, should you want to. You just need to remove the line continuation character. Personally, I feel it looks better this way, as the attribute, which is always enclosed in a pair of less than (<) and greater than (>) characters, is easier to read. The **TransactionOption** enum has the members described in Table 5-1 in alphabetical order.

*Table 5-1. **TransactionOption** Enum Members*

Name	Description
Disabled	This member disables automatic transaction enlisting of a class instance. If you want to use the Microsoft Distributed Transaction Coordinator[a] for transactional support, you need to set the **Transaction** attribute to this value.
NotSupported	This member indicates that a class instance doesn't run within the scope of a transaction. This means that a request to create a new object of the class will be processed by creating the object context without a transaction. This is also true if a transaction exists.
Required	This is the default member, and it indicates that a class instance requires a transaction. This means that it's enlisted in an existing transaction, if one exists, or a transaction is started, if no transaction exists.
RequiresNew	The **RequiresNew** member indicates that the object always requires a new transaction, which means that a new transaction is started for each class instance created.
Supported	This member indicates that a class instance runs within the scope of a transaction, but only if one exists. This means that a request to create a new object of the class will be processed by enlisting the object in an existing transaction, if one exists, or by creating the object context without a transaction, if no transaction exists.

a. Please see your Microsoft documentation for more information on the Microsoft Distributed Transaction Coordinator (DTC). There are a number of examples in SQL Server Books Online that comes with Microsoft SQL Server.

Depending on your needs for automatic transaction enlistment of your class instances, you set the **Transaction** attribute to one of the members of the **TransactionOption** enum listed in Table 5-1. If you don't specify one, like this `<Transaction()>`, the **Required** member is automatically assumed, as it is the default member.

Sign Assembly with Strong Name

The assembly that hosts your class must be signed with a strong name. A *strong name* is a guaranteed unique name that consists of the assembly's identity. This identity is created using the assembly name (usually the name of the VS .NET project), the version number, the culture information, a public key, and a digital signature. The public key is used in combination with a private key, and this public/private key pair can be generated from the command prompt, using the Strong Name tool, Sn.exe. So, to generate the Automatic Transaction Assembly.snk[7] key pair, execute this command from the command prompt:

```
Sn -k "Automatic Transaction Assembly.snk"
```

You need to enclose the file in double quotes, if the file name contains spaces. There are now two ways to sign the assembly: using the Assembly Linker (Al.exe), and using assembly attributes. You'll be using the assembly **AssemblyKeyFileAttribute** attribute, which you add to a code file, such as a class file.[8] In this case, I've added the following line to the CTransactional class:

```
<Assembly: AssemblyKeyFileAttribute("Automatic Transaction Assembly.snk")>
```

The assembly **AssemblyKeyFileAttribute** attribute is part of the **System.Reflection** namespace, which must be imported into your code file. When compiling from the VS .NET IDE, the public/private key pair file, Automatic Transaction Assembly.snk, should be placed in the appropriate folder, which is the same folder as the project file, when your project is a VB .NET project.

TIP   When you load your solution into the VS .NET IDE, it automatically tries to locate any files referenced from within class attributes. So, if you happen to get an error displayed in the Task List about a missing strong key file, make sure the file is located in the same folder as the project file, close down the VS .NET IDE, and reopen it. It seems there's a problem recognizing that the file is actually there, once an error has been reported.

That's all you have to do to create a transactional .NET assembly containing the classes you want to take part in automatic transactions. If you need to make your assembly available to COM-based applications, you need to look this up in the Microsoft documentation.

---

7. The .snk extension is the standard extension for **Strong Name Key** files. However, you can use any name you like.
8. You can and probably should place the attribute in the AssemblyInfo.vb file where it's easy to find for other developers.

Handling Connection and Transaction Exceptions

This section describes how you deal with exceptions when you work with connections and transactions. An exception, which is more or less the same as what used to be called a trappable error, can be caught using the **Try . . . Catch . . . End Try** statement construct. If you are using the **OdbcConnection** class, please look up the property or method in the "OdbcConnection Class Exceptions" section for the correct exception. **OleDbConnection** class exceptions are discussed in the "OleDbConnection Class Exceptions" section, and **SqlConnection** class exceptions are discussed in the "SqlConnection Class Exceptions" section later in this chapter. Please note that only exceptions to noninherited properties and methods are mentioned. So, exceptions caused by the **Equals** method, which is inherited from the **Object** class, are not shown. The list is also not exhaustive, but merely shows the more common exceptions you will encounter.

Why Did You Get an Exception?

For each exception, I show you a piece of code that can help you determine why an exception occurred. This is useful when the code in the **Try** section of a **Try . . . Catch . . . End Try** construct contains multiple procedure calls that can throw an exception. Be aware that this is simple code, and it's only there to help you get an idea of how to proceed with your exception handling. In the examples provided I show you how to find out what method, property, and so on threw the exception. However, some methods and properties can throw more than one type of exception, and this is when you need to set up multiple catch blocks, like this:

```
Try
...
Catch objInvalid As InvalidOperationException
...
Catch objArgument As ArgumentException
...
Catch objE As Exception
End Try
```

One of the most common mistakes is to provide a "faulty" connection string. It often happens that a user needs to type in a user ID and password, which is then passed as part of the connection string, without first being validated. If the user has typed in any special characters, such as a semicolon, an exception is thrown, if you don't catch this yourself. For more information on exception handling, please refer to Chapter 14.

Connection Class Exceptions

When you're working with one of the .NET Data Providers and an exception is thrown that the **OdbcDataAdapter**, **OleDbDataAdapter**, or **SqlDataAdapter** can't handle (see the "The DataAdapter Explained" section in Chapter 8), an **OdbcException**, **OleDbException**, or **SqlException** is thrown. This Exception class, which can't be inherited, is derived from the **SystemException** class. The **OdbcException**, **OleDbException**, or **SqlException** class holds at least one instance of the **OdbcError**, **OleDbError**, or **SqlError** class. It's up to you to traverse through all of the instances of **OdbcError**, **OleDbError**, or **SqlError** classes contained in the **OdbcException**, **OleDbException**, or **SqlException** class, in order to check what errors occurred. Listing 5-20 shows how you can do it. The example catches exceptions that occur when you try to open a connection, but the code in the catch section can be used for any ODBC, OLE DB, or SQL Server exceptions encountered.

*Listing 5-20. Traversing Through an **OdbcException** Class*

```
1 Public Sub TraverseAllOdbcErrors()
2    Dim cnnUserMan As OdbcConnection
3
4    Try
5       ' Instantiate the connection
6       cnnUserMan = New OdbcConnection(PR_STR_CONNECTION_STRING)
7       ' Open the connection
8       cnnUserMan.Open()
9       ' Do your stuff...
10      ' ...
11   Catch objException As OdbcException
12      ' This Catch block will handle all exceptions that
13      ' the OdbcAdapter cannot handle
14      Dim objError As OdbcError
15
16      For Each objError In objException.Errors
17         MsgBox(objException.Message)
18      Next
19   Catch objException As Exception
20      ' This Catch block will catch all exceptions that
21      ' the OdbcAdapter can handle
22      MsgBox(objException.Message)
23   End Try
24 End Sub
```

Listing 5-20 shows you how to extract all instances of the **OdbcError** class from the **Errors** property collection of the **OdbcException** class. Please see the example code, available on the Apress Web site, for examples of doing this with the OLE DB .NET Data Provider and the SQL Server .NET Data Provider.

Examining the OdbcError Class

In Listing 5-20, all I've specified is to display the error message, but there are actually a few more properties in the **OdbcError** class that are of interest. See Table C-16 in Appendix C for a list of all these properties. Incidentally, the **OdbcError** class, which is noninheritable, is inherited directly from the **Object** class. There are no public, noninherited methods or events of the **OdbcError** class.

Examining the OleDbError Class

In Listing 5-20, or rather, the corresponding OLE DB .NET Data Provider example code, I've specified to display the error message, but there are actually a few more properties in the **OleDbError** class that are of interest. See Table C-19 in Appendix C for a list of all these properties. Incidentally, the **OleDbError** class, which is noninheritable, is inherited directly from the **Object** class. There are no public, noninherited methods or events of the **OleDbError** class.

Examining the SqlError Class

In Listing 5-20, or rather, the corresponding SQL Server .NET Data Provider example code, I've specified to display the error message, but there are actually a few more properties in the **SqlError** class that are of interest. See Table C-22 in Appendix C for a list of all these properties. Incidentally, the **SqlError** class, which is noninheritable, is inherited directly from the **Object** class. There are no public, noninherited methods or events of the **SqlError** class.

The **SqlError** class properties are somewhat different from the ones in the **OdbcError** and **OleDbError** classes. This comes from the fact that the SQL Server .NET Data Provider has been tailor-made for use with SQL Server, whereas the ODBC .NET Data Provider and the OLE DB .NET Data Provider are generic ones for use with a number of different data sources. This also means that you can read such properties as the name of a stored procedure, or the exact line number where an error occurred in a stored procedure or a batch of T-SQL statements.

Examining the OdbcException Class

Besides the **Errors** collection, the **OdbcException** class has a few other properties and methods of interest as you can see in Tables C-17 and C-18 in Appendix C. Both tables are in alphabetical order. The **OdbcException** class exposes no events.

Examining the OleDbException Class

Besides the **Errors** collection, the **OleDbException** class has a few other properties and methods of interest as you can see in Tables C-20 and C-21 in Appendix C. Both tables are in alphabetical order. The **OleDbException** class exposes no events.

Examining the SqlException Class

Besides the **Errors** collection, the **SqlException** class has a few other properties and methods of interest as you can see in Tables C-23 and C-24 in Appendix C. Both tables are in alphabetical order. The **SqlException** class exposes no events.

Specific Exceptions

Here I will show you how to deal with some of the most common exceptions thrown when working with the Connection class. All of the examples work with the **SqlConnection** class, but some of these exceptions are also thrown when working with the **OdbcConnection** and **OleDbConnection** classes. Please see the individual sections for more information on what Connection class throws the listed exception.

NOTE   The examples you see here are only to give you an idea of how you can work with the various exceptions of the Connection class. There are many other exceptions that aren't covered here, but you should be able to set up your own exception handlers by looking at how the ones shown are constructed. For general exception handling, please refer to Chapter 14.

BeginTransaction Method Exceptions

The **InvalidOperationException** exception is thrown when you call the **BeginTransaction** method on an invalid or closed connection. You can check if the connection is open, like this:

```
' Check if the connection is open
If cnnUserMan.State = ConnectionState.Open Then
```

The **InvalidOperationException** exception is also thrown if you try to start parallel transactions by calling the **BeginTransaction** method twice, before committing or rolling back the first transaction.

Listing 5-21 shows you how you can check if the exception was thrown because of the **BeginTransaction** method. This only works with the **SqlConnection** class.

*Listing 5-21. Checking If **BeginTransaction** Caused the Exception*

```
1 Public Sub CheckBeginTransactionMethodException()
2    Dim cnnUserMan As SqlConnection
3    Dim traUserMan1, traUserMan2 As SqlTransaction
4
5    ' Instantiate the connection
6    cnnUserMan = New SqlConnection(PR_STR_CONNECTION_STRING)
7    ' Open the connection
8    cnnUserMan.Open()
9
10   Try
11      ' Start parallel transactions
12      traUserMan1 = cnnUserMan.BeginTransaction()
13      traUserMan2 = cnnUserMan.BeginTransaction()
14   Catch objException As InvalidOperationException
15      ' Check if a BeginTransaction method threw the exception
16      If objException.TargetSite.Name = "BeginTransaction" Then
17         MsgBox("The BeginTransaction method threw the exception!")
18      End If
19   End Try
20 End Sub
```

In Listing 5-21, you can see how you can catch an exception thrown by the **BeginTransaction** method of the **SqlConnection** class. Check the example code, available on the Apress Web site, for examples that work with the **OdbcConnection** and **OleDbConnection** classes.

ConnectionString Property Exceptions

The **InvalidOperationException** exception is thrown when the connection is open or broken and you try to set the property. Listing 5-22 shows you how you can check if the **InvalidOperationException** exception was thrown because of the **ConnectionString** property.

*Listing 5-22. Checking If **ConnectionString** Caused the Exception*

```
 1 Public Sub CheckConnectionStringPropertyException()
 2    Dim cnnUserMan As OleDbConnection
 3
 4    ' Instantiate the connection
 5    cnnUserMan = New OleDbConnection(PR_STR_CONNECTION_STRING)
 6    ' Open the connection
 7    cnnUserMan.Open()
 8
 9    Try
10       ' Set the connection string
11       cnnUserMan.ConnectionString = PR_STR_CONNECTION_STRING
12    Catch objException As InvalidOperationException
13       ' Check if setting the ConnectionString threw the exception
14       If objException.TargetSite.Name = "set_ConnectionString" Then
15          MsgBox("The ConnectionString property threw the exception!")
16       End If
17    End Try
18 End Sub
```

In Listing 5-22, you can see how you can catch an exception thrown by the **ConnectionString** property of the **OleDbConnection** class. Check the example code, available on the Apress Web site, for examples that work with the **OdbcConnection** and **SqlConnection** classes.

ConnectionTimeout Property Exceptions

The **ArgumentException** exception is thrown when you try to set the **ConnectionTimeout** property to a value less than 0. Actually, the **ConnectionTimeout** property is read-only, so you can't set it directly. However, you can set this property through the **Connection Timeout** value name in the **ConnectionString** property. Listing 5-23 shows you how you can check if the **ArgumentException** exception was thrown because of the **ConnectionTimeout** property.

*Listing 5-23. Checking If **ConnectionTimeout** Caused the Exception*

```
1 Public Sub CheckConnectionTimeoutPropertyException()
2    Dim cnnUserMan As SqlConnection
3
4    Try
5       ' Instantiate the connection
6       cnnUserMan = New SqlConnection(PR_STR_CONNECTION_STRING & _
7          ";Connection Timeout=-1")
8       ' Open the connection
9       cnnUserMan.Open()
10   Catch objException As ArgumentException
11      ' Check if setting the Connection Timeout to an invalid value
12      'threw the exception
13      If objException.TargetSite.Name = "SetConnectTimeout" Then
14         MsgBox("The Connection Timeout value threw the exception!")
15      End If
16   End Try
17 End Sub
```

Listing 5-23 shows you how you can check if an exception was thrown because of an invalid **ConnectionTimeout** property value. This only works with the **SqlConnection** class.

Database Property and ChangeDatabase Method Exceptions

The **InvalidOperationException** exception is thrown if the connection isn't open when you try to switch databases. Actually, the **Database** property is read-only, so you can't set it directly. However, you can set this property through the **ChangeDatabase** method or using a Transact-SQL statement with the **SqlConnection** class. You can in fact change from the current database to the master database by executing the simple USE master SQL statement using the **ExecuteNonQuery** method of the **SqlCommand** class. The **Database** property is then dynamically updated, and it's after this that an exception can be thrown.

 NOTE Transact-SQL (T-SQL), which is used in SQL Server, is Microsoft's dialect of the ANSI SQL standard. T-SQL is fully ANSI compliant, but it also features many enhancements. You can find an excellent explanation of T-SQL at Garth Wells' site, SQLBOOK.COM, at http://www.sqlbook.com/code_centric--sample_chapters.html. Check out sample Chapter 1.

Listing 5-24 shows you how you can check if the **InvalidOperationException** exception was thrown because of the **Database** property.

*Listing 5-24. Checking If **Database** Caused the Exception*

```
1 Public Sub CheckChangeDatabaseMethodException()
2    Dim cnnUserMan As SqlConnection
3
4    Try
5       ' Instantiate the connection
6       cnnUserMan = New SqlConnection(PR_STR_CONNECTION_STRING)
7       ' Open the connection
8       ' If the following line is commented out, the ChangeDatabase
9       ' exception will be thrown
10      'cnnUserMan.Open()
11      ' Change database
12      cnnUserMan.ChangeDatabase("master")
13   Catch objException As InvalidOperationException
14      ' Check if we tried to change database on an invalid connection
15      If objException.TargetSite.Name = "ChangeDatabase" Then
16         MsgBox("The ChangeDatabase method threw the exception!")
17      End If
18   End Try
19 End Sub
```

Listing 5-24 shows you how you can check if the **InvalidOperationException** exception was thrown because you tried to change the database on a closed **SqlConnection** object. Check the example code for examples that work with the **OdbcConnection** and **OleDbConnection** classes. The **TargetSite.Name** value of the value of the objException object needs to be set to a different value when working with the **OdbcConnection** or **OleDbConnection** classes. This also means that the exception handler won't be unique for the **ChangeDatabase** method, but more of a general exception handler for catching operations performed on a closed connection.

Open Method Exceptions

The **InvalidOperationException** exception is thrown when you try to open an already open or broken connection. When this exception is thrown, simply close the connection and open it again. Listing 5-25 shows you how you can check if the **InvalidOperationException** exception was thrown because of the **Open** method.

*Listing 5-25. Checking If **Open** Caused the Exception*

```
1 Public Sub CheckOpenMethodException()
2    Dim cnnUserMan As OleDbConnection
3
4    Try
5       ' Instantiate the connection
6       cnnUserMan = New OleDbConnection(PR_STR_CONNECTION_STRING)
7       ' Open the connection
8       cnnUserMan.Open()
9       ' Open the connection
10      cnnUserMan.Open()
11   Catch objException As InvalidOperationException
12      ' Check if we tried to open an already open connection
13      If objException.TargetSite.Name = "Open" Then
14         MsgBox("The Open method threw the exception!")
15      End If
16   End Try
17 End Sub
```

In Listing 5-25, you can see how you can check if the **InvalidOperationException** exception was thrown because of using the **Open** method on a closed **OleDbConnection** object. Check the example code, available on the Apress Web site, for examples that work with the **OdbcConnection** and **SqlConnection** classes.

Summary

This chapter introduced you to connections and transactions in general, as well as the Connection and Transaction classes. You saw how to use transactions, automatic and manual and learned just what transaction boundaries are.

This chapter covered the following ground:

- *Connection class:* An explanation of the **OdbcConnection**, **OleDbConnection**, and **SqlConnection** classes

- *Transaction class:* An explanation of the **OdbcTransaction**, **OleDbTransaction**, and **SqlTransaction** classes

- *Error class:* An explanation of the **OdbcError**, **OleDbError**, and **SqlError** classes

- *Exception class:* An explanation of the **OdbcException**, **OleDbException**, and **SqlException** classes

The following chapter covers the Command and Parameter classes in the connected layer of ADO.NET. Learn how to use these classes in connection with the Connection, Transaction, and DataAdapter classes, to manipulate the data in your data source in various ways.

CHAPTER 6

The Command and Parameter Classes

WHEN YOU WANT TO execute action queries against your data source, such as DELETE or UPDATE statements, Command objects are your best bet. Command objects are used to execute commands against your data source, but not just action queries; it can be any kind of query or even a stored procedure. If you need to supply input and or output parameters with your commands, you can use the Parameter class for this very purpose.

Although the Command class can't really be used on its own, meaning you also need at least a Connection object (see Chapter 5 for more information on the Connection class), it's probably the most versatile class of all the classes of the ADO.NET connected layer. The Command class is used for executing queries against your data source, but it's also used by the DataAdapter class (see Chapter 8 for more information) for configuring how the data is being transported from your data source to a **DataSet** and back again. See Chapter 9 for more information on the **DataSet** class. Furthermore, using the Command class is the only way to populate a DataReader. See Chapter 7 for more information on the DataReader class.

Using Command Objects

A *Command object* is used when you need to execute a query against your database. The Command object is the simplest and easiest way of doing this. The three Command classes in ADO.NET that are of interest to us are **OdbcCommand**, **OleDbCommand**, and **SqlCommand**. The **OdbcCommand** class is part of the **Microsoft.Data.Odbc** namespace, the **OleDbCommand** class is part of the **System.Data.OleDb** namespace, and the **SqlCommand** class is part of the **System.Data.SqlClient** namespace.

TIP   If you are uncertain about which namespace a certain class in your code belongs to, then simply move the cursor over this class and the namespace will be displayed in the little tool tip that pops up.

OdbcCommand, OleDbCommand, and SqlCommand

As with the Provider and Connection classes, you should make up your mind if you are going to connect to a Microsoft SQL Server 7.0 or later data source, or an entirely different data source. The **SqlCommand** should be used with SQL Server, the **OdbcCommand** with any other ODBC data source, and the **OleDbCommand** with any other OLE DB data source. Because the **SqlCommand** class has been optimized for use with SQL Server, it outperforms the **OdbcCommand** and **OleDbCommand** classes when connecting to SQL Server. However, if you want, you can use the **OdbcCommand** or **OleDbCommand** classes instead of the **SqlCommand** in much the same way. In Listing 6-1, you can see how to declare and instantiate a **SqlCommand**.

Listing 6-1. Instantiating a SqlCommand

```
1 Public Sub InstantiateCommandObject()
2    Dim cnnUserMan As SqlConnection
3    Dim cmmUserMan As SqlCommand
4    Dim strSQL As String
5
6    ' Instantiate the connection
7    cnnUserMan = New SqlConnection(PR_STR_CONNECTION_STRING)
8    ' Open the connection
9    cnnUserMan.Open()
10   ' Build query string
11   strSQL = "SELECT * FROM tblUser"
12   ' Instantiate the command
13   cmmUserMan = New SqlCommand(strSQL, cnnUserMan)
14 End Sub
```

In Listing 6-1, I instantiate and open the connection on Lines 7 and 9. On Line 11, I build the query string to be used for the command; and on Line 13, I instantiate the Command, with the query string and the instantiated Connection object. The way the Command object is instantiated here is one of four different instantiation procedures available, because the **SqlCommand** constructor is overloaded. See the example code, available on the Apress Web site, for examples of how to do this using the **OdbcCommand** and **OleDBCommand** objects.

The Overloaded Command Constructor

Here are the four different ways you can instantiate an instance of one of the Command classes, **OdbcCommand**, **OleDbCommand**, and **SqlCommand**. The

Connection object, the query string, and the connection string have all been declared elsewhere:

- `cmmUserMan = New OleDbCommand()`: Instantiates `cmmUserMan` with no arguments. If you use this way to instantiate your Command object, you need to set some of the properties, such as **Connection**, before it can be used to execute a command. The following properties are set to initial values when you instantiate:

  `CommandText = ""`

  `CommandTimeout = 30`

  `CommandType = CommandType.Text`

  `Connection = Nothing`

- `cmmUserMan = New OleDbCommand(ByVal strSQL As String)`: Instantiates `cmmUserMan` with the query command text (`strSQL`). You also need to upply a valid and open connection by setting the **Connection** property. The following properties are set to initial values when you instantiate:

  `CommandText = strSQL`

  `CommandTimeout = 30`

  `CommandType = CommandType.Text`

  `Connection = Nothing`

- `cmmUserMan = New OleDbCommand(ByVal strSQL As String, ByVal cnnUserMan As OleDbConnection)`: Instantiates cmmUserMan with the query command text (strSQL) and a valid and open connection, cnnUserMan. The following properties are set to initial values when you instantiate:

  `CommandText = strSQL`

  `CommandTimeout = 30`

  `CommandType = CommandType.Text`

  `Connection = cnnUserMan`

- cmmUserMan = New OleDbCommand(ByVal strSQL As String, ByVal cnnUserMan As OleDbConnection, ByVal traUserMan As OleDbTransaction): Instantiates cmmUserMan with the query command text and a Connection object. cnnUserMan must be a valid and open connection, and traUserMan must be a valid and open transaction that has been opened on cnnUserMan. This version should be used when you have started a transaction with the **BeginTransaction** method of the Connection class. The following properties are set to initial values when you instantiate:

CommandText = strSQL

CommandTimeout = 30

CommandType = CommandType.Text

Connection = cnnUserMan

I've used the **OleDbCommand** class for the preceding examples, but you can replace the OleDb bit with Odbc or Sql, because the constructor overloads are the same for all three classes. Choose the instantiation method that is best suited to the context of your requirement. However, you must always use cmmUserMan = New OleDbCommand(strSQL, cnnUserMan, traUserMan) when a transaction has been started on the Connection object, and you want your command to be part of the transaction.

NOTE   You can't use a Command object on a Connection object where a transaction has already been started, unless you specify the same Transaction object for the Command object. This means that if you want your Command object to be used outside the transaction started on the Connection object, you must use another Connection object with no pending transactions.

Command Class Properties

Tables C-25, C-26, and C-27 in Appendix C list all the public, noninherited Command class properties in alphabetical order and show the equivalent Command class constructor argument (see the preceding section "The Overloaded Command Constructor"). Please note that in most cases the properties are only checked for syntax when you set them. The real validation takes place when you perform one of the **Execute . . .** methods. See the "Executing a Command" section later in this chapter, or Table C-28 in Appendix C for more information on these methods.

Command Class Methods

Table C-28 in Appendix C lists all the public, noninherited class methods for the three Command classes, **OdbcCommand**, **OleDbCommand**, and **SqlCommand** in alphabetical order. You can see by looking at their names that the methods of these classes are straightforward to use. However, the **Prepare** method is one of those methods one tends to forget about. When you deal with stored procedures and/or parameters in your SQL statements, it can often be a good idea to call the **Prepare** method before calling one of the **Execute . . .** methods. This is so because when a statement is prepared and called more than once, the statement is parsed and optimized when first executed, meaning subsequent executions will use the compiled version, giving a performance increase.

Executing a Command

Now you know how to set up and instantiate a Command object, but you really need to execute it as well in order to fully exploit a Command object's potential. As you can see from the various methods of the Command class, the **ExecuteNonQuery**, **ExecuteReader**, **ExecuteScalar**, and **ExecuteXmlReader** methods are the ones you need for this purpose. Actually, this is fairly simple, and if you carefully read the names of the methods, you should have no doubt about which one to use (see Table 6-1).

Table 6-1. Executing a Command

Method Name	When to Use	Example
ExecuteNonQuery	Use this method when you want to execute a non–row-returning command, such as a DELETE statement, or a parameterized statement Although you can use this method with row-returning statements, it doesn't make much sense, as the result set is discarded.	See Listing 6-2, which shows how to delete and insert a row.
ExecuteReader	This method should be used when you want to execute a row-returning command, such as a SELECT statement. The rows are returned in an **OdbcDataReader**, an **OleDbDataReader**, or a **SqlDataReader**, depending on which .NET Data Provider you are using. Please note that the DataReader class is a read-only, forward-only data class, which means that it should only be used for retrieving data for display or other read-only purposes. You can't update data in a DataReader!	See Listing 6-3, which shows how to retrieve all users from a table.
ExecuteScalar	You should use this method when you want only the first column of the first row of the result set returned. If there's more than one row in the result set, they are ignored by this method. This method is faster and has substantially less overhead than the **ExecuteReader** method. So use it when you know you will only have one row returned, or when you are using an aggregate function such as COUNT.	See Listing 6-4, which shows how the number of rows in the tblUser table is returned.
ExecuteXmlReader (**SqlCommand** class only)	This method is similar to the **ExecuteReader** method, but the returned rows must be expressed using XML.	See Listing 6-5, which shows how all the rows in a table are returned as XML. Please note that this method can also be used to retrieve the content of an **ntext** column, in which the text is valid XML data.

In Listing 6-2, you can see how the **ExecuteNonQuery** command is used to first delete a row from the data source and then to insert one using SQL statements.

*Listing 6-2. Using the **ExecuteNonQuery** Method*

```
1 Public Sub ExecuteNonQueryCommand()
2    Dim cnnUserMan As SqlConnection
3    Dim cmmUserMan As SqlCommand
4    Dim strSQL As String
5
6    ' Instantiate the connection
7    cnnUserMan = New SqlConnection(PR_STR_CONNECTION_STRING)
8    ' Open the connection
9    cnnUserMan.Open()
10   ' Build delete query string
11   strSQL = "DELETE FROM tblUser WHERE LoginName='User99'"
12   ' Instantiate and execute the delete command
13   cmmUserMan = New SqlCommand(strSQL, cnnUserMan)
14   cmmUserMan.ExecuteNonQuery()
15   ' Build insert query string
16   strSQL = "INSERT INTO tblUser (LoginName) VALUES('User99')"
17   ' Instantiate and execute the insert command
18   cmmUserMan = New SqlCommand(strSQL, cnnUserMan)
19   cmmUserMan.ExecuteNonQuery()
20 End Sub
```

In Listing 6-2, I use the SQL Server .NET Data Provider, but the code is almost the same for the ODBC .NET Data Provider and the OLE DB .NET Data Provider. See the example code, available on the Apress Web site, for some examples.

In Listing 6-3, you can see how the **ExecuteReader** command is used to retrieve all the rows from the tblUser table in an **OleDbDataReader** object, using a SQL statement.

*Listing 6-3. Using the **ExecuteReader** Method*

```
1 Public Sub ExecuteReaderCommand()
2    Dim cnnUserMan As OleDbConnection
3    Dim cmmUserMan As OleDbCommand
4    Dim drdTest As OleDbDataReader
5    Dim strSQL As String
6
7    ' Instantiate the connection
8    cnnUserMan = New OleDbConnection(PR_STR_CONNECTION_STRING)
```

```
 9    ' Open the connection
10    cnnUserMan.Open()
11    ' Build query string
12    strSQL = "SELECT * FROM tblUser"
13    ' Instantiate and execute the command
14    cmmUserMan = New OleDbCommand(strSQL, cnnUserMan)
15    drdTest = cmmUserMan.ExecuteReader()
16 End Sub
```

In Listing 6-3, I use the OLE DB .NET Data Provider, but the code is almost the same for the ODBC .NET Data Provider, and the SQL Server .NET Data Provider. See the example code, available on the Apress Web site, for some examples.

In Listing 6-4, you can see how the **ExecuteScalar** command is used to the number of rows in the tblUser table, using a SQL statement including the COUNT aggregate function.

*Listing 6-4. Using the **ExecuteScalar** Method*

```
 1 Public Sub ExecuteScalarCommand()
 2    Dim cnnUserMan As OdbcConnection
 3    Dim cmmUserMan As OdbcCommand
 4    Dim intNumRows As Integer
 5    Dim strSQL As String
 6
 7    ' Instantiate the connection
 8    cnnUserMan = New OdbcConnection(PR_STR_CONNECTION_STRING)
 9    ' Open the connection
10    cnnUserMan.Open()
11    ' Build query string
12    strSQL = "SELECT COUNT(*) FROM tblUser"
13    ' Instantiate the command
14    cmmUserMan = New OdbcCommand(strSQL, cnnUserMan)
15    ' Save the number of rows in the table
16    intNumRows = CInt(cmmUserMan.ExecuteScalar().ToString)
17 End Sub
```

In Listing 6-4, I use the ODBC .NET Data Provider, but the code is almost the same for the OLE DB .NET Data Provider, and the SQL Server .NET Data Provider. See the example code, available on the Apress Web site, for some examples.

In Listing 6-5, you can see how the **ExecuteXmlReader** command is used to retrieve all the rows from the tblUser table in an **XmlReader** object, using a SQL statement.

*Listing 6-5. Using the **ExecuteXmlReader** Method*

```
1 Public Sub ExecuteXmlReaderCommand()
2    Dim cnnUserMan As SqlConnection
3    Dim cmmUserMan As SqlCommand
4    Dim drdTest As XmlReader
5    Dim strSQL As String
6
7    ' Instantiate the connection
8    cnnUserMan = New SqlConnection(PR_STR_CONNECTION_STRING)
9    ' Open the connection
10   cnnUserMan.Open()
11   ' Build query string to return result set as XML
12   strSQL = "SELECT * FROM tblUser FOR XML AUTO"
13   ' Instantiate the command
14   cmmUserMan = New SqlCommand(strSQL, cnnUserMan)
15   ' Retrieve the rows as XML
16   drdTest = cmmUserMan.ExecuteXmlReader()
17 End Sub
```

In Listing 6-5, the result set is retrieved as XML, because the FOR XML AUTO clause appears at the end of the query. This instructs SQL Server 2000 to return the result set as XML, but you can only have it returned in an **XmlReader** object, the **SqlDataReader** will not work! I use the SQL Server .NET Data Provider, and this is the only provider that supports the **ExecuteXmlReader** method.

Handling Command Class Exceptions

There are a number of exceptions that can be thrown when you work with the properties and methods of the Command class. The following sections discuss the most common ones and how to deal with them. Please note that the example code listings are only suggestions; they need some work if you want to use them in production-quality code. However, they should give you a good idea of how to progress.

CommandTimeout Property

The **ArgumentException** exception is thrown when you try to set the **Command-Timeout** property to a negative value. Listing 6-6 shows you how you can check if the **ArgumentException** exception was thrown when the command time-out was changed.

Listing 6-6. Check If the Exception Was Caused When Setting Command Time-Out

```
1 Public Sub CheckCommandTimeoutPropertyException()
2    Dim cnnUserMan As OdbcConnection
3    Dim cmmUserMan As OdbcCommand
4    Dim strSQL As String
5
6    Try
7       ' Instantiate the connection
8       cnnUserMan = New OdbcConnection(PR_STR_CONNECTION_STRING)
9       ' Open the connection
10      cnnUserMan.Open()
11      ' Build query string
12      strSQL = "SELECT * FROM tblUser"
13      ' Instantiate the command
14      cmmUserMan = New OdbcCommand(strSQL, cnnUserMan)
15      ' Change command timeout
16      cmmUserMan.CommandTimeout = -1
17   Catch objException As ArgumentException
18      ' Check if we tried to set command timeout to an invalid value
19      If objException.TargetSite.Name = "set_CommandTimeout" Then
20         ' You can choose to have the user set a new timeout value,
21         ' set it to the default value, or just leave it as it is as
22         ' it hasn't changed
23         ' ...
24      End If
25   End Try
26 End Sub
```

In Listing 6-6, I use the ODBC .NET Data Provider, but the code is almost the same for the OLE DB .NET Data Provider, and the SQL Server .NET Data Provider. See the example code, available on the Apress Web site, for some examples.

CommandType Property

The **ArgumentException** exception is thrown if you try to set the property to an invalid command type. Listing 6-7 shows you how you can check if the **ArgumentException** exception was thrown when the command type was changed.

Listing 6-7. Check If the Exception Was Caused When Setting Command Type

```
 1 Public Sub CheckCommandTypePropertyException()
 2    Dim cnnUserMan As SqlConnection
 3    Dim cmmUserMan As SqlCommand
 4    Dim strSQL As String
 5
 6    Try
 7       ' Instantiate the connection
 8       cnnUserMan = New SqlConnection(PR_STR_CONNECTION_STRING)
 9       ' Open the connection
10       cnnUserMan.Open()
11       ' Build query string
12       strSQL = "SELECT * FROM tblUser"
13       ' Instantiate the command
14       cmmUserMan = New SqlCommand(strSQL, cnnUserMan)
15       ' Change command type
16       cmmUserMan.CommandType = CommandType.TableDirect
17    Catch objException As ArgumentException
18       ' Check if we tried to set command type to an invalid value
19       If objException.TargetSite.Name = "set_CommandType" Then
20          ' Perhaps ask the user, or since we know this is because
21          ' we're trying to use a OLE DB .NET Data Provider only
22          ' supported setting, we can change the SQL statement and
23          ' set the CommandType property to Text
24          cmmUserMan.CommandType = CommandType.Text
25          cmmUserMan.CommandText = "SELECT * FROM " & _
26             cmmUserMan.CommandText
27       End If
28    End Try
29 End Sub
```

In Listing 6-7, I use the SQL Server .NET Data Provider, but the code is almost the same for the ODBC .NET Data Provider. See the example code, available on the Apress Web site, for some examples. Since the **TableDirect** is a valid **CommandType** property setting of the **OleDbCommand**, you won't be throwing an exception if you run the example code in Listing 6-7 against the OLE DB .NET Data Provider.

Prepare Method

The **InvalidOperationException** exception is thrown if the connection variable is set to a null value or if the connection isn't open. Listing 6-8 shows you how you can check if the **InvalidOperationException** exception was thrown when preparing the command.

Listing 6-8. Check If Exception Was Thrown When Trying to Prepare the Command

```
 1 Public Sub CheckPrepareMethodException()
 2    Dim cnnUserMan As OleDbConnection
 3    Dim cmmUserMan As OleDbCommand
 4    Dim strSQL As String
 5
 6    Try
 7       ' Instantiate the connection
 8       cnnUserMan = New OleDbConnection(PR_STR_CONNECTION_STRING)
 9       ' Open the connection
10       ' If the following line is commented out, the ValidateCommand exception
11       ' will be thrown
12       'cnnUserMan.Open()
13       ' Build query string
14       strSQL = "SELECT * FROM tblUser"
15       ' Instantiate the command
16       cmmUserMan = New OleDbCommand(strSQL, cnnUserMan)
17       ' Prepare command
18       cmmUserMan.Prepare()
19    Catch objException As InvalidOperationException
20       ' Check if we tried to prepare the command on an invalid connection
21       If objException.TargetSite.Name = "SetStateExecuting" Then
22          ' Open the connection and try again
23          cnnUserMan.Open()
24          cmmUserMan.Prepare()
25       End If
26    End Try
27 End Sub
```

In Listing 6-8, I use the OLE DB .NET Data Provider, but the code is almost the same for the ODBC .NET Data Provider and the SQL Server .NET Data Provider, except for the **TargetSite.Name** value. See the example code, available on the Apress Web site, for some examples.

UpdatedRowSource Property

The **ArgumentException** exception is thrown if the row source update property was set to a value other than an **UpdateRowSource** enum value. Listing 6-9 shows you how to check if the **ArgumentException** exception was thrown.

Listing 6-9. Check If Exception Was Thrown When Trying to Change Row Source Update

```
1 Public Sub CheckUpdatedRowSourcePropertyException()
2    Dim cnnUserMan As OdbcConnection
3    Dim cmmUserMan As OdbcCommand
4    Dim strSQL As String
5
6    Try
7        ' Instantiate the connection
8        cnnUserMan = New OdbcConnection(PR_STR_CONNECTION_STRING)
9        ' Open the connection
10       cnnUserMan.Open()
11       ' Build query string
12       strSQL = "SELECT * FROM tblUser"
13       ' Instantiate the command
14       cmmUserMan = New OdbcCommand(strSQL, cnnUserMan)
15       ' Change Row source Update
16       ' You need to turn Option Strict Off for this to compile
17       cmmUserMan.UpdatedRowSource = 5
18   Catch objException As ArgumentException
19       ' Check if we tried to set the row source update to an invalid value
20       If objException.TargetSite.Name = "set_UpdatedRowSource" Then
21           ' Ask the user or simply set to a valid value. Was the current
22           ' value okay?
23           ' ...
24       End If
25   End Try
26 End Sub
```

In Listing 6-9, I use the ODBC .NET Data Provider, but the code is almost the same for the OLE DB .NET Data Provider, and the SQL Server .NET Data Provider. See the example code, available on the Apress Web site, for some examples.

NOTE   In the code in Listing 6-9 you need to set **Option Strict** to **Off** for Line 17 to compile. **Option Strict** can be turned on or off at the top of each code module or class, or project-wide from the Project Property dialog box. **Option Strict** means that implicit data type conversions are restricted to only widening conversions. Therefore, implicitly you can have, say, a function return an **Integer** to a **Long** variable, but not vice versa.

Using Parameter Objects

The Parameter class, which encompasses **OdbcParameter**, **OleDbParameter**, and **SqlParameter**, is one of those classes in the ADO.NET connected layer that can't be used on its own; it's purpose is to serve as a "helper" class to the Command class. As the class name suggests, it's for adding parameters to the parameters collection of the Command class, which can be accessed through the **Parameters** property.

Parameterized calls is what you call it when you use parameters within a SQL statement, and in this case, the SQL statement of your Command object. Parameterized calls are generally used when executing a SQL statement that doesn't return any rows, but has output parameters, or to improve the performance of a stored procedure call.

I won't be going into too many details concerning the Parameter class here, because you'll see it used in later chapters in connection with the Command objects of the DataAdapter class. However, Table C-31 in Appendix C lists all the public properties of the class. There are no public, noninherited methods or events of the Parameter class. The rest of this chapter will show you the basics of the Parameter class, and how you use it. See the "Setting the Command Properties" section of Chapter 8 for more detailed examples.

Instantiating a Parameter Object

The Parameter object can be instantiated using the overloaded **New** constructor (see the "The Overloaded Parameter Constructor" section next), or you can add them directly to the parameter collection of a Command object, which is accessed through the **Parameter** property.

NOTE   You can also add a parameter to the parameters collection of a Command object, without first instantiating a Parameter object. This is so because the **Add** method of the parameters collection (**OdbcParameterCollection**, **OleDbParameterCollection**, or **SqlParameterCollection**) is overloaded and takes a number of different arguments, ranging from the name and value of the parameter, to the name, data type, size, and source column name of the parameter. In this chapter, I concentrate on instantiating Parameter objects and adding them to the parameters collection.

The Overloaded Parameter Constructor

Here are the six different ways you can instantiate an instance of one of the Parameter classes, **OdbcParameter**, **OleDbParameter**, and **SqlParameter**:

- prmUser = New SqlParameter(): Instantiates prmUser with no arguments.

- prmUser = New SqlParameter(ByVal strParameterName As String, ByVal objValue As Object): Instantiates prmUser with the name of the parameter (strParameterName), and the parameter value (objValue).

- prmUser = New SqlParameter(ByVal strParameterName As String, ByVal intDataType As SqlDbType): Instantiates prmUser with the name of the parameter (strParameterName) and the parameter data type (intDataType).

- prmUser = New SqlParameter(ByVal strParameterName As String, ByVal intDataType As SqlDbType, ByVal intSize As Integer): Instantiates prmUser with the name of the parameter (strParameterName), the parameter data type (intDataType), and the size or width of the parameter (intSize).

- prmUser = New SqlParameter(ByVal strParameterName As String, ByVal intDataType As SqlDbType, ByVal intSize As Integer, ByVal strSourceColumn As String): Instantiates prmUser with the name of the parameter (strParameterName), the parameter data type (intDataType), the size or width of the parameter (intSize), and the name of the source column (strSourceColumn).

- prmUser = New SqlParameter(ByVal strParameterName As String, ByVal intDataType As SqlDbType, ByVal intSize As Integer, ByVal intDirection As ParameterDirection, ByVal blnNullable As Boolean, bytPrecision As Byte, ByVal bytScale As Byte, ByVal strSourceColumn As String, ByVal intSourceVersion As DataRowVersion, ByVal objValue As Object): Instantiates prmUser with the name of the parameter (strParameterName); the parameter data type (intDataType); the size or width of the parameter (intSize); the parameter type or direction (intDirection); a **Boolean** value indicating if the column accepts null values (blnNullable); the precision of the parameter (bytPrecision), meaning the total number of digits, excluding the decimal point; the scale or number of decimal places (bytScale), meaning the number of digits to the right of the decimal point; the name of the source column (strSourceColumn); the parameter source version (intSourceVersion); and the value of the parameter (objValue).

Choose the instantiation method that is best suited to the context of your requirement. Listing 6-10 shows you an example of how to declare and instantiate the various overloads of the Parameter class.

Listing 6-10. Instantiating a Parameter Class

```
1 Public Sub InstantiateParameterObject()
2    Dim prmNoArguments As New SqlParameter()
3    Dim prmNameValueArguments As New SqlParameter("Id", 3)
4    Dim prmNameDataTypeArguments As New SqlParameter("Id", SqlDbType.Int)
5    Dim prmNameDataTypeSizeArguments As New SqlParameter("LoginName", _
6        SqlDbType.VarChar, 50)
7    Dim prmNameDataTypeSizeSourceColumnArguments As New SqlParameter( _
8        "LoginName", SqlDbType.VarChar, 50, "LoginName")
9    Dim prmNameDataTypeSizeDirNullPrecisionScaleSrcColSrcVersionValueArgs _
10       As New SqlParameter("LoginName", SqlDbType.VarChar, 50, _
11       ParameterDirection.Input, True, 0, 0, "LoginName", _
12       DataRowVersion.Current, 3)
13 End Sub
```

I've used the **SqlParameter** class for the constructor examples and Listing 6-10, but you can replace the Sql bits with Odbc or OleDb, because the constructor over-loads are the same for all three classes. Which parameter constructor you should use is really up to you, but with most of them, you still need to set some properties before adding the parameter to the parameter collection of the Command class. It all depends on what data type, type or direction, source column version, and so on you're working with. See the following sections for more information on these properties. Please note that you don't necessarily have to specify all arguments for the various overloads; you can pass a null value (**Nothing**) or the value 0, if that particular argument isn't needed for your parameter. One such argument can be the bytPrecision argument in the last of the overloads shown. If your parameter isn't a floating-point number, then it doesn't make any sense, so just pass the value 0.

> **NOTE** If you don't specify the values for the required parameters, or you specify the wrong values, this will throw an exception when you execute the Command object.

Setting the Data Type of a Parameter

All parameters must have a data type, which you can specify using the **DbType** property. This property must be set to one of the **DbType**[1] enum members, which are .NET data types and not .NET Data Provider specific. The **OdbcType**, **OleDbType**, and **SqlDbType** properties are .NET Data Provider specific, so do you use the .NET-specific property, or the .NET Data Provider–specific one? Well, you can use both really, because they're directly linked, meaning that if you set one, the other one is automatically set to the corresponding value. Therefore, if you set the **DbType** property of an **OdbcParameter** class instance to **String**, the **OdbcType** parameter is set to **Char**. This is quite good as you can have the Parameter class take care of the conversion, if you only know one of the data types, which can be the case when you're working with more than one of the .NET Data Providers.

If you don't explicitly set the **DbType** property, it's automatically set to **String**, which is the default value.

Specifying the Parameter Type

A parameter can be of type input, output, input and output, or the return value of a stored procedure, stored function, built-in function, or user-defined function. You can specify the type by setting the **Direction** property, which must be set to one of the **ParameterDirection** enum members; see Table C-32 in Appendix C for more on these enum members.

---

1. See the MSDN documentation that comes with VS .NET for the various members of the **DbType** enum.

NOTE   Any output value, **ParameterDirection.InputOutput**, **ParameterDirection.Output**, and **ParameterDirection.ReturnValue**, is not populated until the last row of the last result set (if more than one) has been read.

Parameter Mapping

When you use parameters for your SQL statements or stored procedures, it's important to know how the Parameter objects are mapped to the parameters in your SQL statements and stored procedures. You can see how this is done in the "Parameter Object to SQL Statement Parameter Mapping" section next. It's also important that you make sure that it's the right version of the data in your **DataTable** that's used for the parameter value. You can find more information about this in the "Parameter to Data Version Mapping" section later in this chapter. The last thing you might need to check concerning parameter mapping is to specify which column in the data source your Parameter object maps to. See the "Parameter to Source Column Mapping" section later in this chapter for more information.

Parameter Object to SQL Statement Parameter Mapping

When a Parameter object is added to the parameter collection of a Command object (accessed through the **Parameters** property), the Command object needs to know to which parameter in the SQL statement or stored procedure it should map. The SQL Server .NET Data Provider only supports named parameters, whereas the ODBC .NET Data Provider and the OLE DB .NET Data Provider only support positional parameters.

Named parameters are mapped by name, meaning the name of the Parameter object, which is set and read using the **ParameterName** property, must match the name used in the SQL statement or stored procedure. Say you have a SQL statement that looks like this:

```
SELECT * FROM tblUser WHERE FirstName=@FirstName And @LastName=@LastName
```

Then you need two Parameter objects associated with your Command object, named as follows:

```
prmFirstName.ParameterName = "@FirstName"
prmLastName.ParameterName = "@LastName"
```

Because the SQL Server .NET Data Provider uses named parameters, it doesn't matter in what order they're added to the parameter collection of the Command object (see the "Adding Parameter Objects to Parameters Collection" section later in this chapter for more information). Therefore, you can add the `prmLastName` parameter before you add the `prmFirstName`.

Positional parameters are mapped by position, meaning the order in which they appear in the SQL statement or stored procedure (left to right) is mapped to the order in which the parameters are added to the parameters collection. Say you have a SQL statement that looks like this (positional parameters are indicated with a question mark):

```
SELECT * FROM tblUser WHERE FirstName=? AND LastName=?
```

If your SQL statement looks like that, you'll need two Parameter objects, one for each parameter (?) in the SQL statement. I always name my parameters, whether they're named or positional parameters, so the parameters will look like this:

```
prmFirstName.ParameterName = "@FirstName"
prmLastName.ParameterName = "@LastName"
```

These Parameter objects must then be added to the parameter collection, in the same order, as the **ParameterName** property has been set.

TIP Even if you don't have to specify a name for positional Parameter objects, it's always a good idea, because it's easier to find them in the parameters collection of the Command class. If at runtime you have a parameter that you want to know the details of, it's always quite simple to look at the name to get an idea, assuming that you name the parameter according to its purpose.

Parameter to Data Version Mapping

A **DataRow** class holds different versions of the data in the row, such as the original data and the current data. When you use parameters with your Command objects, it's important to specify which version of the **DataRow**, or rather **DataColumn**, you want to use. The source version is specified by setting the **SourceVersion** property, or by specifying it as the source version argument, when instantiating the Parameter object. You must specify the source version using one of the members of the **DataRowVersion** enum, which you can see in Table C-44 in Appendix C.

Actually, it's really only with input parameters that you need to specify the source version, because it's not needed for output parameters for obvious reasons. Generally, you don't have to specify it for SELECT statements, because you really just need the current value as the input. The same goes for most stand-alone Command objects, meaning Command objects that aren't associated with a DataAdapter object (see Chapter 8 for more information), because you generally set the value of the parameter manually. Manually is the keyword here, because when you use the Command object with a DataAdapter object, all the data generally comes from the data source. Therefore, say you have a table with a primary key, whose value is updateable, and this often happens in your **DataTable**. Imagine then that you've changed the primary key value, and instead of updating the data source, you decide to delete the row. The DataAdapter uses the primary key information to look up the row in the data source, but if you changed the value, it can't find the original row, and perhaps it finds a different one, depending on what you new value you assigned. In such a case, you specify that the value used for the Parameter object, should be the original one, which is accessed with the **Original** member of the **DataRowVersion** enum, like this:

```
prmLastName.SourceVersion = DataRowVersion.Original
```

I know that the last name of a person is rarely used as a primary, but it serves as a good example. I'm also assuming that you haven't set up any referential integrity that would disallow the changing of the primary key and/or deletion of the row.

Parameter to Source Column Mapping

If you use different column names in your **DataTable** than in your data source, you need to specify this with your Parameter object. It's not that difficult, but you need to make sure you do it. Say you have the a copy of the tblUser table from the UserMan database in a **DataTable** object, and the FirstName column in the data source is mapped to the First Name column (with a space character) in the **DataTable**. Then you need to set the source column when you instantiate your Parameter object, or set the **SourceColumn** property, like this:

```
prmFirstName.SourceColumn = "FirstName"
```

Using Null Values with Parameters

If you want to specify a null value as the value of your Parameter object, you must use the **DBNull** class, and *not* **Nothing**, because **DBNull** is used to represent a null value. Setting the property to **Nothing** doesn't have the same effect. You can specify it like this:

```
prmUserMan.Value = DBNull.Value
```

Adding Parameter Objects to Parameters Collection

Parameters must be added to the parameters collection of the Command object before you execute the command. There's only one way to add the parameters, and that's using the **Add** method of the parameters collection (**OdbcParameterCollection**, **OleDbParameterCollection**, or **SqlParameterCollection**) of the Command object (**OdbcCommand**, **OleDbCommand**, or **SqlCommand**).

For named parameters, which is supported by the SQL Server .NET Data Provider, it doesn't matter in what order you add them, but for positional parameters, which is supported by the ODBC .NET Data Provider and the OLE DB .NET Data Provider, you must add them in the order they appear in the SQL statement or stored procedure.

This is how you add an instantiated and initialized Parameter object to the parameters collection:

```
cmmUserMan.Parameters.Add(prmFirstName)
```

Summary

This chapter introduced you to command and Parameter objects, and how they're used together when retrieving data from your data source, inserting data into your data source, deleting data from your data source, or updating data in your data source.

This chapter covered the following ground:

- **OdbcCommand**, **OleDbCommand**, and **SqlCommand** classes

- **OdbcParameter**, **OleDbParameter**, and **SqlParameter** classes

The following chapter covers the DataReader classes in the connected layer of ADO.NET.

DataReaders

DATAREADERS ARE USED FOR retrieving read-only data from a data source, and fast. It's much more efficient to use a DataReader than to use a **DataTable** and/or **DataSet**. Some of the reasons that it's faster are that only one row is ever in memory, and that it's a direct stream of data from the data source. This chapter will introduce you to the four different DataReader classes: **OdbcDataReader**, **OleDbDataReader**, **SqlDataReader**, and **XmlReader**.

Using the DataReader Class

The *DataReader* class is a read-only, forward-only data class, and it's very efficient when it comes to memory usage, because only one row is ever in memory at a time. This is in contrast to the **DataTable** class (discussed in Chapter 10), which allocates memory for all rows retrieved.

You can only instantiate a DataReader by using the **ExecuteReader** method of the Command class (see "Executing a Command" in Chapter 6 for details). When you use the DataReader, the associated connection can't perform any other operations. This is because the connection as such is serving the DataReader, and you need to close the DataReader before the connection is ready for other operations. Another thing you definitely need to know is that the DataReader class seems to jam communications at the server by locking rows,[1] leaving queries from other connections hanging and eventually leading to time-outs. The DataReader class is one of the ADO.NET classes that resemble the classic ADO **Recordset** class the most. Well, it is, when you come to think about it, simply a **Recordset** with a read-only, forward-only cursor. One of the differences is how you get the next row (see the "Reading Rows in a DataReader" section later in this chapter).

---

1. This is *not* part of the DataReader description, and I can't really give you a reason as to why and when it happens. Only one thing is sure, don't overdo the use of the DataReader, and if you happen to run into the mentioned problems, redesign your application, because you'll have little if no luck solving it.

OdbcDataReader, OleDbDataReader, and SqlDataReader

As with the Connection and Command classes, there are also three general DataReader classes of interest:[2] **OdbcDataReader** for use with your ODBC data source, **OleDbDataReader** is for use with your OLE DB data source, and **SqlDataReader** is for use with MS SQL Server 7 or later. Please note that if you are using a **SqlConnection** object, then you can't use **OleDbCommand** and/or an **OdbcDataReader** class with the connection. The same goes the other way around. In other words, you can't mix Odbc, OleDb, and Sql data classes; they can't work together!

Declaring and Instantiating a DataReader Object

The DataReader class can't be inherited, which effectively means that you can't create your own data class based on the DataReader class. Therefore, the following example code is wrong:

```
Dim drdTest As New SqlDataReader()
```

It's wrong because it tries to instantiate drdTest using the **New** keyword, but that doesn't work, because the DataReader class doesn't have a public constructor. Listing 7-1 shows you what you need to do to declare and instantiate a **SqlDataReader** object.

*Listing 7-1. Instantiating a **SqlDataReader** Object*

```
 1 Public Sub InstantiateDataReader()
 2    Dim cnnUserMan As SqlConnection
 3    Dim cmmUserMan As SqlCommand
 4    Dim drdUserMan As SqlDataReader
 5    Dim strSQL As String
 6
 7    ' Instantiate the connection
 8    cnnUserMan = New SqlConnection(PR_STR_CONNECTION_STRING)
 9    ' Open the connection
10    cnnUserMan.Open()
11    ' Build query string
12    strSQL = "SELECT * FROM tblUser"
```

---

2. Well, there's actually one more, the **XmlReader** class, discussed in the "XmlReader" section later in this chapter.

```
13    ' Instantiate the command
14    cmmUserMan = New SqlCommand(strSQL, cnnUserMan)
15    ' Instantiate data reader using the ExecuteReader method
16    ' of the command class
17    drdUserMan = cmmUserMan.ExecuteReader()
18 End Sub
```

Listing 7-1 shows you how to instantiate a **SqlDataReader** object, using the **ExecuteReader** method of the **SqlCommand** class. Please note how the Connection is instantiated, and opened, before the Command object is instantiated, set up, and used to populate the DataReader object.

The code is nearly identical for the ODBC .NET Data Provider and the OLE DB .NET Data Provider. You can find examples in the example code available on the Apress Web site.

Nondefault Instantiation of DataReader

When you instantiate a DataReader using the **ExecuteReader** method of the Command class as shown in Listing 7-1, you don't pass any arguments to the method, which means you're using the default values. The **ExecuteReader** method takes one or more of the **CommandBehavior** enum members as the first and only argument. Table C-33 in Appendix C lists the members of the **CommandBehavior** enum. There are members that perform the following actions:

- Closing the connection when you close the DataReader (see the "Closing a DataReader" section later in this chapter)

- Extracting metadata information (see the "Extracting Metadata" section later in this chapter)

- Loading only one column in memory at a time (see the "Reading Images from Data Source" section later in this chapter)

- Returning only a single row and/or result (see the "Reading Rows in a DataReader" and "Handling Multiple Results" sections later in this chapter)

Opening a DataReader

A DataReader isn't opened as such, because it's ready to work with once you instantiate it using the **ExecuteReader** method. See the previous section, "Declaring and Instantiating a DataReader Object," for more information.

Closing a DataReader

Because the DataReader object keeps the connection busy while it's open, it's good practice to close the DataReader once you are done with it. The DataReader is closed using the **Close** method, like this:

```
drdTest.Close()
```

You can use the **IsClosed** property to check if the DataReader is closed, as follows:

```
If Not drdTest.IsClosed Then
```

This little piece of example code will execute the code in the **If . . . Then . . . End If** block if the DataReader is *not* closed!

Because the DataReader object keeps the connection busy while it's open, you might find yourself using a separate Connection object for your DataReader. This is to avoid problems with the connection being busy, when you want to use it for other purposes. In this case, it can be a good idea to have the Connection object closed at the same time you close the DataReader. This can be achieved by specifying the **CommandBehavior.CloseConnection** enum member, when instantiating the DataReader. It's done like this:

```
drdUserMan = cmmUserMan.ExecuteReader(CommandBehavior.CloseConnection)
```

You can find more information about instantiating the DataReader object in the "Declaring and Instantiating a DataReader Object" section earlier in this chapter.

Reading Rows in a DataReader

Since the DataReader class is a forward-only data class, you need to read the rows sequentially from start to finish if you need to read all the returned rows. In Listing 7-2 you can see how to loop through a populated DataReader.

Listing 7-2. Loop Through All Rows in a DataReader

```
1 Public Sub ReadRowsFromDataReader()
2    Dim cnnUserMan As OdbcConnection
3    Dim cmmUserMan As OdbcCommand
4    Dim drdUser As OdbcDataReader
5    Dim strSQL As String
6    Dim lngCounter As Long = 0
7
8    ' Instantiate the connection
9    cnnUserMan = New OdbcConnection(PR_STR_CONNECTION_STRING)
10   ' Open the connection
11   cnnUserMan.Open()
12   ' Build query string
13   strSQL = "SELECT * FROM tblUser"
14   ' Instantiate the command
15   cmmUserMan = New OdbcCommand(strSQL, cnnUserMan)
16   ' Execute command and return rows in data reader
17   drdUser = cmmUserMan.ExecuteReader()
18   ' Loop through all the returned rows
19   Do While drdUser.Read
20      ' Display Id of current row
21      MsgBox(drdUser.GetInt32(0).ToString)
22      ' Increment number of rows
23      lngCounter = lngCounter + 1
24   Loop
25
26   ' Display the number of rows returned
27   MsgBox(CStr(lngCounter))
28 End Sub
```

Listing 7-2 loops through the rows in the **OdbcDataReader**, displays the Id
column value, and counts the number of rows. This is obviously just an example of
how to sequentially go through all the rows returned by the **ExecuteReader** method of
the Command class. The code is nearly identical for the OLE DB .NET Data Provider
and the SQL Server .NET Data Provider. You can find additional examples in the
example code available on the Apress Web site.

If you only want a single row returned, you can use the
CommandBehavior.SingleRow enum member, when calling the
ExecuteReader method, like this:

```
drdUser = cmmUserMan.ExecuteReader(CommandBehavior.SingleRow)
```

Checking for Null Values in Columns

Null values can be a burden to deal with because they can crash your application if you haven't set up your code to appropriately handle them. Null values are empty references or nothing at all, meaning a value that has yet to be defined. It's unlike an empty string, because an empty string is something: a string, although an empty one.

NOTE One thing you should be aware of when dealing with null values in your database is if the ANSI SQL-92 standard is being used by your DBMS. If your DBMS uses ANSI SQL-92, you can't compare a column value to NULL. This is because ANSI SQL-92 dictates that a comparison made in a SELECT statement always returns false when you compare a column value with NULL. In SQL Server you can turn this option on and off using the SET ANSI_NULLS statement. See you DBMS documentation for more information.

When you have instantiated your DataReader and positioned it to a valid row using the **Read** method, you can check the column to see if it contains a null value. This is done by using the **IsDBNull** method, which compares the content of a specific column in the current row with the **DBNull** class. If the column contains a null value, the **IsDBNull** method returns **True**. Otherwise, **False** is returned. Listing 7-3 shows how you can perform the check.

Listing 7-3. Check for Null Value in Column

```
1 Public Sub CheckForNullValueInColumn(ByVal intColumn As Integer)
2    Dim cnnUserMan As OleDbConnection
3    Dim cmmUserMan As OleDbCommand
4    Dim drdUser As OleDbDataReader
5    Dim strSQL As String
6
7    ' Instantiate the connection
8    cnnUserMan = New OleDbConnection(PR_STR_CONNECTION_STRING)
9    ' Open the connection
10   cnnUserMan.Open()
11   ' Build query string
12   strSQL = "SELECT * FROM tblUser"
13   ' Instantiate the command
14   cmmUserMan = New OleDbCommand(strSQL, cnnUserMan)
15   ' Execute command and return rows in data reader
16   drdUser = cmmUserMan.ExecuteReader()
```

```
17    ' Advance reader to first row
18    drdUser.Read()
19    ' Check if the column contains a NULL value
20    If drdUser.IsDBNull(intColumn) Then
21        MsgBox("Column " & CStr(intColumn) & " contains a NULL value!")
22    Else
23        MsgBox("Column " & CStr(intColumn) & " does not contain a NULL value!")
24    End If
25 End Sub
```

In Listing 7-3, you can see how the **IsDBNull** method of the **OleDbDataReader** class is used for checking if a particular column contains a null value. The **IsDBNull** method takes the ordinal position of the column as the only argument. The column array is zero-based, meaning that a table with 5 columns will have an ordinal range of 0 to 4.

The code is nearly identical for the ODBC .NET Data Provider and the SQL Server .NET Data Provider. You can find examples hereof in the example code available on the Apress Web site.

Reading Images from Data Source

Quite often images are saved to a database and you then need to retrieve the images for various display purposes, such as pictures on buttons, and links on Web pages.[3] Unlike standard column values, images are generally stored as an array of bytes in your data source. This also means that you need to do a little more work than just retrieving a simple number or string value. You need to retrieve the bytes from a single column in your data source and save it to a byte array, but you also need to know how many bytes the image has. In classic ADO, you have the **GetChunk** method of the **Recordset** class to retrieve an image from your data source, but there are a few ADO.NET ways of doing it. The DataReader has the **GetBytes** method, and it can be used to get the size of the image as well as retrieving the image and saving it as a byte array. If you already know the exact image size in bytes—for instance, if all your images are the same size—you don't need to query for the size. However, in many cases, you will need to get the size of the stored image, and you can do it like this:

```
Dim lngNumBytes As Long = drdSql.GetBytes(1, 0, Nothing, 0, Integer.MaxValue)
```

---

3. Many programmers swear to a different way of dealing with images: saving them on disk or even as a URL, and then saving a reference to the images in the database. Personally, I can see both approaches working, but be aware that images stored in your database will quickly bloat your database.

This will save the number of bytes in column 2 (the first argument is set to the value 1, the column array is zero-based) of the current row in the DataReader, in the lngNumBytes variable. It's the passing of a null value (**Nothing**) as the third argument that's the real trick here, because not passing the size of the byte array means you'll get the size of the column returned. See Table C-35 in Appendix C for more information on the arguments of the **GetBytes** method. Once you have the size of the image, you can go ahead and retrieve it, as is shown in Listing 7-4.

Listing 7-4. Retrieving Image from DataReader

```
1 Public Sub ReadImageFromDataReader(ByVal intImageId As Integer)
2    Dim cnnImage As SqlConnection
3    Dim cmmImage As SqlCommand
4    Dim drdTest As SqlDataReader
5    Dim strSQL As String
6    Dim fstImage As FileStream
7    Dim bwrTest As BinaryWriter
8    Dim lngTotalNumBytes As Long
9    Dim strFileName As String = "Image.bmp"
10
11   ' Instantiate the connection
12   cnnImage = New SqlConnection(PR_STR_CONNECTION_STRING)
13   ' Open the connection
14   cnnImage.Open()
15   ' Build query string
16   strSQL = "SELECT Picture FROM tblImage WHERE Id=" & intImageId.ToString()
17   ' Instantiate the command
18   cmmImage = New SqlCommand(strSQL, cnnImage)
19   ' Execute command and return row in data reader
20   drdTest = cmmImage.ExecuteReader(CommandBehavior.SequentialAccess)
21
22   ' Check if a row was returned
23   If drdTest.Read() Then
24      ' Get size of image
25      lngTotalNumBytes = drdTest.GetBytes(0, 0, Nothing, 0, Integer.MaxValue)
26
27      ' Create a new file to hold the output
28      fstImage = New FileStream(strFileName, FileMode.CreateNew, _
29         FileAccess.Write)
30      bwrTest = New BinaryWriter(fstImage)
31
32      ' Create byte array with the exact size of the picture
33      Dim arrbytImage(CInt(lngTotalNumBytes)) As Byte
```

```
34        ' Save picture in byte array
35        drdTest.GetBytes(0, 0, arrbytImage, 0, CInt(lngTotalNumBytes))
36
37        ' Write the buffer to file
38        bwrTest.Write(arrbytImage)
39        bwrTest.Flush()
40
41        ' Close the output file
42        bwrTest.Close()
43        fstImage.Close()
44    End If
45    ' Close connection
46    cnnImage.Close()
47 End Sub
```

In Listing 7-4, I instantiate and open a connection on Lines 12 and 14, build the query string to retrieve the picture by Id on Line 16, instantiate a Command object with the connection and query string on Line 18, and on Line 20 the Picture column of the row with the specified Id is returned. Please note that I'm using the **SequentialAccess** member of the **CommandBehavior** enum as the first and only argument of the **ExecuteReader** method. I do this to signal sequential access to the columns. The advantage of doing this is that only one column is ever in memory at one time. You could argue that I'm only returning one column for every row returned anyway, which is correct; but the significance of using the **SequentialAccess** member becomes clear when you have multiple columns returned, including one or more images. You need to change the name of the image column and the table to match your data source.

If anything is returned from the data source, assuming only one row will ever be returned by the query, the size of the image is retrieved on Line 25. The arrbytImage **Byte** array is resized to the exact size of the image on Line 33, and this figure is then used to retrieve the image on Line 35 and saved in the **Byte** array. Just to show you the output, I've also set up the code to save it to a file, using a **BinaryWriter** and a **FileStream** object. You can find more information on these classes in the MSDN Help Documentation.

The code has been written using the SQL Server .NET Data Provider, but the code is nearly identical for the ODBC .NET Data Provider and the OLE DB .NET Data Provider. You can find examples hereof in the example code available on the Apress Web site.

If you have large images in your database, the approach taken in Listing 7-4 might not be the best to use. This is because you retrieve the entire image in one go, which can be a problem depending on your scenario, with bandwidth and timeouts being possible difficulties.

A better method is to retrieve smaller chunks at a time. What size will work best for you is for you to find out, by testing it. Listing 7-5 shows you how to retrieve an image in smaller chunks.

Listing 7-5. Retrieving Image from DataReader in Smaller Chunks

```
1 Public Sub ReadImageFromDataReaderInChunks(ByVal intImageId As Integer)
2     Const INT_IMAGE_BUFFER_SIZE As Integer = 128
3
4     Dim cnnImage As OleDbConnection
5     Dim cmmImage As OleDbCommand
6     Dim drdTest As OleDbDataReader
7     Dim strSQL As String
8     Dim fstImage As FileStream
9     Dim bwrTest As BinaryWriter
10    Dim lngTotalNumBytes As Long
11    Dim strFileName As String = "Image.bmp"
12    Dim lngNumBytesReturned As Long
13    Dim arrbytImage(INT_IMAGE_BUFFER_SIZE - 1) As Byte
14    Dim intImagePos As Integer = 0
15
16    ' Instantiate the connection
17    cnnImage = New OleDbConnection(PR_STR_CONNECTION_STRING)
18    ' Open the connection
19    cnnImage.Open()
20    ' Build query string
21    strSQL = "SELECT Picture FROM tblImage WHERE Id=" & _
22        intImageId.ToString()
23    ' Instantiate the command
24    cmmImage = New OleDbCommand(strSQL, cnnImage)
25    ' Excute command and return row in data reader
26    drdTest = cmmImage.ExecuteReader(CommandBehavior.SequentialAccess)
27
28    ' Create a new file to hold the output
29    fstImage = New FileStream(strFileName, FileMode.CreateNew, _
30        FileAccess.Write)
31    bwrTest = New BinaryWriter(fstImage)
32
33    ' Check if a row was returned
34    If drdTest.Read() Then
35        ' Save image chunk in byte array and save the number of bytes returned
36        lngNumBytesReturned = drdTest.GetBytes(0, 0, arrbytImage, 0, _
37            INT_IMAGE_BUFFER_SIZE)
38
```

```
39        ' Keep reading chunks of the image until only the last chunk remains
40        Do While lngNumBytesReturned = INT_IMAGE_BUFFER_SIZE
41           bwrTest.Write(arrbytImage)
42           bwrTest.Flush()
43
44           ' Move the position of where the image should be read from to the
45           ' byte following the last byte read
46           intImagePos = intImagePos + INT_IMAGE_BUFFER_SIZE
47           ' Save image chunk in byte array and
48           ' save the number of bytes returned
49           lngNumBytesReturned = drdTest.GetBytes(0, intImagePos, _
50               arrbytImage, 0, INT_IMAGE_BUFFER_SIZE)
51        Loop
52
53        ' Write the remaining buffer
54        bwrTest.Write(arrbytImage)
55        bwrTest.Flush()
56
57        ' Close the output file
58        bwrTest.Close()
59        fstImage.Close()
60     End If
61
62     ' Close connection
63     cnnImage.Close()
64 End Sub
```

In Listing 7-5, I instantiate and open a connection on Lines 17 and 19, build the query string to retrieve the picture by Id on Line 21, and instantiate a Command object with the connection and query string on Line 24. On Line 26, the Picture column of the row with the specified Id is returned. You need to change the name of the image column and the table to match your data source.

If anything is returned from the data source, assuming only one row will ever be returned by the query, the image is retrieved in small chunks and saved in the arrbytImage **Byte** array, until the last chunk has been retrieved (Lines 25 through 51), and saved to a file. Notice how the number of bytes is returned by the **GetBytes** method (Lines 26 and 49), and used to move the starting position of where the image should read from (Line 46). Finally, the loop that starts on Line 40 is executed for as long as chunks of the same size, at the size requested, is returned. This is because when a smaller chunk is returned, you've effectively retrieved the last chunk.

The code has been written using the OLE DB .NET Data Provider, but the code is nearly identical for the ODBC .NET Data Provider and the SQL Server .NET Data Provider. You can find examples hereof in the example code available on the Apress Web site.

Extracting Metadata

Sometimes it's not the data itself you want, but rather the metadata. The metadata is data that describes the data in the DataReader. This means information such as the primary key for the table, and column information such as the data type and the column size. This can be useful, if you want to make your forms data driven; for example, you can use the column size of a char column to set the **MaxLength** property of a textbox. This is a good way of ensuring that the data entered into a form is not too long for the data source.

This kind of information can be retrieved with the **GetSchemaTable** method of the DataReader class. This method returns a **DataTable** object that holds the requested information. You can find more information about the **DataTable** class in Chapter 10.

You can use the **GetSchemaTable** method any time you've populated a DataReader using the **ExecuteReader** method of the Command class. However, depending on what you want to achieve, you might want column information only returned and thus avoid the overhead of having any rows selected at the data source and returned. See Listing 7-6 for an example of how to extract the column information.

Listing 7-6. Extract Column Information

```
 1 Public Sub ExtractColumnInformation()
 2    Dim cnnUserMan As SqlConnection
 3    Dim cmmUserMan As SqlCommand
 4    Dim drdUserMan As SqlDataReader
 5    Dim dtbUser As DataTable
 6    Dim dtcColumnInfo As DataColumn
 7    Dim strSQL As String
 8
 9    ' Instantiate the connection
10    cnnUserMan = New SqlConnection(PR_STR_CONNECTION_STRING)
11    ' Open the connection
12    cnnUserMan.Open()
13    ' Build query string
14    strSQL = "SELECT * FROM tblUser"
15    ' Instantiate the command
16    cmmUserMan = New SqlCommand(strSQL, cnnUserMan)
17    ' Instantiate data reader using the ExecuteReader method
18    ' of the command class and return column information only
19    drdUserMan = cmmUserMan.ExecuteReader(CommandBehavior.SchemaOnly)
20    ' Save the column information to a DataTable
21    dtbUser = drdUserMan.GetSchemaTable()
```

```
22
23      ' Display some column information
24      MsgBox("Name = " & dtbUser.Rows(0)("ColumnName").ToString() & vbCrLf & _
25          "Ordinal = " & dtbUser.Rows(0)("ColumnOrdinal").ToString() & vbCrLf & _
26          "Size = " & dtbUser.Rows(0)("ColumnSize").ToString() & vbCrLf & _
27          "Data Type = " & dtbUser.Rows(0)("DataType").ToString() & vbCrLf & _
28          "Key = " & dtbUser.Rows(0)("IsKey").ToString(), _
29          MsgBoxStyle.Information, "Column Information")
30 End Sub
```

In Listing 7-6, I instantiate the `drdUserMan` DataReader object on Line 19, using the **CommandBehavior.SchemaOnly** member (see Table C-33 in Appendix C for more information), which means that no data rows are returned. If you try to use the **Read** method of the DataReader class after it has been instantiated, it will return **False**, as there are no rows to read. However, you use the **GetSchemaTable** method, as on Line 21, to create a **DataTable** object, holding one row for each column specified in the SQL statement (Line 14). The message box displayed by the **MsgBox** function on Lines 24 through 29 is shown in Figure 7-1.

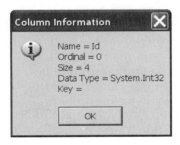

*Figure 7-1. The column information retrieved with **CommandBehavior.SchemaOnly***

In Figure 7-1, you can see the message box displayed by the example code in Listing 7-1, and if you look at the Key field, nothing is shown. That's because information about keys isn't returned when using the **CommandBehavior.SchemaOnly** argument. On Line 19, replace **CommandBehavior.SchemaOnly** with **CommandBehavior.KeyInfo**, and the message box will look like in Figure 7-2. Actually, this is only partly true. In Listing 7-6 I've used the SQL Server .NET Data Provider, but if you use the OLE DB .NET Data Provider, it depends on the OLE DB provider you use. The IBMDADB2 won't return the key information and therefore the message box will display **False**, whether you specify **SchemaOnly** or **KeyInfo**. The same is true if you the ODBC .NET Data Provider; some drivers will support it, and others won't. See the example code, available on the Apress Web site, for examples of retrieving column and key information using these two .NET Data Providers.

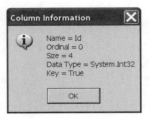

*Figure 7-2. The column information retrieved with **CommandBehavior.KeyInfo***

Handling Multiple Results

The DataReader class can handle multiple results returned by the Command class. This is one advantage the DataReader class has over the ADO "equivalent," a forward-only, read-only **RecordSet**. If the Command class returns multiple results specified using a batch of SQL statements separated by a semicolon, you can use the **NextResult** method to advance to the next result. The code for this is very simple:

```
Dim blnMoreResults = drdTest.NextResult()
```

Please note that you can only move forward, so as much as it would be nice to have a PreviousResult method to move back to a previous result, it just isn't possible. I guess it might just have something to do with the fact that the DataReader class is forward-only, and that it only ever holds one row in memory?

NOTE   If you specified **CommandBehavior.SingleResult** as the first and only argument when you created and instantiated the DataReader with the **ExecuteReader** method of the Command class, there's no need to try to call the **NextResult** method, as only one result set will ever be returned.

DataReader Properties

The DataReader class has the properties shown in ascending order in Table C-34 in Appendix C. There aren't that many properties, but they're all public, and as such, you can use all of them when working with a DataReader instance.

DataReader Methods

Table C-35 in Appendix C lists the noninherited and public methods of the DataReader class in alphabetical order. Please note that all the methods marked with an asterisk (*) require that the data contained in the specified column to be of the same type as the method indicates. This is because no conversion is performed on the content of the specified column. If you try to use any of the methods on a column containing content of a different data type, the **InvalidCastException** exception is thrown. Also, these methods can't be overridden in an inherited class. In the case of the **OdbcDataReader** class, conversions are performed by your ODBC driver. This means that the method will fail if the conversion is not supported by the ODBC driver.

Handling DataReader Exceptions

The properties and methods of the DataReader class can throw the exceptions shown in Table 7-1.

Table 7-1. DataReader Class Exceptions

Name	Description	Thrown by Property/Method
IndexOutOfRangeException	This exception is thrown when using an index argument that doesn't exist within the range, array, or collection.	The **GetOrdinal** method
InvalidCastException	If you try to implicitly cast or convert a database value using one of the Get* methods that retrieve a column value as a specific data type, then this exception is thrown.	All the methods that are used for retrieving the column value as a specific data type, such as the **GetInt32** or **GetString**.
InvalidOperationException	When you try to perform an operation (property or method) that isn't valid in the object's current state, this exception is thrown.	The **GetSchemaTable** method

Table 7-1. DataReader Class Exceptions (Continued)

Name	Description	Thrown by Property/Method
NotSupportedException	This exception is thrown when you try to use an I/O property or method on a DataReader object that is closed or otherwise not connected.	The **FieldCount** property

When to Use the DataReader Class

The DataReader class should be used in cases where you want a minimal overhead in terms of memory usage. Now obviously you do not want to use a DataReader object if you are expecting hundreds of thousands of rows returned, because it could take forever to sequentially loop through all these rows.

If you are looking at only one or even a few rows returned in which you just need to read one or two fields or columns, then the DataReader is definitely a good choice. The DataReader class is read-only, so if you need to update your data, then the DataReader class is obviously *not* a good choice! Another point to make is that the DataReader is a forward-only scrolling, data-aware class. So there's no moving backwards in the returned rows or jumping to the first or last row.[4]

XmlReader

The **XmlReader** class, which is similar to the other three DataReader classes I discussed in the previous sections, is quite obviously for handling data formatted as XML. Actually, the **XmlReader** class, which is part of the **System.Xml** namespace, must be overridden, and this has already been done in the .NET Framework. You can still choose to override the **XmlReader** class yourself, but there are already three classes that all implement the **XmlReader** class, and they are the **XmlNodeReader**, **XmlTextReader**, and the **XmlValidatingReader**.

- *XmlNodeReader:* The **XmlNodeReader** class reads XML data from an **XmlNode**, or an XML DOM subtree. There's no schema or DTD validation, so if that's what you need, you must use the **XmlValidatingReader** class.

---

4. Well, you can close the DataReader and reopen it, effectively making it move to the first row again.

- *XmlTextReader:* This class is for fast, noncached, forward-only character stream access. The class checks for well-formed XML, but there's no schema or DTD validation; if that's what you need, you must use the **XmlValidatingReader** class.

- *XmlValidatingReader:* This class provides XDR, XSD, and DTD schema validation of the XML data.

I won't go into more detail on these three derived XML readers, but I will take a closer look at the parent class, the **XmlReader** class, because it is this class that is to be used with the **ExecuteXmlReader** method of the **SqlCommand** class.

TIP If you want to use the information returned in an **XmlReader** object as hierarchical data, instead of relation data, which is my angle in this section, you should check out the mentioned classes, derived from the **XmlReader** class. However, you should also check out the **XmlDocument** class, and the **Load** method of this class, for working with the data returned from your data source in a true hierarchical manner.

The main difference between the **XmlReader** class and the three other DataReader classes, **OdbcDataReader**, **OleDbDataReader**, and **SqlDataReader**, is that the **XmlReader** works with data in the form of nodes, whereas the other DataReader classes works with rows. This is obviously very simplified, but XML data is of a hierarchical nature with the root node being the table, nodes for rows, and nodes and/or attributes for columns and column values.

XmlReader Properties

The **XmlReader** class has the properties, shown in alphabetical order, in Table C-36 in Appendix C.

XmlReader Methods

Table C-39 in Appendix C lists the noninherited and public methods of the **XmlReader** class in alphabetical order.

Declaring and Instantiating an XmlReader Object

The **XmlReader** class must be overridden, which means that you can't create an instance of the **XmlReader** class. The following sample code is wrong:

```
Dim xrdTest As New XmlReader()
```

It's wrong because it tries to instantiate xrdTest using the **New** keyword. Listing 7-7 shows you how to perform the instantiation correctly.

*Listing 7-7. Instantiating an **XmlReader** Object*

```
 1 Public Sub InstantiateXmlReader()
 2    Dim cnnUserMan As SqlConnection
 3    Dim cmmUserMan As SqlCommand
 4    Dim drdUserMan As XmlReader
 5    Dim strSQL As String
 6
 7    ' Instantiate the connection
 8    cnnUserMan = New SqlConnection(PR_STR_CONNECTION_STRING)
 9    ' Open the connection
10    cnnUserMan.Open()
11    ' Build query string
12    strSQL = "SELECT * FROM tblUser FOR XML AUTO"
13    ' Instantiate the command
14    cmmUserMan = New SqlCommand(strSQL, cnnUserMan)
15    ' Instantiate data reader using the ExecuteXmlReader method
16    ' of the command class
17    drdUserMan = cmmUserMan.ExecuteXmlReader()
18 End Sub
```

In Listing 7-7, you can see how you can instantiate an **XmlReader** object using the **ExecuteXmlReader** method of the **SqlCommand** class. This method is only supported by the SQL Server .NET Data Provider. Notice how I've appended the FOR XML AUTO clause to the SQL statement on Line 12. This is a SQL Server–specific SQL clause that instructs SQL Server to return the requested rows expressed as XML. You can find more information about various ways of having data from SQL Server returned as XML in Chapter 22.

Opening a XmlReader

An **XmlReader** isn't opened as such because it's ready to work with once you instantiate it using the **ExecuteXmlReader** method. See the previous section, "Declaring and Instantiating an XmlReader Object," for more information.

Closing an XmlReader

Because the **XmlReader** object keeps the connection busy while it's open, it's a good practice to close the XML reader once you are done with it. The **XmlReader** is closed using the **Close** method, as follows:

```
xrdTest.Close()
```

Reading Rows in an XmlReader

Since the **XmlReader** is a forward-only data class, you need to read the rows sequentially from start to finish if you need to read all the returned rows. In Listing 7-8, you can see how you loop through a populated XML reader.

*Listing 7-8. Looping Through All Rows in an **XmlReader***

```
1 Public Sub ReadRowsFromXmlReader()
2    Dim cnnUserMan As SqlConnection
3    Dim cmmUserMan As SqlCommand
4    Dim xrdUser As XmlReader
5    Dim strSQL As String
6    Dim lngCounter As Long = 0
7
8    ' Instantiate the connection
9    cnnUserMan = New SqlConnection(PR_STR_CONNECTION_STRING)
10   ' Open the connection
11   cnnUserMan.Open()
12   ' Build query string
13   strSQL = "SELECT * FROM tblUser FOR XML AUTO"
14   ' Instantiate the command
15   cmmUserMan = New SqlCommand(strSQL, cnnUserMan)
16   ' Execute command and return rows in data reader
17   xrdUser = cmmUserMan.ExecuteXmlReader()
```

```
18    ' Loop through all the returned rows
19    Do While xrdUser.Read
20       lngCounter = lngCounter + 1
21    Loop
22
23    ' Display the number of rows returned
24    MsgBox(CStr(lngCounter))
25 End Sub
```

The code in Listing 7-8 loops through the rows in the **XmlReader** and counts the number of rows. This is obviously just an example on how to sequentially go through all the rows returned by the **ExecuteXmlReader** method of the **SqlCommand** class.

Navigating in an XmlReader

There are various ways of navigating in an **XmlReader**, depending on what you want to achieve. This book is all about using databases, which means that this section will be focusing on moving to a specific row or column. The properties and methods referenced in this section can be found in Tables C-36 and C-39 in Appendix C.

After executing the **ExecuteXmlReader** method on the **SqlCommand** class in Listing 7-8, the XML representation of all the rows in the **XmlReader** looks similar to Listing 7-9.

*Listing 7-9. The XML Representation of the tblUser Data in **XmlReader***

```
<?xml version="1.0" encoding="utf-8"?>
<UserMan>
   <tblUser
      Id=1
      FirstName='John'
      LastName='Doe'
      LoginName='UserMan'
      Password='userman'
   </tblUser>
   <tblUser
      Id=2
      LoginName='User1'
      Password='password'
   </tblUser>
```

```
    <tblUser
        Id=3
        LoginName='User2'
        Password='password'
    </tblUser>
    <tblUser
        Id=4
        LoginName='User3'
        Password='password'
    </tblUser>
    <tblUser
        Id=5
        LoginName='User99'
        Password='password'
    </tblUser>
</UserMan>
```

Listing 7-9 shows you what the XML representation of the data from the tblUser table in an **XmlReader** could look like, if written to a text file. First, you have the XML identifier node, followed by the UserMan root node. Within the root node, you have the rows of the tblUser table as separate nodes or elements, with opening (`<tblUser>`) and closing (`</tblUser>`) tags. Each node (in this case, it's the start tag) has a number of attributes that correspond to the columns in the rows with values. Please note that only nonnull attributes are shown.

Actually, there's more to it than you can see in Listing 7-9, but I want to give you an idea of what it can look like to the **XmlReader**, seen with human eyes.

You might also see the elements as start and end tags in the same tag, like this:

```
<tblUser Id=5 LoginName='User99' Password='password' />
```

Within each row or element, you can also have the columns of a particular row represented as elements, one for each nonnull column value, like this:

```
<tblUser>
    <Id>1</Id>
    <FirstName>John</FirstName>
    <LastName>Doe</LastName>
    <LoginName>UserMan</LoginName>
    <Password>userman</Password>
</tblUser>
```

Move to First Row

As I'm sure you're aware by now, the **XmlReader** is a forward-only type of data class, just like the other DataReader classes. This means that you can only go to the first row right after instantiating the **XmlReader** and calling the **Read** method, like this:

```
xrdUser = cmmUserMan.ExecuteXmlReader()
' Go to the first row
xrdUser.Read()
```

Although you can close the **XmlReader**, you can't reopen it, so there's no way you can move back to the first row after you've moved beyond it.

Move to Next Row

For moving to the next row, you call the **Read** method, and you check if the **Boolean** value was **True** (the reader's position was advanced one row) or **False** (the reader can't read the next row, probably because you're at the last row). Call it like this:

```
' Go to the next row
If xrdUser.Read() Then
    'The reader moved to next row, do your stuff
    ...
End If
```

Move to Previous Row

It's not possible to move to the previous row, no matter what state the reader is in, or what position the reader is at.

Move to Last Row

There's no direct way of moving to the last row, so you need to call the **Read** method until it returns **False**, like this:

```
' Go to the last row
While xrdUser.Read()
    ...
End While
' You're now beyond the last row
```

What's wrong with example code shown? Well, when the **Read** method returns **False**, the **XmlReader** is actually positioned after the last row, at the end of the stream. At this position, you can't read any of the column values, because there's no current row. Does this mean that there's no direct way of knowing when you're at the last row in an **XmlReader**? I'm afraid so.

 NOTE   If you really need to know the number of rows returned, and/or need to identify the last row, the **XmlReader** isn't really a good choice. Sure, you can implement other ways of retrieving this, but seeing as this would mean using functionality separate from the **XmlReader**, you can't rely on this always to be accurate. You should really use a **DataTable** for such purposes. See Chapter 10 for more information on the **DataTable** class.

Retrieving Column Values

The column values for the current row can be retrieved in different ways. As is the case with the DataReaders mentioned earlier in this chapter, you can access them directly by ordinal position or by column name, like this:

```
' Access Id column by ordinal
xrdUser(0)
' Access Id column by name
xrdUser("Id")
```

You can also use the **Item** property, which is the default property, to access the column values, like this:

```
' Access Id column by ordinal
xrdUser.Item(0)
' Access Id column by name
xrdUser.Item("Id")
```

When working with an instance of the **XmlReader** class created by the **ExecuteXmlReader** method, I recommend you use the approach shown previously when accessing the column values. It is, however, possible to use some of the XML-specific methods for accessing column, or rather attribute, values, but for most of these properties or methods (listed in Tables C-36 and C-39 in Appendix C), you need to use your own implementation of the **XmlReader** class, or one of the derived classes: **XmlNodeReader**, **XmlTextReader**, or the **XmlValidatingReader**.

See the beginning of the "XmlReader" section earlier in this chapter for a short description of these classes.

Handling XmlReader Exceptions

The methods of the **XmlReader** class typically throw the exceptions shown in Table 7-2.

*Table 7-2. **XmlReader** Exceptions*

Name	Description	Thrown by Property/Method
ArgumentOutOfRangeException	This exception is thrown when an argument is out of range.	**GetAttribute** and **MoveToAttribute** methods
InvalidOperationException	This exception is thrown when you try to perform an operation that isn't valid in the object's current state.	**ResolveEntity** method
XmlException	This exception is thrown if the **XmlReader** object encounters invalid or incorrect XML in the input stream.	**IsStartElement**, **MoveToContent**, **ReadElementString**, **ReadEndElement**, and **ReadStartElement** methods

Summary

This chapter introduced you to the DataReader classes and how they're used for retrieving read-only data from your data source. You also saw how you can navigate between the rows in a DataReader and read the values from the various columns.

The following classes were covered:

OdbcDataReader, **OleDbDataReader**, **SqlDataReader**, and **XmlReader**

The next chapter introduces you to the DataAdapter and CommandBuilder classes.

CHAPTER 8

The DataAdapter and CommandBuilder Classes

IN THIS CHAPTER, you'll be introduced to the DataAdapter and CommandBuilder classes. The DataAdapter is the class that handles populating your disconnected **DataSet** and **DataTable** objects (see Chapters 9 and 10 for more information on these classes), and propagating changes made to these objects back to your data source. The DataAdapter uses Command objects for the various SQL statements, SELECT, INSERT, UPDATE, and DELETE. The Command class is covered in Chapter 6, but you can use the CommandBuilder class to automatically generate the INSERT, UPDATE, and DELETE Command objects, based on the SELECT statement.

The DataAdapter Explained

The DataAdapter class is used for retrieving data from your data source and populating your **DataSet** and related classes such as the **DataTable**; see Chapters 9 and 10 for more information on these disconnected data classes. The DataAdapter class is also responsible for propagating your changes back to the data source. In other words, the DataAdapter is the "connector" class that sits between the disconnected and the connected parts of ADO.NET. It would indeed be very appropriate to say that the DataAdapter class is your toolbox when you want to manipulate data in your data source!

The DataAdapter connects to a data source using a Connection object and then it uses Command objects to retrieve data from the data source and to send data back to the data source. With the exception of the DataReader class, all data access in ADO.NET goes through the DataAdapter. Actually, this can be put differently: All disconnected data access works through the DataAdapter. The DataAdapter is the bridge between the data source and the **DataSet**!

When the DataAdapter needs to retrieve or send data to and from the data source, it uses Command objects. You must specify these Command objects. Now, this is very different from what happens in ADO, where you have little control over the way queries are executed. You specify the Command objects for selecting, updating, and deleting rows in the data source. This is done by creating your Command objects, and then assigning them to the appropriate DataAdapter property: **SelectCommand**, **InsertCommand**, **UpdateCommand**, or **DeleteCommand**.

Please note that in some cases these properties can be automatically generated using the CommandBuilder class. See the "Using the CommandBuilder Class" section later in this chapter.

The DataAdapter class comes in three flavors, the **OdbcDataAdapter** class, the **OleDbDataAdapter** class, and the **SqlDataAdapter** class.

DataAdapter Properties

The DataAdapter class has the properties shown in Table C-40 in Appendix C in alphabetical order. Please note that only the public, noninherited properties are shown. Actually, this isn't entirely true, because only properties that are inherited from base classes like **Object** are left out. This means that properties inherited from the DataAdapter class are shown. The properties listed are the same for the three DataAdapter classes: **OdbcDataAdapter**, **OleDbDataAdapter**, and **SqlDataAdapter**.

DataAdapter Methods

Table C-43 in Appendix C lists the noninherited and public methods of the DataAdapter class in alphabetical order. The methods listed are the same for the three DataAdapter classes, **OdbcDataAdapter**, **OleDbDataAdapter**, and **SqlData-Adapter**, unless otherwise stated.

DataAdapter Events

Table C-45 in Appendix C lists the noninherited and public events of the DataAdapter class in ascending order. The events listed are the same for the three DataAdapter classes: **OdbcDataAdapter**, **OleDbDataAdapter**, and **SqlDataAdapter**.

Instantiating a DataAdapter

As with all other objects, the DataAdapter must be instantiated before you can use it. The DataAdapter class is instantiated using the constructor, which is overloaded. Listing 8-1 shows you an example hereof.

*Listing 8-1. Instantiating an **OdbcDataAdapter***

```
1 Public Sub InstantiateAndInitializeDataAdapter()
2    Const STR_SQL_USER As String = "SELECT * FROM tblUser"
3
4    Dim cnnUserMan As OdbcConnection
5    Dim cmmUser As OdbcCommand
6    Dim dadDefaultConstructor As OdbcDataAdapter
7    Dim dadOdbcCommandArgument As OdbcDataAdapter
8    Dim dadOdbcConnectionArgument As OdbcDataAdapter
9    Dim dadStringArguments As OdbcDataAdapter
10
11   ' Instantiate the connection
12   cnnUserMan = New OdbcConnection(PR_STR_CONNECTION_STRING)
13   ' Instantiate the command
14   cmmUser = New OdbcCommand(STR_SQL_USER)
15
16   ' Instantiate data adapters
17   dadDefaultConstructor = New OdbcDataAdapter()
18   dadOdbcCommandArgument = New OdbcDataAdapter(cmmUser)
19   dadOdbcConnectionArgument = New OdbcDataAdapter(STR_SQL_USER, cnnUserMan)
20   dadStringArguments = New OdbcDataAdapter(STR_SQL_USER,
21     PR_STR_CONNECTION_STRING)
22   ' Initialize data adapters
23   dadDefaultConstructor.SelectCommand = cmmUser
24   dadDefaultConstructor.SelectCommand.Connection = cnnUserMan
25 End Sub
```

If you use the default constructor for the DataAdapter (Lines 6, 17, 23, and 24), you have to specify the Command object for the actions you will perform. This means that if you want to retrieve rows from the data source, you will at least have to set the **SelectCommand** property. See the next section, "Setting the Command Properties," for more information on how to set command properties. On Line 23, I have set the **SelectCommand** property to a valid Command object. However, I could also have specified a SELECT statement for the **CommandText** property of the Command object, like this:

```
dadDefaultConstructor.SelectCommand.CommandText = STR_SQL_USER
```

The other three constructors do not need any further initialization for retrieving rows from your data source. However, if you want to insert, delete, and update your data source, you must specify the corresponding command properties. See the next section, "Setting the Command Properties," for more information on how to do this.

Which method you want to use is really up to you, but if you are using the same connection with all your command objects, why not specify it when you instantiate the DataAdapter?

I have used the **OdbcDataAdapter** class in Listing 8-1, but the code looks similar for the **OleDbDataAdapter** and the **SqlDataAdapter**. This means there's no real difference between instantiating an **OdbcDataAdapter**, an **OleDbDataAdapter**, or a **SqlDataAdapter** object. The real difference between these three classes becomes apparent when you want to populate your **DataSet**. See the "Populating Your DataSet Using the DataAdapter" section in Chapter 9 for more information on how to do this.

Setting the Command Properties

If you use the DataAdapter only to retrieve data from your data source, you don't have to set the command properties of your DataAdapter. This is so if you've already specified the **SelectCommand** property using the DataAdapter constructor (see the "Instantiating a DataAdapter" section earlier in this chapter). However, if you need to insert rows into, update rows in, or delete rows from your data source, or if you haven't set the **SelectCommand** property when instantiating the DataAdapter, you'll have to set these properties before you start using the DataAdapter. The **SelectCommand** is for retrieving rows from the data source, whereas the other three command properties are for updating the data source when the **Update** method is called.

The four command properties are as follows:

- SelectCommand

- InsertCommand

- DeleteCommand

- UpdateCommand

In classic ADO, you don't have this option to explicitly tell the data-aware class how it should update the data source. However, in ADO.NET, it's a different story, and you have full control over how data is passed to and from the data source. If you assign Command objects to the command properties, you'll also be able to control what these objects do, through events like errors. Yes, there's a little more coding involved, but you definitely get to be in the driver's seat when it comes to data source flow control.

With regards to setting the command properties, it's actually quite simple. If you have created Command objects, you only have to assign them to the corresponding property, as shown in Listing 8-2 and Listing 8-3 (shown later).

*Listing 8-2. Set the Command Properties of an **SqlDataAdapter***

```
 1 Public Sub SetDataAdapterCommandProperties()
 2    Const STR_SQL_USER_SELECT As String = "SELECT * FROM tblUser"
 3    Const STR_SQL_USER_DELETE As String = "DELETE FROM tblUser WHERE Id=@Id"
 4    Const STR_SQL_USER_INSERT As String = "INSERT INTO tblUser(ADName, " & _
 5       "ADSID, FirstName, LastName, LoginName, Password) VALUES(@ADName, " & _
 6       "@ADSID, @FirstName, @LastName, @LoginName, @Password)"
 7    Const STR_SQL_USER_UPDATE As String = "UPDATE tblUser SET ADName=" & _
 8       "@ADName, ADSID=@ADSID, FirstName=@FirstName, LastName=@LastName, " & _
 9       "LoginName=@LoginName, Password=@Password WHERE Id=@Id"
10
11    Dim cnnUserMan As SqlConnection
12    Dim cmmUserSelect As SqlCommand
13    Dim cmmUserDelete As SqlCommand
14    Dim cmmUserInsert As SqlCommand
15    Dim cmmUserUpdate As SqlCommand
16    Dim dadUserMan As SqlDataAdapter
17    Dim prmSQLDelete, prmSQLUpdate, prmSQLInsert As SqlParameter
18
19    ' Instantiate the connection
20    cnnUserMan = New SqlConnection(PR_STR_CONNECTION_STRING)
21    ' Instantiate the commands
22    cmmUserSelect = New SqlCommand(STR_SQL_USER_SELECT, cnnUserMan)
23    cmmUserDelete = New SqlCommand(STR_SQL_USER_DELETE, cnnUserMan)
24    cmmUserInsert = New SqlCommand(STR_SQL_USER_INSERT, cnnUserMan)
25    cmmUserUpdate = New SqlCommand(STR_SQL_USER_UPDATE, cnnUserMan)
26
27    ' Instantiate data adapter
28    dadUserMan = New SqlDataAdapter(STR_SQL_USER_SELECT, cnnUserMan)
29    ' Set data adapter command properties
30    dadUserMan.SelectCommand = cmmUserSelect
31    dadUserMan.InsertCommand = cmmUserInsert
32    dadUserMan.DeleteCommand = cmmUserDelete
33    dadUserMan.UpdateCommand = cmmUserUpdate
34
```

```
35      ' Add Delete command parameters
36      prmSQLDelete = dadUserMan.DeleteCommand.Parameters.Add("@Id", _
37          SqlDbType.Int, Nothing, "Id")
38      prmSQLDelete.Direction = ParameterDirection.Input
39      prmSQLDelete.SourceVersion = DataRowVersion.Original
40
41      ' Add Update command parameters
42      cmmUserUpdate.Parameters.Add("@ADName", SqlDbType.VarChar, 100, "ADName")
43      cmmUserUpdate.Parameters.Add("@ADSID", SqlDbType.VarChar, 50, "ADSID")
44      cmmUserUpdate.Parameters.Add("@FirstName", SqlDbType.VarChar, 50, _
45          "FirstName")
46      cmmUserUpdate.Parameters.Add("@LastName", SqlDbType.VarChar, 50, _
47          "LastName")
48      cmmUserUpdate.Parameters.Add("@LoginName", SqlDbType.VarChar, 50, _
49          "LoginName")
50      cmmUserUpdate.Parameters.Add("@Password", SqlDbType.VarChar, 50, _
51          "Password")
52
53      prmSQLUpdate = dadUserMan.UpdateCommand.Parameters.Add("@Id", _
54          SqlDbType.Int, Nothing, "Id")
55      prmSQLUpdate.Direction = ParameterDirection.Input
56      prmSQLUpdate.SourceVersion = DataRowVersion.Original
57
58      ' Add insert command parameters
59      cmmUserInsert.Parameters.Add("@ADName", SqlDbType.VarChar, 100, "ADName")
60      cmmUserInsert.Parameters.Add("@ADSID", SqlDbType.VarChar, 50, "ADSID")
61      cmmUserInsert.Parameters.Add("@FirstName", SqlDbType.VarChar, 50, _
62          "FirstName")
63      cmmUserInsert.Parameters.Add("@LastName", SqlDbType.VarChar, 50, _
64          "LastName")
65      cmmUserInsert.Parameters.Add("@LoginName", SqlDbType.VarChar, 50, _
66          "LoginName")
67      cmmUserInsert.Parameters.Add("@Password", SqlDbType.VarChar, 50, _
68          "Password")
69 End Sub
```

In Listing 8-2, I set up the SQL statements for the **SqlCommand** objects as
constants on Lines 2 through 9, and note how I'm using named parameters in the
SQL statements. This is because the SQL Server .NET Data Provider uses named
parameters exclusively, and not positional parameters. You can find more information about the Parameter classes in Chapter 6. I then declare the **SqlConnection**
object, the **SqlCommand** objects, the **SqlDataAdapter** object, and the **SqlParameter**
objects (Lines 11 through 17).

On Line 20, I instantiate the **SqlConnection** object; you can also choose to open the connection at this stage, but you don't really have to, as the DataAdapter takes care of it for you, including closing it when done. The only thing you have to do before you set up the **SqlCommand** objects is to declare the **SqlConnection** object (Line 11). The **SqlCommand** objects are instantiated on Lines 22 through 25, with the **SqlConnection** object–appropriate SQL statements, and the **SqlDataAdapter** object instantiated on Line 28. On Lines 30 through 33, the **SqlCommand** objects are assigned to the corresponding Command properties of the **SqlDataAdapter**.

On Lines 36 through 39, I instantiate the prmSQLDelete **SqlParameter** object, by adding it to the **Parameters** collection of the dadUserMan's **DeleteCommand** property. Please note that the only parameter added to the **Parameters** collection is the Id column, as an input parameter, using the original value. When deleting a row from the data source, you need to specify and set up the one or more columns that uniquely identify a row in the data source, which is the WHERE clause of the SQL DELETE statement. In this case, the Id column, which is the primary key, is all you need. For deleting a row, the parameter should be an input parameter, and you use the original value, meaning the value that was originally retrieved from the data source. In this case, the parameter is a primary key, which means you won't be changing the value in the **DataSet**; but the parameter can also be a different column that you can change, which is why you need to specify the original value, using the **Original** member of the **DataRowVersion** enum. You can find more information about parameters and different row versions in Chapter 6.

On Lines 42 through 51, I add parameters to the **Parameters** collection of the cmmUserUpdate **SqlCommand** object. I'm adding them to the collection in the same order that they appear in the SQL UPDATE statement, but this isn't a requirement, as SQL Server supports named parameters. Therefore, you can add them in any order you like, as long as the names match those given in the UPDATE statement. Personally, I still like to add them in the "correct" order, as I believe it makes the code easier to read. On Lines 53 through 56, I instantiate the prmSQLUpdate **SqlParameter** object by adding it to the **Parameters** collection of the dadUserMan's **UpdateCommand** property. When updating a row in the data source, you need to specify and set up the one or more columns that uniquely identify a row in the data source, which is the WHERE clause of the SQL DELETE statement. In this case, the Id column, which is the primary key, is all you need. For updating a row, the parameter should be an input parameter, and you use the original value. In this case, the parameter is a primary key, which means you won't be changing the value in the **DataSet**; but because the parameter can be a column with a value that you can change, you need to specify the original value, using the **Original** member of the **DataRowVersion** enum.

On Lines 59 through 68, I add parameters to the **Parameters** collection of the cmmUserInsert **SqlCommand** object. Please note that I'm not adding the Id column to the **Parameters** collection of this **SqlCommand** object, because the Id column is automatically generated by the DBMS when a new row is added to a table. Some DBMSs, like Oracle, don't support this fully, which means you'll have to create workarounds for this. However, SQL Server, IDM DB2 7.2 EE, MySQL, and Microsoft Access do support this. You'll see in later chapters how you can create a workaround for Oracle.

One other thing you might have noticed about the Command and Parameter objects for the INSERT and UPDATE statements is that I haven't specified a row version or a direction. This is because it's not needed, as I'm using default values, which means the row version is the current one, and the direction is Input. You can find more information about parameters, different row versions, and the direction in Chapter 6.

In Listing 8-2, I used the SQL Server .NET Data Provider, which only supports named parameters, as opposed to the two other .NET Data Providers, the ODBC .NET Data Provider and the OLE DB .NET Data Provider, which do not support named parameters. In Listing 8-3, you can see how to set up the very same example code as in Listing 8-2, but for use with the OLE DB .NET Data Provider.

*Listing 8-3. Set the Command Properties of an **OleDbDataAdapter***

```
1 Public Sub SetDataAdapterCommandProperties()
2     Const STR_SQL_USER_SELECT As String = "SELECT * FROM tblUser"
3     Const STR_SQL_USER_DELETE As String = "DELETE FROM tblUser WHERE Id=?"
4     Const STR_SQL_USER_INSERT As String = "INSERT INTO tblUser(ADName, " & _
5         "ADSID, FirstName, LastName, LoginName, Password) " & _
6         "VALUES(?, ?, ?, ?, ?, ?)"
7     Const STR_SQL_USER_UPDATE As String = "UPDATE tblUser SET ADName=?, " & _
8         "ADSID=?, FirstName=?, LastName=?, LoginName=?, Password=? WHERE Id=?"
9
10    Dim cnnUserMan As OleDbConnection
11    Dim cmmUserSelect As OleDbCommand
12    Dim cmmUserDelete As OleDbCommand
13    Dim cmmUserInsert As OleDbCommand
14    Dim cmmUserUpdate As OleDbCommand
15    Dim dadUserMan As OleDbDataAdapter
16    Dim prmSQLDelete, prmSQLUpdate, prmSQLInsert As OleDbParameter
17
18    ' Instantiate the connection
19    cnnUserMan = New OleDbConnection(PR_STR_CONNECTION_STRING)
20    ' Instantiate the commands
21    cmmUserSelect = New OleDbCommand(STR_SQL_USER_SELECT, cnnUserMan)
22    cmmUserDelete = New OleDbCommand(STR_SQL_USER_DELETE, cnnUserMan)
23    cmmUserInsert = New OleDbCommand(STR_SQL_USER_INSERT, cnnUserMan)
24    cmmUserUpdate = New OleDbCommand(STR_SQL_USER_UPDATE, cnnUserMan)
```

```
25
26      ' Instantiate data adapter
27      dadUserMan = New OleDbDataAdapter(STR_SQL_USER_SELECT, cnnUserMan)
28      ' Set data adapter command properties
29      dadUserMan.SelectCommand = cmmUserSelect
30      dadUserMan.InsertCommand = cmmUserInsert
31      dadUserMan.DeleteCommand = cmmUserDelete
32      dadUserMan.UpdateCommand = cmmUserUpdate
33
34      ' Add Delete command parameters
35      prmSQLDelete = dadUserMan.DeleteCommand.Parameters.Add("@Id", _
36          OleDbType.Integer, Nothing, "Id")
37      prmSQLDelete.Direction = ParameterDirection.Input
38      prmSQLDelete.SourceVersion = DataRowVersion.Original
39
40      ' Add Update command parameters
41      cmmUserUpdate.Parameters.Add("@ADName", OleDbType.VarChar, 100, _
42          "ADName")
43      cmmUserUpdate.Parameters.Add("@ADSID", OleDbType.VarChar, 50, _
44          "ADSID")
45      cmmUserUpdate.Parameters.Add("@FirstName", OleDbType.VarChar, 50, _
46          "FirstName")
47      cmmUserUpdate.Parameters.Add("@LastName", OleDbType.VarChar, 50, _
48          "LastName")
49      cmmUserUpdate.Parameters.Add("@LoginName", OleDbType.VarChar, 50, _
50          "LoginName")
51      cmmUserUpdate.Parameters.Add("@Password", OleDbType.VarChar, 50, _
52          "Password")
53
54      prmSQLUpdate = dadUserMan.UpdateCommand.Parameters.Add("@Id", _
55          OleDbType.Integer, Nothing, "Id")
56      prmSQLUpdate.Direction = ParameterDirection.Input
57      prmSQLUpdate.SourceVersion = DataRowVersion.Original
58
59      ' Add insert command parameters
60       cmmUserInsert.Parameters.Add("@ADName", OleDbType.VarChar, 100, _
61          "ADName")
62       cmmUserInsert.Parameters.Add("@ADSID", OleDbType.VarChar, 50, _
63          "ADSID")
64      cmmUserInsert.Parameters.Add("@FirstName", OleDbType.VarChar, 50, _
65          "FirstName")
66      cmmUserInsert.Parameters.Add("@LastName", OleDbType.VarChar, 50, _
67          "LastName")
68      cmmUserInsert.Parameters.Add("@LoginName", OleDbType.VarChar, 50, _
```

```
69        "LoginName")
70  cmmUserInsert.Parameters.Add("@Password", OleDbType.VarChar, 50, _
71        "Password")
72 End Sub
```

There are only minor differences between Listings 8-2 and 8-3, and they are all due to what .NET Data Provider you are using. In Listing 8-3, I'm using positional parameters, which means that the parameters must be added to the **Parameters** collection of the Command object in the same order as they appear in the SQL statement. Although positional parameters are required when you use the ODBC .NET Data Provider or the OLE DB .NET Data Provider, you can still give the parameters a name for making your code easier to read, just as I've done in Listing 8-2.

In Listing 8-3, I used the OLE DB .NET Data Provider, which only supports positional parameters. The ODBC .NET Data Provider also only supports positional parameters, so you can find the very same code for the ODBC .NET Data Provider in the example code.

Populating the DataSet or DataTable

Once you've set up the DataAdapter, you can go ahead and populate the **DataSet** or **DataTable** you want to work with. For this purpose, you have the **Fill** method, which is overloaded and can be used for retrieving data from your data source, or even from a **Record** or **Recordset** object from classic ADO, if you're working with the OLE DB .NET Data Provider. In Chapter 9, which covers the **DataSet** class, you can find various examples of how to use the **Fill** method. The "Populating Your DataSet Using the DataAdapter" section in Chapter 9 also describes how to use it.

Handling Fill Operation Errors

When you execute the **Fill** method of the DataAdapter class, one or more errors can occur. If the errors occur at the client side,[1] the **FillError** event is triggered. You can handle these events by setting up an event handler to intercept the event. If you don't set up an event handler for this event, and an error occurs, an **InvalidCastException** exception is thrown. Listing 8-4 shows you how to set up the event handler.

---

1. If they're generated at the data source, when the data retrieved from the data source is being filled into the **DataSet** or **DataTable** object.

Listing 8-4. Handling Fill Operation Errors

```
1 Private Shared Sub OnFillError(ByVal sender As Object, _
2    ByVal args As FillErrorEventArgs)
3    ' Display a message indicating what table an error occurred in and
4    ' let the user decided whether to continue populating the DataSet
5    args.Continue = (MsgBox("There were errors filling the Data Table: " & _
6       args.DataTable.ToString & ". Do you want to continue?", _
7       MsgBoxStyle.YesNo + MsgBoxStyle.Question, "Continue Updating") _
8       = DialogResult.Yes)
9 End Sub
10
11 Public Shared Sub TriggerFillErrorEvent()
12    Dim dstUser As New DataSet("Users")
13    ' Declare and instantiate connection
14    Dim cnnUserMan As New SqlConnection(PR_STR_CONNECTION_STRING)
15    ' Declare and instantiate data adapter
16    Dim prdadUserMan As New SqlDataAdapter("SELECT * FROM tblUser", _
17       cnnUserMan)
18    ' Set up event handler
19    AddHandler prdadUserMan.FillError, AddressOf OnFillError
20
21    ' Populate the DataSet
22    prdadUserMan.Fill(dstUser, "tblUser")
23 End Sub
```

NOTE The TriggerFillErrorEvent procedure in Listing 8-4 has been declared as Shared, which isn't necessary. However, I took the easy way out for referencing it in the example code. The OnFillError event handler procedure, which is also shared, can be declared only in a class file, not a module, so I decided to make the TriggerFillErrorEvent procedure shared as well, so that I can reference it without having to declare an instance of the class in which the procedure resides.

In Listing 8-4, I have created a procedure to handle the **FillError** event (Lines 1 through 9), and on Lines 11 through 23, I've created the TriggerFillErrorEvent standard procedure for filling the dstUser **DataSet**. In this procedure, I set up the event handler on Line 19, which means that if any errors occur when populating dstUser on Line 22, the OnFillError procedure is invoked. In the OnFillError procedure, I display a message and leave it up to the user to decide if I should continue populating dstUser. This is done by setting the args.Continue property to **True** or **False**, depending on whether the user clicks the Yes or No button in the message box. Although there are other uses for the **FillError** event, its main purpose is to decide if the filling should continue if an error occurs. The TriggerFillErrorEvent procedure doesn't necessarily trigger the FillError event; this only happens when an error occurs.

In Listing 8-4, I used the SQL Server .NET Data Provider, but you can find similar code for the ODBC .NET Data Provider and OLE DB .NET Data Provider in the example code available on the Apress Web site.

Retrieving the SELECT Statement Parameters

When you set up your DataAdapter yourself, you generally know what kind of parameters you use. However, sometimes you might be using a DataAdapter that's being set up dynamically, or you're using a DataAdapter that is being passed to your procedure, meaning that you don't know the parameters for the SELECT statement. Another reason is that you want to know the current value of the parameter(s).

You can find out about the parameters, using the **GetFillParameters** method of the DataAdapter class, like this:

```
Dim arrprmSelect() As Object = dadUserMan.GetFillParameters()
```

This will return all parameters used in the SELECT statement of the Command objects, which is assigned to the **SelectCommand** property of the DataAdapter. The **GetFillParameters** method returns an array of **IDataParameter** objects. You can loop through the array like this:

```
For Each prmSelect In arrprmSelect
    MsgBox(prmSelect.Value.ToString)
Next
```

The prmSelect variable is of data type **OdbcParameter**, **OleDbParameter**, or **SqlParameter**, depending on which .NET Data Provider you're using. The example simply displays the current value of each parameter in the returned array. You can find more information on the Parameter class in Chapter 6. Listing 8-5 shows you a complete example of how to set up the SELECT statement using a single parameter, and later, how you retrieve the parameters in an array.

Listing 8-5. Retrieve SELECT Statement Parameters

```
1 Public Sub GetSelectParameters()
2    Const STR_SQL_USER_SELECT As String = _
3       "SELECT * FROM tblUser WHERE LoginName=@LoginName"
4
5    Dim cnnUserMan As SqlConnection
6    Dim cmmUserSelect As SqlCommand
7    Dim dadUserMan As SqlDataAdapter
8    Dim prmSQLSelect As SqlParameter
9    Dim arrprmSelect() As Object
10   Dim prmSelect As SqlParameter
11
12   ' Instantiate the connection
13   cnnUserMan = New SqlConnection(PR_STR_CONNECTION_STRING)
14   ' Instantiate the select command
15   cmmUserSelect = New SqlCommand(STR_SQL_USER_SELECT, cnnUserMan)
16
17   ' Instantiate data adapter
18   dadUserMan = New SqlDataAdapter(STR_SQL_USER_SELECT, cnnUserMan)
19   ' Set data adapter select command property
20   dadUserMan.SelectCommand = cmmUserSelect
21
22   ' Add Select command parameter
23   prmSQLSelect = dadUserMan.SelectCommand.Parameters.Add("@LoginName", _
24      SqlDbType.VarChar, 50, "LoginName")
25   prmSQLSelect.Direction = ParameterDirection.Input
26   prmSQLSelect.SourceVersion = DataRowVersion.Current
27   prmSQLSelect.Value = "UserMan"
28   ' Retrieve select statement parameters
29   arrprmSelect = dadUserMan.GetFillParameters()
30
31   ' Loop through all the parameters
32   For Each prmSelect In arrprmSelect
33      ' Display some of the properties
34      MsgBox("Name = " & prmSelect.ParameterName & vbCrLf & _
35         "Value = " & prmSQLSelect.Value.ToString & vbCrLf & _
36         "DB Data Type = " & prmSQLSelect.DbType.ToString & vbCrLf & _
37         "Parameter Type = " & prmSQLSelect.Direction.ToString)
38   Next
39 End Sub
```

In Listing 8-5, you can see how the SELECT statement is set up to use a named parameter for the LoginName column value, and then the **GetFillParameters** method is used to retrieve this parameter in an array. Obviously, the example isn't all that useful as it is, but it should give you and idea of how to use the **GetFillParameters** method if you need to find out about the current property values, such as the name, value, and data type, of the parameters used by the **SelectCommand** property.

In Listing 8-5, I used the SQL Server .NET Data Provider, but you can find similar code for the ODBC .NET Data Provider and OLE DB .NET Data Provider in the example code available on the Apress Web site.

Retrieving the Schema from Data Source

If you want to know the schema of a specific table in your data source, or if you need to work with a copy of a specific table in your data source, you can use the **FillSchema** method of the DataAdapter class. This class retrieves the schema from a specific table and adds a **DataTable** object to a **DataSet**. This **DataTable** has the exact same schema as the table in the data source.

When you call the **FillSchema** method, the **SelectCommand** property of the DataAdapter object is being used to determine what schema(s) to extract from the data source.

 NOTE   You don't have to call the **FillSchema** method on the DataAdapter object before you call the **Fill** method. The DataAdapter will retrieve the information from the data source, based on what you request in the SELECT statement associated with the **SelectCommand** property.

Listing 8-6 shows you a simple example of using the **FillSchema** method.

Listing 8-6. Retrieve Simple Table Schema from Data Source

```
1 Public Sub GetSimpleTableSchema()
2    Const STR_SQL_USER_SELECT_ALL As String = _
3       "SELECT * FROM tblUser"
4
5    Dim cnnUserMan As OdbcConnection
6    Dim dadUserMan As OdbcDataAdapter
7    Dim dtbUser As New DataTable()
8    Dim dtcUser As DataColumn
9
```

```
10    ' Instantiate the connection
11    cnnUserMan = New OdbcConnection(PR_STR_CONNECTION_STRING)
12
13    ' Instantiate data adapter
14    dadUserMan = New OdbcDataAdapter(STR_SQL_USER_SELECT_ALL, _
15       cnnUserMan)
16    ' Retrieve table schema from data source
17    dadUserMan.FillSchema(dtbUser, SchemaType.Source)
18
19    ' Loop through all the columns in the data table
20    For Each dtcUser In dtbUser.Columns
21       ' Display the name of the column
22       MsgBox(dtcUser.ColumnName)
23    Next
24 End Sub
```

The **FillSchema** method is overloaded, and you should really check Table 8-1 to see which overload suits your needs. In Listing 8-6, I use the **FillSchema** overload that takes a **DataTable** as the first argument. If you run the example code in Listing 8-6, you will see the message box displayed seven times, each time with the name of the current column in the **Columns** collection of the **DataTable** object. I've used the **Source** member of the **SchemaType** enum because I want to create a new schema in the dtbUser **DataTable**, which is why I don't save the returned **DataTable** object (the **FillSchema** method is a **Function** procedure. See Table 8-1 for more information). You can see the members of the **SchemaType** enum in Table C-46 in Appendix C.

 NOTE The **FillSchema** method doesn't return any rows, only schema information.

In Listing 8-6, I used the ODBC .NET Data Provider, but you can find similar code for the OLE DB .NET Data Provider and SQL Server .NET Data Provider in the example code available on the Apress Web site. Table 8-1 shows a list of the various public overloads of the **FillSchema** method.

*Table 8-1. **FillSchema** Method Overloads*

Overload Signature	Description	Example
FillSchema(ByVal dtbSchema As DataTable, ByVal objSchemaType As SchemaType) As DataTable	This overload configures the schema of the dtbSchema **DataTable** based on the objSchemaType **SchemaType**. The returned **DataTable** holds the schema returned by the method, and it's the same schema as the dtbSchema **DataTable** is configured with if you pass the **Source** member of the **SchemaType** enum as the objSchemaType argument. However, if you pass the **Mapped** member instead (see the members of the **SchemaType** enum in Table C-46 in Appendix C), and the dtbSchema already has a schema before invoking the method, the dtbSchema will be different from the returned **DataTable** object because the schema will be a "merger" between the existing schema and the one retrieved from the data source. This means that you can use the returned **DataTable** for matching against the dtbSchema, and thus you can see which schema information is new and which schema information existed before the call to the **FillSchema** method. If the **CommandText** property of the Command object, assigned to the **SelectCommand** property, retrieves more than one table using batched SQL SELECT statements, it's the last table that will be used.	See Listing 8-6 earlier in this chapter.

Table 8-1. FillSchema Method Overloads (Continued)

Overload Signature	Description	Example
FillSchema(ByVal dstSchema As DataSet, ByVal objSchemaType As SchemaType) As DataTable()	This overload adds a **DataTable** object named *Table* to the dstSchema **DataSet**. The schema of the **DataTable** is configured according to the table in the data source, based on the objSchemaType **SchemaType**. If more than one table is specified in the SELECT statement, they're added to the dstSchema **DataSet**, named *Table, Table1, Table2*, and so on. The returned value is a reference to the array of **DataTable** objects that were added to the **DataSet**. This means that you can use the return value for matching against the dstSchema, and thus you can see which schema information is new and which schema information existed before the call to the **FillSchema** method.	See Listing 8-7 later in this chapter.
FillSchema(ByVal dstSchema As DataSet, ByVal objSchemaType As SchemaType, ByVal strTableName As String) As DataTable()	This overload adds a **DataTable** object named *Table* to the dstSchema **DataSet**. The schema of the **DataTable** is configured according to the table in the data source, based on the objSchemaType **SchemaType**. If more than one table is specified in the SELECT statement, they're added to the dstSchema **DataSet**, named consecutively after the value of the strTableName argument. This means that if strTableName holds the value *tblLog*, the tables will be named *tblLog, tblLog1, tblLog2*, and so on. The returned value is a reference to the array of **DataTable** objects that were added to the **DataSet**. This means that you can use the return value for matching against the dstSchema, and thus you can see which schema information is new, and which schema information did exist before the call to the **FillSchema** method.	See Listing 8-8 later in this chapter.

Instead of having the schema for one table returned in a **DataTable** object, you can have one or more table schemas added to a **DataSet**. Listing 8-7 shows you how you can do this.

*Listing 8-7. Retrieve Table Schema from Data Source in **DataSet***

```
1 Public Sub GetTableSchema()
2    Const STR_SQL_USER_SELECT_LOG As String = _
3       "SELECT * FROM tblLog"
4    Const STR_SQL_USER_SELECT_USER As String = _
5       "SELECT * FROM tblUser"
6
7    Dim cnnUserMan As OleDbConnection
8    Dim dadUserMan As OleDbDataAdapter
9    Dim dstUserMan As New DataSet("UserMan")
10   Dim dtbSchema() As DataTable
11   Dim dtbUser As DataTable
12
13   ' Instantiate the connection
14   cnnUserMan = New OleDbConnection(PR_STR_CONNECTION_STRING)
15
16   ' Instantiate data adapter
17   dadUserMan = New OleDbDataAdapter(STR_SQL_USER_SELECT_LOG, _
18      cnnUserMan)
19   ' Populate the DataSet with the Log table
20   dadUserMan.Fill(dstUserMan, "tblLog")
21   ' Set the Command text to retrieve from User table
22   dadUserMan.SelectCommand.CommandText = _
23      STR_SQL_USER_SELECT_USER
24   ' Retrieve table schema from data source
25   dtbSchema = dadUserMan.FillSchema(dstUserMan, _
26      SchemaType.Source)
27
28   ' Display the name of the tables that
29   ' had a schema returned
30   For Each dtbUser In dtbSchema
31      MsgBox(dtbUser.TableName, MsgBoxStyle.OKOnly, _
32         "DataTable Array Reference")
33   Next
34
35   ' Display the name of the tables in
36   ' the DataSet
37   For Each dtbUser In dstUserMan.Tables
38      MsgBox(dtbUser.TableName, MsgBoxStyle.OKOnly, "DataSet Tables")
39   Next
40 End Sub
```

In Listing 8-7, I used the OLE DB .NET Data Provider, but you can find similar code for the ODBC .NET Data Provider and SQL Server .NET Data Provider in the example code available on the Apress Web site. Anyway, the code in Listing 8-7 populates the dstUserMan **DataSet** with all rows from the tblLog table in the data source. Then the **CommandText** property for the **SelectCommand** is changed to retrieve all rows from the tblUser table (Lines 22 and 23). Finally, the schema for the tblUser table is retrieved and saved to the dstUserMan **DataSet**, in a table named Table. The two iterations on Lines 30 through 33 and Lines 37 through 39 display the names of the tables returned by the **FillSchema** method and the names of the tables in the **DataSet**. When you run the example code, you can see that there's one more table in the **DataSet**, because you populated the **DataSet** with the tblLog table prior to calling the **FillSchema** method.

As you can see from Listing 8-7, the table returned by that particular overload of the **FillSchema** method is named *Table*. Subsequent tables are named *Table1*, *Table2*, and so on, which isn't all that nice. Although you can change the name of the table in the **Tables** collection of the **DataSet** afterwards, it's easier to have the table named according to the names they have in the data source when you call the **FillSchema** method. The third overload of the **FillSchema** method can help you do this, as shown in Listing 8-8.

*Listing 8-8. Retrieve Table Schema from Data Source in **DataSet** with Correct Names*

```
1 Public Sub GetFullTableSchema()
2    Const STR_SQL_USER_SELECT As String = _
3       "SELECT * FROM tblUser;SELECT * FROM tblLog"
4
5    Dim cnnUserMan As SqlConnection
6    Dim dadUserMan As SqlDataAdapter
7    Dim dstUserMan As New DataSet("UserMan")
8    Dim dtbSchema() As DataTable
9    Dim dtbUser As DataTable
10
11   ' Instantiate the connection
12   cnnUserMan = New SqlConnection(PR_STR_CONNECTION_STRING)
13
14   ' Instantiate data adapter
15   dadUserMan = New SqlDataAdapter(STR_SQL_USER_SELECT, _
16      cnnUserMan)
17   ' Retrieve table schema from data source
18   dtbSchema = dadUserMan.FillSchema(dstUserMan, _
19      SchemaType.Source, "tblUser")
20
```

```
21    ' Display the name of the tables
22    For Each dtbUser In dtbSchema
23        MsgBox(dtbUser.TableName)
24    Next
25 End Sub
```

In Listing 8-8, I've used the third overload of the **FillSchema** method, which takes the name of the table as the third argument. This means that instead of naming the table *Table*, it will be given the name stored in the third argument. The only problem with this approach, as you'll find if you run the example code in Listing 8-8, is that if you have the schema for more than one table returned, the tables are named consecutively. This means that the two tables returned in Listing 8-8 will be named *tblUser* and *tblUser1*.

WARNING   The technique described of having the schema from more than one table returned in one go doesn't work with all ODBC drivers or OLE DB providers. Some return the last table in the batch of SQL statements, and others throw an exception. It's up to you to check your driver or provider.

I've used the SQL Server .NET Data Provider for the example code in Listing 8-8, but you can find similar code for the ODBC .NET Data Provider and OLE DB .NET Data Provider in the example code.

NOTE   In all the examples you've seen previously in this chapter with the **FillSchema** method, I haven't explicitly opened the Connection object that is being used by the DataAdapter. This isn't necessary, as the DataAdapter can open the connection and close it afterwards, as long as the Connection object is valid.

Besides returning basic column information, such as data type and name, the **FillSchema** method also returns information such as the primary key and constraints. Please see the following sections for more information.

Setting Primary Key

When the **FillSchema** method returns the schema information for a table, it also tries to configure the primary key for that table. If the primary key column(s) is specified as part of the SELECT statement, the column or columns will be marked as the primary key in the **DataTable**. However, this information isn't always returned, which is why the DataAdapter also tries to look for unique columns. If it finds one or more columns that aren't nullable,[2] and no primary key information is returned, the unique column(s) are used as the primary key. No primary key is set if none of the information described is returned.

The primary key is set by adding the column(s) that makes the primary key to the **PrimaryKey** property of the **DataTable** object.

Setting Constraints

The only constraints that the DataAdapter can add to the **ConstraintCollection** of the **DataTable** object are the primary key (see the previous section) and unique constraints. Therefore, when a column is marked as unique in the data source, the DataAdapter adds the column to the **ConstraintCollection**, and the **Unique** property is set to **True** for the column(s). Any other constraint must be added manually.

Setting Column Properties

There are a number of properties, besides the primary key and unique constraints, that the DataAdapter can set for you when the **FillSchema** method is called:

- *AllowDBNull:* This property is set when the column in the data source allows null values.

- *AutoIncrement:* This property, which refers to IDENTITY columns in SQL Server and IBM DB2 7.2 EE, and AutoNumber columns in Microsoft Access, is set to **True** for the column if auto numbering is set at the data source. However, the **AutoIncrementStep** and **AutoIncrementSeed** properties must be set manually.

- *MaxLength:* This property is set if any maximum length is specified for the column in the data source. This property is generally used for string and binary columns.

---

2. Null values are disallowed.

- *ReadOnly:* If the column in the data source can't be updated, this property is set to **True**.

Please keep in mind that the shown properties are only set if the driver or provider can retrieve the appropriate information from the data source.

Updating the Data Source

When you've manipulated the data in your **DataSet** or **DataTable** object, which has been populated using data from your data source, you generally want to propagate the changes back to the data source. For this purpose, you have the **Update** method. In the "Updating Your Data Source Using the DataAdapter" section in Chapter 9, you can find a description of the **Update** method, as well as various examples of how to use it.

Handling Row Updates

When you update your data source using the **Update** method of the DataAdapter, two events are triggered to which you can respond. The events are **RowUpdating**, which occurs before the data source is updated, and **RowUpdated**, which occurs after the update of the data source.

> **NOTE** The **RowUpdating** and **RowUpdated** events are triggered once for every row that is being sent to the data source for updating.

Listing 8-9 shows you how you can set up and use the two events.

Listing 8-9. Handling Row Updates

```
1 Protected Shared Sub OnRowUpdating(ByVal sender As Object, _
2    ByVal e As SqlRowUpdatingEventArgs)
3    ' Display a message showing all the Command properties
4    ' if a command exists
5    If Not e.Command Is Nothing Then
6        MessageBox.Show("Command Properties:" & vbCrLf & _
7            vbCrLf & "CommandText: " & _
8            e.Command.CommandText & vbCrLf & _
9            "CommandTimeout: " & _
10           e.Command.CommandTimeout.ToString() & _
```

```
11          vbCrLf & "CommandType: " & _
12          e.Command.CommandType.ToString(), _
13          "RowUpdating", MessageBoxButtons.OK, _
14          MessageBoxIcon.Information)
15      End If
16      ' Display a message showing all the Errors properties,
17      ' if an error exists
18      If Not e.Errors Is Nothing Then
19          MessageBox.Show("Errors Properties:" & vbCrLf & _
20              vbCrLf & "HelpLink: " & e.Errors.HelpLink & _
21              vbCrLf & "Message: " & e.Errors.Message & _
22              vbCrLf & "Source: " & e.Errors.Source & _
23              vbCrLf & "StackTrace: " & _
24              e.Errors.StackTrace & vbCrLf & _
25              "TargetSite: " & _
26              e.Errors.TargetSite.ToString, _
27              "RowUpdating", MessageBoxButtons.OK, _
28              MessageBoxIcon.Information)
29      End If
30      ' Display a message showing other misc. properties
31      MessageBox.Show("Misc. Properties:" & vbCrLf & _
32          vbCrLf & "StatementType: " & _
33          e.StatementType.ToString & vbCrLf & _
34          "Status: " & e.Status.ToString, _
35          "RowUpdating", MessageBoxButtons.OK, _
36          MessageBoxIcon.Information)
37  End Sub
38
39  Protected Shared Sub OnRowUpdated(ByVal sender As Object, _
40      ByVal e As SqlRowUpdatedEventArgs)
41      ' Display a message showing all the Command properties
42      ' if a command exists
43      If Not e.Command Is Nothing Then
44          MessageBox.Show("Command Properties:" & vbCrLf & _
45              vbCrLf & "CommandText: " & _
46              e.Command.CommandText & vbCrLf & _
47              "CommandTimeout: " & _
48              e.Command.CommandTimeout.ToString() & _
49              vbCrLf & "CommandType: " & _
50              e.Command.CommandType.ToString(), _
51              "RowUpdated", MessageBoxButtons.OK, _
52              MessageBoxIcon.Information)
53      End If
```

```vb
54     ' Display a message showing all the Errors properties,
55     ' if an error exists
56     If Not e.Errors Is Nothing Then
57       MessageBox.Show("Errors Properties:" & vbCrLf & _
58           vbCrLf & "HelpLink: " & e.Errors.HelpLink & _
59           vbCrLf & "Message: " & e.Errors.Message & _
60           vbCrLf & "Source: " & e.Errors.Source & _
61           vbCrLf & "StackTrace: " & _
62           e.Errors.StackTrace & vbCrLf & _
63           "TargetSite: " & _
64           e.Errors.TargetSite.ToString, _
65           "RowUpdated", MessageBoxButtons.OK, _
66           MessageBoxIcon.Information)
67     End If
68     ' Display a message showing other misc. properties
69     MessageBox.Show("Misc. Properties:" & vbCrLf & _
70         vbCrLf & "StatementType: " & _
71         e.StatementType.ToString & vbCrLf & _
72         "Status: " & e.Status.ToString, _
73         "RowUpdated", MessageBoxButtons.OK, _
74         MessageBoxIcon.Information)
75 End Sub
76
77 Public Shared Sub TriggerRowUpdateEvents()
78     Dim dstUser As New DataSet("Users")
79     ' Declare and instantiate connection
80     Dim cnnUserMan As New SqlConnection(PR_STR_CONNECTION_STRING)
81     ' Declare and instantiate data adapter
82     Dim dadUserMan As New SqlDataAdapter("SELECT * FROM tblUser", _
83         cnnUserMan)
84     ' Declare and instantiate command builder
85     Dim cmbUser As New SqlCommandBuilder(dadUserMan)
86     ' Set up event handlers
87     AddHandler dadUserMan.RowUpdating, AddressOf OnRowUpdating
88     AddHandler dadUserMan.RowUpdated, AddressOf OnRowUpdated
89
90     ' Populate the DataSet
91     dadUserMan.Fill(dstUser, "tblUser")
92     ' Modify second row
93     dstUser.Tables("tblUser").Rows(1)("FirstName") = "Tom"
94     ' Update the data source
95     dadUserMan.Update(dstUser, "tblUser")
96 End Sub
```

In Listing 8-9, you can see how I've set up event handlers for the **RowUpdating** and **RowUpdated** events. Both of the two procedures that handle the events, OnRowUpdating and OnRowUpdated, display the same properties. I am using a CommandBuilder object to generate the **UpdateCommand** property of the DataAdapter, and if you want more information on the CommandBuilder class, please the next section "Using the CommandBuilder Class."

I trigger the two events by modifying the second row of the tblUser **DataTable** (Line 93), and then I use the **Update** method of the DataAdapter class (Line 95). This will always trigger **RowUpdating** event, but not necessarily the **RowUpdated** event. Why is that? Well, if you run the example code in Listing 8-9 twice, and look at some of the properties being displayed in the message box, you'll notice that the second time around, the **Status** property being displayed in the OnRowUpdating procedure has a value of **SkipCurrentRow**. This means that the row won't be updated, because you've not really made any modifications to the row. The original values and the current values are the same. These two events are valuable tools when searching for bugs, if nothing else.

On Lines 5, 18, 43, and 56, I check to see if the **Errors** or **Command** objects have been set before trying to access them. I need to do this because they aren't necessarily set. Basically, the **Errors** object is set if there are any errors; otherwise, it holds a null value. The same can be said about the **Command** object: If the **Status** property is set to **SkipCurrentRow**, the **Command** object holds a null value, because no commands will be executed.

I've used the SQL Server .NET Data Provider for the example code in Listing 8-9, but you can find similar code for the ODBC .NET Data Provider and OLE DB .NET Data Provider in the example code available on the Apress Web site.

 TIP The **RowUpdating** and **RowUpdated** events are most commonly used with optimistic concurrency, to detect and fix problems with rows that have been changed by other connections, after you retrieved the data from the data source. You can find more information and example code in Appendix A.

Using the CommandBuilder Class

The CommandBuilder class is used for generating the following properties of the DataAdapter class automatically:

- InsertCommand

- UpdateCommand

- DeleteCommand

Before moving on, I would like to add that there is no CommandBuilder class per se, but instead you use the **OdbcCommandBuilder**, **OleDbCommandBuilder**, or the **SqlCommandBuilder** class, depending on the DataAdapter you use (**OdbcDataAdapter**, **OleDbDataAdapter**, or **SqlDataAdapter**). The example shown uses the **SqlCommandBuilder** class and related data classes.

When to Use the CommandBuilder Class

The CommandBuilder class can only be used when your **DataTable**[3] maps to a single database table. This means that if your database query is a join of two or more tables, you cannot use the CommandBuilder class; you'll have to write the code yourself. This is the main secret of the CommandBuilder class; it saves you having to write code when dealing with a single table. Nothing more, nothing less! Therefore, it is of no use if your **DataTable**s are generated from more than one database table. The "Setting the Command Properties" section earlier in this chapter describes how to set up the properties needed for performing the INSERT, UPDATE, and DELETE SQL operations.

In addition to the restriction that a **DataTable** must be based on a single database table, the following restrictions apply:

- The CommandBuilder will not work, or rather the automatic generation will fail, if the table and/or column names contain any special characters. These special characters include a period (.), any of the quotation marks (" or '), a space, or any nonalphanumeric character. This is also true if the table or column name containing the special character(s) is enclosed in brackets ([]). However, fully qualified names are supported. The following is a fully qualified name from the UserMan example database in SQL Server: *UserMan.dbo.tblUser.*

---

3. The **DataTable** class, which is discussed in Chapter 10, is used to represent a single table. However, the schema and the values in your **DataTable** can be made up of columns from several tables in your data source by using a join in your SELECT query.

- The CommandBuilder works only with **DataTable**s that aren't related to any other **DataTable**s in your **DataSet**. The CommandBuilder ignores any relationships in your data source, or rather isn't aware of them, which means that if you try to update a table in your data source that has a relationship with another table in your data source, the update might fail. This can happen because you might be trying to update a foreign key value. Basically, you should use the CommandBuilder with single, nonrelated database tables, or write the code for the DataAdapter properties yourself.

Preparing the DataAdapter

You need to set up the DataAdapter properly before you can use the CommandBuilder. This includes setting the **SelectCommand** property, because it is the schema retrieved by this property that is used for determining the syntax for the automatic generation.

Not only do you need to set up the **SelectCommand** property, you also need to make sure that at least one primary key or unique column is returned as part of the SELECT statement. Obviously a SELECT * . . . statement will return the required column if the table holds a unique column, but you need to be aware of this requirement when you specify the columns to retrieve as part of the SELECT statement.

If you use the tblUser table from the UserMan database, the following statement will make the CommandBuilder generate the mentioned properties:

```
SELECT Id, FirstName, LastName, Password FROM tblUser
```

However, if you remove the Id column from the SELECT statement, like this:

```
SELECT FirstName, LastName, Password FROM tblUser
```

the CommandBuilder class can't be used to generate the mentioned properties. Okay, so the first statement will work with the CommandBuilder class, because the Id column, which is the primary key and thus unique, is one of the columns retrieved. The second statement will cause the CommandBuilder to fail, because none of the retrieved columns are unique. "Fail" in this case means that an **InvalidOperationException** exception is thrown.

Another thing you need to be aware of when using the CommandBuilder class is that when it is executed, only properties that have not been set, or rather properties that are equal to **Nothing**, will be automatically generated. However, this can be exploited if for whatever reason you want to set the **UpdateCommand** property yourself and have the CommandBuilder generate the **InsertCommand** and **DeleteCommand** properties for you.

Listing 8-10 does the same as Listing 8-2, but it uses the **SqlCommandBuilder** class instead of setting the properties manually.

*Listing 8-10. Using the **SqlCommandBuilder** Class*

```
1 Public Sub SetDataAdapterCommandPropertiesUsingCommandBuilder()
2   Const STR_SQL_USER_SELECT As String = _
3     "SELECT * FROM tblUser"
4
5   Dim cnnUserMan As SqlConnection
6   Dim cmmUserSelect As SqlCommand
7   Dim dadUserMan As SqlDataAdapter
8   Dim cmbUser As New SqlCommandBuilder(dadUserMan)
9
10  ' Instantiate the connection
11  cnnUserMan = New SqlConnection(PR_STR_CONNECTION_STRING)
12  ' Instantiate the select command
13  cmmUserSelect = New SqlCommand(STR_SQL_USER_SELECT, _
14    cnnUserMan)
15
16  ' Instantiate data adapter
17  dadUserMan = New SqlDataAdapter(STR_SQL_USER_SELECT, _
18    cnnUserMan)
19  ' Set data adapter select command property
20  dadUserMan.SelectCommand = cmmUserSelect
21 End Sub
```

If you compare Listing 8-10 with Listing 8-2, you'll see how much work the CommandBuilder class does for you; you save almost 50 lines of code! However, there's a possibility that using the CommandBuilder will incur a slight increase in performance and resource overhead and runtime, compared to setting the DataAdapter commands manually.

I've used the SQL Server .NET Data Provider for the example code in Listing 8-10, but you can find similar code for the ODBC .NET Data Provider and OLE DB .NET Data Provider in the example code available on the Apress Web site.

NOTE The CommandBuilder class uses the **CommandTimeout**, **Connection**, and **Transaction** properties referenced by the **SelectCommand** property of the DataAdapter class. This means you need to call the **RefreshSchema** method of the CommandBuilder class if you change any of the mentioned properties or change the **SelectCommand** itself. No exception will be thrown if you don't call the method, but the original values will be used, meaning the changes you've made won't be reflected in the automatically generated commands.

Summary

In this chapter, you saw how to use the DataAdapter to populate your **DataSet** and **DataTable** objects, and how changes made to the **DataSet** and **DataTable** can be sent back to your data source. You also saw how you can handle errors that occur during fill operations (populating your **DataSet** or **DataTable**) and update operations (updating the data source with changes from your **DataSet** or **DataTable**) using public event procedures.

Finally, you saw how you can use the CommandBuilder class with some types of SELECT statements to automatically generate the Command objects for inserting into, updating, and deleting from the data source.

The following classes were covered:

- **OdbcDataAdapter, OleDbDataAdapter**, and **SqlDataAdapter**

- **OdbcCommandBuilder, OleDbCommandBuilder**, and **SqlCommandBuilder**

In the next chapter, you'll learn what the **DataSet** class is all about. The next chapter marks the beginning of Part Three of the book, which covers the disconnected layer of ADO.NET.

Part Three

ADO.NET Disconnected
Layer Reference

CHAPTER 9

The DataSet Class

THIS CHAPTER INTRODUCES you to the **DataSet** class, the first of the data-aware classes in the disconnected layer of ADO.NET.

Using the DataSet Class

The **DataSet** class can be a complex one to deal with and understand. Well, at least until you've had a closer look at it and in this chapter I'll discuss the essentials and must-know information. I will go through all aspects of the **DataSet** class, so you can see for yourself how you can use it. The **DataSet** class is part of the **System.Data** namespace.

First things first: A **DataSet** is rather closely related to a relational database in structure. When I say that it resembles a relational database, I mean that the **DataSet** class actually exposes a hierarchical object model (which has nothing to do with hierarchical databases). This object model consists of tables, rows, and columns, and it also contains relations and constraints. In fact, the **DataSet** and **DataTable**[1] classes hold collections containing the following objects:

- **DataSet** class holds the **Tables** collection, which contains objects of data type **DataTable**, and the **Relations** collection, which contains objects of data type **DataRelation**.

- **DataTable** class holds the **Rows** collection, which contains objects of data type **DataRow**, and the **Columns** collection, which contains objects of data type **DataColumn**. The **Rows** collection holds all the rows in the table and the **Columns** collection is the actual schema for the table.

In order to exploit the full potential of the **DataSet** class, you need to use it in conjunction with at least the **DataTable** class.

If nothing else, the **DataSet** class is a local container or in-memory cache for the data you retrieve from the database. You can consider it to be a virtual data store, because all the data retrieved from the database, including the schema for the data, is stored in the disconnected cache, known as the **DataSet**. The real trick of the **DataSet** is that although you're disconnected from the data source, you can

---

1. The **DataTable** class is a disconnected class that resembles a database table in structure.

work with the data in it in much the same way you would with the data in the database. If you are thinking, "Ah, so the data in the **DataSet** is really a copy of the real data," you would be correct, my friend! Now you may be wondering if updating the real data is difficult. Well, yes and no. Yes, because it requires more than just using the good old classic ADO **Recordset** class, but no, because you have several options available for this purpose. I will get to this in a moment.

So, how do you get the data from the database and into the **DataSet**? This is a job for the DataAdapter class, the connected part of ADO.NET. The DataAdapter is the class that either works directly with the data source, as is the case with SQL Server 7.0 or later, or uses the underlying OLE DB provider or ODBC driver to talk to the database. The DataAdapter class is explained in Chapter 8.

One more thing to notice about the **DataSet** class is that it's *not* subclassed; or rather, this is the class, you'll work with, no matter which .NET Data Provider you're dealing with. There is no OdbcDataSet, OleDbDataSet, or SqlDataSet class!

Recordset vs. DataSet

If you are familiar with classic ADO, then you probably know the **Recordset** class, and how it can be used with various cursors, and so on. Although the **Recordset** class doesn't have a direct equivalent in ADO.NET, I'll show you some of the things that make the **DataSet** class and its associated data class, **DataTable**, behave in similar ways to the **Recordset** class. When ADO.NET was on the drawing board, one of the major obstacles was to find a way of making the connected classic ADO **Recordset** class a disconnected class. The result is that the ADO **Recordset** class has been mapped to a few different classes in ADO.NET. This includes the disconnected **DataSet** class, which uses the connected DataAdapter class for retrieving data. Even though classic ADO introduced the concept of a disconnected recordset through Remote Data Services (RDS), the connected part of the setup is still evident behind the scenes.

Simply put, the **DataSet** class is really a collection of disconnected **Recordset** objects, which are exposed using the **DataTable** class. Therefore, if you like using the classic ADO **Recordset** object, but want to use ADO.NET at the same time, you do have the option, and this option is called the **DataTable** class. The **DataTable** class works in much the same way as a classic ADO recordset. See the "Using the DataTable Class" section in Chapter 10 for more details.

Data Source Independence

One of the strengths of a **DataSet** is the fact that it is completely independent of the data source. It is in other words a container, or cache, of data that is copied from the data source. The fact that a **DataSet** is disconnected and thereby independent of the data source makes it ideal for containing data from multiple data sources, such as tables from various databases. The data source independence also makes it ideal for temporary storage of especially relational data, because you can create a **DataSet** from scratch and use it without ever being connected to a data source.

In order to maintain data integrity, most data source changes are usually handled within the confines of a transaction; however, it's not a good idea to have pending transactions open on a data source for long periods. This is exactly the situation you're faced with when information is being updated on a Web site or by a service on another computer, or when you need to support users on the road. This kind of application is commonly referred to as a *disconnected application*. With disconnected applications, you generally don't need to worry about the connection to the data source abruptly disappearing, leaving any changes you've made on the client stranded. The concept of data source independence is your friend in need, when an open data source connection isn't a good solution as in the cases stated previously. You will, however, have to ensure that data source integrity is maintained, when the changes made to the data in the **DataSet** are ultimately propagated back to the data source. However, there are no concerns about long-term locking at the data source when the **DataSet** is originated.

XML Is the Format

When data is moved from a data source, such as a database, to the **DataSet** (or the other way around), the format used to facilitate this is XML. This is one of key concepts of ADO.NET; everything is XML based! Because the format is XML, not only can you transfer **DataSet**s across process and machine boundaries, but you can also transfer **DataSet**s across networks that use a firewall! That's right, XML makes this possible! Now you truly have a way of manipulating data coming across the Internet from any data source that understands XML.

Okay, so the format used for transferring the data is XML, but this is not the only place ADO.NET uses XML. XML is the underlying serialization format for all data in ADO.NET, meaning if you need to persist or serialize your data to a file, the format used is XML. This means that you can read the persisted file using any XML-capable reader.

One point should be made very clear before you continue: Although the underlying or fundamental data format in ADO.NET is XML, the data in a **DataSet** is *not* expressed using XML. The ADO.NET data APIs automatically handle the creation of XML data when you exchange data between **DataSet**s and data sources, but the data inside the **DataSet** is in a format that is much more efficient to work with. Therefore, you don't actually have to know anything about XML in order to use ADO.NET. However, I would recommend that you learn at least the basics of XML, because it's such an integral part of Visual Studio .NET. You can learn a great deal from this book:

> *XML Programming Using the Microsoft XML Parser,* by Soo Mee Foo and Wei Meng Lee. Apress, February 2002. ISBN: 1-893115-42-9.

Typed vs. Untyped Data sets

A **DataSet** can be *typed* or *untyped*. The difference is that the typed **DataSet** has a schema and the untyped **DataSet** doesn't. You can choose to use either kind of **DataSet** in your application, but you need to know that there's more support for the typed **DataSet**s in Visual Studio, and as such, there are more tools for your convenience.

A typed **DataSet** gives you easier access to the content of table fields through strongly typed programming. Strongly typed programming uses information from the underlying data scheme. This means you're programming directly against your declared objects and not the tables you're really trying to manipulate. A typed **DataSet** has a reference to an XML schema file. This schema file (.xsd) describes the structure of all the tables contained within the **DataSet**. A typed **DataSet** is based on a class file that is derived from the **DataSet** class.

CROSS-REFERENCE   See Chapter 13 for more information on how to create a typed **DataSet**.

In Listing 9-1 you can see how strong typing changes the way you would normally access the content of a column in a table.

Listing 9-1. Strong Typing vs. Weak Typing

```
1 ' Display value from ADO Recordset
2 MsgBox(rstUser.Fields("FirstName").Value.ToString())
3 ' Display value from ADO.NET DataSet using strong typing
4 MsgBox(dstUser.tblUser(0).FirstName.ToString())
5 ' Display value from ADO.NET DataSet using weak typing
6 MsgBox(dstUser.Tables("tblUser").Columns("FirstName").ToString())
```

As you can see from Listing 9-1, the syntax is much simpler when you use strong typing. Simply reference the table and field by using the table name and field name directly (see Line 4). The rstUser **Recordset** and the dstUser **DataSet** have been declared, instantiated, and opened or populated elsewhere.

DataSet Properties

The **DataSet** class has the properties shown in Table D-1 in Appendix D, in alphabetical order. Please note that only the public, noninherited properties are shown.

DataSet Methods

Table D-2 in Appendix D lists the noninherited and public methods of the **DataSet** class in alphabetical order.

DataSet Events

The **DataSet** class only has one noninherited event, the **MergeFailed** event. This event can be used when you merge a **DataSet** with an array of **DataRow** objects, another **DataSet**, or a **DataTable**, and you want to handle possible merge failures. The event is triggered when the schema of the data classes being merged are conflicting and the **EnforceConstraints** property has been set to **true**. One such conflict can be when two tables in the **DataSet** have different primary keys. See the "Handling DataSet Merge Failures" section later in this chapter for more information and an example.

Instantiating a DataSet

There isn't much fuss to instantiating a **DataSet** object. It can be done when declaring it, or later when needed. Another thing you might want to consider when declaring and/or instantiating the object is to name it. If you have a number of dynamically created **DataSet** objects, it's so much easier to recognize the different **DataSet**s by name. Please see Listing 9-2 for an example.

Listing 9-2. Instantiating a DataSet

```
1 Public Sub InstantiateDataSet()
2    ' Declare and instantiate
3    Dim dstUnnamed1 As New DataSet()
4    Dim dstNamed1 As New DataSet("UserManDataSet")
5
```

```
6      ' Declare
7      Dim dstUnnamed2 As DataSet
8      Dim dstNamed2 As DataSet
9
10     ' Instantiate
11     dstUnnamed2 = New DataSet()
12     dstNamed2 = New DataSet("UserManDataSet")
13
14     ' Name DataSets
15     dstUnnamed1.DataSetName = "Unnamed1"
16     dstUnnamed2.DataSetName = "Unnamed2"
17 End Sub
```

As you can see from Listing 9-2, there are a few ways of declaring, instantiating, and naming your **DataSet**s. I recommend always naming your DataSets, because it's so much easier to work with, especially when you have a number of dynamically created **DataSet**s, or if you have a collection or array of **DataSet**s. Giving a **DataSet** a name is also useful when it's persisted as XML, because the XML document element is then given a name you can recognize.

Populating Your DataSet Using the DataAdapter

Once you have set up the DataAdapter and the **DataSet**, you need to populate the **DataSet**. The **Fill** method of the DataAdapter class is used for populating and refreshing the **DataSet** object. The **Fill** method is overloaded, and there are more method versions for the **OleDbDataAdapter** class than the **OdbcDataAdapter** and **SqlDataAdapter** classes. This is because the **OleDbDataAdapter** class supports populating a **DataSet** from an ADO **Recordset** object or an ADO **Record** object. Yes, that's right—you can mess about with the good old ADO **Recordset** object and the somewhat newer ADO **Record** object. In Table D-6 in Appendix D, I show you the various public versions of the **Fill** method.

Since I won't be going over how to use the classic ADO **Recordset** and the classic ADO classes in general, perhaps this is a good time to show you a complete code example, which opens an ADO **Recordset** and uses this **Recordset** to fill a **DataSet**. Listing 9-3 demonstrates how to do this.

*Listing 9-3. Populating a **DataSet** from an ADO **Recordset***

```
1 Public Sub FillDataSetFromRecordset()
2    Const STR_CONNECTION_STRING As String = "Provider=SQLOLEDB;" & _
3       "Data Source=10.8.1.12;User ID=UserMan;Password=userman;" & _
4       "Initial Catalog=UserMan"
5    Const STR_SQL_USER_SELECT As String = _
6       "SELECT * FROM tblUser"
7
8    Dim cnnUserMan As OleDbConnection
9    Dim dadUserMan As OleDbDataAdapter
10   Dim dstUserMan As DataSet
11
12   Dim rstUser As ADODB.Recordset
13   Dim cnnADOUserMan As ADODB.Connection
14
15   Dim intNumRows As Integer
16
17   ' Instantiate and open the connections
18   cnnUserMan = New OleDbConnection(STR_CONNECTION_STRING)
19   cnnUserMan.Open()
20   cnnADOUserMan = New ADODB.Connection()
21   cnnADOUserMan.Open(STR_CONNECTION_STRING)
22
22   ' Instantiate data adapter
23   dadUserMan = New OleDbDataAdapter(STR_SQL_USER_SELECT, _
24      cnnUserMan)
25
26   ' Instantiate dataset
27   dstUserMan = New DataSet()
28   ' Instantiate recordset
29   rstUser = New ADODB.Recordset()
30
31   ' Populate recordset
32   rstUser.Open(STR_SQL_USER_SELECT, cnnADOUserMan)
33   ' Fill dataset
34   intNumRows = dadUserMan.Fill(dstUserMan, rstUser, _
35      "tblUser")
36 End Sub
```

In Listing 9-3, I make use of some classic ADO classes, and in order to do this, you must add a reference to the classic ADO COM libraries from your project. See Appendix B for information on how to this. There isn't much wizardry to the code in Listing 9-3; I open two connections, one ADO.NET connection and one classic ADO connection. I then instantiate the DataAdapter and the **Recordset**, populate the **Recordset** set, and then use the **Recordset** to populate the **DataSet**. You can use a classic ADO **Record** object instead of the **Recordset** object and/or you can populate a **DataTable** instead of a **DataSet**. See Table D-6 in Appendix D for more information on how you can do this using the **Fill** method of the DataAdapter. The example code in Listing 9-3 uses the OLE DB .NET Data Provider, and this is the only provider that supports populating a **DataSet** using a classic ADO **Recordset** object.

As stated earlier, Table D-6 in Appendix D shows you how to use the various overloads of the DataAdapter's **Fill** method, but Listings 9-4, 9-5, 9-6, and 9-10, shown later in this chapter, also show you examples of populating a **DataSet**.

 CROSS-REFERENCE   You can also find some information about working with the DataAdapter class used for populating a **DataSet** and/or **DataTable** object in the "The DataAdapter Explained" section in Chapter 8.

Clearing Data from a DataSet

When you have added tables, relations, constraints, and so on to a **DataSet**, or what makes up the structure in your **DataSet**, you frequently need a way of clearing all the data from the **DataSet**. This can easily be accomplished using the **Clear** method, as shown here:

```
dstUser.Clear()
```

Keep in mind that it's not possible to undo this action! If you need to clear the **DataSet** completely, meaning data and schema, you need to call the **Reset** method. See the "Clearing a DataSet" section next.

Clearing a DataSet

If you need to clear everything from your **DataSet**, meaning both the data and the schema, you can call the **Reset** method, as shown here:

```
dstUser.Reset()
```

Keep in mind that it's not possible to undo this action! If you just need to clear the data from your **DataSet**, you need to call the **Clear** method. See the "Clearing Data from a DataSet" section earlier in this chapter.

Copying a DataSet

Sometimes it's necessary to copy a **DataSet** for various reasons. If you need to manipulate some data for testing purposes, or perhaps to provide an undo facility, copying a **DataSet** is a good way of leaving the original data intact. Depending on what you actually need to do, there are two ways you can approach this: Copy just the data structure, or copy the data structure and the data within it. The next sections describe each of these methods.

Copying the Data Structure of a DataSet

When you need to copy, or rather clone, the structure of a **DataSet**, you can use the **Clone** method, as shown here:

```
dstClone = dstUser.Clone()
```

This will copy of the data structure from the dstUser **DataSet** to the dstClone **DataSet**.

Copying the Data and Structure of a DataSet

When you need a complete copy of the data structure and the data contained therein from a **DataSet**, you can use the **Copy** method, as shown here:

```
dstCopy = dstUser.Copy()
```

This will create an exact copy (dstCopy) of the dstUser **DataSet**.

Merging Data in a DataSet with Other Data

From time to time, you'll probably want to combine data from a **DataSet** and data that exist in another form. For example, say you have a **DataSet** (destination **DataSet**) that you filled with a data structure and data using the **Fill** method of the DataAdapter, and you want to combine this with a **DataSet** or **DataTable** (source data object) that you have created programmatically. Once you are done manipulating the data, you want to merge the data in the two objects. You can achieve this by merging the data into the **DataSet**. Data in the form of an array of **DataRow** objects, a **DataTable** object, or a **DataSet** object can be merged using the **Merge** method of the **DataSet**. The resulting merged **DataSet** replaces the data in the **DataSet**, which executes the **Merge** method. See Listings 9-4, 9-5, and 9-6, later in this section, for some examples of the using the **Merge** method.

One thing to note about the **Merge** method is that it's to be used for objects that have the same or similar schema. When you call the **Merge** method, the schemas for the two data objects are compared, and if they're the same, the merging is started. If they're not the same, meaning the source data object(s) have columns defined that don't exist in the destination **DataSet**, they're handled according to the member of the **MissingSchemaAction** enum, which you can pass as the third argument for some of the **Merge** method overloads. See Table D-7 in Appendix D for more information on the members of the **MissingSchemaAction** enum.

Any constraints defined on the data objects are disabled during the merge, and reenabled at the end of the merge. When the constraints are reenabled, a **ConstraintException** exception is thrown if any of the new data conflicts with the constraints. Such a conflict can, and most often will, occur if you try to merge the same data more than once. See the "Handling DataSet Merge Failures" section later in this chapter for an example of how to handle merge failures. The invalid data is *not* rejected; it's actually kept in the destination **DataSet**, but the **EnforceConstraints** property is set to **False**, and all the rows with invalid data are marked in error. This means that the **HasErrors** property of the **DataRow** objects with invalid data is set to **True**. When this property is set to **False** on a **DataRow** object, the same property is also set to **False** on the **DataTable** in which it exists (if any), and the **DataSet** in which the table resides (if any).You can find more information about the **DataTable** class in Chapter 10 and the **DataRow** class in Chapter 11.

Some of the overloads of the **Merge** method take a second argument, the blnPreserveChanges argument. This **Boolean** argument is used to indicate if changes in the destination **DataSet** should be preserved after the call to the **Merge** method. If you pass the value **False** (which is the default value) for this argument, both the original and current column values in the destination **DataSet** are overwritten with the column values from the source **DataSet**. If you instead pass the value **True**, only the original column values in the destination **DataSet** are overwritten with the original column values from the source **DataSet**. You can find more information about the different row and column versions in Chapter 11.

In Listing 9-4, the dstUser **DataSet** is merged with an array of **DataRow** objects (arrdrwUser). First, I populate the **DataSet** on Line 20, and then I create a new **DataRow** object (drwUser) on Line 22, with the same schema as the rows in the tblUser table of the **DataSet**. On Lines 23 through 26, the columns of the new **DataRow** object are modified, and the DataRow itself added to the arrdrwUser array. Finally, this array is merged with the **DataSet**.

*Listing 9-4. Merging a **DataSet** Object with an Array of **DataRow** Objects*

```
1 Public Sub MergeDataSetWithDataRows()
2    Dim cnnUserMan As SqlConnection
3    Dim cmmUser As SqlCommand
4    Dim dadUser As SqlDataAdapter
5    Dim dstUser As DataSet
6    Dim dtbUser As DataTable
7    Dim arrdrwUser(0) As DataRow
8    Dim drwUser As DataRow
9
10   ' Instantiate the connection
11   cnnUserMan = New SqlConnection(PR_STR_CONNECTION_STRING)
12   ' Instantiate the command, data set and data table
13   cmmUser = New SqlCommand("SELECT * FROM tblUser", cnnUserMan)
14   dstUser = New DataSet()
15   dtbUser = New DataTable()
16   ' Instantiate and initialize the data adapter
17   dadUser = New SqlDataAdapter("SELECT * FROM tblUser", cnnUserMan)
18   dadUser.SelectCommand = cmmUser
19   ' Fill the data set
20   dadUser.Fill(dstUser, "tblUser")
21   ' Create new row and fill with data
22   drwUser = dstUser.Tables("tblUser").NewRow()
23   drwUser("LoginName") = "NewUser1"
24   drwUser("FirstName") = "New"
25   drwUser("LastName") = "User"
26   arrdrwUser.SetValue(drwUser, 0)
27   ' Merge the data set with the data row array
28   dstUser.Merge(arrdrwUser)
29 End Sub
```

In Listing 9-5, I set up two **DataSet** object, dstUser and dstCopy, populate the dstUser one, copy the dstUser **DataSet** into dstUser, and finally I merge the two

DataSet's into one again (Line 23). If you run the example code as shown, nothing much will happen, but if you manipulate the data and/or schema in one or both of the **DataSet** objects, you will see a different outcome. One of your options is to specify what should happen if you change the schema of the dstCopy **DataSet**. You can do this by passing a member of the **MissingSchemaAction** enum to the **Merge** method.

*Listing 9-5. Merging Two **DataSet** Objects*

```
1 Public Sub MergeDataSets()
2    Dim cnnUserMan As SqlConnection
3    Dim cmmUser As SqlCommand
4    Dim dadUser As SqlDataAdapter
5    Dim dstUser As DataSet
6    Dim dstCopy As DataSet
7
8    ' Instantiate the connection
9    cnnUserMan = New SqlConnection(PR_STR_CONNECTION_STRING)
10   ' Instantiate the command and data set
11   cmmUser = New SqlCommand("SELECT * FROM tblUser", cnnUserMan)
12   dstUser = New DataSet()
13   ' Instantiate and initialize the data adapter
14   dadUser = New SqlDataAdapter("SELECT * FROM tblUser", cnnUserMan)
15   dadUser.SelectCommand = cmmUser
16   ' Fill the data set
17   dadUser.Fill(dstUser, "tblUser")
18   ' Copy the data set
19   dstCopy = dstUser.Copy()
20   ' Do your stuff with the data sets
21   ' ...
22   ' Merge the two data sets
23   dstUser.Merge(dstCopy)
24 End Sub
```

In Listing 9-6, I set up a **DataSet** object, dstUser, and a DataTable object, dtbUser, populate both data objects (Lines 18 and 19), and merge the two data objects into one, dstUser, (Line 23). If you run the example code as shown, nothing much will happen, but if you manipulate the data and/or schema in either the **DataSet** object or the **DataTable** object, you will see a different outcome. One of your options is to specify what should happen if you change the schema of the dtbUser **DataTable**. You can do this by passing a member of the **MissingSchemaAction** enum to the **Merge** method.

*Listing 9-6. Merging a **DataSet** Object with a **DataTable** Object*

```
 1 Public Sub MergeDataSetWithDataTable()
 2    Dim cnnUserMan As SqlConnection
 3    Dim cmmUser As SqlCommand
 4    Dim dadUser As SqlDataAdapter
 5    Dim dstUser As DataSet
 6    Dim dtbUser As DataTable
 7
 8    ' Instantiate the connection
 9    cnnUserMan = New SqlConnection(PR_STR_CONNECTION_STRING)
10    ' Instantiate the command, data set and data table
11    cmmUser = New SqlCommand("SELECT * FROM tblUser", cnnUserMan)
12    dstUser = New DataSet()
13    dtbUser = New DataTable()
14    ' Instantiate and initialize the data adapter
15    dadUser = New SqlDataAdapter("SELECT * FROM tblUser", cnnUserMan)
16    dadUser.SelectCommand = cmmUser
17    ' Fill the data set and data table
18    dadUser.Fill(dstUser, "tblUser")
19    dadUser.Fill(dtbUser)
20    ' Do your stuff with the data set and the data table
21    ' ...
22    ' Merge the data set with the data table
23    dstUser.Merge(dtbUser)
24 End Sub
```

Please note that in Listings 9-4 through 9-6, I have chosen to create the data structure and fill the **DataTable** using the DataAdapter's **Fill** method. You can obviously create the data structure yourself and fill it with data from a variety of sources before you merge it with the **DataSet**. See Chapter 10 for more information on how to do this.

Handling DataSet Merge Failures

When you perform a merge, like the examples shown in the previous section, one or more errors can occur. Exceptions can be caught using a **Try . . . Catch . . . End Try** construct, but problems like primary key conflicts trigger the **MergeFailed** event instead. Therefore, if you set up an event handler that can respond to merge failures, as well as placing the call to the **Merge** method in a **Try** block, you'll have a better chance of catching all merge related failures. Listing 9-7 shows you how to set up and handle merge failures.

Listing 9-7. Handling Merge Failures

```
1 Private Shared Sub OnMergeFailed(ByVal sender As Object, _
2   ByVal args As MergeFailedEventArgs)
3   ' Display a message detailing the merge conflict
4   MsgBox("There were errors when merging the data sets:" & vbCrLf & _
5       vbCrLf & args.Conflict & " The conflict happened in table " & _
6       args.Table.TableName & ".")
7 End Sub
8
9 Public Shared Sub HandleMergeFailures()
10   Dim drwNew As DataRow
11   ' Declare and instantiate data sets
12   Dim dstUser As New DataSet("Users")
13   Dim dstCopy As New DataSet("UsersCopy")
14   Dim dstClone As New DataSet("UsersClone")
15
16   ' Declare and instantiate connections
17   Dim cnnUserMan As New SqlConnection(PR_STR_CONNECTION_STRING)
18   ' Declare and instantiate data adapters
19   Dim prdadUserMan As New SqlDataAdapter("SELECT * FROM tblUser", _
20       cnnUserMan)
21
22   ' Set up event handler
23   AddHandler dstUser.MergeFailed, AddressOf OnMergeFailed
24
25   ' Populate the dataset
26   prdadUserMan.Fill(dstUser, "tblUser")
27   ' Close the connection
28   cnnUserMan.Close()
29   ' Copy DataSet
30   dstCopy = dstUser.Copy()
31
32   Try
33     ' Add new string column to user table in
34     ' dataset copy
35     dstCopy.Tables("tblUser").Columns.Add("NewColumn", _
36         Type.GetType("System.String"))
37     ' Merge the DataSets
38     dstUser.Merge(dstCopy, True, MissingSchemaAction.Error)
39   Catch objE As Exception
40     MsgBox("An exception was thrown when merging the data sets:" & _
41         vbCrLf & vbCrLf & objE.Message)
42   End Try
```

```
43
44    ' Clone dataset
45    dstClone = dstUser.Clone
46    ' Do your stuff
47    ' ...
48    ' Merge the data sets
49    dstUser.Merge(dstClone, True)
50 End Sub
```

In Listing 9-7, I populate three **DataSets**, the original (dstUser), a copy (dstCopy), and a clone (dstClone). The original **DataSet** is populated with all rows and columns from the tblUser table in the UserMan database on Line 26. After copying the structure and data from the original **DataSet** to the copy, I add a new column the schema of the copy **DataSet**, and try to merge it with the original **DataSet** on Line 38. Because I specify that columns missing from the destination **DataSet** (dstUser) should throw an exception (**MissingSchemaAction.Error**), the message box on Lines 40 and 41 is displayed. When doing a merge, I generally recommend that you set up an exception handler, because there are a number of issues that can throw an exception, such as constraint violations, missing columns in the destination **DataSet**, incompatible data types, and so on.

Problems with primary keys conflicts will cause the **MergeFailed** event to be triggered if you've set up and declared the event handler procedure. You can see the OnMergeFailed procedure on Lines 1 through 7 that is called if a primary key conflict arises, because I've set up the event handler on Line 23.

Detecting and Handling Changes to Data in a DataSet

Sometimes it's necessary to know if the data in your **DataSet** has been changed. Changes in this context include new rows and deleted rows, as well as modified rows. The **DataSet** class has the **HasChanges** method that can be used for this purpose. This method actually exists for the individual **DataTable** objects in the **Tables** collection, but if you just want to know if any of the data in the **DataSet** has changed, you need to use the **DataSet**'s method. The **GetChanges** method is used to retrieve the changed rows from a **DataSet**, and this method is particularly useful when you extract the changed rows from a **DataSet** and copy them to a separate **DataSet**, before propagating the changed rows back to the data source. Unless all the rows in the original **DataSet** have changed, this will help reduce network traffic. The **HasChanges** method is overloaded, and you can see how to use the various versions in Listing 9-8.

*Listing 9-8. Detecting and Handling Data Changes in a **DataSet** Object*

```
 1 Public Sub DetectDataSetChanges()
 2    Dim cnnUserMan As SqlConnection
 3    Dim cmmUser As SqlCommand
 4    Dim dadUser As SqlDataAdapter
 5    Dim dstUser As DataSet
 6    Dim dstAllChanges, dstChanges As DataSet
 7    Dim dstAdditions, dstDeletions As DataSet
 8
 9    ' Instantiate the connection
10    cnnUserMan = New SqlConnection(PR_STR_CONNECTION_STRING)
11    ' Instantiate the command and data set
12    cmmUser = New SqlCommand("SELECT * FROM tblUser", cnnUserMan)
13    dstUser = New DataSet()
14    ' Instantiate and initialize the data adapter
15    dadUser = New SqlDataAdapter("SELECT * FROM tblUser", cnnUserMan)
16    dadUser.SelectCommand = cmmUser
17    ' Fill the data set
18    dadUser.Fill(dstUser, "tblUser")
19    ' Do your stuff with the data set
20    ' ...
21    ' Check if any errors exist in the DataSet
22    If Not dstUser.HasErrors Then
23      ' Check if any data has changed in the data set
24      If dstUser.HasChanges() Then
25        ' Save all changes in a new data set
26        dstAllChanges = dstUser.GetChanges()
27        ' Save all modified rows in a new data set
28        dstChanges = dstUser.GetChanges(DataRowState.Modified)
29        ' Save all added rows in a new data set
30        dstAdditions = dstUser.GetChanges(DataRowState.Added)
31        ' Save all deleted rows in a new data set
32        dstDeletions = dstUser.GetChanges(DataRowState.Deleted)
33      End If
34    Else
35      ' Deal with errors in DataSet
36    End If
37 End Sub
```

In Listing 9-8, I've populated the dstUser **DataSet** with all the rows from the tblUser table in the data source. After making changes to the data in the **DataSet**, I check to see if there are any errors to the data in the **DataSet**. This is considered good programming practice, as it will help reduce the number of exceptions being thrown if you handle these errors before trying to propagate the changes back to the data source. You can also perform this check after isolating the changed rows. If there are no errors to the data, I move on to retrieve the changed rows in the original **DataSet**, and have them copied to a new **DataSet**. On Lines 26, 28, 30, and 32, you can see how I use four different ways of retrieving the changed data; dstAllChanges gets a copy of all changed rows (inserted, modified, and deleted), dstChanges gets a copy of all modified rows, dstAdditions gets a copy of all inserted/added rows, and dstDeletions gets a copy of all deleted rows.

Obviously, this doesn't do anything to the data in itself, but once you have the changes isolated, you can manipulate the data and check for errors (if you haven't already). This is particularly useful when you want to update the data source. Don't forget that the **DataSet** is disconnected from the data source and any changes will not be propagated back to the data source until you explicitly update the data source!

Accepting or Rejecting Changes to Data in a DataSet

When changes have been made to data in the **DataSet**, you can choose to reject or accept them. The **DataSet** class has two methods for doing this: the **AcceptChanges** and **RejectChanges** methods. One thing you have to note about these methods is that they work on the data in the **DataSet** and *not* in the data source itself. This goes back to the fact that the **DataSet** is disconnected, and as such doesn't interact directly with the data source.

One reason for rejecting changes to the data in the **DataSet** can be that you have user feedback on the updates and perhaps the user wants to reject the changes he or she has been making. See the "The RejectChanges Method" section later in this chapter. A reason for accepting changes in the **DataSet** can be that the **DataSet** is used as a temporary data store that has been built from scratch, like in Listing 9-9, shown later. In this kind of situation, you might have made a number of changes and now you need to make another batch of changes, but you want to make sure you can distinguish the new changes from all nonchanged rows. This can be done by calling the **AcceptChanges** method before making the second batch of changes. See the "The AcceptChanges Method" section next.

 NOTE If you call either of the **AcceptChanges** or **RejectChanges** methods, you also "reset" the **HasChanges** method, meaning it will return **False**.

The AcceptChanges Method

When using this method, any changes to a row in a **DataTable** in the **Tables** collection will be accepted. This is done by calling the **AcceptChanges** method on each of the **DataTable** objects in the table collection. When the **AcceptChanges** method is called on a **DataTable**, the **DataTable** invokes the **AcceptChanges** method on each **DataRow** object in the **Rows** collection. What happens then is the **RowState** property of each data row is examined. If the row state is **Added** or **Modified**, then the **RowState** property is changed to **Unchanged**. Rows with **Deleted** row state are removed from the respective **DataTable**. If a **DataRow** is being edited when the **AcceptChanges** method is called, the row in question will successfully exit edit mode. See Listing 9-9 in the next section for an example of how **AcceptChanges** can be used and how it affects a **DataSet**. If you call **AcceptChanges** just before calling the **Update** method of the DataAdapter, no changes will be written back to the data source because you have just accepted the changes and they are now marked **Unchanged**!

NOTE If a **DataSet** contains any **ForeignKeyConstraint** objects, the **AcceptRejectRule** property is enforced once the **AcceptChanges** method is called. The **AcceptRejectRule** property is used to determine if the changes or deletions should be cascaded across a relationship. Please see the "What Is a Foreign Key?" section in Chapter 2 for more information on foreign keys.

The RejectChanges Method

When using the **RejectChanges** method, any changes to a row in a **DataTable** in the **Tables** collection will be rejected. This is done by calling **RejectChanges** on each of the **DataTable** objects in the table collection. When the **RejectChanges** method is called on a **DataTable**, the **DataTable** invokes the **AcceptChanges** method on each **DataRow** object in the **Rows** collection. What happens then is the **RowState** property of each data row is examined. If the row state is **Added**, then the row is removed from the respective **DataTable**. The **RowState** property for rows with **Modified** and **Deleted** row states is changed to **Unchanged** and the original content of the rows restored. If a **DataRow** is being edited when the **RejectChanges** method is called, the row in question will cancel edit mode. See Listing 9-9 for an example of how **RejectChanges** can be used and how it affects a **DataSet** object.

*Listing 9-9. Accepting or Rejecting Changes to the Data in a **DataSet** Object*

```
1 Public Sub AcceptOrRejectDataSetChanges()
2    Dim cnnUserMan As SqlConnection
3    Dim cmmUser As SqlCommand
4    Dim dadUser As SqlDataAdapter
5    Dim dstUser, dstChanges As DataSet
6    Dim drwUser As DataRow
7    Dim intCounter As Integer
8
9    ' Instantiate the connection
10   cnnUserMan = New SqlConnection(PR_STR_CONNECTION_STRING)
11   ' Instantiate the command and the data set
12   cmmUser = New SqlCommand("SELECT * FROM tblUser", cnnUserMan)
13   dstUser = New DataSet()
14   ' Instantiate and initialize the data adapter
15   dadUser = New SqlDataAdapter("SELECT * FROM tblUser", cnnUserMan)
16   dadUser.SelectCommand = cmmUser
17   ' Fill the data set
18   dadUser.Fill(dstUser, "tblUser")
19   ' Create a new data row with the schema from the user table
20   drwUser = dstUser.Tables("tblUser").NewRow()
21   ' Enter values in the data row columns
22   drwUser("LoginName") = "NewUser1"
23   drwUser("FirstName") = "New"
24   drwUser("LastName") = "User"
25   ' Add the data row to the user table
26   dstUser.Tables("tblUser").Rows.Add(drwUser)
27   ' Check if any data has changed in the data set
28   If dstUser.HasChanges() Then
29      ' Save all changed rows in a new data set
30      dstChanges = dstUser.GetChanges()
31      ' Check if the changed rows contains any errors
32      If dstChanges.HasErrors() Then
33         ' Display the row state of all rows before rejecting changes
34         For intCounter = 0 To dstUser.Tables(0).Rows.Count - 1
35            MsgBox("HasErrors=True, Before RejectChanges, RowState=" & _
36               dstUser.Tables(0).Rows(intCounter).RowState.ToString & _
37               ", LoginName=" & _
38               dstUser.Tables(0).Rows(intCounter)("LoginName").ToString)
39         Next
```

```
40          ' Reject the changes to the data set
41          dstUser.RejectChanges()
42          ' Display the row state of all rows after rejecting changes
43          For intCounter = 0 To dstUser.Tables(0).Rows.Count - 1
44            MsgBox("HasErrors=True, After RejectChanges, RowState=" & _
45              dstUser.Tables(0).Rows(intCounter).RowState.ToString & _
46              ", LoginName=" & _
47              dstUser.Tables(0).Rows(intCounter)("LoginName").ToString)
48          Next
49        Else
50          ' Display the row state of all rows before accepting changes
51          For intCounter = 0 To dstUser.Tables(0).Rows.Count - 1
52            MsgBox("HasErrors=False, Before AcceptChanges, RowState=" & _
53              dstUser.Tables(0).Rows(intCounter).RowState.ToString & _
54              ", LoginName=" & _
55              dstUser.Tables(0).Rows(intCounter)("LoginName").ToString)
56          Next
57          ' Accept the changes to the data set
58          dstUser.AcceptChanges()
59          ' Display the row state of all rows after accepting changes
60          For intCounter = 0 To dstUser.Tables(0).Rows.Count - 1
61            MsgBox("HasErrors=False, After AcceptChanges, RowState=" & _
62              dstUser.Tables(0).Rows(intCounter).RowState.ToString & _
63              ", LoginName=" & _
64              dstUser.Tables(0).Rows(intCounter)("LoginName").ToString)
65          Next
66        End If
67      End If
68  End Sub
```

Listing 9-9 shows how to use the **AcceptChanges** and **RejectChanges** methods of the **DataSet** class. It also shows you how to check for changes and errors in the changed rows. As the example stands, the **HasErrors** method returns **False**, which means that the changes are accepted. You can manipulate the example code so that the changes are rejected and the **RejectChanges** method will be used instead.

Updating Your Data Source Using the DataAdapter

When you have finished manipulating the data in your **DataSet**, it's time to update the data source. This is done using the **Update** method of the DataAdapter class. This method is responsible for examining the **RowState** property of each of the **DataRow** objects in the **DataRowsCollection**, which can be accessed using the

Rows property. The **Rows** property is a member of each of the **DataTable** objects contained in the **Tables** collection of the **DataSet**. Therefore, the DataAdapter starts by looping through all the tables in the **Tables** collection in the **DataSet**, and for each table it loops through the **DataRowsCollection** collection to examine the **RowState** property. If a row has been inserted, updated, or deleted, the DataAdapter uses one of the command properties to handle the update. This means that the **InsertCommand** property is used if you are inserting a new row, the **UpdateCommand** property is used if you are updating an existing row, and the **DeleteCommand** is used if you are deleting an existing row.

In Listing 9-10, I set up a DataAdapter, a **DataSet**, and some Command objects to manipulate the tblUser table in the UserMan database. Then I add, modify, and delete a row from the table. I then use the **HasChanges** method to check if there are any changes to the data in the **DataSet**. If so, I specify that all the changed rows be loaded into the dstChanges **DataSet** using the **GetChanges** method. The changes are rejected if there are any errors; otherwise, the data source is updated using the **Update** method. The code in Listing 9-10 doesn't handle exceptions thrown when I try to update the data source, but check out Chapter 14 for example code and recommendations on how to handle exceptions.

Listing 9-10. Propagating Changes Back to the Data Source

```
1 Public Sub UpdateDataSet()
2     Const STR_SQL_USER_SELECT As String = _
3         "SELECT * FROM tblUser"
4     Const STR_SQL_USER_DELETE As String = _
5         "DELETE FROM tblUser WHERE Id=@Id"
6     Const STR_SQL_USER_INSERT As String = "INSERT INTO tblUser(" & _
7         "ADName, ADSID, FirstName, LastName, LoginName, Password) " & _
8         "VALUES(@ADName, @ADSID, @FirstName, @LastName, @LoginName, " & _
9         "@Password)"
10    Const STR_SQL_USER_UPDATE As String = "UPDATE tblUser SET " & _
11        "ADName=@ADName, ADSID=@ADSID, FirstName=@FirstName, " & _
12        "LastName=@LastName, LoginName=@LoginName, Password=@Password " & _
13        "WHERE Id=@Id"
14
15    Dim cnnUserMan As SqlConnection
16    Dim cmmUserSelect As SqlCommand
17    Dim cmmUserDelete As SqlCommand
18    Dim cmmUserInsert As SqlCommand
19    Dim cmmUserUpdate As SqlCommand
20    Dim dadUserMan As SqlDataAdapter
21    Dim prmSQLDelete, prmSQLUpdate, prmSQLInsert As SqlParameter
22    Dim dstUserMan, dstChanges As DataSet
23    Dim drwUser As DataRow
```

```
24
25      ' Instantiate the connection
26      cnnUserMan = New SqlConnection(PR_STR_CONNECTION_STRING)
27      ' Instantiate the commands
28      cmmUserSelect = New SqlCommand(STR_SQL_USER_SELECT, cnnUserMan)
29      cmmUserDelete = New SqlCommand(STR_SQL_USER_DELETE, cnnUserMan)
30      cmmUserInsert = New SqlCommand(STR_SQL_USER_INSERT, cnnUserMan)
31      cmmUserUpdate = New SqlCommand(STR_SQL_USER_UPDATE, cnnUserMan)
32
33      ' Instantiate data adapter
34      dadUserMan = New SqlDataAdapter(STR_SQL_USER_SELECT, cnnUserMan)
35      ' Set data adapter command properties
36      dadUserMan.SelectCommand = cmmUserSelect
37      dadUserMan.InsertCommand = cmmUserInsert
38      dadUserMan.DeleteCommand = cmmUserDelete
39      dadUserMan.UpdateCommand = cmmUserUpdate
40
41      ' Add Delete command parameters
42      prmSQLDelete = dadUserMan.DeleteCommand.Parameters.Add("@Id", _
43          SqlDbType.Int, Nothing, "Id")
44      prmSQLDelete.Direction = ParameterDirection.Input
45      prmSQLDelete.SourceVersion = DataRowVersion.Original
46
47      ' Add Update command parameters
48      cmmUserUpdate.Parameters.Add("@ADName", SqlDbType.VarChar, 100, _
49          "ADName")
50      cmmUserUpdate.Parameters.Add("@ADSID", SqlDbType.VarChar, 50, _
51          "ADSID")
52      cmmUserUpdate.Parameters.Add("@FirstName", SqlDbType.VarChar, 50, _
53          "FirstName")
54      cmmUserUpdate.Parameters.Add("@LastName", SqlDbType.VarChar, 50, _
55          "LastName")
56      cmmUserUpdate.Parameters.Add("@LoginName", SqlDbType.VarChar, 50, _
57          "LoginName")
58      cmmUserUpdate.Parameters.Add("@Password", SqlDbType.VarChar, 50, _
59          "Password")
60
61      prmSQLUpdate = dadUserMan.UpdateCommand.Parameters.Add("@Id", _
62          SqlDbType.Int, Nothing, "Id")
63      prmSQLUpdate.Direction = ParameterDirection.Input
64      prmSQLUpdate.SourceVersion = DataRowVersion.Original
65
```

```
66    ' Add insert command parameters
67    cmmUserInsert.Parameters.Add("@ADName", SqlDbType.VarChar, 100, _
68       "ADName")
69    cmmUserInsert.Parameters.Add("@ADSID", SqlDbType.VarChar, 50, _
70       "ADSID")
71    cmmUserInsert.Parameters.Add("@FirstName", SqlDbType.VarChar, 50, _
72       "FirstName")
73    cmmUserInsert.Parameters.Add("@LastName", SqlDbType.VarChar, 50, _
74       "LastName")
75    cmmUserInsert.Parameters.Add("@LoginName", SqlDbType.VarChar, 50, _
76       "LoginName")
77    cmmUserInsert.Parameters.Add("@Password", SqlDbType.VarChar, 50, _
78       "Password")
79
80    ' Instantiate dataset
81    dstUserMan = New DataSet()
82    ' Populate the data set
83    dadUserMan.Fill(dstUserMan, "tblUser")
84
85    ' Add new row
86    drwUser = dstUserMan.Tables("tblUser").NewRow()
87    drwUser("FirstName") = "New User"
88    drwUser("LastName") = "New User LastName"
89    drwUser("LoginName") = "NewUser"
90    drwUser("Password") = "password"
91    dstUserMan.Tables("tblUser").Rows.Add(drwUser)
92
93    ' Update an existing row (with index 3)
94    dstUserMan.Tables("tblUser").Rows(3)("FirstName") = "FirstName"
95    dstUserMan.Tables("tblUser").Rows(3)("LastName") = "LastName"
96    dstUserMan.Tables("tblUser").Rows(3)("LoginName") = "User3"
97
98    ' Delete row with index 4
99    dstUserMan.Tables("tblUser").Rows(4).Delete()
100
101   ' Check if any data has changed in the data set
102   If dstUserMan.HasChanges() Then
103      ' Save all changed rows in a new data set
104      dstChanges = dstUserMan.GetChanges()
105      ' Check if the changed rows contains any errors
106      If dstChanges.HasErrors() Then
107         ' Reject the changes
108         dstUserMan.RejectChanges()
```

```
109      Else
110         ' Update the data source
111         dadUserMan.Update(dstChanges, "tblUser")
112      End If
113   End If
114 End Sub
```

In Listing 9-10, I use the SQL Server .NET Data Provider that uses named parameters, but please see Chapter 8 for how to work positional parameters using the ODBC .NET Data Provider or the OLE DB .NET Data Provider, or the example code, available on the Apress Web site, for examples hereof. In the preceding example, the **Update** method is responsible for ensuring that the data source is "informed" of the changes that have occurred in the disconnected **DataSet**. This is achieved by the insert, delete, and update commands that are defined in the code. It is important to note that any concurrency issues must be resolved in these commands. Concurrency is covered in Appendix A, and I suggest you read this appendix if you work in an environment with a high contention for your data.

Summary

This chapter introduced you to the **DataSet** class, including the properties, methods, and events hereof.

The following ground was covered:

- Populating a **DataSet**

- Copying and cloning a **DataSet**

- Clearing a **DataSet**

- Merging data in a **DataSet** with data from other data objects

- Accepting or rejecting changes to a **DataSet**

- Detecting and extracting changes to a **DataSet**

- Propagating changes in a **DataSet** back to the data source

The following chapter introduces you to the **DataTable** and **DataView** classes, and how you can use these classes together with the **DataSet** class.

CHAPTER 10

The DataTable and DataView Classes

IN THIS CHAPTER, you'll be introduced to the **DataTable** and **DataView** classes. The **DataTable** is the primary building block of the ADO.NET disconnected layer, and the **DataView** class is a helper class to the **DataTable** class.

Using the DataTable Class

The **DataTable** class is used for manipulating the contents of a table contained in the **Tables** collection of the **DataSet** class, or as a stand-alone table object. The **DataTable** class is part of the **System.Data** namespace, and it's really an in-memory cache of the data from exactly one table. One last thing to notice about the **DataTable** class is that, like the **DataSet** class, it's *not* subclassed—in other words, this class will work with whatever provider you are dealing with.

NOTE　There is no OdbcDataTable, OleDbDataTable, or SqlDataTable class.

DataTable Properties

The **DataTable** class has the properties shown in alphabetical order in Table D-8 in Appendix D. Please note that only the public, noninherited properties are shown.

DataTable Methods

Table D-9 in Appendix D lists the noninherited and public methods of the **DataTable** class in alphabetical order.

DataTable Events

Table D-10 in Appendix D lists the noninherited and public events of the **DataTable** class in alphabetical order. These events make it possible to programmatically intercept and react to changes to the values in your **DataTable** objects, in a number of ways. Please see the sections listed in the Example column for example code and more information about a specific event.

Declaring and Instantiating a DataTable

There are various ways to instantiate a **DataTable** object. You can use the overloaded class constructors or you can reference a specific table in the **Tables** collection of a **DataSet**. Here is how you instantiate a **DataTable** when you declare it:

```
Dim dtbNoArgumentsWithInitialize As New DataTable()
Dim dtbTableNameArgumentWithInitialize As New DataTable("TableName")
```

You can also declare it and then instantiate it when you need to, as follows:

```
Dim dtbNoArgumentsWithoutInitialize As DataTable
Dim dtbTableNameArgumentWithoutInitialize As DataTable

dtbNoArgumentsWithoutInitialize = New DataTable()
dtbTableNameArgumentWithoutInitialize = New DataTable("TableName")
```

I have used two different constructors, one with no arguments and one that takes the table name as the only argument. If you don't give your **DataTable** a name, it will be given the name *Table1* if you add it to a **DataSet**, because a **DataTable** must have a unique name[1] in the **DataTableCollection** of the **DataSet**.

Your other option is to first declare the **DataTable** object, and then have it reference a table in the **Tables** collection of a populated **DataSet**, like this:

```
Dim dtbUser As DataTable

dtbUser = dstUser.Tables("tblUser")
```

---

1. Subsequent tables without a name that are added to the table collection are given the name *Table2*, *Table3*, and so forth.

Building Your Own DataTable

Sometimes you need storage for temporary data that has a table-like structure, meaning several groups of data sequences with the same structure. Because of the table-like structure, a **DataTable** is an obvious choice for storage, although not your only one. Listing 10-1 demonstrates how to create a data structure from scratch, like the one in the tblUser table in the UserMan database.

*Listing 10-1. Building Your Own **DataTable***

```
1 Public Sub BuildDataTable()
2     Dim dtbUser As DataTable
3     Dim dclUser As DataColumn
4     Dim arrdclPrimaryKey(0) As DataColumn
5
6     ' Instantiate DataTable
7     dtbUser = New DataTable("tblUser")
8
9     ' Create table structure
10    ' Id column
11    dclUser = New DataColumn()
12    dclUser.ColumnName = "Id"
13    dclUser.DataType = Type.GetType("System.Int32")
14    dclUser.AutoIncrement = True
15    dclUser.AutoIncrementSeed = 1
16    dclUser.AutoIncrementStep = 1
17    dclUser.AllowDBNull = False
18    ' Add column to DataTable structure
19    dtbUser.Columns.Add(dclUser)
20    ' Add column to Primary key array
21    arrdclPrimaryKey(0) = dclUser
22    ' Set primary key
23    dtbUser.PrimaryKey = arrdclPrimaryKey
24
25    ' ADName column
26    dclUser = New DataColumn()
27    dclUser.ColumnName = "ADName"
28    dclUser.DataType = Type.GetType("System.String")
29    ' Add column to DataTable structure
30    dtbUser.Columns.Add(dclUser)
31
```

```
32    ' ADSID column
33    dclUser = New DataColumn()
34    dclUser.ColumnName = "ADSID"
35    dclUser.DataType = Type.GetType("System.String")
36    ' Add column to DataTable structure
37    dtbUser.Columns.Add(dclUser)
38
39    ' FirstName column
40    dclUser = New DataColumn()
41    dclUser.ColumnName = "FirstName"
42    dclUser.DataType = Type.GetType("System.String")
43    ' Add column to DataTable structure
44    dtbUser.Columns.Add(dclUser)
45
46    ' LastName column
47    dclUser = New DataColumn()
48    dclUser.ColumnName = "LastName"
49    dclUser.DataType = Type.GetType("System.String")
50    ' Add column to DataTable structure
51    dtbUser.Columns.Add(dclUser)
52
53    ' LoginName column
54    dclUser = New DataColumn()
55    dclUser.ColumnName = "LoginName"
56    dclUser.DataType = Type.GetType("System.String")
57    dclUser.AllowDBNull = False
58    dclUser.Unique = True
59    ' Add column to DataTable structure
60    dtbUser.Columns.Add(dclUser)
61
62    ' Password column
63    dclUser = New DataColumn()
64    dclUser.ColumnName = "Password"
65    dclUser.DataType = Type.GetType("System.String")
66    dclUser.AllowDBNull = False
67    ' Add column to DataTable structure
68    dtbUser.Columns.Add(dclUser)
69 End Sub
```

The example code in Listing 10-1 uses the **DataColumn** class, which is covered in Chapter 11, as well as the **DataTable** class. I've declared and instantiated the **DataTable** (see the "Declaring and Instantiating a DataTable" section earlier in this chapter), but you obviously need a little more to have a complete **DataTable**, meaning a **DataTable** with the same schema as the table in your data source you're trying to build a copy of.

Please see the following sections for a more detailed description of the example code in Listing 10-1, and how you can build a **DataTable** object in general.

Matching Schemas

If you want to build a **DataTable** that is an exact copy of an existing table in your data source, you can use the **WriteXmlSchema** method of the **DataSet** to compare the existing table with the **DataTable** you've built. To do so, retrieve the schema of the existing table using the **FillSchema** method of the DataAdapter, and save the schema with the **WriteXmlSchema**. Then build your **DataTable**, add it to a **DataSet**, and save the schema with the **WriteXmlSchema** method. I know it's easier just to copy the schema from an existing table, but there are times when this isn't possible; in such instances, this is one way of making sure that you have an actual copy of an existing table. This is obviously something you'd use at development time, and not at runtime. However, in general, writing the schema of your table(s) as an XML file really is a good idea, because you can quickly spot if anything is wrong about the schema. It's also useful content for the project documentation.

Adding Columns to a DataTable

When you build the structure of a **DataTable** yourself, or when you want to add extra columns to an existing **DataTable** schema, you first need to declare and instantiate the columns, which is done using the **New** constructor, as shown on Lines 4 and 12 in Listing 10-1.

Then you need to set the various properties of the **DataColumn** before the column is added to the **DataTable**'s **DataColumnCollection**. General **DataColumn** properties are covered in Chapter 11, but please see the "Setting DataTable Keys and Constraints" section next for more information on how to set the key and constraint properties. At a minimum, you need to set the name and the data type of the **DataColumn**.

Anyway, when you've created and initialized the **DataColumn** object, you need to add it to the **DataTable**'s column collection, which is done through the **Columns** property, as shown here:

```
dtbUser.Columns.Add(dclUser)
```

In Listing 10-1, note how I've added the columns in the exact same order as they appear in the tblUser table in the UserMan database. Although this isn't necessary, because you can refer to the various columns by name, it's still important, as some programmers refer to the columns by their ordinal number.

You can add columns to a **DataTable** that already holds one or more rows of data, even if the column you add doesn't allow null values. This means that the column will be added to the **DataTable** schema, but null values will be inserted in the column in all existing rows. No exception is thrown at this point; but if you later try to populate the **DataTable** again, a **ConstraintException** exception is thrown, because the new column doesn't allow null values, and this is checked when the **Fill** method finishes. If you append the following code to Listing 10-1, you'll see the error message for a **ConstraintException** exception displayed:

```
70    Dim cnnUserMan As SqlConnection
71    Dim dadUser As SqlDataAdapter
72
73    ' Instantiate and open the connection
74    cnnUserMan = New SqlConnection(PR_STR_CONNECTION_STRING)
75    cnnUserMan.Open()
76    ' Instantiate and initialize the data adapter
77    dadUser = New SqlDataAdapter("SELECT * FROM tblUser", cnnUserMan)
78    ' Fill the DataTable
79    dadUser.Fill(dtbUser)
80
81    ' New column
82    dclUser = New DataColumn()
83    dclUser.ColumnName = "NewColumn"
84    dclUser.DataType = Type.GetType("System.Int32")
85    dclUser.AllowDBNull = False
86    ' Add column to DataTable structure
87    dtbUser.Columns.Add(dclUser)
88
89    Try
90        ' Fill the DataTable
91        dadUser.Fill(dtbUser)
92    Catch objE As ConstraintException
93        MsgBox(objE.Message)
94    End Try
```

The lesson here is that you should be careful when adding columns to a **DataTable** with existing data.

Removing Columns from a DataTable

When you've built your own **DataTable** or created it using the **FillSchema** or **Fill** methods of the DataAdapter, it's sometimes necessary to remove a column. If the table contains a column with, say, a 50KB string in each row, and the column is not part of the proposed operation, then it's a good idea to remove the column from the **DataTable** for performance reasons. Anyway, removing a **DataColumn** object from a **DataTable**'s column collection is done through the **Columns** property, using the **Remove** or **RemoveAt** method of the **DataColumnCollection**. The **Remove** method takes a **DataColumn** object as its only argument, so if you want to remove the ADName column, it can be done like this:

```
Dim dclUser As DataColumn = dtbUser.Columns("ADName")
dtbUser.Columns.Remove(dclUser)
```

The **RemoveAt** method takes an **Integer** value for the column ordinal as its only argument, like this:

```
dtbUser.Columns.RemoveAt(1)
```

This will also remove the ADName column from the **DataTable** schema.

NOTE   The one thing to keep in mind is that you can't remove primary columns from a **DataTable**. Primary keys are discussed in the "Primary Keys" section later in this chapter.

Setting DataTable Keys and Constraints

Most tables need one or more keys and some constraints to work the way you want them to. You can find more information about keys and constraints in Chapter 2, but here's a short description:

- Constraints are generally used to make sure you only add the right data to a column and/or row in your table. Some columns are unique, meaning that the values in those columns must be unique throughout all the rows in the table. That's a unique constraint.

- Primary keys are used to uniquely identify a row in the table. This means that a primary key must be unique, and in most cases, an index is built using the primary key, making it easier to look up a specific row.

- Foreign keys are used as part of a relationship between a parent table and a child table. Data relations are covered in Chapter 12, but for now just understand that you need a primary key in the parent table and a foreign key in the child table to establish a relationship between two tables.

Primary Keys

In Listing 10-1, you saw how I added a primary key to the **DataTable**. The primary key is set using an array (arrdclPrimaryKey) of **DataColumn** objects, and in the case of Listing 10-1, it's just the Id column that makes up the primary key. arrdclPrimaryKey is then assigned to the **PrimaryKey** property. Therefore, the lesson here is that you need to create an array of **DataRow** objects, instantiate and initialize the individual **DataRow** objects that make up the primary key, and then add them to the DataRow array, like this:

```
Dim arrdclPrimaryKey(0) As DataColumn
dclUser = New DataColumn()
dclUser.ColumnName = "Id"
dclUser.DataType = Type.GetType("System.Int32")
' Add column to DataTable structure
dtbUser.Columns.Add(dclUser)
' Add column to Primary key array
arrdclPrimaryKey(0) = dclUser
' Set primary key
dtbUser.PrimaryKey = arrdclPrimaryKey
```

Now, if you look carefully, you'll see that before adding the Id column to the primary key array, I add it to the columns collection of the **DataTable**. This is necessary because you can't use as primary keys columns that don't belong to the same table.

Foreign Keys

In a data source, a foreign key is generally built using an index, and by creating a relationship with a primary key in the parent table. However, since you don't build an index in a **DataTable**, you only need to create the relationship. Although this is covered in detail in Chapter 12, I will give you a quick rundown here. The **ConstraintCollection** collection class of a **DataTable**, which is accessed through the **Constraints** property, contains both unique constraints in the form of **UniqueConstraint** objects and foreign key constraints in the form of **ForeignKeyConstraint** objects.

The **UniqueConstraint** objects are easy to deal with because you simply set the **Unique** property of a **DataColumn** object to **True**, and it's automatically added to the **ConstraintCollection**. The **ForeignKeyConstraint** objects are also automatically added to the **ConstraintCollection**, but this happens when you add a **DataRelation** object to the **DataRelationCollection** of a **DataSet**. As stated earlier, this is covered in Chapter 12, but if you look at what I just said, foreign keys can only be created as part of a relationship between two **DataTable**s that are part of a **DataSet**. It makes sense really, but you do need to be aware of this, because if you design your application with one **DataSet** holding just one **DataTable**, you'll have problems with your relationships, and you'll need to handle this yourself.

Both **UniqueConstraint** objects and **ForeignKeyConstraint** objects can be added manually to the **ConstraintCollection** by calling the **Add** method, as well as automatically, as described previously.

Setting Culture Information

Culture information is information about the calendar and the language used in a particular country or region. It also contains information about how numbers and dates should be formatted, and how strings should be sorted. It's only the last thing mentioned that is of real interest when dealing with **DataSet** and **DataTable** objects. The reason why it's important to set the right culture for a **DataSet** and/or **DataTable** is that it's used when sorting, filtering, and comparing the data in your **DataTable**s.

The culture information is set using the **Locale** property of the **DataSet** and **DataTable** classes, and if you don't explicitly specify one, the locale or culture for the current system is used. This will probably suffice in most cases, but if you're working with international character sets on a multilingual Web site, you'll have to set this property explicitly to the right culture.

NOTE A **DataTable** automatically inherits the setting of the **Locale** property from the **DataSet**, if it belongs to one. However, you can override the setting in a **DataTable**, which also indicates that you can have different cultures in the various **DataTable**s in a **DataSet**.

Say I need to store Danish text in one of my **DataTable**s, and I want to be able to search and sort this information. Now, if I don't set the culture to Danish, I can still search and sort the information, but I'll get a different result than expected.

Table 10-1 shows the current content of the rows in my **DataTable**, which has the same schema as the tblUser table in the UserMan database.

Table 10-1. Content of DataTable with tblUser Schema

Id	ADName	ADSID	FirstName	LastName	LoginName	Password
1	-	-	John	Doe	UserMan	userman
2	-	-	-	-	User1	password
3	-	-	-	-	User2	password
4	-	-	-	-	User3	password
5	-	-	-	-	User99	password
6	-	-	Øjvind	Ærebar	Åndelig	adgangskode
7	-	-	Åge	Ødipus	Ængstelig	adgangskode
8	-	-	Ærmer	Ågdolf	Ømhed	adgangskode

As you can see from Table 10-1, I've just added three extra rows (Ids 6, 7, and 8) to the default[2] content of the tblUser table. However, as you can see, I've used some of the special Danish characters in the FirstName, LastName, and LoginName columns. These three special characters are

æ or Æ, ø or Ø, and å or Å

The order shown is the order in which they appear in the Danish alphabet, after the standard English characters. Therefore, if you apply a sort order to a **DataView** that is based on the data in a **DataTable** that holds the rows shown in Table 10-1, you'll see different results, depending on the culture your **DataTable** is using. Listing 10-2 shows you how you can test this.

Listing 10-2. Test Culture Settings

```
1 Public Sub TestCultureSettings()
2    Dim cnnUserMan As SqlConnection
3    Dim dadUser As SqlDataAdapter
4    Dim dtbUser As DataTable
5    Dim intCounter As Integer
6
```

---

2. As the database is installed with one of the scripts from the example code

```
7    ' Instantiate and open the connection
8    cnnUserMan = New SqlConnection(PR_STR_CONNECTION_STRING)
9
10   cnnUserMan.Open()
11   ' Instantiate the data adapter
12   dadUser = New SqlDataAdapter("SELECT * FROM tblUser", cnnUserMan)
13   ' Set the culture of the current thread as this will be used when
14   ' you instantiate the DataTable
15   Thread.CurrentThread.CurrentCulture = New CultureInfo("en-US")
16   ' Instantiate DataTable
17   dtbUser = New DataTable("tblUser")
18   ' Set culture to US
19   dtbUser.Locale = New CultureInfo("en-US")
20   ' Fill the DataTable
21   dadUser.Fill(dtbUser)
22   ' Apply sorting to the default view
23   dtbUser.DefaultView.Sort = "LastName DESC"
24
25   ' Loop through all the rows in the default view
26   For intCounter = 0 To dtbUser.DefaultView.Count - 1
27       ' Display the Id of the current row in the default view
28       MsgBox(dtbUser.DefaultView(intCounter).Row("Id").ToString(), _
29           MsgBoxStyle.Information, dtbUser.Locale.DisplayName)
30   Next
31   ' Set culture to Danish
32   dtbUser.Locale = New CultureInfo("da-DK")
33
34   ' Loop through all the rows in the default view
35   For intCounter = 0 To dtbUser.DefaultView.Count - 1
36       ' Display the Id of the current row in the default view
37       MsgBox(dtbUser.DefaultView(intCounter).Row("Id").ToString(), _
38           MsgBoxStyle.Information, dtbUser.Locale.DisplayName)
39   Next
40 End Sub
```

In Listing 10-2, I instantiate and open a Connection object, instantiate a DataAdapter object, and then I "cheat" by setting the culture of the current thread to US English. I have no idea what kind of regional settings you're using on your machine, so I need to do this to make sure the **DataTable** is instantiated using a US English culture for the purpose of running the example code. I'm not totally sure as to why it isn't enough to set the **Locale** property of the DataTable object, as I do on Line 19, but it doesn't work without it.

Anyway, when you run the example code, the first group of message boxes displayed will show the value of Id column in this order:

7, 1, 8, 6, 2, 3, 4, 5

This is obviously wrong, because if I sort the rows in the **DefaultView** by LastName in descending order, as done on Line 23, then Rows 6, 7, and 8, which all have one of those extended characters as the first character of the first name, should definitely come before any of the other rows. This is because they're either null (Rows 2 through 5), or start with a standard English character (Row 1).

The second group of message boxes displayed when you run the example code will show the value of Id column in this order:

8, 7, 6, 1, 2, 3, 4, 5

This is the correct if you're using the Danish sort order, which makes sense since it's Danish text. The same kind of problems can occur when you search and filter the rows in your **DataTable** or **DataView**, so be sure you know what culture or locale you should be working with, which depends on the text stored in your data source.

Locales and cultures are really outside the scope of this book, so this is the only detailed information you'll find here; but if you need more information, I can recommend this book:

Internationalization and Localization Using Microsoft .NET, by Nick Symmonds. Apress, January 2002. ISBN: 1-59059-002-3.

Using Case-Sensitive Data

By default, most data sources and ADO.NET implement case-insensitive data structures, meaning that sorting and searching text columns is done without comparing the case of the letters. This means that the lowercase letter *a* is the same as the uppercase letter *A*, as far as the data source and ADO.NET is concerned. Searching is generally faster this way, and personally I've only had to use case-sensitive searches in a very small number of cases. However, if that's what you need, you can switch case sensitivity on in your **DataTable** by setting the **CaseSensitive** property to **True**. The default is **False**, if your **DataTable** isn't part of a **DataSet**. If your **DataTable** is part of a **DataSet**, it's initially set to the value of the same property of the **DataSet**. You set the property like this:

```
dtbUser.CaseSensitive = True
```

Populating a DataTable

Populating a **DataTable** can be done in various ways. You can manually add rows to the **DataTable** by creating a **DataRow** object, set the column values, and then add it to the **DataTable** using the **Add** method of the **Rows** property. Listing 10-1 contains an example of how to create your own **DataTable**.

Otherwise, you can use the **Fill** method of the DataAdapter class for this purpose, as demonstrated in Listing 10-3.

*Listing 10-3. Populating a **DataTable***

```
1 Public Sub PopulateDataTable()
2    Dim cnnUserMan As SqlConnection
3    Dim dadUser As SqlDataAdapter
4    Dim dtbUser As DataTable
5
6    ' Instantiate and open the connection
7    cnnUserMan = New SqlConnection(PR_STR_CONNECTION_STRING)
8    cnnUserMan.Open()
9    ' Instantiate and initialize the data adapter
10   dadUser = New SqlDataAdapter("SELECT * FROM tblUser", cnnUserMan)
11   ' Instantiate DataTable
12   dtbUser = New DataTable("tblUser")
13   ' Fill the DataTable
14   dadUser.Fill(dtbUser)
15 End Sub
```

As you can see from Listing 10-3, I'm using the **Fill** method of the DataAdapter to populate a **DataTable**. It's not that different from the way you populate a **DataSet**, so have a look at Chapter 9, where you can see detailed coverage of the **Fill** method, and Table D-6 in Appendix D.

 NOTE   The **Fill** method of the **DataAdapter** doesn't add any metadata to the **DataTable**, except the column name. This means that if you have a new **DataTable** without a schema, and you depend on this schema for later operations on the **DataTable**, you should call the **FillSchema** method of the DataAdapter before you call the **Fill** method.

Manually Adding Rows to a DataTable

The **DataTable** built in Listing 10-1, or the one created automatically in Listing 10-3, can be used for storage by using the **Add** method of the **Rows** collection of the **DataTable**. The **Add** method is overloaded, taking a **DataRow** object as the only argument, and the other taking an array of **Object** objects. You use them like this:

```
1 ' Declare data row
2 Dim drwUser As DataRow
3 ' Instantiate data row with correct schema
4 drwUser = dtbUser.NewRow()
5 ' Set column values
6 drwUser("LoginName") = "NewLogin"
7 drwUser("Password") = "password"
8 ' Add row to DataTable
9 dtbUser.Rows.Add(drwUser)
10
11 ' Add row to DataTable using Object array
12 dtbUser.Rows.Add(New Object(6) {Nothing, Nothing, Nothing, _
13    Nothing, Nothing, "NewLogin", "password"})
```

Both the calls to the **Add** method (Lines 9, and 12 and 13) add the same row to the **DataTable**. The reason why I have to add a value to the Password column is that the default value, which is *password*, is not retrieved from the data source using the **Fill** or **FillSchema** method of the DataAdapter. There are three columns in the schema for the tblUser table in the UserMan database that don't allow null values—namely, the Id, LoginName, and Password columns. Okay, so I pass a value for the LoginName and Password columns, but what about the Id column? Well, the Id column is an **AutoIncrement** column, meaning the value is automatically added. Unlike the default value for the Password column, this information is retrieved when you use the **FillSchema** method.

Clearing Data from a DataTable

When you have added relations, constraints, and so on to a **DataTable**, or what makes up the structure in your **DataTable**, you frequently need a way of clearing all or some of the data from the **DataTable**. There are two ways of doing this: removing one row, or removing all rows in one go. See the following two sections for more information.

Deleting All Rows from a DataTable

Removing all rows from a **DataTable** is quite easy, and it can be accomplished using the **Clear** method, as shown here:

```
dtbUser.Clear()
```

That's all there is to it. Now you have a **DataTable** object with the schema left intact, but no data in it. It's generally quicker to do this than to instantiate a new **DataTable** object and use the **FillSchema** method of the DataAdapter to create the schema of the **DataTable**. This is especially true if your **DataTable** has any relations defined. Please be aware that if the **DataTable** has an enforced relationship with one or more child **DataTable**s, and there is at least one related row in a child table, an exception is thrown, if any child rows are orphaned.[3] An enforced relationship means that constraints, such as a relationship linking a parent and a child table through a primary key in the parent table and a foreign key in the child table, are enforced. This is true when the **EnforceConstraints** property of the **DataSet**, to which the **DataTable** belongs, is set to **True** (default). Chapter 12 discusses data relations; but to be sure that you don't throw an exception when clearing your **DataTable**, set up an exception handler, as demonstrated in Listing 10-4.

*Listing 10-4. Clearing a **DataTable** in a Safe Manner*

```
Try
    ' Clear the data from the DataTable
    dtbUser.Clear()
Catch objDataException As DataException
    ' There was a problem clearing the DataTable,
    ' probably because of a problem with
    ' orphaned rows in a child table
    MsgBox(objDataException.Message)
End Try
```

Obviously, the example code in Listing 10-4 doesn't resolve the problem, but at least you catch the exception, and then it's up to you to add the necessary code, depending on how you've set up your relations. Data relations are covered in detail in Chapter 12.

---

3. An orphaned row is a row in a child table with a foreign key that no longer matches a row in the parent table.

Deleting a Single Row from a DataTable

Once you've added rows to your **DataTable**, whether it was built manually or created automatically by the **Fill** or **FillSchema** method of the DataAdapter, it's sometimes necessary to delete one or more rows, but not all of them, from the **DataRowCollection** of a **DataTable**. This can be done through the **Rows** property, using the **Remove** or **RemoveAt** methods. The **Remove** method takes a **DataRow** object as its only argument, so if you want to remove the first row in the **DataTable**, it can be done like this:

```
Dim drwUser As DataRow = dtbUser.Rows(0)
dtbUser.Rows.Remove(drwUser)
```

The **RemoveAt** method takes an **Integer** value for the row ordinal as its only argument, like this:

```
dtbUser.Rows.RemoveAt(0)
```

This will also remove the first row from the **DataTable**.

 NOTE   If you try to remove rows from a parent **DataTable** that will result in orphaned rows in a related child table, an exception is thrown.

Copying a DataTable

It is sometimes necessary to copy a **DataTable**—for example, if you need to manipulate some data for testing purposes, or work on a copy of a **DataTable** in order to leave the original data intact. Depending on what you actually need to do, there are two ways you can approach this: You can copy just the data structure (similar to working with a **DataSet**), or you can copy the data structure and the data within it. See the example code for both techniques in the next two sections.

Copying the Data Structure of a DataTable

If you need to copy the data structure of a **DataTable**, without copying the data in it, you can use the **Clone** method, like this:

```
Dim dtbClone As DataTable = dtbUser.Clone()
```

Copying the Data and Structure of a DataTable

When you need a complete copy of the data structure and data contained therein from a **DataTable**, you can use the **Copy** method for this purpose, as shown here:

```
Dim dtbCopy As DataTable = dtbUser.Copy()
```

Searching a DataTable

The **DataTable** class doesn't have any direct methods for finding a specific row as such. In classic ADO, you have the **Recordset** class, which supports the concept of a cursor, and therefore has methods for placing the cursor at a specific row. This isn't so with the **DataTable** class in ADO.NET, although you do have the **Select** method. The **Select** method isn't really for searching as such, as the functionality to search is built into the **DataView** class, which is covered in the "Using the DataView Class" section later in this chapter. However, Listing 10-5 shows you how you can search and retrieve rows from a **DataTable** using the **Select** method.

*Listing 10-5. Searching in a **DataTable** Class Using **Select***

```
1  Public Sub SearchDataTableUsingSelect()
2     Dim cnnUserMan As SqlConnection
3     Dim cmmUser As SqlCommand
4     Dim dadUser As SqlDataAdapter
5     Dim dtbUser As DataTable
6     Dim arrdrwSelect() As DataRow
7     Dim drwSelect As DataRow
8
9     ' Instantiate and open the connection
10    cnnUserMan = New SqlConnection(PR_STR_CONNECTION_STRING)
11    cnnUserMan.Open()
12    ' Instantiate the command and DataTable
13    cmmUser = New SqlCommand("SELECT * FROM tblUser", cnnUserMan)
14    dtbUser = New DataTable()
15    ' Instantiate and initialize the data adapter
16    dadUser = New SqlDataAdapter("SELECT * FROM tblUser", cnnUserMan)
17    dadUser.SelectCommand = cmmUser
18    ' Create the DataTable schema
19    dadUser.FillSchema(dtbUser, SchemaType.Source)
20    ' Fill the DataTable
21    dadUser.Fill(dtbUser)
22    ' Search the DataTable
23    arrdrwSelect = dtbUser.Select("FirstName = 'John' AND LastName='Doe'")
```

```
24
25    ' Loop through all the selected rows
26    For Each drwSelect In arrdrwSelect
27      ' Display the Id of the retrieved rows
28      MsgBox(drwSelect("Id").ToString())
29    Next
30 End Sub
```

In Listing 10-5, all rows with a FirstName of *John* and a LastName of *Doe* are returned in the **DataRow** array. You can work on the **DataRow** objects in the arrdrwSelect array, but of course, the **DataRow** objects are now separate objects. However, although they're separate objects, they're still references to the **DataRow** objects in the **DataTable**, so be careful if you try to manipulate the data in the returned rows, because you're also updating the **DataTable** at the same time.

 NOTE When you set up the search criteria, it's generally important to ensure unique return values. One way, and probably the best way, to ensure this is to use the primary key columns as the search criteria.

Anyway, as you can see, the **Select** method is there for you, if you want to work an array of **DataRow** objects extracted from your **DataTable**, based on your search criteria and optionally the state of the row. The rows can also be sorted, if you specify sort order and direction.

Your only other option is to look at the **DefaultView** property, with which you can apply a view to the data in your **DataTable**. This property returns or sets a **DataView** object, which has a **RowFilter** property that works pretty much the same as the **Filter** property of a classic ADO **Recordset** object. See Listing 10-6 for an example that filters all the users in the tblUser table with the LastName of *Doe* and a FirstName of *John*.

Listing 10-6. Searching in a DataTable Class Using DefaultView

```
1 Public Sub SearchDataTableUsingDefaultView()
2    Dim cnnUserMan As SqlConnection
3    Dim cmmUser As SqlCommand
4    Dim dadUser As SqlDataAdapter
5    Dim dtbUser As DataTable
6    Dim intCounter As Integer
7
```

```
8     ' Instantiate and open the connection
9     cnnUserMan = New SqlConnection(PR_STR_CONNECTION_STRING)
10    cnnUserMan.Open()
11    ' Instantiate the command and DataTable
12    cmmUser = New SqlCommand("SELECT * FROM tblUser", cnnUserMan)
13    dtbUser = New DataTable()
14    ' Instantiate and initialize the data adapter
15    dadUser = New SqlDataAdapter("SELECT * FROM tblUser", cnnUserMan)
16    dadUser.SelectCommand = cmmUser
17    ' Fill the DataTable
18    dadUser.Fill(dtbUser)
19    ' Filter the DataTable view
20    dtbUser.DefaultView.RowFilter = _
21       "LastName = 'Doe' AND FirstName='John'"
22
23    ' Loop through all the rows in the DataTable view
24    For intCounter = 0 To dtbUser.DefaultView.Count - 1
25       MsgBox(dtbUser.DefaultView(intCounter).Row("LastName").ToString())
26    Next
27 End Sub
```

In Listing 10-6, I use the **DefaultView** property to specify a row filter that filters all rows except the ones with a LastName of *Doe* and a FirstName of *John*. Please note that the number of visible rows in the **DataTable** itself does *not* change when you filter the **DataTable** view as in the preceding listing. If you were to check the number of rows in the **DataTable** (using dtbUser.Rows.Count()) before and after the filtering, the number would be the same. Although the filter is applied to the **DataTable**, the results or rather filtering is only "visible" in the **DataView**. If you work directly with the **DataTable** after having specified a row filter on the **DefaultView**, you'd see no change at all. This is the whole secret to the **DataTable** class; if you need to work with a subset of the data contained in the **DataTable**, you either use the **Select** method, or you work on a **DataView**, generally through the **DefaultView** property. What I'm implying here is that you can have as many views of the data in your **DataTable** as you want, but I'll leave that for the "Using the DataView Class" section later in this chapter.

Copying Rows in a DataTable

Sometimes you need to copy one or more rows from one table to another, or even duplicate one or more rows in the same table. This is indeed possible and can even be done using different methods of the **DataTable** class. See Listing 10-7 for an example of how to copy rows in a **DataTable**.

*Listing 10-7. Copying Rows in a **DataTable***

```
 1 Public Sub CopyRowsInDataTable()
 2    Dim cnnUserMan As SqlConnection
 3    Dim cmmUser As SqlCommand
 4    Dim dadUser As SqlDataAdapter
 5    Dim dtbUser As DataTable
 6    Dim cmbUser As SqlCommandBuilder
 7    Dim intCounter As Integer
 8
 9    ' Instantiate and open the connection
10    cnnUserMan = New SqlConnection(PR_STR_CONNECTION_STRING)
11    cnnUserMan.Open()
12    ' Instantiate the command and DataTable
13    cmmUser = New SqlCommand("SELECT * FROM tblUser", cnnUserMan)
14    dtbUser = New DataTable()
15    ' Instantiate and initialize the data adapter
16    dadUser = New SqlDataAdapter("SELECT * FROM tblUser", cnnUserMan)
17    dadUser.SelectCommand = cmmUser
18    cmbUser = New SqlCommandBuilder(dadUser)
19    ' Fill the DataTable
20    dadUser.Fill(dtbUser)
21
22    ' Copy a row from the same table using ImportRow method
23    dtbUser.ImportRow(dtbUser.Rows(0))
24    ' Make sure the Update method detects the new row
25    dtbUser.Rows(dtbUser.Rows.Count - 1)("LoginName") = "NewLogin1"
26
27    ' Copy the first row from the same table using the LoadDataRow
28    ' If you change the last argument of this method to true, the
29    ' RowState property will be set to Unchanged
30    dtbUser.LoadDataRow(New Object(6) {Nothing, dtbUser.Rows(0)("ADName"), _
31       dtbUser.Rows(0)("ADSID"), dtbUser.Rows(0)("FirstName"), _
32       dtbUser.Rows(0)("LastName"), "NewLogin2", _
33       dtbUser.Rows(0)("Password")}, False)
34
35    ' Loop through all the rows in the DataTable,
36    ' displaying the Id and RowState value
37    For intCounter = 0 To dtbUser.Rows.Count - 1
38       MessageBox.Show(dtbUser.Rows(intCounter)("Id").ToString() & _
39          " " & dtbUser.Rows(intCounter).RowState.ToString())
40    Next
41
42    ' Update the data source
43    dadUser.Update(dtbUser)
44 End Sub
```

In Listing 10-7, you can see how to copy one or more rows in a **DataTable**. I am using the **ImportRow** method on Line 23 to import a row from the same table, but you can just as well import a row from a different table, as long as the schema is compatible with the **DataTable** in which you're trying to import the row. There is, however, one problem with the **ImportRow** method, or one thing you should be aware of: The **ImportRow** method copies everything as it is, it doesn't change anything. This means that if the row's **RowState** property is set to **Unchanged**, the **Update** method of the DataAdapter class (Line 43) won't detect the new row, even if you just added it. Basically, you'll have to change a value in the row after importing it as is done on Line 25. Now the **RowState** property value changes to **Modified**. The **Update** method on Line 43 will then detect a change, but will it add the new row? No, it will update the original row, because the Id of the new row is still the same and the **RowState** is **Modified**. You can see that from the message boxes, if you run the example code. What I'm trying to say here is that you shouldn't be using the **ImportRow** method to copy a row. It's too much hassle if you're going to propagate the changes back to the data source. The method is just fine for temporary data storage or even for output to a different data source.

You can use the **LoadDataRow** method instead as I have done on Lines 30 through 33, where I simply copy the content of the first row into the new row. I pass **Nothing** in the case of the Id, because this is automatically generated by the data source.

Handling Column Changes

Sometimes it's desirable to be able to control the process of updating the values in the columns and rows of your **DataTable**. Unlike classic ADO, ADO.NET gives you very good control over the process. Basically, two events are tied to the column value change process: **ColumnChanging** and **ColumnChanged**. As you've probably guessed from the event names, you can use the former for controlling the process before the column value is changing, and the latter for controlling the process when the column value has changed. Both events give you access to the following properties: the **DataColumn** in which a value is being or has been changed (**Column** property), the new value for the **DataColumn** (**ProposedValue** property), and the **DataRow** in which the **DataColumn** is located (**Row** property). See Listing 10-8 for an example of how to set up and handle the column changes.

Listing 10-8. Handling Column Changes in a **DataTable**

```
1 Private Shared Sub OnColumnChanging(ByVal sender As Object, _
2    ByVal e As DataColumnChangeEventArgs)
3    ' Display a message showing some of the Column properties
4    MsgBox("Column Properties:" & vbCrLf & vbCrLf & _
5       "ColumnName: " & e.Column.ColumnName & vbCrLf & _
6       "DataType: " & e.Column.DataType.ToString() & vbCrLf & _
7       "CommandType: " & e.Column.Table.TableName & vbCrLf & _
8       "Original Value: " & e.Row(e.Column.ColumnName, _
9       DataRowVersion.Original).ToString() & vbCrLf & _
10      "Proposed Value: " & e.ProposedValue.ToString(), _
11      MsgBoxStyle.Information, "ColumnChanging")
12 End Sub
13
14 Private Shared Sub OnColumnChanged(ByVal sender As Object, _
15    ByVal e As DataColumnChangeEventArgs)
16    ' Display a message showing some of the Column properties
17    MsgBox("Column Properties:" & vbCrLf & vbCrLf & _
18       "ColumnName: " & e.Column.ColumnName & vbCrLf & _
19       "DataType: " & e.Column.DataType.ToString() & vbCrLf & _
20       "CommandType: " & e.Column.Table.TableName & vbCrLf & _
21       "Original Value: " & e.Row(e.Column.ColumnName, _
22       DataRowVersion.Original).ToString() & vbCrLf & _
23       "Proposed Value: " & e.ProposedValue.ToString(), _
24       MsgBoxStyle.Information, "ColumnChanged")
25 End Sub
26
27 Public Shared Sub TriggerColumnChangeEvents()
28    Dim dadUserMan As SqlDataAdapter
29    Dim dtbUser As New DataTable("tblUser")
30    ' Declare and instantiate data adapter
31    dadUserMan = New SqlDataAdapter("SELECT * FROM tblUser", _
32       PR_STR_CONNECTION_STRING)
33    ' Set up event handlers
34    AddHandler dtbUser.ColumnChanging, AddressOf OnColumnChanging
35    AddHandler dtbUser.ColumnChanged, AddressOf OnColumnChanged
36
37    ' Populate the DataTable
38    dadUserMan.Fill(dtbUser)
39    ' Modify first row, this triggers the Column Change events
40    dtbUser.Rows(0)("FirstName") = "Tom"
41 End Sub
```

In Listing 10-8, I have the `TriggerColumnChangeEvents` procedure (Lines 27 through 41), which sets up the event handlers for the **ColumnChanging** and **ColumnChanged** events (Lines 34 and 35). On Line 40, I trigger these events by setting the FirstName column of the first row to a new value, "Tom". This invokes the **OnColumnChanging** and **OnColumnChanged** procedures in that order. These procedures (Lines 1 through 25) display the properties that are accessible from the **DataColumnChangeEventArgs** argument. Basically, you have the opportunity to inspect all the properties of the column, who's value has changed, and even retrospectively change it should you want to do so. For example, you could force a value to be lowercase if the change included uppercase characters. See the "Using the DataColumn Class" section in Chapter 11 for more information on the **DataColumn** class. You can also access the **DataRow** that the column belongs to, through the **Row** property. Thus cross-column validation checks can be performed. Finally, because you have access to all these properties before and after the change, you're in full control of the change process, and you can apply any logic to the change procedures. However, I would like to point out that business logic should generally be placed elsewhere, like in the data source.

Handling Row Changes

As is the case with changes to the value in a particular column, it certainly can be desirable to be able to control the process of updating the rows of your **DataTable**. Two events are tied to the row change process: **RowChanging** and **RowChanged**. As you can gather from the event names, you can use the former for controlling the process before the row is changed and the latter for controlling the process after the row has been changed. Both events give you access to the following properties: the **DataRow** in which the change occurs (**Row** property), and a **DataRowAction** enum member that indicates what action is being processed (**Action** property). See Listing 10-9 for an example of how to set up and handle the row changes.

*Listing 10-9. Handling Row Changes in a **DataTable***

```
1 Private Shared Sub OnRowChanging(ByVal sender As Object, _
2    ByVal e As DataRowChangeEventArgs)
3    ' Display a message showing some of the Row properties
4    MsgBox("Row Properties:" & vbCrLf & vbCrLf & _
5       "RowState: " & e.Row.RowState.ToString() & vbCrLf & _
6       "Table: " & e.Row.Table.TableName & vbCrLf & _
7       "Action: " & e.Action.ToString(), _
8       MsgBoxStyle.Information, "RowChanging")
9 End Sub
10
```

```
11 Private Shared Sub OnRowChanged(ByVal sender As Object, _
12    ByVal e As DataRowChangeEventArgs)
13    ' Display a message showing some of the Row properties
14    MsgBox("Row Properties:" & vbCrLf & vbCrLf & _
15       "RowState: " & e.Row.RowState.ToString() & vbCrLf & _
16       "Table: " & e.Row.Table.TableName & vbCrLf & _
17       "Action: " & e.Action.ToString(), _
18       MsgBoxStyle.Information, "RowChanged")
19 End Sub
20
21 Public Shared Sub TriggerRowChangeEvents()
22    Dim dtbUser As New DataTable("tblUser")
23    ' Declare and instantiate data adapter
24    Dim dadUserMan As New SqlDataAdapter("SELECT * FROM tblUser", _
25       PR_STR_CONNECTION_STRING)
26    ' Set up event handlers
27    AddHandler dtbUser.RowChanging, AddressOf OnRowChanging
28    AddHandler dtbUser.RowChanged, AddressOf OnRowChanged
29
30    ' Populate the DataTable
31    dadUserMan.Fill(dtbUser)
32    ' Modify first row, this triggers the Column Change events
33    dtbUser.Rows(0)("FirstName") = "Tom"
34 End Sub
```

In Listing 10-9, I have the TriggerRowChangeEvents procedure (Lines 21 through 34), which sets up the event handlers for the **RowChanging** and **RowChanged** events (Lines 27 and 28). On Line 33, I trigger these events by setting the FirstName column of the first row to a new value, "Tom". This invokes the **OnRowChanging** and **OnRowChanged** procedures in that order, just like what happens with the column change events in Listing 10-8. These procedures (Lines 1 through 19) display the properties that are accessible from the **DataRowChangeEventArgs** argument. You have the opportunity to inspect all of the properties of the row, which is being changed, and even ignore the change should you want to do so. See the "Using the DataRow Class" section in Chapter 11 for more information on the **DataRow** class. Finally, because you have access to all of the properties before and after the change, you're in full control of the change, and you can apply any logic to the change procedures. However, I would like to point out that business logic generally should be placed elsewhere, like in the data source.

One thing that is different for the row change events compared to the column change events is the number of times they're being called. Try out the example code and notice how the **Action** and **RowState** property changes for every call. It's interesting.

Handling Row Deletions

Like the column changes and row changes, you can also control the process of deleting the rows of your **DataTable**. Two events are tied to the row deletion process: **RowDeleting** and **RowDeleted**. You can use the former for controlling the process before the row is deleted and the latter for controlling the process after the row has been deleted. Both events give you access to the following properties: the **DataRow** in which the change occurs (**Row** property), and a **DataRowAction** enum member that indicates what action is being processed (**Action** property). See Listing 10-10 for an example of how to set up and handle the row changes.

*Listing 10-10. Handling Row Deletions in a **DataTable***

```
1 Private Shared Sub OnRowDeleting(ByVal sender As Object, _
2    ByVal e As DataRowChangeEventArgs)
3    ' Display a message showing some of the Row properties
4    MsgBox("Row Properties:" & vbCrLf & vbCrLf & _
5       "RowState: " & e.Row.RowState.ToString() & vbCrLf & _
6       "Table: " & e.Row.Table.ToString() & vbCrLf & _
7       "Action: " & e.Action.ToString(), _
8       MsgBoxStyle.Information, "RowDeleting")
9 End Sub
10
11 Private Shared Sub OnRowDeleted(ByVal sender As Object, _
12    ByVal e As DataRowChangeEventArgs)
13    ' Display a message showing some of the Row properties
14    MsgBox("Row Properties:" & vbCrLf & vbCrLf & _
15       "RowState: " & e.Row.RowState.ToString() & vbCrLf & _
16       "Table: " & e.Row.Table.ToString() & vbCrLf & _
17       "Action: " & e.Action.ToString(), _
18       MsgBoxStyle.Information, "RowDeleted")
19 End Sub
20
21 Public Shared Sub TriggerRowDeleteEvents()
22    Dim dtbUser As New DataTable("tblUser")
23    ' Declare and instantiate data adapter
24    Dim dadUserMan As New SqlDataAdapter("SELECT * FROM tblUser", _
25       PR_STR_CONNECTION_STRING)
26    ' Set up event handlers
27    AddHandler dtbUser.RowDeleting, AddressOf OnRowDeleting
28    AddHandler dtbUser.RowDeleted, AddressOf OnRowDeleted
29
```

```
30     ' Populate the DataTable
31     dadUserMan.Fill(dtbUser)
32     ' Delete second row, this triggers the row delete events
33     dtbUser.Rows(1).Delete()
34 End Sub
```

In Listing 10-10, I have the `TriggerRowDeleteEvents` procedure (Lines 21 through 33), which sets up the event handlers for the **RowDeleting** and **RowDeleted** events (Lines 27 and 28). On Line 33, I trigger these events by deleting the second row. This invokes the **OnRowDeleting** and **OnRowDeleted** procedures in that order, just as it happens with the column change events in Listing 10-8 and the row change events in Listing 10-9. The event procedures (Lines 1 through 19) display the properties that are accessible from the **DataRowChangeEventArgs** argument. You have the opportunity to inspect all row properties that are being deleted. See the "Using the DataRow Class" section in Chapter 11 for more information on the **DataRow** class. Finally, because you have access to all these properties before and after the change, you're in full control of the change, and you can apply any logic to the change procedures. However, I would like to point out that business logic generally should be placed elsewhere, like in the data source.

Using the DataView Class

The **DataView** class is used for having more than just one view, the default view (**DataTable.DefaultView**), of your **DataTable** objects. The **DataView** class is part of the **System.Data** namespace, and as stated, this class is for creating an alternative view of your **DataTable**. You can use this class for filtering, sorting, alphabetizing, searching, navigating, and even editing the rows in your **DataTable**, and you can create as many **DataView** objects on a **DataTable** as you like. A **DataView** is excellent for creating partial views of a **DataTable**, to deliver the different options selected by the user in the presentation layer. Some users may see all of the columns in a **DataTable**, whereas others are only interested in a few columns, or possibly are not allowed to see some of the columns.

DataView objects are often used as the data source for data grids and other UI elements, as they allow greater flexibility with sorting and filtering of the rows, without requerying the database.

Like the **DataSet** and the **DataTable** class, the **DataView** is not subclassed; or rather, this class will work with whichever provider you are dealing with.

 NOTE   There is no OdbcDataView, OleDbDataView, or SqlDataView class!

DataView Properties

The **DataView** class has the properties shown in Table D-12 in Appendix D, in alphabetical order. Please note that only the public, noninherited properties are shown.

DataView Methods

Table D-13 in Appendix D lists the noninherited and public methods of the **DataView** class in ascending order.

DataView Event

The **DataView** class only has one noninherited event: the **ListChanged** event. This event is triggered when the list that the **DataView** manages has changed. Changes include additions, deletions, and updates to items in the list. The **ListChanged** event gives you access to the following properties: the type of change that has taken place, indicated by a member of the **ListChangedType** enum (**ListChangedType** property), and the old and new list index, indicated by the two integer properties **OldIndex** and **NewIndex**. See Listing 10-11 for an example of how to set up the **DataView** list changes.

*Listing 10-11. Handling **DataView** List Changes*

```
1 Protected Shared Sub OnListChanged(ByVal sender As Object, _
2    ByVal args As System.ComponentModel.ListChangedEventArgs)
3    ' Display a message showing some of the List properties
4    MsgBox("List Properties:" & vbCrLf & vbCrLf & _
5       "ListChangedType: " & args.ListChangedType.ToString() & vbCrLf & _
6       "OldIndex: " & args.OldIndex.ToString() & vbCrLf & _
7       "NewIndex: " & args.NewIndex.ToString(), _
8       MsgBoxStyle.Information, "ListChanged")
9 End Sub
10
11 Public Shared Sub TriggerListChangeEvent()
12    Dim dtbUser As New DataTable("tblUser")
13    ' Declare and instantiate data adapter
14    Dim dadUserMan As New SqlDataAdapter("SELECT * FROM tblUser", _
15       PR_STR_CONNECTION_STRING)
16
```

```
17    ' Populate the DataTable
18    dadUserMan.Fill(dtbUser)
19    ' Declare and instantiate data view
20    Dim dvwUser As New DataView(dtbUser)
21    ' Set up event handler
22    AddHandler dvwUser.ListChanged, New _
23       System.ComponentModel.ListChangedEventHandler(AddressOf OnListChanged)
24    ' Trigger list change event by adding new item/row
25    dvwUser.AddNew()
26 End Sub
```

In Listing 10-11, I have the TriggerListChangeEvent procedure (Lines 11 through 26), which sets up the event handler for the **ListChanged** event (Lines 22 and 23). On Line 25, I trigger the event by adding a new row to the **DataView**. This invokes the OnListChanged procedure (Lines 1 through 9), which displays the properties that are accessible from the **ListChangedEventArgs** argument. You're probably wondering why the underlying **DataTable** is referred to as a list, but my guess is that, besides being a list in an abstract kind of way, the .NET Framework tends to "reuse" a lot of classes and enums. This is also the case here, where the argument **ListChangedEventArgs** comes from the **System.ComponentModel** namespace. If you have a better explanation, do let me know; you can reach me at carstent@dotnetservices.biz.

Declaring and Instantiating a DataView

There are various ways to instantiate a **DataView** object. You can use the overloaded class constructors, or you can reference the **DefaultView** property of the **DataTable** object. Here is how you instantiate a **DataView** when you declare it:

```
Dim dvwNoArgumentsWithInitializer As New DataView()
Dim dvwTableArgumentWithInitializer _
   As New DataView(dstUser.Tables("tblUser"))
```

You can also declare it and then instantiate it when you need to, like this:

```
Dim dvwNoArgumentsWithoutInitializer As DataView
Dim dvwTableArgumentWithoutInitializer As DataView

dvwNoArgumentsWithoutInitializer = New DataView()
dvwTableArgumentWithoutInitializer = _
   New DataView(dstUser.Tables("tblUser"))
```

I've used two different constructors, one with no arguments and one that takes the **DataTable** as the only argument. The other option is to first declare the **DataView** object and then have it reference the **DefaultView** property of the **DataTable** object, as shown here:

```
Dim dvwUser As DataView
dvwUser = dstUser.DefaultView()
```

Searching a DataView

There are several ways in which you can find one or more rows that match a criterion. I've already shown one way in the **DataTable** section, using the **RowFilter** property of the **DataView** class. Please see Listing 10-6 for an example of this. You can also use the **Find** method for finding a specific row or the **FindRows** method for finding one or more rows that match a given criterion. Please see the following sections for more information.

NOTE   When you use the **Find** or **FindRows** method of the **DataView** class, you must keep in mind that they work on the visible rows, and not necessarily all the rows in the **DataView**. By visible rows, I mean the rows that match the criteria set using the **RowFilter** property, if any.

Locating a Single Row

The **Find** method, which is overloaded, takes an object or an array of objects as the only argument. See Listing 10-12 for some example code that finds the user with an Id of 1 in the tblUser table in the UserMan database.

*Listing 10-12. Searching in a **DataView** Class Using **Find***

```
1 Public Sub SearchDataViewUsingFind()
2     Dim dadUser As SqlDataAdapter
3     Dim dtbUser As DataTable
4     Dim dvwUser As DataView
5     Dim intIndex As Integer
6
```

```
 7    ' Instantiate the DataTable
 8    dtbUser = New DataTable()
 9    ' Instantiate and initialize the data adapter
10    dadUser = New SqlDataAdapter("SELECT * FROM tblUser", _
11       PR_STR_CONNECTION_STRING)
12    ' Fill the DataTable
13    dadUser.Fill(dtbUser)
14    ' Create the new data view
15    dvwUser = dtbUser.DefaultView
16    ' Specify a sort order key and direction
17    dvwUser.Sort = "Id ASC"
18    ' Find the user with an id of 1
19    intIndex = dvwUser.Find(CObj(1))
20    MsgBox(dvwUser(intIndex).Row("LastName").ToString())
21 End Sub
```

In Listing 10-12, you can see how the first row in the tblUser table is found through the **Find** method. The **Find** method works by specifying a sort order on Line 17, which is a required step, and then you pass an object or an array of objects as the only argument to the **Find** method. The value(s) must be of the same sub–data type as the sort key column(s) you're searching. In Listing 10-12, this means the Integer data type, because the Id column in the tblUser table is an integer. This also means that you can only use the **Find** method to search on the specified sort key. The return value is the index or ordinal position of the row that was found. **Nothing** is returned if a row matching the criterion wasn't found.

If you want to search for a specific row, based on the values in more than one column, you can do it like this:

```
1 ' Specify a sort order keys and direction
2 dvwUser.Sort = "LastName ASC, FirstName ASC"
3 ' Find the user with LastName of Doe and FirstName of John
4 intIndex = dvwUser.Find(New Object() {CObj("Doe"), CObj("John")})
```

Therefore, the only argument of the **Find** method must correspond directly to the number of columns specified in the **Sort** property.

To sum it up, the **Find** method is for locating a specific row by searching in the specified sort key column(s). If you need to find more than one row, you should use the **FindRows** method. See the next section for more information on this method.

Finding Several Rows

If you need to locate more than one row using a sort order key, you can use the
FindRows method. Listing 10-13 shows you how to do so.

*Listing 10-13. Searching in a **DataView** Class Using **FindRows***

```
1 Public Sub SearchDataViewUsingFindRows()
2    Dim dadUser As SqlDataAdapter
3    Dim dtbUser As DataTable
4    Dim dvwUser As DataView
5    Dim arrdrvRows() As DataRowView
6    Dim drvFound As DataRowView
7
8    ' Instantiate the DataTable
9    dtbUser = New DataTable()
10   ' Instantiate and initialize the data adapter
11   dadUser = New SqlDataAdapter("SELECT * FROM tblUser", _
12     PR_STR_CONNECTION_STRING)
13   ' Fill the DataTable
14   dadUser.Fill(dtbUser)
15   ' Create the new data view
16   dvwUser = dtbUser.DefaultView
17   ' Specify a sort order
18   dvwUser.Sort = "LastName ASC"
19   ' Find the users with no LastName
20   arrdrvRows = dvwUser.FindRows(CObj(DBNull.Value))
21
22   ' Loop through collection
23   For Each drvFound In arrdrvRows
24      ' Display LoginName column value
25      MsgBox(drvFound("LoginName").ToString)
26   Next
27 End Sub
```

In Listing 10-13, I use the **FindRows** method for locating all rows in the
DataView with no LastName, meaning all rows where the LastName column
contains a null value. The return value from the **FindRows** method is an array of
DataRowView objects, and to some extent, this method can be used much the
same way as the **Select** method of the **DataTable** class.

NOTE Instead of specifically setting the **Sort** property of the **DataView** when you use the **Find** or **FindRows** methods, you can also set the **ApplyDefaultSort** property of the **DataView** class. See the next section, "Sorting a DataView," for more information.

Sorting a DataView

When you access the rows in a **DataTable**, they're ordered as they were retrieved from your data source. However, using the **DefaultView** property of the **DataTable**, you can change the way they're sorted. Actually, you don't change the way the **DataTable** is sorted, only the way the rows are accessed using the **DefaultView** property. See Listing 10-14 for example code that sorts the rows by LastName in ascending order.

Listing 10-14. Sorting Rows in a DataView

```
1 Public Sub SortDataView()
2    Dim dadUser As SqlDataAdapter
3    Dim dtbUser As DataTable
4    Dim intCounter As Integer
5
6    ' Instantiate the DataTable
7    dtbUser = New DataTable()
8    ' Instantiate and initialize the data adapter
9    dadUser = New SqlDataAdapter("SELECT * FROM tblUser", _
10      PR_STR_CONNECTION_STRING)
11   ' Fill the DataTable
12   dadUser.Fill(dtbUser)
13   ' Sort the DataTable view after LoginName in ascending order
14   dtbUser.DefaultView.Sort = "LoginName ASC"
15
16   ' Loop through all the rows in the data view,
17   ' displaying the LoginName
18   For intCounter = 0 To dtbUser.DefaultView.Count - 1
19      MsgBox(dtbUser.DefaultView(intCounter)("LoginName").ToString())
20   Next
21 End Sub
```

In Listing 10-14, you can see how you can use the **DefaultView** property of a **DataTable** to sort the rows by LoginName in ascending order. If you want to sort in descending order, you simply change the ASC on Line 14 to DESC.

NOTE The **ApplyDefaultSort** property of the **DataView** class can be used to specify that the default sort order should be applied. The default sort order uses the primary key for the sorting, if one exists. If no primary key columns exist in the **DataView**, or if the **Sort** property is set to any value other than **Nothing** or an empty string, the **ApplyDefaultSort** property is ignored. So, once you set the **Sort** property to a specific sort order, the **ApplyDefaultSort** property is ignored, until you set it to an empty string or **Nothing**.

Manipulating Rows in a DataView

Just as you can manipulate the rows in the **DataTable**, you can also manipulate the rows in an associated **DataView**. It makes sense, really, as you'll often find yourself using a **DataView** to group any number of rows from the **DataTable**, and it certainly makes it easier if you can manipulate the rows in the **DataView** directly, rather than having to access the underlying **DataTable**.

When you manipulate data (meaning add, update, or delete data), constraints from the underlying **DataTable** are upheld. This means that an exception is thrown if you try to add a row with null values in columns that don't allow null values. Listing 10-15 shows an example of how you can manipulate data in **DataView**.

*Listing 10-15. Manipulating Data in a **DataView***

```
1 Public Sub ManipulateRowsInDataView()
2    Dim dadUser As SqlDataAdapter
3    Dim dtbUser As DataTable
4    Dim drvUser As DataRowView
5
6    ' Instantiate the DataTable
7    dtbUser = New DataTable()
8    ' Instantiate and initialize the data adapter
9    dadUser = New SqlDataAdapter("SELECT * FROM tblUser", _
10       PR_STR_CONNECTION_STRING)
11   ' Fill the DataTable
12   dadUser.FillSchema(dtbUser, SchemaType.Source)
13   dadUser.Fill(dtbUser)
```

```
14    ' Make sure we can manipulate the rows in the default view
15    dtbUser.DefaultView.AllowDelete = True
16    dtbUser.DefaultView.AllowEdit = True
17    dtbUser.DefaultView.AllowNew = True
18    ' Apply row filter
19    dtbUser.DefaultView.RowFilter = "LastName IS NULL"
20
21    Try
22        ' Update existing row
23        dtbUser.DefaultView(0).BeginEdit()
24        dtbUser.DefaultView(0)("LastName") = "NewLastName"
25        dtbUser.DefaultView(0).EndEdit()
26        ' Delete existing row
27        dtbUser.DefaultView.Delete(2)
28        ' Insert new row
29        drvUser = dtbUser.DefaultView.AddNew()
30        ' Begin edit of the new row
31        drvUser.BeginEdit()
32        ' Add values to the new row
33        drvUser("LoginName") = "NewLogin"
34        drvUser("Password") = "password"
35        drvUser("LastName") = "NewLastName2"
36        ' End row edit and update row in data view
37        drvUser.EndEdit()
38    Catch objE As DataException
39        MsgBox(objE.Message)
40    End Try
41 End Sub
```

In Listing 10-15, I add the tblUser table schema to a new **DataTable**, and populate it with all the current rows from the tblUser table. I then set up the default view of the dtbUser **DataTable** on Lines 15 through 17, meaning I explicitly allow deleting, editing, and inserting of rows in the **DataView**. On Line 19, a filter is applied to the **DataView**, resulting in only rows in the **DataTable** that have no LastName being visible in the **DataView**.

In the **Try** block, I update the first row in the **DataView** on Line 24 by setting the LastName column to "NewLastName", but first I call the **BeginEdit** method on the **DataRowView** object returned by dtbUser.DefaultView(0). This means that I begin editing the very first row in the **DataView**. After I've updated the row, I call **EndEdit** to end the edit and update the **DataView**. If I wanted to undo the changes, I'd have to call the **CancelEdit** method to end the edit and cancel the changes made.

NOTE   When you want to update rows in a **DataView**, whether they've just been added or already contain data, you need to call the **BeginEdit** method before you start editing the row, and call the **EndEdit** method after you've applied your changes. If you don't, the **DataView** isn't updated, even if no exception is thrown when you try.

On Line 27, I delete the third row in the **DataView**, and this is all it takes to delete a row. You don't have to begin an edit operation or anything like that, you just have to make sure the pass row index exists, or an exception is thrown.

I add a new row to the **DataView** on Line 29, begin editing the new row, which at this stage contains default values according to the schema of the underlying **DataTable**, change the values of the desired columns, and end the edit on Line 37.

The reason why I've put all the row manipulation statements in the **Try** block is that if any of the corresponding manipulation properties are set to **False**, an exception is thrown. Therefore, if you were to comment out Line 15, Line 27 would throw an exception, because deletions won't be allowed. You can test this yourself by commenting out Line 16 or 17, or by setting the **AllowDelete** property to **False** on Line 15.

Question on Visible Rows in DefaultView

How many visible rows are there in the **DefaultView** of the dtbUser **DataTable**, after you've run the example code in Listing 10-15? Assume that you have the initial data in your tblUser database, which means that four rows are visible after the filtering on Line 19. Take your time and think about it before you run the code. This is a bit tricky at first but obvious once you know the result (think **RowFilter** . . .). You can append the following code to the procedure to test it:

```
Dim intCounter As Integer
' Loop through all the rows in the data view,
' displaying the LoginName
For intCounter = 0 To dtbUser.DefaultView.Count - 1
    MsgBox(dtbUser.DefaultView(intCounter)("LoginName").ToString())
Next
```

Summary

This chapter introduced you to the **DataTable** class and its related class, the **DataView** class. The **DataTable** class is the disconnected data-aware class of ADO.NET that resembles a table in your data source. The **DataView** class works with the data in a **DataTable** class, and you can use the **DataView** class to present different views of the data in the **DataTable**, which can be very useful for UI controls that need to sort and filter data on the fly based upon user input, without having to requery the data source.

The following chapter introduces you to the **DataRow** and **DataColumn** classes.

CHAPTER 11

The DataRow and DataColumn Classes

THIS CHAPTER IS a short introduction to the **DataRow** and **DataColumn** classes of the disconnected ADO.NET layer. A number of related topics have already been covered indirectly in the previous two chapters, but this chapter will serve as a general and formal introduction.

The **DataRow** together with the **DataColumn** class are in fact the primary building blocks of the **DataTable** class. This makes sense really, because when you have a table in a database it consists of rows and columns. So why make this object model any different? See the "Using the DataRow Class" and "Using the DataColumn Class" sections later in this chapter for a detailed description of both classes.

The **DataRow** class is the data brick of the **DataTable** class, and the **DataColumn** class is the structure brick of the **DataTable** class. One or more **DataColumn** objects make up the structure of a **DataTable**, and one or more **DataRow** objects make up the data in a **DataTable**.

Using the DataRow Class

The **DataRow** class is used for representing a single row in the **DataTable** class. **DataRow** objects in a **DataTable** are part of the **DataRowCollection** class, which is referenced using the **Rows** property of the **DataTable** class.

DataRow Properties

In Table D-14 in Appendix D, you can see a description of all the noninherited, public properties of the **DataRow** class.

DataRow Methods

Table D-15 in Appendix D, shows you all the noninherited, public methods of the **DataRow** class.

DataRow Events

The **DataRow** class doesn't expose any events.

Declaring and Instantiating a DataRow

There is only one way to instantiate a **DataRow** object, because the **DataRow** class doesn't have a public constructor, which means you rely on the **DataTable** to help you out. The **NewRow** method of the **DataTable** is what you need, like this:

```
Dim drwUser As DataRow

drwUser = dtbUser.NewRow()
```

Manipulating DataRows

When you have a **DataTable** object, you need to fill it with data and that data resides in **DataRow** objects in the **DataRowCollection** of the **DataTable**. You saw in the previous section how a **DataRow** object is declared and instantiated, and in Chapter 10 you saw how to add a **DataRow** to the **DataRowCollection** of the **DataTable** and delete a **DataRow** from that very same collection. In the "Using the DataColumn Class" section later in this chapter, I cover how to manipulate the values of a specific column in a **DataRow**, which is basically all there is to manipulating the data in a **DataRow**. However, there's more to it than that, because a **DataRow** also has various states it can be in (see the "Looking at the State of a DataRow" section later in this chapter), and it can contain more than one version of the data stored (see the "Checking for Versions of a DataRow" section later in this chapter). Depending on what you're trying to do, it's often a requirement that you work with both the state and version of a **DataRow**.

Editing a DataRow

A **DataRow** object can be edited directly, or you can choose to put it in edit mode before you start changing the column values. When you edit the column values directly, meaning you simply assign a new value to one or more columns, the **DataRow** is changed immediately, and so is the row state (see the "Looking at the State of a DataRow" section next). Direct editing is done like this:

```
drwUser("FirstName") = "John"
```

That's all you need to do, assuming the **DataRow** has been instantiated and actually holds a **DataColumn** by the name FirstName that accepts a string value. In many cases, it makes sense to perform direct editing, because it's the easiest to do; but there will be times when you want put the **DataRow** in edit mode first.

 NOTE   Even direct editing of the column values on a **DataRow** uses the edit mode. When you change the value of a column directly, the **BeginEdit** method is implicitly called on the **DataRow**, the original column is saved in the **Original** version, and the new value is saved in the **Proposed** version of the **DataRow**. Then, the **EndEdit** method is called, the new value is copied to the **Current** version, and the **Proposed** version is removed from the **DataRow**. All this happens very quickly, so you don't get to "see" it, but it does happen, which is why you're reading this note. Do keep in mind though that even if there are no proposed values, it's not the same as accepting the values, which happens when you call **AcceptChanges** on the **DataRow**, because you'll have an **Original** and a **Current** version after a direct edit.

One reason for explicitly using edit mode is event triggering, when changing more than just one column value in the **DataRow**. The row and column events are disabled when you're in edit mode, and not triggered until you end the edit mode. You enter edit mode by calling the **BeginEdit** method, and end it by calling the **EndEdit** mode, like this:

```
' Begin edit mode
drwUser.BeginEdit()
' Change the column value
drwUser("FirstName") = "John"
' End the edit mode
drwUser.EndEdit()
```

If you want to discard any changes made in edit mode, when still in edit mode, you can call the **CancelEdit** method, which means that the edit mode is cancelled, and all proposed values are discarded. The **CancelEdit** method is called like this:

```
drwUser.CancelEdit()
```

TIP The fact that you can cancel proposed changes to the column values in a **DataRow**, while still in edit mode, is one very good reason to use it when exposed to user input. If the user wants to cancel the changes made to a single row, say in a grid, you call the **CancelEdit** method. It's obviously possible to do this without using explicit edit mode, but in my experience it's easier to use it.

So, let's sum up what versions of the column values in a **DataRow** exist, and when, because not all values exist at all times. Table 11-1 explains these details.

*Table 11-1. Description and Scope of **DataRow** Versions*

DataRow Version Member	Description	Scope
Current	This is the version of the **DataRow** that contains the current values, meaning the values you get, if you retrieve a value, without specifying a particular version. If no changes have been made since the **DataRow** was populated, or since the **AcceptChanges** method was last called, this version is the same as the **Original** version.	This version always exists.
Default	This version specifies the default column values, if any, as dictated by the **DataTable** schema.	This version always exists.
Original	This version contains the original values, as they were when the **DataRow** was populated or when the **AcceptChanges** method was last called. If no changes have been made since the **DataRow** was populated, or since the **AcceptChanges** method was last called, this version is the same as the **Current** version.	This version always exists.
Proposed	This version holds the proposed values, meaning the values you assign as column values, when you're in edit mode.	This version only exists when the **DataRow** is in edit mode, meaning after the **BeginEdit** method has been called, but before the **CancelEdit** or **EndEdit** method is called.

Using Explicit Edit Mode

You've already seen how to call, cancel, and end edit explicit mode, and you've seen a few reasons as to why you'd want to use it. However, you haven't seen what happens to the various **DataRow** versions at the different stages in explicit edit mode. Let's assume that the **DataRow** is populated like the first row in the tblUser table in the UserMan database, which means that the Password column, which is the only one we're interested in, holds the value *userman*.

Table 11-2 shows you how the values move around the different row versions when you change column values in explicit edit mode.

Table 11-2. Explicit Edit Mode Stages

Stage	Original	Proposed	Current	Default
Before explicit edit mode	userman	-	userman	password
In explicit edit mode, after calling **BeginEdit**	userman	-	userman	password
In explicit edit mode, after changing the value in Password column value to "test"	userman	test	userman	password
After calling **CancelEdit**	userman	-	userman	password
After calling **EndEdit**	userman	-	test	password

The rows in Table 11-2 show you how the column values of different row versions of a **DataRow** changes, when you use explicit edit mode for changing the column values. Figure 11-1 illustrates the explicit edit mode stages.

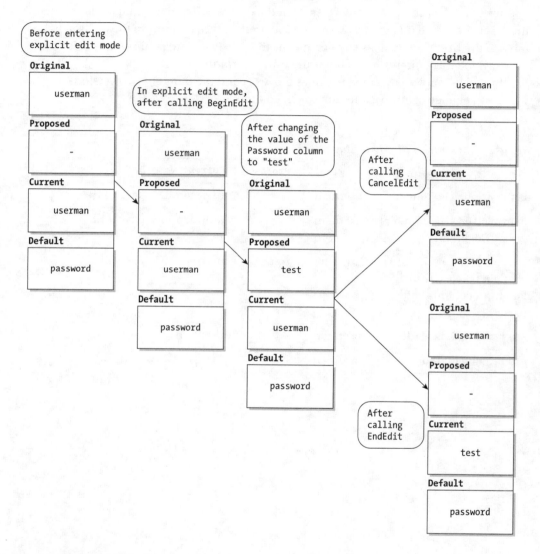

Figure 11-1. Explicit edit mode stages

Accepting DataRow Changes

If you work with a copy of the data in your data source, and you're not going to propagate the changes made back to the data source, you'll want to manually accept the changes made to a **DataRow**. The **AcceptChanges** method is automatically called on the **DataSet** and/or **DataTable** when you call the **Update** method of the DataAdapter class, and then called for each **DataRow** in the **DataTable**. This means that you shouldn't be calling the **AcceptChanges** method yourself, before calling the **Update** method, because the DataAdapter won't be able to detect the changes and will therefore not propagate the changed data to the data source.

 NOTE The **AcceptChanges** method is exposed by the **DataSet**, **DataTable**, and **DataRow** classes, and when you call this method on a parent object, it's automatically called on the child objects. So, if you call it on the **DataSet**, it's automatically called on all **DataTable** objects in the **DataSet**, and then called on all **DataRow** objects within each **DataTable**.

It's the **RowState** property of a **DataRow** that enables the **AcceptChanges** method to detect if any column values in the **DataRow** have changed. However, the **AcceptChanges** method not only reads the **RowState** property, it also changes the row state of changed and inserted rows to **Unchanged**, and removes rows marked as deleted from the row collection of a **DataTable**, if the **DataRow** belongs to one.

Rejecting DataRow Changes

When you've made changes to a **DataRow** object that you want to undo, you must call the **RejectChanges** method, before the **AcceptChanges** method is called. The reason why you must call it before the **AcceptChanges** method is that **AcceptChanges** changes the row state of all the rows to **Unchanged**, and thus the **RejectChanges** method won't be able to detect the changes made. It's the **RowState** property of a **DataRow** that makes the method able to detect if any column values in the **DataRow** have changed. However, the **RejectChanges** method not only reads the **RowState** property, it also changes the row state of changed and deleted rows to **Unchanged**, and removes rows marked as added from the row collection of a **DataTable**, if the **DataRow** belongs to one.

Looking the State of a DataRow

Every **DataRow** object has a state, which can be read through the **RowState** property. This property is read-only, so you can't set it directly, because it's set indirectly when calling methods of the **DataRow** and the **DataRowCollection** of the **DataTable** class, as you'll see later in this section. The **RowState** property returns a member of the **DataRowState** enum (see Table D-3 in Appendix D), and this member tells you the current state your **DataRow** is in. This section describes the general flow of states for some of the more trivial ways of working with the **DataRow**.

The states for a new **DataRow** are as follows:

- *Detached:* The **DataRow** has just been instantiated.

- *Added:* The **DataRow** has been added to a **DataTable**.

- *Unchanged:* The **AcceptChanges** method has been called on the **DataRow**.

After instantiating a **DataRow** using the **NewRow** method of the **DataTable** class, the state will always be **Detached**, even if you change any of the column values. The same is true when the **DataRow** has a state of **Added**; it doesn't matter if you change any of the column values, the state will still be **Added**. Not until the **AcceptChanges** method is called on the **DataRow**, and the state set to **Unchanged**, will changes to the column values be reflected through the row state.

When column values in existing **DataRow** are changed, the following states can result:

- *Unchanged:* The **DataTable**, in which the **DataRow** resides, has just been populated, and no changes have been made to the **DataRow**.

- *Modified:* One or more of the column values in the **DataRow** has been changed.

The **DataRow** returns to the Unchanged state after the **AcceptChanges** or **RejectChanges** method is called on the **DataRow**.

A number of row state combinations can exist, depending on how you perform your data manipulations, but there are few things to bear in mind:

- **DataRow** objects that haven't been added to the **DataRowCollection** of a **DataTable** object always have a row state of **Detached**. This also means that if you have a **DataRow** object that references a row in the **DataRowCollection** of a **DataTable**, and this row is deleted, including the call to the **AcceptChanges** method, the row state will be set to **Detached** because it's no longer part of the collection.

- Calling the **AcceptChanges** or **RejectChanges** method on the **DataRow** will always reset the row state, generally to **Unchanged**, unless the row state is **Detached**.

- **DataRow** objects that have been added to the **DataRowCollection** of a **DataTable** object will have a row state of **Added**, until the **AcceptChanges** method is called.

- You can't change the column values of **DataRow** objects with a row state of **Deleted**; a **DeletedRowInaccessibleException** exception will be thrown if you try.

- If you call the **AcceptChanges** method on a row with a row state of **Deleted**, the row will be removed from the collection;[1] but if you call the **RejectChanges** method, the row state is reset to **Unchanged**. This is also true even if you made changes to the column values of the **DataRow** before you called the **Delete** method.

Listing 11-1 shows you how the **RowState** changes when manipulating the column values of a **DataRow** object.

*Listing 11-1. Manipulating **RowState***

```
1 Public Sub ManipulateRowState()
2    Dim cnnUserMan As SqlConnection
3    Dim dadUser As SqlDataAdapter
4    Dim dtbUser As New DataTable("tblUser")
5    Dim drwNewRow, drwExisting As DataRow
6
7    ' Instantiate the connection
8    cnnUserMan = New SqlConnection(PR_STR_CONNECTION_STRING)
9    ' Instantiate and initialize the data adapter
10   dadUser = New SqlDataAdapter("SELECT * FROM tblUser", cnnUserMan)
11
12   ' Fill the DataTable
13   dadUser.Fill(dtbUser)
14
15   ' Set RowState to Detached
16   drwNewRow = dtbUser.NewRow()
17   MsgBox(drwNewRow.RowState.ToString)
18   ' No changes to the row state when changing column values
19   ' if row state is Detached
20   drwNewRow(3) = "FirstName"
21   MsgBox(drwNewRow.RowState.ToString)
22
23   ' Row state is Unchanged, because no changes since
24   ' DataTable was loaded or populated
25   drwExisting = dtbUser.Rows(1)
26   MsgBox(drwExisting.RowState.ToString)
```

---

1. If the row is referenced through a **DataRow** object as shown in Listing 11-1, and not directly through the **DataRowCollection** of a **DataTable**, the row state will be change to **Detached**.

```
27    ' Set row state to modified
28    drwExisting(3) = "FirstName"
29    MsgBox(drwExisting.RowState.ToString)
30    ' Reset row state
31    drwExisting.AcceptChanges()
32    MsgBox(drwExisting.RowState.ToString)
33    ' Change row state to Deleted
34    drwExisting.Delete()
35    MsgBox(drwExisting.RowState.ToString)
36    ' Reset row state
37    drwExisting.RejectChanges()
38    MsgBox(drwExisting.RowState.ToString)
39    ' Change row state to Deleted
40    drwExisting.Delete()
41    ' Remove row from collection
42    drwExisting.AcceptChanges()
43    MsgBox(drwExisting.RowState.ToString)
44 End Sub
```

In Listing 11-1, you can see how the **RowState** property of a **DataRow** object changes when you perform various actions on the **DataRow** and the **DataTable** in which it resides.

 NOTE   It's rather important that you're aware of the way the **RowState** property "works," because it might give you a few surprises when you start working explicitly with **DataRow** objects. It certainly surprised me a few times. In fact, I think that the **RowState** property is by far the single biggest issue when looking for bugs when your code doesn't perform as expected.

Working with Different Versions of a DataRow

Every **DataRow** object can hold more than one version of the data contained in the columns that make up the **DataRow**. This can be a source of confusion and lead to code that doesn't perform the way it should do. However, if you look at it logically, it's not all that bad, just confusing. Listing 11-2 shows you when the various versions of a **DataRow** can be accessed.

Listing 11-2. Checking Accessible Row Versions

```
1 Public Sub CheckAccessibleRowVersions()
2    Dim cnnUserMan As SqlConnection
3    Dim dadUser As SqlDataAdapter
4    Dim dtbUser As New DataTable("tblUser")
5    Dim drwExisting As DataRow
6
7    ' Instantiate the connection
8    cnnUserMan = New SqlConnection(PR_STR_CONNECTION_STRING)
9    ' Instantiate and initialize the data adapter
10   dadUser = New SqlDataAdapter("SELECT * FROM tblUser", cnnUserMan)
11
12   ' Fill the DataTable
13   dadUser.Fill(dtbUser)
14
15   ' Reference row in table
16   drwExisting = dtbUser.Rows(1)
17   ' Display accesible row versions
18   MsgBox("Current Row version = " & drwExisting.HasVersion( _
19      DataRowVersion.Current).ToString & vbCrLf & _
20      "Default Row version = " & drwExisting.HasVersion( _
21      DataRowVersion.Default).ToString & vbCrLf & _
22      "Original Row version = " & drwExisting.HasVersion( _
23      DataRowVersion.Original).ToString & vbCrLf & _
24      "Proposed Row version = " & drwExisting.HasVersion( _
25      DataRowVersion.Proposed).ToString, _
26      MsgBoxStyle.Information, "Accessible Row Versions - No Edit Mode")
27   ' Enter edit mode
28   drwExisting.BeginEdit()
29   ' Display accesible row versions
30   MsgBox("Current Row version = " & drwExisting.HasVersion( _
31      DataRowVersion.Current).ToString & vbCrLf & _
32      "Default Row version = " & drwExisting.HasVersion( _
33      DataRowVersion.Default).ToString & vbCrLf & _
34      "Original Row version = " & drwExisting.HasVersion( _
35      DataRowVersion.Original).ToString & vbCrLf & _
36      "Proposed Row version = " & drwExisting.HasVersion( _
37      DataRowVersion.Proposed).ToString, _
38      MsgBoxStyle.Information, "Accessible Row Versions - In Edit Mode")
39   ' End edit mode
40   drwExisting.CancelEdit()
41   drwExisting.EndEdit()
```

```
42    ' Display accesible row versions
43    MsgBox("Current Row version = " & drwExisting.HasVersion( _
44       DataRowVersion.Current).ToString & vbCrLf & _
45       "Default Row version = " & drwExisting.HasVersion( _
46       DataRowVersion.Default).ToString & vbCrLf & _
47       "Original Row version = " & drwExisting.HasVersion( _
48       DataRowVersion.Original).ToString & vbCrLf & _
49       "Proposed Row version = " & drwExisting.HasVersion( _
50       DataRowVersion.Proposed).ToString, _
51       MsgBoxStyle.Information, "Accessible Row Versions - After Edit Mode")
52 End Sub
```

In Listing 11-2, you can see when the various row versions are accessible, which is good to know when you write your code. Please note that rows 40 and 41 both end edit mode, and although they're normally used for different purposes, they'll both result in the same values being displayed in the following message box. So, the **HasVersion** method of the **DataRow** class can be used to detect if the **DataRow** object, on which you call the method, holds a specific version of the data. The **HasVersion** method only takes one argument and that's a member of the **DataRowVersion** enum, which you can see described in Table C-44 in Appendix C.

Basically, you can use the **HasVersion** method for detecting if a specific version of the row is accessible, and you can use it for comparing values from different **DataRow** versions.

Listing 11-2 shows you how you can detect if a particular version of a **DataRow** exists, but to compare to different versions of a specific column in a **DataRow** object, you do the following:

```
If drwExisting("FirstName", DataRowVersion.Proposed).ToString = _
   drwExisting("FirstName", DataRowVersion.Current).ToString Then
```

This code compares the proposed value for the FirstName column with the current version. You can use this kind of comparison to cancel edits where the proposed value and current or original values are the same. If you cancel enough edits this way, you'll save some network bandwidth when it's time to update the data source.

Working with DataRow Errors

When working with data in your **DataRow** objects, errors occasionally occur. An example of such might be when you update the data source with changes from your **DataSet** and/or **DataTable**, and another user has changed the same values as you're trying to change since the time you retrieved the data from the data source.

In such a case, a so-called concurrency exception is thrown and the **DataRow** is marked in error. (You can read more about concurrency and locking in Appendix A.) You can also set up custom errors, perhaps for validating the data in the **DataRow**. It can be the case that a given column needs to be validated against an external service before the data is persisted.

At least noncustom errors in **DataRow** objects should be detected and fixed before you try to update your data source.

Table 11-3 shows the various properties and methods you can use for working with **DataRow** errors.

*Table 11-3. **DataRow** Error Properties and Methods*

Name	Description
ClearErrors	This method clears all errors in the **DataRow** object. This means that the **RowError** property is set to an empty **String**, and all column errors are cleared.
GetColumnError	You can use this method to retrieve the error description for a specific column in the **DataRow**, by passing the name of a column, the ordinal position, or a **DataColumn** object. You can use the **SetColumnError** method to set the error description.
GetColumnsInError	This method returns all the columns in a **DataRow** that are in error as an array of **DataColumn** objects.
HasErrors	This property returns a **Boolean** value indicating if the **DataRow** has errors.
RowError	This property returns or sets the error description for the **DataRow**.
SetColumnError	You can use this method to set the error description for a specific column in the **DataRow**, passing the error description, and the name of a column, the ordinal position, or a **DataColumn** object. You can use the **GetColumnError** method to retrieve the error description.

Setting Custom DataRow Errors

You can set custom **DataRow** errors in two ways:

- Set the **RowError** property to any **String** value, except an empty one.

- Call the **SetColumnError** method, passing the column to indicate an error for, and the error description.

Which method you should use, if not both, really depends on the circumstances. The **SetColumnError** method is the best to indicate a problem with a specific column, whereas the **RowError** property can be used to specify a general problem with the row as a whole. See Listing 11-3 later for an example.

Detecting DataRow Errors

There are many times when you need to know if a certain **DataRow** is in error, and for this purpose, you can use the **HasErrors** method. In general, it's always a good idea to check before you try to update your data source, or before displaying data to a user. Having said that, there are two things to note:

- The **HasErrors** method should be called on the **DataSet** and/or **DataTable** before you try to update your data source. This will check the individual **DataTable** objects in the **DataSet**, and the individual **DataRow** objects in the **DataTable**.

- If the user is to correct the rows in error (perhaps he or she made the errors), you should obviously display the rows in error. Sometimes though, it's better to retrieve the rows in error and only display these rows to the user.

The **HasErrors** method returns **True**, if either of the following two conditions is met:

- The **RowError** property is different from an empty **String** ("").

- Any of the **DataColumn** objects has been marked in error.

Remember, always call **HasErrors** before checking individual rows for errors. It can save you a fair amount of time, depending on the number of columns and rows you're processing. See Listing 11-3 in the next section for an example.

Fixing DataRow Errors

Although it's possible to ignore errors in your **DataRow**, the idea is that you should fix them, maybe using a user's input. (See Listing 11-3 for an example.) In Appendix A, you can see how to catch and deal with concurrency violations, which are the most common type of noncustom **DataRow** errors. Once you've fixed the error(s) in a **DataRow** object, you need to indicate that the row no longer has any errors. See the "Clearing DataRow Errors" section next for more information.

Listing 11-3. Working with DataRow Errors

```
 1 Public Sub WorkWithDataRowErrors()
 2    Dim cnnUserMan As SqlConnection
 3    Dim dadUser As SqlDataAdapter
 4    Dim dtbUser As New DataTable("tblUser")
 5    Dim drwExisting As DataRow
 6
 7    ' Instantiate the connection
 8    cnnUserMan = New SqlConnection(PR_STR_CONNECTION_STRING)
 9    ' Instantiate and initialize the data adapter
10    dadUser = New SqlDataAdapter("SELECT * FROM tblUser", cnnUserMan)
11
12    ' Fill the DataTable
13    dadUser.Fill(dtbUser)
14
15    ' Reference row in table
16    drwExisting = dtbUser.Rows(1)
17    ' Indicate a row error
18    drwExisting.RowError = "This row is in error"
19    MsgBox(drwExisting.HasErrors)
20    ' Reset the row error
21    drwExisting.RowError = ""
22    MsgBox(drwExisting.HasErrors)
23    ' Indicate a column error
24    drwExisting.SetColumnError(0, "This column is in error")
25    MsgBox(drwExisting.HasErrors)
26    ' Reset the column error
27    drwExisting.SetColumnError(0, "")
28    MsgBox(drwExisting.HasErrors)
29
```

```
30      ' Set row error
31      drwExisting.RowError = "This row is in error."
32      ' Detect row error
33      If drwExisting.HasErrors Then ' Fix the error(s)
34          ' Retrieve columns in error
35          Dim arrdtcError() As DataColumn = drwExisting.GetColumnsInError()
36          Dim dtcError As DataColumn
37          ' Loop through error column, if any
38          For Each dtcError In arrdtcError
39              ' Do what's needed to fix column error
40              ' ...
41          Next
42          ' Check for a general row error
43          Select Case drwExisting.RowError
44              Case ""
45                  ' No general row error, so do nothing
46              Case "This row is in error."
47                  ' Do what's needed to fix error
48                  ' ...
49              Case Else
50                  ' Do what's needed to fix error
51                  ' ...
52          End Select
53
54          ' Clear the errors
55          drwExisting.ClearErrors()
56      End If
57 End Sub
```

In Listing 11-3, you can see how **DataRow** errors are set, detected, and fixed. In particular, Lines 30 through 56 can be used as a skeleton for dealing with your own custom errors.

Clearing DataRow Errors

Once you've fixed the errors in a **DataRow**, you should call the **ClearErrors** method to indicate that the row is no longer in error. The **ClearErrors** method doesn't take any arguments, and it's called like this:

```
drwUser.ClearErrors()
```

This clears all errors, both custom and noncustom, from the **DataRow**.

NOTE You should be careful with this method, because it also clears errors set by the DataAdapter. If you clear errors that were set on a previous call to a DataAdapter method, such as **Update**, and the errors haven't been fixed, you simply risk having the errors set again. It's a waste of resources at best, and a potential data corruption problem at worst.

Custom errors can also be cleared manually, using one the following methods:

- Set the **RowError** property to an empty **String**.

- Call the **SetColumnError** with an empty **String** for the error description argument, for each **DataColumn** in the **DataRow** marked in error.

See Listing 11-3 for an example.

Using the DataColumn Class

The **DataColumn** class is used for representing the schema of a single column in the **DataRow** class. The **DataColumn** class is also said to be the fundamental building block for creating a **DataTable**. Well, you really need to use the **DataColumn** class in conjunction with the **DataRow** class.

The schema of a column consists of information about the data type, if the column can contain null values, if it's unique or read-only, and if there are other restrictions on what can be inserted as a value other than the restrictions placed by the data type, and so on.

NOTE If you want to read the values in a column of a **DataRow**, you need to use the **DataRow** class and not the **DataColumn** class. The **DataColumn** class is for specifying and reading the schema.

DataColumn Properties

In Table D-16 in Appendix D, you can see a description of all the noninherited, public properties of the **DataColumn** class. This table lists the various column properties that you need to set, depending on what type of column you're creating.

DataColumn Methods

The **DataColumn** class doesn't expose any public, noninherited methods.

DataColumn Events

The **DataColumn** class doesn't expose any noninherited events.

Declaring and Instantiating a DataColumn

There are four ways to instantiate a **DataColumn** object using the column constructor, as demonstrated in Listing 11-4.

*Listing 11-4. Declaring and Instantiating a **DataColumn***

```
1 Public Sub InstantiateDataColumn()
2    Dim dtcDefaultValues As New DataColumn()
3    Dim dtcColumnName As New DataColumn("ColumnName")
4    Dim dtcColumnNameAndDataType As New DataColumn("ColumnName", _
5        Type.GetType("System.String"))
6    Dim dtcColumnNameAndDataTypeAndExpression As New DataColumn( _
7        "ColumnName", Type.GetType("System.String"), "ColumnName + _
8        'Extra Text'")
9    Dim dtcColumnNameAndDataTypeAndExpressionAndMappingType As New _
10       DataColumn("ColumnName", Type.GetType("System.Int32"), _
11       "ColumName + 10", MappingType.Attribute)
12 End Sub
```

Which constructor you choose to use is really a matter of preference, because you can set the properties, which you specify in the constructor, after you've instantiated the **DataColumn** object. The constructor used on Line 2 is the simplest, and in most cases, you'll need to specify the properties afterwards. The constructor used on Lines 9 through 11 is for specifying the mapping type, which is used when the **DataSet**, in which the **DataTable** the **DataRow** is contained, is saved as an XML document.

Using AutoIncrement DataColumns

AutoIncrement columns, which you might know from SQL Server, Microsoft Access, or IBM DB2, can also be used with the **DataColumn** class. **AutoIncrement** must be set to **True** if you want to use integer values that are automatically incremented when you add a new row to a **DataTable**.

The following properties are used when you work with **AutoIncrement** columns:

- *AutoIncrement:* This property is set to a **Boolean** value, with **False** as the default value, to determine if the **DataColumn** uses incrementing values.

- *AutoIncrementSeed:* This is the starting value, or seed, that is used if no **DataRow** objects exist in the **DataTable**. 1 is the default value.

- *AutoIncrementStep:* This is the value that the number is incremented by when a new row is inserted. 1 is the default value.

You can employ the **FillSchema** method of the DataAdapter to generate the **DataColumn** objects that make up the schema in your **DataTable** object(s). However, if you have any **AutoIncrement** columns in your data source you want to copy in your **DataTable**, or if you want to build a **DataTable** to be used for creating a table in your data source, you'll explicitly have to set the seed and the increment value. These values aren't transferred, so the seed is set to 0, and the increment value to 1.

Besides the properties already mentioned, it's also a good idea to set the **ReadOnly** property to **True**, and the **AllowDBNull** property to **False**. However, this is only necessary if you create the **DataColumn** object yourself, because if you use the **FillSchema** method, then these properties are appropriately set. Listing 11-5 shows you how it works.

*Listing 11-5. Working with **AutoIncrement DataColumn** Objects*

```
1 Public Sub WorkWithAutoIncrementColumns()
2    Dim cnnUserMan As SqlConnection
3    Dim dadUser As SqlDataAdapter
4    Dim dtbUser As New DataTable("tblUser")
5    Dim dclId As DataColumn
6
7    ' Instantiate the connection
8    cnnUserMan = New SqlConnection(PR_STR_CONNECTION_STRING)
9    ' Instantiate and initialize the data adapter
10   dadUser = New SqlDataAdapter("SELECT * FROM tblUser", cnnUserMan)
11
12   ' Fill the DataTable Schema
13   ' (this will set the AutoIncrement, AllowDBNull, and ReadOnly
14   ' properties)
15   dadUser.FillSchema(dtbUser, SchemaType.Source)
```

```
16    ' Fill the DataTable
17    ' (this won't set the AutoIncrement, AllowDBNull, and ReadOnly
18    ' properties)
19    dadUser.Fill(dtbUser)
20
21    ' Reference column in table
22    dclId = dtbUser.Columns("Id")
23    ' Display AutoIncrement properties
24    MsgBox("AutoIncrement = " & dclId.AutoIncrement.ToString & vbCrLf & _
25       "AutoIncrementSeed = " & dclId.AutoIncrementSeed.ToString & vbCrLf & _
26       "AutoIncrementStep = " & dclId.AutoIncrementStep.ToString, _
27       MsgBoxStyle.Information, "AutoIncrement DataColumn")
28    ' Set autoincrement properties
29    ' (not needed when FillSchema is used)
30    dclId.AutoIncrement = True
31    dclId.AutoIncrementSeed = 1
32    dclId.AutoIncrementStep = 1
33    ' Display AutoIncrement properties
34    MsgBox("AutoIncrement = " & dclId.AutoIncrement.ToString & vbCrLf & _
35       "AutoIncrementSeed = " & dclId.AutoIncrementSeed.ToString & vbCrLf & _
36       "AutoIncrementStep = " & dclId.AutoIncrementStep.ToString, _
37       MsgBoxStyle.Information, "AutoIncrement DataColumn")
38    ' Set other related properties
39    ' (only needed when you create the column yourself)
40    dclId.AllowDBNull = False
41    dclId.ReadOnly = True
42 End Sub
```

In Listing 11-5, you can see how a **SqlDataAdapter** and a **SqlConnection** object are declared and instantiated. On Line 15, I create the schema of the dtbUser **DataTable** object by calling the **FillSchema** method of the **SqlDataAdapter**, which copies the schema of the tblUser table from the UserMan database. This saves you the steps taken on Lines 30, 31, 32, 40, and 41. Try to run the example code in Listing 11-5 with and without the call to the **FillSchema** method.

Dealing with Null Values

Null values can be problematic to work with, especially when they show up unexpectedly. I guess one should never trust the values read from a data source not to be null values, unless the data source schema disallows null values. You might have some business logic that doesn't allow insertion of null values in certain columns, but if your data source does allow null values in these very same columns, you can never be sure if a null value will be returned. So, to avoid exceptions when your application has been deployed, make sure you can handle null values both to and from the data source. Although most of this section really belongs in the earlier discussion on **DataRow**s, I've chosen to put it here, because this is more than likely the place you'll look anyway. To some extent, it also makes sense.

The **DataRow** class supports the **IsNull** property that returns a **Boolean** value, indicating whether the specified **DataColumn** allows null values to be stored in the column (see Line 31 of Listing 11-6). Although I recommend using the **IsNull** property for checking columns for null values, which is what happens in a typed **DataSet**, there are also other options.

Listing 11-6. Working with Null Value Columns

```
 1 Public Sub WorkWithNullValueColumns()
 2    Dim cnnUserMan As SqlConnection
 3    Dim dadUser As SqlDataAdapter
 4    Dim dtbUser As New DataTable("tblUser")
 5    Dim drwUser As DataRow
 6    Dim dclId As DataColumn
 7
 8    ' Instantiate the connection
 9    cnnUserMan = New SqlConnection(PR_STR_CONNECTION_STRING)
10    ' Instantiate and initialize the data adapter
11    dadUser = New SqlDataAdapter("SELECT * FROM tblUser", cnnUserMan)
12
13    ' Fill the DataTable Schema
14    ' (this will set the AllowDBNull property)
15    dadUser.FillSchema(dtbUser, SchemaType.Source)
16    ' Fill the DataTable
17    ' (this won't set the AllowDBNull property)
18    dadUser.Fill(dtbUser)
19
20    ' Reference row in table
21    drwUser = dtbUser.Rows(1)
22
23    ' Reference Id column in table
24    dclId = dtbUser.Columns("Id")
25    ' Disallow null values in Id column
26    ' (only needed when you create the column yourself,
27    ' or you don't use FillSchema)
28    dclId.AllowDBNull = True
```

```
29
30     ' Check if the LastName column holds a null value
31     If drwUser.IsNull("LastName") Then
32        MsgBox("DataColumn value is Null")
33     Else
34        MsgBox(drwUser("LastName"))
35     End If
36
37     ' This will throw an exception if a null value
38     ' is stored in the LastName column
39     MsgBox(drwUser("LastName"))
40     ' Make sure a null value in a string column
41     ' doesn't throw an exception
42     MsgBox(drwUser("LastName").ToString)
43 End Sub
```

If you're reading values from string data columns, you can use the **ToString** method to return an empty string, in case the value in the **DataColumn** is a null value. (See Line 42 of Listing 11-6.) In classic ASP you work with variables of data type **Variant**, a now extinct data type that has been replaced by the **Object** data type in the .NET Framework. This also means that in classic ASP you can do the following to avoid problems with null values in data columns:

```
strUser = rstUser("LoginName") & ""
strUser = rstUser.Fields("LoginName").Value & ""
```

If you ever worked with ASP, I'm sure you've seen at least one of the two ways just shown for retrieving a column value. By adding the empty string ("") to the column value, you avoid null values, because in the case of a null value in the data column, an empty string is saved in the variable. If you work with variables of data type **Object**, you can use the **ToString** method in your .NET code to achieve the same result. Basically, it's the same code as for variables of data type **String**. However, if you work with nonstring data columns and you don't save the retrieved value in a variable of data type **Object**, you need to add a little more code. I suggest you use the **IsNull** property of the **DataRow** class, but you can also choose to work with data type conversions, should that fit your style of coding better.

Summary

This chapter introduced you to the **DataRow** and **DataColumn** classes. The following ground was covered:

- Instantiating a **DataRow** object

- Editing a **DataRow** object using implicit or explicit edit mode

- Accepting and rejecting **DataRow** changes

- Working with the state of a **DataRow** object

- Working with the different versions of a **DataRow** object

- Setting, detecting, and fixing **DataRow** errors

- Using **AutoIncrement** columns

- Dealing with null values

The following chapter looks at how you can use relationships between **DataTable**s in your **DataSet**.

CHAPTER 12

Data Relations

A DATA RELATION or a data relationship is when two tables have content that is related, and as such are linked. Linked isn't the right word, because you can generally access one table without accessing the other as well; but if you think in terms of accessing all the related data in one go, then its okay to use "link" to describe it. In Chapter 2, you can find more information about data relationships, which is part of relational database design. In this chapter, you'll see how ADO.NET works with data relations.

Using the DataRelation Class

The **DataRelation** class is used for representing a parent/child relationship between two **DataTable** objects. This is done through "linking" the primary key, represented by the **DataColumn** object in a **DataTable**, to a foreign key in a second **DataTable**. The relationships can be cascading, meaning that changes to the parent table, such as deletions, can be cascaded to the child table, effectively making sure no child rows are ever orphaned or left stranded.

The **DataRelation** objects of a **DataTable** are contained in the **DataRelationCollection**, which you can access through a **DataTable's** **ParentRelations** or **ChildRelations** property. In a **DataSet**, you can access all **DataRelation**s through the **Relations** property.

 NOTE When you create and set up a **DataRelation** object, the data in the linking columns in both the parent and child **DataTable**s are verified, making sure that the relation can be made between the two **DataTable** objects. If there is data in any of the columns that violate the constraints that the relation enforces, an exception is thrown. The exception is one of the following:

ArgumentNullException, thrown when one or both of the related columns contains a **null** value.

InvalidConstraintException, thrown if the two related **DataTable**s aren't located in the same **DataSet**, or if the data types of the related columns are different.

DataRelation Class Properties

Table D-18 in Appendix D shows you all the noninherited, public properties of the **DataRelation** class. Except for the **Nested** and **RelationName** properties, they're all read-only and can only be set indirectly, as when the **DataRelation** object is instantiated.

DataRelation Class Methods

The **DataRelation** class exposes no events.

DataRelation Class Events

There are no public, noninherited methods of the **DataRelation** class.

Declaring and Instantiating a DataRelation

There are five ways to instantiate a **DataRelation** object using the **New** constructor:

- Instantiate using the name of the **DataRelation** and the parent and child **DataColumn** objects. The **DataColumn** objects must belong to a **DataTable**. This is the simplest of all the constructors, and you should use it when you want to create a relationship between two tables, each with a single-column key: a primary key in the parent table and a foreign key in the child table.

- Instantiate using the name of the **DataRelation**, the parent and child **DataColumn** objects, and a **Boolean** value indicating if constraints should be created. The **DataColumn** objects must belong to a **DataTable**. Use this constructor when you want to create a relationship between two tables, each with a single-column key—a primary key in the parent table and a foreign key in the child table—and you specifically want to specify whether constraints should be created for the relationship or not.

- Instantiate using the name of the **DataRelation** and two arrays of **DataColumn** objects, one with parent and one with child objects. The **DataColumn** objects must all belong to a **DataTable**, and the objects in the two arrays must match, meaning the first object in the parent array must match the first object in the child array, and so on. Use this constructor when you want to create a relationship between two tables, each with a composite[1] key: a primary key in the parent table and a foreign key in the child table

- Instantiate using the name of the **DataRelation** and two arrays of **DataColumn** objects, one with parent and one with child objects. The **DataColumn** objects must all belong to a **DataTable**, and the objects in the two arrays must match, meaning the first object in the parent array must match the first object in the child array, and so on. Use this constructor when you want to create a relationship between two tables, each with a composite key—a primary key in the parent table and a foreign key in the child table—and you specifically want to identify whether constraints should be created for the relationship or not.

- Instantiate using the name of the **DataRelation**, the name of the parent **DataTable**, the name of the child **DataTable**, and two arrays with the name(s) of **DataColumn** objects, one with parent and one with child object names, and a **Boolean** value indicating if the relationship(s) are nested. This constructor is provided for design time support and is not intended to be used from "standard" applications, only from designer tools or VS .NET IDE add-ins.

You can find an example of the five ways to instantiate a **DataRelation** object in Listing 12-1.

*Listing 12-1. Declaring and Instantiating a **DataRelation***

```
1 Public Sub InstantiateDataRelation()
2    ' Declare parent and child columns for use in relationship
3    Dim dtcParentColumn As New DataColumn("ParentColumn")
4    Dim dtcChildColumn As New DataColumn("ChildColumn")
5    ' Declare and initialize array of parent and child
6    ' columns for use in relationship
7    Dim arrdtcParentColumn(1) As DataColumn
8    Dim arrdtcChildColumn(1) As DataColumn
9
```

---

1. A composite key is a key made up of more than one column.

```
10    arrdtcParentColumn(0) = New DataColumn("ParentColumn1")
11    arrdtcParentColumn(1) = New DataColumn("ParentColumn2")
12    arrdtcChildColumn(0) = New DataColumn("ChildColumn1")
13    arrdtcChildColumn(1) = New DataColumn("ChildColumn2")
14
15    ' This constructor will fail, unless you add the
16    ' specified parent and child columns to a table
17    Dim dtrParentColumnAndChildColumn As New _
18       DataRelation("RelationName", dtcParentColumn, _
19       dtcChildColumn)
20    ' This constructor will fail, unless you add the
21    ' specified parent and child columns to a table
22    Dim dtrParentColumnAndChildColumnAndConstraints As New _
23       DataRelation("RelationName", dtcParentColumn, _
24       dtcChildColumn, False)
25
26    ' This constructor will fail, unless you add the
27    ' specified arrays of parent and child columns to a table
28    Dim dtrParentColumnsAndChildColumns As New _
29       DataRelation("RelationName", arrdtcParentColumn, _
30       arrdtcChildColumn, False)
31    ' This constructor will fail, unless you add the
32    ' specified arrays of parent and child columns to a table
33    Dim dtrParentColumnsAndChildColumnsAndConstraints As New _
34       DataRelation("RelationName", arrdtcParentColumn, _
35       arrdtcChildColumn, False)
36
37    ' This constructor takes string values for all arguments
38    ' except for the last argument, Nested. This argument is
39    ' used for indicating if this relation is used in connection
40    ' with hierarchical data, like an XML document
41    Dim dtrStringsAndNested As New _
42       DataRelation("RelationName", "ParentTableName", _
43       "ChildTableName", New String(0) {"PrimaryKeyColumn1"}, _
44       New String(0) {"ForeignKeyColumn1"}, False)
45 End Sub
```

In Listing 12-1, you can see the five different constructors for the **DataRelation** class. Lines 3 through 13, are simply used for declaring and instantiating columns and arrays of columns used when instantiating the relationships. All five constructors take the name of the relationship as the first argument, but this is really the only thing they all have in common. Please note that it's possible to pass an empty

String "" as the first argument, in which case the **DataRelation** object is given a default name when it's added to the **DataRelationCollection** of the **DataSet**.

The constructor used on Lines 17 through 19 for the dtrParentColumnAndChildColumn **DataRelation** object takes a single parent and child column as arguments. You should use this constructor when you're creating a relationship between two tables, where you have single column primary and foreign keys. Please see the "What Are Keys?" section in Chapter 2, if you need more information on primary and foreign keys.

The constructor used on Lines 41 through 44 is really only for use for design time support, and as such should only be used when creating controls or macros.

Now, you want an example of how to create relationships, don't you? That's a rhetorical question, so in Listing 12-2, I've created the UserMan example database from scratch, using a **DataSet** object, four **DataTable** objects, and **DataRow**, **DataColumn**, and **DataRelation** objects.

*Listing 12-2. Building the UserMan Database as **DataSet***

```
 1 Public Sub BuildUserManDatabase()
 2    ' Declare and instantiate DataSet
 3    Dim dstUserMan As New DataSet("UserMan")
 4    ' Declare and instantiate tables in DataSet
 5    Dim dtbUser As New DataTable("tblUser")
 6    Dim dtbRights As New DataTable("tblRights")
 7    Dim dtbUserRights As New DataTable("tblUserRights")
 8    Dim dtbLog As New DataTable("tblLog")
 9    ' Declare table elements
10    Dim dclUser, dclRights, dclUserRights, dclLog As DataColumn
11    Dim arrdclUserPrimaryKey(), arrdclRightsPrimaryKey(), _
12       arrdclUserRightsPrimaryKey(), arrdclLogPrimaryKey() _
13       As DataColumn
14    ' Declare table relations
15    Dim dtrUser2Log, dtrUser2UserRights, _
16       dtrRights2UserRights As DataRelation
17
18    ' Set up DataSet for saving to XML
19    dstUserMan.Namespace = "UserMan"
20    dstUserMan.Locale = New CultureInfo("En-US", True)
21    dstUserMan.Prefix = "Development"
22
```

```
23    ' Create user table structure
24    ' Create Id column
25    dclUser = New DataColumn("Id", Type.GetType("System.Int32"), "", _
26      MappingType.Element)
27    ' Make the Id column an auto increment column, incrementing by 1
28    ' every time a new row is added to the table, with a seed of 1
29    dclUser.AutoIncrement = True
30    dclUser.AutoIncrementSeed = 1
31    dclUser.AutoIncrementStep = 1
32    ' Disallow null values in column
33    dclUser.AllowDBNull = False
34    ' Add Id column to user table structure
35    dtbUser.Columns.Add(dclUser)
36    ' Create single-column primary key
37    ReDim arrdclUserPrimaryKey(0)
38    ' Add Id column to PK array
39    arrdclUserPrimaryKey(0) = dclUser
40    ' Set primary key
41    dtbUser.PrimaryKey = arrdclUserPrimaryKey
42
43    ' Create ADName column
44    dclUser = New DataColumn("ADName", Type.GetType("System.String"))
45    dclUser.MaxLength = 100
46    ' Add column to user table structure
47    dtbUser.Columns.Add(dclUser)
48
49    ' Create ADSID column
50    dclUser = New DataColumn("ADSID", Type.GetType("System.String"))
51    dclUser.MaxLength = 50
52    ' Add column to user table structure
53    dtbUser.Columns.Add(dclUser)
54
55    ' Create FirstName column
56    dclUser = New DataColumn("FirstName", Type.GetType("System.String"))
57    dclUser.MaxLength = 50
58    ' Add column to user table structure
59    dtbUser.Columns.Add(dclUser)
60
61    ' Create LastName column
62    dclUser = New DataColumn("LastName", Type.GetType("System.String"))
63    dclUser.MaxLength = 50
64    ' Add column to user table structure
65    dtbUser.Columns.Add(dclUser)
66
```

```
67     ' Create LoginName column
68     dclUser = New DataColumn("LoginName", Type.GetType("System.String"))
69     ' Disallow null values in column
70     dclUser.AllowDBNull = False
71     ' Disallow duplicate values in column
72     dclUser.Unique = True
73     dclUser.MaxLength = 50
74     ' Add column to user table structure
75     dtbUser.Columns.Add(dclUser)
76
77     ' Create Password column
78     dclUser = New DataColumn("Password", Type.GetType("System.String"))
79     ' Disallow null values in column
80     dclUser.AllowDBNull = False
81     dclUser.MaxLength = 50
82     ' Add column to user table structure
83     dtbUser.Columns.Add(dclUser)
84
85     ' Add User table to dataset
86     dstUserMan.Tables.Add(dtbUser)
87
88     ' Create Rights table structure
89     ' Create Id column
90     dclRights = New DataColumn("Id", _
91       Type.GetType("System.Int32"), "", MappingType.Element)
92     ' Make the Id column an auto increment column, incrementing by 1
93     ' every time a new row is added to the table, with a seed of 1
94     dclRights.AutoIncrement = True
95     dclRights.AutoIncrementSeed = 1
96     dclRights.AutoIncrementStep = 1
97     ' Disallow null values in column
98     dclRights.AllowDBNull = False
99     ' Add Id column to Rights table structure
100    dtbRights.Columns.Add(dclRights)
101    ' Create single-column primary key
102    ReDim arrdclRightsPrimaryKey(0)
103    ' Add Id column to PK array
104    arrdclRightsPrimaryKey(0) = dclRights
105    ' Set primary key
106    dtbRights.PrimaryKey = arrdclRightsPrimaryKey
107
```

```
108     ' Create Name column
109     dclRights = New DataColumn("Name", Type.GetType("System.String"))
110     dclUser.MaxLength = 50
111     ' Add column to Rights table structure
112     dtbRights.Columns.Add(dclRights)
113
114     ' Create Description column
115     dclRights = New DataColumn("Description", Type.GetType("System.String"))
116     dclUser.MaxLength = 255
117     ' Add column to Rights table structure
118     dtbRights.Columns.Add(dclRights)
119
120     ' Add Rights table to dataset
121     dstUserMan.Tables.Add(dtbRights)
122
123     ' Create Log table structure
124     ' Create Id column
125     dclLog = New DataColumn("Id", _
126        Type.GetType("System.Int32"), "", MappingType.Element)
127     ' Make the Id column an auto increment column, incrementing by 1
128     ' every time a new row is added to the table, with a seed of 1
129     dclLog.AutoIncrement = True
130     dclLog.AutoIncrementSeed = 1
131     dclLog.AutoIncrementStep = 1
132     ' Disallow null values in column
133     dclLog.AllowDBNull = False
134     ' Add Id column to Log table structure
135     dtbLog.Columns.Add(dclLog)
136     ' Create single-column primary key
137     ReDim arrdclLogPrimaryKey(0)
138     ' Add Id column to PK array
139     arrdclLogPrimaryKey(0) = dclLog
140     ' Set primary key
141     dtbLog.PrimaryKey = arrdclLogPrimaryKey
142
143     ' Create Logged column
144     dclLog = New DataColumn("Logged", Type.GetType("System.DateTime"))
145     ' Add column to Log table structure
146     dtbLog.Columns.Add(dclLog)
147
148     ' Create Description column
149     dclLog = New DataColumn("Description", Type.GetType("System.String"))
150     dclLog.MaxLength = 255
151     ' Add column to Log table structure
152     dtbLog.Columns.Add(dclLog)
```

```
153
154    ' Create UserId column
155    dclLog = New DataColumn("UserId", Type.GetType("System.Int32"), "", _
156       MappingType.Element)
157    ' Disallow null values in column
158    dclLog.AllowDBNull = False
159    ' Add UserId column to Log table structure
160    dtbLog.Columns.Add(dclLog)
161
162    ' Add Log table to dataset
163    dstUserMan.Tables.Add(dtbLog)
164
165    ' Create UserRights table structure
166    ' Create UserId column
167    dclUserRights = New DataColumn("UserId", _
168       Type.GetType("System.Int32"), "", MappingType.Element)
169    ' Disallow duplicate values in column
170    dclUserRights.Unique = True
171    ' Add Id column to UserRights table structure
172    dtbUserRights.Columns.Add(dclUserRights)
173
174    ' Create composite primary key
175    ReDim arrdclUserRightsPrimaryKey(1)
176    ' Add UserId column to PK array
177    arrdclUserRightsPrimaryKey(0) = dclUserRights
178
179    ' Create RightsId column
180    dclUserRights = New DataColumn("RightsId", _
181       Type.GetType("System.Int32"), "", MappingType.Element)
182    ' Disallow null values in column
183    dclUserRights.AllowDBNull = False
184    ' Add RightsId column to UserRights table structure
185    dtbUserRights.Columns.Add(dclUserRights)
186
187    ' Add RightsId column to PK array
188    arrdclUserRightsPrimaryKey(1) = dclUserRights
189    ' Set primary key
190    dtbUserRights.PrimaryKey = arrdclUserRightsPrimaryKey
191
192    ' Add UserRights table to dataset
193    dstUserMan.Tables.Add(dtbUserRights)
194
```

```
195    ' Create table relations
196    dtrUser2Log = New DataRelation("User2Log", dtbUser.Columns("Id"), _
197        dtbLog.Columns("UserId"), True)
198    dtrUser2UserRights = New DataRelation("User2UserRights", _
199        dtbUser.Columns("Id"), dtbUserRights.Columns("UserId"), True)
200    dtrRights2UserRights = New DataRelation("Rights2UserRight", _
201        dtbRights.Columns("Id"), dtbUserRights.Columns("RightsId"), True)
202    ' Add relationships to DataSet
203    dstUserMan.Relations.Add(dtrUser2Log)
204    dstUserMan.Relations.Add(dtrUser2UserRights)
205    dstUserMan.Relations.Add(dtrRights2UserRights)
206 End Sub
```

In Listing 12-2, you can see how I gradually build the entire UserMan database, table by table, column by column. I set up the primary and foreign keys and add the tables to the dstUserMan **DataSet**. Finally, I create the relations between the tables and these to the **DataSet**.

Now, even if the preceding code actually runs, it can be quite hard to "see" what happens, but don't despair; you simply add this line of code to the example code in Listing 12-2 after Line 205 to write the **DataSet** schema to a text file in XML format:

```
dstUserMan.WriteXmlSchema("C:\\UserManDatabase.xml")
```

You can open the file in Internet Explorer to see the XML document with color-coding of the nodes, elements, and attributes. You can then compare it to an XML document created the same way, but where the **DataSet** is generated using the **DataAdapter** class' **Fill** method. See the "Populating the DataSet or DataTable" section in Chapter 8 for more information on how to populate a **DataSet**.

Using Constraints with Relationships

When you have relationships between any two tables, data in either of the two tables will more than likely be updated or deleted at some stage, and new data inserted. Inserting new data in the parent table isn't that difficult when concerned with relationships; you only have to make sure that you insert a row with a unique parent key. See more about parent key constraints in the "Parent Key Constraints" section next. Child tables are a little trickier, meaning that inserted, updated, and deleted rows must adhere to all the foreign key constraints defined for the relations. See the "Child Key Constraints" section later in this chapter.

Parent Key Constraints

In any **DataRelation**, there is one *parent key constraint*, which is accessed through the **ParentKeyConstraint** property. This property returns a **UniqueConstraint** object (see Table D-19 in Appendix D for a list of **UniqueConstraint** class properties), which ensures that all columns that are part of the **UniqueConstraint** object hold values that are unique across all rows in a **DataTable**.

> **NOTE** The unique constraint representing the parent key constraint is automatically set and added to the **ConstraintCollection** of the parent **DataTable**, when you add a **DataRelation** object to a **DataSet**; see Line 73 through 79 in Listing 12-3, later in this section. However, this is only true if the constraint hasn't already been set on the parent **DataTable**. This is the case when you use the primary key as the parent key constraint.

The **ParentKeyConstraint** property isn't set until you add the **DataRelation** object to the **DataSet** that contains the two related **DataTable** objects.

> **NOTE** A parent key constraint doesn't have to be set on the primary key in the parent table. You can use the **IsPrimaryKey** property of the **DataRelation** class to check if the parent key constraint has been set on the primary key. See Line 81 of Listing 12-3 later in this section for an example.

So summing up, a parent key constraint in an ADO.NET data relationship is nothing more than a unique constraint. This also means that if you add a **DataColumn** from your parent table in the **DataRelation** object that isn't unique or rather doesn't have the **Unique** property set to **True**, it will automatically be set to **True** when the **DataRelation** is added to the **DataSet**. Listing 12-3 shows you how to work with parent key constraints.

Listing 12-3. Working with Parent Key Constraints

```
1 Public Sub ParentKeyConstraints()
2     ' Declare and instantiate DataSet
3     Dim dstUserMan As New DataSet("UserMan")
4     ' Declare and instantiate tables in DataSet
5     Dim dtbUser As New DataTable("tblUser")
6     Dim dtbLog As New DataTable("tblLog")
```

```
 7    ' Declare table elements
 8    Dim dclUser, dclLog As DataColumn
 9    Dim arrdclUserPrimaryKey(), arrdclLogPrimaryKey() _
10      As DataColumn
11    ' Declare table relations
12    Dim dtrUser2Log As DataRelation
13
14    ' Create user table structure
15    ' Create Id column
16    dclUser = New DataColumn("Id", Type.GetType("System.Int32"), "", _
17      MappingType.Element)
18    ' Make the Id column an auto increment column, incrementing by 1
19    ' every time a new row is added to the table, with a seed of 1
20    dclUser.AutoIncrement = True
21    dclUser.AutoIncrementSeed = 1
22    dclUser.AutoIncrementStep = 1
23    ' Disallow null values in column
24    dclUser.AllowDBNull = False
25    ' Add Id column to user table structure
26    dtbUser.Columns.Add(dclUser)
27    ' Create single-column primary key
28    ReDim arrdclUserPrimaryKey(0)
29    ' Add Id column to PK array
30    arrdclUserPrimaryKey(0) = dclUser
31    ' Set primary key
32    dtbUser.PrimaryKey = arrdclUserPrimaryKey
33
34    ' Add User table to dataset
35    dstUserMan.Tables.Add(dtbUser)
36
37    ' Create Log table structure
38    ' Create Id column
39    dclLog = New DataColumn("Id", _
40      Type.GetType("System.Int32"), "", MappingType.Element)
41    ' Make the Id column an auto increment column, incrementing by 1
42    ' every time a new row is added to the table, with a seed of 1
43    dclLog.AutoIncrement = True
44    dclLog.AutoIncrementSeed = 1
45    dclLog.AutoIncrementStep = 1
46    ' Disallow null values in column
47    dclLog.AllowDBNull = False
48    ' Add Id column to Log table structure
49    dtbLog.Columns.Add(dclLog)
```

```
50    ' Create single-column primary key
51    ReDim arrdclLogPrimaryKey(0)
52    ' Add Id column to PK array
53    arrdclLogPrimaryKey(0) = dclLog
54    ' Set primary key
55    dtbLog.PrimaryKey = arrdclLogPrimaryKey
56
57    ' Create UserId column
58    dclLog = New DataColumn("UserId", Type.GetType("System.Int32"), "", _
59        MappingType.Element)
60    ' Disallow null values in column
61    dclLog.AllowDBNull = False
62    ' Add UserId column to Log table structure
63    dtbLog.Columns.Add(dclLog)
64
65    ' Add Log table to dataset
66    dstUserMan.Tables.Add(dtbLog)
67
68    ' Create table relations
69    dtrUser2Log = New DataRelation("User2Log", dtbUser.Columns("Id"), _
70        dtbLog.Columns("UserId"), True)
71    ' This next line of code  will throw an exception, because
72    ' the property hasn't been set yet
73    'MsgBox(dtrUser2Log.ParentKeyConstraint.ConstraintName.ToString)
74
75    ' Add relationships to DataSet
76    dstUserMan.Relations.Add(dtrUser2Log)
77    ' Now, after adding the DataRelation to the DataSet, you can
78    ' read the ParentKeyConstraint property
79    MsgBox(dtrUser2Log.ParentKeyConstraint.ConstraintName.ToString)
80    ' Check if the parent key constraint has been set on a primary key
81    MsgBox(dtrUser2Log.ParentKeyConstraint.IsPrimaryKey.ToString)
82 End Sub
```

In Listing 12-3, I reuse some of the code from Listing 12-2 for building the parent **DataTable** object, which has a schema of a single column, and a child table, which has a schema of two columns; these are added to a **DataSet**, and then linked with a **DataRelation** object, which is also added to the **DataSet**.

Child Key Constraints

Child key constraints are constraints that are used to maintain referential integrity between data in the parent and child tables in a relationship. You can find more information about referential integrity in Chapter 2. Basically, a child key constraint determines what action to take when a row in the parent table of a relationship is deleted or updated. Of course, the affected parent table row must have at least one related row in the child table. Child key constraints are really instances of the **ForeignKeyConstraint** class, and they can be accessed using the **ChildKeyConstraint** property of the **DataRelation** class.

 NOTE   The foreign key constraint is automatically set and added to the **ConstraintCollection** of the child **DataTable** when you add a **DataRelation** object to a **DataSet**; see Line 73 through 87 in Listing 12-4 later in this section.

By default, changes, meaning updates and deletions, in the parent table aren't reflected in or cascaded to the child table (see Lines 90 through 92 in Listing 12-4 later in this section). This is hardly ever the right course of action, as it will leave related rows in the child table orphaned or stranded. This means that the stranded rows in the child table no longer have a related row in the parent table, but generally, the whole idea of the child table and the relationship is to avoid this. To avoid this, you need to set the appropriate action to be taken when rows in the parent table are updated or deleted. There are three properties of a **ForeignKeyConstraint** class that help you set the action to take, and they are

- AcceptRejectRule

- DeleteRule

- UpdateRule

AcceptRejectRule is the main property as it controls the two others. If **AcceptRejectRule** is set to the **None** member of the **AcceptReject** enum (see Table D-21 in Appendix D for an overview of the **AcceptReject** enum members), the **DeleteRule** and **UpdateRule** are never triggered, because the changes to the rows in the parent table aren't cascaded to the child table. Therefore, if you want changes in the parent table to cascade to the child table, you must set **AcceptRejectRule** to the **Cascade** member of the **AcceptReject** enum (see Lines 95 and 96 in Listing 12-4).

Listing 12-4. Working with Child Key Constraints

```
 1 Public Sub ChildKeyConstraints()
 2    ' Declare and instantiate DataSet
 3    Dim dstUserMan As New DataSet("UserMan")
 4    ' Declare and instantiate tables in DataSet
 5    Dim dtbUser As New DataTable("tblUser")
 6    Dim dtbLog As New DataTable("tblLog")
 7    ' Declare table elements
 8    Dim dclUser, dclLog As DataColumn
 9    Dim arrdclUserPrimaryKey(), arrdclLogPrimaryKey() _
10       As DataColumn
11    ' Declare table relations
12    Dim dtrUser2Log As DataRelation
13    ' Declare rows
14    Dim drwUser, drwLog As DataRow
15
16    ' Create user table structure
17    ' Create Id column
18    dclUser = New DataColumn("Id", Type.GetType("System.Int32"), "", _
19       MappingType.Element)
20    ' Make the Id column an auto increment column, incrementing by 1
21    ' every time a new row is added to the table, with a seed of 1
22    dclUser.AutoIncrement = True
23    dclUser.AutoIncrementSeed = 1
24    dclUser.AutoIncrementStep = 1
25    ' Disallow null values in column
26    dclUser.AllowDBNull = False
27    ' Add Id column to user table structure
28    dtbUser.Columns.Add(dclUser)
29    ' Create single-column primary key
30    ReDim arrdclUserPrimaryKey(0)
31    ' Add Id column to PK array
32    arrdclUserPrimaryKey(0) = dclUser
33    ' Set primary key
34    dtbUser.PrimaryKey = arrdclUserPrimaryKey
35
36    ' Add User table to dataset
37    dstUserMan.Tables.Add(dtbUser)
38
```

```
39    ' Create Log table structure
40    ' Create Id column
41    dclLog = New DataColumn("Id", _
42       Type.GetType("System.Int32"), "", MappingType.Element)
43    ' Make the Id column an auto increment column, incrementing by 1
44    ' every time a new row is added to the table, with a seed of 1
45    dclLog.AutoIncrement = True
46    dclLog.AutoIncrementSeed = 1
47    dclLog.AutoIncrementStep = 1
48    ' Disallow null values in column
49    dclLog.AllowDBNull = False
50    ' Add Id column to Log table structure
51    dtbLog.Columns.Add(dclLog)
52    ' Create single-column primary key
53    ReDim arrdclLogPrimaryKey(0)
54    ' Add Id column to PK array
55    arrdclLogPrimaryKey(0) = dclLog
56    ' Set primary key
57    dtbLog.PrimaryKey = arrdclLogPrimaryKey
58
59    ' Create UserId column
60    dclLog = New DataColumn("UserId", Type.GetType("System.Int32"), "", _
61       MappingType.Element)
62    ' Disallow null values in column
63    dclLog.AllowDBNull = False
64    ' Add UserId column to Log table structure
65    dtbLog.Columns.Add(dclLog)
66
67    ' Add Log table to dataset
68    dstUserMan.Tables.Add(dtbLog)
69
70    ' Create table relations
71    dtrUser2Log = New DataRelation("User2Log", dtbUser.Columns("Id"), _
72       dtbLog.Columns("UserId"), True)
73    Try
74       ' This next line of code  will throw an exception, because
75       ' the ChildKeyConstraint property hasn't been set yet
76       MsgBox(dtrUser2Log.ChildKeyConstraint.ConstraintName.ToString)
77    Catch objE As NullReferenceException
78       MsgBox(obje.Message, MsgBoxStyle.Information, _
79          "Accessing ChildConstraint property")
80    End Try
81
```

```
82    ' Add relationships to DataSet
83    dstUserMan.Relations.Add(dtrUser2Log)
84    ' Now, after adding the DataRelation to the DataSet, you can
85    ' read the ChildKeyConstraint property
86    MsgBox("ChildKeyConstraint Name = " & _
87       dtrUser2Log.ChildKeyConstraint.ConstraintName.ToString)
88    ' Display the default action to take in the relation,
89    ' for updated and deleted rows in the parent table
90    MsgBox("ChildKeyConstraint AcceptRejectRule = " & _
91       dtrUser2Log.ChildKeyConstraint.AcceptRejectRule.ToString, _
92       MsgBoxStyle.Information, "Default Value")
93    ' Make sure updated and deleted rows in the parent table are cascaded
94    ' to the child table
95    dtrUser2Log.ChildKeyConstraint.AcceptRejectRule = _
96       AcceptRejectRule.Cascade
97    ' Display the explicit action to take in the relation,
98    ' for updated and deleted rows in the parent table
99    MsgBox("ChildKeyConstraint AcceptRejectRule = " & _
100      dtrUser2Log.ChildKeyConstraint.AcceptRejectRule.ToString, _
101      MsgBoxStyle.Information, "Explicit Value")
102   ' Display the default action to take in the child table,
103   ' for updated and deleted rows in the parent table
104   MsgBox("ChildKeyConstraint DeleteRule = " & _
105      dtrUser2Log.ChildKeyConstraint.DeleteRule.ToString & vbCrLf & _
106      "ChildKeyConstraint UpdateRule = " & _
107      dtrUser2Log.ChildKeyConstraint.UpdateRule.ToString, _
108      MsgBoxStyle.Information, "Default Value")
109   ' Make sure updated rows in the parent table are changed accordingly
110   ' in the child table, and rows related to deleted rows, are
111   ' set to null in the child table
112   dtrUser2Log.ChildKeyConstraint.UpdateRule = Rule.Cascade
113   dtrUser2Log.ChildKeyConstraint.DeleteRule = Rule.SetNull
114   ' Display the explicit action to take in the child table,
115   ' for deleted rows in the parent table
116   MsgBox("ChildKeyConstraint DeleteRule = " & _
117      dtrUser2Log.ChildKeyConstraint.DeleteRule.ToString & vbCrLf & _
118      "ChildKeyConstraint UpdateRule = " & _
119      dtrUser2Log.ChildKeyConstraint.UpdateRule.ToString, _
120      MsgBoxStyle.Information, "Explicit Value")
121   ' Add data to the parent table
122   drwUser = dtbUser.NewRow()
123   dtbUser.Rows.Add(drwUser)
```

```
124    ' Display number of rows in parent table
125    MsgBox("Rows #" & dtbUser.Rows.Count.ToString, _
126        MsgBoxStyle.Information, "Parent Table")
127    ' Add related data to the child table
128    drwLog = dtbLog.NewRow()
129    ' We need to specify the id of an existing row
130    ' in the parent table or an exception is thrown,
131    ' because of the ForeignKeyConstraint
132    drwLog("UserId") = drwUser("Id")
133    dtbLog.Rows.Add(drwLog)
134    ' Display number of rows in child table
135    MsgBox("Rows #" & dtbLog.Rows.Count.ToString, _
136        MsgBoxStyle.Information, "Child Table")
137    Try
138        ' Delete the row from the parent table
139        ' This will throw an exception, because the ForeignKeyConstraint
140        ' specifies that the value of foreign key column should be set
141        ' to null
142        dtbUser.Rows.Remove(drwUser)
143    Catch objE As NoNullAllowedException
144        ' Allow null values in the UserId column
145        ' Disallow null values in column
146        dtbLog.Columns("UserId").AllowDBNull = True
147        ' Delete row
148        dtbUser.Rows.Remove(drwUser)
149    End Try
150
151    ' Check if the UserId column of the related row in the child
152    ' table has been set to null
153    If dtbLog.Rows(0)("UserId") Is DBNull.Value Then
154        MsgBox("The UserId column of related row in child table is null.")
155    End If
156 End Sub
```

Once the **AcceptRejectRule** property is set to **Cascade**, as on Lines 95 and 96 in Listing 12-4, all deletions and updates of rows in the parent table are by default cascaded to the child table, because the **DeleteRule** and **UpdateRule** properties are set to the **Cascade** member of the **Rule** enum by default. (See Table D-22 in Appendix D for an overview of the **Rule** enum members.) This is in most cases the most appropriate course of action, because your data will stay synchronized. However, you can also specify that you want the related rows set to null (**SetNull**), as on Line 113 in Listing 12-4, or to the default column value of the related row. When you choose to set the related rows to null, it's only the foreign key column(s) that are set to null. Please note that although it's always possible to specify this kind of action, a **NoNullException** exception will be thrown if the foreign key column(s) disallow null values. Anyway, inserting null values is one way of leaving maintenance for later, and returning to the more current duties in your application. You can then have a maintenance application deleting all the rows in the child table(s), where the foreign key has been set to null.

NOTE It's really your business logic and part of your data maintenance plan that should help you decide which rules to apply with your constraints.

Relational Navigation

In a **DataSet** with **DataTable** and **DataRelation** objects defined, you need to be able to move around from a parent table to a child table and back, and this can be done using some of the properties of the **DataRelation** object. If you take the example code in Listing 12-2, and add some rows to the tables, as shown in Listing 12-5, you can move around between the data.

Listing 12-5. Adding Rows to In-Memory UserMan Database

```
1 Public Sub AddRowsToUserManDatabase()
2    Dim dstUserMan As DataSet
3    Dim drwUser, drwUserRights, drwRights As DataRow
4
5    ' Build in-memory database
6    BuildUserManDatabase(dstUserMan)
7    ' Add rows to user table
8    dstUserMan.Tables("tblUser").Rows.Add(New Object(6) _
9       {Nothing, Nothing, Nothing, "John", "Doe", "UserMan", "userman"})
10   dstUserMan.Tables("tblUser").Rows.Add(New Object(6) _
11      {Nothing, Nothing, Nothing, Nothing, Nothing, "User1", "password"})
12   dstUserMan.Tables("tblUser").Rows.Add(New Object(6) _
13      {Nothing, Nothing, Nothing, Nothing, Nothing, "User2", "password"})
14   dstUserMan.Tables("tblUser").Rows.Add(New Object(6) _
15      {Nothing, Nothing, Nothing, Nothing, Nothing, "User3", "password"})
16   dstUserMan.Tables("tblUser").Rows.Add(New Object(6) _
17      {Nothing, Nothing, Nothing, Nothing, Nothing, "User99", "password"})
```

```
18    ' Add rows to rights table
19    dstUserMan.Tables("tblRights").Rows.Add(New Object(2) _
20       {Nothing, "AddUser", _
21       "Gives the user the right to add users to the database"})
22    dstUserMan.Tables("tblRights").Rows.Add(New Object(2) _
23       {Nothing, "DeleteUser", _
24       "Gives the user the right to delete users from the database"})
25    dstUserMan.Tables("tblRights").Rows.Add(New Object(2) _
26       {Nothing, "ClearLog", _
27       "Gives the user the right to clear the log"})
28    ' Add rows to user rights table
29    dstUserMan.Tables("tblUserRights").Rows.Add(New Object(1) {1, 1})
30    dstUserMan.Tables("tblUserRights").Rows.Add(New Object(1) {1, 2})
31    dstUserMan.Tables("tblUserRights").Rows.Add(New Object(1) {1, 3})
32 End Sub
```

The example code shown in Listing 12-5 adds the same rows to your in-memory UserMan database, as the accompanying SQL scripts do to the UserMan database in your data source. Listing 12-6 shows you how you can look up related rows in a child table using various properties of the parent **DataTable** and the **DataRelation** object.

Listing 12-6. Navigating Related Rows

```
 1 Public Sub NavigateRelatedRows()
 2    Const STR_PARENT_TABLE_NAME As String = "tblUser"
 3
 4    Dim dstUserMan As DataSet
 5    Dim dtrUser As DataRelation
 6    Dim arrdclParent(), dclParent As DataColumn
 7    Dim arrdclChild(), dclChild As DataColumn
 8    Dim drwParent, drwChild As DataRow
 9    Dim arrdrwParent, arrdrwChild() As DataRow
10    Dim strRelated As String
11
12    ' Retrieve populated in-memory database
13    AddRowsToUserManDatabase(dstUserMan)
14    ' Locate all relations that the parent user table is part of
15    For Each dtrUser In dstUserMan.Relations
16      If dtrUser.ParentTable.TableName = STR_PARENT_TABLE_NAME Then
17          ' Build related data string
18          strRelated += "Child table: " & _
19             dtrUser.ChildTable.TableName & vbCrLf & vbCrLf
```

```
20        ' Look up parent key
21        strRelated += "Parent Key = "
22        ' Find all parent key columns
23        For Each dclParent In dtrUser.ParentColumns()
24            strRelated += dclParent.ColumnName & ", "
25        Next
26
27        ' Remove last separating comma and add hyphen
28        strRelated = strRelated.Remove(strRelated.Length - 2, 2) & " -- "
29
30        ' Look up child key
31        strRelated += "Child Key = "
32        ' Find all child key columns
33        For Each dclChild In dtrUser.ChildColumns()
34            strRelated += dclChild.ColumnName & ", "
35        Next
36
37        ' Remove last separating comma and add CR
38        strRelated = strRelated.Remove(strRelated.Length - 2, 2) & _
39            vbCrLf & vbCrLf
40
41        ' Find related rows in child table
42        For Each drwParent In dstUserMan.Tables(STR_PARENT_TABLE_NAME).Rows
43            ' Look up related columns
44            arrdrwChild = drwParent.GetChildRows(dtrUser)
45            ' Check if any child rows exist
46            If arrdrwChild.GetLength(0) > -1 Then
47                ' Display parent key column values
48                strRelated += vbTab & "Parent Key Column Value(s) : "
49                For Each dclParent In dtrUser.ParentColumns()
50                    strRelated += drwParent(dclParent.ColumnName).ToString & _
51                        ", "
52                Next
53
54                ' Remove last separating comma and add CR
55                strRelated = strRelated.Remove(strRelated.Length - 2, 2) & _
56                    vbCrLf
57
58                ' Display child key column values
59                strRelated += vbTab & "Child Key Column Value(s) : "
60                For Each drwChild In drwParent.GetChildRows(dtrUser)
61                    For Each dclChild In dtrUser.ChildColumns()
62                        strRelated += drwChild(dclChild.ColumnName).ToString & _
63                            ", "
```

```
64                     Next
65                 Next
66
67                 ' Remove last separating comma and add CR
68                 strRelated = strRelated.Remove(strRelated.Length - 2, 2) & _
69                     vbCrLf
70             End If
71
72             strRelated += vbCrLf
73         Next
74     End If
75 Next
76
77 ' Display related data
78 MsgBox(strRelated, MsgBoxStyle.Information, STR_PARENT_TABLE_NAME & _
79     " Relationships")
80 End Sub
```

In Listing 12-6, you can see how I go through all the relationships defined in the dstUserMan **DataSet**, singling out the ones where the parent table is the tblUser table. I then retrieve the name of the child table, and the name and values of the parent key and child key column(s). Now, the value(s) of the child key columns are pretty obvious, since they should match the parent key columns, because they're lookup keys, right? However, this should serve as an example of how you can dynamically look up primary and child key column names and values.

Summary

This chapter introduced you to how data relations are handled in ADO.NET. You saw how you can build the UserMan database from scratch, using ADO.NET building blocks. You also saw how constraints, in the form of **UniqueConstraint** and **ForeignKeyConstraint** objects, work with the **DataRelation** class. Finally, you saw how you can navigate in relational data, meaning between child and parent tables, and vice versa.

The following chapter takes you through the various data-related features of the IDE, such as how to create database projects, triggers, and stored procedures.

Part Four

Working with Databases in the VS .NET IDE

CHAPTER 13

Presenting the IDE from a Database Viewpoint

THIS CHAPTER INTRODUCES you to the Integrated Development Environment (IDE) and more specifically how IDEs relate to databases. I'll be discussing how you create database projects and how you let the various designers do the hard work for you—in other words, how you perform tasks from the IDE that you would otherwise do through code or using other external tools.

In this chapter, I've included several hands-on exercises that will take you through creating a database project and adding scripts, queries, and command files. Just look for the Exercise items that appear throughout this text.

Using the Server Explorer

The Server Explorer is located on the left-hand side of the IDE, and it's displayed if you move the mouse cursor over the Server Explorer tab[1] or if you press Ctrl+Alt+S. The Server Explorer is hidden again if you click any other part of the IDE, such as the Code Editor. The Server Explorer window contains a tree view of the data connections that have been created and the servers to which you have connected.

 NOTE The resources shown in the Server Explorer window are NOT specific to the project that is currently open.

When you open up the Visual Studio .NET IDE for the first time, the Server Explorer doesn't display any data connections or servers. Figure 13-1, however,

---

1. You'll have to hover the mouse over the actual Server Explorer icon if the Toolbar tab is currently displayed. The Server Explorer and the toolbar share the same tabbing area on the left side of the IDE.

shows you the Server Explorer with one server added. You'll see in the coming sections how you can add a server and a data connection to the Server Explorer.

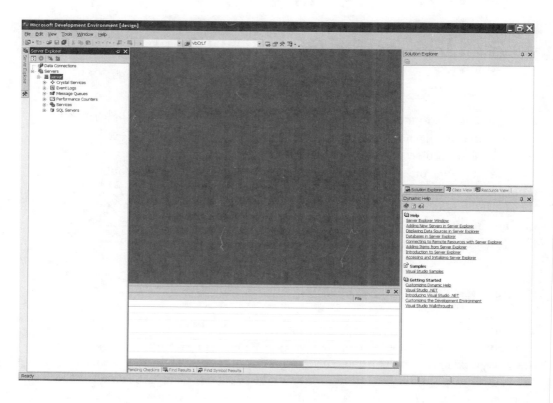

Figure 13-1. The Server Explorer window

Handling Data Connections

If you need to manipulate a database or create a strongly typed **DataSet**, you have to create a data connection first. Depending on your access privileges, you can perform most database tasks from the Server Explorer.

Adding a Data Connection

You can add a data connection by right-clicking the Data Connections node and selecting Add Connection from the pop-up menu. This brings up the Data Link Properties dialog box. You might need to click the Provider tab to see the dialog box shown in Figure 13-2.

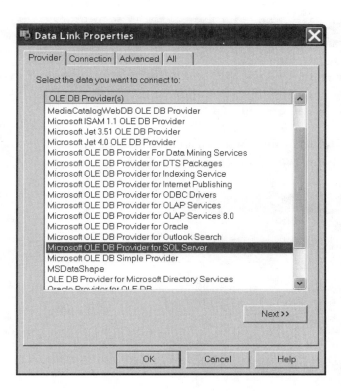

Figure 13-2. Provider tab in Data Link Properties dialog box

On the Provider tab of the Data Link Properties dialog box, you must select the appropriate provider for the data source you are going to connect to, and click Next. This brings the Connection tab to the front.

Exercise

On the Provider tab of the Data Link Properties dialog box, select Microsoft OLE DB Provider for SQL Server.

On the Connection tab, you must enter the appropriate details concerning the database to which you are connecting, that is, the user name and password for a user that has access rights to the database. See the following exercise for an example.

Exercise

1. On the Connection tab of the Data Link Properties dialog box, you must enter the following text:

   USERMANPC (or the name of your SQL Server)

   See Figure 13-3. The password is userman and you must replace USERMANPC with the name of your SQL Server.

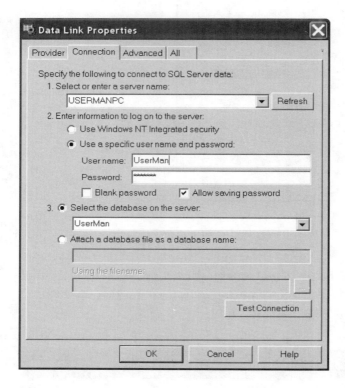

Figure 13-3. SQL Server setup on the Connection tab in Data Link Properties dialog box

2. Click OK, or try clicking the Test button first to see if there are any problems connecting to the data source.

Automatically Generating a Data Connection

Instead of creating a new data connection as described in the previous sections, you can also have it created automatically by the VS .NET IDE, if you work with SQL Server 7.0 or later. What you need to do is to expand the server that holds your SQL Server database under the Servers node in the Server Explorer (see the "Handling Servers" section later in this chapter for more information on working with servers in the Server Explorer). When you've expanded the server, expand the SQL Servers node and the SQL Server instance you want to connect to. Then you need to expand the database, and from the database node, you can drag a database object (table, view, stored procedure) onto a form in design view.[2] This will automatically generate the connection of type **SqlConnection**, and it will be automatically added to your code. Depending on what the database object does (meaning if it is row returning or not), a **SqlCommand** object or **SqlDataAdapter** object is also created for you.

This procedure is good when you really only need the connection for a single database object—the object you dragged onto your form.

Deleting a Data Connection

When a data connection is no longer relevant to you, you should delete it from the Server Explorer, because it can quickly become "overcrowded." There are three ways in which you can delete a data connection from the Server Explorer. First, you must select the appropriate data connection node in the tree view and then do one of the following:

- Press the Delete key.

- Right-click the tree-view node and select the Remove command from the pop-up menu.

- Select the Remove command from the Edit menu.

Please note that this procedure only deletes the connection, and not the database to which you are connecting! If you need to delete a SQL Server database, please see the "Deleting/Dropping a SQL Server Database" section later in this chapter.

---

2. This works with both Windows Forms and Web Forms.

Creating Database Objects

If you want to create database objects such as tables, diagrams, views, stored procedures, or functions, you can do this by first selecting the corresponding tree-view node. In this case corresponding tree-view node means the Tables node, or the Stored Procedures node in the database you want to create a table in, and so on. Next, right-click the node, and select the New Table command, or the New Stored Procedure command, and so on from the pop-up menu. Check out Part Six of this book for more information on how to create database objects. Chapter 2 holds information on how to design a relational database the "right" way.

Handling Servers

Under the Servers node in the Server Explorer you can add any server to which you have access. You should add at least all the servers that the current project will be accessing, because it's easier to control and manipulate the servers once they are shown with their resources in the Server Explorer window.

Adding a Server

You can add a server by right-clicking the Servers node and selecting Add Server from the pop-up menu. The Add Server dialog box, shown in Figure 13-4, appears.

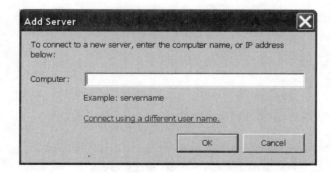

Figure 13-4. Add Server dialog box

In the Add Server dialog box you can add a server by typing the name of the server in the Computer textbox. The name can be specified in two different ways:

- Using the name (URL or UNC file path) if the server is on a local network—for example, USERMANPC

- Using the IP address of the server—for example, 192.129.192.15

Exercise

Type the name of your server in the Name textbox of the Add Server dialog box and click OK.

If you want to connect to the server as a different user, you must click the option Connect using a different user name. This brings up the Connect As dialog box as shown in Figure 13-5.

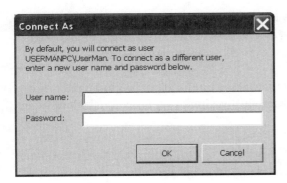

Figure 13-5. Connect As dialog box

The Connect As dialog box has two textboxes you must fill in:

- *User Name:* Type the name of the user you want to connect as. If this user is in a different domain, you must also specify the domain name; use the format *DomainName\UserName*.

- *Password:* Type the password that corresponds to the user name entered. Leave this textbox empty if the user doesn't have a password.

Once you have added a server to the Server Explorer, you can view all the resources this server has to offer by expanding the tree node (click the + icon next to the node if it isn't already expanded). See Figure 13-1 earlier.

There are a number of different resources on a server, but I will only cover the ones that are database related, including message queues and SQL Servers.

Using Server Resources

The following sections describe how to use the database-related resources on the server of your choice.

Using Message Queues

Chapter 21 covers message queues extensively, so I won't go into too many details here. Having said this, I will show you how to create, manipulate, and delete a message queue from the Server Explorer. Another thing you need to be aware of is that you can only access message queues on a server with a dependent message queue. This means workgroup message queue setup is not supported. A workgroup setup is an independent message queue, which means that it's not dependent on a server for storage of messages.

Three types of message queues can be seen in the Server Explorer, although which message you can actually see depends on your permissions:

- *Private queue:* This is a queue registered on the local computer and is not part of a directory service. Generally this kind of queue cannot be located by other applications.

- *Public queue:* This is a queue registered in the directory service. This queue can be located by any other message queuing application.

- *System queue:* This kind of queue is generally used by the OS for internal messaging.

If you need more information on the various message queues you can create, please see Chapter 21. Figure 13-6 shows you the expanded Message Queue node in the Server Explorer.

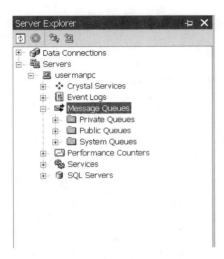

Figure 13-6. Expanded Message Queue node in the Server Explorer

Creating a Message Queue

Right-click the queue node where you want to create the new queue, and select Create Queue from the pop-up menu. This brings up the Create Message Queue dialog box as shown in Figure 13-7.

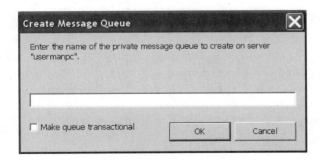

Figure 13-7. Create Message Queue dialog box

You give the message queue a name by typing it in the textbox. Select the Make queue transactional check box to accept only those messages that are part of a transaction. Note that you need permissions to create a message queue on the server to which you are connected. Click OK to create the queue.

Deleting a Message Queue

If a message queue is no longer of use to you, you can delete it. This is done by right-clicking the message queue and selecting Remove from the pop-up menu, or by selecting it and pressing the Delete key. A confirmation of the deletion is required. All messages in the queue will be deleted permanently.

Deleting Messages from a Message Queue

If you need to clear one or more messages from a queue, there are two ways of doing so from the Server Explorer. You can delete one at a time or you can delete all messages from a queue. Clearing all messages from a queue is done by expanding the queue node and right-clicking the Queue messages node. Select Clear Messages from the pop-up menu and then confirm the deletion. A single message is cleared from the queue by selecting it, right-clicking it, and selecting Remove from the pop-up menu.

Using SQL Server Databases

You can use the SQL Server resources to see if a specific server actually hosts a SQL Server. Click the + icon to expand the SQL Servers node. If you click a SQL Server, the SQL Server Login dialog box pops up if the service isn't already running. This is in contrast to using Data Connections, where the SQL Server service must be started for you to add a connection! Please see the next section for information on how to add a SQL Server instance to a server.

Registering a SQL Server Instance

If you haven't registered an instance of SQL Server on the server you've expanded under the Servers node in the Server Explorer, you can do so by right-clicking the SQL Servers node and selecting Register SQL Server Instance from the pop-up menu. This brings up the Register SQL Server Instance dialog box as shown in Figure 13-8.

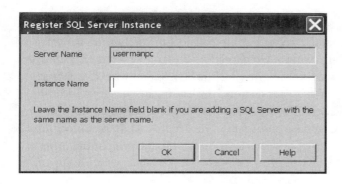

Figure 13-8. Register SQL Server Instance dialog box

In Figure 13-8, you can see the Register SQL Server Instance dialog box, which is used for registering an instance of SQL Server on the selected server. If your SQL Server instance is named the same as your server,[3] all you have to do is click the OK button. However, if you have given it a different name from that of your server, you need to type it in the Instance Name textbox and click OK. This adds the specified SQL Server instance to the SQL Servers node in the Server Explorer.

NOTE Although the registering and unregistering of SQL Server instances looks and feels like the same process in the Enterprise Manager, the two have nothing to do with each other, meaning the actions you perform in the Server Explorer don't show in Enterprise Manager and vice versa.

Unregistering a SQL Server Instance

If you've registered an instance of SQL Server that you no longer need, or if for any other reason you don't want the SQL Server instance to show up under the SQL Servers node in the Server Explorer, you can unregister it by right-clicking the SQL Servers node and selecting Unregister SQL Server Instance from the pop-up menu. Please be aware that you're not required to confirm this action, meaning as soon as you've selected the command from the pop-up menu, the instance is unregistered.

---

3.   For SQL Servers prior to version 2000, the instance name is always the same as the server name.

Creating a SQL Server Database

If you haven't created the database you want to connect to yet, here's a way of doing it. In the Server Explorer window, expand the server on which the SQL Server is running, expand SQL Servers, and right-click the SQL Server where you want to create a database. (Please see the earlier section, "Registering a SQL Server Instance," if your SQL Server instance isn't shown.) This brings up a pop-up menu from which you select the New Database command. The Create Database dialog box appears, as shown in Figure 13-9, and this is where you specify the initial properties for the database.

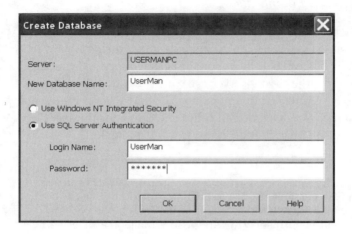

Figure 13-9. Create Database dialog box

If you have ever used the Server Explorer in SQL Server 7.0 or later, you'll probably recognize the content of this dialog box:

- *Server:* This is the name of the server that hosts the SQL Server. If you need to change this, you have to cancel this dialog box and bring up the same dialog box on the required server.

- *New Database Name:* This is the name you want to give your new database. The name must conform to the limitations imposed by the target file system.

- *Use Windows NT Integrated Security:* Select this option if you want to use Windows NT authentication for connecting to the SQL Server. Whatever user you are connected as will be used for authentication on the server that hosts the SQL Server. (I won't be demonstrating the use of this option in this book.)

- *Use SQL Server Authentication:* Select this option if you want to use SQL Server's own authentication. With this option, you have to create a login to use if you are not going to use the system administrator account, sa.

- *Login Name:* This is where you must indicate the name of the login you want to use. This textbox is not enabled if you use Windows NT authentication.

- *Password:* Enter the password that corresponds to the login name. This textbox is not enabled if you use Windows NT authentication.

---

sa

sa is the system administrator login for Microsoft SQL Server. It's generally the only account on SQL Servers used for development purposes. If you log in as sa, you have the rights to perform any valid task, such as creating and deleting databases and users. However, when you test your application, you should always test the database access using the user credentials that your application will be using. It's worth noting that when you install SQL Server, the sa user account has a blank password by default. sa or any other SQL Server login can only be used if your SQL Server setup employs mixed mode authentication, meaning Windows and SQL Server authentication. See your SQL Server documentation for information on user authentication.

I cover connecting to SQL Server databases earlier in this chapter in the "Handling Data Connections" section. When you create a database this way, it has one disadvantage worth noting: If you need to re-create the database, you don't have a script to do it; you need to do it manually again.

Exercise

You might already have created a UserMan database on your SQL Server. However, if you'd like to create a new database, simply follow these instructions on how to fill in the Create Database dialog box:

1. Type or select the name of your server in the Server combo box.

2. Type **Test** in the New Database Name textbox.

3. Select the Use SQL Server Authentication option.

4. Type a login name that has create database privileges in the Login Name textbox.

5. Type the corresponding password for the login account used in Step 4.

6. Click OK to create the new database and have the display refreshed so that it includes the new database. Your display should refresh automatically, but you can refresh it manually by right-clicking the node of the SQL Server node you want to refresh, and clicking the Refresh menu item. Alternatively you can select the desired SQL Server node and click the Refresh menu item in the View menu.

 NOTE   When you create a SQL Server database this way, all the default values for a new database will be used. These values are set on the server. If you want to create a database with non-default values or properties, you must either do so in code using a CREATE DATABASE SQL statement or from the SQL Server Enterprise Manager Microsoft Management Console (MMC) snap-in. Alternatively you can create your database as shown and then change some of the default values, like where the database and/or log files are located, through code using an ALTER DATABASE SQL statement.

You cannot create a file-based database, like a Microsoft Access JET database, using the Server Explorer.[4] For this purpose, you need to use the corresponding

---

4.   There are many other limitations, such as connecting to a MySQL database on a Linux machine, or an Oracle database on a Netware server. Although I have managed to create connections to other DBMSs, such as Oracle, MySQL, and IBM DB2 on Windows, I think it's safe to say that the only truly reliable connection is SQL Server on a Windows server.

front-end tool (Microsoft Access in this case). You can also execute a
CREATE DATABASE SQL statement from code using the appropriate provider
or driver.

Deleting/Dropping a SQL Server Database

You cannot delete or drop a SQL Server database automatically from the Server
Explorer window. You need to do this from the SQL Server Enterprise Manager or
through code using a DROP DATABASE SQL statement.

Exercise

If you created the Test database in the previous exercise, and you want to delete or
drop it again, work through the instructions in the following tip.

TIP   Actually, it's possible to delete or drop a SQL Server database from
the Server Explorer window, if you have the rights to access the master
database and the permissions to drop a database. If you do, you can do
the following:

1. Open a database other than the master database on the server in question.
   This has to be a database in which you have a login name that has the right
   permissions, as just described.

2. Expand the Tables node and right-click a table.

3. Select the Retrieve Data from Table command from the pop-up menu.

4. Click the Show SQL Pane button on the Query Toolbar (check the Tool Tip).

5. Delete the SELECT * SQL statement from the SQL Pane.

6. Type **USE master** and click the Run Query button on the Query toolbar.

7. Click OK in the resulting dialog box.

8. Delete the content of the SQL Pane and type **DROP DATABASE**
   databasename (where *databasename* is the actual name of the
   database you want to delete or drop) and click Run Query.

9. Click OK.

Deleting a Server

If a server becomes obsolete to you, you should delete it from the Server Explorer. There are three ways in which you can delete a server from the current project. First you must select the appropriate node in the tree view, and then do one of the following:

- Press the Delete key.

- Right-click the tree-view node and select the Remove command from the pop-up menu.

- Select the Remove command from the Edit menu.

Looking at Database Projects

A database project is used for storing connections, SQL scripts, and command files (such as those for batching scripts and/or scheduled script execution). Besides this, through a database project you can also use Visual SourceSafe for handling the various versions of your database objects. In other words, a database project is for manipulating your database objects directly!

You can create a database project by following these steps:

1. Select the File/New/Project menu command or press Ctrl+Shift+N. This brings up the New Project dialog box, as shown in Figure 13-10.

2. In the New Project dialog box, expand the Other Projects node and select Database Projects.

3. Give the project a name by typing the name in the Name textbox, and specify the location in the Location textbox.

4. Specify if the new project should be added to the current solution or if the current solution should be closed and a new one created. Select the Add to Solution option or the Close Solution option to specify which you want. Please note that the Add to Solution option and the Close Solution option are only available if you currently have a project open.

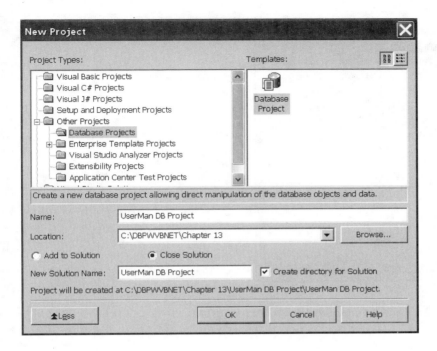

Figure 13-10. The New Project dialog box

Exercise

In the New Project dialog box type **UserMan DB Project** in the Name textbox. Save the project to your hard disk.

5. In the New Solution Name textbox, you can give the solution a different name than that specified in the Name textbox. By default, the name from the Name textbox is assumed and displayed in the New Solution Name textbox. Please note that this textbox is only enabled once you select the Create directory for Solution check box. This check box, which is selected by default, creates a new directory or folder with the name specified for your solution. The New Solution Name textbox and the Create directory for Solution check box are only shown if you click the More button to expand the dialog box. Once expanded, the button caption changes to Less.

6. Click OK. Now the Add Database Reference dialog box appears. This dialog box is shown in Figure 13-11.

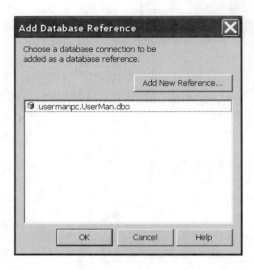

Figure 13-11. The Add Database Reference dialog box

The Add Database Reference dialog box has a list of all the data connections from the Server Explorer; see the "Handling Data Connections" section earlier in this chapter for details. Select the desired data connection. If the database connection you want to reference is not shown on the list, you can add it by clicking Add New Reference. This will bring up the Data Link Properties dialog box, which is described in the "Adding a Data Connection" section earlier in this chapter. Click OK and the new project will now appear in the Solution Explorer.

7. If you need to add more database references to your project, right-click the Database References node in the Solution Explorer and select New Database Reference from the pop-up menu.

NOTE When you add a database reference that doesn't exist under Data Connections in the Server Explorer to a database project, it's automatically added to the Data Connections node.

If you have more than one database reference in your project, you can set one of them to be the default reference. As a result of specifying a default reference, when you create for example a script, the list of tables to add to the script will consist of tables from the default database. In addition, the default database reference is the one used when you run scripts and queries within your project. You can set the default database reference by right-clicking the root project folder and selecting Set Default Reference from the pop-up menu. This brings up the Set Default Reference dialog box, which looks very similar to the Add Database Reference dialog box in Figure 13-11. Select the database you want as your default, and click OK. After you do so, you will notice the Database References node in the Solution Explorer has changed. You can also right-click the desired database reference in the Solution Explorer, and select Set as Project Default from the pop-up menu. The default database reference has a new icon, indicating that it's the default reference.

Creating a Database Project Folder

If you look in the Solution Explorer for a database project (make sure the database project is expanded), you can see that three subfolders have already been created. These folders are used for grouping your database objects as described here:

- The Change Scripts folder is for holding delete and update scripts, and so on.

- The Create Scripts is for creation scripts (tough one to guess, eh?), such as those for creating a database or a table.

- The Queries folder is for scripts that return rows or single/scalar values and the like.

If you need more folders or just want to create your own set of folders for grouping your database objects, then feel free to do so. All you need to do is right-click a database project node in the Solution Explorer and select New Folder from the pop-up menu. The new folder is automatically added to the Solution Explorer. You can give the new folder a meaningful name and create subfolders as you would in any normal file system. Please also note that you can create a default database reference to every folder you have in your project, which means you can make more than one folder for create scripts or change scripts or any other kind of folder. The point is that you can then have a folder for each of these categories for each of the different database connections in your project.

TIP Although you can group your database objects any way you want, following a commonsense folder-naming scheme, like the one used for the default folders, and making sure that the database objects are placed in the appropriate folders is the best approach. This will make it a lot easier to find a specific database object, and obviously it will also make it easier to create command files that only contain scripts from one folder.

Deleting a Database Project Folder

You can delete folders as well as you can create them for your database objects. You do this by right-clicking the folder you want to delete, selecting Remove from the pop-up menu, and confirming the deletion of the folder. Actually, you can choose to just remove the folder from the project or to delete the folder from your hard disk as well as remove it from the project.

CAUTION You have to be careful when you delete a folder, because all database objects in the folder will be deleted as well.

Adding Database Objects to a Database Project

You can add both new and existing database objects to your database project. See the following sections for information on how to do either task.

Adding New Database Objects

If you want to add a new database object to any of the folders in a project, including the project root folder, right-click the desired folder and select Add New Item from the pop-up menu. Actually, there are other options for this purpose on the pop-up menu, but the Add New Item command covers both the Add SQL Script and Add Query commands. After you make the selection, the Add New Item dialog box pops up (see Figure 13-12).

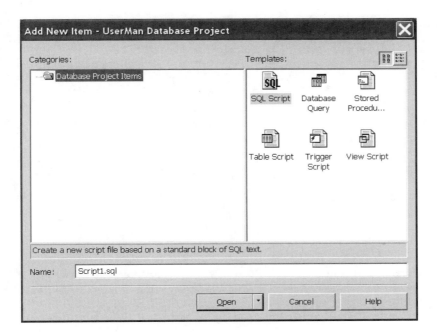

Figure 13-12. The Add New Item dialog box

As you can see from Figure 13-12, there are a few different database objects that can be added to your database project. When you add a new database object to your project, it must be based on a template. Available templates are shown in the right-hand pane of the Add New Item dialog box. Except for the Database Query template, they all open up the SQL Editor for editing once you click Open. (See the "Script Editing Using the SQL Editor" section later in this chapter for more information on how to use this feature.) If you create a new database object based on the Database Query template, the Query Designer is opened once you click Open. (See the "Designing Queries with the Query Designer" section later in this chapter for more information on how to use the Query Designer.)

The Query Designer and the SQL Editor overlap in a few areas when it comes to creating scripts or queries. What I mean is that some things can be achieved by using either of the two, and which one you choose is simply a matter of preference. The Query Designer, with its drag-and-drop features, is easier to use, whereas you can perform more complex tasks using the SQL Editor. Table 13-1 lists the templates available and describes which template is best for creating certain database objects as well as which tool to use.

Table 13-1. Database Object Templates

Template Name	Default Tool	Description
Database Query	Query Designer	Use a database query for creating row-returning queries, delete and update queries, make/create table queries, and insert queries. You can use the SQL Editor for this purpose as well, but the Query Designer is perfectly designed for this task. It's much simpler because of its query grid and the drag-and-drop features.
SQL Script	SQL Editor	You should use the SQL Script template when you want to create a script that isn't covered by any of the other templates.
Stored Procedure Script	SQL Editor	Use the Stored Procedure template to create stored procedures for fast server-side processing of repeating queries or functions. See Chapter 16 for more information on stored procedures.
Table Script	SQL Editor	Use the Table Script template to make CREATE TABLE SQL scripts. Personally, I think it's easier to use the Query Designer for this purpose, but sometimes you might add an existing create table script and then you can use the SQL Editor to edit it. It's your call.
Trigger Script	SQL Editor	The Trigger Script template should be used to create triggers for server-side processing or validation of data manipulation. See Chapter 18 for more information on triggers.
View Script	SQL Editor	The View Script template should be used for creating views that make row-returning queries faster. See Chapter 17 for more information on views.

Running Scripts in the IDE

Once you have a created a script, like the Create UserMan database script from the UserMan database project, you can actually test it in the IDE. Right-click the script in the Solution Explorer and select Run from the pop-up menu. This will execute the script on the default database. If you want to execute the script on a different database, select Run On from the aforementioned pop-up menu. This brings up the Run On dialog box, as shown in Figure 13-13.

Figure 13-13. The Run On dialog box

The Run On dialog box is quite similar to the Add Database Reference dialog box in Figure 13-11, but with one exception, the temporary reference (represented by <temporary reference>). You can use this temporary reference to create a temporary database connection, which is only created for running the script and is destroyed as soon as the script ends. This is ideal for dial-up connections, which you don't want the IDE to keep open after running the script.

Once you have selected the reference you require, click OK to run the script on the selected reference.

Adding a Command File

If you want to execute several scripts at a time, it's a good idea to put them all in a single command file, (which is a Windows file with the *.cmd extension). This way you can execute a batch of scripts at any time by executing the command file. Actually, since a command file can be executed at the command line, it's also a good candidate for scheduled execution. This means that it even makes sense to put one script in a command file.

You create a command file by right-clicking the folder in the Solution Explorer in which you want the command file to be placed. The Create Command File dialog box appears after you select Create Command File from the pop-up menu (see Figure 13-14).

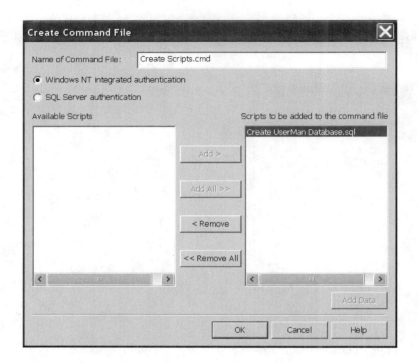

Figure 13-14. The Create Command File dialog box

In the Create Command File dialog box you can give the command file a name and choose which scripts should be part of the command file. The scripts listed under Available Scripts are taken from the folder in which you are creating the command file. You cannot select scripts from folders other than subfolders. This is one reason why it's so important to organize your scripts in the correct folders. (This goes for queries as well!)

The last thing you need to do is to choose if you want to use Windows NT authentication or SQL Server authentication. If you choose Windows NT authentication, the scripts will be executed with the permissions of the logged-in user or the user account assigned to the scheduler service. However, if you choose SQL Server authentication, you must provide the login name and password at the command prompt when you execute the script. Click OK when you're done, and the command file is placed in the folder you right-clicked when you first began creating the file.

When you execute the command file, you need to supply the name of the server and the name of the database, like this:

```
CommandFileName.cmd ServerName DatabaseName
```

Adding Existing Database Objects

If you have already created one or more of the database objects that you want to add to your project, all you have to do is add them using the pop-up menu. Right-click the folder you want to add the object to, and select Add Existing Item from the pop-up menu. This brings up the Add Existing Item dialog box, in which you can browse and select the database objects. You can select more than one database object from the same folder at one time by holding down the Ctrl key when clicking the objects you want. Click Open once you have selected the desired object(s). The selected objects are added to your project immediately and shown in the updated Solution Explorer window.

NOTE   There's no validation of the existing items you add to your project, so it's up to you to add the correct types of database objects.

Designing Databases with Visio for Enterprise Architect

The Enterprise Architect edition of VS .NET comes with Visio for VS .NET. This stand-alone tool can be used for modeling and documenting your application and database using the Unified Modeling Language (UML). Figure 13-15 shows you a reverse-engineered Visio database model diagram of the UserMan database. Visio is a great tool for creating and documenting your databases, but you can also use it for reverse-engineering an existing database and updating it from a Visio document.

However, database design using UML and Visio is really beyond the scope of an intermediate reader and as such isn't covered in this book; but do look for the following book, if you want to get involved with UML and Visio.

Enterprise Development with VS .NET, UML, and MSF, by Carsten Thomsen and John Erik Hansen. Apress, January 2003. ISBN: 1-59059-042-2.

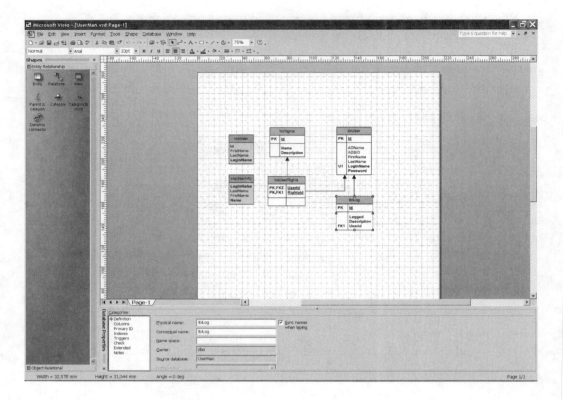

Figure 13-15. A Visio database model diagram

You can find more information about this title here:

`http://www.apress.com/book/bookDisplay.html?bID=105`.

The rest of this chapter exclusively covers how to work with databases from within the VS .NET IDE.

Designing Databases with the Database Designer

The Database Designer is a visual tool for designing your SQL Server and Oracle databases. Unfortunately, this tool can't be used to create databases in any other databases than the ones mentioned. You can use it for creating tables, including columns, keys, indexes, constraints, and relationships between tables. The Database Designer creates a diagram through which you can visualize your database objects as you add and manipulate them. The database diagram depicts the database graphically, showing the database structure. This means that a database diagram can only hold database objects from one database. In other words, you can have several diagrams in one database, but only one database in any diagram.

Creating a Database Diagram

The *database diagram* is a visual tool for creating your database. You can add or create tables, add relationships between tables, and perform just about all the tasks you normally would when you design your database. You can create a database diagram from the Server Explorer. Expand the Data Connections node and the database for which you want to create the diagram. Right-click the Database Diagrams node and select New Diagram from the pop-up menu. This brings up the Add Table dialog box, as shown in Figure 13-16. In this dialog box you can select the tables from the database that you want on the diagram. Select the desired table(s) and click Add. Click Close to close the dialog box and continue with the diagram.

 NOTE Database diagrams are NOT available for Microsoft Access (JET Engine), MySQL, or DB2 databases, only for SQL Server and Oracle databases!

Exercise

Create a new database diagram and add all the tables in the UserMan database that start with tbl.

Figure 13-16. The Add Table dialog box

When the diagram opens, the tables you selected are automatically added to the diagram, and if you have set up relations between any of the tables, they are automatically shown as well (see Figure 13-17).

In Figure 13-17 you can see the diagram for the UserMan database. There are four tables, all named as indicated at the top of each table box:

- tblUser

- tblRights

- tblUserRights

- tblLog

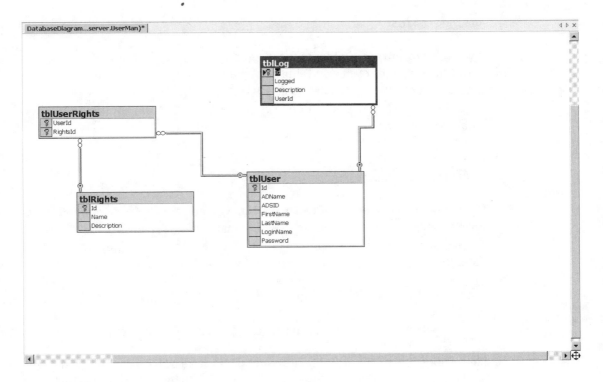

Figure 13-17. A database diagram

The columns of each table are shown below the table name, meaning UserId and RightsId are the columns of the tblUserRights table. The tables are related, and you can see the relationships displayed in Figure 13-17 as the lines connecting the tables. These lines are solid, indicating that the DBMS enforces referential integrity (see Chapter 2 for more information about referential integrity). If a line is dotted, it means that referential integrity isn't enforced for that particular relationship. The parent table for the relationship is the table with the key as an endpoint, and the child table is the one with the figure eight on its side (∞) as an endpoint. All the relationships in the UserMan database are one-to-many relationships (key-∞). The primary key field(s) in each table is marked with a key in the left-hand column of each table.

Adding Tables

If you need to add more tables to the diagram, you can right-click any blank space in the diagram and select Add Table from the pop-up menu. This brings up the Add Table dialog box shown in Figure 13-16. Select the tables you want on the diagram and click Add. Click Close to close the dialog box and continue with the database diagram.

Deleting and Removing Tables

If you have added a table to the diagram that you don't really need, all you have to do is remove it. Well, there's more to it than that, because removing a table from the diagram is one thing, deleting a table from the database is a completely different story. Here is what you do to remove a table from a diagram:

1. Right-click the table in question.

2. Select Remove Table from Diagram from the pop-up menu.

Please note that no confirmation is required for this task! If on the other hand you actually want to delete the table from the database, then this is how you do it:

1. Right-click the table in question.

2. Select Delete Table from Database from the pop-up menu.

3. Click Yes in the confirmation dialog box.

Creating a New Table

If you haven't already created the table you want to add to the database diagram, you can create it from within the diagram. Right-click any blank space on the diagram and select New Table from the pop-up menu. This brings up the Choose Name dialog box in which you need to enter the name of the new table. Click OK when done entering the name. When you have entered the name and clicked OK, the new table is displayed on the database diagram.

For each field, or column, in the new table you can specify a column name, data type, and length, and indicate whether the column allows Null values. So to add a new column, simply fill in these attributes as appropriate under Column Name, Data Type, Length, and Allows Nulls, and move to the next row (see Figure 13-18).

I know this may seem a little weird and confusing, what with the columns that make up a table being represented as rows in this table design view, but just hang in there, and you'll get it eventually

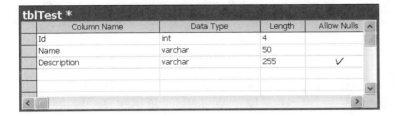

Figure 13-18. Column attributes.

Exercise

Fill in the column attributes as shown in Figure 13-18 and press Ctrl+S to save the table and diagram.

One of the first things you may notice is that the Data Type Column attribute is DBMS specific. This means the drop-down list of data types is filled with valid data types for the database the diagram is created in.

Once you are done entering the columns and the column attributes, press Ctrl+S to save the diagram and to create the new table. Although it's convenient to create and edit tables with the Database Designer database diagram, it can be of greater help to use the Table Designer. See the "Using the Table Designer" section later in this chapter for more information.

Adding Relationships

Relationships are used for indicating relations between data in different tables. Once you have created your tables, all you need to do is create relationships by dragging a field from a table to the related field in another table. This brings up the Create Relationship dialog box, where you can define your relationship. In Figure 13-17, you can see the relationships between the tables in the UserMan database as the lines or links connecting the tables on the database diagram.

CROSS-REFERENCE See Chapter 2 for a more detailed description of relationships.

Deleting Relationships

If a relationship has become obsolete for some reason, you can delete it by right-clicking the relationship and selecting Delete Relationship from Database from the resulting pop-up menu. You are required to confirm this deletion. As with all other changes you make to the database diagram, the deletion isn't saved to the database until you save the diagram.

Editing Database Properties

If you need to change the properties of the database, such as the keys of a table or the relationship between two tables, you simply right-click any table or relationship and select Property Pages from the pop-up menu. This brings up the Property Pages dialog box, where you can edit the owner, keys, indexes, and constraints of a table and the relationships between tables.

Database Diagram Overview

I am sure you have had the same problems as me in previous versions of Microsoft database tools: Once you have added many tables to a diagram, it's nearly impossible to get the full overview of the diagram. Well, there are actually a few features available to help you:

- *Zoom in to view just one table or so, or zoom out to view the entire diagram*: You can zoom using the shortcut menu; right-click any blank space on the diagram, select Zoom from the pop-up menu, and specify the percentage you want to zoom to. The current zoom percentage is checked on the menu if you have previously changed the zoom percentage. One command on the Zoom submenu is of special interest: the To Fit command. This command will automatically choose the zoom percentage that will let you view the entire database diagram in the current view.

- *Move the view port, or rather change the viewable area of the diagram:* Locate the view port icon in the lower-right corner of the diagram (see Figure 13-19). If you click the view port icon, you can see the entire diagram in the overview window, as shown in Figure 13-20. If you hold down the left mouse button, you can move the view port around the diagram. The view port is the dotted rectangle you can see in the middle of the overview window when you first click the view port icon.

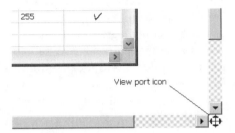

Figure 13-19. The database diagram view port icon

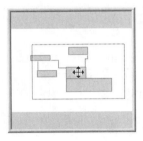

Figure 13-20. The database diagram overview window

Exercise

Zoom the database diagram to 200% and click the view port icon. Hold down the left mouse button and move the view port around the database diagram. Once you have selected the right area of the diagram, let go of the mouse button. Now the area of the database diagram you can see should be the same as the one you just selected using the overview window.

- *Arrange all tables so that related tables sit together nice and orderly:* Right-click any blank space on the diagram, and select Arrange Tables from the pop-up menu.

- *Show relationship names:* Right-click any blank space on the diagram, and select Show Relationship Labels from the pop-up menu. This will display a name label next to the relationship.

- *Add descriptive free text labels to the diagram:* Right-click any blank space on the diagram, and then select New Text Annotation from the pop-up menu. This will open a text field where you right-clicked the diagram. When you have finished typing your text, you simply click any other part of the diagram to finish editing the text annotation. Use these text annotations to add descriptive text that makes your diagram easier to read. These text annotations are NOT part of the database in any way. If you need to edit an existing text annotation, just click the text on the diagram, and the text field opens up for editing.

- *Change the table view:* If you want to see more or fewer table attributes than what is displayed, you can select the table(s) in question and right-click one of the selected tables. Next, select Table View from the pop-up menu and click the desired view in the submenu. Standard view is very useful when designing a database, whereas the Column Names view is good as an overview.

- *Automatically size the tables:* If the size of one or more tables doesn't fit the number of rows and/or columns, you can select the table(s) in question, right-click one of the selected tables, and then click Autosize Selected Tables from the pop-up menu.

Saving the Database Diagram

When you have the database diagram open, you can press Ctrl+S any time to save the diagram. The diagram is validated before it's saved to the database. If any existing data violates any new relationships and/or constraints, the diagram cannot be saved.[5] A dialog box detailing the error will appear. You will have to correct the error before you can save the diagram and thus save the changes to the database. Although the diagram can be seen under the Diagram node in the Server Explorer, it isn't actually an object on its own. The diagram is saved to the system table dtproperties in your database. This table doesn't show up under the Tables node in the Server Explorer, but you can see it using the Enterprise Manager that comes with SQL Server. Don't try to edit this table manually, only through the diagram itself. If you try to edit it manually, you might end up destroying other diagrams and objects in the database.

Using the Table Designer

The Table Designer is by far the most comprehensive tool for creating a new table in a database. Although you can use the Database Designer to add a new table to a diagram and thus the database, you have a much better overview of a table when you use the Table Designer. However, there's nothing stopping you from creating the initial database, including all the tables in a database diagram, and then editing the table design of each of the tables individually in the Table Designer afterward.

To create a new table using the Table Designer, you must open up Server Explorer; expand the desired database, and right-click the Tables node in this database. Selecting New Table from the pop-up menu brings up the Table Designer, as shown in Figure 13-21.

At first the Table Designer looks similar to the table view you see when you use the New Table feature of the Database Designer (see the "Adding Tables" section earlier in this chapter), but it's a little more sophisticated.

---

5. This means that you have to either change the relationship to accommodate the existing data, which is most often the solution, or alternatively change/delete the conflicting data. In some cases, changing or deleting existing data is the right solution, because the data should never have been added to the table, as it's invalid.

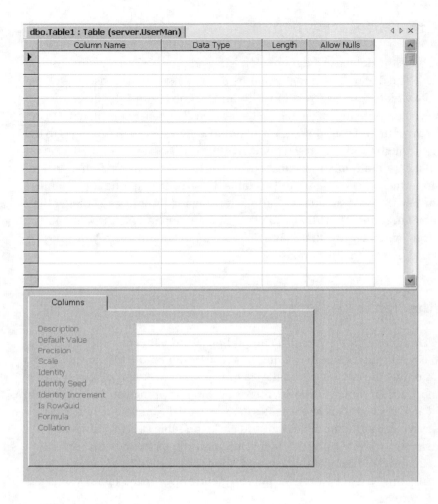

Figure 13-21. The Table Designer

Adding Columns

To add a new column to your table, you simply type the name of the column in the Column Name column. The Data Type attribute must also be filled in with the desired data type for the column. Please note that the data types in the drop-down list box are DBMS specific, which means that the list only contains data types that are valid for the database you are connected to. The Length attribute is also required when you specify a data type that can have varying lengths such as the **varchar** data type of SQL Server. The Allow Nulls attribute is always checked by default when you create a new column (by typing in the name of the column). If a column allows Null values, it cannot be a key field, so be sure you clear this attribute for your key field before you start adding data to a table, as it can be quite hard to change this attribute afterwards.

What I've described so far is pretty much the same as using the Database Designer to add a new table. Here is the big difference: the Columns attributes pane at the bottom of the Table Designer[6] (see Figure 13-21). The Columns attributes pane varies depending on the database to which you are connected. In the case of Figure 13-21, I am using SQL Server 2000. Some attributes are the same, however, as is the case with the following:

- *Description:* Use this attribute to add a description of the column, such as what kind of values it holds. This can be very valuable to someone taking over your database at a later stage in the life of the database or even valuable to yourself when working on a large project.

- *Default Value:* This value is used for specifying a value that will be saved with rows that don't contain a value for this particular column. This can be used in place of allowing Null values, which can be hard to handle from code.

Setting the Primary Key

You can set the primary key by right-clicking the grid next to the Column Name column for the column you want to have as the primary key. See the "What Is a Primary Key?" section in Chapter 2 for more information about primary keys. Next, click Set Primary Key to set the column as the primary key (see Figure 13-22). If you need to have a composite primary key, then you have to select all the columns that make up the primary key before you right-click the grid next to the Column Name column. You can select several columns the same way you would select multiple items on a list, that is, by holding down Ctrl when selecting the columns one by one. If the columns are contiguous, you can select the first column, and then hold down the Shift key and select the last column before you right-click the grid next to the Column Name column.

---

6. The Columns attributes pane can be accessed from within a database diagram, however, if you open the Properties dialog box for a table on the diagram.

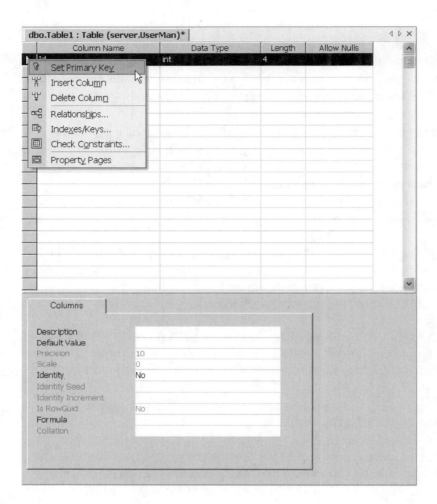

Figure 13-22. Setting the primary key

Adding Indexes and Keys

It's often a good idea to create an index on a column that is used for searching a table. See the "What Is an Index?" section in Chapter 2 for more information about indexes. You can create an index by right-clicking anywhere on the table grid in the Table Designer and selecting Indexes/Keys from the pop-up menu. This brings up the Property Pages dialog box with the Indexes/Keys tab shown (see Figure 13-23). Please note that the tab looks different if you have already created an index and/or primary key. The Selected Index list box in this case is then populated and one of the existing indexes is selected. Another thing to observe is that the content of this tab is also DBMS specific, so it changes depending on the database you are connected to. The Indexes/Keys tab in Figure 13-23 shows a connection to a SQL Server database.

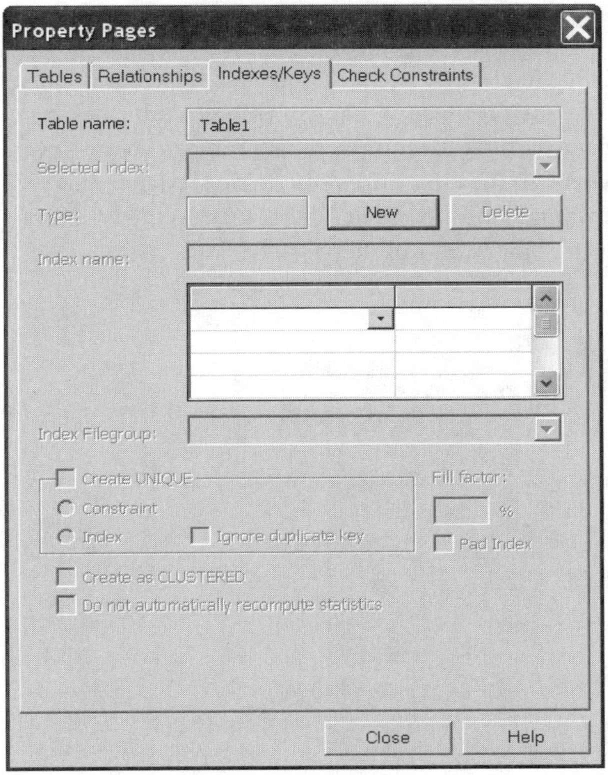

Figure 13-23. The Indexes/Keys tab of the Property Pages dialog box

To create a new index, you click the New button. This enables some of the text-boxes and check boxes on the tab. Start out by giving your index a name in the Index name textbox, and then add the columns that make up the index in the grid below the Index name textbox. For each column you add to the grid, you must specify if the sorting order is ascending or descending. This obviously depends on the data in the index and how it will be searched. The other options shown in Figure 13-23 are SQL Server specific, and I recommend you read the help files for SQL Server, if you are in doubt about these options. Once you click Close, the index is saved. Well, this is not quite true, as it's only saved to memory. This means the index won't be saved to the database until you save the diagram. Just to avoid confusion any more than necessary, only the primary key is designated as a key. So if you want to add a foreign key to use in a relationship, you just add an index to the column(s) in question.

Adding Constraints

Sometimes the values in a particular column in your table must be in a particular range. If so, it's a good idea to create a constraint that will enforce your rules, or ensure that the values are indeed within the required range. You can create a constraint by right-clicking anywhere on the table grid in the Table Designer and selecting Check Constraints from the pop-up menu. This brings up the Property Pages dialog box with the Check Constraints tab shown (see Figure 13-24).

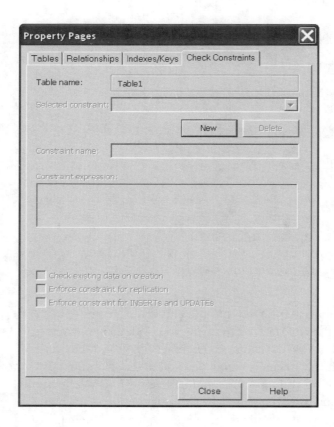

Figure 13-24. The Check Constraints tab of the Property Pages dialog box

To create a new constraint, click the New button. This enables some of the textboxes and check boxes on the tab. Start out by giving your constraint a name in the Constraint name textbox, and then type the constraint expression in the Constraint expression textbox. Here's an example of a constraint:

```
Test <> ''
```

This means the field Test cannot hold an empty string. Following is a description of the check box options on the tab:

- *Check existing data on creation:* When the table is saved, any existing data is validated to see if it conflicts with the constraint. Unlike an index, it's possible to have values in a table that don't conform to a column constraint.

- *Enforce constraint for replication:* This option enforces the constraint when the table is replicated to another database.

- *Enforce constraint for INSERTs and UPDATEs:* This option enforces the constraint when data is inserted or updated. This means that an insert or update will fail if it doesn't conform to the constraint.

The constraint is saved to memory when you click Close. Constraints are a good option when you work with column-level integrity, more commonly known as domain integrity. However, business rules, which can be enforced by constraints, can also be enforced by triggers. A *trigger* is really a special kind of stored procedure that is automatically invoked, just like a constraint. See Chapters 16 and 18 for more information about stored procedures and triggers. A trigger can perform any task that a constraint can and more. However, there is more overhead in invoking a trigger, so basically if your business rule can be enforced using a constraint, you should use a constraint. If not, look into using a trigger.

One advantage a trigger has over a constraint is that it can compare or validate a value in a row against a value in a column located in a different table. It's fair to state that a trigger can contain more complex logic than a constraint.

Creating a Relationship

Although the Table Designer should be the preferred tool for creating a table, it's not the easiest way to create a relationship. Once you have created your tables using the Table Designer, you should open up a database diagram and use the Database Designer to create your relationships. For information on how to do this, see the "Adding Relationships" section earlier in this chapter.

Designing Queries with the Query Designer

The Query Designer is to queries what the Table Designer is to tables, a visual tool that makes it easy to create your queries. This should be your preferred tool for creating even the simplest of queries, because it has drag-and-drop features as well as a text pane in which you can type your query manually. Here is how you create a simple select query in the UserMan example database (if you are uncertain on how to perform the following tasks, please see the "Adding New Database Objects" section earlier in this chapter):

1. Open up the UserMan database project if it isn't already open in the IDE.

2. Add a new query named Select Users.

3. Add the tblUser table to the query.

The Query Designer should now look like Figure 13-25. The top part where the table is placed is called the Diagram pane. The part beneath this is called the Grid pane, followed by a pane displaying free text, which is called the SQL pane. The Results pane resides in the bottom part of the designer.

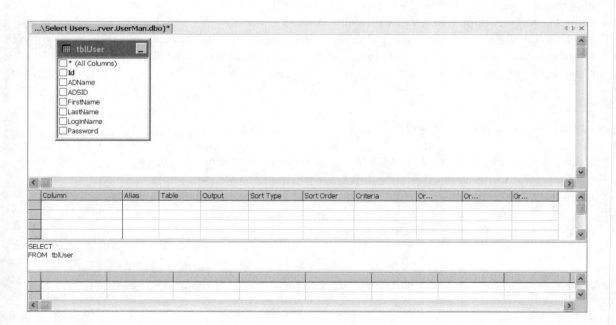

Figure 13-25. The Query Designer

Taking a Closer Look at the Query Designer Panes

As mentioned in the preceding section, there are four panes in the Query Designer:

- Diagram pane

- Grid pane

- SQL pane

- Results pane

These panes all have a function to perform, but with the exception of the Results pane, they overlap in functionality. The Diagram, Grid, and SQL panes allow successively greater complexity in the query, though they overlap in functionality for very simple queries, and if you look at the other two panes when you edit one pane, you will find that these three panes stay synchronized. I guess it's really a matter of preference which pane you use. See the following sections on what each of the panes can do for you.

The Diagram Pane

The Diagram pane, which is the top part of the Query Designer, is where you add and show the tables used in the query. You can add tables by dragging them from the Server Explorer, or by right-clicking anywhere in the Diagram pane and selecting Add Table from the pop-up menu. For each table in the Diagram pane, you can select which columns are parts of the query. This is done by checking the check box next to the column name. If you want all rows output, simply check the option * (All Columns). You can also right-click the table, choose Select All Columns on the pop-up menu, and toggle the check marks by pressing the Space key.

 CAUTION If you check all the columns in a table as well as the option * (All Columns), you will get all the rows as output of your query twice.

Removing Tables

Right-click a table and select Remove from the pop-up menu to remove the table from the Diagram pane. The number of tables allowed in the Diagram pane depends on the query type. A SELECT, Make Table, and INSERT Results query can hold any number of tables, whereas the UPDATE, DELETE, and INSERT VALUES queries can only hold one table. If the tables in the Diagram pane are related or if there are relationships between any two of the tables, they are shown on the diagram. However, you can't change or delete the relationships in the Query Designer. Actually, this is not quite true. If any two tables have an inner or outer join, and you remove this join from the Diagram pane, the join is changed to a cross-join. A cross-join outputs all selected columns from the tables in question in all possible combinations. In other words, you cannot delete a join/relationship between two tables using the Diagram pane. You only change the join in the Diagram pane to affect how the query will behave, and not in the database itself. You need to use the Table Designer or the Database Designer if you want to change a relationship between two tables.

Changing the Join Type

You can also change the join type by right-clicking the join and selecting Property Pages from the pop-up menu. In the Property Pages dialog box you can change the join to include all rows from one or both of the joined tables or simply just the selected columns in the tables. This is also called a LEFT OUTER JOIN or RIGHT OUTER JOIN, FULL OUTER JOIN or INNER JOIN. In addition, you can change the way the tables are joined by changing the column comparison symbol to one of the following: = (equal to), <> (not equal to), < (less than), <= (less than or equal to), > (greater than), or >= (greater than or equal to). I am of course talking about the column in each table that is used for joining the tables. When the Property Pages dialog box is not shown, you can see from the join itself how the tables are joined. In the middle you can see the comparison sign, and if the join is an OUTER JOIN, a box is added to the diamond shape. See Figure 13-26 for examples of the various combinations of diamond and rectangle shapes that represent joins.

Figure 13-26. Various join types depicted in the Diagram pane

The four join shapes in Figure 13-26 depict the following, from left to right:

Full Outer Join, joining columns not equal

Full Outer Join, joining columns equal

Left Outer Join, joining columns equal

Inner Join, joining columns equal

Besides the joins mentioned, there is also the cross-join, which is when you have every single row in the left table combined with all rows in the right table. Basically, this means that the result of a cross-join, also called the Cartesian product, is the number of rows in the left table multiplied by the number of rows in the right table.

If you have many tables in the Diagram pane, then you can choose to show only the name of a table and thus save some real estate onscreen for more tables. This is done by right-clicking the table and selecting Name Only from the pop-up menu. Right-click the table and click Column Names to show the full table again.

Grouping and Sorting the Output

The output can be sorted (ordered) and grouped as in any normal SQL statement using the Diagram pane. Sorting the columns is done by right-clicking the column in a table and selecting Sort Ascending or Sort Descending. A sort symbol is placed next to the column name when you want output sorted by a specific column. You can cancel the sorting by right-clicking the column in the table and clicking the checked sort order.

Grouping is done nearly the same way as sorting, except you need to click the Group By button on the Query toolbar first. In Figure 13-27 the Group By button is the second from the right. Once the Group By button is pressed, you can select the columns you want to group by. When a column is part of the output grouping, a grouping symbol like the one the Group By button displays is placed to the far right of the column name. You can remove a grouping by pressing the Group By button again. Please note that the grouping is done in the order you select the columns. As in any SQL query, at least all output columns must be part of the grouping.

Figure 13-27. The query toolbar

If you are in doubt about how to create a SQL statement in the SQL pane, then using the Diagram pane is a good way to learn, because you can see what effect a change in the Diagram pane has on the corresponding SQL statement in the SQL pane.

The Grid Pane

Recall that the Grid pane allows you to make the same changes as in the Diagram pane and the SQL pane. However, there is one difference to the Grid pane:

You cannot add tables to it. So in order to add tables to the query, you must use the functionality of the Diagram pane or the SQL pane. Okay, when I say the functionality isn't there, I mean there is no pop-up menu with an Add Table command for the Grid pane, but you can actually use the Add Table command on the Query menu to add a table.

 NOTE When you enter data in the various columns, the data is validated, or verified, as soon as you move to another row or column.

The Grid pane holds a number of named columns (what a surprise, eh?), and in Table 13-2 you can see a description of each these named columns. Please note that not all columns are visible for all the different query types. Check the Valid Query Types column to see if the column is valid for a particular query.

Table 13-2. Grid Pane Columns Explained

Column Name	Valid Query Types	Description
Column	All query types	This is the name of the column in the table referenced in the Table column.
Alias	SELECT, INSERT Results, and Make Table	If you give a column an alias, the alias is what the output column will be named. Use the Alias column to give your output a more descriptive name. Aliases are also used for computed columns, or when including the same column twice for whatever reason. This is the same as the AS SQL clause in the SQL pane.
Table	SELECT, INSERT Results, UPDATE, DELETE, and Make Table	This is where you select the name of the table into which your column is placed. You can only select tables from the drop-down list. If you need to add more tables, use the Add Table command on the Query menu. If the column is computed, this column should be left blank.
Output	SELECT, INSERT Results, and Make Table	This column indicates if the column is to be output as part of the result.
Sort Type	SELECT, INSERT Results, and Make Table	If you leave this column empty, the output is not sorted. To specify a sort order, choose Ascending or Descending from the drop-down list. This is the same as the ORDER BY clause in the SQL pane, ASC for ascending or DESC for descending.

Table 13-2. Grid Pane Columns Explained (Continued)

Column Name	Valid Query Types	Description
Sort Order	SELECT, INSERT Results, and Make Table	This is where you specify in which order the columns are sorted, if you want to sort by more than one column. The columns will be sorted first by the column starting with 1, and then by the column with number 2, and so on. This is the same as the list of columns following the ORDER BY clause in the SQL pane.
Group By	SELECT, INSERT Results, and Make Table	This is the same as the GROUP BY clause in the SQL pane.
Criteria	SELECT, INSERT Results, UPDATE, DELETE, and Make Table	You don't specify the column name, because you add the criteria to the row with the correct table column. If you need to add more than one criteria using the Or operator, you put each criteria in a separate Or . . . column. If you need to add criteria using the And operator, you do it in the same column, like this: > 1 AND < 5. This means that the result set will hold rows where the column (indicated in the Column Name column) is greater than 1 and less than 5. Sub-SELECT statements also show in this column.
Or . . .	SELECT, INSERT Results, UPDATE, DELETE, and Make Table	This is for adding more than one criterion. You just keep adding one criterion in each of the Or . . . columns until you have added all your criteria for that table.
Append	INSERT Results	This is for appending the results of a row-returning query to an existing table. The result value in the Column column is appended to the column named in the Append column in the destination table. Normally this column is filled out by the Query Designer, if it's able to figure out what destination column matches the source column (Column).
New Value	UPDATE and INSERT VALUES	This dictates the new value for the column specified in the Column column. The new value can be an expression that will be evaluated or a literal value.

If you are in doubt about how to create a SQL statement in the SQL pane, then the grid pane is a good way to learn, because you can see what effect a change in the Grid pane has on the corresponding SQL statement in the SQL pane. Live and learn . . .

The SQL Pane

The SQL pane is for entering your queries in free text based on the SQL standard for the database to which you are connected. Most relational databases these days rely on the ANSI SQL standard as the base with added functionality. I am not going into details about the SQL standards, as that is a subject for a whole book on its own. If you need specifics on one dialect of a SQL standard, I can only recommend you read the help files and/or documentation that come with your database, or alternatively buy yourself a copy of a book that covers the subject. However, there are also a number of online tutorials on the subject, and here are URLs to some of them:

- http://ioc.unesco.org/oceanteacher/resourcekit/Module2/Database/DBMS/Sql/sql.html

- http://spectral.mscs.mu.edu/javadev/databases/sqltut.html

- http://www.sqlcourse.com/

You can do anything in the SQL pane that you can do in the Grid and Diagram panes. One major difference though is that you need to verify the SQL syntax before these other two panes are updated based on the contents of the SQL pane. (See the "Verifying the SQL Syntax" section later in this chapter for details.) Actually, you can also move to either the Diagram or Grid pane in order to accomplish an update of these panes, but it's not verified as such. You can type the name of an invalid column in a SELECT statement, and this will be shown in the Grid pane. So use the Verify SQL Syntax facility frequently when you are editing your queries using the SQL pane. It will save you a lot of hassle.

The Results Pane

The Results pane is quite different from the other three panes in the Query Designer, because it's not intended for editing your query. As the name implies, it's simply an output window. The Results pane is only for row-returning queries, such as SELECT queries and scalar queries with aggregate functions like SELECT COUNT(*) FROM TableName.

In the case of a row-returning query, other than a GROUP BY query, if such a query has returned rows from a single table, it's actually possible to use the Results pane to add new rows to the source table. If you are familiar with Microsoft Access or SQL Server's Query Analyzer, then you probably recognize the grid in the Results pane, and you also know that you can add a new row by typing the column values in the last row in the grid (the one marked with an asterisk). If you want to edit the values returned by the query, you can do so by typing the new value in the desired column. Once you have entered the column values, you simply move to another row, and the Query Designer will try to update the database immediately. If an error occurs when updating, a message box will be displayed, detailing the error. Once you click OK, the cursor is placed in the row in the grid where the error occurred.

Hiding and Showing the Various Panes

All the panes can be hidden, but at least one of the panes has to be visible when the Query Designer is shown. A pane can be hidden by right-clicking the pane and selecting Hide Pane from the pop-up menu. Actually, you can also hide the panes using the Query toolbar shown in Figure 13-27, which appears by default when you open the Query Designer. If the toolbar isn't showing, you can use one of the menu commands in the View ➤ Panes menu. The first four buttons from the left on the toolbar are for hiding and showing the Query Designer panes. The tool tips help you figure out which button does what; to view a tool tip, position the mouse pointer over a button and keep it there for a little while. These buttons are the only way you can show a pane once it's hidden—you cannot use a command on a pop-up menu to show a pane as you can to hide it.

Verifying the SQL Syntax

If you want to make sure that your query is valid, you can use the Verify SQL Syntax facility. This is only necessary if you are using the SQL pane to edit your query, as the other panes automatically verify your changes. You can perform the task by clicking the Verify SQL Syntax button on the Query toolbar or by clicking Verify SQL Syntax on the Query menu. Alternatively, you can right-click the SQL pane and select Verify SQL Syntax from the pop-up menu. A message box appears when the query has been validated. It simply tells you that your query is valid or that your query needs to be changed according to the explanation shown in the message box.

Typical errors are typos, like in Figure 13-28. If your query is invalid, you may get more information by clicking the Help button in the message box displayed in Figure 13-29.

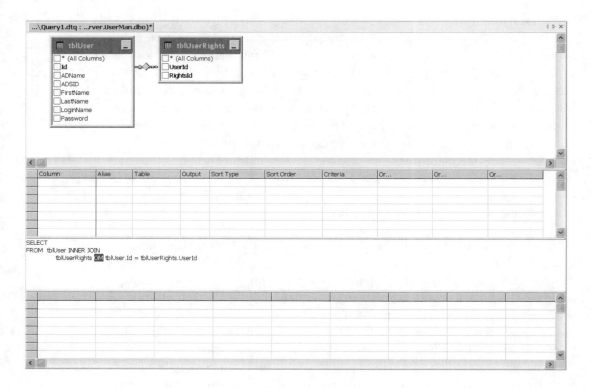

Figure 13-28. A typo makes this invalid SQL script.

Figure 13-29. Error message dialog box with Help button

Executing a Query

When you have finished building your query, you might want to execute it. You can execute, or run, your query by clicking the Run Query button on the Query toolbar, by clicking the Run command on the Query menu, or by right-clicking a blank space in the Diagram pane and selecting Run from the pop-up menu.

CAUTION Queries cannot be undone, so if you are deleting rows from one or more tables, make sure they are expendable!

The query won't execute if the SQL syntax in the SQL pane is invalid. If you are uncertain if your query is correct, then try verifying the syntax before you run the query. See the "Verifying the SQL Syntax" section earlier in this chapter for details.

Examining the Various Query Types

By default, the query created is a SELECT query, but you can change the query type by clicking the Change Type button on the Query toolbar. You can also change the query type using the Change Type command on the Query menu. In the following sections you will find a short description and example (in the form of SQL statement queries) of all the query types offered by the IDE. Here's a list of them:

- SELECT

- UPDATE

- DELETE

- Make Table

- INSERT

SELECT Query

The SELECT query is always used for returning rows from one or more tables in the database. Sometimes the SELECT statement is combined with or part of an INSERT query to append the result to an existing table (INSERT Results query) or add the result to a new table (Make Table query, covered shortly).

This is the SELECT query in its very simplest form: `SELECT * FROM tblUser`. This query returns all rows in the tblUser table. All columns (*) are output. Please note that unless you have a specific reason for always wanting all columns, you should avoid the asterisk as good programming practice; you only have to ask, "Do I want all the additional fields that a developer at a later stage might add to this table, rather than specific fields I need for the current task?"

UPDATE Query

The UPDATE query is for updating column values in specific rows in the destination table. The query `UPDATE tblUser SET FirstName='Peter'` updates all rows in the tblUser table and sets the FirstName column to "Peter". If you only want to update specific rows, you need to include the WHERE clause, like this:

```
UPDATE tblUser SET FirstName='Peter' WHERE FirstName='John'
```

This will only update the rows where the FirstName column holds the value "John". If you need to update more than one column in each row that matches the criteria in the WHERE clause, you can separate the columns with a comma, like this:

```
UPDATE tblUser SET FirstName='Peter', LastName='Johnson' WHERE FirstName='John'
```

You can only update rows in one table at a time.

DELETE Query

If you want to delete certain rows from a table, this is your best choice. The DELETE query is quite simple and here is an example: `DELETE FROM tblUser`. This will delete all rows in the tblUser table. As with the update query, you can select which rows to delete using the WHERE clause, like this:

```
DELETE tblUser WHERE FirstName='John'
```

This will delete all rows where the FirstName column holds the value "John". You can only delete rows from one table at a time.

Make Table Query

The Make Table query is actually a little more complex than the name implies. Although a table is created when you use this query, it also selects some rows that are inserted into the new table. The INTO keyword in the following example is what makes the difference; it creates a new table and copies all the rows from the tblUser into the new table (tblTest).

```
SELECT * INTO tblTest FROM tblUser
```

As you can see from the example, the SELECT statement is used for retrieving the rows from the tblUser table that are inserted into the new tblTest table. An error occurs if tblTest already exists in the database. If you need to append the result to an existing table, you need to use an INSERT Results query.

The Make Table query is very good for copying certain rows and/or columns from a source database into a temporary table, where you can manipulate it without messing up the "real" data. It can also be used for backing up data from one or more tables and then restoring it later on. If you wish to only create a copy of the table schema, you can do so with a statement like this:

```
SELECT * INTO tblTest FROM tblUser WHERE 1=2
```

This little trick won't be copying any data, because 1 never equals 2. However, you can only create one table at a time with a Make Table query.

 NOTE Copying a table in this manner doesn't copy the extended column attributes, such as default values or descriptions.

INSERT Queries

There are actually two INSERT queries, one for inserting the result of a row-returning query into another table and one for inserting values into a table.

INSERT Results Query

The INSERT Results query is for appending rows to an existing table. If you need to add rows to a new table, then you must use the Make Table query. The INSERT Results query is structured like this:

```
INSERT INTO tblUser (LoginName, FirstName, LastName, Password) _
 SELECT LoginName, FirstName, LastName, Password FROM tblTest
```

In this query I retrieve the columns LoginName, FirstName, and LastName from the table tblTest, and I append it to the tblUser table. The column names in the source table tblTest do NOT have to be same as in the destination table tblUser, but the order of which the columns appear obviously matters.

You can retrieve rows from as many tables as you like, as long as the number of columns match the number of columns in the destination table. There is always only one destination table.

INSERT VALUES Query

The INSERT VALUES query is quite similar to the UPDATE query in the way the SQL statement is constructed:

```
INSERT INTO tblUser (LoginName, FirstName, LastName, Password) _
 VALUES('peterj', 'Peter', 'Johnson', 'password')
```

This query will insert a row into the tblUser table with the values "peterj", "Peter", "Johnson", and "password" for the columns LoginName, FirstName, LastName, and Password. The order of the values (VALUES) must match how the columns, specified in the first set of parentheses, are ordered. You can leave out the field names and the parentheses after the table name, if you specify values for all the columns in the order in which they appear in the database. It's not recommended to use this kind of query while developing your application, because the table design will more than likely be altered at least a few times.

 NOTE You can only insert one row into the destination table at a time.

Script Editing Using the SQL Editor

The SQL Editor is a text editor, and it's the same editor that is used for writing your VB .NET code. This means it has the same facilities as the code editor, such as color-coding and line numbering. However, there is no IntelliSense! You can change the default behavior of the editor by opening up the Options dialog box, by clicking Options on the Tools menu. See Figure 13-30 for a view of the Options dialog box with the Text Editor node expanded.

As you can see from Figure 13-30, there are several options available for customization for different SQL dialects such as PL/SQL (Oracle) and various versions of T-SQL (Microsoft SQL Server). There are also some options under the Database Tools node that are relevant to the SQL Editor.

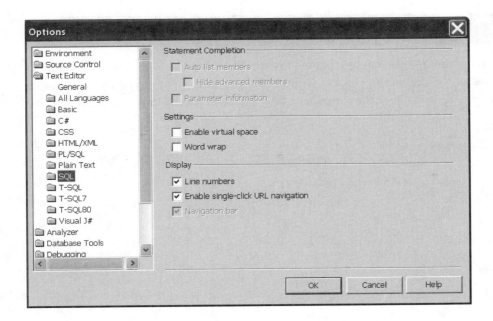

Figure 13-30. The Options dialog box with the Text Editor node expanded

Using the Query Editor to Produce SQL Statements

If you are like me, you can't remember the syntax for all the various SQL statements there are, but instead of looking up syntax in the help files for your database, you can use the Query Editor for this purpose. You can access the Query Editor without leaving the SQL Editor by right-clicking anywhere in the SQL Editor and selecting Insert SQL from the pop-up menu. This brings up the Query Editor, or rather the Query Builder as it's called when invoked from within the SQL Editor.

Although you can right-click anywhere in the SQL Editor to bring up the Query Builder, perhaps I should point out that the text generated using the Query Builder is placed where you right-click in order to select the Insert SQL command. So make sure that you place the mouse cursor where you want the SQL text inserted before you right-click. When you are done using the Query Builder, close the window and you will be prompted to save the content. Click Yes, if you want the generated text inserted into your script or click No if you don't want to save the text. If you click No, the generated text is discarded, and you cannot retrieve it again! See the "Designing Queries with the Query Designer" section earlier in this chapter for information on using the Query Editor/Query Builder.

Exercise

Add a Table Script in the Create Scripts folder named Create SQL Server Table. See the "Adding New Database Objects" section earlier in this chapter for more information on how to add new database objects to your database project. Once the script has been created, it should look like Figure 13-31.

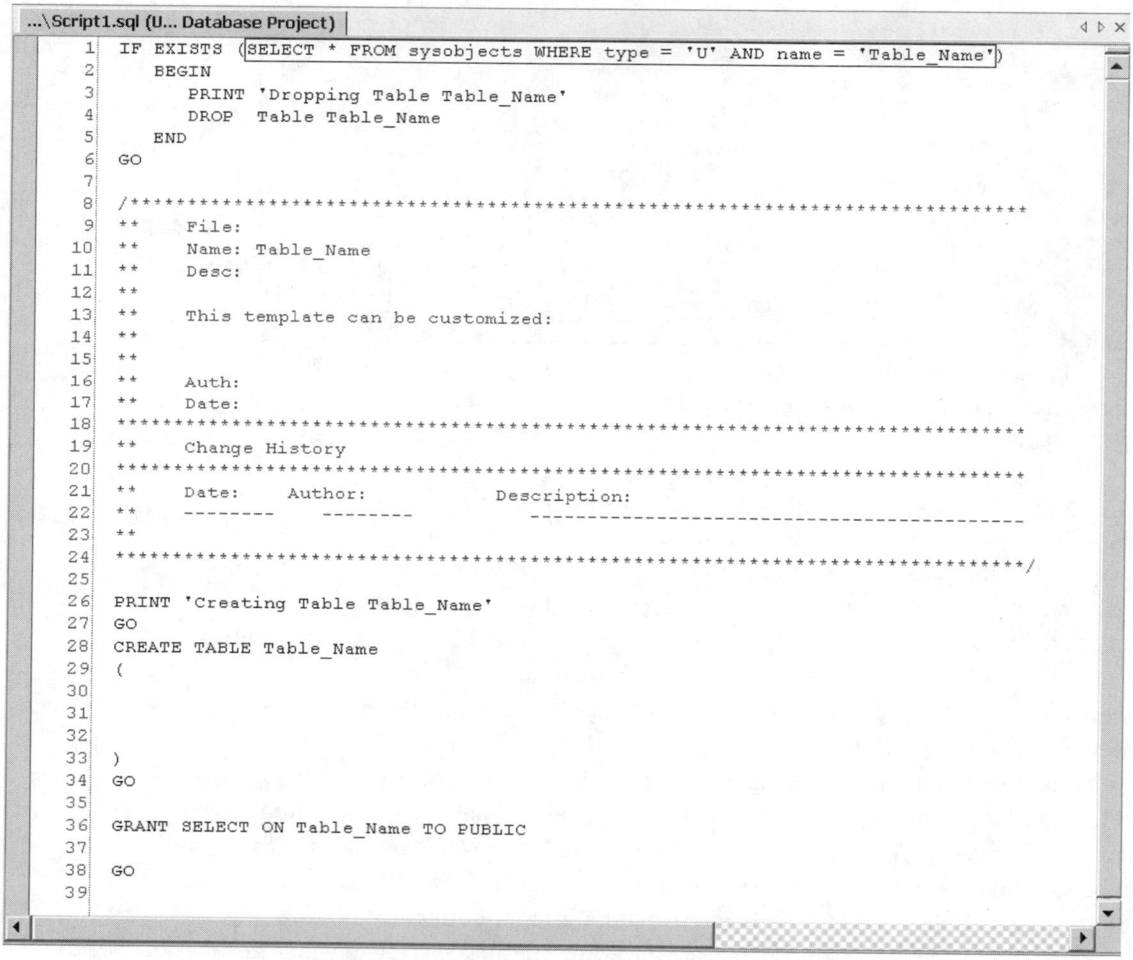

```
...\Script1.sql (U... Database Project)
 1   IF EXISTS (SELECT * FROM sysobjects WHERE type = 'U' AND name = 'Table_Name')
 2      BEGIN
 3         PRINT 'Dropping Table Table_Name'
 4         DROP   Table Table_Name
 5      END
 6   GO
 7
 8   /****************************************************************************
 9   **    File:
10   **    Name: Table_Name
11   **    Desc:
12   **
13   **    This template can be customized:
14   **
15   **
16   **    Auth:
17   **    Date:
18   ****************************************************************************
19   **    Change History
20   ****************************************************************************
21   **    Date:     Author:            Description:
22   **    --------   --------            -------------------------------------
23   **
24   ****************************************************************************/
25
26   PRINT 'Creating Table Table_Name'
27   GO
28   CREATE TABLE Table_Name
29   (
30
31
32
33   )
34   GO
35
36   GRANT SELECT ON Table_Name TO PUBLIC
37
38   GO
39
```

Figure 13-31. The SQL editor with the Create SQL Server Table script open

Exercise

Use the Replace functionality (Ctrl+H) of the Text Editor to replace all occurrences of the string Table_Name with tblTest. After the starting parentheses, "(", below the CREATE TABLE statement, and before the closing parentheses, ")", type in the following text:

```
Id int PRIMARY KEY NOT NULL IDENTITY, Test varchar(50) DEFAULT('Test').
```

Saving a Script

Once you are done editing your script, or even better, once you have done some work you don't want to lose due to unforeseen circumstances, you should save your script. This is as easy as pressing Ctrl+S. You can also access the save functionality using the menus. Select the Save Create Scripts ➤ Create SQL Server Table.sql command on the File menu. This menu command is obviously dynamically created, so if you called your script something different, then the menu command looks different. The script is saved to the folder that was selected in the Solution Explorer when you added the script to your project.

Exercise

Save your script.

Editing and Using Script Templates

I have chosen to create a script for Microsoft SQL Server simply because the default template is the SQL Server one. You can change the templates by editing them using any text editor that can save in plain text, such as Notepad. The templates are located in the \Program Files\Microsoft Visual Studio .NET\ Common7\Tools\Templates\Database Project Items folder. If you placed Visual Studio .NET on a different drive and/or in a different folder when you ran Setup, you obviously need to change the path to the templates accordingly.

Running SQL Scripts

When you have created your script, you can run the script by right-clicking it in the Solution Explorer and selecting Run On from the pop-up menu. Select the desired database connection or reference from the Run On dialog box and click OK. The script now runs against the selected database connection.

This is a nice little improvement over previous versions of Microsoft Visual Database Tools where you had to explicitly assign a connection to a script. Now you can assign a connection to a script before running it. Mind you, not all scripts are compatible with any database connection or reference.

However, this is not the only way to run a script. If you have a script open in the SQL Editor, you can right-click anywhere in the editor and select Run from the pop-up menu. Mind you, if you haven't saved the changes to your script, you will be prompted to do so before the script is run.

When the script is running, all output from the script is written to the output window, which is located just below the SQL Editor by default. It's always a good idea to examine the output to see if the script was executed correctly.

Creating Typed DataSets

If you want to work with typed **DataSet**s, you have to create the typed **DataSet** manually or at least with the help of some tools. (See Chapter 9 for an explanation of typed versus untyped **DataSet**s.) You cannot create a typed **DataSet** from code!

There are a number of steps required in order to generate a typed **DataSet**:

1. Retrieve or create the schema.

2. Generate the **DataSet** class.

3. Create an instance of the newly generated and derived **DataSet** class.

Therefore, what you can glean from the preceding steps is that a typed **DataSet** is really nothing more than a class that wraps the data access and provides you with strong typing, or the IntelliSense feature and compile-time syntax checking, and so on.

There are three tools you can use to create a typed DataSet (actually only two, because the DataSet Designer and the XML Designer are really the same):

- Component Designer

- DataSet Designer

- XML Designer

I will show you how to create a typed **DataSet** in the following sections.

Using the XML Designer to Create a Typed DataSet

Although you can use the XML Designer to create a schema, it's easier to use the DataSet Designer. The DataSet Designer is really the XML Designer with a little extra functionality added, so do yourself a favor and use the DataSet Designer. Because most of the functionality is duplicated in the XML Designer and the DataSet Designer, I will only cover how to use the DataSet Designer to create your typed **DataSet**s.

Using the DataSet Designer to Create a Typed DataSet

You can actually use the DataSet Designer to create a new schema from scratch and thus also use it to create a new table or even a new database. I am not going to go through that particular task in this book, but instead I will concentrate on creating a schema based on an existing table.

Exercise

Open up the Typed DataSet Project located in the Chapter 13\Typed DataSet Project folder.

If you have a project open that is *not* a database project, you can add a new **DataSet** if you right-click the project in the Solution Explorer and select the Add New Item command from the Add submenu. In the Add New Item dialog box select the DataSet template and give the **DataSet** a name before you click Open.

Exercise

Open the UserManDataSet.xsd schema and make sure you have it open in DataSet schema view and not XML view. You can change views by clicking the tabs at the bottom of the UserManDataSet.xsd window. See Figure 13-32.

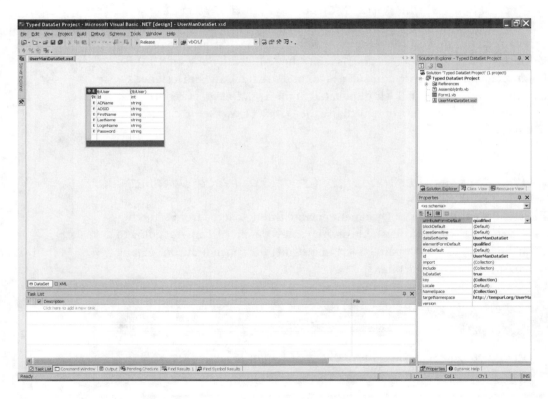

Figure 13-32. The UserManDataSet.xsd DataSet schema file

Exercise

Open the Server Explorer, expand the UserMan database node and the Tables node, and drag the tblUserRights table over to the DataSet Designer window and drop it. Now you have two tables in the DataSet Designer window. Press Ctrl+S to save the schema file to disk. Now you need to build the **DataSet** or rather the VB .NET **DataSet** class file. This is done by pressing Ctrl+Shift+B, or selecting the Build Solution menu command in the Build menu, which starts the build process. Now you have created a typed **DataSet**! Actually, what you've created is an assembly in the form of a DLL. Within your own project, you don't have to build the solution before using the typed **DataSet**. The DLL is output to the obj\Debug\TempPE or obj\Release\TempPE subfolder[a] in the folder where your project file is located. The assembly DLL file is named using the name of the typed DataSet, followed by a dot, the name of the programming language it's coded in, and then the DLL extension. In our case, this means a name of UserManDataSet.vb.dll.

a.   This depends on whether you're using a Debug or Release configuration.

 CAUTION   The **DataSet** class file is not visible in the Solution Explorer, and you should not edit this file even though it's accessible in the same folder as the schema file. Any changes will be overwritten the next time you build your solution!

Using a Typed DataSet

In the typed DataSet project, I've added a button to the Form1 Windows form, and in the click event of this file, I've shown you how to use a typed **DataSet**.

The example code in the Form1 Windows form class file, which is shown in Listing 13-1, demonstrates how I use the strong typing in the Button1_Click event.

Listing 13-1. The `Button1_Click` *Event*

```
1 Private Sub Button1_Click(ByVal sender As System.Object, _
2   ByVal e As System.EventArgs) Handles Button1.Click
3   Dim dadUserMan As SqlDataAdapter
4   Dim cnnUserMan As SqlConnection
5   Dim dstUserMan As New UserManDataSet()
6
7   ' Instantiate and open connection
8   cnnUserMan = New SqlConnection("Data Source=USERMANPC;" & _
9     "Initial Catalog=UserMan;User Id=UserMan;Password=userman")
10  cnnUserMan.Open()
11  ' Initialize and instantiate Data Adapter
12  dadUserMan = New SqlDataAdapter("SELECT * FROM tblUser", cnnUserMan)
13  ' Fill DataSet
14  dadUserMan.Fill(dstUserMan, "tblUser")
15  ' Display the login name for the first row in the user table
16  MsgBox(dstUserMan.tblUser(0).LoginName.ToString)
17 End Sub
```

In Listing 13-1, you can see that `UserManDataSet` typed **DataSet** is part of our project as a class, because I can create an instance of this class, as shown on Line 5.

Line 16 of the listing shows how you can access a typed **DataSet** using the actual table and column names.

Summary

This chapter took you on a journey through all the features of the IDE that are database related. You had a look at the Server Explorer, which holds server resources. The data connections and message queues were the ones specifically discussed. The exercises for this chapter took you through all the steps required to create a database project with database references, scripts, queries, and command files.

You saw how to use the Database Designer to create database diagrams and the Table Designer for creating tables with keys and indexes, constraints, and relationships. I dived into using the SQL Editor for creating scripts and stored procedures. I then demonstrated how to create a typed **DataSet**.

The next chapter demonstrates how to handle exceptions in your applications.

Part Five

Exception Handling
and Debugging

CHAPTER 14

Exception Handling

ANY APPLICATION NEEDS to handle errors that occur at runtime. Unfortunately it can be difficult to resolve all the possible errors that can occur. However, it's always a good idea to try to create code that can resolve or foresee most events and exceptions, so that the user doesn't have to worry about them. You should then attempt to catch the rest of them and display an error message with detailed information to the user about how to continue from this point. The overall purpose of exception handlers is to allow the application to gracefully recover from things going awry. This is especially important when dealing with relational databases. Since you are passing through multiple layers of technology, there are many places that an application can break. Although this chapter is about handling data-related exceptions, I will cover the basics for handling all kinds of exceptions briefly.

Now, let's get one thing straight before moving on: For the discussions in this chapter, exceptions include errors, therefore from this point on, when I use the word *exception*, I'm referring to both.

One question that I often hear is this: "Do I need exception handling in all my procedures?" My answer is always a firm NO, because some procedures are so simple and they don't use variables that can overflow or something similar. These procedures might call a few other very simple procedures, and in such cases, you know that no application exceptions will occur. Don't put an exception handler in these types of procedures; it's a waste, and even if it represents a rather small overhead, there's still a performance penalty to pay! Obviously knowing when to use an exception handler is a matter of experience and perhaps preference, but if you're in doubt, just stick one in there!

Visual Basic .NET has two programmatic ways of dealing with runtime exceptions: structured exception handling (SEH) and unstructured exception handling (UEH). I absolutely dislike UEH, which is the only type of exception handling in previous versions of Visual Basic. Although I've seen a number of people create some well-functioning exception handlers with UEH, the code for doing so was generally very messy. Anyway, I just thought that you'd like to know my preferences before we move on. SEH is covered in the first part of this chapter, and UEH in the last part.

Using Both Types of Exception Handling

Although it is possible to use both unstructured and structured exception handling, I recommend that you don't. It will only make your code more difficult to read, maintain, and debug. One thing to notice though is that a single procedure cannot contain both unstructured and structured exception handling. So if you are set on using both approaches, you can only use either one or the other (**XOr**) in a single procedure.

Structured Exception Handling

SEH works like this: It marks blocks of code as *guarded*, which means that if any line of code within the block throws an exception, it will be caught by one of the associated exception handlers. The guarded block of code is marked using the **Try . . . Catch** statements, and as such, the guarded code must be inserted between these statements. These statements are part of the **Try . . . Catch . . . Finally . . . End Try** construct. This construct gives you a control structure that monitors the code in the guarded block, catches exceptions when they are thrown, and addresses these through a so-called filter handler. The control structure also separates the code that potentially throws exceptions from your "normal" code. I personally like this approach, as I think it makes your code easy to read.

Listing 14-1 shows you how the **Try . . . Catch . . . Finally . . . End Try** construct is put together.

*Listing 14-1. The **Try . . . Catch . . . Finally . . . End Try** Construct*

```
' The Try statement on the next line marks the beginning of guarded code
Try
... ' This is the guarded block of code
Catch [(objException As Exception)]{
... ' This is where you place your exception handling code that can
    ' resolve and recover from exceptions.
Finally
... ' This block of code is always executed
End Try
```

The **Try** statement, which doesn't take any arguments, is mandatory if you want to use exception handling. Besides this statement, you also need at least either a **Catch** or **Finally** statement. Here is what the different code blocks do:

- *Try block:* This is where you place the lines of code you want to monitor, because they might throw an exception.

- *Catch block(s):* The **Catch** block is optional, and you can have as many **Catch** blocks as you like, but the filter must be different for each **Catch** block. The **Catch** block is optional only if you specify the **Finally** block. In Listing 14-1, I'm catching all exceptions in the one **Catch** block, whether the optional filter is specified or not. I'll get to the exception filtering in the "Handling Exceptions in the Exception Handler" and "Filtering Exceptions" sections later in this chapter. In these blocks you place your exception handling code—code that can possibly resolve the exceptions by examining the exception (`objException As Exception` in Listing 14-1) and let execution continue without notifying a possible user. The **Catch** block is also called the *fault handler.*

- *Finally block:* The **Finally** block, which is optional, is where you put the lines of code that should run immediately after all exception processing has ended. You may be thinking, "Wait a minute, why not just place those lines of code after the end of the exception handler?" Well, my friend, you could do that, but it doesn't make your code easier to read, does it? By placing it in the **Finally** block, you indicate that this code has something to do with the guarded code in the **Try** block. Oh, I nearly forgot: If you place the code after the exception handler, it won't be executed if there is a **Return** statement in the **Catch** block that processes the exception. Place the code in the **Finally** block, and it will run. Therefore, any code that really needs to run, whether or not an exception is thrown in the **Try** block, goes here! The **Finally** block is also called the *finally handler.*

NOTE   There is only a small performance penalty in placing code in the **Try** block.

When you deal with guarded blocks of code, there are three types of exception handlers:

- *Fault handler:* This is the same as the **Catch** block when no filter has been specified.

- *Filter handler:* The filter handler is the same as the **Catch** block when a filter has been specified. Actually, there are two types of filter handlers:

- *Type-filter handler:* This filter handler is used for handling exceptions of a specified class and any subclasses thereof.

- *User-filter handler:* The user-filter handler is used for handling exceptions of any exception class when you want to specify requirements for the exception. This is done using the **When** keyword.

- *Finally handler:* This is the same as the **Finally** block.

Using Catch Blocks the Right Way!

In Listing 14-1 I use a catch-all exception handler to catch all exceptions, which is really only because the code example serves as an overview. However, it's not considered good programming practice to do this. Although you can and in many cases should use a catch-all **Catch** block, you should never place a catch-all **Catch** block anywhere but the very end of a set of **Catch** blocks, and only if you have more than **Catch** block, because this block will catch all exceptions. The idea of exception handling is to catch an exception and then try to recover from it, which is why you should use as many **Catch** blocks as necessary to specify all the different types of exceptions that might potentially be thrown. If you do this, it's easier to write the code to recover from a specific exception, such as a "file not found" exception. Often you can use a loop to retry the offending line of code after having changed what you expect is the problem, or simply because you know that executing the offending line of code will have a different outcome if retried. One such example is locking at the data source.

Enabling Structured Exception Handling

Well, perhaps the preceding heading is inaccurate, because you don't really "enable" exception handling. Instead, you place the code you believe might throw an exception in a guarded block, called the **Try** block. All code placed in this block is monitored, and any exceptions thrown are passed to the fault handler in your **Try ... Catch ... Finally ... End Try** construct. Please see the beginning of the "Structured Exception Handling" section earlier in this chapter for more information.

Using Two or More Structured Exception Handlers in One Procedure

It's possible to have more than one structured exception handler in the same procedure. You simply encapsulate your code in the **Try . . . Catch . . . Finally . . . End Try** construct wherever you feel the need. In many cases, this is probably overkill, because it's possible to filter the various exceptions, determine the reason for an exception being thrown, and then recover from it, even if you have many lines of code in the **Try** block. I guess it's a matter of preference and making your code readable. Listing 14-2 shows you how two exception handlers can coexist in the same procedure.

Listing 14-2. Two Exception Handlers in One Procedure

```
1 Public Sub TwoStructuredExceptionHandlers()
2    Dim lngResult As Long
3    Dim lngValue As Long = 0
4
5    Try   ' First exception handler
6       lngResult = 8 / lngValue
7    Catch objFirst As Exception
8       MsgBox(objFirst.Message)
9    End Try
10
11   Try   ' Second exception handler
12      lngResult = 8 / lngValue
13   Catch objSecond As Exception
14      MsgBox(objSecond.Source)
15   End Try
16 End Sub
```

There is no hocus-pocus to Listing 14-2; it's simply plain code showing you it is indeed possible to have more than one structured exception handler in the same procedure.

Examining the Exception Class

The **Exception** class holds information about the last thrown exception. This is why it's usually a good idea to check the properties of this class when you catch an exception in your exception handler. Table 14-1 lists these properties.

*Table 14-1. **Exception** Class Properties*

Name	Description
HelpLink	The **HelpLink** property returns or sets a link to the help file that is associated with the exception. The data type for this property is **String**, and it must be specified using a URL or a URN.
InnerException	This read-only property returns a reference to the inner exception. This property is often used when an exception handler catches a system exception and stores this information in the **InnerException** property in a new exception object. This new exception object is then used to throw a new exception, one that is user friendly. If the exception handler that catches the new exception wants to know the original exception, it can examine the **InnerException** property. If there's no inner exception, this property is set to **Nothing**.
Message	This read-only property, which can be overridden in your own derived exception class, is of data type **String**. It returns the error message text that describes the exception in detail.
Source	The **Source** property returns or sets a **String** value that holds the name of the application or the object that threw the exception. If this property is not set, the returned value is a **String** holding the name of the assembly in which the exception was thrown. The **Source** property is a good place to include precise error location information when you create and/or throw your own exceptions. Information to include can be the application name, procedure name, procedure line number, module line number, and anything else you can think of that pinpoints the location of the error as precisely as possible.

Table 14-1. **Exception** *Class Properties (Continued)*

Name	Description
StackTrace	This read-only property, which can be overridden, returns the stack trace. The stack trace pinpoints the location in your code where the exception was thrown, down to the exact line number. The returned value is data type **String**. The stack trace is captured immediately before an exception is thrown.
TargetSite	The **TargetSite** property is read-only and returns an object of data type **MethodBase**. The returned object contains the method that threw the exception. However, if the exception-throwing method is unavailable, the method is obtained from the stack trace. **Nothing** is returned if the method is unavailable and the stack trace is set to **Nothing**.

The **Exception** class also has the public, noninherited methods described in Table 14-2.

Table 14-2. **Exception** *Class Methods*

Name	Description
GetBaseException()	This overridable method returns a reference to the original exception that was thrown, meaning the exception that caused a chain of exceptions. The returned object is of type **Exception**.
GetObjectData(ByVal objInfo As SerializationInfo, ByVal objContext As StreamingContext)	The **GetObjectData** method sets objInfo with all the information about the thrown exception that must be serialized.

Handling Exceptions in the Structured Exception Handler

When an exception is thrown, your code needs to handle it. If you can resolve or recover from the exception, you can continue execution, and if not, you have to let the user know and/or perhaps log the exception.

The **Catch** block is where you deal with the thrown exceptions. In its simplest form, the **Catch** block is also called the *fault handler*. The simplest form is not to specify any filter and simply catch all exceptions, as shown in Listing 14-3.

*Listing 14-3. The **Catch** Block in Its Simplest Form (Fault Handler)*

```
1 Public Sub SimpleCatchBlock()
2    Dim lngResult As Long
3    Dim lngValue As Long = 0
4
5    Try
6        lngResult = 8 / lngValue
7    Catch
8        MsgBox("Catch")
9    End Try
10 End Sub
```

In Listing 14-3, there is only one **Catch** block, and it will receive all exceptions that are thrown in the **Try** block. The problem with this form is you haven't specified that you want a copy of the **Exception** object. This means you don't have any access to the exception that was thrown. However, if you do specify an **Exception** object as part of the **Catch** statement, as in Listing 14-4, you have full access to the thrown exception.

*Listing 14-4. The **Catch** Block with Exception Object*

```
1 Public Sub CatchBlockWithDefaultExceptionObject()
2    Dim lngResult As Long
3    Dim lngValue As Long = 0
4    Dim objE As Exception
5
6    Try
7        lngResult = 8 / lngValue
8    Catch objE
9        MsgBox(objE.ToString)
10    End Try
11 End Sub
```

Listing 14-4 specifies that you want all exceptions and that you want the property values from the thrown exception stored in the objE variable. Actually, there's an easier way to do this. All you have to do is to delete Line 4, and replace Line 8 with this:

```
8    Catch objE As Exception
```

The objE variable is instantiated as an object of type **Exception** and the values from the thrown exception are then stored in objE. If you want to specify exactly what kind of exception is handled by a particular **Catch** block, you need to filter the exceptions. See "Filtering Exceptions" later in this chapter for more information on how to filter exceptions.

NOTE   If you have more than one **Catch** block in your exception handler, they will be tried one by one by the CLR when an exception is thrown from the code in the corresponding **Try** block. When I say tried, I mean that the various **Catch** statements will be examined in top-to-bottom fashion, as in a **switch** construct, and when a **Catch** statement matches the exception, this **Catch** block is executed. If none of the **Catch** statements matches the exception, the CLR will display a standard message to the user detailing the exception.

Okay, once you've caught an exception, what do you do with it? In order to be able to recover from an exception, you need to know what kind of exception has been thrown. Table 14-3 shows a list of some of the standard exception types of interest that the CLR provides.

Table 14-3. Standard Exception Types

Exception Type	Base Type	Description	Example
Exception	**Object**	This is the base class for all exceptions. See "Examining the Exception Class" for more information.	See one of the subclasses for more information.
SystemException	**Exception**	The **SystemException** class is the base class for all exceptions thrown by the CLR. It's thrown by the CLR for exceptions that are recoverable by the user application. This means nonfatal exceptions. This class adds no new functionality to the class it's derived from (**Exception**) and generally, you shouldn't throw exceptions of this type.	See one of the subclasses for more information.
IndexOutOfRangeException	**SystemException**	This exception is thrown by the CLR, when you try to access a nonexistent element in an array, meaning an element with an index that is out-of-bounds. This class cannot be inherited.	See Listing 14-5 later in this chapter.
NullReferenceException	**SystemException**	The **NullReferenceException** exception is thrown by the CLR if you try to reference an invalid object. An invalid object has a null reference or is set to **Nothing**.	See Listing 14-6 later in this chapter.

Table 14-3. Standard Exception Types (Continued)

Exception Type	Base Type	Description	Example
InvalidOperationException	**SystemException**	This exception is thrown by a method if the object that the method belongs to is in an invalid state.	See Listing 14-7 later in this chapter.
ArgumentException	**SystemException**	This exception type is the base class for all argument exceptions. You should use one the subclassed exceptions when throwing an exception if one exists.	See one of the subclasses for more information.
ArgumentNullException	**ArgumentException**	This exception is thrown by methods of an object, when you supply a null value for an argument that doesn't allow the argument to be **Nothing**.	See Listing 14-8 later in this chapter.
ArgumentOutOfRangeException	**ArgumentException**	The **ArgumentOutOfRangeException** is thrown by a method when one or more of the arguments aren't within the valid range.	See Listing 14-9 later in this chapter.

In Listing 14-5 I try to set the third element (Line 5) of the reference to the arrlngException array, but there are only two elements in the array (Line 2), so an **IndexOutOfRangeException** exception is thrown.

*Listing 14-5. Throwing an **IndexOutOfRangeException** Exception*

```
1 Public Sub ThrowIndexOutOfRangeException()
2    Dim arrlngException(2) As Long
3
4    Try
5        arrlngException(3) = 5
6    Catch objE As Exception
7        MsgBox(objE.ToString)
8    End Try
9 End Sub
```

In Listing 14-6 I try to reference the objException object, but this object has been destroyed, so a **NullReferenceException** exception is thrown.

*Listing 14-6. Throwing a **NullReferenceException** Exception*

```
1 Public Sub ThrowNullReferenceException()
2    Dim objException As New Exception()
3
4    Try
5       objException = Nothing
6       MsgBox(objException.Message)
7    Catch objE As Exception
8       MsgBox(objE.ToString)
9    End Try
10 End Sub
```

On Line 15 in Listing 14-7, I try to execute a non–row-returning query using the cmmUser command, but the command requires an open-and-ready connection. Because the connection (cnnUserMan) is busy serving the DataReader while it is open, an **InvalidOperationException** exception is thrown.

*Listing 14-7. Throwing an **InvalidOperationException** Exception*

```
1 Public Sub ThrowInvalidOperationException()
2    Dim cnnUserMan As SqlConnection
3    Dim cmmUser As SqlCommand
4    Dim drdUser As SqlDataReader
5
6    Try
7       ' Instantiate and open the connection
8       cnnUserMan = New SqlConnection(PR_STR_CONNECTION_STRING)
9       cnnUserMan.Open()
10      ' Instantiate command
11      cmmUser = New SqlCommand(PR_STR_SQL_USER_SELECT, cnnUserMan)
12      ' Instantiate and populate data reader
13      drdUser = cmmUser.ExecuteReader()
14      ' Execute query while data reader is open
15      cmmUser.ExecuteNonQuery()
16   Catch objE As Exception
17      MsgBox(objE.ToString)
18   End Try
19 End Sub
```

On Line 20 in Listing 14-8, I try to update the data source using the DataAdapter, but the **DataSet** supplied as the only argument hasn't been set yet. Therefore, because the **DataSet** object is **Nothing**, an **ArgumentNullException** exception is thrown.

*Listing 14-8. Throwing an **ArgumentNullException** Exception*

```
1 Public Sub ThrowArgumentNullException()
2    Dim cnnUserMan As SqlConnection
3    Dim cmmUser As SqlCommand
4    Dim dstUser As DataSet
5    Dim dadUser As SqlDataAdapter
6
7    Try
8       ' Instantiate and open the connection
9       cnnUserMan = New SqlConnection(PR_STR_CONNECTION_STRING)
10      cnnUserMan.Open()
11      ' Instantiate command
12      cmmUser = New SqlCommand()
13      ' Instantiate data adapter
14      dadUser = New SqlDataAdapter(cmmUser)
15      ' Update data source
16      dadUser.Update(dstUser)
17   Catch objE As Exception
18      MsgBox(objE.ToString)
19   End Try
20 End Sub
```

In Listing 14-9, on Line 4, I try to display the first 200 characters from the connection string, but there aren't that many characters in the connection string, which is why an **ArgumentOutOfRangeException** exception is thrown.

*Listing 14-9. Throwing an **ArgumentOutOfRangeException** Exception*

```
1 Public Sub ThrowArgumentOutOfRangeException()
2    Try
3       ' Display the first 200 chars from the connection string
4       MsgBox(PR_STR_CONNECTION_STRING.Substring(1, 200))
5    Catch objE As Exception
6       MsgBox(objE.ToString)
7    End Try
8 End Sub
```

Now you know what kind of standard exceptions you can expect to catch. How do you deal with them in the **Catch** block? Well, it depends on what exception you're talking about and how you catch it. First, you need to look at how you can filter the exceptions so that you make sure that the right **Catch** block handles the right exception. See the next section for more information.

Filtering Exceptions

When you set up your exception handler, it's always good to know what kind of exceptions you can expect, although this isn't always possible. However, depending on the code you put in the **Try** block, it can be quite easy to predict some of the possible exceptions that can be thrown. If you make a call to a method that takes one or more arguments, and the values you pass are variables, it's conceivable that one of the arguments is out of range or even set to **Nothing**. This will throw a standard exception, which you can handily filter using a type filter. Other times you might want to apply user-defined criteria when you're filtering your exceptions. Please note that both of these types of filtering can work together.

Type-Filtering Exceptions

Type filtering works by filtering the exceptions by type or class to be technically correct. If you specify a class in a **Catch** statement, the **Catch** block will handle the class and all of its subclasses. See Listing 14-10 for some example code.

Listing 14-10. Type-Filtering Exceptions

```
1 Public Sub TypeFilterExceptions()
2    Dim arrlngException(2) As Long
3    Dim objException As Exception
4    Dim lngResult As Long
5    Dim lngValue As Long = 0
6
7    Try
8        arrlngException(3) = 5
9        MsgBox(objException.Message)
10       lngResult = 8 / lngValue
11   Catch objE As NullReferenceException
12       MsgBox("NullReferenceException")
13   Catch objE As IndexOutOfRangeException
14       MsgBox("IndexOutOfRangeException")
15   Catch objE As Exception
16       MsgBox("Exception")
17   End Try
18 End Sub
```

In Listing 14-10, there are three potential exceptions in the **Try** block. Only one of the lines of code will ever be executed, because the code will throw an exception and then you enter the exception handler. You need to comment out those lines of code you don't want to throw an exception and then run the code.

However, Listing 14-10 shows you how to include more than one **Catch** block, and they each have a different task to do, or rather different types of exceptions to handle. When the first line of code (Line 8) in the **Try** block is executed, an exception is thrown. This means the CLR looks at the available handlers for this block of code. It starts with Line 11, but seeing there is no match between the exception that Line 8 throws (**IndexOutOfRangeException**), it then looks at Line 13, which is a match. As a result, a message box will appear displaying the message "IndexOutOfRangeException".

Notice that I have created a "generic" exception handler at the bottom on Line 15 to catch any exceptions that haven't been caught by the other handlers. You don't have to do this, and it isn't always appropriate to have one, but in some cases where you are uncertain about the exceptions that are thrown, it can be a good idea to include this catch-all handler. When it catches an unhandled exception, you can display a message to the user, log the exception, or do whatever you fancy with it.

User-Filtering Exceptions

Type filtering is a very good way of filtering your exceptions, but sometimes it's just not enough. Imagine you're referencing two objects of the same data type and you know that they sometimes are null (**Nothing**). You can type-filter the exception, which will be a **NullReferenceException**, but how do you tell which of the two objects caused the exception to be thrown? Take a look at Listing 14-11.

Listing 14-11. User-Filtering Exceptions

```
 1 Public Sub UserFilterExceptions()
 2    Dim objException1 As New Exception()
 3    Dim objException2 As Exception
 4
 5    Try
 6       MsgBox(objException1.Message)
 7       MsgBox(objException2.Message)
 8    Catch objE As NullReferenceException When objException1 Is Nothing
 9       MsgBox("objException NullReferenceException1")
10    Catch objE As NullReferenceException When objException2 Is Nothing
11       MsgBox("objException NullReferenceException2")
12    End Try
13 End Sub
```

Listing 14-11 contains two **Catch** blocks that type-filter on the same exception type, the **NullReferenceException**. Now, in order to know which object caused the exception to be thrown, I have added some user filtering after the type filtering. The **When** keyword specifies a user-defined criteria that must be met before this particular **Catch** block can handle the exception.

In this case, I simply check if the object has been instantiated. The user filter can be virtually any criteria.

Creating Your Own Exception

Sometimes it's necessary to create your own custom exception. Perhaps you are creating a class or component from which you want to throw a custom exception. In such cases, you need to create a class that inherits from the **ApplicationException** class. The **ApplicationException** class is the base exception class for exceptions thrown by user applications. Mind you, this is only true when a nonfatal exception is thrown (see Listing 14-12).

Listing 14-12. Creating Your Own Custom Exception Class

```
1 Public Class UserManException
2    Inherits ApplicationException
3
4    Private prstrSource As String = "UserManException"
5
6    Public Overrides ReadOnly Property Message() As String
7      Get
8          Message = "This exception was thrown because you..."
9      End Get
10   End Property
11
12   Public Overrides Property Source() As String
13     Get
14         Source = prstrSource
15     End Get
16
17     Set(ByVal Value As String)
18         prstrSource = Value
19     End Set
20   End Property
21 End Class
```

In Listing 14-12, you can see how to create your own custom exception classes. The sample code shown overrides two of the inherited properties; all other properties and methods are taken from the base class, the **ApplicationException** class. This is a very simple exception class, but it does show the basics for creating your own exception classes.

Throwing a Structured Exception

If you need to throw an exception, you can use the **throw** statement for this very purpose. The **throw** statement is quite often used for testing your exception handler using this format:

```
Throw expression
```

The required argument *expression* is the exception you want to throw. The following code will raise a new **IndexOutOfRangeException** exception:

```
Throw New IndexOutOfRangeException()
```

Now, throwing an exception is very easy, and as such, it can be used for general communication. However, as the name suggests, exceptions are for exceptional circumstances. So don't use it for general communication purposes. It's guaranteed to confuse the heck out of whoever looks at your code. If you're dealing with classes, then simply create events to handle the communication with the client or use callbacks.

Handling Data-Related Exceptions

Now that I've covered the basics of exception handling, it's time to look at how you can use it with data-related exceptions. If you follow my earlier instructions on NOT putting too much code in the same guarded block, it's actually quite easy to figure out which data-related procedure or object throws the exception. Listing 14-13 demonstrates how to catch **SqlConnection** class exceptions.

*Listing 14-13. Catch **SqlConnection** Class Exceptions*

```
1 Public Sub CatchSqlConnectionClassExceptions()
2    Dim cnnUserMan As SqlConnection
3
4    Try
5       ' Instantiate the connection
6       cnnUserMan = New SqlConnection(PR_STR_CONNECTION_STRING & _
7          ";Connection Timeout=-1")
8    Catch objException As ArgumentException
9       If objException.TargetSite.Name = "SetConnectTimeout" Then
10         MsgBox(objException.StackTrace)
11      End If
12   End Try
13 End Sub
```

In Listing 14-13, I try to instantiate the **SqlConnection** with an invalid **Connection Timeout** value. This obviously throws an **ArgumentException**, which I can catch. Because I know that this kind of exception is fairly common and I know that other lines of code can throw it, I also check to see if it was a **Connection Timeout** exception (Line 9). Okay, I know the example is rather short, but I am sure you can see where I am heading with this. All the information you need is in the **Exception** object or a subclassed object, so you have to just dig it out!

NOTE It's bad programming practice to rely on exception handling where you can easily avoid an exception by validating the input. This is the case with Listing 14-13, where you should be able to validate the value for the **Connection Timeout** value name. However, Listing 14-13 serves as an example of how to catch anticipated exceptions, in cases where there can be an overhead in validating input.

It's all about filtering the exceptions, as I have shown earlier on in this chapter. I could go on in this chapter and show you how to catch and filter every method of every data-related class in ADO.NET, but why not just stick to a rule of thumb? What you do is look up a particular method and check what kind of exceptions it can throw. You set up your exception handler to type-filter those exceptions, and then if necessary perform an extra check on the **TargetSite.Name**. This will make sure you process an exception with the right exception handler!

Common Data-Related Exceptions

As with general application exceptions, some data-related exceptions are very common, and you can avoid many of these if only you look for them when developing your application. These common data-related exceptions include, but aren't limited to, the following:

- Connection exceptions; invalid connection string values

- Unexpected null values in columns

- Time-out exceptions; queries take too long, server is down, and so on

- Invalid characters in queries; not handling apostrophes in string comparisons

- Empty result sets, causing application logic to fail

Some of these exceptions are already explained in Chapters 3 through 12, with example code showing how to deal with them.

CLR Handling of Structured Exceptions

If you've read the previous part of the chapter, I'm sure you have a pretty good idea of how the CLR handles exceptions, but here is a quick run-through of how it works.

First, the CLR uses guarded blocks of code and exception objects to handle exceptions. If and when an exception is thrown, the CLR creates an exception object and fills it with information about the exception.

In every executable there is an information table for exceptions, and every method in the executable has an associated array in this information table. This array holds information about the exception handling, but it can be empty. Every element in this array has a description of a guarded code block, all the exception filters that are associated with the code, and all the exception handlers.

The exception table is very efficient, and therefore it sacrifices neither processor time nor memory consumption. You obviously use more resources when an exception is thrown, but if no exception is thrown the overhead is the same as with "normal" code.

So when an exception is thrown, the CLR starts the exception process. This two-step process begins with the CLR searching through the array. The CLR looks for the first guarded block of code, which guards the currently executing line of code, and contains an exception handler and a filter that is associated with the exception.

The second step in this process depends on whether or not such a match is found. If a match is found, the CLR creates the exception object that describes the exception, and then executes all the finally and/or fault statements between the line of code where the exception was thrown and the statement that handles the exception. You must be aware that the order of the exception handlers is very important, because the innermost exception handler is always evaluated first.

If no match is found, all of the calling methods are searched, meaning that the caller of the current method is searched, whereby the calling method becomes the current method, and this goes on all the way up the stack. If after this search still no match is found, the CLR aborts the application after dumping the stack trace.

Unstructured Exception Handling

Unstructured exception handling is exactly what the name suggests, unstructured. Although you can organize it to look fairly nice and not make too many jumps in your code, it's still unstructured. Unstructured exception handling (UEH) should be well known to most Visual Basic programmers. Up until now, with the release of Visual Basic .NET, this has been the only built-in mechanism for trapping and handling runtime exceptions. Although you can continue to use unstructured exception handling in VB .NET, I can only recommend it as a means of upgrading old code and simply dumping your old code. This is because unstructured exception handling easily results in code that can be extremely difficult to maintain not to mention debug. Whenever exception handling is discussed elsewhere in this book, it is built using structured exception handling.

Enabling Unstructured Exception Handling

In order to enable unstructured exception handling, you must use the **On Error GoTo <*Label*>** statement (see Listing 14-14) or the **On Error GoTo <*LineNumber*>** statement (see Listing 14-15), where <*Label*> is a defined label in the current procedure and <*LineNumber*> is a line number in the current procedure.

Listing 14-14. Enabling Unstructured Exception Handling with a Label

```
1    Public Sub EnableUnstructuredExceptionHandling1()
2        ' Enable local exception handling
3        On Error GoTo Err_EnableUnstructuredExceptionHandlingFromLabel
4
5        Exit Sub
6 Err_EnableUnstructuredExceptionHandlingFromLabel:
7    End Sub
```

Listing 14-15. Enabling Unstructured Exception Handling with a Line Number

```
1    Public Sub EnableUnstructuredExceptionHandling2()
2       ' Enable local exception handling
3       On Error GoTo 5
4
5       Exit Sub
6  5:
7    End Sub
```

In Listings 14-14 and 14-15, the line numbers shown are the ones displayed by the IDE, not line numbers supplied by the programmer.

A compile-time error occurs if you haven't defined the label in the current procedure or if the line number doesn't exist in the current procedure, as shown in Listings 14-14 and 14-15. Hence, you can't use either of the **On Error GoTo** *<Label>* or **On Error GoTo** *<LineNumber>* statements to jump to a different procedure.

 NOTE   When I talk about line numbers in this context, I'm not referring to the line numbers that the IDE visually displays. This is an optional feature of the text editor. I'm talking about the line numbers you can add yourself, like any other label. Basically, the line number in this case is a label. You can see this from Listing 14-15, where the line number 5, shown on line 6 of the example, has been typed in as a label with the name "5". The colon after the name indicates a label.

As you can see from Listings 14-14 and 14-15, I've enabled the exception handler on the very first line in the procedure. This is *not* a requirement, but it is advisable to keep it near the beginning of the procedure. Mind you, if you are one of those programmers that tend to have procedures made up of hundreds of lines of code, you might want to include more than one exception handler in the same procedure. Actually, I think you should break your procedure into smaller procedures if you do have procedures of that length!

Keep in mind that the exception handler is only active from the line where you enable it, meaning that any exception that occurs because of the code in your procedure before the exception handler is enabled will be trapped by the CLR, and you won't be able to respond to and/or resolve the exception.

Separating Exception Handler from Normal Code

When you have an unstructured exception handler in your procedure, it is necessary to separate it from your normal code, because otherwise the exception handler code might be executed even if no exception was thrown. In Listings 14-14 and 14-15, I have separated the exception handler from the normal code by placing it at the end of the procedure and by adding the **Exit Sub** statement on the line before the exception handler label/line number. If I hadn't done that, the exception handler code would be executed with the normal code.

Having More Than One Unstructured Exception Handler in the Same Procedure

Since it is possible for you to have more than one unstructured exception handler in your code, it can quickly become a problem with the readability of your procedure (see Listing 14-16).

Listing 14-16. Two Unstructured Exception Handlers in the Same Procedure

```
1    Public Sub EnableUnstructuredExceptionHandling3()
2        ' Enable local exception handling 1
3        On Error GoTo Err_EnableUnstructuredExceptionHandlingFromLabel1
4
5        ' Enable local exception handling 2
6        On Error GoTo Err_EnableUnstructuredExceptionHandlingFromLabel2
7
8  Err_EnableUnstructuredExceptionHandlingFromLabel1:
9        Exit Sub
10 Err_EnableUnstructuredExceptionHandlingFromLabel2:
11     End Sub
```

Listing 14-16 contains two unstructured exception handlers, Err_EnableUnstructuredExceptionHandlingFromLabel1 and Err_EnableUnstructuredExceptionHandlingFromLabel2. When there's only one, it's advisable to place the label or line number that begins the exception handler after the last line of "normal" code, that is, non–exception-handling code. It makes your code easier to read, because it is out of the way and as such doesn't interfere with your normal code.

The problem with having more than one unstructured exception handler in the same procedure is the number of labels and where you need to place them. Listing 14-16 contains only two exception handlers, which I've placed at the end of the procedure in the order they're enabled in the procedure. I had to put an extra **Exit Sub** statement in the code, because otherwise the second exception handler will also be executed when the first exception handler is executed. My point is that even if you do have the label and the **Exit Sub** statements, your code gets more and more complicated to read the more exception handlers you add. I do realize this is a matter of opinion, but I fail to see why anyone would consider this approach easier to maintain than using structured exception handlers.

Another thing I mentioned is that UEH also makes your code harder to debug, not for the CLR, but for you when you step through the code. You will be branching to one label and back and then to another label and back. It's hard enough stepping into all your custom procedures, don't you think?

One last thing to notice about having more than one unstructured exception handler in your code is this: Only exceptions that are thrown from the code from the line where you enable the first exception handler until the line just before you enable the next exception handler will be handled by the first exception handler. In Listing 14-16, this means exceptions that are thrown on Line 4 will result in Line 9 being executed. If the exception is thrown on Line 7, execution will continue on Line 11. Now, consider what happens if you produce so-called spaghetti code and therefore jump from the second exception handler to code that is located within the block of code that is served by the first exception handler. Take a look at Listing 14-17 to discover the result.

Listing 14-17. Jumping from Code in One Exception Handler to Another

```
1    Public Sub EnableUnstructuredExceptionHandling4()
2        Dim intResult As Integer
3        Dim intValue As Integer
4
5        On Error GoTo Err_EnableUnstructuredExceptionHandlingFromLabel1
6        GoTo SecondExceptionHandlerBlock
7 FirstExceptionHandlerBlock:
8        intValue = 0
9        intResult = 9 / intValue
10
11       On Error GoTo Err_EnableUnstructuredExceptionHandlingFromLabel2
12 SecondExceptionHandlerBlock:
13       intValue = 0
14       intResult = 9 / intValue
15
16       Exit Sub
```

```
17 Err_EnableUnstructuredExceptionHandlingFromLabel1:
18      MsgBox("Err_EnableUnstructuredExceptionHandlingFromLabel1")
19      Exit Sub
20 Err_EnableUnstructuredExceptionHandlingFromLabel2:
21      GoTo FirstExceptionHandlerBlock
22    End Sub
```

In Listing 14-17, which is really messed up, I enable two exception handlers (Lines 5 and 11). After enabling the exception handler `Err_EnableUnstructuredExceptionHandlingFromLabel1`, I jump to the `SecondExceptionHandlerBlock` label on Line 12, and within the block of code served by the `Err_EnableUnstructuredExceptionHandlingFromLabel2` exception handler I throw an exception by dividing by 0 (Line 14). This means the CLR continues execution from the first line of code in the second error handler, which is Line 21. Now this line of code simply jumps to the `FirstExceptionHandlerBlock` label, which means that Lines 8 and 9 are executed. Line 9 throws an exception by dividing by 0. What happens then? Will the first or second exception handler be invoked? Try running the example code.

I wanted to make the three following points by creating this messy example:

- Don't write spaghetti code with **GoTo** statements. These statements can easily be replaced by more naturally flowing code.

- Keep exception handling as simple as possible.

- Don't use unstructured exception handling. Use structured exception handling all the time.

Okay, the message box is actually shown, which means that the CLR knows what lines of code belong to what exception handler. Therefore, even if a second exception handler has been enabled, executing lines of code served by the first exception handler will invoke the first exception handler and NOT the second. If you knew this already, good for you, but if not, did you guess right?

Using Parent Exception Handlers

If you have a procedure that enables an unstructured exception handler, the parent exception handler is the one that will be invoked. This is the case if any of the procedures you call within the block of code that is served by the exception handler throws an exception (see Listing 14-18).

Listing 14-18. Using Parent Exception Handers

```
1    Public Sub UsingParentExceptionHandling()
2        On Error GoTo Err_EnableUnstructuredExceptionHandling
3
4        UsesParentExceptionHandling()
5
6        Exit Sub
7  Err_EnableUnstructuredExceptionHandling:
8        MsgBox("Err_EnableUnstructuredExceptionHandling")
9    End Sub
10
11   Public Sub UsesParentExceptionHandling()
12       Dim intResult As Integer
13       Dim intValue As Integer
14
15       intValue = 0
16       intResult = 9 / intValue
17   End Sub
```

Listing 14-18 enables the `Err_EnableUnstructuredExceptionHandling` exception handler on Line 2 in the `UsingParentExceptionHandling` procedure. Within the block of code that is served by this exception handler, the `UsesParentExceptionHandling` procedure is called, which doesn't enable any exception handlers. This means when Line 18 in this procedure is executed, an exception is thrown. Because this procedure doesn't have its own exception handler, the CLR looks to see if the calling procedure does have one, and it does indeed. As a result, this exception handler is called, which means that the message box containing the text "Err_EnableUnstructuredExceptionHandling" will appear.

Disabling Unstructured Exception Handling

If you want to disable exception handling in the current procedure, you can execute the **On Error GoTo 0** statement. This disables all exception handlers in the current procedure. Please note that this statement does *not* tell the CLR to jump to a line with line number 0 if an exception is thrown. This is also true even if your procedure actually has a line with the number 0, as shown Line 11 in Listing 14-19.

Listing 14-19. Disabling Unstructured Exception Handling

```
1    Public Sub DisableUnstructuredExceptionHandling()
2        ' Enable structured exception handling
3        On Error GoTo 5
4
5        ' Disable structured exception handling
6        On Error GoTo 0
7
8        Exit Sub
9 5:
10       Exit Sub
11 0:
12       MsgBox("Line Number 0 has been reached!")
13   End Sub
```

 CAUTION   Disabling all exception handlers using the **On Error GoTo 0** statement can be fatal, meaning you have no control over what happens if an exception is thrown. You generally don't know the potential side-effects of doing so, so I advise you generally don't use this statement, unless you have a very compelling reason for doing so.

Disabling structured exception handling in one procedure like in Listing 14-19 also disables unstructured exception handling in general, not just in the procedure where you execute the **On Error GoTo 0** statement. This means you will have to enable exception handling before any exceptions thrown are handed to your application and not handled by the CLR.

Disabling Unstructured, Local Exceptions

If you want to disable any exceptions thrown in a procedure, meaning the exceptions will be ignored, you can use the **On Error GoTo -1** statement. This instructs the CLR to ignore any exceptions in the current procedure and any procedures it might call that don't have an exception handler. The CLR does actually try to clean up after the exception, but it won't hand any exceptions to your application and it won't show a message box detailing the exception.

NOTE   In line with the behavior of the **On Error GoTo 0** statement, the **On Error GoTo -1** statement does *not* tell the CLR to jump to the line with line number -1 if an exception is thrown. This is also true even if your procedure has a line with number -1. Please note that the disabling of the exception handling is only valid for the current procedure, because as soon as the procedure ends, normal exception handling is turned back on.

Ignoring Exceptions and Continuing Execution

Sometimes it can be a good idea to just ignore an error and continue execution without interruption, and the **On Error Resume Next** statement can help you do just that. If you place this statement in a procedure, execution will continue on the line following the one that caused the exception (see Listing 14-20).

Listing 14-20. Ignoring Exceptions

```
 1 Public Sub IgnoreExceptions()
 2    Dim intResult As Integer
 3    Dim intValue As Integer
 4
 5    On Error Resume Next
 6
 7    ' Throw an exception
 8    intValue = 0
 9    intResult = 9 / intValue
10
11    MsgBox("Was an exception thrown?", MsgBoxStyle.Question)
12 End Sub
```

When an exception is thrown on Line 9 in Listing 14-20, execution will continue on Line 10 and thus the message box will be displayed. Because of this behavior, you definitely want to make sure that any **On Error Resume Next** statements in your code are commented out, because otherwise you won't catch many exceptions!

One thing to notice about the **On Error Resume Next** statement is that it only applies to the procedure in which it is placed. If you call another procedure, this other procedure will not inherit the ignored behavior. If the called procedure enables an exception handler, this handler will catch any exceptions thrown in the called procedure. However, if the called procedure does not enable an exception handler, execution halts in the called procedure and the exception is propagated back to the calling procedure, where it is ignored.

Handling Exceptions in the Exception Handler

Once you have enabled your exception handler, it is time to create some code that handles the exceptions when they are thrown. If you can resolve an exception, you can continue execution, and if not, you have to let the user know and perhaps log the exception.

If you can resolve the exception, you can use the **Resume** statement to continue execution from the line of code that threw the exception, and as a result this line will be executed again (see Listing 14-21).

Listing 14-21. Resolving Exceptions

```
1    Public Sub ResolveException()
2        On Error GoTo Err_EnableUnstructuredExceptionHandling
3
4        Exit Sub
5 Err_EnableUnstructuredExceptionHandling:
6        ' Resolve exception
7        ...
8
9        ' Continue execution by retrying the offending line of code
10       Resume
11    End Sub
```

Other times it's not feasible to continue execution from the line of code that threw the exception, but you have taken other actions in your exception handler and want execution to continue without executing the offending line of code. You can do this by using the **Resume Next** statement. It will start the execution from the line of code immediately following the offending line (see Listing 14-22).

Listing 14-22. Working Around an Exception

```
1    Public Sub WorkingAroundAnException()
2        On Error GoTo Err_EnableUnstructuredExceptionHandling
3
4        Exit Sub
5    Err_EnableUnstructuredExceptionHandling:
6        ' Take other actions to work around the exception
7        ...
8
9        ' Continue execution from the following line
10       Resume Next
11   End Sub
```

One really important thing to know about the unstructured exception handler is that if a new exception is thrown by the code that is part of the exception handler, Lines 6 through 10 in Listing 14-22, the exception handler cannot handle the exception, and it is propagated back to the calling procedure. This can cause some unexpected results, so it is important that you construct your exception handler in a way that eliminates or at least minimizes the risk of throwing a new exception.

Examining the Err Object

The **Err** object holds information about the last occurring exception. This is why you should check the properties of this object whenever you catch an exception in your exception handler.

 NOTE   The **Err** object can only be used to handle exceptions that have been caught using the **On Error GoTo** *<Label>* statement.

Because the **Err** object is "flushed" every time a new exception is thrown, it is important that you save any information from this object that you want to hang on to. The **Err** object has the properties described in Table 14-4.

Table 14-4. **Err** *Object Properties*

Name	Description
Description	This property returns or sets a **String** value that describes the exception that is thrown.
Erl	This property returns the line number on which the exception was thrown.
HelpContext	The **HelpContext** property is used to indicate a specific help topic in the file specified by the **HelpFile** property. If both the **HelpFile** and the **HelpContext** properties are valid, or if both the help file exists and the topic exists in this help file, the help topic is shown.
HelpFile	The **HelpFile** property returns or sets the fully qualified path to a valid help file. This help file is shown when the user presses the F1 key on the keyboard or clicks the Help button when the error message dialog box is shown. You should use the **HelpFile** property in conjunction with the **HelpContext** property to make sure that a particular exception number points to the right help topic.
LastDLLError	This read-only property returns the system-generated exception that was thrown when you called a DLL. This property is only set when you call the DLL from within your VB code. System calls to DLLs that throw exceptions are not reflected in this property. The problem with this property is that it does NOT raise an exception when it is set. This means you should check this property immediately after making a call to a DLL in order to ensure you catch any exception thrown.
Number	The **Number** property is the default property of the **Err** object, and it returns or sets a numeric value that indicates the exception that is thrown.
Source	This property returns or sets a **String** value that indicates what object generated or threw the exception.

The **Err** object also has the two noninherited methods described in Table 14-5.

Table 14-5. Err Object Methods

Name	Description	Example
Clear()	The **Clear** method is used for clearing the **Err** object, meaning all the properties are reset. This method is automatically invoked when any of the following statements are encountered: **Resume, Resume Next, Resume <*LineNumber*>, Exit Sub, Exit Function, Exit Property**, and all **On Error xxx** statements.	`Err.Clear()`
Raise(ByVal vintNumber As Integer, Optional yVal vobjSource As Object = Nothing, Optional ByVal vobjDescription As Object = Nothing, Optional ByVal vobjHelpFile As Object = Nothing, Optional ByVal vobjHelpContext As Object = Nothing)	You use the **Raise** method to raise an exception in your application. This can be particularly helpful when you try to test your exception handler, or if you want to let a calling procedure know that something went wrong. All arguments except for `vintNumber` are optional. Check the corresponding properties for an explanation. Please note that if you don't set all the properties and any of the properties you don't set already have a value, these values will be used as part of the exception you raise. Always use the **Clear** method and manually set the properties in order to make sure you don't raise an exception with invalid values.	`Err.Raise(vbObjectError + 9)`

The **Err** object is a global object, meaning you do not have to create an instance of it in order to use it. Simply call any of the properties or methods like this:

```
Dim intExceptionNum As Integer = Err.Number
Err.Clear()
```

Raising an Unstructured Exception

If for some reason you want an exception thrown, you can use the **Raise** method of the **Err** object to do just this. Actually, the **Error** statement will also throw an exception, but it is an older statement and only supplied for backwards compatibility, so don't use it.

There are two main reasons for raising an exception: to test an exception handler and to notify the caller that an exception was thrown in your object. Whatever your reason, it is fairly simple to raise an exception.

Raising a System Exception

If you want to simulate a system exception, use one of the reserved numbers for system exceptions. This means that you have to call the **Raise** method with a number between 0 and 512, as shown in Listing 14-23.

Listing 14-23. Raising a System Exception

```
1 Public Sub RaiseSystemException(ByVal vintExceptionNum As Integer)
2    Err.Raise(vintExceptionNum)
3 End Sub
```

If you call the RaiseSystemException procedure with a vintExceptionNum argument value of 5, you will raise the dreaded "Invalid procedure call or argument" exception. This exception is usually caused when you pass an invalid number of arguments to a procedure. See your documentation for other system error numbers.

Raising a Valid User Exception

If you want to raise an exception that the receiving exception should recognize as user defined, you can add the value of the **vbObjectError** constant to your error number. This constant has a value of –2147221504, which makes it suitable for simulating a user exception when you raise an exception (see Listing 14-24).

Listing 14-24. Raising a User-Defined Exception

```
1 Public Sub RaiseUserException(ByVal vintExceptionNum As Integer)
2    Err.Raise(vbObjectError + vintExceptionNum)
3 End Sub
```

In Listing 14-24, you can call the RaiseUserException procedure with any number, even numbers that would normally overlap the system error numbers (0 through 512). This is because the **vbObjectError** constant is added to the passed value before the exception is raised. When you have raised an exception like this, and your own exception handler is set to handle the exception, it is important that you determine if the exception is a user-defined one or if it is a system exception. See the next section, "Determining if a User-Defined Exception Was Thrown" for information on how to do this.

Determining if a User-Defined Exception Was Thrown

So, you have caught an exception in your exception handler. Now you need to know if it's a system exception (numbers 0 through 512) or if it's one of your own. All you need to do is work backwards and subtract the **vbObjectError** constant from the **Number** property of the **Err** object (see Listing 14-25).

Listing 14-25. Determining a User-Defined Exception

```
1 Public Sub DetermineUserException(ByVal vlngExceptionNum As Long)
2    Dim lngExceptionNum As Long
3
4    lngExceptionNum = vlngExceptionNum - vbObjectError
5
6    ' Determine if this is a user-defined exception number
7    If lngExceptionNum > 0 And lngExceptionNum < 65535 Then
8       MsgBox("User-defined Exception")
9    Else
10      MsgBox("Visual Basic Exception")
11   End If
12 End Sub
```

Listing 14-25 saves the difference between the vlngExceptionNum argument value and the **vbObjectError** constant in the lngExceptionNum variable. Line 7 compares the saved value to see if it's in the range 0 through 65,535. If it is, then the exception number is user defined; otherwise, it is a Visual Basic system error.

Catching Exceptions That Occur in DLLs

When you call DLLs through an API call using the **Declare** statement, it's always a good idea to check if anything went wrong in the procedure you called. Because DLLs do not raise exceptions, you need to check the return value; if it's an unexpected value, you should check the **LastDLLError** property of the **Err** object. When I talk about DLLs in this context, I am referring to "plain-vanilla" Windows DLLs, not ActiveX or COM DLLs.

Handling Data-Related Exceptions

Now that I've covered the basics of unstructured exception handling, it's time to look at how you can use this type of handling with data-related exceptions. Listing 14-26 shows an example.

Listing 14-26. Handling Data-Related Exceptions

```
1    Public Sub CatchOpenConnectionException()
2       Const strConnection As String = "Data Source=USERMANPC1;" & _
3         "User ID=UserMan;Password=userman;Initial Catalog=UserMan"
4
5       Dim cnnUserMan As SqlConnection
6
7       On Error GoTo Err_EnableUnstructuredExceptionHandling
8
9       ' Instantiate and open the connection
10      cnnUserMan = New SqlConnection(strConnection)
11      cnnUserMan.Open()
12
13      Exit Sub
14   Err_EnableUnstructuredExceptionHandling:
15      MsgBox(Err.Description  & vbCrLf & Err.Erl & vbCrLf & Err.Number & _
16        vbCrLf & Err.Source)
17   End Sub
```

If you run the example code in Listing 14-26, you will see a message box that displays the following values:

Timeout expired	(Err.Description)
0	(Err.Erl)
5	(Err.Number)
SQL Server Managed Provider	(Err.Source)

If you look at these values, there isn't even one of them that is unique. Any of these can be duplicated by a different exception, so it can be hard to resolve this exception. Listing 14-26 only instantiates and opens the connection, but in most procedures you will do at least a little more than that.

How are you going to determine what caused the exception when the property values of the **Err** object are not unique? Here are some potential answers:

- You can enable a new exception handler for every block of code that can be logically grouped (such as an object instantiation and opening).

- You can use the value from the **Erl** property. This way you know the exact offending line of code, assuming you have set up your code with line number labels.

- You can check the **Number** property.

Okay, so what is wrong with these suggestions? Well, they would clutter your code and make it very hard to read. Using the **Erl** property would mean that you have to change the exception handler every time you add or remove a line in your procedure, and furthermore you have to have a line number label on at least every nonblank line. Finally, the **Number** property is *not* unique, meaning that quite a few exceptions will cause the **Number** property to be 5. Refer back to Listing 14-24 and the text that explains this listing.

Actually, if you are willing to add some extra code to your exception handler, you can determine what caused the exception, but my point here (again) is that it simply takes too much coding. Therefore, in this case you could combine the value of the **Source** and **Description** properties to determine the cause of the exception. It's a time-out, but why?

Now, here's a little revelation: You can actually get the values from the **Exception** object as you can when you use structured exception handling. So why didn't I tell you this until now? Well, the way I see it, if you're going to use this new **Exception** object, which is much more detailed in its information than the **Err** object, why not go all the way and simply use structured exception handling? You will also get the benefit of having much more control over your exception handler and the exceptions. Do yourself a favor, forget about unstructured exception handling!

Summary

This chapter has shown you how to use structured exception handling as well as unstructured exception handling for catching exceptions in your data processing applications. I also gave you some very clear advice on why you should leave the unstructured exception handling behind with your VB6-or-earlier–compatible code.

This chapter also discussed the following points:

- The **Err** object holds information about exceptions when you use the unstructured exception handling.

- If you use structured exception handling, you will be dealing with the **Exception** class, or subclasses thereof.

In the next chapter, you see how you can use the **Debug** and **Trace** classes to further improve your exception handling.

CHAPTER 15

Using the Debug and Trace Classes

THE DEBUG AND TRACE classes are very good utility classes for profiling and tracing your applications at runtime. They're not specific to database applications, but they are unique and small utility classes that any .NET developer should know about. That's why you're reading this chapter. This chapter will serve as an introduction to these classes, but it's by no means an exhaustive listing of all capabilities of the two classes. That is way beyond the scope of this book.

Using the Debug Class

The **Debug** class, which can be found in the **System.Diagnostics** namespace, can be used for debugging your code while you're developing it. Any calls to methods or properties in the **Debug** class won't be compiled into the release version of your application. You're probably thinking, "Okay, so far so good, but what is the **Debug** class, and what can it actually do for me?" Well, the **Debug** class has a number of properties and methods that can be used during development and debugging, such as making assertions. *Asserting* means that you test for a specific condition (such as if an object is **Nothing**), and if the condition is **False**, a message is displayed. This message can be user supplied. It's a bit like all those **MsgBox** function calls I've placed throughout the example code, after checking a certain condition with an **If . . . Then** statement. However, the difference is that the assertion, which is made with a call to the **Assert** method of the **Debug** class, isn't included in the release version of your software by default. With regard to exception handling, this makes it a perfect tool to include in your exception handlers, displaying potentially more information about thrown exceptions than you want the user of your software to see once it has been released.

Enabling Debugging

In order to use the **Debug** class, you must enable it before use. This can be done in various ways: Either you enable it locally in a file, or you enable it globally for your project.

To enable it locally, you simply add the following line to the top of the file in which you want to use the **Debug** class:

```
#Const DEBUG = 1
```

Globally, you can enable it in two different ways: by adding the /d:DEBUG=TRUE flag to the command line compiler command, or by specifying it in the Project Property Pages dialog box, as shown in Figure 15-1.

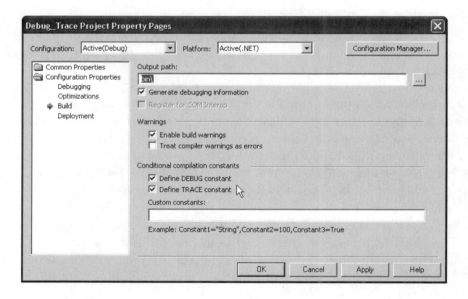

Figure 15-1. Project Property Pages dialog box

Figure 15-1 shows you the Project Property Pages dialog box, which can be opened by right-clicking your project in Solution Explorer, and selecting Properties from the pop-up menu, or by selecting the Properties command from the Project menu. In Figure 15-1, you can see the Build node, and the Define DEBUG constant check box in the Conditional compilation constants section has been selected. This means that all calls to the **Debug** class in your project code will be compiled.

NOTE   Enabling calls to the **Debug** class as shown here has nothing to do with general debugging, which when enabled creates a PDB[1] file in addition to the standard executable. If you look at the Configuration list box in Figure 15-1, you can see that general debugging is enabled, but you can disable this and manually add the DEBUG constant to the Conditional Compilation Constant item textbox.

You can actually add calls to the **Debug** class properties and methods in your code, without enabling these calls as shown previously, but that means the calls won't be compiled with the rest of the code.

Another thing you need to do is to add the following statement to the top of the files in which you're using the **Debug** class:

```
Imports System.Diagnostics
```

Strictly speaking, you don't have to do this, but if you don't, you'll have to add the full namespace path to the class when using it, like this:

```
System.Diagnostics.Debug.Assert(blnAssertion)
```

Whether or not you enable the **Debug** class locally or project-wide is really all your decision, but keep in mind that enabling the local use of the **Debug** class overrides the global setting. This means that you can have one or more files in your project in which the **Debug** class use is enabled, whereas other files won't have it enabled, even if there are calls to the **Debug** class in these files.

Disabling Debugging

Well, there isn't really much to say about this, because all you have to do is to remove the `/d:DEBUG =TRUE` flag from the command line when compiling, or remove it from the project Property Pages dialog box, which you can see in Figure 15-1. However, if any of the files in your project has enabled the use of the **Debug** class locally, this will be compiled into your executable, regardless of the setting on the command line or in the Project Property Pages dialog box.

---

1.   This is short for Program Database file, and it contains symbols for debugging your code using a debugger.

Using Debug Assertions

You can use the **Assert** method of the **Debug** class to check for certain conditions at runtime and have a message box displayed, if a condition evaluates to **False**. You need to keep this in mind, because this isn't an **If . . . Then** construct with which you can choose to perform an action whether the condition evaluates to **True** or **False**. Assertions only act if the condition evaluates to **False**. Generally, this shouldn't be a problem, because you simply form your conditions to conform to this, but you need to be aware of it.

The **Assert** method has three overloads, and you can see them in Table 15-1.

*Table 15-1. **Assert** Method Overloads*

Definition	Description
Assert(blnCondition)	This overload, which is the simplest, only accepts the condition for which to test. This also means you won't see a user-supplied message, only the call stack, which is supplied by the CLR.
Assert(blnCondition, strMessage)	This overload takes two arguments, the `blnCondition` condition and the message to display, if the condition evaluates to **False**. The CLR-supplied call stack is also shown in the message box, below the text in `strMessage`.
Assert(blnCondition, strMessage, strDetailedMessage)	This overload takes three arguments, the `blnCondition` condition, the message to display, and a detailed message. If the condition evaluates to **False**, the two messages are shown, with `strMessage` at the top, `strDetailedMessage` just below it on a new line, and finally the call stack supplied by the CLR.

The message box displayed has three buttons that let you decide what to do: Abort, Retry, and Ignore. Abort allows you to quit the application; Retry lets you attempt once more to debug the application; and Ignore, well, means you want to ignore the assertion. In addition, the message boxes referenced in Table 15-1 are only shown when you're running in user interface mode (default trace output), but you can have the trace output sent to a log file instead. You need to set this up in the configuration file for your application. I won't be covering this, but there are some good examples in the VS .NET documentation.

Listing 15-1. Using Debug Assertions

```
1 Public Sub TestDebugAssert()
2    Dim dstUser As New DataSet()
3    Dim dstLog As New DataSet()
4
5    Try
6       ' Do your stuff
7       ' ...
8       ' Destroy Log dataset
9       dstLog.Dispose()
10      dstLog = Nothing
11      ' This obviously throws the
12      ' NullReferenceException exception
13      MsgBox(dstLog.DataSetName)
14   Catch objNullReference As NullReferenceException
15      ' Check if both our object instances are null
16      Debug.Assert((dstUser Is Nothing And dstLog Is Nothing), _
17          "Assert Message")
18   Catch objE As Exception
19      ' Handle all other exceptions here
20   End Try
21 End Sub
```

In Listing 15-1, I instantiate two **DataSet** objects, and then in the exception handler destroy the dstLog **DataSet** object on Line 10. This means that the reference to this object on Line 13 will throw a **NullReferenceException** exception. Now, my application logic is that if one of the **DataSet** objects is **Nothing**, then the other must be too, so this is what I have as my condition in the call to the **Debug.Assert** method on Lines 16 and 17 in the **Catch** block. If you run the example code in Listing 15-1 as it is, the assert message will appear. I know this is a very simple example, but it should give you an idea as to how the **Assert** method can be used from within your exception handler. However, you should also take a look at the **Fail** method, presented later in this chapter.

What to Watch Out For

Although the **Debug** class is great for finding problems in your code at development time, there is one thing you need to look out for. You need to make sure you don't place function calls as part of your condition, because this might change a variable here and there and finally end up having an impact on the execution of your application. This is all fine if you want it this way. You need to keep in mind, however, that unless you have locally enabled the use of the **Debug** class, the **Assert** method won't be compiled into your released software, making it all too possible that the behavior of your application will be different from what you expect when running it in the IDE.

Using Debug Error Messages

The **Debug** class has one method that is well suited for exception handling and that's the **Fail** method. This method displays an error message and as such doesn't do anything that the **MsgBox** function can't do if you're running in the IDE. However, the **Fail** method only displays a message during development, meaning it's a great tool for debugging when setting up exception handlers. Listing 15-2 illustrates what I'm trying to say.

Listing 15-2. Using Debug Error Messages

```
 1 Public Sub TestDebugFail()
 2    Try
 3       ' Do your stuff here
 4       ' ...
 5       Throw New Exception("I'm not really expected!")
 6    Catch objNullReference As NullReferenceException
 7       ' Handle the NullReferenceException here
 8    Catch objIndexOutOfRange As IndexOutOfRangeException
 9       ' Handle the IndexOutOfRangeException here
10    Catch objE As Exception
11       Debug.Fail("Fail Message", _
12          "An unexpected exception has been thrown." & _
13          vbCrLf & vbCrLf & objE.Message)
14    End Try
15 End Sub
```

In Listing 15-2, I've set up an exception handler that expects that the code in the **Try** block can throw exceptions of types **NullReferenceException** and **IndexOutOfRangeException**. These two exception types have their own catch block that handles them, but what about other exception types? Well, they're caught by the **Catch** block with the general **Exception** object, meaning this **Catch** block will handle all other exceptions thrown in the **Try** block. However, in many cases, this can be the kind of exception you really don't expect to see, and you certainly don't want your end users to see a message displayed at this point, so you basically have to put the call to the **Fail** method in there. This gives you one of two advantages:

- Your messages won't be displayed in the release version of your application.

- You can enable the **Debug** class in the release version of your application, but have it write to a log file instead of the screen. You can then use the log file later when bug fixing.

The **Fail** method has two overloads, and they look similar to the **Assert** method overloads. One takes one **String** argument, and the other accepts two **String** arguments, **Message** and **Detailed Message**. If you log the output from the **Assert** methods, you might want to use the overload with the two strings, because then you can use the **Message** argument as the title of the exception you've caught to make it easier for the reviewer of the log file to scan it by means of the title. If the reviewer then comes across an unknown or unexpected title, he or she can read the detailed message. That's one possibility, anyway.

Debug Class Methods and Properties

The **Debug** class has other methods and a handful of properties, but none are as important as the **Assert** and **Fail** methods. I encourage you to have a look at the **Debug** class in the VS .NET documentation, especially if you need information on how to

- Save the output to a file instead of showing it onscreen.

- Format the output (using the **Indent** and **Unindent** methods, and **IndentSize** property).

 NOTE   The **Debug** class and all of its methods and properties are **Shared**, so you don't have to declare an instance of the **Debug** class in order to use it.

Using the Trace Class

The **Trace** class, which can be found in the **System.Diagnostics** namespace, is used just like the **Debug** class, which is described previously in this chapter. Actually, the **Trace** class is identical to the **Debug** class, and they're different on one account only, the default behavior. The calls to the properties and methods of the **Trace** class are compiled with your application by default, whereas the properties and methods of the **Debug** class aren't.

Okay, so why should you use one over the other? Now, there's a real good question! The idea of having both classes is that the **Debug** class is active when you define DEBUG (see the "Enabling Debugging" section earlier in this chapter), and the **Trace** class is active when you define TRACE. I believe Microsoft expects you to use DEBUG for your debug builds and TRACE for all builds. I can see one good thing about this, and that is it makes your code easier to read, in my opinion, if you stick to the idea of where and when to use either of the classes.

So, if you want to use the **Trace** class, please refer to the "Using the Debug Class" section at the start of this chapter.

Summary

This chapter has shown you the **Debug** and **Trace** classes from the **System.Diagnostics** namespace. The **Debug** class can be used when developing and debugging your code; by default, it won't be compiled into the release version of your software unless you specify otherwise.

The next chapter will tell you how to deal with stored procedures on the server. In other words, you will be shown how to process your data on the server, instead of letting the client do it. If you implement this correctly, it can lead to performance and/or security improvements.

Part Six

Server-Side Processing

CHAPTER 16

Using Stored Procedures

Using Stored Procedures, Stored Functions, and Server-Side Processing in General

IN THIS CHAPTER, I discuss one specific way of doing server-side processing: stored procedures and stored functions. Server-side processing, which is when you let a server process your queries and the like, is probably a concept you have heard of, and it's the subtopic of this chapter. Well, to some extent anyway. The good thing about server-side processing is that you can use the power and resources of your server for doing purely data-related processing and thus leave your client free to do other stuff, and your network clearer of data that the client doesn't want. It's not always appropriate to do so, but in many cases, you can benefit from it.

This chapter includes several hands-on exercises that will take you through creating stored procedures and functions. See the Exercise items that appear throughout the text.

Although this chapter primarily focuses on SQL Server 2000 features, some of the functionality can certainly be reproduced in the other DBMSs I cover in this book:

- *SQL Server 7.0:* All functionality shown in this chapter can be reproduced.

- *Microsoft Access:* Microsoft Access doesn't support stored procedures.

- *Oracle:* Oracle supports all the server-side processing described in this chapter.

- *IBM DB2 7.2 EE:* This version of DB2 supports all the server-side processing described in this chapter.

- *MySQL:* For the examples in this book, I have been using MySQL version 3.23.51, which doesn't support stored procedures, meaning there is no example code for MySQL in this chapter. However, at the time of writing (August 2002), version 4.? of MySQL is described on http://www.mysql.com, and according to the plans and description, version 4.? is supposed to support stored procedures. Even when this means of server-side processing is available in MySQL, it's still not possible to create any of these items from within the VS .NET IDE.

The code for this chapter has examples for all the listed DBMSs where appropriate. Besides stored procedures and stored functions, I also discuss optimization issues that relate and often lead to the use of stored procedures. However, optimization issues aren't a stored procedures–only topic, but more of a general database topic. It's included here in this first of the three server-side processing chapters, because optimization often means including server-side processing of at least some of your data.

Optimization Issues

When I talk about optimizing performance of an application, there are a number of things to consider, but let's just make one thing clear before I go on: I am only talking distributed applications and not stand-alone applications that sit nicely on a possibly disconnected single PC. These stand-alone applications are also called *single tier* or *monolithic applications.*[1] The applications I discuss here use a network of some sort to access data and business services.

Okay, now that the basics are out of the way, I can focus on the obstacles that can lead to decreasing performance and how you need to know these obstacles well when you start the optimization process. You should keep such obstacles in mind when you design your application. However, the various resources, such as network bandwidth, processor power, available RAM, and so on, most often change over time. This means that you'll have to check these resources and tune your application as needed. In order to track these resources, you need to establish a baseline, which is used when comparing new values. The baseline is a point in time when you measure all the resources you want to track and you then write down the measurable values for future comparison with new values. Typically, the baseline is established after setting up a new system, or just before you start optimizing.

Table 16-1 lists some of the varying factors that can influence the performance of your application, which could be a topic for an entire book. However, although

---

1. Stand-alone applications don't have to be single tier, but they generally are.

I only describe these factors briefly, I want you to be aware of the resources mentioned; they have great influence on what server-side processing resources you should choose when you design your application. In general it's often the client queries and not the server itself that create the biggest performance problems.

Table 16-1. Performance Resources Optimization

Resource Name	Description
Network resources	When speaking of network resources, I am referring to the actual bandwidth of the network. Consider your network setup—whether you are on a LAN or you are accessing resources over a WAN such as the Internet, and so on. If you have a low bandwidth, it's obvious that you want to transfer as little data across the network as possible. If on the other hand you have plenty of bandwidth, you might want to transfer large amounts of data across the network. However, best practices prescribe that you only transfer the data needed across your network, even when you have wide bandwidth.
Local resources	If you have the raw power available on your local box, it can be good to do most of the data processing there. Mind you, it all depends on the available bandwidth and the processing resources on the server.
Server resources	Server-side processing is desirable, if the server has resources to do so. Another thing you should consider is whether it has the resources to serve all your clients, if you let the server do some of the data processing.
Data distribution	Although strictly speaking this isn't a resource as such, it's definitely another issue you might need to consider. If your data comes from different and even disparate data sources, it often doesn't make too much sense to have one server process data from all the data sources, just to send the result set to the client. In most cases it makes sense to have all the data delivered directly to the client.
Borrowed resources	When using concepts like grid computing and Web services, you need to consider the effects of resources that aren't under your control.[a] These resources are borrowed from someone else, and can greatly influence the performance of your applications.

Table 16-1. Performance Resources Optimization (Continued)

Resource Name	Description
Fabric resources/ nonattached resources	Essentially this refers to such concepts as a storage area network (SAN) or network-attached storage (NAS), both of which are familiar to drive storage users, but are also becoming useful for other types of peripheral devices.
Glitch factor	One example of a glitch factor is noise introduced into a network connection. This can and often does reduce the performance of the network, which is something you may have to take into account. One way of dealing with this is to specify performance as a range of values and not a fixed value. In many cases, distributed applications have very little control over the glitch factor, because some resources are borrowed, while others pass through public networks. Another thing to keep in mind about glitch factors is that they can also occur as the result of one-time application errors, which are nonrepeatable, system stability, user load, and hardware errors.
Security	This is a catch-22, because the more secure you make an application, the slower it tends to run, and if you optimize it, it often leads to a less secure application.

a. The Web services might be running locally, but the idea of using Web services constitutes remote access.

Table 16-1 just provides a quick overview of performance issues. Table 16-2 shows you some different application scenarios.

Table 16-2. Different Application Scenarios

Client Machine	Server	Network	Recommendation
Limited processing resources	Plenty of processing resources	Limited bandwidth	Now, this one is obvious. You should use the raw processing power of the server to process the data and only return the requested data. This will save resources on the network and on the client.
Plenty of processing resources	Plenty of processing resources	Limited bandwidth	Hmm, processing could be done on either the client or the server, but it really depends on the amount of data you need to move across the network. If it's a limited amount of data, processing on either side will do, but if it's a lot of data, then let the server do the processing. Another solution could be to store the data locally and then use replication or batch processing to update the server.
Plenty of processing resources	Limited processing resources	Limited bandwidth	In this case, processing should be done on the client, but it really depends on the amount of data you need to move across the network. If it's a limited amount of data, the client should do the processing; but if it's a lot of data, you might consider letting the server do some of the processing, or even better, upgrade your server.
Plenty of processing resources	Limited processing resources	Plenty of bandwidth	Okay, don't think too hard about this one—processing should be done on the client.

I could add plenty more scenarios to the list, but I think you get the picture. You'll rarely encounter a situation that matches a straightforward scenario with a simple answer. It's your job to know about all the potential issues when you design your application and have to decide on where to process your data. Quite often different aspects of an application have different data/processing needs, so the answer may vary even within a single application. One book that will help you with many common problems you may encounter with SQL Server is this one:

> *SQL Server: Common Problems, Tested Solutions,* by Neil Pike. Apress, October 2000. ISBN: 1-893115-81-X.

Troubleshooting Performance Degradation

When you realize that you have performance problems or when you just want to optimize your server, you need one or more tools to help. SQL Server and Windows NT/2000 provides a number of tools you can use when troubleshooting, and here are a few of them:

- Database Consistency Checker (DBCC) (SQL Server)

- Performance Monitor (Windows NT/2000/XP)

- Query Analyzer (SQL Server)

- System Stored Procedures (SQL Server)

I'll briefly describe what you can use these tools for and give you links for obtaining more information.

Database Consistency Checker

The *Database Consistency Checker* (DBCC) is used for checking the logic as well as the consistency of your databases using T-SQL DBCC statements. Furthermore, many of the DBCC statements can also fix the problems detected when running. DBCC statements are T-SQL enhancements and as such must be run as SQL scripts. One example of a DBCC statement is

```
DBCC CHECKDB
```

This DBCC statement is used for checking the structural integrity of the objects in the database you specify. It can also fix the problems found when running. There are many DBCC statements, and this isn't the place to go over these, but check SQL Server Books Online (included with SQL Server) for more information about DBCC.

Performance Monitor

The *Performance Monitor* (perfmon) is used for tracking and recording activity on your machine or rather any machine within your enterprise. Perfmon comes with Windows NT/2000/XP and is located in the Administrative Tools menu, but you can also run it from a command prompt, or the Run facility of Windows Start Menu, by executing perfmon. Any of the Windows platforms mentioned produces counters that can be tracked or polled by perfmon at regular intervals if needed. SQL Server also comes with counters that can be tracked or polled by perfmon. Some of the more general counters are used for polling processor time, disk access, memory usage, and so on. Arguably the best of all is the ability to save a session of all activity recorded or polled within any given period. You can then play back a saved session, whenever appropriate. This is especially important when you want to establish a baseline against which to compare future session recordings.

Check your Windows NT/2000/XP documentation for more information about perfmon.

Query Analyzer

The *Query Analyzer* is an external tool that comes with SQL Server for analyzing and optimizing your queries. You can find it in the menus created by SQL Server Setup.

Query Analyzer can be used for validating your queries in the form of script files and queries you type yourself in the query window. Besides validating a query, you can get Query Analyzer to analyze it by running it. The analysis includes an execution plan, statistics, and a trace of the query being executed. Queries can get complicated, and many do when joining tables, and it isn't always obvious how much processing a particular query will take. There's normally more than one way to get to complex data, so the trace is invaluable in optimizing your data requests.

See SQL Server Books Online (included with SQL Server) for more information about Query Analyzer. You can actually invoke the Query Analyzer part of the SQL Server Books Online help text from within Query Analyzer by pressing F1.

System Stored Procedures

The *System Stored Procedures* is a set of stored procedures that comes with SQL Server for database administrators to use for maintaining and administering SQL Server. There are a large number of system stored procedures, including two XML ones, and I certainly can't cover them here. However, I can mention some of their functionality: they let you see who's logged on to the system, administer registration with Active Directory, set up replication, set up full-text search, create and edit maintenance plans, and administer a database in general.

See SQL Server Books Online (comes with SQL Server) for more information about the system stored procedures.

Using Stored Procedures and Functions

A *stored procedure* is one or more precompiled SQL statement(s) that are stored on the database server. The SQL statements are always executed on the database server. Stored procedures have long been a good way of letting the server process your data. They can significantly reduce the workload on the client, and once you get to know them, you'll wonder how you ever managed without them.

There is certainly more to a stored procedure than just mentioned, but I do think this is the most significant aspect of a stored procedure. Think about it: It's a way of grouping a batch of SQL statements, storing it on the database server, and executing it with a single call. The fact that the stored procedure is precompiled will save you time as well when executed. Furthermore, the stored procedure can be executed by any number of users, meaning you might save a lot of bandwidth just by calling the stored procedure instead of sending the whole SQL statement every time.

A stored procedure can contain any SQL statement that your database server can understand. This means you can use stored procedures for various tasks, such as executing queries—both so-called action queries, such as DELETE queries, and row-returning queries, such as SELECT statements.

Another task you can use a stored procedure for is database maintenance. Use it to run cleanup SQL statements when the server is least busy and thus save the time and effort of having to do this manually. I won't cover maintenance tasks in this chapter, but they're important, and you should be aware of the various tasks you can perform with stored procedures. If you're like me, you have been or are working for a small company that doesn't have a database administrator, in which case you're in charge of keeping the database server running. Granted, it's not an ideal situation, but you certainly get to know your DBMS in different ways than you would just being a programmer, and that's not bad at all.

To sum it up: A stored procedure is one or more precompiled SQL statements that are stored on the database server. All processing takes place on the server, and any result requested by a client is then returned in a prepared format.

Why Use a Stored Procedure?

You should use a stored procedure in the following cases (please note that other cases do apply, depending on your circumstances):

- Executing one or more related SQL statements on a regular basis.

- Hiding complex table structures from client developers.

- Returning the result of your SQL statements because you have a limited bandwidth on your network.

- Delegating data processing to the server because you have limited processing resources on your client.

- Confronting security issues. You can force all access to a table through stored procedures and revoke direct access to the underlying tables. All the user/developer has permission to do is to execute the stored procedures.

- Ensuring processes are run, on a scheduled basis, without user intervention.

Granted, there can be substantially more work in setting up a stored procedure than in just executing the SQL statement(s) straight from the client, but my experience has confirmed that the extra work saves you at least the extra time once you start coding and using your application. Even SQL Server itself and other major DBMSs use stored procedures for maintenance and other administrative tasks.

One last thing I want to mention is the fact that if you base a lot of your data calls on stored procedures, it can be much easier to change the data calls at a later date. You can simply change the stored procedure and not the application itself, meaning you don't have to recompile a business service or even your client application, depending on how you have designed your application. On the negative side, stored procedures are often written using database-vendor–specific SQL extensions, which means that they're hard to migrate to a different RDBMS. This of course is only a real concern if you're planning to move to another RDBMS.

Planning a Move to a Different RDBMS

If you're planning to move to another RDBMS from SQL Server, or just want to make it as easy as possible should management decide so in the future, it'll probably be a good idea to look up the following T-SQL statements in the SQL Server Books Online Help Documentation:

- **SET ANSI_DEFAULTS**: This statement sets the ANSI defaults on for the duration of the query session, trigger, or stored procedure

- **SET FIPS_FLAGGER**: This statement can be used to check for compliance with the ANSI SQL-92 standard.

If you use these statements appropriately, they can certainly help ease the move from SQL Server to another ANSI SQL-92–compliant RDBMS.

Creating and Running a Stored Procedure

Creating a stored procedure is fairly easy, and you're probably used to working with the Enterprise Manager that comes with SQL Server or a different stored procedure editor for SQL Server or Oracle. If this is the case, you may want to check out the facilities in the Server Explorer in the VS .NET IDE. Amongst other things, it's much easier to run and test a stored procedure directly from the text editor. Anyway, here's how you would create a stored procedure for the example UserMan database:

1. Open up the Server Explorer window.

2. Expand the UserMan database on your database server.

3. Right-click the Stored Procedures node and select New Stored Procedure.

This brings up the Stored Procedure text editor, which incidentally looks a lot like your VB .NET code editor. Except for syntax checking and other minor stuff, they're exactly the same (see Figure 16-1).

```
dbo.StoredPro...RVER.UserMan)*               ◁ ▷ ×
   1│ CREATE PROCEDURE dbo.StoredProcedure1
   2│ /*
   3│     (
   4│         @parameter1 datatype = default value,
   5│         @parameter2 datatype OUTPUT
   6│     )
   7│ */
   8│ AS
   9│     /* SET NOCOUNT ON */
  10│     RETURN
  11│
```

Figure 16-1. Stored procedure editor with SQL Server default template

NOTE   With SQL Server, it's only possible to use T-SQL for your stored procedures. However, the upcoming version of SQL Server, code-named Yukon, will have support for the .NET programming languages. Knowing this, perhaps you'll want to create your stored procedures in C# or VB .NET when Yukon is released.

Creating a Simple Stored Procedure

Once you've created a stored procedure, you need to give it a name. As you can see from your stored procedure editor, the template automatically names it StoredProcedure1. If you're wondering about the dbo prefix, it simply means that the stored procedure is created for the dbo user. In SQL Server terms, dbo stands for **data**base **o**wner, and it indicates who owns the database object, which is a stored procedure in this case. If you've been working with SQL Server for a while, you probably know the term *broken ownership chain*. An ownership chain is the dependency of a stored procedure upon tables, views, or other stored procedures.

Generally, the objects that a view or stored procedure depend on are also owned by the owner of the view or stored procedure. In such a case, there are no problems, because SQL Server doesn't check permissions in this situation. (It doesn't really have to, does it?) However, when one or more of the dependent database objects are owned by a different user than the one owning the view or stored procedure, the ownership chain is said to be broken. This means that SQL Server has to check the permissions of any dependent database object that has a different owner. This can be avoided if all of your database objects are owned by the same user, such as dbo.

Okay, let's say you've deleted the `StoredProcedure1` name and replaced it with `SimpleStoredProcedure`. To save the stored procedure before continuing, press Ctrl+S. If you saved your stored procedure at this point, you'd notice that you don't have to name it using a Save As dialog box, because you've already named it. The editor will make sure that the stored procedure is saved on the database server with the name you've entered, which in this case is `SimpleStoredProcedure`. If you first save your stored procedure, then change the name, and save it again, the stored procedure will be saved with the new name. However, the old stored procedure is still there too, which means you probably want to delete it. So, hold off saving your initial stored procedure until you've named it in the stored procedure text.

Although you can see your stored procedure in the Stored Procedure folder of the SQL Server Enterprise Manager and the Stored Procedure node in the Server Explorer, there isn't actually an area in your database designated for just stored procedures. The stored procedure is saved to the system tables as are most other objects in SQL Server.

As soon as you have saved it, the very first line of the stored procedure changes. The SQL statement CREATE PROCEDURE is changed so that the first line reads

```
ALTER PROCEDURE dbo.SimpleStoredProcedure
```

Why? Well, you just saved the newly created stored procedure, which means that you can't create another with the same name. Changing CREATE to ALTER takes care of that. It's that simple. In case you're wondering what happens when you change the name of your stored procedure and the SQL statement still reads ALTER PROCEDURE . . . , I can tell you the editor takes care of it for you and creates a new procedure. Try it and see for yourself! Basically, this means that CREATE PROCEDURE is never actually needed; one can simply use ALTER PROCEDURE, even on brand new procedures. However, this can be a dangerous practice, if you inadvertently change the name of your stored procedure to the name of an already existing one.

The `SimpleStoredProcedure` shown in Figure 16-1 doesn't actually do a lot, does it? Okay, I'll show you how to change that, but first let's cover some of the basics of how a stored procedure is written. In Figure 16-1 you can see two parts of the stored procedure: The first part is the header, and then there is the actual stored procedure itself. The header consists of all text down to and including Line 7. Basically the header declares how the stored procedure should be called, how many arguments to include and what type of arguments, and so on. Since this is a very simple procedure, I don't want any arguments, so I'll leave the commented-out text alone.

If you haven't changed the default editor settings, text that is commented out or any comments you have inserted yourself are printed in green. In a SQL Server stored procedure, comments are marked using start and end tags: /* for the comment start tag and */ for the comment end tag. This has one advantage over the way you insert comments in your VB .NET code in that you don't have to have a comment start tag on every line you want to comment out. You only need to have both a start and end tag.

The second part of the stored procedure is the part that starts with the AS clause on Line 8. The AS clause indicates that the text that follows is the body of the stored procedure, the instructions on what to do when the stored procedure is called and executed.

Now that you know a little about how a stored procedure is put together, it's time to edit it. See the exercise that follows.

Exercise

Create a stored procedure, name it **SimpleStoredProcedure**, and save it as described earlier. Type the following text on Line 10 in the SimpleStoredProcedure in place of the RETURN statement:

```
SELECT COUNT(*) FROM tblUser
```

Now the stored procedure should look like the example in Figure 16-2. The stored procedure will return the number of rows in the tblUser table. Please note that it's generally good practice to keep the RETURN statement as part of your stored procedure, but I'm taking it out and leaving it for an explanation later, when I discuss return values and how they're handled in code.

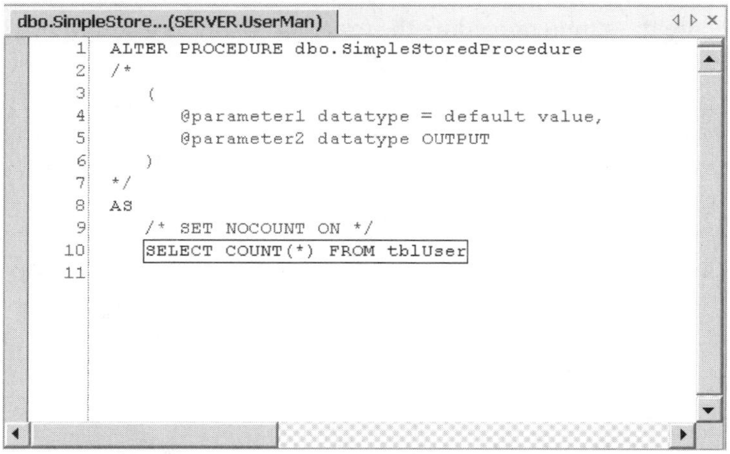

```
dbo.SimpleStore...(SERVER.UserMan)                    ◁ ▷ ✕
    1    ALTER PROCEDURE dbo.SimpleStoredProcedure
    2    /*
    3        (
    4            @parameter1 datatype = default value,
    5            @parameter2 datatype OUTPUT
    6        )
    7    */
    8    AS
    9        /* SET NOCOUNT ON */
   10        SELECT COUNT(*) FROM tblUser
   11
```

Figure 16-2. Stored procedure that returns the number of rows in the tblUser table

Don't forget to save the changes using Ctrl+S.

Running a Simple Stored Procedure from the IDE

Of course, there's no point in having a stored procedure that just sits there, so here's what you do to run it: If you have the stored procedure open in the stored procedure editor window, you can right-click anywhere in the editor window and select Run Stored Procedure from the pop-up menu. If you do this with the stored procedure you created in the exercise in the previous section, the Output window, located just below the editor window, should display the output from the stored procedure as shown in Figure 16-3.

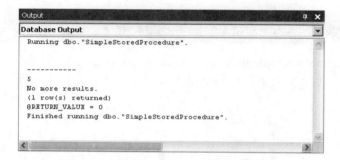

Figure 16-3. The Output window with output from SimpleStoredProcedure

If you have closed down the stored procedure editor window, you can run the stored procedure from the Server Explorer. Expand the database node, right-click the Stored Procedures node, and select Run Stored Procedure from the pop-up menu. This will execute the stored procedure the exact same way as if you were running it from the editor window.

Running a Simple Stored Procedure from Code

Okay, now that you have a fully functional stored procedure, you can try to run it from code. Listing 16-1 shows you some very simple code that will run the stored procedure. The example code in this listing uses data classes that were introduced in Chapters 5 and 6.

Listing 16-1. Running a Simple Stored Procedure

```
 1 Public Sub ExecuteSimpleSP()
 2    Dim cnnUserMan As SqlConnection
 3    Dim cmmUser As SqlCommand
 4    Dim lngNumUsers As Long
 5
 6    ' Instantiate and open the connection
 7    cnnUserMan = New SqlConnection(PR_STR_CONNECTION_STRING)
 8    cnnUserMan.Open()
 9
10    ' Instantiate and initialize command
11    cmmUser = New SqlCommand("SimpleStoredProcedure", cnnUserMan)
12    cmmUser.CommandType = CommandType.StoredProcedure
13
14    lngNumUsers = CLng(cmmUser.ExecuteScalar)
15    MsgBox(lngNumUsers.ToString)
16 End Sub
```

The code in Listing 16-1 retrieves the return value from the stored procedure. Now, this isn't usually all you want from a stored procedure, but it merely demonstrates what a simple stored procedure looks like. The stored procedure itself could just as well have had a DELETE FROM tblUser WHERE LastName='Johnson' SQL statement. If you want to execute this from code, you need to know if the stored procedure returns a value or not. It doesn't in this case, so you need to use the **ExecuteNonQuery** method of the **SqlCommand** class.

Exercise

Create a new stored procedure and save it with the name **uspGetUsers**. Type in the following text in place of the RETURN statement:

```
SELECT * FROM tblUser
```

Now the stored procedure should look like the one in Figure 16-4. This stored procedure will return all rows in the tblUser table.

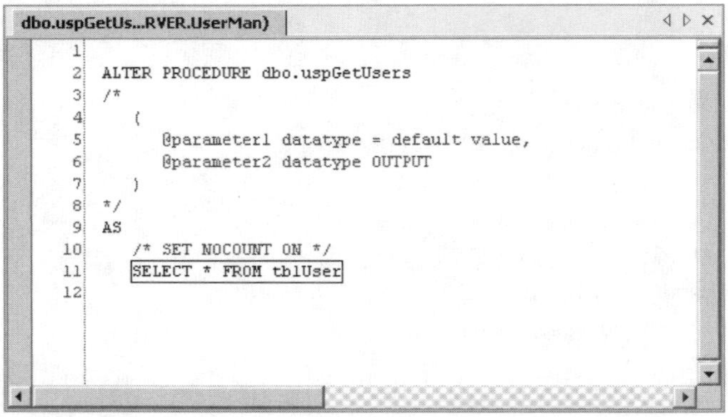

Figure 16-4. The uspGetUsers *stored procedure*

Don't forget to save the changes using Ctrl+S.

What you need now is some code to retrieve the rows from the stored procedure (see Listing 16-2).

Listing 16-2. Retrieving Rows from a Stored Procedure

```
1 Public Sub ExecuteSimpleRowReturningSP()
2    Dim cnnUserMan As SqlConnection
3    Dim cmmUser As SqlCommand
4    Dim drdUser As SqlDataReader
5
6    ' Instantiate and open the connection
7    cnnUserMan = New SqlConnection(PR_STR_CONNECTION_STRING)
8    cnnUserMan.Open()
9
```

```
10     ' Instantiate and initialize command
11     cmmUser = New SqlCommand("uspGetUsers", cnnUserMan)
12     cmmUser.CommandType = CommandType.StoredProcedure
13
14     ' Retrieve all user rows
15     drdUser = cmmUser.ExecuteReader()
16 End Sub
```

The example in Listing 16-2 retrieves the rows returned from the stored procedure by using the **ExecuteReader** method of the **SqlCommand** class. Please note that this method and the related **ExecuteXmlReader** method are the only options for retrieving rows as the result of a function call with the Command class.

Creating a Stored Procedure with Arguments

I'm sure you know arguments[2] from your daily programming, and there is no conceptual difference between those arguments and the ones used with stored procedures. Arguments are a great way of saving lines of code, and this is especially true if you have two or more stored procedures essentially performing the same task, such as deleting all rows with a specific ID.

Another reason for using arguments with stored procedures is to make the stored procedure behave differently, depending on the input from the arguments. One argument might hold the name of a table, view, or another stored procedure from which to extract data.

 TIP   In SQL Server you can use the EXECUTE sp_executesql statement and system stored procedure with arguments of type **ntext**, **nchar**, or **nvarchar** to execute parameterized queries. See the SQL Server Books Online Help Documentation for more information.

Arguments in stored procedures can be either input or output. If you include an input argument, you don't have to specify anything after the data type, but if you use an output argument, you need to specify the OUTPUT keyword after the data type.

---

2. I'm using the word *argument* here, but I might as well call it *parameter*, as T-SQL does. However, the two words are synonymous in this case.

Exercise

Create a new stored procedure and save it with the name
uspGetUsersByLastName. Type in the following text in place
of the RETURN statement:

```
SELECT * FROM tblUser
WHERE LastName = @strLastName
```

Uncomment the lines with arguments, and insert the following text instead of the
existing arguments:

```
@strLastName varchar(50)
```

The stored procedure should look like the one in Figure 16-5. This stored procedure will return all rows in the tblUser table where the LastName column
matches the strLastName argument.

```
dbo.uspGetUs...RVER.UserMan)                    ◁ ▷ ×
 1
 2   ALTER PROCEDURE dbo.uspGetUsersByLastName
 3      (
 4          @strLastName varchar(50)
 5      )
 6
 7   AS
 8      /* SET NOCOUNT ON */
 9      SELECT * FROM tblUser
10      WHERE LastName = @strLastName
11
```

Figure 16-5. The uspGetUsersByLastName *stored procedure*

Don't forget to save your changes using Ctrl+S.

NOTE   I only cover the absolute basics of how to create a stored procedure in this chapter. If you need more information, I suggest you look
up the CREATE PROCEDURE statement in the Books Online help application that comes with SQL Server.

Running a Stored Procedure with Arguments from the IDE

Try and run the stored procedure you created in the last exercise and see how the argument affects how it's run. You can try running the stored procedure from either the editor window or the Server Explorer window. The Run dialog box asks you for a value for the strLastName argument. Type **Doe** in the textbox and click OK. Now all users with the last name of Doe are returned as the result of the stored procedure.

Using a Stored Procedure with Arguments

The uspGetUsersByLastName stored procedure seems to work, so try and run it from code. Listing 16-3 shows how you would do this.

Listing 16-3. Retrieving Rows from a Stored Procedure with an Input Argument

```
1 Public Sub GetUsersByLastName()
2    Dim cnnUserMan As SqlConnection
3    Dim cmmUser As SqlCommand
4    Dim drdUser As SqlDataReader
5    Dim prmLastName As SqlParameter
6
7    ' Instantiate and open the connection
8    cnnUserMan = New SqlConnection(PR_STR_CONNECTION_STRING)
9    cnnUserMan.Open()
10
11   ' Instantiate and initialize command
12   cmmUser = New SqlCommand("uspGetUsersByLastName", cnnUserMan)
13   cmmUser.CommandType = CommandType.StoredProcedure
14   ' Instantiate, initialize and add parameter to command
15   prmLastName = cmmUser.Parameters.Add("@strLastName", _
16     SqlDbType.VarChar, 50)
17   ' Indicate this is an input parameter
18   prmLastName.Direction = ParameterDirection.Input
19   ' Set the value of the parameter
20   prmLastName.Value = "Doe"
21
22   ' Return all users with a last name of Doe
23   drdUser = cmmUser.ExecuteReader()
24 End Sub
```

In Listing 16-3, a **SqlParameter** object specifies the input parameter of the stored procedure. On Lines 15 and 16, I ask the command object to create and associate a parameter with the `@strLastName` argument. The value of this parameter is set to "Doe", which effectively means that only rows containing a last name of Doe are returned.

As you can see, I have specified that the parameter is an input argument using the **ParameterDirection** enum, although you don't really have to, because this is the default. Don't worry too much about parameter and argument; they are essentially the same thing. Chapter 6 tells you more about the Command and Parameter classes.

Creating a Stored Procedure with Arguments and Return Values

So far I have created stored procedures that return a single value or a result set (rows) and a stored procedure that takes an input argument. In many cases, this is all you want, but sometimes it's not enough. What if you want a value and a result set returned at the same time? Actually, you may want several values and a result set, but I'm sure you get the idea. In such instances, you can use output arguments.

Actually, you can return as many different values and results sets as you want by including multiple SELECT statements after the AS clause, but I personally think this approach looks messy. If I return rows and one or more values, I generally use OUTPUT arguments for the values. I guess that to some extent this is a matter of preference. However, you should be aware that including an OUTPUT parameter is a faster approach than having it returned in a **DataSet** object, but sometimes you might need the richer functionality of the **DataSet** class, once the values have been returned.

Instead of using the following example code to return a scalar value, two result sets, and another scalar value in that order, as shown here:

```
...
AS
    SELECT 19
    SELECT * FROM tblUser
    SELECT * FROM tblUserRights
    SELECT 21
```

I would use something like this:

```
...
AS
    SELECT * FROM tblUser
    SELECT * FROM tblUserRights
```

The two return values should then be returned as OUTPUT arguments. However, it's your call, my friend, as to which approach you prefer to use. Please note that OUTPUT arguments can also serve as INPUT arguments by default, meaning you can actually supply a value in the OUTPUT argument when calling the stored procedure, and get a different value back—just like a value passed by reference from one procedure to another.

Exercise

Create a new stored procedure and save it with the name **uspGetUsersAndRights**. This stored procedure should return the value 55 for the OUTPUT argument lngNumRows, and then all rows in the tblUser table and all rows in the tblUserRights table. The stored procedure should look like the one in Figure 16-6.

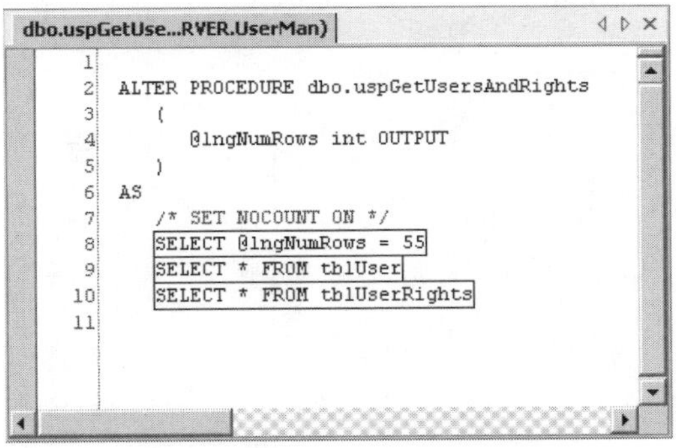

Figure 16-6. The uspGetUsersAndRights *stored procedure*

In the uspGetUsersAndRights stored procedure, shown in Figure 16-6, you can see that the @lngNumRows **int** argument is set to the value 55 on Line 8. However, using a default value for the argument you can achieve the same result, by changing Line 4 like this:

```
@lngNumRows int = 55 OUTPUT
```

This means that if for some reason you don't set the value of this parameter when calling the stored procedure or within the stored procedure itself, it'll return 55 as the output value. Default argument values also work for input arguments, and they're specified the same way, using the equal sign followed by the default value, right after the data type.

Running a Stored Procedure with Arguments and Return Values from the IDE

If you've created and saved the stored procedure in the previous exercise, test it by running it. You can try running the stored procedure from either the editor window or the Server Explorer window. The Output window, located just below the editor window, will display the output from the stored procedure, and it should look similar to the output in Figure 16-7, if you supply the value 55 for the @lngNumRows input parameter.

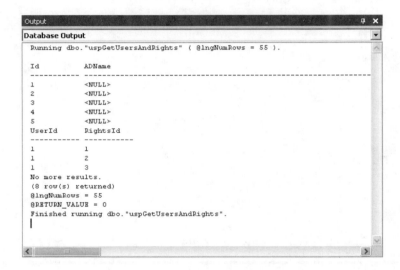

Figure 16-7. The Output window with output from the uspGetUsersAndRights *stored procedure*

NOTE Syntax testing of your stored procedure is done when you save it, and I have a feeling you have already encountered this. If not, just know that's how it is—syntax errors are caught when you try to save your stored procedure. However, the current error messages displayed when a syntax error is caught usually leaves you guessing as to what is wrong. This is a major problem that needs to be addressed by Microsoft IMHO.

Using a Stored Procedure with Arguments and Return Values

Listing 16-4 shows the code to execute the uspGetUsersAndRights stored procedure programmatically. See the "Auto-Generating Stored Procedure Code" section later in this chapter for basic information on how to let the VS .NET shell create most of the code for you automatically.

Listing 16-4. Retrieving Rows and Output Values from a Stored Procedure

```
1 Public Sub GetUsersAndRights()
2    Dim cnnUserMan As SqlConnection
3    Dim cmmUser As SqlCommand
4    Dim drdUser As SqlDataReader
5    Dim prmNumRows As SqlParameter
6
7    ' Instantiate and open the connection
8    cnnUserMan = New SqlConnection(PR_STR_CONNECTION_STRING)
9    cnnUserMan.Open()
10
11   ' Instantiate and initialize command
12   cmmUser = New SqlCommand("uspGetUsersAndRights", cnnUserMan)
13   cmmUser.CommandType = CommandType.StoredProcedure
14   ' Instantiate, initialize and add parameter to command
15   prmNumRows = cmmUser.Parameters.Add("@lngNumRows", SqlDbType.Int)
16   ' Indicate this is an output parameter
17   prmNumRows.Direction = ParameterDirection.Output
18   ' Get first batch of rows (users)
19   drdUser = cmmUser.ExecuteReader()
20
21   ' Display the last name of all user rows
22   Do While drdUser.Read()
23      MsgBox(drdUser("LastName").ToString)
24   Loop
25
26   ' Get next batch of rows (user rights)
27   If drdUser.NextResult() Then
28      ' Display the id of all rights
29      Do While drdUser.Read()
30         MsgBox(drdUser("RightsId").ToString)
31      Loop
32   End If
33 End Sub
```

In Listing 16-4 two result sets are returned, and therefore I use the **NextResult** method of the DataReader class to advance to the second result set on Line 27. Otherwise, this stored procedure works pretty much the same as one with input parameters, although the parameter direction is specified as an output on Line 17.

Retrieving a Value Specified with RETURN

In a stored procedure you can use the RETURN statement to return a scalar value. However, this value cannot be retrieved using the **ExecuteScalar** method of the Command class, as it would when you use the SELECT statement (refer back to Figure 16-2). Of course there is a way of retrieving this value, which I show you after the following exercise.

Exercise

Create a new stored procedure and save it with the name **uspGetRETURN_VALUE**. This stored procedure should return the value 55 as the RETURN_VALUE. The stored procedure should look like the one in Figure 16-8.

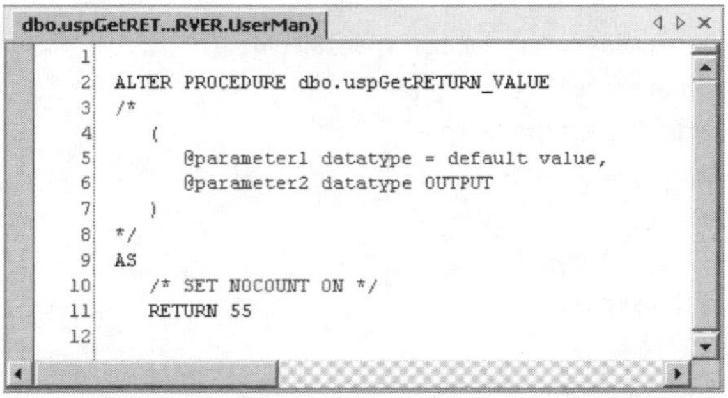

```
dbo.uspGetRET...RVER.UserMan)                      ◁ ▷ ✕
 1
 2   ALTER PROCEDURE dbo.uspGetRETURN_VALUE
 3   /*
 4      (
 5          @parameter1 datatype = default value,
 6          @parameter2 datatype OUTPUT
 7      )
 8   */
 9   AS
10      /* SET NOCOUNT ON */
11      RETURN 55
12
```

Figure 16-8. The uspGetRETURN_VALUE *stored procedure*

Listing 16-5 shows you how to retrieve the value from code.

Listing 16-5. Retrieving RETURN_VALUE from a Stored Procedure

```
1 Public Sub GetRETURN_VALUE()
2    Dim cnnUserMan As SqlConnection
3    Dim cmmUser As SqlCommand
4    Dim prmNumRows As SqlParameter
5    Dim lngResult As Long
6
7    ' Instantiate and open the connection
8    cnnUserMan = New SqlConnection(PR_STR_CONNECTION_STRING)
9    cnnUserMan.Open()
10
11    ' Instantiate and initialize command
12    cmmUser = New SqlCommand("uspGetRETURN_VALUE", cnnUserMan)
13    cmmUser.CommandType = CommandType.StoredProcedure
14    ' Instantiate, initialize and add parameter to command
15    prmNumRows = cmmUser.Parameters.Add("@RETURN_VALUE", _
16       SqlDbType.Int)
17    ' Indicate this is a return value parameter
18    prmNumRows.Direction = ParameterDirection.ReturnValue
19    ' Get RETURN_VALUE
20    lngResult = CLng(cmmUser.ExecuteScalar())
21 End Sub
```

In Listing 16-5 the **ExecuteScalar** method gets the RETURN_VALUE from a stored procedure. Normally, you would use this method to return the value in the lngResult variable, but this variable will contain the default value, 0, in this case. However, because I have specified the **Direction** property of the prmNumRows parameter with the **ReturnValue** member of the **ParameterDirection** enum, I can simply look at the **Value** property of the parameter after executing the command.

Auto-Generating Stored Procedure Code

Instead of doing all the hard work yourself; you can let the VS .NET shell do it for you. Just drag a stored procedure from the Server Explorer to a form in your application. The VS .NET shell then creates the Connection and Command objects for you, set up and ready to use. All you need to do is to execute the Command object and take care of the return values and result set(s), if any.

The auto-generated code is placed in the InitializeComponent procedure of your form.

Changing the Name of a Stored Procedure

If you change the name of your stored procedure in the editor window, the stored procedure is saved with the new name when you save (Ctrl+S). However, if you're not using this method to copy an existing stored procedure, you should be aware that the old stored procedure still exists. Therefore, you'll have to delete it if you don't want it.

Viewing Stored Procedure Dependencies

In SQL Server Enterprise Manager, you can see what tables and other objects your stored procedure uses or is dependent on. Open up Enterprise Manager, expand your SQL Server, expand databases and your database, select the Stored Procedures node, right-click the stored procedure you want to see the dependencies for, and select All Task Display Dependencies from the pop-up menu. This brings up the Dependencies dialog box, where you can see what database objects your stored procedure depends on and vice versa. This is also called the *ownership chain*.

Running Oracle Stored Procedures

Oracle stored procedures and stored functions are different from those of SQL Server. That's why I've chosen to explain the Oracle stored procedures in a separate section. When discussing what you can do with stored procedures/functions in Oracle compared to stored procedures in SQL Server, it's pretty much the same, but the implementation is quite different.

SQL Server stored procedures can return a value, just like a function in VB .NET, whereas in Oracle you have stored procedures and stored functions. This means that if you want a return value that isn't a parameter, you must use a stored function. In this chapter, you won't see how to create stored procedures and stored functions in Oracle. However, you can use the Oracle Database Project located in the example code, which you can download from the Apress Web site (http://www.apress.com) or the UserMan site (http://www.userman.dk), to create the tables, stored procedures, views, and triggers used by the Oracle example code. Please consult your Oracle documentation if you need more information on how to implement stored procedures and stored functions in Oracle.

When you use ADO.NET and ADO for that matter, you can't use the **ExecuteScalar** method of the Command class to retrieve a return value, as shown in Listings 16-1 and 16-5 and discussed in the "Retrieving a Value Specified with RETURN" section. This is also true if you execute a stored function. You need to return any return values in output parameters, just as I've demonstrated in Listing 16-4. If all you need to do is to return a value, as in Listing 16-1, which is what the Oracle stored function in Listing 16-6 does, you can do so as shown in Listing 16-7, which is really more or less the same code as in Listing 16-1.

Listing 16-6. A Simple Oracle Stored Function

```
1 CREATE OR REPLACE FUNCTION SIMPLESTOREDFUNCTION
2 RETURN NUMBER
3 AS
4    lngNumRows NUMBER;
5 BEGIN
6    SELECT COUNT(*) INTO lngNumRows FROM TBLUSER;
7    RETURN lngNumRows;
8 END SIMPLESTOREDFUNCTION;
```

Listing 16-7. Running a Simple Oracle Stored Function

```
1 Public Sub ExecuteSimpleOracleSF()
2    Dim cnnUserMan As OleDbConnection
3    Dim cmmUser As OleDbCommand
4    Dim prmNumRows As OleDbParameter
5    Dim objReturnValue As Object
6
7    ' Instantiate and open the connection
8    cnnUserMan = New OleDbConnection(PR_STR_CONNECTION_STRING)
9    cnnUserMan.Open()
10
11   ' Instantiate and initialize command
12   cmmUser = New OleDbCommand("SimpleStoredFunction", cnnUserMan)
13   cmmUser.CommandType = CommandType.StoredProcedure
14   ' Instantiate output parameter and add to parameter
15   ' collection of command object
16   prmNumRows = cmmUser.CreateParameter()
17   prmNumRows.Direction = ParameterDirection.ReturnValue
18   prmNumRows.DbType = DbType.Int64
19   prmNumRows.Precision = 38
20   prmNumRows.Size = 38
21   cmmUser.Parameters.Add(prmNumRows)
22
23   ' Retrieve and display value
24   objReturnValue = cmmUser.ExecuteScalar()
25   MsgBox(cmmUser.Parameters(0).Value.ToString())
26 End Sub
```

In Listing 16-6 you can see an Oracle stored function that returns the number of rows in the tblUser table. Listing 16-7 shows you how to access this stored function and retrieve the return value.

In Listing 16-7 I've actually used the **ExecuteScalar** method of the Command class on Line 24, but if you look carefully, you'll see that I don't use the value returned from the function call (`objReturnValue`) as in Listing 16-1. However, I do retrieve the return value in the `prmNumRows` parameter, which is instantiated, initialized, and set up as a return value on Lines 12–21, and display it after executing the command on Line 25. I use **ExecuteScalar** method, because it has the least overhead of any of the **Execute** methods of the Command class. Therefore, even if you don't use the return value from the **ExecuteScalar** method, which is always **Nothing** when calling an Oracle stored function or stored procedure, you can still get the return value from the stored function. The trick is to add a parameter to the command object and make sure you set the **Direction** property of the parameter object to the **ReturnValue** member of the **ParameterDirection** enum, as is shown on Line 17.

If you want to use an Oracle stored procedure instead of a stored function, like the one shown in Listing 16-8, to retrieve one or more simple data types using output parameters, you can use the example code shown in Listing 16-9.

Listing 16-8. A Simple Oracle Stored Procedure

```
1 CREATE OR REPLACE PROCEDURE  SIMPLESTOREDPROCEDURE
2 (lngNumRows OUT NUMBER)
3 AS
4 BEGIN
5   SELECT COUNT(*) INTO lngNumRows FROM TBLUSER;
6 END SIMPLESTOREDPROCEDURE;
```

The Oracle stored procedure in Listing 16-8 accepts one output parameter (`lngNumRows`) and sets this parameter to the number of rows in the tblUser table when executed. You can see how you can call this stored procedure from code in Listing 16-9.

Listing 16-9. Running a Simple Oracle Stored Procedure

```
1 Public Sub ExecuteSimpleOracleSP()
2    Dim cnnUserMan As OleDbConnection
3    Dim cmmUser As OleDbCommand
4    Dim prmNumRows As OleDbParameter
5    Dim objReturnValue As Object
6
7    ' Instantiate and open the connection
8    cnnUserMan = New OleDbConnection(PR_STR_CONNECTION_STRING)
9    cnnUserMan.Open()
10
11   ' Instantiate and initialize command
12   cmmUser = New OleDbCommand("SimpleStoredProcedure", cnnUserMan)
13   cmmUser.CommandType = CommandType.StoredProcedure
14   ' Instantiate output parameter and add to parameter
15   ' collection of command object
16   prmNumRows = cmmUser.CreateParameter()
17   prmNumRows.Direction = ParameterDirection.Output
18   prmNumRows.DbType = DbType.Int64
19   prmNumRows.Precision = 38
20   prmNumRows.Size = 38
21   cmmUser.Parameters.Add(prmNumRows)
22
23   ' Retrieve and display value
24   objReturnValue = cmmUser.ExecuteScalar()
25   MsgBox(cmmUser.Parameters(0).Value.ToString())
26 End Sub
```

In Listing 16-9, I again use the **ExecuteScalar** method of the Command class on Line 24 for retrieving a value from a stored procedure. The example code in Listing 16-9 really isn't all that different from Listing 16-7, but it does show you how to call a stored procedure instead of a stored function.

The Oracle stored procedures and stored functions and the example code to execute them shown so far only deal with simple return values. If you need to return result sets, such as in Listings 16-2, 16-3, and 16-4, you need to use cursors in the stored procedures.[3]

Listing 16-10 shows a stored procedure that returns a result set using cursors.

---

3. You can also use cursors with a stored function, but since I won't be using the function return value from this point on, I'll concentrate on using stored procedures.

Listing 16-10. Oracle Stored Procedure Returning Result Set

```
1 CREATE OR REPLACE PACKAGE PKGTBLUSER
2 AS
3   TYPE CUR_TBLUSER IS REF CURSOR RETURN TBLUSER%ROWTYPE;
4 END PKGTBLUSER;
5
6 CREATE OR REPLACE PROCEDURE USPGETUSERSBYLASTNAME
7   (ROWS OUT PKGTBLUSER.CUR_TBLUSER, strLastName IN VARCHAR2)
8 IS
9 BEGIN
10 OPEN ROWS FOR SELECT * FROM TBLUSER
11 WHERE LASTNAME = strLastName;
12 END USPGETUSERSBYLASTNAME;
```

In Listing 16-10, you can see how I first create a package definition (Lines 1 through 4) in my Oracle database; in this package, I define the CUR_TBLUSER cursor type to be of data type **REF CURSOR**,[4] which returns rows from the tblUser table. The package definition only holds the type declaration, which is used in the stored procedure. Please note that the notion of Oracle package definitions and package bodies are beyond the scope of this book, although you can certainly use a package body instead of the stored procedure shown on Lines 6 through 12. Please see your Oracle documentation for more information on packages.

You need to declare the cursor type in a package, because you're using it as the data type for one of the parameters in the USPGETUSERSBYLASTNAME stored procedure. You can't declare a data type in the parameters section of a stored procedure, which is why you need it declared elsewhere. If you look at the parameters declaration on Line 7, you can see that I need to use the full path to the data type, PKGTBLUSER.CUR_TBLUSER. Lines 10 and 11 of Listing 16-10 is where the rows that match the passed last name criterion are retrieved with the CUR_TBLUSER cursor and saved in the ROWS output parameter. Listing 16-11 shows you how to retrieve the result set from the stored procedure.

---

4. This is short for REFERENCE CURSOR, and basically it's used as a pointer to the original data. Please see your Oracle documentation for more information.

Listing 16-11. Retrieving Result Set from Oracle Stored Procedure

```
1 Public Sub OracleGetUsersByLastName()
2    Dim cnnUserMan As OleDbConnection
3    Dim cmmUser As OleDbCommand
4    Dim prmLastName As OleDbParameter
5    Dim drdUser As OleDbDataReader
6
7    ' Instantiate and open the connection
8    cnnUserMan = New OleDbConnection(PR_STR_CONNECTION_STRING)
9    cnnUserMan.Open()
10
11   ' Instantiate and initialize command
12   cmmUser = New OleDbCommand("USPGETUSERSBYLASTNAME", cnnUserMan)
13   cmmUser.CommandType = CommandType.StoredProcedure
14   ' Instantiate, initialize and add parameter to command
15   prmLastName = cmmUser.Parameters.Add("strLastName", OleDbType.VarChar, 50)
16   ' Indicate this is an input parameter
17   prmLastName.Direction = ParameterDirection.Input
18   ' Set the type and value of the parameter
19   prmLastName.Value = "Doe"
20   ' Retrieve rows
21   drdUser = cmmUser.ExecuteReader()
22   ' Loop through the returned rows
23   While drdUser.Read()
24      ' Display the last name of all user rows
25      MsgBox(drdUser("LastName").ToString())
26   End While
27 End Sub
```

In Listing 16-11, you can see how I set up the command object on Lines 12 and 13, and then prepare the prmLastName input parameter with the value of "Doe". I then call the **ExecuteReader** method of the Command class, which returns the DataReader with all users having a last name of Doe. If you compare the stored procedure in Listing 16-10 and the example code in Listing 16-11, you'll see that there's a mismatch of the number of parameters. The stored procedure has two parameters, the last name input parameter and the result set output parameter. However, I only set up one parameter in Listing 16-11 and that's the last name input parameter. The Command object takes care of returning the result set as the return value of the function call (**ExecuteReader**) instead of as an output parameter. It almost works the same as with the SQL Server example code in Listing 16-3.

> **NOTE** It doesn't matter where you place the **ROWS OUT** parameter in the stored procedure parameter declaration—that is, whether you place it first as is done in Listing 16-10, or last like this:
>
> ```
> (strLastName IN VARCHAR2, ROWS OUT PKGTBLUSER.CUR_TBLUSER)
> ```

There are other ways of calling a stored procedure in your Oracle database, such as using the ODBC {call storedprocedurename} syntax, but I've chosen to show you the way that looks and feels as close to the one used for calling SQL Server procedures.

Running DB2 Stored Procedures

IBM DB2 stored procedures are different from those of SQL Server, just as the Oracle ones are, which is why I've chosen to explain them in this section. As is the case with Oracle, when discussing what you can do with stored procedures in DB2 compared to stored procedures in SQL Server, it's pretty much the same, but the implementation is quite different.

SQL Server stored procedures can return a value, just like a function in VB .NET, whereas in DB2, your stored procedures can only pass error codes in the form of integer values as the return value. This means that if you want a return value that isn't a parameter, you can only return an integer. I won't be showing you how to create stored procedures in DB2, but you can use the DB2 UserMan database script, which you can download from the Apress Web site (http://www.apress.com) or the UserMan site (http://www.userman.dk), to create the tables, stored procedures, views, and triggers used by the DB2 example code. Please consult your DB2 documentation if you need more information on how to implement stored procedures in DB2.

When you use ADO.NET and ADO for that matter, you can't use the **ExecuteScalar** method of the Command class to retrieve a return value, as shown in Listings 16-1 and 16-5 and discussed in the "Retrieving a Value Specified with RETURN" section. You need to return any return values in output parameters, just as I've demonstrated in Listing 16-4. If all you need to do is to return a value, as in Listing 16-1, which is what the DB2 stored procedure in Listing 16-12 does, you can do so as shown in Listing 16-13, which is really more or less the same code as in Listing 16-1.

Listing 16-12. A Simple DB2 Stored Procedure with Return Value

```
1 CREATE PROCEDURE SimpleStoredFunc()
2 LANGUAGE SQL
3    RETURN (SELECT COUNT(*) FROM tblUser)
```

Listing 16-13. Running a Simple DB2 Stored Procedure with Return Value

```
1 Public Sub ExecuteSimpleDB2SPWithReturnValue()
2    Dim cnnUserMan As OleDbConnection
3    Dim cmmUser As OleDbCommand
4    Dim prmNumRows As OleDbParameter
5    Dim objReturnValue As Object
6
7    ' Instantiate and open the connection
8    cnnUserMan = New OleDbConnection(PR_STR_CONNECTION_STRING)
9    cnnUserMan.Open()
10
11   ' Instantiate and initialize command
12   cmmUser = New OleDbCommand("SimpleStoredFunc", cnnUserMan)
13   cmmUser.CommandType = CommandType.StoredProcedure
14   ' Instantiate output parameter and add to parameter
15   ' collection of command object
16   prmNumRows = cmmUser.CreateParameter()
17   prmNumRows.Direction = ParameterDirection.ReturnValue
18   prmNumRows.DbType = DbType.Int32
19   cmmUser.Parameters.Add(prmNumRows)
20
21   ' Retrieve and display value
22   objReturnValue = cmmUser.ExecuteScalar()
23   MsgBox(cmmUser.Parameters(0).Value.ToString())
24 End Sub
```

In Listing 16-12, you can see a DB2 stored procedure that returns the number of rows in the tblUser table. I've named this stored procedure SimpleStoredFunc as in a stored function, because I want to differentiate between this stored procedure and the one in Listing 16-14, shown a little later. Please note that due to the restrictions on the number of characters you can use with DB2 objects, I can't call the stored procedure SimpleStoredFunction as I did with the Oracle one earlier in this chapter. You can see in Listing 16-13 how you can access this stored procedure and retrieve the return value.

In Listing 16-13, I've actually used the **ExecuteScalar** method of the Command class on Line 22, but if you look carefully, you'll see that I don't use the value returned from the function call (objReturnValue) as in Listing 16-1. However, I do retrieve the return value in the prmNumRows parameter, which is instantiated, initialized, and set up as a return value on Lines 12 through 19, and display it after executing the command on Line 23. I use **ExecuteScalar** method, because it has the least overhead of any of the **Execute** methods of the Command class. Therefore, even if you don't use the return value from the **ExecuteScalar** method, which is always **Nothing**, when calling an DB2 stored procedure, you can still get the return value from the stored procedure. The trick is to add a parameter to the command object and make sure you set the **Direction** property of the parameter object to the **ReturnValue** member of the **ParameterDirection** enum, as is shown on Line 17.

If you want to return anything but an integer value, you must use output parameters, like the one shown in Listing 16-14, to retrieve one or more simple data types using output parameters. To do so, you can use the example code shown in Listing 16-15.

Listing 16-14. A Simple DB2 Stored Procedure

```
1 CREATE PROCEDURE SimpleStoredProc(OUT strLastName VARCHAR(50))
2    READS SQL DATA
3    LANGUAGE SQL
4 BEGIN
5    DECLARE v_LastName VARCHAR(50);
6    SELECT LastName INTO v_LastName FROM tblUser WHERE Id=1;
7    SET strLastName = v_LastName;
8 END
```

Listing 16-15. Running a Simple DB2 Stored Procedure

```
1 Public Sub ExecuteSimpleDB2SP()
2    Dim cnnUserMan As OleDbConnection
3    Dim cmmUser As OleDbCommand
4    Dim prmLastName As OleDbParameter
5    Dim objReturnValue As Object
6
7    ' Instantiate and open the connection
8    cnnUserMan = New OleDbConnection(PR_STR_CONNECTION_STRING)
9    cnnUserMan.Open()
10
11    ' Instantiate and initialize command
12    cmmUser = New OleDbCommand("SIMPLESTOREDPROC", cnnUserMan)
13    cmmUser.CommandType = CommandType.StoredProcedure
```

```
14    ' Instantiate output parameter and add to parameter
15    ' collection of command object
16    prmLastName = cmmUser.CreateParameter()
17    prmLastName.Direction = ParameterDirection.Output
18    prmLastName.DbType = DbType.String
19    prmLastName.Size = 50
20    cmmUser.Parameters.Add(prmLastName)
21
22    ' Retrieve and display value
23    objReturnValue = cmmUser.ExecuteScalar()
24    MsgBox(cmmUser.Parameters(0).Value.ToString())
25 End Sub
```

The DB2 stored procedure in Listing 16-14 accepts one output parameter (strLastName) and sets this parameter to the LastName of the row in the tblUser table with an ID of 1. You can see how you can call this stored procedure from code in Listing 16-15.

In Listing 16-15, I again use the **ExecuteScalar** method of the Command class on Line 23 for retrieving a value from a stored procedure. The example code on Listing 16-15 really is somewhat different from Listing 16-13, and it shows you how to return a noninteger value.

The DB2 stored procedures, and the example code to execute them shown so far, only deal with simple return values. If you need to return result sets, such as in Listings 16-2, 16-3, and 16-4, you need to use cursors in the stored procedures.

Listing 16-16 shows a stored procedure that returns a result set using cursors.

Listing 16-16. DB2 Stored Procedure Returning Result Set

```
1 CREATE PROCEDURE uspGetUsersByLastName(IN strLastName VARCHAR(50))
2    DYNAMIC RESULT SETS 1
3    LANGUAGE SQL
4    BEGIN
5       DECLARE UserCursor CURSOR WITH RETURN TO CALLER
6           FOR SELECT * FROM tblUser
7           WHERE LastName=strLastName;
8       OPEN UserCursor;
9    END /
```

In Listing 16-16, you can see how I declare the UserCursor CURSOR, which returns rows from the tblUser table. If you need any information on how to create stored procedures and/or using cursors with DB2, please refer to your documentation.

Lines 5 through 8 of Listing 16-16 is where the rows that match the passed last name criterion are retrieved with the `UserCursor` cursor, and returned to the caller with the OPEN statement on Line 8. Listing 16-17 shows you how to retrieve the result set from the stored procedure.

Listing 16-17. Retrieving Result Set from DB2 Stored Procedure

```
1 Public Sub DB2GetUsersByLastName()
2    Dim cnnUserMan As OleDbConnection
3    Dim cmmUser As OleDbCommand
4    Dim prmLastName As OleDbParameter
5    Dim drdUser As OleDbDataReader
6
7    ' Instantiate and open the connection
8    cnnUserMan = New OleDbConnection(PR_STR_CONNECTION_STRING)
9    cnnUserMan.Open()
10
11   ' Instantiate and initialize command
12   cmmUser = New OleDbCommand("uspGetUsersByLastName", cnnUserMan)
13   cmmUser.CommandType = CommandType.StoredProcedure
14   ' Instantiate, initialize and add parameter to command
15   prmLastName = cmmUser.Parameters.Add("strLastName", OleDbType.VarChar, 50)
16   ' Indicate this is an input parameter
17   prmLastName.Direction = ParameterDirection.Input
18   ' Set the type and value of the parameter
19   prmLastName.Value = "Doe"
20
21   ' Retrieve rows
22   drdUser = cmmUser.ExecuteReader()
23   ' Loop through the returned rows
24   While drdUser.Read()
25      ' Display the last name of all user rows
26      MsgBox(drdUser("LastName").ToString())
27   End While
28 End Sub
```

In Listing 16-17, you can see how I set up the command object on Lines 12 and 13, and then prepare the `prmLastName` input parameter with the value of "Doe". I then call the **ExecuteReader** method of the Command class, which returns the DataReader with all users having a last name of Doe.

There are other ways of calling a stored procedure in your DB2 database, such as using the ODBC {call storedprocedurename} syntax, but I've chosen to show you the way that looks and feels as close to the one used for calling SQL Server procedures.

Summary

In this chapter, I discussed when and why to use various server-side objects for server-side processing of your data. I demonstrated stored procedures and functions, and showed you how to create, run, and execute a stored procedure and function from code.

I went into enough details about stored procedures and functions to cover just what a VB .NET programmer needs to know, but if you're also responsible for coding a SQL Server database and you need more information and example code, I can certainly recommend you read this Apress book:

> *Code Centric: T-SQL Programming with Stored Procedures and Triggers*, by Garth Wells. Apress, February 2001. ISBN: 1-893115-83-6.

You can find more information about this title here:
`http://www.apress.com/book/bookDisplay.html?bID=73`.

The next chapter is also about server-side processing, namely how, when, and why to use views.

Using Views

IN THIS CHAPTER, I discuss one specific way of doing server-side processing: views. If you need to know about server-side processing in general, I suggest you read the beginning of Chapter 16.

This chapter includes hands-on exercises that will take you through creating views. See the Exercise items that appear throughout the text.

Although this chapter primarily focuses on SQL Server 2000 features, some of the functionality can certainly be reproduced in the other DBMSs I cover in this book:

- *SQL Server 7.0:* All functionality shown in this chapter can be reproduced.

- *Microsoft Access:* Microsoft Access doesn't support views as such. However, views can be reproduced as queries in Microsoft Access, but you can't do this from within the VS .NET IDE; you have to use other means, like the Microsoft Access front-end.

- *Oracle:* Oracle supports all the server-side processing described in this chapter.

- *MySQL:* For the examples in this book, I have been using MySQL version 3.23.51, which doesn't support views, meaning there is no example code for MySQL in this chapter. However, at the time of writing (August 2002), version 4.? of MySQL is described on http://www.mysql.com, and according to the plans and description, version 4.? is supposed to support views. Even when this means of server-side processing is available in MySQL, it's still not possible to create any of these items from within the VS .NET IDE.

The code for this chapter has examples for all the listed DBMSs where appropriate.

Using Views

A *view* is, as the word suggests, a display of data in your database. Perhaps it helps to think of a view as a virtual table. It can be a subset of a table or an entire table, or it can be a subset of several joined tables. Basically, a view can represent just about any subset of data in your database, and you can include other views in a view. Including a view in another view is called *nesting,* and it can be a valuable way of grouping display data. However, nesting too deeply can also result in performance problems and can certainly make it a real challenge to track down errors. There isn't really any magic to a view or any big secrets that I can let you in on; it's simply just a great tool for manipulating your data. In the rest of this section, I am going to look at why, when, where, and how you should use a view.

 NOTE   The example code shown in this section is SQL Server only, but if you take a look at the accompanying example code, you'll see that it works exactly the same with Microsoft Access queries. Only the SQL Server .NET Data Provider has been changed to the OLE DB .NET Data Provider. The same goes for Oracle and DB2 views. See the example code on the Apress Web site, which is almost identical to the Microsoft Access code. Views aren't supported in MySQL 3.23.51.

View Restrictions

A view is almost identical to a row-returning query, with just a few exceptions. Some of the restrictions are detailed here:

- COMPUTE and COMPUTE BY clauses cannot be included in your view.

- ORDER BY clauses aren't allowed in a view, unless you specify the TOP clause as part of the SELECT statement. However, you can index a view with SQL Server 2000.

- The INTO keyword cannot be used to create a new table.

- Temporary tables can't be referenced.

There are other restrictions, so please check with your SQL Server documentation and/or Help Files.

Why Use a View?

Like stored procedures, views are used for server-side processing of your data; however, whereas stored procedures mainly are used for security and performance reasons, views are generally used to secure access to your data and to hide complexity of queries that contain many joins. You may want to use a view for a variety of reasons:

- *Security:* You don't want your users to access the tables directly, and with the help of a view, you can restrict users to seeing only the parts of a table they are allowed to see. You can restrict access to specific columns and/or rows and thus make it easy for your users to use for their own queries.

- *Encryption:* You can encrypt a view so that no one can see where the underlying data comes from. Mind you, this is an irreversible action, meaning that the textual SQL statements that form the view can't be retrieved again!

- *Aggregated data:* Views are often used on large scale systems to provide aggregated data.

There are other reasons for creating a view, but the mentioned reasons are certainly two of the most common.

Creating a View

It's easy to create a view. If you are used to working with the SQL Server's Server Manager, you should check out what the Server Explorer has to offer you. Here's how you create a view using the UserMan database as an example:

1. Open up the Server Explorer window.

2. Expand the UserMan database on your database server.

3. Right-click the Views node and select New View.

This brings up the View Designer, which in fact is the same as the Query Designer.

 NOTE The Query Designer is described in detail in Chapter 13. Although the View Designer and Query Designer have the same look and feel, you cannot create views that don't adhere to the view restrictions mentioned in the "View Restrictions" section.

The Add Table dialog box is also shown when the View Designer is displayed. In this dialog box, simply select the tables you want to retrieve data from and click Add. Click Close when all the required tables have been added.

As you start selecting in the Diagram pane the columns that should be output when the view is run, the SQL pane and the Grid pane change accordingly. When you are done selecting the columns to output, you should save the view using Ctrl+S.

Exercise

Create a new view. This view should contain the following tables: tblUser, tblRights, and tblUserRights. The following fields should be output: `tblUser.LoginName`, `tblUser.FirstName`, `tblUser.LastName`, and `tblRights.Name`. Save the view under the name **viwUserInfo**. The new view should look like the one in Figure 17-1.

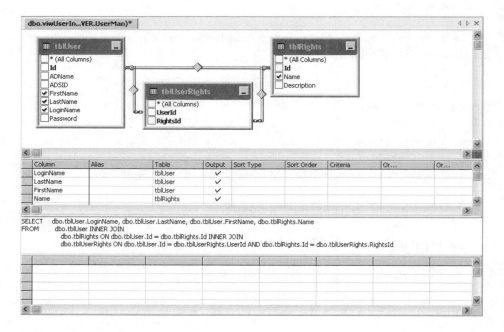

Figure 17-1. The `viwUserInfo` *view*

Running a View from the IDE

"Running a view" is perhaps not the most appropriate phrase when you think about it. On the other hand, the view does have to retrieve the data from all the tables referenced in the view, so I guess this phrase will have to do.

Anyway, you can run a view from the View Designer by right-clicking a blank area of the View Designer and selecting Run from the pop-up menu. The data retrieved by the view is then displayed in the Results pane of the View Designer.

Exercise

Run the `viwUserInfo` view from the View Designer. The Results pane now displays rows like the ones in Figure 17-2. Notice that the Name field of the tblRights table seems a bit confusing, because it doesn't really show what Name means. Therefore, in the Grid pane, you should add the text **RightsName** to the Alias column in the Name row. Run the view again and notice how the new column name appears in the Results pane. Save the view with Ctrl+S.

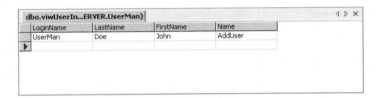

Figure 17-2. The results of running the `viwUserInfo` *view*

Using a View from Code

Actually, it's very easy to use a view in code, because a view is referenced like any standard table in your database, which means that you can retrieve data using a Command object or a DataAdapter that fills a **DataSet**, and so on.

NOTE   Please see Chapter 9 for specific information on how to manipulate data in a table.

Retrieving Read-Only Data from a View in Code

The simplest use of a view is for display purposes, like when you just need to display some information from one or more related tables. Because in the example code I don't have to worry about updates, I don't have to set up anything particular.

Listing 17-1 demonstrates how to return all rows from a view and populate a DataReader.

Listing 17-1. Retrieving Rows in a View

```
1 Public Sub RetrieveRowsFromView()
2    Dim cnnUserMan As SqlConnection
3    Dim cmmUser As SqlCommand
4    Dim drdUser As SqlDataReader
5
6    ' Instantiate and open the connection
7    cnnUserMan = New SqlConnection(PR_STR_CONNECTION_STRING)
8    cnnUserMan.Open()
9
10   ' Instantiate and initialize command
11   cmmUser = New SqlCommand("SELECT * FROM viwUserInfo", cnnUserMan)
12
13   ' Get rows
14   drdUser = cmmUser.ExecuteReader()
15 End Sub
```

Listing 17-1 is just like any other row-returning query, except that a view is queried instead of a table.

Manipulating Data in a View from Code

Listing 17-1 shows you how to retrieve data from a view into a data reader, and this means the data cannot be updated, because the data reader doesn't allow updates. However, it's possible to update data in a view. The problem with this is that various versions of SQL Server support different levels of update support for views. If you only have one table in a view, this isn't a problem at all; however, if you have multiple tables in a view, only SQL Server 2000 supports updating rows in more than one of the source tables. Besides the mentioned problems, you'll certainly run into even bigger problems if you need to migrate to a different RDBMS. Generally I would discourage updating data in views.

Exercise

Create a new view. This view should contain the tblUser table. The following fields should be output: Id, FirstName, LastName, and LoginName. Save the view under the name **viwUser**. The new view should look like the one in Figure 17-3.

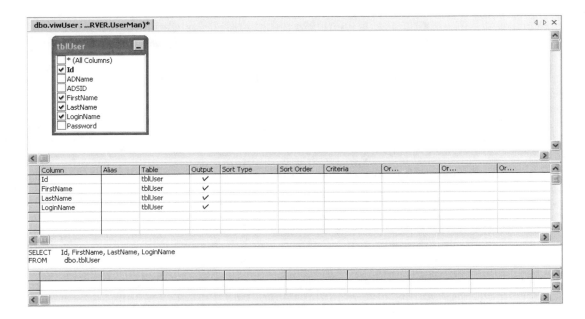

Figure 17-3. The viwUser *view*

This view, which can be located on SQL Server 7.0 as well as SQL Server 2000, can be manipulated using the code in Listing 17-2.

Listing 17-2. Manipulating Data in a View Based on a Single Table

```
1 Public Sub ManipulateDataInAViewBasedOnSingleTable()
2   Const STR_SQL_USER_SELECT As String = _
3     "SELECT * FROM viwUser"
4   Const STR_SQL_USER_DELETE As String = _
5     "DELETE FROM viwUser WHERE Id=@Id"
6   Const STR_SQL_USER_INSERT As String = _
7     "INSERT INTO viwUser(FirstName, LastName, LoginName, Logged, " & _
8     "Description) VALUES(@FirstName, @LastName, @LoginName)"
9   Const STR_SQL_USER_UPDATE As String = "UPDATE viwUser SET " & _
10    "FirstName=@FirstName, LastName=@LastName, LoginName=@LoginName " & _
11    "WHERE Id=@Id"
12
13  Dim dstUser As DataSet
14
15  Dim cnnUserMan As SqlConnection
16  Dim cmmUser As SqlCommand
17  Dim dadUser As SqlDataAdapter
18
19  Dim cmmUserSelect As SqlCommand
20  Dim cmmUserDelete As SqlCommand
21  Dim cmmUserInsert As SqlCommand
22  Dim cmmUserUpdate As SqlCommand
23
24  Dim prmSQLDelete, prmSQLUpdate, prmSQLInsert As SqlParameter
25
26  ' Instantiate and open the connection
27  cnnUserMan = New SqlConnection(PR_STR_CONNECTION_STRING)
28  cnnUserMan.Open()
29
30  ' Instantiate and initialize command
31  cmmUser = New SqlCommand("SELECT * FROM viwUser", cnnUserMan)
32  ' Instantiate the commands
33  cmmUserSelect = New SqlCommand(STR_SQL_USER_SELECT, cnnUserMan)
34  cmmUserDelete = New SqlCommand(STR_SQL_USER_DELETE, cnnUserMan)
35  cmmUserInsert = New SqlCommand(STR_SQL_USER_INSERT, cnnUserMan)
36  cmmUserUpdate = New SqlCommand(STR_SQL_USER_UPDATE, cnnUserMan)
37  ' Instantiate command and DataSet
38  cmmUser = New SqlCommand(STR_SQL_USER_SELECT, cnnUserMan)
39  dstUser = New DataSet()
40
41  dadUser = New SqlDataAdapter()
42  dadUser.SelectCommand = cmmUserSelect
```

```
43    dadUser.InsertCommand = cmmUserInsert
44    dadUser.DeleteCommand = cmmUserDelete
45    dadUser.UpdateCommand = cmmUserUpdate
46
47    ' Add parameters
48    prmSQLDelete = dadUser.DeleteCommand.Parameters.Add("@Id", _
49       SqlDbType.Int, 0, "Id")
50    prmSQLDelete.Direction = ParameterDirection.Input
51    prmSQLDelete.SourceVersion = DataRowVersion.Original
52
53    cmmUserUpdate.Parameters.Add("@FirstName", SqlDbType.VarChar, 50, _
54       "FirstName")
55    cmmUserUpdate.Parameters.Add("@LastName", SqlDbType.VarChar, 50, _
56       "LastName")
57    cmmUserUpdate.Parameters.Add("@LoginName", SqlDbType.VarChar, 50, _
58       "LoginName")
59    prmSQLUpdate = dadUser.UpdateCommand.Parameters.Add("@Id", _
60       SqlDbType.Int, 0, "Id")
61    prmSQLUpdate.Direction = ParameterDirection.Input
62    prmSQLUpdate.SourceVersion = DataRowVersion.Original
63
64    cmmUserInsert.Parameters.Add("@FirstName", SqlDbType.VarChar, 50, _
65       "FirstName")
66    cmmUserInsert.Parameters.Add("@LastName", SqlDbType.VarChar, 50, _
67       "LastName")
68    cmmUserInsert.Parameters.Add("@LoginName", SqlDbType.VarChar, 50, _
69       "LoginName")
70
71    ' Populate the DataSet from the view
72    dadUser.Fill(dstUser, "viwUser")
73
74    ' Change the last name of user in the second row
75    dstUser.Tables("viwUser").Rows(1)("LastName") = "Thomsen"
76    dstUser.Tables("viwUser").Rows(1)("FirstName") = "Carsten"
77    ' Propagate changes back to the data source
78    dadUser.Update(dstUser, "viwUser")
79 End Sub
```

In Listing 17-2, a DataAdapter and a **DataSet** are set up to retrieve and hold data from the viwUser view. The LastName column of row 2 is then updated as well as the data source with the changes in the **DataSet**. This simple demonstration was designed to show you how to work with views based on a single table.

Summary

In this chapter, I demonstrated views, and showed you how to how to create, run, and use a view from code, including updating the view.

I went into enough details about views to cover just what a VB .NET programmer basically needs to know. However, the information presented in this chapter is far from exhaustive, and I recommend you read some specific material on the DBMS you're working with.

The next chapter is also about server-side processing, namely how, when, and why to use triggers.

CHAPTER 18

Using Triggers

IN THIS CHAPTER, I discuss one specific way of doing server-side processing: triggers. If you need to know about server-side processing in general, I suggest you read the beginning of Chapter 16.

This chapter includes a hands-on exercise that will take you through creating triggers.

Although this chapter primarily focuses on SQL Server 2000 features, some of the functionality can certainly be reproduced in the other DBMSs I cover in this book:

- *SQL Server 7.0:* All functionality shown in this chapter can be reproduced. However, SQL Server 7.0 doesn't support the INSTEAD OF triggers described in "Using Triggers."

- *Microsoft Access:* Microsoft Access doesn't support triggers.

- *IBM DB2 7.2 EE:* This version of DB2 supports all the server-side processing described in this chapter.

- *Oracle:* Oracle supports all the server-side processing described in this chapter.

- *MySQL:* For the examples in this book, I have been using MySQL version 3.23.51, which doesn't support triggers, meaning there is no example code for MySQL in this chapter. However, at the time of writing (August 2002), version 4.? of MySQL is described on http://www.mysql.com, and according to the plans and description, version 4.? is supposed to support triggers. Even when this means of server-side processing is available in MySQL, it's still not possible to create any of these items from within the VS .NET IDE.

The code for this chapter has examples for all the listed DBMSs where appropriate.

Using Triggers

A *trigger* is actually a stored procedure that automatically invokes (triggers) when a certain change is applied to your data. As a developer you probably know what an event is, and if you do, well you almost have the definition of a trigger. Triggers are the final server-side processing functionality that I'll discuss in this part of the book. Until SQL Server 2000 was released, triggers were a vital part of enforcing referential integrity, but with the release of SQL Server 2000, you now have that capability built in. In the rest of this section I'll show you what a trigger is and when and how you can use it, but there is little VB .NET programming involved with using triggers, because they operate entirely internally, only passing status or error indicators back to the client.

Triggers respond to data modifications using INSERT, UPDATE, and DELETE operations. Basically, you can say that a trigger helps you write less code; you can incorporate business rules as triggers and thus prevent the inclusion of data that is invalid because it violates your business rules.

SQL Server implements AFTER triggers, meaning that the trigger is invoked after the modification has occurred. However, this doesn't mean that a change can't be rolled back, because the trigger has direct access to the modified row and as such can roll back any modification. When SQL Server 2000 was released, you also got support for the notion of BEFORE triggers, which you might know from the Oracle or DB2 RDBMS. In SQL Server 2000, they're called INSTEAD OF triggers.

 NOTE The example code shown in this chapter is SQL Server only, but if you take a look at the accompanying example code on the Apress Web site, you'll see that Oracle and DB2 after triggers work almost the same as SQL Server triggers, although the syntax is different. Only the SQL Server .NET Data Provider has been changed to the OLE DB .NET Data Provider. Triggers aren't supported in Microsoft Access or MySQL 3.23.51.

Why Use a Trigger?

Triggers are automatic, so you don't have to apply the business logic in your code. Here's a perfect situation for a business rule: You need to check if a member of an organization has paid his or her annual fee, and therefore is allowed to order material from the organization's library. An INSERT trigger can perform the lookup in the members table when a member tries to order material, and check if the member has paid the annual fee. This is exactly what makes a trigger more useful than a constraint in some situations, because a trigger can access columns in other tables, unlike a constraint, which can only access columns in the current table or row. If your code is to handle your business rule, this will mean that you need to look up the member's information in the members table before you can insert the order in the orders table. With the trigger, this lookup is done automatically, and an exception is thrown if you try to insert an order for library material if the member hasn't paid his or her annual fee. Furthermore, you don't have to rely on another front-end code developer to know what the business rules are.

In short, use a trigger for keeping all your data valid, or for complying with your business rules. Think of triggers as an extra validation tool that you can use while making sure you have also set up referential integrity.

NOTE   With SQL Server 2000, you shouldn't use triggers for referential integrity (see Chapter 2), because you can set that up with the Database Designer. See Chapter 13 for information on the Database Designer.

Creating a Trigger

It's quite easy to create a trigger. This can be done using the Server Manager that comes with SQL Server, but I'll use the Server Explorer. Here's how you create a trigger for the example UserMan database:

1. Open up the Server Explorer window.

2. Expand the UserMan database on your database server.

3. Expand the Tables node.

4. Right-click the table for which you want to create a trigger and select New Trigger from the pop-up menu.

This brings up the trigger text editor, which is more or less the same editor you use for your VB .NET code (see Figure 18-1).

```
dbo.tblUser _T...ERVER.UserMan)                    ◁ ▷ ×
   1   CREATE TRIGGER tblUser_Trigger1
   2   ON dbo.tblUser
   3   FOR /* INSERT, UPDATE, DELETE */
   4   AS
   5       /* IF UPDATE (column_name) ...*/
   6   |
```

Figure 18-1. Trigger editor with default template

In the trigger editor, you can see that the template automatically names a new trigger `Trigger1` prefixed with the name of the table. Actually, if another trigger with this name already exists, the new trigger is named `Trigger2`, and so on.

Once you are done editing your trigger, you need to save it by pressing Ctrl+S. As soon as you have saved it, the very first line of the stored procedure changes. The SQL statement CREATE TRIGGER is changed so that the first line reads as follows:

`ALTER TRIGGER dbo....`

NOTE   The trigger editor performs syntax checking when you save your trigger, meaning if the syntax of your trigger is invalid, you aren't allowed to save it to your database.

When a trigger has been saved to the database, you can locate it under the table to which it belongs in the Server Explorer.

The `tblUser_Update` trigger is invoked when updating a row in the user table. The trigger first tests to see if the LastName column is updated. If it is, then the trigger checks to see if the FirstName column is empty, because if it is the update is rolled back and an exception is raised. Please note that this trigger is designed to work with only one updated or inserted row at a time. If more rows are inserted at the same time, the trigger will have to be redesigned to accommodate this. However, this trigger only serves as a demonstration. The functionality of this trigger can easily be implemented using constraints, because the check I perform is done in the same table. If I had looked up a value in a different table, then the trigger would be your only choice.

A trigger with the same functionality in DB2 looks similar to Listing 18-1, and in Oracle, it looks similar to Listing 18-2.

Exercise

Create a new trigger for the tblUser table and save it with the name
tblUser_Update. This is an update trigger, so you need to change the text on Line 3
to **FOR UPDATE**. Replace the text on Line 5 and down with the following:

```
DECLARE @strFirstName varchar(50)
/* Get the value for the FirstName column */
SELECT @strFirstName = (SELECT FirstName FROM inserted)
/* Check if we're updating the LastName column.
If so, make sure FirstName is not NULL */
IF UPDATE (LastName) AND @strFirstName IS NULL
BEGIN
    /* Roll back update and raise exception */
    ROLLBACK TRANSACTION
    RAISERROR ('You must fill in both LastName and FirstName', 11, 1)
END
```

Now the stored procedure should look like the one in Figure 18-2.

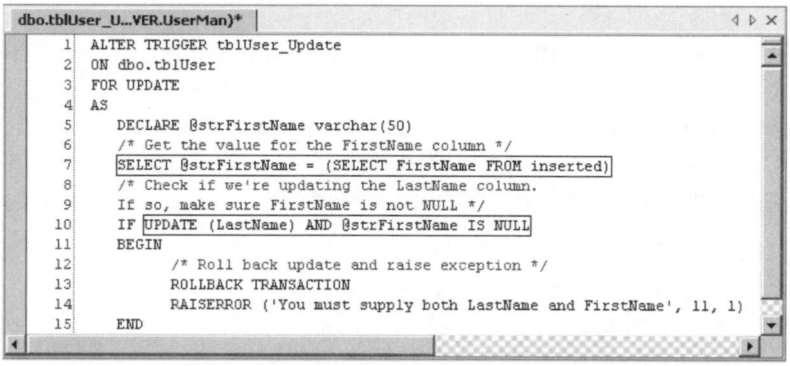

```
dbo.tblUser_U...VER.UserMan)*                               ◁ ▷ ✕
  1   ALTER TRIGGER tblUser_Update
  2   ON dbo.tblUser
  3   FOR UPDATE
  4   AS
  5       DECLARE @strFirstName varchar(50)
  6       /* Get the value for the FirstName column */
  7       SELECT @strFirstName = (SELECT FirstName FROM inserted)
  8       /* Check if we're updating the LastName column.
  9       If so, make sure FirstName is not NULL */
 10       IF UPDATE (LastName) AND @strFirstName IS NULL
 11       BEGIN
 12           /* Roll back update and raise exception */
 13           ROLLBACK TRANSACTION
 14           RAISERROR ('You must supply both LastName and FirstName', 11, 1)
 15       END
```

Figure 18-2. The tblUser_Update *trigger*

Don't forget to save the changes using Ctrl+S.

Listing 18-1. The tblUser_Update *Trigger for DB2*

```
1 CREATE TRIGGER tblUser_Update
2 NO CASCADE BEFORE UPDATE ON tblUser
3 REFERENCING NEW AS NEWUSER
4 FOR EACH ROW MODE DB2SQL
5 WHEN (NEWUSER.LastName IS NULL OR NEWUSER.FirstName IS NULL)
6    SIGNAL SQLSTATE '75002' ('You must supply both LastName and FirstName') /
```

Listing 18-2. The tblUser_Update *Trigger for Oracle*

```
1 CREATE OR REPLACE TRIGGER USERMAN.TBLUSER_UPDATE
2 AFTER UPDATE ON USERMAN.TBLUSER
3 FOR EACH ROW
4 BEGIN
5    /* Check if we're updating the LastName column and if FirstName is NULL */
6    IF (:OLD.LASTNAME <> :NEW.LASTNAME) OR (:NEW.FIRSTNAME IS NULL) THEN
7       /* Roll back update and raise exception */
8       Raise_application_error(-20201,
9          'You must supply both LastName and FirstName');
10    END IF;
11 END TBLUSER_UPDATE;
```

Please see your SQL Server, DB2, or Oracle documentation, if you need more information on how to create triggers. Listing 18-3 shows you how to execute the new trigger, demonstrating how to catch an exception in code raised by a trigger.

Listing 18-3. Invoking Trigger and Catching Exception Raised

```
1 Public Sub TestUpdateTrigger()
2    Const STR_SQL_USER_SELECT As String = _
3       "SELECT * FROM tblUser"
4
5    Dim dstUser As DataSet
6 #If SQLSERVER Then
7    Const STR_SQL_USER_DELETE As String = _
8       "DELETE FROM tblUser WHERE Id=@Id"
9    Const STR_SQL_USER_INSERT As String = _
10      "INSERT INTO tblUser(FirstName, LastName, LoginName) " & _
11      "VALUES(@FirstName, @LastName, @LoginName)"
12   Const STR_SQL_USER_UPDATE As String = "UPDATE tblUser " & _
13      "SET FirstName=@FirstName, LastName=@LastName, " & _
14      "LoginName=@LoginName WHERE Id=@Id"
15
```

```
16    Dim cnnUserMan As SqlConnection
17    Dim cmmUser As SqlCommand
18    Dim dadUser As SqlDataAdapter
19
20    Dim cmmUserSelect As SqlCommand
21    Dim cmmUserDelete As SqlCommand
22    Dim cmmUserInsert As SqlCommand
23    Dim cmmUserUpdate As SqlCommand
24
25    Dim prmSQLDelete, prmSQLUpdate As SqlParameter
26
27    ' Instantiate and open the connection
28    cnnUserMan = New SqlConnection(PR_STR_CONNECTION_STRING)
29    cnnUserMan.Open()
30
31    ' Instantiate and initialize command
32    cmmUser = New SqlCommand("SELECT * FROM tblUser", cnnUserMan)
33    ' Instantiate the commands
34    cmmUserSelect = New SqlCommand(STR_SQL_USER_SELECT, cnnUserMan)
35    cmmUserDelete = New SqlCommand(STR_SQL_USER_DELETE, cnnUserMan)
36    cmmUserInsert = New SqlCommand(STR_SQL_USER_INSERT, cnnUserMan)
37    cmmUserUpdate = New SqlCommand(STR_SQL_USER_UPDATE, cnnUserMan)
38    ' Instantiate command and DataSet
39    cmmUser = New SqlCommand(STR_SQL_USER_SELECT, cnnUserMan)
40    dstUser = New DataSet()
41
42    dadUser = New SqlDataAdapter()
43    dadUser.SelectCommand = cmmUserSelect
44    dadUser.InsertCommand = cmmUserInsert
45    dadUser.DeleteCommand = cmmUserDelete
46    dadUser.UpdateCommand = cmmUserUpdate
47
48    ' Add parameters
49    prmSQLDelete = dadUser.DeleteCommand.Parameters.Add("@Id", _
50        SqlDbType.Int, 0, "Id")
51    prmSQLDelete.Direction = ParameterDirection.Input
52    prmSQLDelete.SourceVersion = DataRowVersion.Original
53
54    cmmUserUpdate.Parameters.Add("@FirstName", SqlDbType.VarChar, 50, _
55        "FirstName")
56    cmmUserUpdate.Parameters.Add("@LastName", SqlDbType.VarChar, 50, _
57        "LastName")
58    cmmUserUpdate.Parameters.Add("@LoginName", SqlDbType.VarChar, 50, _
59        "LoginName")
60    prmSQLUpdate = dadUser.UpdateCommand.Parameters.Add("@Id", _
```

```
 61      SqlDbType.Int, 0, "Id")
 62    prmSQLUpdate.Direction = ParameterDirection.Input
 63    prmSQLUpdate.SourceVersion = DataRowVersion.Original
 64
 65    cmmUserInsert.Parameters.Add("@FirstName", SqlDbType.VarChar, 50, _
 66      "FirstName")
 67    cmmUserInsert.Parameters.Add("@LastName", SqlDbType.VarChar, 50, _
 68      "LastName")
 69    cmmUserInsert.Parameters.Add("@LoginName", SqlDbType.VarChar, 50, _
 70      "LoginName")
 71 #Else
 72    Const STR_SQL_USER_DELETE As String = _
 73      "DELETE FROM tblUser WHERE Id=?"
 74    Const STR_SQL_USER_INSERT As String = _
 75      "INSERT INTO tblUser(FirstName, LastName, LoginName) " & _
 76      "VALUES(?, ?, ?)"
 77    Const STR_SQL_USER_UPDATE As String = "UPDATE tblUser " & _
 78      "SET FirstName=?, LastName=?, LoginName=? WHERE Id=?"
 79
 80    Dim cnnUserMan As OleDbConnection
 81    Dim cmmUser As OleDbCommand
 82    Dim dadUser As OleDbDataAdapter
 83
 84    Dim cmmUserSelect As OleDbCommand
 85    Dim cmmUserDelete As OleDbCommand
 86    Dim cmmUserInsert As OleDbCommand
 87    Dim cmmUserUpdate As OleDbCommand
 88
 89    Dim prmSQLDelete, prmSQLUpdate As OleDbParameter
 90
 91    ' Instantiate and open the connection
 92    cnnUserMan = New OleDbConnection(PR_STR_CONNECTION_STRING)
 93    cnnUserMan.Open()
 94
 95    ' Instantiate and initialize command
 96    cmmUser = New OleDbCommand("SELECT * FROM tblUser", cnnUserMan)
 97    ' Instantiate the commands
 98    cmmUserSelect = New OleDbCommand(STR_SQL_USER_SELECT, cnnUserMan)
 99    cmmUserDelete = New OleDbCommand(STR_SQL_USER_DELETE, cnnUserMan)
100    cmmUserInsert = New OleDbCommand(STR_SQL_USER_INSERT, cnnUserMan)
101    cmmUserUpdate = New OleDbCommand(STR_SQL_USER_UPDATE, cnnUserMan)
102    ' Instantiate command and DataSet
103    cmmUser = New OleDbCommand(STR_SQL_USER_SELECT, cnnUserMan)
104    dstUser = New DataSet()
105
```

```
106     dadUser = New OleDbDataAdapter()
107     dadUser.SelectCommand = cmmUserSelect
108     dadUser.InsertCommand = cmmUserInsert
109     dadUser.DeleteCommand = cmmUserDelete
110     dadUser.UpdateCommand = cmmUserUpdate
111
112     ' Add parameters
113     prmSQLDelete = dadUser.DeleteCommand.Parameters.Add("@Id", _
114         OleDbType.Integer, 0, "Id")
115     prmSQLDelete.Direction = ParameterDirection.Input
116     prmSQLDelete.SourceVersion = DataRowVersion.Original
117
118     cmmUserUpdate.Parameters.Add("@FirstName", OleDbType.VarChar, 50, _
119         "FirstName")
120     cmmUserUpdate.Parameters.Add("@LastName", OleDbType.VarChar, 50, _
121         "LastName")
122     cmmUserUpdate.Parameters.Add("@LoginName", OleDbType.VarChar, 50, _
123         "LoginName")
124     prmSQLUpdate = dadUser.UpdateCommand.Parameters.Add("@Id", _
125         OleDbType.Integer, 0, "Id")
126     prmSQLUpdate.Direction = ParameterDirection.Input
127     prmSQLUpdate.SourceVersion = DataRowVersion.Original
128
129     cmmUserInsert.Parameters.Add("@FirstName", OleDbType.VarChar, 50, _
130         "FirstName")
131     cmmUserInsert.Parameters.Add("@LastName", OleDbType.VarChar, 50, _
132         "LastName")
133     cmmUserInsert.Parameters.Add("@LoginName", OleDbType.VarChar, 50, _
134         "LoginName")
135 #End If
136
137     ' Populate the DataSet from the view
138     dadUser.Fill(dstUser, "tblUser")
139
140     ' Change the name of user in the second row
141     dstUser.Tables("tblUser").Rows(2)("LastName") = "Thomsen"
142     dstUser.Tables("tblUser").Rows(2)("FirstName") = DBNull.Value
143
144     Try
145         ' Propagate changes back to the data source
146         dadUser.Update(dstUser, "tblUser")
147     Catch objE As Exception
148         MsgBox(objE.Message)
149     End Try
150 End Sub
```

In Listing 18-3, the second row is updated, and the LastName column is set to "Thomsen" and the FirstName to **Nothing**. This will invoke the update trigger that throws an exception, which is caught in the code, and an error message is displayed. As you can see from Listing 18-3, I've mixed the example code, so depending on the setting of the #Const SQLSERVER compiler directive, you'll be using the SQL Server .NET Data Provider, or the OLE DB .NET Data Provider. Check the full listing in the example code, which can be used with DB2, Oracle, and SQL Server.

This should give you a taste for using triggers, and they really aren't that hard to work with. Just make sure you have a well-designed database that doesn't use triggers for purposes that can easily be achieved by other means such as referential integrity.

Viewing Trigger Source

In SQL Server Enterprise Manager you can see the source for your triggers. Open up Enterprise Manager, expand your SQL Server, and expand databases and your database. Next, select the Tables node, right-click the table you have created the trigger for, and select All Task Manager Triggers from the pop-up menu. This brings up the Triggers Properties dialog box, where you can see and edit the triggers for the selected table.

In the Server Explorer in the VS .NET IDE, you can also view the trigger source by expanding your database, expanding the Tables node, expanding the table with the trigger, and double-clicking the trigger.

Please see your Oracle or DB2 documentation for information on how to view the trigger source.

Summary

In this chapter I discussed how to create various server-side objects for server-side processing of your data. I demonstrated stored procedures, views, and triggers, and showed you how to create, run, and execute a stored procedure from code; how to create, run, and use a view from code, including updating the view; and finally how to create triggers.

I went into enough details about stored procedures, views, and triggers to cover just what a VB .NET programmer needs to know. However, if you are also responsible for coding the SQL Server database and you need more information and example code, I can certainly recommend you read this book:

> *Code Centric: T-SQL Programming with Stored Procedures and Triggers* by Garth Wells. Apress, February 2001. ISBN: 1-893115-83-6.

You can find more information about this book here: `http://www.apress.com/book/bookDisplay.html?bID=73`.

The next chapter is about hierarchical databases. I'll discuss how you use the LDAP protocol to access a network directory database like the Active Directory, and you'll see how to access information stored on Exchange Server 2000.

Part Seven

Hierarchical Databases

CHAPTER 19

Hierarchical Databases

IN THIS CHAPTER, I will discuss the Lightweight Directory Access Protocol (LDAP) directory service protocol, and how it can be used for connecting to Active Directory, Microsoft's network directory service. Active Directory is a hierarchical database, and you can find a general description of such a database in Chapter 2.

Looking at LDAP

Since you'll be accessing Active Directory in the example application, I believe providing some brief background on Active Directory and LDAP is in order. Active Directory is a network directory service, like the Domain Name System (DNS) and Novell Directory Services (NDS). A *network directory service* holds information on objects such as users, printers, clients, servers, and so on. In short, a network directory service holds information that is used to manage or access a network. This chapter contains hands-on exercises that will take you through accessing Active Directory.

Active Directory was first introduced with the Microsoft Windows 2000 operating system. Active Directory is an X.500-compliant network directory based on open standards protocols such as LDAP. Because Active Directory is X.500 compliant, it is a hierarchical database with a treelike structure. When the specifications for the X.500 directory were under development, an access protocol for accessing a network directory based on the X.500 specification was needed, and thus the Directory Access Protocol (DAP) was created. However, the specification for DAP was too overwhelming and the overhead too big, which resulted in very few clients and/or applications being able to connect to DAP. If you need more information about the X.500 directory standard as it is defined by the International Organization for Standardization (ISO) and the International Telecommunication Union (ITU), you can visit http://www.isi.salford.ac.uk/staff/dwc/Version.Web/Contents.htm.

The challenge of the DAP specification being too overwhelming was met by a group of people at the University of Michigan who realized that reducing the DAP overhead could result in faster retrieval of the same directory information and much smaller clients. This group created a new protocol specification, LDAP.

NOTE See Chapter 2 for information on how a hierarchical database is structured.

LDAP runs directly over the TCP/IP stack. The network directory service needs to host an LDAP service if you want to use LDAP to access the directory, though, which means that LDAP is client-server based.

These days LDAP is becoming the de facto standard for clients to access directory information. This is true for clients working over both the Internet and intranets, with standard LAN directory access now also moving toward LDAP.

One of the most important aspects of the LDAP protocol standard is that it gives us an API that is common and, most notably, platform independent. As a result, applications that access a directory service such as Microsoft Active Directory or Novell Directory Services (NDS) will be a lot easier and less expensive to develop.

NOTE   The LDAP directory service protocol gives you access to an existing directory; it cannot create a new directory.

Exploring Active Directory

The fact that Active Directory server is currently available only with Windows 2000 means you need at least a Windows 2000 Server, with Active Directory installed, in order to follow this discussion. However, Windows .NET Servers[1] should be available not too long after you read this.

Not only is Active Directory accessible, but it is also extendable, which is significant. If you have an object that you want to expose to a network, you can extend the schema of Active Directory and make it available to anyone who can access the Active Directory implementation in question. The schema in Active Directory defines all the object classes and attributes that can be stored in the directory. This doesn't mean that all the objects defined in the schema are actually present in Active Directory, but the schema allows them to be created if you have the proper rights. For each object class, the schema also defines where the object can be created in the directory tree by specifying the class' valid or legal parents. Furthermore, the content of a class is defined by a list of attributes that the class must or may contain. This means that an Active Directory object is a named set of attributes. This set of attributes is distinct and is used to describe a user or printer, for instance. Anything on the network that is a physical entity can be specified as an object in Active Directory.

---

1.   Windows .NET Servers are the next version of Windows 2000 or, to be more accurate, they are the server version of Windows XP.

As I won't go into much more detail about Active Directory, you should check out the information at http://www.microsoft.com/windows2000/technologies/directory/default.asp if you want more specifics about Active Directory.

So to sum up quickly: Active Directory is a network directory service, based on the X.500 specifications that can be accessed using the client-server–based LDAP directory service protocol.

Accessing Active Directory Programmatically

Active Directory can, of course, be accessed programmatically from VB .NET, as is the case with previous versions of Windows programming languages such as Visual Basic 6.0. However, unlike these previous versions of programming languages, VB .NET, or rather the .NET Framework, has some built-in features that let you access Active Directory without having to go through the Windows API. The **System.DirectoryServices** namespace has everything you need for this purpose.

Examining the System.DirectoryServices Namespace

The **System.DirectoryServices** namespace holds a number of classes that let you access Active Directory. Table 19-1 lists some of the classes in this namespace that I show you in this chapter or use in the example code.

*Table 19-1. **System.DirectoryServices** Classes*

Class Name	Description
DirectoryEntries	This collection class contains the child entries of an Active Directory entry (**DirectoryEntry.Children** property). Please note that the collection only contains immediate children.
DirectoryEntry	The **DirectoryEntry** class encapsulates an object or a node in the Active Directory database hierarchy.
DirectorySearcher	This class is used for performing queries against Active Directory using the LDAP protocol.
PropertyCollection	This collection holds all the properties of a single **DirectoryEntry** class (**DirectoryEntry.Properties** property).

*Table 19-1. **System.DirectoryServices** Classes (Continued)*

Class Name	Description
PropertyValueCollection	The **PropertyValueCollection** collection holds values for a **DirectoryEntry** property (**DirectoryEntry.Properties.Values** property).
ResultPropertyCollection	This collection holds the properties of a **SearchResult** object (**SearchResultCollection(0).Properties** property).
ResultPropertyValueCollection	The **ResultPropertyValueCollection** collection holds values for a **SearchResult** object.
SearchResult	This class encapsulates a node in the Active Directory database hierarchy. This node is returned as the result of a search performed by an instance of the **DirectorySearcher** class. Use the **SearchResult** class with the **FindOne** method of the **DirectorySearcher** class.
SearchResultCollection	This collection contains the instances of the **SearchResult** class that are returned when querying the Active Directory hierarchy using the **DirectorySearcher.FindAll** method.

In order to use the **DirectoryEntry** and **DirectorySearcher** classes, you need to be aware of the following restrictions:

- The Active Directory Services Interface Software Development Kit (ADSI SDK) or the ADSI runtime must be installed on your computer. If you're running Windows 2000 or Windows XP, it's installed by default. If you're running an earlier version of Windows, you can install the SDK by downloading it from the Microsoft Web site: http://www.microsoft.com/windows2000/techinfo/howitworks/activedirectory/adsilinks.asp.

- A directory service provider, such as Active Directory or LDAP, must be installed on your computer.

I won't explain all the classes in the **System.DirectoryServices** namespace, but the **DirectoryEntry** class is quite important, so I discuss this class in the following section.

Studying the DirectoryEntry Class

Recall that the **DirectoryEntry** class encapsulates an object in the Active Directory database hierarchy. You can use this class for binding to objects in Active Directory or for manipulating object attributes. This class and the helper classes can be used with the following providers: **IIS, LDAP, NDS**, and **WinNT**. More providers will probably follow. As you may have guessed, I will demonstrate the use of LDAP to access Active Directory in this chapter. Table 19-2 shows you the noninherited, public properties of the **DirectoryEntry** class.

Table 19-2. DirectoryEntry Class Properties

Property Name	Description
AuthenticationType	This property returns or sets the type of authentication to be used. The value must be a member of the **AuthenticationTypes** enum. The default value is **None**, and the following are the other values of the enum: **Anonymous, Delegation, Encryption, FastBind, ReadonlyServer, Sealing, Secure, SecureSocketsLayer, ServerBind**, and **Signing**.
Children	This read-only property returns a **DirectoryEntries** class (collection) that holds the child entries of the node in the Active Directory database hierarchy. Only immediate children are returned.
Guid	The **Guid** property returns the globally unique identifier of the **DirectoryEntry** class. If you're binding to an object in Active Directory, you should use the **NativeGuid** property instead. This property is read-only.
Name	This read-only property returns the name of the object. The value returned is the name of the **DirectoryEntry** object as it appears in the underlying directory service. Note that the **SchemaClassName** property, together with this property, is what makes the directory entry unique; in other words, these two names make it possible to tell one directory entry apart from its siblings.
NativeGuid	The **NativeGuid** property returns the globally unique identifier of the **DirectoryEntry** class as it is returned from the provider. This property is read-only.

Table 19-2. DirectoryEntry Class Properties (Continued)

Property Name	Description
NativeObject	This read-only property returns the native ADSI object. You can use this property when you want to work with a COM interface.
Parent	The **Parent** property returns the **DirectoryEntry** object's parent in the Active Directory database hierarchy. This property is read-only.
Password	This property returns or sets the password that is used when the client is authenticated. When the **Password** and **Username** properties are set, all other instances of the **DirectoryEntry** class that are retrieved from the current instance will automatically be created with the same values for these properties.
Path	The **Path** property returns or sets the path for the **DirectoryEntry** class. The default is an empty **string**. This property is used for uniquely identifying the object in a network.
Properties	This property returns a **PropertyCollection** class holding the properties that have been set on the **DirectoryEntry** object.
SchemaClassName	The **SchemaClassName** property returns the name of the schema that is used for the **DirectoryEntry** object.
SchemaEntry	This property returns the **DirectoryEntry** object that is holding the schema information for the current **DirectoryEntry** object. The **SchemaClassName** property of a **DirectoryEntry** class determines the properties that are valid, both mandatory and optional, for the **DirectoryEntry** instance.
UsePropertyCache	This property returns or sets a **Boolean** value that indicates if the cache should be committed after each operation or not. The default value is **True**.
Username	The **Username** property returns or sets the user name that is used for authenticating the client. When the **Password** and **Username** properties are set, all other instances of the **DirectoryEntry** class that are retrieved from the current instance will automatically be created with the same values for these properties.

To sum up what the **DirectoryEntry** class contains, check out its methods. Table 19-3 shows you the noninherited, public methods of the **DirectoryEntry** class.

Table 19-3. **DirectoryEntry** *Class Methods*

Method Name	Description	Example
Close()	This method closes the **DirectoryEntry** object. This means that any system resources used by the **DirectoryEntry** object are released at this point; or rather, they await garbage collection.	`objAD.Close()`
CommitChanges()	The **CommitChanges** method saves any changes you have made to the **DirectoryEntry** object to the Active Directory database.	`objAD.CommitChanges()`
CopyTo() As DirectoryEntry	This overloaded method is used for creating a copy of the **DirectoryEntry** object as a child of objADParent, with or without a new name (strNewName).	`objADCopy = objAD.CopyTo(objADParent)` `objADCopy = objAD.CopyTo(objADParent, strNewName)`
DeleteTree()	The **DeleteTree** method does exactly what it says: It deletes the **DirectoryEntry** object and the entire subtree (if any) from the Active Directory database hierarchy.	`objAD.DeleteTree()`

*Table 19-3. **DirectoryEntry** Class Methods (Continued)*

Method Name	Description	Example
Exists(ByVal strPath As String)	This **Shared** method is used for searching at strPath to see if an entry exists. A **Boolean** value is returned, but because the method is **Shared**, you can call this method from the type as well as an instantiated object.	`DirectoryEntry.Exists(strPath)`
Invoke(ByVal strMethodName As String, ByVal ParamArray arrArgs() As Object) As Object	This method calls the strMethodName method on the native Active Directory with the arrArgs **ParamArray** arguments. The return value of the invoked method is returned.	
MoveTo()	This overloaded method is used for moving the **DirectoryEntry** object to the objADParent parent, with or without a new name (strNewName).	`objAD.MoveTo(objADParent)` `objAD.MoveTo(objADParent, strNewName)`
RefreshCache()	This overloaded method loads property values for the **DirectoryEntry** object into the property cache. Either all property values are loaded or just the ones specified with the arrstrProperties argument.	`objAD.RefreshCache()` `objAD.RefreshCache(arrstrProperties)`
Rename(string strNewName)	The **Rename** method renames or changes the name of the **DirectoryEntry** object to strNewName.	`objAD.Rename(strNewName)`

Looking at the LDAP Syntax

In order to bind to or search Active Directory, you need to know about the LDAP syntax used for binding and querying, so let's take a closer look at it.

Each object in Active Directory is identified by two names when you use LDAP for access: the relative distinguished name (RDN) and the distinguished name (DN). The DN actually consists of both the RDN and all of its parents/ancestors. Here is an example:

- The RDN for the UserMan object is `CN=UserMan`.

- The DN for the UserMan object in my Active Directory can look like this: `\C=DK\O=UserMan\OU=developers\CN=UserMan`.

Each node in the hierarchy is separated by a backslash (\). The DN is unique across the directory service. This means that for each node the object name is unique. If you look at the DN, the common name (CN) `UserMan` must be unique in the developer's node. The organizational unit (OU) `developers` must be unique in the `UserMan` node, and so on. The O in `O=UserMan` represents an organization, and the C in `C=DK` represents a country, Denmark in this case. For the United States, you'd use `C=US`. Sometimes I use commas and sometimes a slash (forward or backward slash) as the separator. Actually, you can use both kinds, but you have to be aware that the order in which the DN is put together changes. For example, if you use a comma as the delimiter, the DN starts with the end object or the object that is lowest in the hierarchy, and then you traverse up the tree node until you have added the top-level node. On the other hand, if you use a slash as the delimiter, the reverse order is expected:

```
LDAP://DC=dk/DC=userman/CN=Users/CN=UserMan
```

I can't tell you which separator to use—in most cases it's simply a matter of preference.

The prefixes mentioned are called *monikers*, and they're used to identify the object category. CN is the most common moniker of them all. This moniker is used by most of the objects below an OU node in the hierarchy. Table 19-4 shows some of the most common monikers.

Table 19-4. Common Monikers

Moniker Name	Description	Example
Common name (CN)	The most common of all the monikers is logically called common name. It is used for most of the objects below the O or OU nodes or objects.	CN=UserMan
Country (C)	This moniker is used to describe the top-level node.	C=DK C=US
Domain component (DC)	The DC moniker is used to describe a domain. Because you're not allowed to use periods in a relative distinguished name (RDN), you need to use two DC monikers to describe your domain.	DC=userman, DC=dk
Organization (O)	The O moniker is used for describing an organization, and usually this is the company name.	O=UserMan
Organizational unit (OU)	If your organization has more units, the OU moniker is used to describe these.	OU=developers

Here is an example of a complete LDAP path for the UserMan user on my system:

```
LDAP://CN=UserMan,CN=Users,DC=userman,DC=dk
```

Actually, I've changed the domain name, but I'm sure you get the picture. The example starts by indicating that LDAP is the protocol (LDAP://) I want to use followed by a comma-delimited list of RDNs to make up the DN. Translating the query into plain English, the path looks for the user UserMan belonging to the Users group in the userman.dk domain.

Binding to an Object in Active Directory

To do anything in Active Directory using a class from the **System.DirectoryServices** namespace, you must first bind to an object. Not that it's hard to do the binding, but if you're new to LDAP and specifically to LDAP syntax, you're in for a surprise. Make sure you read the "Looking at the LDAP Syntax" section earlier in this chapter before you start binding to Active Directory. Check out Listing 19-1 for a very simple example of how to bind to a specific user object in Active Directory.

Listing 19-1. Binding to an Object in Active Directory

```
1 Public Sub BindToUserManObjectInAD()
2    Dim objEntry As DirectoryEntry
3
4    objEntry = New DirectoryEntry( _
5        "LDAP://CN=UserMan,CN=Users,DC=userman,DC=dk", _
6        "Administrator", "AdminPwd")
7 End Sub
```

In Listing 19-1, I've instantiated the **DirectoryEntry** object and bound it to the UserMan user object in Active Directory. I have also specified the user Administrator and the password for this account. You will have to change these credentials to an account on your system with at least read access to Active Directory. As you can see, it is pretty simple once you know what object to bind to.

Searching for Object(s) in Active Directory

When you want to search for a specific object in Active Directory, you can use an instance of the **DirectorySearcher** class, as shown in Listing 19-2.

Listing 19-2. Searching for a Specific Object in Active Directory

```
1 Public Sub SearchForSpecificObjectInAD()
2    Dim objEntry As DirectoryEntry
3    Dim objSearcher As DirectorySearcher
4    Dim objSearchResult As SearchResult
5
6    ' Instantiate and bind to Users node in AD
7    objEntry = New DirectoryEntry("LDAP://CN=Users,DC=userman,DC=dk", _
8        "UserMan", "userman")
9
```

```
10      ' Set up to search for UserMan on the Users node
11      objSearcher = New DirectorySearcher(objEntry, "(&(objectClass=user)" & _
12         "(objectCategory=person)(userPrincipalName=userman@userman.dk))")
13
14      ' Find the user
15      objSearchResult = objSearcher.FindOne()
16
17      ' Check if the user was found
18      If Not objSearchResult Is Nothing Then
19         ' Display path for user
20         MsgBox("Users Path: " & objSearchResult.Path)
21      Else
22         MsgBox("User not found!")
23      End If
24 End Sub
```

In Listing 19-2, I include an instance of the **DirectorySearcher** object to locate the UserMan user on the Users node. I use the **FindOne** method to return exactly one result that matches the **userPrincipalName**. Please see Table 19-5 later in this chapter for more information on **userPrincipalName**. If more objects are found when searching, only the first object found is returned. If you want more objects returned, you need to use the **FindAll** method. See Listing 19-3 for some example code.

Listing 19-3. Searching for All Objects of a Specific Class in Active Directory

```
1 Public Sub SearchForAllUserObjectsInAD()
2    Dim objEntry As DirectoryEntry
3    Dim objSearcher As DirectorySearcher
4    Dim objSearchResult As SearchResult
5    Dim objSearchResults As SearchResultCollection
6
7    ' Instantiate and bind to root node in AD
8    objEntry = New DirectoryEntry( _
9       "LDAP://DC=userman,DC=dk", "UserMan", "userman")
10
11   ' Set up to search for UserMan on the Users node
12   objSearcher = New DirectorySearcher(objEntry, _
13      "(&(objectClass=user)(objectCategory=person))")
14
```

```
15    ' Find all objects of class user
16    objSearchResults = objSearcher.FindAll()
17
18    ' Check if any users were found
19    If Not objSearchResults Is Nothing Then
20        ' Loop through all users returned
21        For Each objSearchResult In objSearchResults
22            ' Display path for user
23            MsgBox("Users Path: " & objSearchResult.Path)
24        Next
25    Else
26        MsgBox("No users were found!")
27    End If
28 End Sub
```

In Listing 19-3, all objects in Active Directory of the user class and person category are returned.

Returning Nondefault Active Directory Object Properties

In Listing 19-3, a number of objects are returned using the **FindAll** method of the **DirectorySearcher** class. However, what you don't see from the example code is that not all properties of the objects were returned. By default, only the **adsPath** and **Name** properties are returned. If you want other properties returned, you have to specify them, as shown in Listing 19-4.

 TIP   If you need a list of LDAP display names that can represent a user in Active Directory, please visit http://msdn.microsoft.com/library/ default.asp?url=/library/en-us/netdir/adschema/w2k2/ DN_computer.asp?frame=true.

Listing 19-4. *Returning Nondefault Properties from an Active Directory Node or Object*

```
1 Public Sub ReturnNonDefaultNodeProperties()
2    Dim objEntry As DirectoryEntry
3    Dim objSearcher As DirectorySearcher
4    Dim objSearchResult As SearchResult
5    Dim objValue As Object
6    Dim strName As String
7
8    ' Instantiate and bind to Users node in AD
9    objEntry = New DirectoryEntry( _
10       "LDAP://CN=Users,DC=userman,DC=dk", _
11       "UserMan", "userman")
12
13   ' Set up to search for UserMan on the Users node
14   objSearcher = New DirectorySearcher(objEntry, _
15      "(&(objectClass=user)(objectCategory=person)" & _
16      "(userPrincipalName=userman@userman.dk))", _
17      New String(2) {"sn", "telephoneNumber", "givenName"})
18
19   Try
20      ' Find the user
21      objSearchResult = objSearcher.FindOne()
22   Catch objE As Exception
23      ' Catch any mistakes made when setting up
24      ' the DirectoryEntry object, like wrong domain
25      MsgBox(objE.Message)
26   End Try
27
28   ' Check if the user was found
29   If Not objSearchResult Is Nothing Then
30      ' Display all returned user properties
31      ' Loop through all the properties returned
32      For Each strName In objSearchResult.Properties.PropertyNames
33         ' Loop through all the values for each property
34         For Each objValue In objSearchResult.Properties(strName)
35            ' Display the property and value
36            MsgBox("Property Name: " & strName.ToString() & _
37            " - Value: " + objValue.ToString())
38         Next
39      Next
40   Else
41      MsgBox("User not found!")
42   End If
43 End Sub
```

In Listing 19-4, I specify the extra properties I want returned with the object found. This is done on Line 17, where a **String** array consisting of three properties is added as an argument to the **DirectorySearcher** constructor. Please note that although you've specified these extra properties, they're only returned if they have a value. This means that the **telephoneNumber** property is only returned if a phone number has been entered for the user. Alternatively, you can add the objects by using the **Add** or **AddRange** methods of the **PropertiesToLoad** property, as follows:

```
1 ' Add properties one by one
2 objSearcher.PropertiesToLoad.Add("sn")
3 objSearcher.PropertiesToLoad.Add("telephoneNumber")
4 objSearcher.PropertiesToLoad.Add("givenName")
5 ' Add properties in one go
6 objSearcher.PropertiesToLoad.AddRange(New String(2) _
7    {"sn", "telephoneNumber", "givenName"})
```

The following links provide more information on how to construct your LDAP query filter:

- *Creating a query filter:* http://msdn.microsoft.com/library/ default.asp?url=/library/en-us/netdir/ad/creating_a_query_filter.asp

- *Searching filter syntax:* http://msdn.microsoft.com/library/ default.asp?url=/library/en-us/netdir/adsi/search_filter_syntax.asp

- *Understanding LDAP dialect:* http://msdn.microsoft.com/library/ default.asp?url=/library/en-us/netdir/adsi/ldap_dialect.asp

Manipulating Object Property Values

Often, it's okay to just read the data returned from the Active Directory. However, sometimes you may want to manipulate the data as well. Once you have bound to an object, you can actually edit, delete, or add the object's property values.

Checking for the Existence of a Property

One of the first things you need to learn is to check whether a certain property has been returned with the object. For this purpose you would use the **Contains** method of the **Properties** collection. This method and collection are part of the **DirectoryEntry** and the **SearchResult** classes. Here is how you check to see if the **telephoneNumber** property was returned:

```
If objEntry.Properties.Contains("telephoneNumber") Then
If objSearchResult.Properties.Contains("telephoneNumber") Then
```

If you don't check whether a property is in the **Properties** collection before accessing it, you risk throwing an exception!

Using a Local Cache for the Properties

When you work with instances of the **DirectoryEntry** class, the properties and the property values are by default cached locally. This means access to the **DirectoryEntry** object is faster, because any change will only be applied to the local cache and not committed to the Active Directory database. The properties are cached when you first read a property.

The default behavior can, however, be changed using the **UsePropertyCache** property. The default value is **True**, which means properties are cached locally. If you set this property to **False**, all changes to the cache will be committed to the Active Directory database after each operation.

If there has been a change to the Active Directory database, you can update the cache by calling the **RefreshCache** method. However, if you've made changes to the content of the cache, you should call the **CommitChanges** method before you call **RefreshCache**. Otherwise, you will overwrite the noncommitted changes in the cache.

Editing an Existing Property

Editing an existing property of an object in the Active Directory is quite easy. See Listing 19-5 for an example.

Listing 19-5. Editing an Existing User Property

```
1 Public Sub EditUserProperty()
2    Dim objEntry As DirectoryEntry
3
4    ' Bind to UserMan user object
5    objEntry = New DirectoryEntry( _
6       "LDAP://CN=UserMan,CN=Users,DC=userman,DC=dk", _
7       "Administrator", "AdminPwd")
8
9    ' Check if the user already had an e-mail address
10   If objEntry.Properties.Contains("mail") Then
```

```
11        ' Change the e-mail address for the user
12        objEntry.Properties("mail")(0) = "userman@userman.dk"
13        ' Commit the changes to the AD database
14        objEntry.CommitChanges()
15    End If
16 End Sub
```

The example code in Listing 19-5 binds to the UserMan Active Directory object on Lines 5 through 7, and on Line 12, I change the e-mail address of the user. The changes are committed on Line 14. Please note that on Line 10, I check to see if the property already exists in the property collection before I try to edit it.

Adding a New Property

If you want to add a new property to an existing object in Active Directory, you can use the **Add** method of the **DirectoryEntry** class. See Listing 19-6 for some example code.

Listing 19-6. Adding a New User Property

```
1 Public Sub AddNewUserProperty()
2    Dim objEntry As DirectoryEntry
3
4    ' Bind to UserMan user object
5    objEntry = New DirectoryEntry( _
6        "LDAP://CN=UserMan,CN=Users,DC=userman,DC=dk", _
7        "Administrator", "AdminPwd")
8
9    ' Check if the user already had an e-mail address
10   If Not objEntry.Properties.Contains("mail") Then
11       ' Add new e-mail address
12       objEntry.Properties("mail").Add("userman@userman.dk")
13       ' Commit the changes to the AD database
14       objEntry.CommitChanges()
15   End If
16 End Sub
```

In Listing 19-6, I add an e-mail address to the UserMan user by calling the **Add** method of the objEntry object. This happens on Line 12, but before I can do that I have to bind to the UserMan user object in Active Directory, and this is done on Lines 5 through 7. Finally, I use the **CommitChanges** method on Line 14 to propagate the changes back to the Active Directory database. Listings 19-5 and 19-6 are obvious candidates for a single piece of code, as shown in Listing 19-7.

Listing 19-7. Manipulating a User Property

```
1 Public Sub ManipulateUserProperty()
2    Dim objEntry As DirectoryEntry
3
4    ' Bind to UserMan user object
5    objEntry = New DirectoryEntry( _
6       "LDAP://CN=UserMan,CN=Users,DC=userman,DC=dk", _
7       "Administrator", "AdminPwd")
8
9    ' Check if the user already had an e-mail address
10   If objEntry.Properties.Contains("mail") Then
11      ' Add new e-mail address
12      objEntry.Properties("mail")(0) = "userman@userman.dk"
13   Else
14      ' Add new e-mail address
15      objEntry.Properties("mail").Add("userman@userman.dk")
16   End If
17
18   ' Commit the changes to the AD database
19   objEntry.CommitChanges()
20 End Sub
```

Listing 19-7 is simply a piece of example code where I have made one function out of Listings 19-5 and 19-6. Basically it checks if the UserMan user already has an e-mail address. If the user already has an e-mail address, it is edited, and if not, it is added.

Updating the Active Directory Database

If the **UsePropertyCache** property of a **DirectoryEntry** object is set to **False**, you don't have to worry about committing your changes to the Active Directory database, as on Line 19 in Listing 19-7, because it's done automatically. However, if the **UsePropertyCache** property is set to **True**, which is the default, you must manually commit the changes. You can do this by calling the **CommitChanges** method of the **DirectoryEntry** class.

NOTE If you've changed any information that resides in your cache, because the **UsePropertyCache** property is set to **True**, you can abort these changes by calling the **RefreshCache** method of the **DirectoryEntry** class, which will overwrite any information in the cache.

Accessing Active Directory Using the OLE DB .NET Data Provider

Although you can achieve just about anything in relation to Active Directory with the classes in the **System.DirectoryServices** namespace, it can be a lot easier to use the OLE DB .NET Data Provider instead, because it allows you to implement standard SQL syntax to extract the wanted data. See Listing 19-8 for an example.

Listing 19-8. Using OLE DB .NET to Access Active Directory

```
1 Public Sub AccessADWithOleDb()
2   Dim cnnAD As OleDbConnection
3   Dim cmmAD As OleDbCommand
4   Dim drdAD As OleDbDataReader
5
6   ' Instantiate and open connection
7   cnnAD = New OleDbConnection( _
8       "Provider=ADsDSOObject;User Id=UserMan;Password=userman")
9   cnnAD.Open()
10  ' Instantiate command
11  cmmAD = New OleDbCommand("SELECT cn, AdsPath FROM " & _
12      "'LDAP://userman.dk' WHERE objectCategory='person' " & _
13      "AND objectClass='user' AND cn='UserMan'", cnnAD)
14
15  ' Retrieve rows in data reader
16  drdAD = cmmAD.ExecuteReader()
17 End Sub
```

Listing 19-8 shows you how to retrieve all rows from Active Directory for the userman.dk domain with the user name UserMan. You need to change the user ID and password on Line 8 to match a user with read access to your Active Directory. On Line 12, you will need to change the domain name to match the name of the domain to which you are connecting.

The **objectCategory** and **objectClass** references on Lines 11 and 12 are standard LDAP-style query calls, and they ensure that only user objects are searched.

Specifying an OLE DB Provider for the Connection

There is only one provider to use with the OLE DB .NET Data Provider for accessing Active Directory, **ADsDSOObject**, which you can see on Line 8 in Listing 19-8.

Basically, you can use the following code to open a connection to Active Directory:

```
Dim cnnAD As New OleDbConnection("Provider=ADsDSOObject")
cnnAD.Open()
```

Obviously, you need to be logged onto a system that uses Active Directory with an account that has permission to read from Active Directory, but it's really that simple! If you aren't logged on or you don't have read access to Active Directory, you can always use the syntax specified on Line 8 in Listing 19-8.

Specifying What Domain to Access with the LDAP Protocol

When you try to access Active Directory after opening an **OleDbConnection**, you need to specify the protocol and the domain name of the Active Directory to access. This is done where you would normally specify the table name in a SELECT statement, like this:

```
FROM 'LDAP://userman.dk'
```

As you can see, I have put the protocol name and domain name in single quotes. This is a must—if you don't do this, an exception will be thrown. Specifying the protocol is the same as it is when you use your browser: You specify either HTTP or FTP followed by a colon and two slashes (://).

See Listing 19-8 for a complete example of how to construct a SELECT statement that retrieves rows from Active Directory.

Specifying What Information to Retrieve from Active Directory

As in any other SELECT statement, you can tell the command which "columns" you want returned.

Table 19-5 shows a list of some of the information you can retrieve from Active Directory. Please note that this list is not exhaustive, but merely a starting point for how to get user information. The User Properties Dialog Box Equivalent column refers to the information you can find using the Active Directory Users and Computers MMC snap-in. You then double-click the user you want to see information for and the user dialog box pops up. Figures 19-1 and 19-2 show you the General and Account tabs of the user properties dialog box in the Active Directory Users and Computers MMC snap-in.

Table 19-5. User Information "Columns"

Name	Description	User Properties Dialog Box Equivalent
adsPath	This is the full path to the object, including the protocol header.	None
mail	This is the user's e-mail account. Please note that this has nothing to do with any e-mail accounts created in Exchange Server.	General tab, E-mail textbox. See Figure 19-1.
objectSid	This represents the user's security identifier (SID). Please note that this is returned as an array of bytes. You need to convert the SID if you want to display it in a human readable format (S-1-5-21-…).	None
samAccountName	This is the name used by the Security Account Manager (SAM).	Account tab, User logon name (pre–Windows 2000) textbox. See Figure 19-2.
userPrincipalName	The user principal name (UPN) is an Internet-style login name for a user. The UPN is based on the Internet standard RFC 822, and is most often the same as **mail**.	Account tab, User logon name textbox and drop-down list. This is most often the same as the user's e-mail address as it comes from the concept of one logon name to access all services.

Figure 19-1. General tab of the user properties dialog box

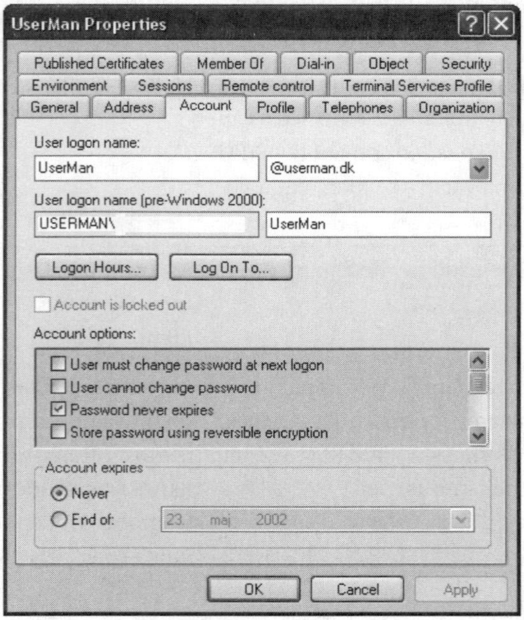

Figure 19-2. Account tab of the user properties dialog box

Figure 19-1 shows you the General tab of the user properties dialog box in the Active Directory Users and Computers MMC snap-in. Figure 19-2 shows you the Account tab of the user properties dialog box in the Active Directory Users and Computers MMC snap-in.

Please note that you cannot specify the asterisks (*) to retrieve all "columns" as you would in a standard SQL statement. If you do, the query will only return **adsPath**. Refer to the SQL Dialect at this address: `http://msdn.microsoft.com/library/default.asp?url=/library/en-us/netdir/adsi/sql_dialect.asp`.

If you want more information about the Active Directory schema, its objects, the objects' attributes, and so on, visit this address: `http://msdn.microsoft.com/library/default.asp?url=/library/en-us/netdir/ad/about_the_active_directory_schema.asp`.

Updating an Active Directory Object

The current OLE DB provider for ADSI, the one that comes with MDAC 2.6 and 2.7, is read-only, meaning you cannot issue an UPDATE statement. Microsoft says this will change, but I haven't found any information detailing if this is to change with ADSI in Windows .NET or if ADSI with Windows 2000 and Windows XP is also part of these plans. Stay alert, my friend!

Retrieving the SID for a User

You've probably noticed that the tblUser table in the UserMan database holds two columns that are named ADName and ADSID. They're there to hold the SID (**objectSid**) and the SAM account name (**samAccountName**) for the user (see Table 19-5 for a description of **objectSid** and **samAccountName**). Take a look at Listing 19-9 to see how to retrieve these two values for the UserMan user. You obviously need to have added the UserMan user to Active Directory on your network for this to work.

Listing 19-9. Retrieving the SAM Account Name and SID from Active Directory

```
1 Public Sub GetSIDAndSAMAccountNameFromAD()
2     Dim cnnAD As OleDbConnection
3     Dim cmmAD As OleDbCommand
4     Dim drdAD As OleDbDataReader
5     Dim strSAMAccountName As String
6     Dim strSID As String
7
```

```
8     ' Instantiate and open connection
9     cnnAD = New OleDbConnection( _
10        "Provider=ADsDSOObject;User Id=UserMan;Password=userman")
11    cnnAD.Open()
12    ' Instantiate command
13    cmmAD = New OleDbCommand("SELECT objectSid, samAccountName FROM " & _
14      "'LDAP://userman.dk' WHERE objectCategory='person' " & _
15      "AND objectClass='user' AND cn='UserMan'", cnnAD)
16
17    ' Retrieve rows in DataReader
18    drdAD = cmmAD.ExecuteReader()
19    ' Go to first row
20    drdAD.Read()
21    ' Get SAM Account name
22    strSAMAccountName = drdAD("samAccountName").ToString
23    ' Get SID
24    strSID = drdAD("objectSid").ToString
25 End Sub
```

In Listing 19-9, the SID and SAM account name are retrieved from Active Directory using the OLE DB provider for Microsoft Directory Services. Once returned, I save the values in local variables. In Chapter 26, I will expand on this example and show you how to save the values to your UserMan database.

Summary

This chapter contains very brief technology background on LDAP and Active Directory, and how they are used in conjunction. I discussed the **System.DirectoryServices** namespace and the classes it encompasses, specifically showing you the **DirectoryEntry** class and its properties and methods.

I also explained how to establish a connection programmatically using the classes in the **System.DirectoryServices** namespace and using the OLE DB .NET Data Provider.

I can conclude by saying that although Active Directory is a unique way of storing some of your data, it will not replace your relational database. Active Directory is for storing data objects long term and only objects that are changed infrequently.

In the next chapter, I give you a look at how to access the mailbox folder contents on a Microsoft Exchange Server 2000, and how you add Exchange Server as a linked server to a SQL Server and create views on the mailbox content, thus making it possible to execute standard SQL queries on the linked server.

CHAPTER 20

Exchange Server

MICROSOFT EXCHANGE SERVER 2000 is classified as a hierarchical database. One very simple reason for this is its treelike folder structure. Exchange Server 2000 uses Active Directory for storing setup and other non–mail-related information. This means that you can access Exchange Server information using the techniques described in Chapter 19, but this is *not* recommended. Microsoft warns about doing it this way, and it's understandable, because you can damage not only your Exchange Server setup, but also your Active Directory setup. Trust me, I know. The Microsoft Exchange Server coverage here is by no means exhaustive, but it should serve as an overview with example code and references to more information. One book I can recommend is this one:

Programming Microsoft Outlook and Microsoft Exchange, by Thomas Rizzo. Microsoft Press, June 2000. ISBN: 0735610193.

Anyway, there are other means of accessing your Exchange Server data besides using Active Directory, such as the following:

- Using Microsoft OLE DB Exchange Server Provider (ExOLEDB)

- Using Microsoft OLE DB Provider for Internet Publishing (MSDAIPP)

- Accessing Exchange Server as a linked server from SQL Server

You can find descriptions of and example code for using these protocols in the sections that follow. There's a 120-day trial version of Exchange Server 2000 available at http://www.microsoft.com/exchange/evaluation/trial/default.asp. You can also order a CD-ROM with the trial version, if you don't want to download it. Please note that this is by no means a thorough walk-through of these access methods, but merely a teaser on how to do them. If you're used to using the Microsoft Collaboration Data Objects (CDO) for formatting and sending messages, I can only recommend that you look into using the classes in the **System.Web.Mail** namespace instead. The classes in this namespace use the CDO for the Windows 2000 (CDOSYS) messaging component. Listing 20-1 shows you a very simple example of sending a message.

Listing 20-1. Sending a Mail Message Using SMTP

```
1 Public Sub SendMessageUsingCDOSYS()
2    Dim msgMail As New MailMessage()
3
4    ' Prepare message
5    msgMail.From = "UserMan <userman@userman.dk>"
6    msgMail.To = "Carsten Thomsen <carstent@userman.dk>"
7    msgMail.Body = "This is the e-mail body"
8    msgMail.Subject = "This is the e-mail subject"
9
10   ' Set the SMTP server (you can use an IP address,
11   ' NETBIOS name or a FQDN)
12   SmtpMail.SmtpServer = "10.8.1.19"
13   SmtpMail.SmtpServer = "EXCHANGESERVER"
14   SmtpMail.SmtpServer = "exchangeserver.userman.dk"
15
16   ' Send the prepared message using the
17   ' specified SMTP server
18   SmtpMail.Send(msgMail)
19 End Sub
```

In Listing 20-1 you can see how an instance of the **MailMessage** class (msgMail) is instantiated on Line 2, and prepared by setting the **From, To, Body,** and **Subject** properties (Lines 5 through 8). On Lines 12 through 14, I use different ways of specifying which SMTP server to use for sending the message. As you can see, I've provided you with three different ways of specifying the SMTP server, but you can also choose not to set the **SmtpServer** property, in which case the **SmtpMail** class assumes that you want to use the local SMTP server. Line 18 sends the prepared message using the **Send** method. Please note that the **SmtpMail** class is **Shared,** and therefore you can use it without creating an instance of it.

The example code shown will only work on Windows 2000, Windows XP, or a Windows .NET Server, but you don't need to have an Exchange Server. The mentioned platforms all have a built-in SMTP service that you can use for sending messages. You need to make sure this service is running and correctly set up. You can set up the service from your IIS. Please see the documentation for more information.

If you get the "Could not access 'CDO.Message' object" error message (see Figure 20-1) when you run the example code in Listing 20-1, the problem more than likely has to do with relaying permissions of the SMTP service on the machine you use for sending the message.

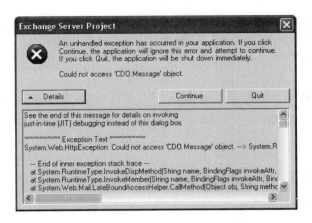

Figure 20-1. "Could not access 'CDO.Message' object" error message

In Figure 20-1, you can see the "Could not access 'CDO.Message' object" error message, which you might get when you run the example code in Listing 20-1. If VS .NET has been properly installed, this error message probably has to do with permissions, and there are different ways of fixing this. The easiest way is to simply allow relaying,[1] but I can't recommend this unless you have a test machine on a dial-up account or similar "security" measures that prevent everyone on the Internet from using your SMTP server for relaying their spam messages. You can also allow relaying to certain machines, which is just as easy to implement from within the Internet Information Services (IIS) MMC snap-in:

1. Open up IIS.

2. Right-click the SMTP service (usually called Default SMTP Virtual Server), and click Properties on the pop-up menu.

3. Click the Access tab.

4. Click the Relay button. Now the Relay Restrictions dialog box is shown, as you can see in Figure 20-2.

---

1. *Relaying* here in it's simplest form means that someone else can use your SMTP mail server to send mail messages.

Figure 20-2. The Relay Restrictions dialog box

5. Select All except the list below option button to allow relaying in general, or select the Only the list below option button to give relaying permissions to specific machines, a group of machines, or entire domains.

6. Click the Add button if you selected the Only the list below option button, and add the machine, group of machines, or domain you want to allow the relaying for. I opted for allowing a single machine, based on the IP address 10.8.1.16, as shown in Figure 20-2.

7. Click OK to close the Relay Restrictions dialog box once you've added the machine(s) or domain to the allow relay list or selected the All except the list below option button.

In Figure 20-2, you can see how I've added the 10.8.1.16 IP address to the allow relay list of the SMTP Virtual Server service on my machine. Try running the example code again to see if that fixed your problem.

As mentioned earlier, there are other ways of fixing this, but the other options, such as authentication, are beyond the scope of this chapter.

Using the Microsoft OLE DB Exchange Server Provider

The Microsoft OLE DB Exchange Server Provider (ExOLEDB) is intended for use only on the machine that hosts Microsoft Exchange Server 2000. This means that it is a server-side–only provider, and you can only use it for accessing a local Exchange

Server. If you need to access Exchange Server 2000 from a client, look into using the OLE DB Provider for Internet Publishing. See the "Using the Microsoft OLE DB Provider for Internet Publishing" section later in this chapter.

The ExOLEDB provider ships with Exchange Server 2000 and *not* with any of the MDACs available for download. (See Chapter 4 for more information on MDAC.) I guess this makes sense, since it can only be run from the local Exchange Server anyway. However, the real problem with the ExOLEDB provider is that it is OLE DB 2.5 compliant. This means that you can't use it with the OLE DB .NET Data Provider, which requires a later version. At the time of this writing, Exchange Server Service Pack (SP) 2 is out, but it only features a version 2.5–compliant OLE DB provider. Rumors have it that Microsoft will ship either an add-on or an SP that will let you access your Exchange Server using truly managed code. This add-on or SP was supposed to ship in the second quarter of 2002. If it hasn't happened, I'm sure you'll find plenty of support for the .NET Framework in the next version of Exchange Server.

Now, I won't leave you empty-handed with regard to the OLE DB Exchange Server Provider, because you can always use classic ADO through COM Interop. See Appendix B for more information. Listing 20-2 is a very simple example that shows you how to retrieve all the contacts for the UserMan user.

Listing 20-2. Retrieving Contacts for UserMan User from Exchange Server 2000

```
1 Public Sub RetrieveContactsUsingExOLEDB()
2     Dim cnnExchange As New ADODB.Connection()
3     Dim rstExchange As New ADODB.RecordsetClass()
4     Dim strFile As String = _
5         "file://./backofficestorage/userman.dk/mbx/userman"
6
7     cnnExchange.Provider = "ExOLEDB.DataSource"
8
9     Try
10        ' Open the connection, keeping in mind that
11        ' the ExOLEDB provider doesn't authenticate
12        ' the passed user id and password arguments
13        cnnExchange.Open(strFile, , , -1)
14        ' Open the recordset
15        rstExchange.Open("SELECT ""DAV:displayname"" AS Name " & _
16            "FROM SCOPE('shallow traversal of ""Contacts""')", cnnExchange, _
17            CursorTypeEnum.adOpenForwardOnly, LockTypeEnum.adLockReadOnly, 0)
18        ' Loop through all the returned rows (contacts)
```

```
19      While Not rstExchange.EOF
20          ' Display Contact name
21          MsgBox(rstExchange.Fields("Name").Value.ToString())
22          ' Move to the next row
23          rstExchange.MoveNext()
24      End While
25   Catch objE As Exception
26      MsgBox(objE.Message)
27   End Try
28 End Sub
```

This example shows you how to open a connection to an Exchange Server 2000 using the OLE DB Exchange Server Provider and classic ADO for retrieving all contacts for the UserMan user.

Using the Microsoft OLE DB Provider for Internet Publishing

The Microsoft OLE DB Provider for Internet Publishing (MSDAIPP) is a client-side–only provider, which means that you can't use it for accessing Exchange Server 2000 from the machine that hosts your Exchange Server 2000. If you need to access Exchange Server 2000 from the machine that hosts Exchange Server 2000, look into using the OLE DB Exchange Server Provider. See the "Using the Microsoft OLE DB Exchange Server Provider" section earlier in this chapter.

The MSDAIPP provider is, as the full name suggests, used for accessing documents located in Internet Information Server (IIS) virtual directories, but it can also be used for accessing data in an Exchange Server 2000 Web store remotely. MSDAIPP uses the WebDAV protocol.

One final point to note about this provider is that it uses the Hypertext Transfer Protocol (HTTP) for the transport, which means that the Data Source value in the connection string must be specified using a URL. In Listing 20-3 you can see how the MSDAIPP provider can be used to retrieve all items in a particular folder.

Listing 20-3. Retrieving Contents of Exchange Server 2000 Folder

```
1 Public Sub MSDAIPPShowFolderProperties()
2    Dim cnnExchange As New OleDbConnection()
3    Dim cmmExchange As New OleDbCommand()
4    Dim drdExchange As OleDbDataReader
5
6    Dim strFolder As String
7    Dim intColumn As Integer
```

```
8
9    ' Set up connection string to bind to the userman folder
10   cnnExchange.ConnectionString = "Provider=MSDAIPP.dso;Data Source=" & _
11     "http://exchangeserver/exchange/userman;" & _
12     "User ID='Administrator';Password=AdminPwd;"
13
14   ' Open the connection
15   cnnExchange.Open()
16   ' Initialize the command
17   cmmExchange.Connection = cnnExchange
18   cmmExchange.CommandType = CommandType.TableDirect
19   ' Return all rows
20   drdExchange = cmmExchange.ExecuteReader()
21
22   ' Loop through all the returned rows (folders)
23   While drdExchange.Read()
24       ' Initialize folder string
25       strFolder = ""
26       ' Loop through all the columns (properties)
27       For intColumn = 0 To drdExchange.FieldCount - 1
28           ' Read folder property name and value
29           strFolder += drdExchange.GetName(intColumn) & _
30               "=" & drdExchange(intColumn).ToString & vbCrLf
31       Next
32
33       ' Display folder properties
34       MsgBox(strFolder)
35   End While
36 End Sub
```

In Listing 20-3, you can see how the property names and values for all items in a particular folder are returned in a DataReader object. Please note that all items are returned, including hidden ones. Run the code to see the various properties that are returned. Here's a quick rundown of the code:

- Lines 10 through 12 set up the connection string for the **OleDbConnection** object, with the MSDAIPP provider specified as Provider=MSDAIPP.dso. The name of the data source, which in this case is an Exchange Server, is specified using Data Source=http://exchangeserver. You obviously need to change this to the name or IP address of your Exchange Server, and don't forget to add the port number (for example, http://exchangeserver:86) if the Web server on the machine that hosts your Exchange Server accepts HTTP requests on a different port such as 86. After the server name, you must specify /exchange, because this is the name of the Exchange Server's virtual directory, and then you need to specify the mailbox you want to access (/userman). This needs to be changed so it matches a mailbox on your system. Finally, you need to supply the user ID and password of a user on your system that has access rights to the specified mailbox. Change the User ID and Password values accordingly. If you supply the wrong user credentials, you'll be required to enter them in an input box displayed by your browser.

- Line 15 opens the connection.

- Line 17 sets the **Connection** property of the **OleDbCommand** object equal to the open connection.

- Line 18 sets the **CommandType** property to the **TableDirect** member of the **CommandType** enum. This way, all rows from the folder specified will be returned.

- Line 20 returns all rows in the specified folder in an **OleDbDataReader** object.

- Lines 23 through 35 loop through all elements in the specified folder and display all properties for each element.

In the example code in Listing 20-3, all elements, meaning all folders, are retrieved from the userman folder/mailbox. You can just as easily add /Inbox to the Data Source value in the connection string specified on Line 11 to retrieve all items/messages in the Inbox folder. If you add /Contacts to the Data Source value, you retrieve all contacts for the specified mailbox. Basically, you can specify any existing folder from the specified mailbox folder.

Accessing Exchange Server as a Linked Server from SQL Server

If your Exchange Server 2000 is located on the same machine as your SQL Server, you can use SQL Server for linking to your Exchange Server and this way create views on the Exchange Server Web store that can be queried like any regular table in your database.

NOTE Because the OLE DB Exchange Server Provider (ExOLEDB) is only intended for use on the machine that hosts Microsoft Exchange Server 2000, your SQL Server also needs to be located on the Exchange Server machine.

The first thing you need to do is set up the Exchange Server as a linked server from your SQL Server. Then you can create views that access the linked server. See the following sections for more information.

Setting Up Exchange Server as a Linked Server

You can set up a linked server by executing the **sp_addlinkedserver** system stored procedure. Basically, this system stored procedure is used for setting up linked servers so you can create distributed queries, meaning queries that you can run on databases on more than one server at a time. You just need a linked Exchange Server, and you can link to it by executing the T-SQL statement in Listing 20-4. You can execute it from Query Analyzer or Enterprise Manager, or whatever tool you normally execute your SQL Server queries from.

Listing 20-4. Adding a Linked Exchange Server with T-SQL

```
1 EXEC sp_addlinkedserver 'ExchangeServer',
2 '@srvproduct = 'Microsoft Exchange OLE DB Provider',
3 '@provider = 'ExOLEDB.DataSource',
4 @datasrc = 'file://./backofficestorage/userman.dk/mbx/UserMan'
5 @provstr = 'User Id=userman@userman.dk;Password=userman;'
```

The T-SQL example code shown in Listing 20-4 will add ExchangeServer as a linked server to your SQL Server (Line 1). You can give it any name you want as long as it doesn't conflict with a different linked server, or even the name of your SQL Server.

On Line 3, I specify that I want to use the ExOLEDB provider, and on Line 4, I specify the data source, meaning the full path to the mailbox I want to access, which is UserMan in this case. Visit http://msdn.microsoft.com/library/ default.asp?url=/library/en-us/wss/wss/_exch2k_the_file_url_scheme.asp to see how to construct your Exchange Server file paths.

Line 5 of Listing 20-4 is the OLE DB provider string, and this one is important if you don't want to get a 7304 error message when you try to access the linked server. You pass the user ID in the format *mailbox@domainname* and the password for the mailbox or Windows login.

NOTE   The Exchange Server mailbox you're accessing not only must be created from the Active Directory Users and Computers MMC snap-in, but you also need to log onto the mailbox at least once for the mailbox to be physically created on your system. You can use Microsoft Outlook to log onto the mailbox.

You can find more information about the system stored procedure **sp_addlinkedserver** in SQL Server Books Online that comes with your SQL Server. Instead of executing the T-SQL statement shown earlier, you can create a linked server from Enterprise Manager. Here's how you create the same linked server you did with the T-SQL script earlier, but this time using the Enterprise Manager:

1. Open Enterprise Manager.

2. Expand the Security node below your database server.

3. Right-click the Linked Servers node, and select New Linked Server from the pop-up menu.

This brings up the Linked Server Properties dialog box shown in Figure 20-3.

Figure 20-3. Linked Server Properties dialog box

Figure 20-3 shows you the General tab of the Linked Server Properties dialog box with the Provider name, Product name, and Data source options already filled in. However, as you can see in Figure 20-3, you can't fill in the provider string as you did with the T-SQL statement. Don't worry, there's a way around this. You can select the Security tab, which is shown in Figure 20-4, and give the same user credentials as you did with the T-SQL statement in Listing 20-4.

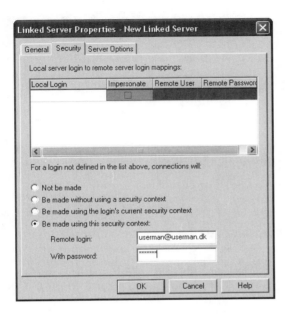

Figure 20-4. Security tab of the Linked Server Properties dialog box

In Figure 20-4, you can see the Security tab of the Linked Server Properties dialog box with the Be made using this security context option selected and the Remote login and With password textboxes filled in with the correct user credentials. This corresponds to the security values set on Line 5 of Listing 20-4, meaning the user ID has the same value as the Remote login textbox, and the Password has the same value as the With password textbox.

Once you click the OK button after having supplied the correct information, you can see the folders in the mailbox you connect to in the details pane if you select the Tables node (see Figure 20-5). If you receive a 7304 or 7309 error message when you select the Tables node, you have entered invalid user credentials.

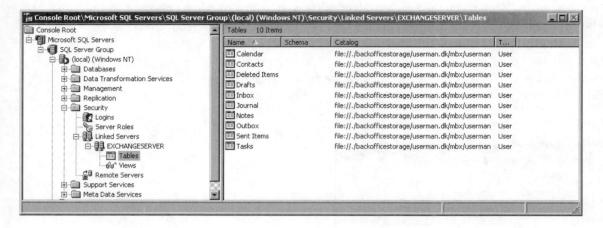

Figure 20-5. Exchange Server mailbox folders shown as tables in Enterprise Manager

Figure 20-5 shows the various mailboxes in the UserMan mailbox displayed as tables in the Enterprise Manager.

Dropping a Linked Exchange Server

You can drop the linked server by executing this T-SQL statement:

```
EXEC sp_dropserver 'ExchangeServer'
```

You can find more information about the **sp_dropserver** system stored procedure in SQL Server Books Online.

You can also drop a linked server from the Enterprise Manager by selecting it under the Linked Server's node and choosing Delete from the pop-up menu. You're required to confirm this irreversible action.

Creating Views on the Linked Exchange Server

Once you've set up your Exchange Server as a linked server from your SQL Server, you can create views on the folders in the catalog you've connected to. If you create a view, or a stored procedure for that matter, you take the pain out of querying the information stored in your Exchange Server. When I say pain, I mean that for someone who's used to dealing with standard ANSI SQL-92 queries it can be quite a task to create and set up queries that extract information from Exchange Server. Basically, you can set up a number of queries that will provide your users with all the information they need from the Exchange Server, and this way they'll never have to worry about how an Exchange Server query is constructed. Listing 20-5 shows you a view that extracts information from the Contacts folder in the UserMan mailbox on the Exchange Server.

Listing 20-5. SQL Server View Extracting Information
from Exchange Server 2000 Mailbox

```
1 CREATE VIEW viwUserManContacts AS
2 SELECT CONVERT(nvarchar(30), "urn:schemas:contacts:givenname") AS FirstName,
3        CONVERT(nvarchar(30), "urn:schemas:contacts:sn") AS LastName,
4        CONVERT(nvarchar(100), "urn:schemas:contacts:email1") AS Email
5 FROM OpenQuery(EXCHANGESERVER, 'SELECT
6        "urn:schemas:contacts:givenname",
7        "urn:schemas:contacts:sn",
8        "urn:schemas:contacts:email1"
9   FROM SCOPE(''shallow traversal of "./Contacts"'')')
```

In Listing 20-5, you can see how the view extracts information (first name, last name, and e-mail address) from the Contacts folder. Listing 20-5 doesn't show you that it's from the UserMan mailbox, but this was specified in the "Setting Up Exchange Server as a Linked Server" section earlier in this chapter.

See Chapter 17 for more information on how to create views on SQL Server. If you want to know more about the way you specify the columns to retrieve in your views, please consult the Microsoft Exchange Server documentation.

Now that you've created a view, you can access the information from the view using any standard SQL query, such as SELECT * FROM viwUserManContacts, which will return all the rows/contacts from the UserMan mailbox on the linked Exchange Server. The columns returned are FirstName, LastName, and Email.

Summary

In this chapter, I gave you a look at how to access the mailbox folder contents on a Microsoft Exchange Server 2000 using various protocols. I showed you how to add Exchange Server as a linked server to a SQL Server, creating views on the mailbox content and thus making it possible to execute standard SQL queries on the linked server.

The next chapter is about message queues and how you can use them for connectionless programming.

Part Eight

Message Queueing

CHAPTER 21

Message Queues

Using Message Queues for Connectionless Programming

MESSAGE QUEUES ARE GREAT whenever you don't have a permanent connection or are working in loosely coupled situations. They're also handy when you simply want to dump your input and return to your application without waiting for the output from whatever application or server will be processing your input. You can make message queues the basis of a fail-safe application that uses them whenever your regular database fails. This can help ensure that no data is lost and you have very little or no downtime at all, if you use transactional queues. Obviously not all applications can use message queues to such advantage, but for storing or accepting customer input it can be a great solution. One example springs to mind that wouldn't benefit from using message queues, and that is a banking transaction, which needs to be processed in real-time.

Microsoft's messaging technology is called *Message Queuing*. Mind you, in line with other traditional Microsoft marketing stunts, this technology has had other names before Windows 2000 was shipped. However, the release that ships with Windows 2000 is built upon a previous version of the technology and includes the Active Directory (AD) integration. AD integration is good because it's now easier to locate public message queues across your domain, and it ensures easy Enterprise-wide backup.

The .NET Framework base classes include native support for MSMQ 2.0 in the **System.Messaging** namespace. This chapter doesn't provide any coverage of MSMQ 1.0, which is used in Windows NT 4.0 networks.

Is MSMQ Dead?

Microsoft Message Queue Server (MSMQ) is the name Microsoft gave version 1.0 of its message queuing technology. It was originally included with the Enterprise Edition of Windows NT 4. With version 2.0 it became an add-on to any server version of Windows NT 4, and it was part of the Windows NT Option Pack. The Windows NT Option Pack could be freely downloaded from the Microsoft Web site. Since then the message queuing technology has been integrated into the OS, as is the case with Windows 2000 and Windows XP, and the upcoming Windows .NET Server. Not only has MSMQ been integrated into the OS, it has been extended in numerous ways. One extension is the integration with Active Directory instead of being SQL Server based.

So to answer the question, "Is MSMQ Dead?" the answer is yes and no. Yes, because it's no longer a stand-alone product, and no because the features of the original MSMQ have been incorporated into the OS as a service called Message Queuing. MSMQ 3.0 has been introduced with Windows XP Professional, and it's covered in the "MSMQ 3.0 Features" section later in this chapter.

Installing Message Queuing

In order to use any of the functionality described in this chapter, you must make sure that Message Queuing is installed on your development machine, as well as on any remote server you want to use for your message queuing. As described in the "Is MSMQ Dead?" sidebar earlier in this chapter, you must install it separately from the Windows NT Option Pack if you're running Windows NT 4. Message Queuing is a component of the OS if you're running Windows 2000, Windows XP, or Windows .NET Server, although it's not installed by default. To install it, select the Add or Remove Programs option in Control Panel. This brings up the Add or Remove Programs dialog box, in which you must click the Add/Remove Windows Components button to bring up the Windows Components Wizard as shown in Figure 21-1. Scroll down the Components list, select the Message Queuing component,[1] and click Next to install it.

---

1. On a Windows .NET Server—well, RC1 anyway—you need to select the Web Application Server component, which includes IIS and Message Queuing. Then click Details to be able to select the Message Queuing component.

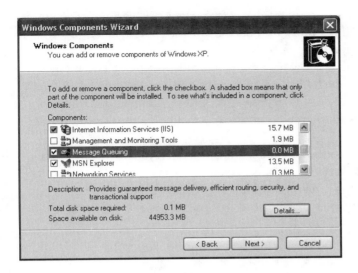

Figure 21-1. Windows Components Wizard

In Figure 21-1 you can see the Windows Component Wizard with the Message Queuing component selected. Depending on what platform you're installing on, you can choose to install a Message Queuing server, a dependent client, or an independent client. Please see the following list for options available to the supported platforms:

- *Windows 2000 Professional:* On this platform you can choose either an independent client or a dependent client of an existing Message Queuing network.

- *Windows 2000 Server:* On a Windows 2000 Server, you're asked if you want to create a Message Queuing server, or a dependent client of an existing Message Queuing network. If no existing server is found on your network, you can only choose to install a Message Queuing server. (See Figure 21-2 later.)

- *Windows XP:* On this platform, you can choose an independent client, or a dependent client of an existing Message Queuing network. See also http://support.microsoft.com/default.aspx?scid=kb;en-us;Q317329.

- *Windows .NET Server:* Again, you can choose an independent client or a dependent client of an existing Message Queuing network.

As you can see from the previous list, newer versions of the Windows operating system, Windows XP and Windows .NET Server, don't support installing a Message Queuing server. However, you can still connect to a Message Queuing server on a Windows 2000 Server. This is due to the new version of Message Queuing, version 3.0, which doesn't work with the notion of a server. Instead you work with dependent and independent clients. See the "Dependent Client vs. Independent Client vs. Server" section later in this chapter for more information on the three different installation types.

In Figure 21-2 you can see what options you have when you install the Message Queuing component on a Windows 2000 Server. On this particular network, no existing Message Queuing server was found, so you can only install a new server and not a dependent client.

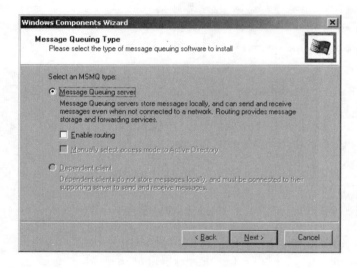

Figure 21-2. Selecting type of Message Queuing component on Windows 2000 Server

Workgroup vs. Active Directory Mode

When installing Message Queuing you can choose to work in workgroup or Active Directory mode. If you ever installed one or more machines on a network, you probably already know the difference. In workgroup mode (which isn't supported by MSMQ 1.0), when you connect to other peers, there's no central place to look for other clients and/or queues. This is in contrast to Active Directory mode, which saves setup and other information in Active Directory. This information can be used for looking up queues that are part of the Message Queuing network. There's overhead involved in using an Active Directory–based Message Queuing network, and Microsoft actually recommends installing in workgroup mode with Message Queuing 3.0 due to performance issues. However, there are a number of reasons you'd want to use Active Directory mode, if your network runs on Active Directory, including the following:

- Enterprise-wide backup when Active Directory is backed up

- Increased support for MSMQ 1.0 and Message Queuing 2.0 installations

- Different formats for accessing a message queue

With Message Queuing 3.0 you need to select the Active Directory Integration subcomponent when installing Message Queuing, if you want to work in Active Directory mode. Remove the selection if you want to run in workgroup mode. Figure 21-3 shows you the Message Queuing 3.0 subcomponents.

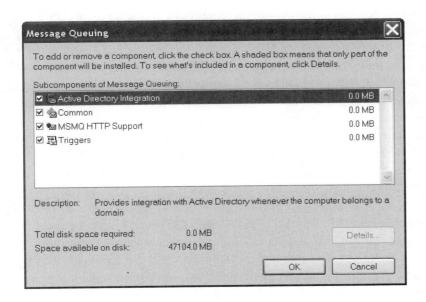

Figure 21-3. Message Queuing 3.0 subcomponents

In Figure 21-3 you can see the Message Queuing 3.0 subcomponents for a Windows XP installation. On a Windows .NET Server you'll also have the Routing Support component.

Dependent Client vs. Independent Client vs. Server

Now, this is confusing to say the least. Well, it is if you read the Microsoft documentation, but I hope I can manage to shed some light on the subject.

In brief, MSMQ 1.0, which runs on Windows NT, has two different types of servers: controller servers and routing servers. Now, the controller server uses SQL Server for storing a copy of the message queue network infrastructure, also called the Message Queue Information Store (MQIS). The routing server doesn't host an MQIS, but simply provides routing functionality to other servers and clients on the MSMQ network. Besides the two types of servers, MSMQ also has two types of clients, a dependent and an independent client. The dependent client can only send and receive messages when it's connected to a MSMQ server, whether controller or routing server, whereas the independent client has a local message store and can therefore send messages while offline (that is, not connected to an MSMQ server).

Then came Message Queuing 2.0, and now the server message store is no longer SQL Server based, but instead a part of Active Directory, which means you can now install in workgroup mode and in Active Directory mode. (See the "Workgroup vs. Active Directory Mode" section earlier in this chapter.) The Message Queuing 2.0 Server installs on a Windows 2000 Server, with or without routing capabilities (see Figure 21-2). So, Message Queuing 2.0 only has one server type, but it optionally supports routing. Independent and dependent clients are also supported by Message Queuing 2.0. As with MSMQ 1.0, the dependent client can only send and receive messages when connected to a server, whereas the independent client has its own local message store. This means that you can send messages while offline, exactly as you can with MSMQ 1.0 independent clients. However, a Message Queuing 2.0 independent client is really the same as a server without routing enabled. I guess that because the optional routing functionality can only be installed on a Windows 2000 Server, Microsoft chose to call it a server, in line with MSMQ 1.0.

In Message Queuing 3.0, Microsoft has changed this slightly again, because now there's no server; you have dependent and independent clients. When you install Message Queuing 3.0 on a Windows .NET Server, you can optionally install routing functionality for your independent client. So, even if the installation types are more or less the same as in Message Queuing 2.0, Microsoft has chosen to remove the notion of a server in Message Queuing 3.0.

Connectionless Programming

Connectionless programming involves using a queue to hold your input to another application or server. Connectionless in this context means you don't have a permanent connection to the application or server. Instead, you log your input in a queue, and the other application or server then takes it from the queue, processes it, and sometimes puts it back in the same or a different queue. This is how an independent Message Queuing client operates.

The opposite of connectionless is *connection oriented,* and basically any standard database system these days falls into this category. You've probably heard these two terms in relation to Transmission Control Protocol/Internet Protocol (TCP/IP). The User Datagram Protocol (UDP) part of the protocol is connectionless, and the TCP part is connection oriented. However, a major difference exists between message queuing and the UDP protocol. Whereas the UDP protocol does not guarantee delivery, and a packet sent over the network using the UDP transport protocol can be lost, the message queue doesn't lose any packets. The reason why a message queue is said to be connectionless is that your client doesn't "speak" directly with your server. There is no direct connection, as there is with a standard database. Actually, Message Queuing does support dependent clients, and in a rather loose sense this is a connection-oriented setup.

Now that you have an understanding of connectionless programming in this context, let's move on to an overview of the **MessageQueue** class.

Taking a Quick Look at the MessageQueue Class

The **MessageQueue** class is part of the **System.Messaging** namespace. That namespace also holds the **Message** class, which is used in conjunction with the **MessageQueue** class. The **System.Messaging** namespace holds a number of classes that are exclusively used for accessing and manipulating message queues.

The **MessageQueue** class is a wrapper around **Message Queuing**, which is an optional component of Windows 2000 and Windows NT. At any rate, you need to make sure you've installed Message Queuing on a server on your network before you can try the examples in this chapter.

When to Use a Message Queue

Use a message queue in your application if you need to perform any of these tasks:

- *Storing less-important information in a message queue while your DBMS is busy serving customers during the day:* The information in the message queue is then batch-processed when the DBMS is less busy. This is ideal for processing all real-time requests and storing all other requests in a message queue for later processing.

- *Queuing data for later processing, because of the nature of the data at the time of entry:* Some data can't be processed by your system at the time of data entry, because other data necessary for processing the entered data simply doesn't exist at this time and would thus mean that the processing would fail. However, later on, like at the end of the day, the data required to do the processing is available and you can process the entered data. One example of this is when you request an interaccount transfer, and the funds aren't available when the request is made, but they will be at the end of the day.

- *Connecting to a DBMS over a WAN, such as the Internet, and the connection isn't always available for whatever reason:* You can do two things when you design your application. You can set up your application to access the DBMS the usual way, and if you get a time-out or another connection failure, you store the request in a message queue. You then start a component that checks for when the DBMS is available, and when it is, it will forward the requests that are stored in the message queue and return a possible result to your application. At this point your application can resume normal operation and shut down the message queue component. The other possibility is to design your application as an offline one, meaning that all DBMS requests are stored in a local message queue and forwarded by your message queue component to the DBMS.

- *Exchanging data with a mainframe system, like SAP:* You can use a message queue to hold SAP IDocs. These are then sent to and received from the SAP system by the queue manager/component. Anyone who ever worked with SAP will know that real-time communications with SAP are often a problem, because the server is frequently overloaded at specific intervals during the day. So basically you use the message queue for storing and forwarding requests to and from the SAP system. Recall that SAP is originally a mainframe system, but these days SAP is often found running on midsize computers or PCs, and the five most popular platforms for R/3 are Windows NT, Sun Solaris, HP-UX, AS/400, and AIX.

I am sure you can come up with a few applications yourself that would benefit from message queuing based on your current or previous work experience.

Why Use a Message Queue and Not a Database Table?

A message queue can be of good use in many situations, but what makes it different from using a database table? When you call a DBMS, it's normally done synchronously, but with a message queue, it's generally done asynchronously. This means it's generally faster to access a message queue than to access a database table. With synchronous access the client application has to wait for the server to respond, whereas with asynchronous access a query or the like is sent to the server, and the client application then continues its normal duties. When the server has finished processing the query, it'll notify you and pass you the result. Please note that this is not the normal message queue setup—you need to set this up specifically.

When you use a database table, you must comply with a fairly strict format for adding data. There are certain fields that must be supplied, and you don't really have the ability to add extra information. Although the same can be said about message queues, when it comes to supplying certain fields, it's much easier to supply extra information that you have a hard time storing in a database table. Even if the data stored in the message queue eventually hits a database table, which it does in most cases, you have an application that takes care of processing the data, and then storing the data in a database. However, when you do the processing, you can have your processing logic validate whatever extra information you have in the messages held in the message queue and store the data in the messages based on the extra information. This can be the time of entry or other constraints that dictate which table the data is stored in.

This approach is valid for Windows Forms and Web Forms, though it depends on the *application type*. Distributed applications, client-server applications on a local network, and stand-alone applications constitute some of the different application types. If your application isn't distributed and you're accessing a standard DBMS on a local server or on your client, there's probably no reason for using a message queue. On the other hand, if your DBMS is busy during the day, you can store the requests and messages in a message queue for batch processing when the DBMS is less busy.

In short, application infrastructure and business requirements in general determine whether you should use message queuing. Having said this, I realize that sometimes it's a good idea to work with a tool for a while so that you can get to know the situations in which you should use it. Therefore, if you're new to message queuing, make sure you try the example code that follows later on in this chapter.

A message queue works using the *First In, First Out* (FIFO) principle, which means that the first message in the queue is the message you'll retrieve if you use the **Receive** or **Peek** method of the **MessageQueue** class. See the "Retrieving a Message" and "Peeking at Messages" sections later in this chapter for more information on these methods.

Now, FIFO is the principle applied to how the messages are placed in the queue, but the priority takes precedence over the arrival time, so it's possible to place a message at the top of the message queue even if other messages are already in the queue. If I were to make up a SELECT statement that describes how the messages are inserted into a queue and returned to you, it would look something like this:

```
SELECT * FROM MessageQueue ORDER BY Priority, ArrivalTime
```

Obviously this statement is just an example, but it does show you how the messages are ordered, first by priority and then by arrival time. Priority isn't normally something you would set, so most messages would have the same priority, but there may be times when it's necessary to "jump" the queue. See "Prioritizing Messages" later in this chapter for more information on how to prioritize your messages.

How to Use a Message Queue

Of course, you need to set up the message queue before you can use it in your application. Even if you already have a queue to connect to, it's a good idea to know how to set one up, so first I'll show you how. Please note that you can't view or manage public queues if you're in a workgroup environment. Public queues only exist in a domain environment. See your Windows NT, Windows 2000, or Windows XP documentation for installing Message Queuing, and optionally see the "Installing Message Queuing" section earlier in this chapter. If you're running in workgroup mode, you can't use Server Explorer to view a queue, not even private ones. I'll get to private and public queues in the next section.

Private Queue vs. Public Queue

You need to know a distinction between the two types of queues you can create before continuing. There are private and public queues, and Table 21-1 compares some of the features of both types of message queues.

Table 21-1. Private vs. Public Message Queues

Private Message Queue	Public Message Queue
Not published in the Message Queue Information Service (MQIS) database	Published in the Message Queue Information Service (MQIS) database
Can only be created on the local machine	Must be registered with the Directory Service
Can be created and deleted offline, meaning not connected to Active Directory	Must be created and deleted while you're online, meaning connected to Active Directory
Can't be located by other message queuing applications, unless they are provided the full path of the message queue	Can be located by other message queuing applications through the Message Queue Information Service (MQIS) database
Is persistent, but backup, although possible, isn't an easy task	Is persistent, and can be backed up on an Enterprise level with the Active Directory

Creating the Queue Programmatically

Chapter 13 covers how to create a message queue from Server Explorer, but if you want to do it programmatically, please read on.

It's easy to create a message queue programmatically. Listings 21-1 and 21-2 show you two different ways of creating a private queue on the local machine, USERMANPC.

Listing 21-1. Creating a Private Message Queue Using the Machine Name

```
1 Public Sub CreatePrivateQueueWithName()
2    MessageQueue.Create("USERMANPC\Private$\UserMan")
3 End Sub
```

Listing 21-2. Creating a Private Message Queue Using the Default Name

```
1 Public Sub CreatePrivateQueue()
2    MessageQueue.Create(".\Private$\UserMan")
3 End Sub
```

In Listing 21-1, I specify the machine as part of the path argument, whereas I simply use a period in Listing 21-2. The period serves as a shortcut for letting the **MessageQueue** object know that you want it created on the local machine. The other thing you should notice is that I prefix the queue with Private$. This must be done to indicate that the queue is private. Exclusion of the prefix indicates you're creating a public queue. The different parts of the path are separated using the backslash, as in a standard DOS file path:

```
MachineName\Private$\QueueName
```

A public queue is created more or less the same way, except you leave out the \Private$ part of the path. You can also use the period to specify that you want it created on the local machine, as shown in Listing 21-3.

Listing 21-3. Creating a Public Message Queue Using the Default Name

```
1 Public Sub CreatePublicQueue()
2    MessageQueue.Create(".\UserMan")
3 End Sub
```

As stated, the period could have been substituted with the name of the local machine or indeed the name of a different machine on which you want to create the queue.

 NOTE   If you try to create an already existing message queue, a **MessageQueueException** exception is thrown.

There are two overloaded versions of the **MessageQueue** class's **Create** method, and you've seen the simpler one. The other one takes a second argument, a **Boolean** value indicating whether the message queue is transactional. I'll go into message queue transactions in the "Making Message Queues Transactional" section later on in this chapter, but for now take a look at Listing 21-4, which shows you how to make the queue transactional.

Listing 21-4. Creating a Transactional Private Message Queue

```
1 Public Sub CreateTransactionalPrivateQueue()
2    MessageQueue.Create(".\Private$\UserMan", True)
3 End Sub
```

In Listing 21-4, a private message queue named UserMan is created on the local machine with transaction support. If you run the example code in Listing 21-4, you might want to remove it afterwards, as it might otherwise have an impact on the rest of the examples in this chapter.

Displaying or Changing the Properties of Your Message Queue

Some of the properties of your message queue can be changed after you've created it. You can do this by using the Computer Management MMC snap-in[2] that's part of the Administrative Tools under Windows 2000 and Windows XP. When you've opened the Computer Management snap-in, do the following:

1. Expand the Services and Applications node.

2. Expand the Message Queuing node.

3. Expand the node with the requested queue and select the queue.

4. Right-click the queue and select Properties from the pop-up menu. This brings up the queue's Properties dialog box (see Figure 21-4).

---

2. It's also possible to right-click the queue in Server Explorer and select Properties from the pop-up menu to see the properties in the Properties window of the VS .NET IDE. However, this window doesn't show as many of the properties as does the Computer Management MMC snap-in.

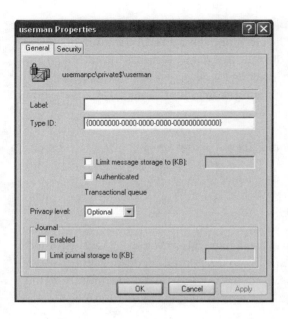

Figure 21-4. The Properties dialog box for the message queue

As you can see from Figure 21-4, one of the options that can't be changed after the queue has been created is whether the queue is transactional or not. This makes it all the more important for you to know if you'll need transaction support before you create the queue.

NOTE   One advantage the Computer Management MMC snap-in has over Server Explorer when it comes to public message queues is that you can use it when you're not connected to the AD Domain Controller, because it caches the queues. This isn't possible with Server Explorer.

Assigning a Label to Your Message Queue

If you want to bind to your message queue using a label, you first need to assign a label to the queue. Looking back at Figure 21-4, notice you can type the text for your label in the Label textbox. One thing you have to remember is that it isn't necessary for the label to be unique across all your message queues, but you are guaranteed problems if you try to bind and send messages to a queue using the same label. So the lesson learned here is make sure your label is unique!

You can also change the label of a message queue programmatically. See Listing 21-5 for some sample code.

Listing 21-5. Changing the Label of an Existing Queue

```
1 Public Sub ChangeQueueLabel()
2    Dim queUserMan As New MessageQueue(".\Private$\UserMan")
3
4    queUserMan.Label = "USERMAN1"
5 End Sub
```

In Listing 21-5, the so-called friendly name, which is defined by the machine and queue name, is used to bind to an existing private queue on the local machine. A friendly name is a name that makes it easier for humans to read and interpret it. In the case of the example code in Listing 21-5, the friendly name tells you that the queue is created on the local machine (.), it's private (Private$), and the name of it is UserMan. You must use the friendly name to bind to the message queue if you want to change the label programmatically! Line 4 is where the actual changing of the label takes place simply by setting the **Label** property.

Retrieving the ID of a Message Queue

If you want to bind to your public message queue using its ID, you can retrieve this using the Computer Management MMC snap-in. See the "Displaying or Changing the Properties of Your Message Queue" section earlier in this chapter for more information on how to display message queue properties. If you refer back to Figure 21-4, you can see the ID just below the Type ID textbox! Mind you, this ID is only available if you're connected to the AD Domain Controller. If you're not connected, you can't view the properties for a public message queue. If you try to view the ID for a private message queue, this space is simply blank.

You can also retrieve the ID of a message queue programmatically, as shown in Listing 21-6.

Listing 21-6. Retrieving the ID of an Existing Queue

```
1 Public Sub RetrieveQueueId()
2    Dim queUserMan As New MessageQueue(".\UserMan")
3    Dim uidMessageQueue As Guid
4
5    uidMessageQueue = queUserMan.Id
6 End Sub
```

As you can see from Listing 21-6, the ID is a GUID, so you need to declare your variable to be data type **Guid** if you want to store the ID. You must be connected to the AD Domain Controller in order to retrieve the ID of a message queue; otherwise, an exception is thrown. If you try to retrieve the ID of a private message queue, an "empty" GUID is returned: 00000000-0000-0000-0000-000000000000. You can display a GUID using the **ToString** method of the **Guid** class.

Binding to an Existing Message Queue

Once you've created a message queue or if you want to access an existing queue, you can bind to it, as described in the following sections.

Binding Using the Friendly Name

Listing 21-7 shows you three different ways of binding to an existing queue, using the **New** constructor, a so-called friendly name (.\Private$\UserMan) or the path of the queue, and the name assigned to the queue when it was created.

Listing 21-7. Binding to an Existing Queue

```
 1 Public Sub BindToExistingQueue()
 2    Dim queUserManNoArguments As New MessageQueue()
 3    Dim queUserManPath As New _
 4       MessageQueue(".\Private$\UserMan")
 5    Dim queUserManPathAndAccess As New _
 6       MessageQueue(".\Private$\UserMan", True)
 7
 8    ' Initialize the queue
 9    queUserManNoArguments.Path = ".\Private$\UserMan"
10 End Sub
```

Line 2 is the simplest way, but it requires an extra line of code because you haven't actually told the message queue object what queue to bind to. Line 9 takes care of specifying the queue using the **Path** property. On Lines 5 and 6, I have specified the queue as well as the read-access restrictions. When the second argument is set to **True**, as is the case with the example in Listing 21-7, exclusive read access is granted to the first application that accesses the queue. This means that no other instance of the **MessageQueue** class can read from the queue, so be careful when you use this option.

Binding Using the Format Name

Since you can't create or bind to a message queue on a machine in workgroup mode, you need to access a queue on a machine that is part of Active Directory. However, this creates a problem when the message queue server you want to access can't access the primary domain controller. Because Active Directory is used for resolving the path, you won't be able to use the syntax shown in Listing 21-7 to bind to a message queue.

Thankfully, there's a way around this. Instead of using the friendly name syntax as in the previous listings, you can use the format name or the label for this purpose. Listing 21-8 shows you how to bind to existing queues using the format name.

Listing 21-8. Binding to an Existing Queue Using the Format Name

```
1 Public Sub BindToExistingQueueUsingFormat()
2    Dim queUserManFormatTCP As New _
3       MessageQueue("FormatName:DIRECT=TCP:10.8.1.18\Private$\UserMan")
4    Dim queUserManFormatOS As New _
5       MessageQueue("FormatName:DIRECT=OS:USERMANPC\UserMan")
6    Dim queUserManFormatPublic As New _
7       MessageQueue( _
8       "FormatName:Public=AB6B9EF6-B167-43A4-8116-5B72D5C1F81C")
9 End Sub
```

In Listing 21-8, I bind to the private queue named UserMan on the machine with the IP address 10.8.1.18 using the TCP protocol, as shown on Lines 2 and 3. On Lines 4 and 5, I bind the public queue named UserMan on the machine with name USERMANPC. There is also an option of binding using the SPX protocol. If you want to use the SPX network protocol, you must use the following syntax:

```
FormatName:DIRECT=SPX:NetworkNumber;HostNumber\QueueName
```

The last format name shown in Listing 21-8 is on Lines 6 through 8, where I use the ID of the message queue as the queue identifier.

You can connect to both public and private queues with all format name options, so in the sample code in Listing 21-8 you could swap the public and private queue binding among the three different format names. The ID used in the example code is fictive, and it will look different on your network. The ID, which is a GUID, is generated at creation time by the MQIS. See the "Retrieving the ID of a Message Queue" section earlier in this chapter for more information on how to get the ID of your message queue.

Binding Using the Label

One last way to bind to an existing message queue is to use the label syntax. This syntax can't be used when you're offline, only when connected to the Active Directory Domain Controller. Listing 21-9 shows you how to connect to the message queue with the UserMan label. See "Assigning a Label to Your Message Queue" earlier in this chapter for more information on how to set the label of a message queue.

Listing 21-9. Binding to an Existing Queue Using the Label

```
1 Public Sub BindToExistingQueueUsingLabel()
2    Dim queUserManLabel As New MessageQueue("Label:Userman")
3 End Sub
```

That rounds up how to bind to a message queue. Now it gets interesting, because next I'll show you how to send, retrieve, and otherwise deal with messages.

Sending a Message

Sending a message is obviously one of the most important aspects of a message queue. If you can't send a message, why have a message queue? Let's take a look at the simplest form of sending a message to a queue. The **Send** method of the **MessageQueue** class is used for this purpose, as demonstrated in Listing 21-10.

Listing 21-10. Sending a Simple Message to a Message Queue

```
1 Public Sub SendSimpleMessage()
2    Dim queUserMan As New MessageQueue(".\Private$\UserMan")
3
4    ' Send simple message to queue
5    queUserMan.Send("Test")
6 End Sub
```

After binding to the private UserMan queue on the local machine, I send a **String** object containing the text "Test" to the queue. Obviously this isn't exactly useful, but you can apply this example to testing whether something is actually sent to the queue. As you've probably guessed, the **Send** method is overloaded, and I've used the version that only takes one argument and that is an object.

If you execute the code in Listing 21-10, you can see the resulting message using Server Explorer or the Computer Management MMC snap-in. Expand the private UserMan message queue and select the Queue Messages node. Now the

Computer Management snap-in should look like what is shown in Figure 21-5; if you're using Server Explorer, it should resemble Figure 21-6. Please note that in Server Explorer, you need to expand the Queue Messages node to see the messages in the queue, as done in Figure 21-6.

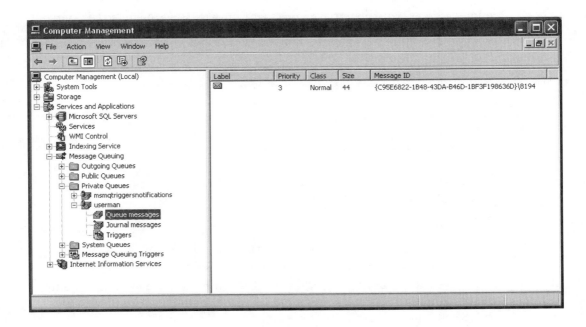

Figure 21-5. Computer Management with Queue Messages node selected

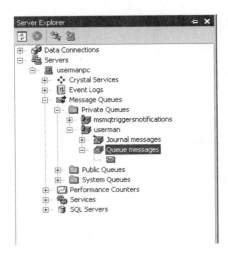

Figure 21-6. Server Explorer with Queue Messages node selected

Retrieving a Message

Obviously it's a very good idea to be able to retrieve the messages that have been posted to a message queue. Otherwise the messages simply stack up in your message queue server and do absolutely no good to anyone. There are actually a number of ways you can retrieve a message from a message queue, so let's start out with retrieving the message sent in Listing 21-10. See Listing 21-11 for the code that retrieves the first message from the message queue.

Listing 21-11. Retrieving the First Message from a Message Queue

```
1 Public Sub RetrieveSimpleMessage()
2    Dim queUserMan As New MessageQueue(".\Private$\UserMan")
3    Dim msgUserMan As Message
4
5    ' Retrieve first message from queue
6    msgUserMan = queUserMan.Receive()
7 End Sub
```

In Listing 21-11 I bind to the private UserMan message queue and retrieve the first message from the queue. When the message is retrieved from the message queue, it's also removed from the queue. If you need to read a message from the queue without removing it, you should take a look at the "Peeking at Messages" section later in this chapter for more information.

Although the example code in Listing 21-11 will retrieve the first message from the message queue, there isn't a lot you can do with it. If you try to access any of the properties of the msgUserMan message, an exception is thrown because you haven't set up a so-called formatter that can read the message. A message can take on a variety of different forms, so it's a must that you set up a formatter before you retrieve a message from the queue. See the next section, "Setting Up a Message Formatter," for more information on how to do this.

Receive and Peek

The **Receive** and **Peek** methods of the **MessageQueue** class are synchronous, meaning that they will block all other activity in your application or thread until the method has been executed. If there are no messages in the message queue, the **Receive** and **Peek** methods will wait until a message arrives in the queue. One option to overcome this potential problem is to call the **Receive** and **Peek** methods on a thread of their own, which means it won't block the rest of your application. Please see your VS .NET documentation for information on how to use threads with your application.

If you need asynchronous access, you must use the **BeginReceive** method instead. Actually, you can specify a time-out value when you call the **Receive** or **Peek** methods to make sure you don't wait indefinitely. Both of these overloaded methods have a version that takes a **TimeSpan** argument. This means the method will return if a message is found in the queue or when the time specified in the **TimeSpan** argument has elapsed. No exception is thrown if the time elapses.

Setting Up a Message Formatter

Recall that you need to set up a formatter in order to be able to read the messages that you retrieve from your message queue. This is a fairly easy yet important task. A message formatter is employed for serializing and deserializing objects that are used as the body of a message.

The **Formatter** property of the **MessageQueue** class is used for this very purpose. When you instantiate an instance of the **MessageQueue** class, a default formatter is created for you, but this formatter can't be used to read from the queue, only to write or send to the queue. This means you have to either change the default formatter or set up a new formatter.

See Listing 21-12 for example code that can retrieve and read the message sent in Listing 21-10. Mind you, if you've already retrieved that message from the queue, the queue is now empty, and you need to send another message before you try to receive messages again. If the message queue is empty, the **Receive** method will await the arrival of a new message in the queue, or time out if a timeout period has been specified.

Listing 21-12. Setting Up a New Formatter and Retrieving the First Message from a Queue

```
1 Public Sub RetrieveMessage()
2    Dim queUserMan As New MessageQueue(".\Private$\UserMan")
3    Dim msgUserMan As Message
4    Dim strBody As String
5
6    ' Set up the formatter
7    queUserMan.Formatter = New XmlMessageFormatter( _
8       New Type() {GetType(String)})
9
10   ' Retrieve first message from queue
11   msgUserMan = queUserMan.Receive
12   ' Save the message body
13   strBody = msgUserMan.Body.ToString
14 End Sub
```

In Listing 21-12, I specify that the formatter should be of type **XmlMessageFormatter**. This is the default formatter for a message queue, and it's used for serializing and deserializing the message body using XML format. I've also specified that the message formatter should accept message bodies of data type **String**. This is done on Lines 7 and 8. If I hadn't done this, I wouldn't be able to access the message body.

Generally, you should use the same formatter for sending and receiving, but because this is a very simple example, the formatter isn't needed for sending to the message queue. Now, let's see in which situations the **Formatter** property is really useful. In Listing 21-13, I set up the formatter so it will be able to read to different types of message bodies: a body of data type **String** and of data type **Integer**. This is done by adding both data types to the **Type** array as the only argument to the **XmlMessageFormatter** constructor.

Listing 21-13. Sending and Retrieving Different Messages from One Message Queue

```
1 Public Sub SendDifferentMessages()
2    Dim queUserMan As New MessageQueue(".\Private$\UserMan")
3    Dim msgUserMan As New Message()
4
5    ' Set up the formatter
6    queUserMan.Formatter = New XmlMessageFormatter( _
7       New Type() {GetType(String), GetType(Integer)})
8
9    ' Create body as a text message
10   msgUserMan.Body = "Test"
11   ' Send message to queue
12   queUserMan.Send(msgUserMan)
13   ' Create body as an integer
14   msgUserMan.Body = 12
15   ' Send message to queue
16   queUserMan.Send(msgUserMan)
17 End Sub
18
19 Public Sub RetrieveDifferentMessages()
20   Dim queUserMan As New MessageQueue(".\Private$\UserMan")
21   Dim msgUserMan As Message
22   Dim strBody As String
23   Dim intBody As Integer
24
25   ' Set up the formatter
26   queUserMan.Formatter = New XmlMessageFormatter( _
27      New Type() {GetType(String), GetType(Integer)})
28
```

```
29    ' Retrieve first message from queue
30    msgUserMan = queUserMan.Receive
31    ' Save the message body
32    strBody = msgUserMan.Body.ToString
33    ' Retrieve next message from queue
34    msgUserMan = queUserMan.Receive
35    ' Save the message body
36    intBody = msgUserMan.Body
37 End Sub
```

In Listing 21-13, I use the SendDifferentMessages procedure to send two messages to the queue: one with a body of data type **String** and one with a body of data type **Integer**. In the RetrieveDifferentMessages procedure, I retrieve these two messages in the same order they were sent to the message queue. The fact that you can send messages with a different body is what makes a message queue even more suitable than a database table for data exchange situations in which the data exchanged has very different structures.

In the example code in Listing 21-13, I've used data types **String** and **Integer** as the body formats that can be deserialized when the messages are read from the queue, but you can in fact use any base data type as well as structures and managed objects. If you need to pass older COM/ActiveX objects, you should use the **ActiveXMessageFormatter** class instead. You can also use the **BinaryMessageFormatter** class for serializing and deserializing messages using binary format, as opposed to the XML format used by the **XmlMessageFormatter** class.

Peeking at Messages

Sometimes it isn't desirable to remove a message from the queue after you've had a look at the contents, as will happen when you use the **Receive** method of the **MessageQueue** class. Here are some reasons why you may want to leave the message in the queue:

- You have two or more clients reading the messages. If so, you obviously need some sort of plan to have the message removed eventually.

- You're waiting for a specific message, perhaps a message with a certain label or body.

- You take periodic snapshots of the first message in the queue, perhaps for statistics.

Anyway, use the **Peek** method, as it does exactly the same as the **Receive** method except for removing the message from the queue. In addition, repeated calls to the **Peek** method will return the same message, unless a new message with a higher priority is inserted into the queue. See the "Prioritizing Messages" section later in this chapter for more information on that topic.

Listing 21-14 is actually a nearly complete copy of Listing 21-12, except for the call to the **Peek** method on Line 11. So if you want to look at the first message in the queue, the **Peek** and **Receive** methods work exactly the same, except for the removal of the message. See the "Clearing Messages from the Queue" section later in this chapter for details about removing messages.

Listing 21-14. Peeking at a Message in the Queue

```
 1 Public Sub PeekMessage()
 2    Dim queUserMan As New MessageQueue(".\Private$\UserMan")
 3    Dim msgUserMan As Message
 4    Dim strBody As String
 5
 6    ' Set up the formatter
 7    queUserMan.Formatter = New XmlMessageFormatter( _
 8       New Type() {GetType(String)})
 9
10    ' Peek at first message from queue
11    msgUserMan = queUserMan.Peek
12    ' Save the message body
13    strBody = msgUserMan.Body.ToString
14 End Sub
```

Picking Specific Messages from a Queue

A message queue is designed with a stack-like structure in mind. It doesn't have any search facilities as such, meaning that messages are retrieved from the top of the stack, or rather the top of the message queue. However, it's possible to pick specific messages from your queue. To do so, use the **ReceiveById** method, which takes a message ID as its only argument. The message ID is generated by Message Queuing, and it's assigned to an instance of the **Message** class when it's sent to the queue. Listing 21-15 shows you how to retrieve the ID from a message and later use that ID to retrieve this message, even though it isn't at the top of the message queue.

Listing 21-15. Retrieving a Message from the Queue by Message ID

```
 1 Public Sub RetrieveMessageById()
 2     Dim queUserMan As New MessageQueue(".\Private$\UserMan")
 3     Dim msgUserMan As New Message()
 4     Dim strId As String
 5
 6     ' Set up the formatter
 7     queUserMan.Formatter = New XmlMessageFormatter( _
 8        New Type() {GetType(String)})
 9
10     ' Create body as a text message
11     msgUserMan.Body = "Test 1"
12     ' Send message to queue
13     queUserMan.Send(msgUserMan)
14
15     ' Create body as a text message
16     msgUserMan.Body = "Test 2"
17     ' Send message to queue
18     queUserMan.Send(msgUserMan)
19     strId = msgUserMan.Id
20
21     ' Create body as a text message
22     msgUserMan.Body = "Test 3"
23     ' Send message to queue
24     queUserMan.Send(msgUserMan)
25
26     msgUserMan = queUserMan.ReceiveById(strId)
27     MsgBox("Saved Id=" & strId & vbCrLf & "Retrieved Id=" & msgUserMan.Id)
28 End Sub
```

In Listing 21-15, I bind to the existing private UserMan queue, set up the formatter to accept data type **String**, create three messages, and send them to the queue. Just after the second message is sent to the queue, the message ID is saved, and then this ID is used to retrieve the associated message. This message is second in the message queue. On Line 27, I simply display the saved message ID and the retrieved message to show that they are the same.

If you use the **ReceiveById** or indeed the **PeekById** method, you must be aware that an **InvalidOperationException** exception is thrown if the message does not exist in the queue. Therefore, whenever you employ one of these methods, you should use a structured error handler, as demonstrated in Listing 21-16.

Listing 21-16. Retrieving a Message by Message ID in a Safe Manner

```
 1 Public Function RetrieveMessageByIdSafe(ByVal vstrId As String) As Message
 2    Dim queUserMan As New MessageQueue(".\Private$\UserMan")
 3    Dim msgUserMan As New Message()
 4
 5    ' Set up the formatter
 6    queUserMan.Formatter = New XmlMessageFormatter( _
 7       New Type() {GetType(String)})
 8
 9    Try
10       msgUserMan = queUserMan.ReceiveById(vstrId)
11    Catch objE As InvalidOperationException
12       ' Message not found, return a Null value
13       RetrieveMessageByIdSafe = Nothing
14
15       Exit Function
16    End Try
17
18    ' Return message
19    RetrieveMessageByIdSafe = msgUserMan
20 End Function
```

Listing 21-16 catches an attempt to locate a nonexisting message by ID and simply returns a null value to the caller. If the passed message ID can be found in the queue, the retrieved message is returned to the caller.

The ID of a message is of data type **String**, but it's internally an ID formatted as a GUID as you can see from Listing 21-15. At any rate, the **Id** property of a message is read-only, so you can't assign your own IDs to your messages. I guess this is one way of ensuring all messages are unique. Your only option is to save the ID of a particular message and then later use this ID to retrieve the message.

NOTE   The **PeekById** method works the same as the **ReceiveById** method, except that the message isn't removed from the message queue.

Retrieving All Messages in a Queue

Instead of retrieving the messages in a queue individually, you can also use the **GetAllMessages** method to retrieve all the messages in the queue as an array of **String**s. The messages in the array are ordered the way they appear in the queue, meaning the first element in the array is the top or first message in the queue. The **GetAllMessages** method is called like this:

```
Dim arrstrMessages() As Object = queUserMan.GetAllMessages()
```

This returns all messages in the queUserMan queue in the arrstrMessages array. However, unlike the other **Receive** methods, this method doesn't remove the messages from the queue, nor does it return message objects that you can manipulate. The **GetAllMessages** method can only be used to retrieve a snapshot of the message queue at any given time. The snapshot is, as the word suggests, static, and won't reflect changes made to the queue after calling the **GetAllMessages** method.

Sending and Retrieving Messages Asynchronously

Sometimes it's desirable to be able to send and receive your messages in asynchronous fashion. This makes sure your application isn't held up until delivery or retrieval has been completed. In order to use asynchronous communication with a message queue, you need to set up an event handler that deals with the result of the asynchronous operation. This can be done as shown on Lines 22 and 23 in Listing 21-17.

Listing 21-17. Receiving a Message Asynchronously Using an Event Handler

```
1 Public Sub MessageReceiveCompleteEvent(ByVal vobjSource As Object, _
2  ByVal vobjEventArgs As ReceiveCompletedEventArgs)
3    Dim msgUserMan As New Message()
4    Dim queUserMan As New MessageQueue()
5
6    ' Make sure we bind to the right message queue
7    queUserMan = CType(vobjSource, MessageQueue)
8
9    ' End async receive
10   msgUserMan = queUserMan.EndReceive(vobjEventArgs.AsyncResult)
11 End Sub
12
```

```
13 Public Sub RetrieveMessagesAsync()
14    Dim queUserMan As New MessageQueue(".\Private$\UserMan")
15    Dim msgUserMan As New Message()
16
17    ' Set up the formatter
18    queUserMan.Formatter = New XmlMessageFormatter( _
19       New Type() {GetType(String)})
20
21    ' Add an event handler
22    AddHandler queUserMan.ReceiveCompleted, AddressOf _
23       MessageReceiveCompleteEvent
24
25    queUserMan.BeginReceive(New TimeSpan(0, 0, 10))
26 End Sub
```

In Listing 21-17 I have first set up the procedure that will receive the **ReceiveComplete** event. This procedure takes care of binding to the passed queue, which is the queue used to begin the retrieval, and then the asynchronous retrieval is ended by calling the **EndReceive** method. This method also returns the message from the queue.

In the RetrieveMessagesAsync procedure, I set up the message queue, and on Lines 22 and 23, I add the event handler that calls the MessageReceiveCompleteEvent procedure on completion of the message retrieval. Finally, the asynchronous message retrieval is started by calling the **BeginReceive** method on Line 25. I have specified that the call should time-out after 10 seconds using a new instance of the **TimeSpan** class.

Listing 21-17 makes use of the **BeginReceive** and **EndReceive** methods, but you can use the example code with only very few modifications if you want to peek instead of receiving the messages from the queue (see Listing 21-18).

Listing 21-18. Peeking Asynchronously Using an Event Handler

```
1 Public Sub MessagePeekCompleteEvent(ByVal vobjSource As Object, _
2  ByVal vobjEventArgs As PeekCompletedEventArgs)
3    Dim msgUserMan As New Message()
4    Dim queUserMan As New MessageQueue()
5
6    ' Make sure we bind to the right message queue
7    queUserMan = CType(vobjSource, MessageQueue)
8
9    ' End async peek
10   msgUserMan = queUserMan.EndPeek(vobjEventArgs.AsyncResult)
11 End Sub
```

```
12
13 Public Sub PeekMessagesAsync()
14    Dim queUserMan As New MessageQueue(".\Private$\UserMan")
15    Dim msgUserMan As New Message()
16
17    ' Set up the formatter
18    queUserMan.Formatter = New XmlMessageFormatter( _
19        New Type() {GetType(String)})
20
21    ' Add an event handler
22    AddHandler queUserMan.PeekCompleted, AddressOf _
23        MessagePeekCompleteEvent
24
25    queUserMan.BeginPeek(New TimeSpan(0, 0, 10))
26 End Sub
```

Clearing Messages from the Queue

Messages can be removed from a message queue in two ways: You can remove them one by one, or you can clear the whole queue in one go.

Removing a Single Message from the Queue

Removing a single message from the queue can only be done programmatically, not using either Server Explorer or Computer Management.

You can use the **Receive** method to remove messages from the queue. Although this method is generally used to retrieve messages from the queue, it also removes the message. See the "Retrieving a Message" section earlier in this chapter for more information.

The **ReceiveById** method also removes a message. Alternatively, you can use the **PeekById** method to find a specific message and then use **ReceiveById** to remove it. See the "Picking Specific Messages from a Queue" section earlier in this chapter for more information on how to use the **ReceiveById** and **PeekById** methods.

Removing All Messages from the Queue

Removing all messages from the queue can be done either manually using Server Explorer or Computer Management, or programmatically.

CAUTION   Clearing all messages from a queue is an irreversible action, and once you confirm the deletion, the messages are permanently lost. So be careful when you perform this action!

Removing All Messages Manually

If you want to manually remove all messages from a queue, you can use either Server Explorer or Computer Management. Select the Queue Messages node (refer back to Figures 21-5 and 21-6), right-click this node, and select All Tasks/Purge (Computer Management) or Clear Messages (Server Explorer) from the pop-up menu. Then click Yes or OK in the confirmation dialog box to clear all messages from the queue.

Removing All Messages Programmatically

If you want to clear all messages from a queue programmatically, you can use the **Purge** method for this purpose, as shown here:

```
queUserMan.Purge()
```

The **Purge** method of the **MessageQueue** class works with any number of messages in the queue, meaning no exception is raised if the queue is empty when you call this method.

Prioritizing Messages

Every now and then, it's important that a particular message be read ASAP. Normally when you send a message, it ends up at the end of the message queue, because messages are sorted by arrival time. However, since messages are primarily sorted by priority, you can specify a higher than default priority to make sure that your message is placed in the message queue before messages with the default priority.

 NOTE   Setting the priority of a message doesn't work with transactional message queues, because the order in which messages are sent and retrieved from a queue is important to a transaction handler.

You can set the priority of a message using the **Priority** method of the **Message** class. See Listing 21-19 for a code example that sends two messages to the queue, one with normal priority and one with highest priority.

Listing 21-19. Sending Messages with Different Priorities

```
1 Public Sub SendPriorityMessages()
2    Dim queUserMan As New MessageQueue(".\Private$\UserMan")
3    Dim msgFirst As New Message()
4    Dim msgSecond As New Message()
5
6    ' Set up the formatter
7    queUserMan.Formatter = New XmlMessageFormatter( _
8       New Type() {GetType(String), GetType(Integer)})
9
10   ' Create first body
11   msgFirst.Body = "First Message"
12   ' Send message to queue
13   queUserMan.Send(msgFirst)
14
15   ' Create second body
16   msgSecond.Body = "Second Message"
17   ' Set priority to highest
18   msgSecond.Priority = MessagePriority.Highest
19   ' Send message to queue
20   queUserMan.Send(msgSecond)
21 End Sub
22
23 Public Sub RetrievePriorityMessage()
24   Dim queUserMan As New MessageQueue(".\Private$\UserMan")
25   Dim msgUserMan As Message
26
27   ' Set up the formatter
28   queUserMan.Formatter = New XmlMessageFormatter( _
29      New Type() {GetType(String)})
30
31   ' Retrieve first message from queue
32   msgUserMan = queUserMan.Receive
33   ' Display the message body
34   MsgBox(msgUserMan.Body.ToString)
35 End Sub
```

If you run the code in Listing 21-19, you'll see that setting the priority of the second message to highest ensures that it goes to the top of the message queue.

The message box will display the text "Second Message". If your message queue isn't transactional, the text displayed will be "First Message".

The priority of the second message is set on Line 18. When you set the **Priority** property of a **Message** object, it must be set to a member of the **MessagePriority** enum. The default is **Normal**.

Locating a Message Queue

Sometimes you don't know the path to a particular queue or you just need to verify that a specific queue still exists. Let's start with the easy task, how to check if a particular queue exists:

```
Dim blnExists MessageQueue.Exists(strPath)
```

You can use the **Exists** method of the **MessageQueue** class. Because this is a public shared function, you don't actually have to instantiate a message queue object in order to use this method.

Now this is pretty simple, because you already know the path. However, sometimes you don't know the path, just the name of the machine where message queuing is installed. See Listing 21-20 for an example of how to retrieve a list of all the private queues on a specific machine.

Listing 21-20. Retrieving All Private Queues on a Machine

```
 1 Public Sub BrowsePrivateQueues()
 2    Dim arquePrivate() As MessageQueue = _
 3       MessageQueue.GetPrivateQueuesByMachine("USERMANPC")
 4    Dim queUserMan As MessageQueue
 5
 6    ' Display the path of all the private queues on the machine
 7    For Each queUserMan In arquePrivate
 8       MsgBox(queUserMan.Path)
 9    Next
10 End Sub
```

In Listing 21-20, I retrieve all the message queues on the USERMANPC machine and display their labels. As you can see from Line 2, all the queues are saved in an array of **MessageQueue** class instances. If you need the public queues instead, simply replace the **GetPrivateQueuesByMachine** method call with a call to the **GetPublicQueuesByMachine** method.

The public queues can also be located on the whole network instead of just one machine. There are three different methods that can be used to locate public queues network-wide:

- **GetPublicQueues**

- **GetPublicQueuesByCategory**

- **GetPublicQueuesByLabel**

See Listings 21-21, 21-22, and 21-23 for code that shows you how to use these methods.

Listing 21-21. Retrieving All Public Queues on a Network

```
1 Public Sub BrowsePublicQueuesNetworkWide()
2    Dim arrquePublic() As MessageQueue = _
3       MessageQueue.GetPublicQueues()
4    Dim queUserMan As MessageQueue
5
6    ' Display the name of all the public queues on the network
7    For Each queUserMan In arrquePublic
8       MsgBox(queUserMan.QueueName)
9    Next
10 End Sub
```

Listing 21-22. Retrieving All Public Queues on a Network by Category

```
1 Public Sub BrowsePublicQueuesByCategoryNetworkWide()
2    Dim arrquePublic() As MessageQueue = _
3       MessageQueue.GetPublicQueuesByCategory(New _
4       Guid("00000000-0000-0000-0000-000000000001"))
5    Dim queUserMan As MessageQueue
6
7    ' Display the name of all the public queues
8    ' on the network within a specific category
9    For Each queUserMan In arrquePublic
10      MsgBox(queUserMan.QueueName)
11   Next
12 End Sub
```

Listing 21-23. Retrieving All Public Queues on a Network by Label

```
 1 Public Sub BrowsePublicQueuesByLabelNetworkWide()
 2    Dim arrquePublic() As MessageQueue = _
 3       MessageQueue.GetPublicQueuesByLabel("USERMAN")
 4    Dim queUserMan As MessageQueue
 5
 6    ' Display the machine name for all the public queues
 7    ' on the network with a specific label
 8    For Each queUserMan In arrquePublic
 9       MsgBox(queUserMan.MachineName)
10    Next
11 End Sub
```

Listing 21-21 uses the **GetPublicQueues** method to retrieve all public queues on the network and then displays the name of each queue.

Listing 21-22 retrieves all public queues on a network by category using the **GetPublicQueuesByCategory** method. For each returned message queue in the "00000000-0000-0000-0000-000000000001" category, I display the queue name. The category being referred to is the same as the Type ID in Figure 21-4 and the **Category** property of the **MessageQueue** class. This is a way for you to group your message queues, particularly for administrative purposes.

Listing 21-23 shows you how to find all the public queues on the network that have the "USERMAN" label (case insensitive). The name of the machine where each queue is located is then displayed one by one.

Removing a Message Queue

Now and then you might need to remove a message queue from a machine, and for this purpose you have several options. A message queue can be deleted either manually using Server Explorer or Computer Management or programmatically.

 CAUTION   Clearing a message queue is an irreversible action, and once you confirm the deletion, the queue and all its messages are permanently lost!

Removing a Message Queue Manually

If you want to manually remove a queue, you can use either Server Explorer or Computer Management. Select the queue node (see Figure 21-7), right-click this node, and select Delete from the pop-up menu. Then click Yes in the confirmation dialog box to remove the message queue and all its messages.

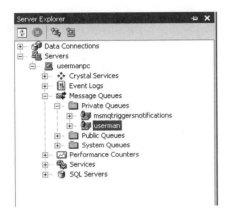

Figure 21-7. Server Explorer with message queue selected

Removing a Message Queue Programmatically

If you want to remove a queue programmatically, you can use the shared **Delete** method for this purpose, like this:

```
MessageQueue.Delete(strPath)
```

strPath is the path of the message queue. Keep in mind that if the queue doesn't exist, an exception is thrown, so I can only recommend that you don't use the example code without being sure the queue actually exists. See how to use the **Exists** method in the "Locating a Message Queue" section earlier in this chapter. Alternatively, you can set up a structured error handler like the one in Listing 21-24.

Listing 21-24. Removing a Message Queue in a Safe Manner

```
1 Public Sub RemoveMessageQueueSafely(ByVal vstrPath As String)
2    Try
3        MessageQueue.Delete(vstrPath)
4    Catch objE As Exception
5        MsgBox(objE.Message)
6    End Try
7 End Sub
```

In Listing 21-24 I catch any exception being thrown when I try to remove the message queue specified using the strPath argument. I'm only displaying the error message, but I am sure you can take it from there.

Controlling Message Queue Storage Size

Depending on how soon messages are retrieved from your message queue after they've been sent there, the queue can take up a lot of storage.

Generally, you shouldn't be clearing your queues, because you might destroy messages that need to be processed by a client. However, you can solve this by specifying a maximum limit in kilobytes. If you look at Figure 21-4, you can see the General tab of the Message Queue Properties dialog box. Check the Limit message storage to (KB) check box and type the size in the textbox to the right of the check box.

Programmatically you can do this using the **MaximumQueueSize** property of the **MessageQueue** class, as follows:

```
queUserMan.MaximumQueueSize = 15
```

When you set the storage limit, all messages that are sent to a message queue where the limit has been reached are rejected, and a negative acknowledgment message is sent to the administration queue on the client that sends the message.

Making Message Queues Transactional

As with normal database access, it's possible to make your message queues transactional. This means you can send several messages as a single transaction, and then act upon the result of the transmission of these messages by determining if you should commit or roll back the messages. Whether a message queue is transactional or not is determined at creation time. You can't change this after the queue has been created.

There are two types of transactions when it comes to message queues: internal and external. Please see the following sections for a brief description of each.

Internal Transactions

The term *internal transactions* refers to transactions that you manage manually or explicitly and only involve messages sent between a client and a message queue. This means that no other resources, such as database manipulation, can be part of an internal transaction, and that you must explicitly begin and then commit or roll back a transaction. Internal transactions are handled by the Message Queuing's Transaction Coordinator.

Internal transactions are faster than external transactions, which are discussed next.

External Transactions

External transactions are exactly what the name suggests: external. External transactions are also implicit or automatic. Resources other than message queue resources are part of external transactions. These can be database access, Active Directory access, and so on. The Microsoft Distributed Transaction Coordinator (MS DTC), and not the Message Queuing's Transaction Coordinator, is the standard coordinator used for external transactions, but as a developer you can choose to create your own coordinator.

External transactions are slower than internal transactions. In this chapter, I'll only cover internal transactions, since external transactions fall outside the scope of this book, and could indeed by themselves be the subject of an entire book. See the "Automatic Transactions" section in Chapter 5 for a brief introduction to how to use automatic or external transactions.

Creating a Transactional Message Queue

If you're creating your queue programmatically, see Listing 21-4 for an example of how to make it transactional. If you want to create your transactional message queue using Server Explorer, Chapter 13 gives you the details. Of course it's also possible to use the Computer Management MMC snap-in. Open the snap-in and follow these steps:

1. Expand the Services and Applications node.

2. Expand the Message Queuing node.

3. Select either the Public Queues or the Private Queues node.

4. Right-click the node and select New/Public Queue or New/Private Queue from the pop-up menu. This brings up the Queue Name dialog box.

5. Give the message queue a name by typing one in the Name textbox, and make sure you check the Transactional check box before you click OK to create the message queue.

Starting a Transaction

Because internal transactions are explicit or manual, you must begin a transaction from code before you start sending and retrieving messages that are to be part of the transaction. Actually, the very first thing you should check is if your message queue is transactional. This can be done using the **Transactional** property, which returns a **Boolean** value indicating if the queue is transactional or not:

```
If queUserMan.Transactional Then
```

The next thing you need to do is to create an instance of the **MessageQueueTransaction** class. The constructor for this class isn't overloaded, so it's created like this:

```
Dim qtrUserMan As New MessageQueueTransaction()
```

Now it's time to start the transaction, and this is done using the **Begin** method of the **MessageQueueTransaction** class, as follows:

```
qtrUserMan.Begin()
```

You may be wondering how you can reference this transaction object from the message queue object. I understand if you're confused, but it's really not that difficult. You simply pass the transaction object when you send or retrieve a message, like this:

```
msgUserMan = queUserMan.Receive(qtrUserMan)
```

or

```
queUserMan.Send(msgUserMan, qtrUserMan)
```

As you can see from these short examples, you do as you normally would when you write your code without transactions, with the exception that you pass the transaction object when you perform an operation that needs to be part of the transaction. Mind you, the transaction object can only be used with one message queue, meaning that you can't use the same transaction object with two different message queues.

Ending a Transaction

When you've started a transaction, you must also end it. That's pretty logical if you ask me. However, how the transaction should be ended isn't quite so direct. If you don't run into any problems during the operations that are part of the transaction, you'll normally commit the transaction or apply the changes to the message queue(s). If you do run into a problem with any of the transactional operations, you'll normally abort the transaction as soon as the problem occurs. When I refer to problems, I'm not only talking about exceptions that are thrown by the **MessageQueue** object, but also other operations external to the message queue operations that can make you abort the transaction. For example, say you're sending messages to a queue as a result of processing rows from a database, and you come across unexpected data. In this situation, you may want to abort all of the messages you've already sent.

Committing a Transaction

Committing a transaction is straightforward, and it's done using the **Commit** method of the **MessageQueue** class, as follows:

```
qtrUserMan.Commit()
```

The **Commit** method isn't overloaded and it doesn't take any parameters. However, an **InvalidOperationException** exception is thrown if you try to commit a transaction that hasn't been started (via the **Begin** method).

Aborting a Transaction

In situations where you have to abort a transaction, you can use the **Abort** method of the **MessageQueue** class, like this:

```
qtrUserMan.Abort()
```

The **Abort** method isn't overloaded and it doesn't take any parameters. However, like the **Commit** method, an **InvalidOperationException** exception is thrown if you try to abort a transaction that hasn't been started (via the **Begin** method).

Using the MessageQueueTransaction Class

I have just gone over all the methods that are important to managing a transaction, but there is one property that I haven't mentioned, and that is the **Status** property. This read-only property returns a member of the **MessageQueueTransactionStatus** enum that tells you the status of the transaction. The **Status** property can be read from the time you create your instance of the **MessageQueueTransaction** class until the object has been destroyed. You can see the **MessageQueueTransactionStatus** enum members in Table 21-2.

*Table 21-2. Members of the **MessageQueueTransactionStatus** Enum*

Member Name	Description
Aborted	The transaction has been aborted. This can be done by the user with the **Abort** method.
Committed	The transaction has been committed. This is done using the **Commit** method.
Initialized	The transaction object has been instantiated, but no transaction has yet been started. In this state you should not pass the transaction object to the message queue methods.
Pending	The transaction has been started and is now pending an **Abort** or **Commit**. When the transaction is pending, you can pass the transaction object to the message queue methods.

See Listing 21-25 for an example of how to use transactions combined with a structured exception handler. The example code can only be run if you've created a private transactional message queue named UserMan on the local machine.

Listing 21-25. Using Message Queue Transactions

```
 1 Public Sub UseMQTransactions()
 2    Dim qtrUserMan As New MessageQueueTransaction()
 3    Dim queUserMan As New MessageQueue(".\Private$\UserMan")
 4    Dim msgUserMan As New Message()
 5
 6    ' Set up the queue formatter
 7    queUserMan.Formatter = New XmlMessageFormatter( _
 8       New Type() {GetType(String)})
 9
10    ' Clear the message queue
11    queUserMan.Purge()
12    ' Start the transaction
13    qtrUserMan.Begin()
14
15    Try
16       ' Create message body
17       msgUserMan.Body = "First Message"
18       ' Send message to queue
19       queUserMan.Send(msgUserMan, qtrUserMan)
20
21       ' Create message body
22       msgUserMan.Body = "Second Message"
23       ' Send message to queue
24       queUserMan.Send(msgUserMan, qtrUserMan)
25
26       ' Retrieve message from queue
27       'msgUserMan = queUserMan.Receive(qtrUserMan)
28       ' Display message body
29       'MsgBox(msgUserMan.Body)
30
31       ' Commit transaction
32       qtrUserMan.Commit()
33
34       ' Retrieve message from queue
35       msgUserMan = queUserMan.Receive(qtrUserMan)
36       ' Display message body
37       MsgBox(msgUserMan.Body)
38
39       ' Retrieve message from queue
40       msgUserMan = queUserMan.Receive(qtrUserMan)
```

```
41        ' Display message body
42        MsgBox(msgUserMan.Body)
43     Catch objE As Exception
44        ' Abort the transaction
45        qtrUserMan.Abort()
46     End Try
47 End Sub
```

In Listing 21-25, I've demonstrated how you can send transactional messages to a message queue. When you run the code, you'll see two message boxes displaying "First Message" and "Second Message". After sending the messages to the queue (Lines 19 and 24), I commit the transaction, which means the messages are actually placed in the queue. If you notice, I have wrapped the sending and receiving part in a structured exception handler, just in case something goes wrong. If this is the case, the **Catch** block (Lines 43 through 46) will abort the transaction. The Lines 27 and 29 have been commented out, but if you were to uncomment these lines and run the example code, your application would stop responding and await the arrival of a message in the queue; they haven't been placed in the queue yet, because you haven't actually committed the transaction at this point. This is something to keep in mind as a developer, because transactional messages won't be sent to a queue until you actually commit the transaction. In this case it causes the application to hang indefinitely or at least until another client sends a message to the queue. Please see the "Receive and Peek" sidebar at the beginning of this chapter for options to avoid this kind of application blocking.

Looking at System-Generated Queues

So far, I've only been looking at user-created queues, but there's another group of queues that needs attention: the system-generated queues. These queues are maintained by **Message Queuing**. The following queues are system queues:

- Dead-letter message queues

- Journal message queues

- Transactional dead-letter message queues

The two dead-letter message queues, seen in Server Explorer in Figure 21-8 on the System Queues node, are used for storing messages that can't be delivered. One queue holds the nontransactional messages and the other one holds the transactional ones. See the next section for an explanation of the journal messages queues.

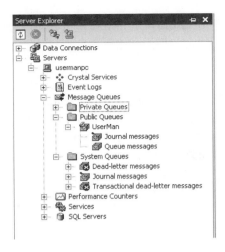

Figure 21-8. The system and journal queues

Using Journal Storage

Journal storage is a great facility for keeping copies of messages that are sent to or removed from a message queue. It can be very helpful if for some reason you need to resend a message. The message delivery might have failed, and you receive a negative acknowledgement as a result. Because an acknowledgement does not contain the message body, you can't use this message to resend the original message. However, you can use it to find a copy of the original message in the journal messages queue.

Every message queuing client (machine) has a global journal queue called the *system journal*. The system journal stores copies of all messages sent *from* the remote message queuing client, if journaling is enabled on the message being sent (see the "Enabling Journaling on a Message" section later in this chapter). This is true whether the message is delivered or not, but only if you send the message from a remote client. Messages sent to a local queue, whether it's a private or public message queue and whether journaling has been enabled on the messages being sent, are *not* stored in the system journal. This is one reason developers prefer working with a remote queue, even if all the messages are handled on the local machine.

Besides the system journal, all message queues have their own journal queue. The journal queue associated with each message queue stores copies of all messages removed, or rather taken from the message queue, but only if journaling is enabled on the message queue. See the next section, "Enabling Journaling on a Message Queue," for more information on how to enable journaling on a message queue.

Enabling Journaling on a Message Queue

Journaling can be enabled on a message queue either manually or programmatically. If you want to do it manually, you can do it from the Computer Management MMC snap-in. In Figure 21-4, you can see the Properties dialog box for an existing queue or a queue that is about to be created. If you want to enable journaling, you should check the Enabled check box in the Journal group and click Apply.

You can also programmatically enable journaling on an existing queue by setting the **UseJournalQueue** property of an existing message queue to **True**, like this:

```
Dim queUserMan As New MessageQueue("USERMANPC\\UserMan")
queUserMan.UseJournalQueue = True
```

Once you've enabled journaling on a message queue, all messages that are removed, or rather taken from the message queue, are copied to the message queue journal. In Listing 21-26 in the upcoming section, you can see how message queue journaling can be used.

Enabling Journaling on a Message

It's also possible to use journaling on a per-message basis instead of on the message queue, and this is done programmatically, by setting the **UseJournalQueue** property of an existing message to **True** before sending it to the queue, like this:

```
msgUserMan.UseJournalQueue = True
```

In Listing 21-26, you can see how message journaling can be used, but please be aware that the example code shown only works if the message queue isn't transactional.

Listing 21-26. Explaining Message Journaling

```
1 Public Sub EnableMessageJournaling()
2    Dim queUserMan As New MessageQueue("USERMANPC\UserMan")
3    Dim queUserManJournal As New _
4       MessageQueue("USERMANPC\UserMan\Journal$")
5    Dim queSystemJournal As New MessageQueue(".\Journal$")
6    Dim msgUserMan As New Message()
7
```

```
8      ' Enable journaling on message queue
9      queUserMan.UseJournalQueue = True
10
11     ' Set up the formatter
12     queUserMan.Formatter = New XmlMessageFormatter( _
13        New Type() {GetType(String)})
14
15     ' Create message body
16     msgUserMan.Body = "Message"
17     ' Enable message journaling
18     msgUserMan.UseJournalQueue = True
19     ' Send message to remote UserMan queue
20     queUserMan.Send(msgUserMan)
21
22     ' Retrieve message from remote UserMan queue
23     msgUserMan = queUserMan.Receive()
24
25     ' Retrieve message from local system journal
26     msgUserMan = queSystemJournal.Receive()
27     ' Retrieve message from remote UserMan journal
28     msgUserMan = queUserManJournal.Receive()
29 End Sub
```

On Lines 2 through 5, in Listing 21-26, I bind to three different message queues:

- The public UserMan queue on the remote USERMANPC machine (Line 2)

- The journal queue for the public UserMan queue on the remote USERMANPC machine (Lines 3 and 4)

- The system journal queue on the local machine (Line 5)

After binding to the message queues, I set up the message formatter (Lines 12 and 13), create the first message body (Line 16), and enable message journaling on the message (Line 18). The message is then sent to the public UserMan queue on USERMANPC (Line 20), and because it's sent to a remote message queue and journaling is enabled on the queue (Line 9), a copy of the message is saved in the local system journal.

On Line 22, I retrieve the message sent to the UserMan queue on USERMANPC, and because journaling is enabled on this queue, a copy of the message is saved in the UserMan journal queue. On Lines 25 and 27, I retrieve the two copies of the message that have been saved to the local system journal and the remote UserMan journal.

NOTE The **UseJournalQueue** property works differently on the **Message** class than on the **MessageQueue** class. On the **Message** class, setting this property to **True** ensures that a copy of the message is saved to the local system journal, while setting this property to **True** on the **MessageQueue** class ensures that a copy of the message is saved to the system journal on the remote machine that the **MessageQueue** object binds to.

Retrieving a Message from Journal Storage

Now, enabling journaling is easy enough, but how do you actually retrieve the messages from the journal when needed? Well, you can access these journal queues and other system queues by specifying the correct path to the queue. For example, the following code accesses the journal storage for the private message queue UserMan on the local machine:

```
Dim queUserMan As New MessageQueue(".\Journal$")
```

See Listing 21-26 earlier in this chapter for a more detailed example of how this works.

Controlling Journal Storage Size

Messages that are sent to either of the types of journals, system journal or queue journal, stay in the journal queue until you remove them. Well, this is true for messages in all message queues, but the point is that you're likely to retrieve messages from a standard message queue yourself, whereas messages in the journal queue are left there.

Generally, you should clear out the journal queues you use at a regular interval depending on how long you want to be able to go back in time to retrieve an old message. However, you can still run into problems with space in your journal, and you can solve this by specifying a maximum limit in kilobytes. If you look at Figure 21-4, you can see the Journal frame on the General tab of the message queue Properties dialog box. If you check the Enabled check box, you can also specify a maximum storage size in kilobytes if you check the Limit journal storage to (KB) check box and type the desired size in the textbox to the right of the check box.

Programmatically you can specify a maximum storage size using the **MaximumJournalSize** property of the **MessageQueue** class, like this:

```
queUserMan.MaximumJournalSize = 15
```

You obviously need to enable journaling in order to limit the storage size of the journal.

Securing Your Message Queuing

So far in this chapter, you've been shown how to create private and public queues, both transactional and nontransactional ones, and you've seen how you send and receive messages to and from a queue, including peeking at messages without removing them from the queue. However, I've yet to mention Message Queuing security, which is what I'm going to cover in this section.

Message Queuing uses built-in features of the Windows OS for securing messaging. This includes the following:

- Authentication

- Encryption

- Access control

- Auditing

Using Authentication

Authentication is the process by which a message's integrity is ensured and the sender of a message can be verified. This can be achieved by setting the message queue's **Authenticate** property to **True**. The default value for this property is **False**, meaning no authentication is required. When this property is set to **True**, the queue will only accept authenticated messages—nonauthenticated messages are rejected. In other words, the message queue on the server requires messages to be authenticated, not just the message queue object you use to set the **Authenticate** property. Basically this means that when you set the property, you affect all other message queue objects that are working on the same message queue. You can programmatically enable authentication, like this:

```
Dim queUserMan As New MessageQueue("USERMANPC\UserMan")
queUserMan.Authenticate = True
```

You can also request authentication by setting this property from the Computer Management MMC snap-in. See Figure 21-4 and the "Displaying or Changing the Properties of Your Message Queue" section for more information on how to set the properties of an existing message queue. In Figure 21-4, you can see the Authenticated check box, which you need to enable before clicking OK to request that messages on this queue be authenticated.

If a message isn't authenticated, it's rejected and therefore lost. However, you can specify that the rejected message be placed in the dead-letter queue, as shown in Listing 21-27.

Listing 21-27. Rejecting a Nonauthenticated Message

```
1 Public Sub RejectNonauthenticatedMessage()
2    Dim queUserMan As New MessageQueue(".\Private$\UserMan")
3    Dim msgUserMan As New Message()
4
5    ' Enable queue authentication
6    queUserMan.Authenticate = True
7    ' Set up the queue formatter
8    queUserMan.Formatter = New XmlMessageFormatter( _
9       New Type() {GetType(String)})
10
11   ' Create message body
12   msgUserMan.Body = "Message Body"
13   ' Make sure a rejected message is placed in
14   ' the dead-letter queue
15   msgUserMan.UseDeadLetterQueue = True
16
17   ' Send message to queue
18   queUserMan.Send(msgUserMan)
19 End Sub
```

In Listing 21-27 the **UseDeadLetterQueue** property is set to **True**, meaning that if the message is rejected for whatever reason, it's placed in the dead-letter queue (see Figure 21-9).

NOTE   When you set the **UseDeadLetterQueue** property of the **Message** class, the message ends up in the dead letter queue if it's rejected by the message queue itself, but this also happens if you delete the message from the queue.

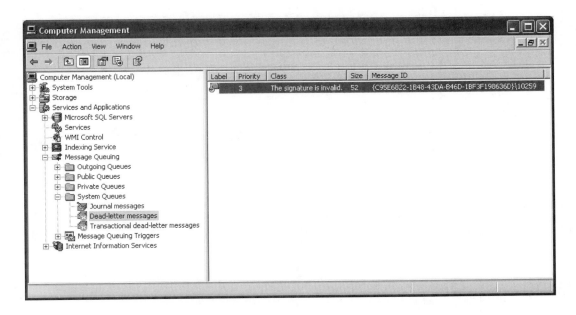

Figure 21-9. A rejected nonauthenticated message in the dead-letter queue

Rejecting Messages When Time Elapses

In Figure 21-9, you can see that the message in the dead-letter queue has been rejected because of an invalid signature. You can also specify a specific time interval that the message is allowed to stay in the queue for retrieval. When the specified time expires, the message is moved to the dead letter queue as demonstrated in Listing 21-28.

In Listing 21-28 the message must be picked up from the queue no later than 20 seconds after being placed there (Line 12). Otherwise, it's automatically moved to the dead-letter queue, because of Line 15.

NOTE   The **TimeToBeReceived** property only works with public queues. If the **UseDeadLetterQueue** property is set to **False**, the message is simply discarded and not placed in the dead-letter queue. When working with the **TimeToBeReceived** property, please be aware that the clock starts ticking as soon as you send it, meaning that if the message for some reason takes 10 seconds to reach the queue, and the **TimeToBeReceived** property has been set to 20 seconds, the message will only stay in the queue for 10 seconds.

Listing 21-28. Removing a Message from a Queue If Specified Time Elapses

```
1 Public Sub SendDeadLetterMessage()
2   Dim queUserMan As New MessageQueue(".\UserMan")
3   Dim msgUserMan As New Message()
4
5   ' Set up the formatter
6   queUserMan.Formatter = New XmlMessageFormatter( _
7     New Type() {GetType(String)})
8
9   ' Create message body
10  msgUserMan.Body = "Message"
11  ' Set max time to be in queue
12  msgUserMan.TimeToBeReceived = New TimeSpan(0, 0, 20)
13  ' Make sure that a dead-letter ends up in
14  ' dead-letter queue
15  msgUserMan.UseDeadLetterQueue = True
16  ' Send message to queue
17  queUserMan.Send(msgUserMan)
18 End Sub
```

Another way of dealing with rejected messages is to request notification of the message rejection. Setting the **AcknowledgeType** and **AdministrationQueue** properties does this (see Listing 21-29).

Listing 21-29. Receiving Rejection Notification in the Admin Queue

```
1 Public Sub PlaceNonauthenticatedMessageInAdminQueue()
2   Dim queUserManAdmin As New MessageQueue( _
3     ".\Private$\UserManAdmin")
4   Dim queUserMan As New MessageQueue(".\Private$\UserMan")
5   Dim msgUserMan As New Message()
6
7   ' Enable queue authentication
8   queUserMan.Authenticate = True
9   ' Set up the queue formatter
10  queUserMan.Formatter = New XmlMessageFormatter( _
11    New Type() {GetType(String)})
12
```

```
13    ' Create message body
14    msgUserMan.Body = "Message Body"
15    ' Make sure a rejected message is placed in the admin queue
16    msgUserMan.AdministrationQueue = queUserManAdmin
17    ' These types of rejected messages
18    msgUserMan.AcknowledgeType = _
19       AcknowledgeTypes.NotAcknowledgeReachQueue
20
21    ' Send message to queue
22    queUserMan.Send(msgUserMan)
23 End Sub
```

In Listing 21-29, I've set up the private queue UserManAdmin to receive notification of rejection. Please note that you need to have created this message queue as a nontransactional queue before you run the example code.

As is the case with the code in Listing 21-27, the code in Listing 21-29 rejects the messages that you send. That seems okay, because you requested that all messages should be authenticated, but you "forgot" to authenticate your message.

Setting the **AttachSenderId** property to **True** does this, because it results in Message Queuing setting the **SenderId** property. However, this isn't enough, because you also need to set the **UseAuthentication** property to **True**. This ensures the message is digitally signed before it's sent to the queue. Likewise, the digital signature that Message Queuing has assigned is used for authenticating the message when it's received. Listing 21-30 shows you how to send an authenticated message.

Listing 21-30. Sending an Authenticated Message

```
1 Public Sub AcceptAuthenticatedMessage()
2    Dim queUserMan As New MessageQueue(".\Private$\UserMan")
3    Dim msgUserMan As New Message()
4
5    ' Enable queue authentication
6    queUserMan.Authenticate = True
7    ' Set up the queue formatter
8    queUserMan.Formatter = New XmlMessageFormatter( _
9       New Type() {GetType(String)})
10
```

```
11      ' Make sure a rejected message is placed in
12      ' the dead-letter queue
13      msgUserMan.UseDeadLetterQueue = True
14      ' Make sure that message queuing attaches the
15      ' sender id and is digitally signed before it is sent
16      msgUserMan.UseAuthentication = True
17      msgUserMan.AttachSenderId = True
18      ' Create message body
19      msgUserMan.Body = "Message Body"
20
21      ' Send message to queue
22      queUserMan.Send(msgUserMan)
23 End Sub
```

In Listing 21-30, I set the **UseAuthentication** and **AttachSenderId** properties of the **Message** object to **True** in order to ensure that the message is digitally signed and can be authenticated by Message Queuing. In this situation the message queue, unlike in the examples in Listings 21-28 and 21-29, won't reject the message, even if it only accepts authenticated messages. If authentication has already been set up on the message queue, you can leave out Lines 5 and 6.

Now it's obviously good to know if a message has been authenticated or not, but you don't actually have to check anything to find out. If you've set up authentication on the message queue, all messages in the queue will have been authenticated when they arrived in the queue, meaning you can trust any message you receive from the queue.

Using Encryption

Encryption is another way of securing messages sent between message queuing computers. With encryption, anyone trying to spy on the traffic on the network between the message queuing computers will receive encrypted messages. Now, while someone might be able to decrypt your messages, encryption certainly makes it harder to obtain sensitive information.

Some overhead is involved when you encrypt your messages at the sending end and decrypt them at the receiving end, but if your network is public and you're sending sensitive information, you should definitely consider using encrypted messages. Table 21-3 shows you the properties that can be set in order to use encryption with your message queues and messages.

Table 21-3. Encryption Properties

Class	Property	Description
Message	EncryptionAlgorithm	This property is used to specify the encryption algorithm used for encrypting the message. The property can only be set to one of the **EncryptionAlgorithm** enum members, with **Rc2** being the default value and the most secure option.
Message	UseEncryption	You must set this property to **True** if you want to encrypt your message, or **False** (default) to specify a nonencrypted message. If the **EncryptionRequired** property on the message queue has been set to **Body**, you must set this property to **True**; otherwise, the message will be rejected.
Message-Queue	EncryptionRequired	This property must be set to a member of the **EncryptionRequired** enum. This enum has three members: **Body**, which makes sure that all messages that are sent to the queue must be encrypted. If you send a nonencrypted message to a queue with encryption enabled, the message is rejected. **None** (default), which makes sure that no messages that are sent to the queue can be encrypted. If you send an encrypted message to a queue with encryption disabled, the message is rejected. **Optional**, which means the queue will accept both encrypted and nonencrypted messages.

As is the case with authentication, encryption requirements can be applied to the queue, meaning that all nonencrypted messages will be rejected by the queue. Set the **EncryptionRequired** property of the **MessageQueue** object to **EncryptionRequired.Body**, like this:

```
queUserMan.EncryptionRequired = EncryptionRequired.Body
```

I set the **EncryptionRequired** property of the **MessageQueue** object to **EncryptionRequired.Body**. As a result, the body of any message sent to the queue must be encrypted; otherwise, it's rejected. Instead of setting the encryption property of the message queue programmatically, you can also set it from the Computer Management MMC snap-in (see Figure 21-10), or by selecting the queue in Server Explorer, right-clicking, and selecting Properties from the pop-up menu.

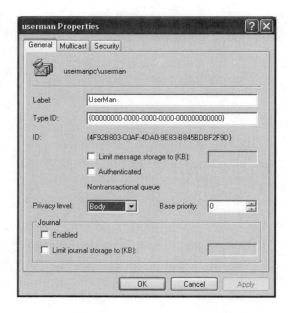

Figure 21-10. The privacy level set to Body

 NOTE   Message Queue encryption is also called *privacy*, meaning a private message, not to be confused with a private message queue.

In Figure 21-10, Body has been selected from the Privacy level drop-down list, which has the same results as programmatically setting the **EncryptionRequired** property to **EncryptionRequired.Body**. Please note that I've unchecked the Authentication check box in this example. This doesn't mean that you can't use encryption and authentication at the same time; I have simply done so to simplify the code in the following listings.

Unlike with authentication, it's possible to use encryption even if the message queue doesn't require it, but only if the privacy level is set to Optional. This can be done from the Computer Management MMC snap-in or programmatically, as follows:

```
' Set message body encryption to optional
queUserMan.EncryptionRequired = EncryptionRequired.Optional
```

If you specify Optional as the privacy level, you can send encrypted and non-encrypted messages to the message queue. However, if you set the privacy level to None, you can only send nonencrypted messages to the queue. If you send an encrypted message to a queue with a privacy level of None, the message is rejected. If you send messages over an unsecured network, it's inappropriate in most cases to use a privacy level of None. If you happen to be building a chat-like messaging system with simple text messages that aren't important, it'll more than likely be okay; otherwise, it's a good idea to consider using encryption for your messages. Listing 21-31 demonstrates how you might send and receive encrypted messages.

Listing 21-31. Sending and Receiving Encrypted Messages

```
1 Public Sub SendAndReceiveEncryptedMessage()
2    Dim queUserMan As New MessageQueue("USERMANPC\UserMan")
3    Dim msgUserMan As New Message()
4
5    ' Require message body encryption
6    queUserMan.EncryptionRequired = EncryptionRequired.Body
7    ' Set up the queue formatter
8    queUserMan.Formatter = New XmlMessageFormatter( _
9      New Type() {GetType(String)})
10
11    ' Make sure that message is encrypted before it is sent
12    msgUserMan.UseEncryption = True
13    ' Create message body
14    msgUserMan.Body = "Message Body"
15
16    ' Send message to queue
17    queUserMan.Send(msgUserMan)
18
```

```
19    ' Retrieve message from queue
20    msgUserMan = queUserMan.Receive()
21    ' Show decrypted message body
22    MsgBox(msgUserMan.Body.ToString)
23 End Sub
```

In Listing 21-31, I encrypt a message, send it to the queue, and receive it from the queue. During the transport to and from the queue, the message body is encrypted, but the message is automatically decrypted by the receiving **MessageQueue** object. This means decryption of an encrypted message is always performed automatically when the message is received.

Using Access Control

Controlling access to the message queue is probably the best way to secure your messages. As with most other Windows operations, such as creating new users, the reading and writing of messages can be access controlled. Access control happens when a user tries to perform an operation, such as reading a message from a queue. Each user under Windows NT, Windows 2000, Windows XP Professional, and Windows .NET Server has an Access Control List (ACL), which contains all the operations the user can perform. The ACL is checked when the user tries to read a message. If the user has read access, the user can read the message from the queue. However, if the user isn't allowed to read from the queue, the read is disallowed.

Access control can be applied at the message queue level or even at the message level, but it can also be applied at the Message Queuing level, meaning that all message queues in the Active Directory will abide by the permissions you set. Take a look at Figure 21-11, where you can see the Access Control List for the UserMan user of the UserMan domain. The permissions shown are for the UserMan private message queue.

You can bring up the ACL by opening the Computer Management MMC snap-in, selecting the private UserMan queue, right-clicking the queue, and selecting Properties from the pop-up menu. This brings up the Properties dialog box, in which you must select the Security tab to get to the ACL (see Figure 21-11).

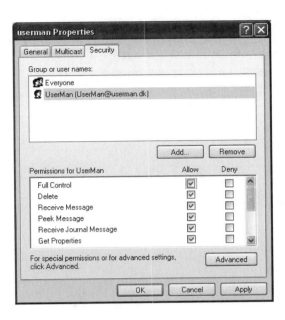

Figure 21-11. The User Properties dialog box with Security tab selected

As you can see from the ACL in Figure 21-11, there are permissions for just about anything you can do with the message queue, such as write, read, and peek at messages. Next to the operation there are two check boxes, one for allowing the operation and one for denying the operation. All you have to do is select the user or group you want to set the permissions for in the listbox in the top part of the dialog box. If the user or group isn't listed, you can add it by clicking the Add button. If you need to remove a user or group, you can select it and click the Delete button.

You need to be careful when you set the permissions for groups especially, because as always with ACLs in Windows, the more restrictive permission takes precedence. For instance, if you set the Delete operation to Allow for the UserMan user and then set the same permission for the Everyone group to Deny, the UserMan user is denied the right to delete the message queue. All users in the domain are part of the Everyone group, so you need to be especially careful with this option. Setting group and user permissions is really outside the scope of this book, so if you need more information on how ACLs work and permissions are set with respect to users and groups, you should look at the documentation that comes with your Windows OS.

Using the SetPermissions Method

Instead of setting the user permissions from Computer Management, you can also perform this task programmatically using the **SetPermissions** method of your **MessageQueue** object. Listing 21-32 shows you how to do it.

Listing 21-32. Setting User Permissions Programmatically

```
1 Public Sub SetUserPermissions()
2    Dim queUserMan As New MessageQueue(".\Private$\UserMan")
3    Dim msgUserMan As New Message()
4    Dim aclUserMan As New AccessControlList()
5
6    ' Give UserMan user full control over
7    ' private UserMan queue
8    queUserMan.SetPermissions("UserMan", _
9       MessageQueueAccessRights.FullControl)
10   ' Give UserMan user full control over private
11   ' UserMan queue
12   queUserMan.SetPermissions(New _
13      MessageQueueAccessControlEntry(New Trustee("UserMan"), _
14      MessageQueueAccessRights.FullControl))
15   ' Deny UserMan deleting the private UserMan queue
16   queUserMan.SetPermissions("UserMan", _
17      MessageQueueAccessRights.DeleteQueue, _
18      AccessControlEntryType.Deny)
19   ' Deny UserMan all access rights on the private UserMan queue
20   aclUserMan.Add(New AccessControlEntry(New _
21      Trustee("UserMan"), _
22      GenericAccessRights.All, StandardAccessRights.All, _
23      AccessControlEntryType.Deny))
24   queUserMan.SetPermissions(aclUserMan)
25 End Sub
```

In Listing 21-32 I've used all four overloads of the **SetPermissions** method. The first two (Lines 8 and 9, and 12 through 14) take the name of the user or group and the rights to assign to this user or group. They're basically the same and can only be used to assign rights to a user or group, not revoke rights. Lines 8 and 9 show how to use a member of the **MessageQueueAccessRights** enum to specify the rights that are to be granted to the UserMan user, whereas Lines 12 through 14 show how to use a **MessageQueueAccessControlEntry** object. The next overloaded version of the method (Lines 16 through 18) can be used to allow, deny, revoke, or set a specific permission for a particular user or group. The last version of the method (Lines 20 through 23) can be used to allow, deny, revoke, or set generic and standard access rights for a user or group. Actually, the last overload can be used for changing permissions for several users and/or groups in one go. You simply need to add as many Access Control Entries (ACE) as necessary to the ACL (Line 20) before you set the permission using the ACL (Line 24).

I have only constructed the example code in Listing 21-32 for you to see how all four of the overloaded versions of the **SetPermissions** method can be used. You shouldn't be using them at the same time. If a conflict occurs between the rights you assign or revoke, only the last rights assigned or revoked will count, unless preceded by a complementary Deny rights setting.

Using Auditing

In the context of this chapter, auditing is used for logging access to a message queue. This allows you to check the Event Log to see who has been accessing it, or even better, who has been trying to access it and been denied the access. Auditing really falls beyond the scope of this book, as it's a generic tool used for logging access to any kind of service or object in the Windows OS, so I'll only touch on it briefly here.

You can set up auditing from the Computer Management MMC snap-in. Select the message queue you want to audit or indeed all of Message Queuing by selecting the node by this name. Right-click the selected node and select Properties from the pop-up menu. This brings up the Properties dialog box, in which you should select the Security tab. On the Security tab, click the Advanced button. This brings up the Access Control Settings dialog box. Select the Auditing tab to bring up the dialog box shown in Figure 21-12. Normally there are no auditing entries on the list, but in Figure 21-12, I have added an entry that logs when any user (Everyone group) fails to send a message to the message queue.

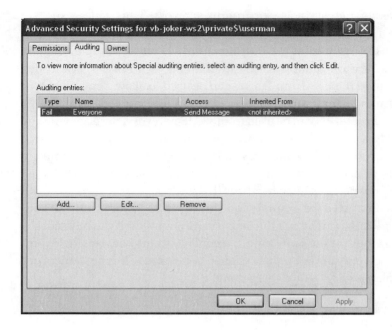

Figure 21-12. The Access Control Settings dialog box

There are two types of audits: Success and Failure. Try playing around with these audits and don't forget to check the entries added to Event Log (the Application Log). You can view the Event Log using the Event Viewer.

If you want further information about auditing or Message Queuing security in general, I suggest you read the documentation for your Windows OS.

MSMQ 3.0 Features

MSMQ 3.0, which was introduced with Windows XP Professional,[3] presents new features and removes some of the features supported by MSMQ 2.0, which is described previously in this chapter. Some of the new features are

- Messaging across the Internet

- One-to-many messaging

- Programmable management, deployment, and programming model enhancements

- Triggers

---

3. Windows XP Personal Edition is not supported.

These four enhancements are briefly described in the following sections. However, you also need to be aware that some of the features described previously in this chapter are no longer supported. The following features have been deprecated in MSMQ 3.0 or are not supported:

- The MSMQ Exchange connector is no longer supported.

- The IPX protocol is no longer supported.

- The MSMQ3.0 dependent client only supports MSMQ 2.0 level functionality, because of its dependence on a MSMQ 2.0 server.

Adding MSMQ 3.0 Functionality

You need to make sure that you've installed all the features discussed in this section before you go on. When you install Message Queuing, as described in the "Installing Message Queuing" section earlier in this chapter, everything is installed by default. However, it's probably a good idea to check your installation. Do as described in the "Installing Message Queuing" section, and when you've selected the Message Queuing component in the Windows Components Wizard (Figure 21-1), click the Details button. This brings up the Message Queuing dialog box, as shown in Figure 21-13.

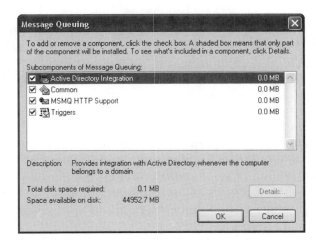

Figure 21-13. The Message Queuing dialog box

Make sure all subcomponents are selected in the Message Queuing dialog box,[4] and click OK. Click Next in the Windows Component Wizard dialog box to install the missing components, if any.

The **System.Messaging** namespace only supports MSMQ 2.0, and not MSMQ 3.0, which means you have to use it through COM Interop. Appendix B briefly covers COM Interop, but to get started, you need to add a reference to the COM library. You can do this by right-clicking the References node in the Solution Explorer, and selecting Add Reference from the pop-up menu. This brings up the Add Reference dialog box, in which you need to select the COM tab, as shown in Figure 21-14.

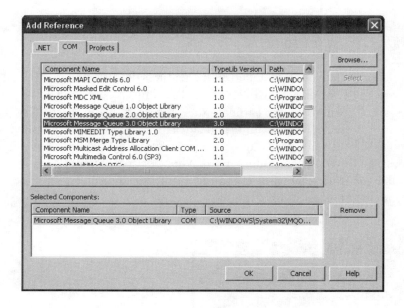

Figure 21-14. Adding MSMQ 3.0 reference to project

When you have the COM tab selected in the Add Reference dialog box, you need to scroll down the component list, select the Microsoft Message Queue 3.0 Object Library, and click the Select button. This will add the MSMQ 3.0 component to the Selected Components list as shown in Figure 21-14. Click OK to close the dialog box. All you need to do now is to import the MSMQ namespace in your class and/or module files, like this:

```
Imports MSMQ
```

4. I'll be discussing all of the components in the upcoming sections, so if you want to follow the examples and discussions, you need to install all of them. Alternatively, you can choose to install each component as we go along.

Well, strictly speaking you don't have to, as you can prefix all classes, enums, and so on with the MSMQ namespace, but I think it's easier to import the namespace at the top of the code files in which you use the classes and enums of the namespace.

Working with MSMQ 3.0 Classes

If you ever worked with MSMQ 2.0 in a programming language before VB .NET, such as VB 6, it won't be that different working with MSMQ 3.0. However, if your only exposure to message queuing is through the **System.Messaging** namespace, it's somewhat different. I won't be discussing the classes and enums in MSMQ 3.0 in details, but I will give you a quick rundown of the most important ones in Table 21-4, just to give you something to compare to the classes and enums in the **System.Messaging** namespace.

Table 21-4. MSMQ 3.0 Classes

MSMQ 3.0 Class Name	Description	System.Messaging Namespace Equivalent
MSMQApplication	This class can be used for retrieving information about the message queuing service on a machine, and performing global administrative tasks, such as deleting empty message files on a computer.	-
MSMQMessage	This is the message class.	**Message**
MSMQQueue	This is the actual message queue class.	**MessageQueue**
MSMQDestination	Instances of this class represent one or more message queues to which you can send messages directly and specify response message queues.	-
MSMQQueueManagement	This class is for monitoring the state of a message queue.	-
MSMQQueueInfo	This is the message queue management class used for manipulating (such as creating and deleting a queue) a single message queue.	**MessageQueue**

NOTE All the MSMQ 3.0 classes mentioned in Table 21-4 have "Class" appended to them when you use them in managed code. Therefore, the **MSMQQueue** class becomes **MSMQQueueClass** in your code.

If you need more information about message queuing in general, and/or MSMQ 3.0 functionality, you can find it at this address: http://msdn.microsoft.com/library/default.asp?url=/library/en-us/msmq/ msmq_ref_queueinfo_0t2d.asp.

As stated earlier, I won't be going into details about the various classes, but I will show you some example code that resembles the example code presented earlier in this chapter, where classes from the **System.Messaging** namespace were used. If you need to create a queue programmatically, please refer to listings used previously. Listing 21-33 sends a message to the private UserMan message queue on the machine with the IP address of 10.8.1.16.

Listing 21-33. Sending a Simple Message Using MSMQ 3.0

```
 1 Public Sub SendSimpleMessageMSMQ30()
 2    Dim msg30 As New MSMQMessageClass()
 3    Dim qud30 As New MSMQDestinationClass()
 4
 5    ' Bind to message queue by setting the
 6    ' format name
 7    qud30.FormatName = "DIRECT=TCP:10.8.1.16\PRIVATE$\userman"
 8    ' Prepare and send message
 9    msg30.Body = "Test Body"
10    msg30.Send(qud30)
11 End Sub
```

In Listing 21-33 I use a **MSMQMessage** and a **MSMQDestination** object for sending a message directly to the UserMan message queue on the machine with IP address 10.8.1.16, without using Active Directory. I bypass Active Directory by specifying a direct format name on Line 7. I then prepare the message by setting the **Body** property, and send it to the destination queue. The **Send** method of the **MSMQMessage** class automatically opens the destination queue, sends the message, and closes the queue again. Therefore, there's no need for you to explicitly call the **Open** and **Close** methods of the **MSMQDestination** object. I will be using this direct approach in the rest of this chapter.

Messaging across the Internet

Now with MSMQ 3.0, the HTTP protocol is supported, in addition to the proprietary TCP-based MSMQ protocol. This gives you the advantage of passing through a firewall when the message queue you have created is set up to receive messages via the HTTP protocol. Actually, this requires very little on your behalf, as it is done automatically if you followed the instructions in the "Adding MSMQ 3.0 Functionality" section earlier in this chapter. However, you might want to check if MSMQ has been set up in IIS before you go on. Open up IIS, expand the machine on which you have MSMQ installed (typically the local computer), expand the Web sites node, and expand the Default Web Site node. Once you've done this, you should see the MSMQ virtual directory under the Default Web Site node, as shown in Figure 21-15. If it's there, your IIS will accept incoming message queue requests. There's nothing else you need to do.

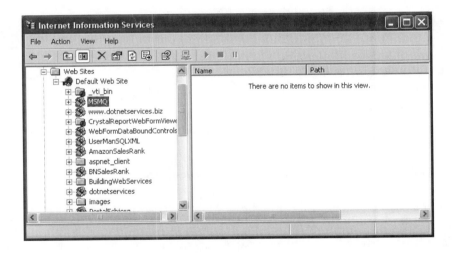

Figure 21-15. MSMQ 3.0 set up in IIS

Now, the MSMQ virtual directory in IIS simply hooks up to the message queues on the machine on which IIS is running. This means that you can access any message queue on this machine, for which you have the right permissions, using the HTTP protocol.

NOTE   You can't browse to the MSMQ virtual directory, or rather you can, but there's nothing to see in your browser.

Listing 21-34 shows you how you can specify a direct format name for the destination queue, in order to use the HTTP protocol to send a message.

Listing 21-34. Sending a Simple Message Using MSMQ 3.0 over HTTP

```
 1 Public Sub SendMessageViaHTTPMSMQ30()
 2    Dim msg30 As New MSMQMessageClass()
 3    Dim qud30 As New MSMQDestinationClass()
 4
 5    ' Bind to message queue by setting the
 6    ' format name
 7    qud30.FormatName = "DIRECT=HTTP://10.8.1.16/MSMQ/PRIVATE$/userman"
 8    ' Prepare and send message
 9    msg30.Body = "Test Body"
10    msg30.Send(qud30)
11 End Sub
```

As you can see from Listing 21-34, this is much the same code as in Listing 21-33, except for the use of the HTTP protocol. The syntax for specifying a machine using the HTTP protocol is

```
HTTP://{machine}/MSMQ/{queue}
```

The HTTP:// bit is always written like this, followed by the machine that hosts the queue. You can specify the machine in any way you'd normally locate a Web server in your browser; I'm using the IP address. /MSMQ/ must always be specified as shown, followed by the name of the queue. In Listing 21-34, I'm using the private UserMan queue, and if you want to access a private queue, you need to put PRIVATE$/ in front of the queue name, just as you do when using the TCP-based MSMQ protocol.

All messages sent via the HTTP protocol will automatically be formatted as SOAP-based messages.

Sending Messages to More Than One Queue

A great new feature of MSMQ 3.0 is the ability to send a message to more than one message queue with just one command. This new one-to-many messaging model provides three different ways of sending messages to multiple destinations:

- Multiple format names

- Multicast addresses

- Distribution lists

I will discuss and show you example code for using the first two methods, which can be employed without Active Directory access. However, at the current time of writing, I'm having problems with the beta version of Windows .NET Server, meaning I can't get it to work as I want. This means that I can't set up the distribution list in Active Directory for use when sending multiple messages. Please see the link to more MSMQ 3.0 information, shown in the "Working with MSMQ 3.0 Classes" section earlier in this chapter. You can find more information about distribution lists here, once Windows .NET Server is ready for prime time or MSMQ 3.0 can be used with the Windows 2000 Active Directory, if ever.

Sending to Multiple Destinations Using Private List

Using multiple format names, the first option for sending to multiple destinations, is very simple and it's really only a matter of extending the simple code you've already seen. You specify the format names as seen in the previous listings, separating each with a comma. Listing 21-35 shows you how you can specify direct format names for the destination queues in order to send a message to multiple destinations.

*Listing 21-35. Sending a Message to Multiple Destinations Using **FormatName***

```
1 Public Sub SendMessageToMultipleDestUsingFormatNameMSMQ30()
2     Dim msg30 As New MSMQMessageClass()
3     Dim qud30 As New MSMQDestinationClass()
4
5     ' Bind to destination queues by specifying the
6     ' format names
7     qud30.FormatName = "DIRECT=HTTP://10.8.1.16/MSMQ/PRIVATE$/userman," & _
8         "DIRECT=TCP:10.8.1.16\PRIVATE$\userman1," & _
9         "DIRECT=OS:USERMANPC\userman"
```

```
10     ' Prepare and send message
11     msg30.Body = "Test Body"
12     msg30.Send(qud30)
13 End Sub
```

In Listing 21-35 you can see how a private list can be used to send a message to multiple destinations. Please note how the three format names are all different, which is obviously another great benefit of this functionality.

NOTE   When setting the **FormatName** property, make sure you use the correct slash. The forward slash (/) works with the HTTP protocol, and the backward slash (\) works with the TCP-based MSMQ protocol. If you don't use the correct one, an exception is thrown.

Sending to Multiple Destinations Using Multicast

Your second option for sending to multiple destinations is to assign a valid multicast address (IP address) to all the message queues you want to associate with a single multicast address. The multicast address must be a valid multicast address, which means it must be in the IP class D address range, from 224.0.0.0 through 239.255.255.255. Multicasting can be done to any message queue, private as well as public. However, keep in mind that this is an MSMQ 3.0 feature and that public queues are stored in your network's Active Directory. This means that the public queue information is stored on a Windows 2000 domain controller, which ultimately means that it supports MSMQ 2.0. If you try to set a multicast address on an MSMQ 2.0 message queue, a **COMException** exception is thrown.

Anyway, Listing 21-36 shows you how you can assign a multicast address to a message queue and then send a message to all queues with this multicast address.

Listing 21-36. Sending a Message to Multiple Destinations Using Multicast

```
1 Public Sub SendMessageToMultipleDestUsingMulticastMSMQ30()
2    Dim msg30 As New MSMQMessageClass()
3    Dim qud30 As New MSMQDestinationClass()
4    Dim qui30 As New MSMQQueueInfo()
5
```

```
 6    ' Set up queues with multicast address
 7    qui30.PathName = ".\PRIVATE$\userman"
 8    qui30.MulticastAddress = "224.0.0.255:0"
 9    qui30.Update()
10    qui30.PathName = ".\PRIVATE$\userman1"
11    qui30.MulticastAddress = "224.0.0.255:0"
12    qui30.Update()
13    qui30.PathName = "USERMANPC\userman"
14    qui30.MulticastAddress = "224.0.0.255:0"
15    qui30.Update()
16
17    ' Bind to destination queues by specifying the
18    ' format names
19    qud30.FormatName = "MULTICAST=224.0.0.255:0"
20    ' Prepare and send message
21    msg30.Body = "Test Body"
22    msg30.Send(qud30)
23 End Sub
```

In Listing 21-36 you can see how I first set the path of the queue and then the multicast address I want to assign to the queue, and finally I call the **Update** method on the **MSMQDestination** class instance. This will assign the new multicast address to a queue, and if you need to reset the multicast address, you simply assign an empty string to it, like this:

```
qui30.MulticastAddress = ""
```

Don't forget to call the **Update** method when you set the **MulticastAddress** property. Line 15 in Listing 21-36 will throw an exception if you're running a Windows 2000–based Active Directory, because it only supports MSMQ 2.0. You can only use multicasting with public queues and a Windows .NET Server.

Multicast addresses can also be assigned using the Computer Management MMC snap-in if you open the Properties dialog box for the message queue you want to assign a multicast address for, as shown in Figure 21-16.

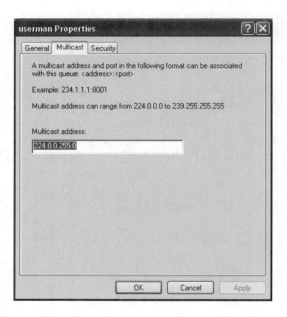

Figure 21-16. Assigning a multicast address from Computer Management

Programmable Management

Previously it was only possible to perform many administrative tasks manually and not programmatically. Monitoring the state of the outgoing and destination message queues is one of those tasks, and with the new **MSMQManagement** and **MSMQQueueManagement** classes, you can now perform the monitoring programmatically. The outgoing message queue is a queue created automatically by Message Queuing for each remote destination queue when sending messages to remote queues.

The **MSMQManagement** class is and must be instantiated using the **Init** method. This method takes two of three arguments:

- The name of the machine hosting the queue (the local machine is used if omitted)

- The path of the queue

- The format name of the queue

You can choose to specify the machine name as the first argument, but you can also leave it out, in which case the local machine is assumed. However, you must specify only one of the other two arguments, not both. If you specify both, an exception is thrown. The machine name is used to indicate an outgoing queue or a destination queue.

The **MSMQManagement** class has a number of properties that can be used to return valuable information about the queue, such as whether the queue is local or remote, if the queue is a foreign queue (meaning not an MSMQ queue), how many messages are in a queue, and how many bytes they take up.

The **MSMQQueueManagement** class has two properties, **BytesInJournal** and **JournalMessageCount**, which return valuable information about a queue journal. See the "Using Journal Storage" section earlier in this chapter for more information about journaling.

The **MSMQApplication** class is also one of those classes that can be used for administrative purposes. However, unlike the other classes mentioned, this class is for administrating the Message Queuing service on a machine. Therefore, you should use this class when you want to perform global administrative message queue tasks on a specific machine.

Using Message Queue Triggers

Triggers are a most welcome addition to the MSMQ functionality, because they make it so much easier to receive confirmation about incoming messages in a destination queue. Message queuing triggers were actually introduced as a stand-alone service with MSMQ 2.0, but they are now an integral part of MSMQ 3.0. This brings us to the first step, ensuring that the Message Queuing Triggers service is running. Open up the Services application from the Administrative Tools menu. Then make sure the Message Queuing Triggers service is running, as shown in Figure 21-17.

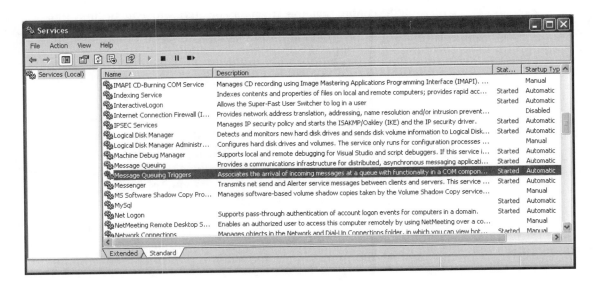

Figure 21-17. Ensuring the Message Queuing Triggers service is running

Once the Message Queuing Triggers service is running, you can create a trigger manually from the Computer Management MMC snap-in. See the following sections on trigger types, rules, and how to create your triggers.

 NOTE It's not possible to create triggers and rules programmatically. It must all be done manually.

You can use triggers on all message queues, including the system-generated ones, such as the journal and dead letter queue. In fact, this is probably one of most appropriate actions, so to speak, for a trigger—to react if a message ends up in the dead letter queue.

Once you've created a trigger, it will monitor the queue with which it's associated, and evaluate the trigger rules. If the rules evaluate to true, the associated action is performed.

Trigger Types

There are two types of message queue triggers: serialized and nonserialized. With serialized triggers, the messages in the associated queue are processed in the order they arrive in the queue, meaning one at a time. Nonserialized triggers process them as fast as possible, which means two or more messages can be processed at the same time if you have more than one trigger associated with the queue in which the messages arrive.

When you have more than one trigger associated with a queue, they must all be of the same type, serialized or nonserialized.

Trigger Actions

When a rule associated with a trigger evaluates to true, the action associated with the rule is executed. The action must be performed by a COM component or an executable file. I have created a very simple VB .NET Class Library project for testing purposes named MSMQTrigger. Now, that's original, don't you think? This project has a single class file named CTrigger.vb, and this file contains the code in Listing 21-37.

Listing 21-37. CTrigger *Class*

```
1 Imports System.Data.SqlClient
2
3 Public Class CTrigger
4    Private Const PR_STR_CONNECTION_STRING As String = _
5        "Data Source=10.8.1.12;User ID=UserMan;Password=userman;" & _
6        "Initial Catalog=UserMan"
7
8    Public Sub DeleteRows(ByVal LastName As String)
9        Dim cnnUserMan As SqlConnection
10       Dim cmmUserMan As SqlCommand
11       Dim strSQL As String
12
13       ' Instantiate the connection
14       cnnUserMan = New SqlConnection(PR_STR_CONNECTION_STRING)
15       ' Open the connection
16       cnnUserMan.Open()
17       ' Build delete query string
18       strSQL = "DELETE FROM tblUser WHERE LastName='" & LastName & "'"
19       ' Instantiate and execute the delete command
20       cmmUserMan = New SqlCommand(strSQL, cnnUserMan)
21       cmmUserMan.ExecuteNonQuery()
22    End Sub
23 End Class
```

The example code in Listing 21-37 simply deletes all users from the tblUser table in the UserMan SQL Server database with the passed last name. Simple, but it will help you see how easy it is to set up business rules with MSMQ triggers. Now, the class library must be compiled to a DLL with a COM wrapper, because that's all the Message Queuing Triggers service can invoke. You can find more information about COM Interop in Appendix B, but for now, it's enough to make sure the DLL is registered for COM Interop. Open up the project, right-click the project file in Solution Explorer, and click Properties on the pop-up menu. This brings up the Property Pages dialog box, in which you need to select the Build node under the Configuration Properties node, as shown in Figure 21-18. Then make sure the Register for COM Interop option is selected as shown. Click OK, and build the solution by pressing Ctrl+Shift+B or by selecting the Build ➤ Build Solution menu command. This builds the MSMQTrigger DLL and registers it in the Registry so it can be used as a regular COM component. The ProgID given to the CTrigger class is MSMQTrigger.CTrigger, and the method is DeleteRows, as shown in Listing 21-37.

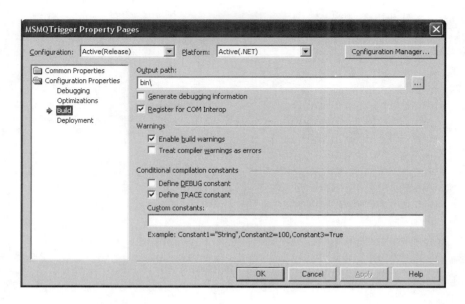

Figure 21-18. Project Property Pages dialog box

Rules

All triggers have a set of rules, and each rule has a condition or logical expression that is evaluated; depending on the evaluation, the trigger invokes a COM component or an executable. These are the conditions that triggers can have:

- What a message label contains or doesn't contain

- What a message body contains or doesn't contain

- What priority a message has (equal to, different from, less than, and greater than)

- What application-specific number a message has (equal to, different from, less than, and greater than)

- What the computer ID of the sending machine is equal to or different from

These conditions can be combined in a number of ways.

Creating a Rule

In order to create a rule, you must perform the following steps:

1. Open up the Computer Management MMC snap-in.

2. Expand the Services and Applications node.

3. Expand the Message Queuing and Message Queuing Triggers node.

4. Select and right-click the Rules node, and select New ➤ Rule from the pop-up menu, as shown in Figure 21-19.

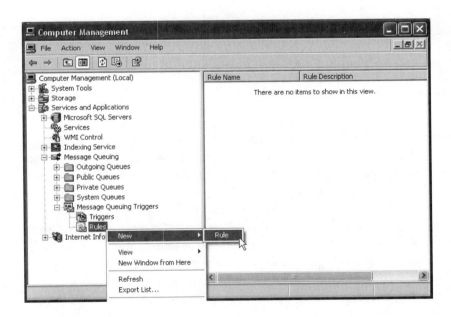

Figure 21-19. Creating a new trigger rule

This brings up the New Rule dialog box, in which you must type a name and optionally a description for the rule, as seen in Figure 21-20.

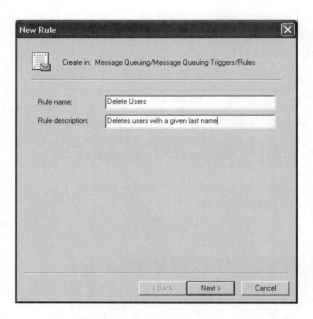

Figure 21-20. New Rule dialog box

Once you've typed the name and optionally the description, click Next. On the next page of the dialog box, you need to add at least one condition to the Condition list by selecting the condition on the New condition list and entering the appropriate condition text, as shown in Figure 21-21.

In Figure 21-21, you can see how the rule will evaluate to true if a message in the associated queue has a body that contains the word "DeleteUser". Click Add to add the condition to the condition list. You can add as many conditions as you want. Click Next to advance to next stage of the rule creation. Then select the Invoke COM component option, type the ProgID (MSMQTrigger.CTrigger) of your class/ component in the Component ProgID textbox, and the method name (DeleteRows) in the Method name textbox. Now, because your example code in the DeleteRows procedure in Listing 21-37 expects a **String** argument for the last name of the users to be deleted, you need to specify this as a parameter. Click the Parameters button. This brings up the Invocation Parameters dialog box, in which you can add the input parameters for the method to be invoked by the rule. I've chosen to add an input parameter based on the content of the message label, as shown in Figure 21-22. Click OK to close the Invocation Parameters dialog box, and click Finish to finish the rule creation.

Figure 21-21. Adding a new rule condition

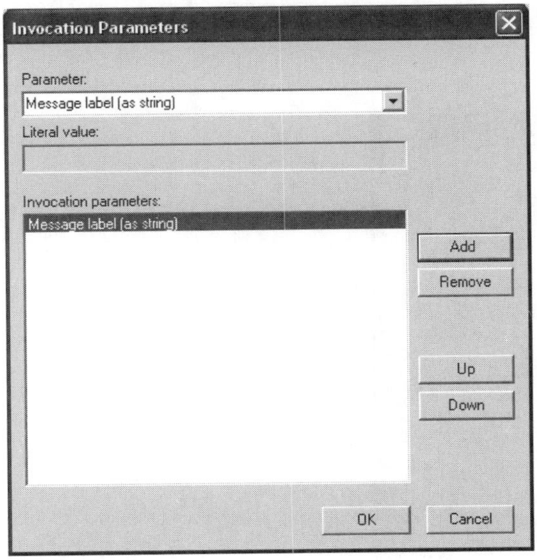

Figure 21-22. Adding an input parameter to a rule

After setting up a rule, you need to associate it with one or more triggers. See the next section for more information on creating a trigger, including associating a rule.

Creating a Trigger

To create a trigger, you must open up the Computer Management MMC snap-in, expand the Services and Applications node, and expand the Message Queuing and Message Queuing Triggers nodes. Now you have to choose whether you want to create the trigger on a user-generated queue or on a system-generated queue. If you want to create it on a system-generated queue, right-click the Triggers node and select New ➤ Trigger from the pop-up menu. From the New Trigger dialog box shown, you have the option of creating a trigger that reads messages in a system-generated queue or a user-generated queue. However, if you want to create a trigger that reads messages in a user-generated queue, it's much easier to create the trigger on that particular queue directly. Expand the queue in question, right-click the Triggers node, and select New ➤ Trigger from the pop-up menu. This brings up the New Trigger dialog box shown in Figure 21-23. The difference between this version of the New Trigger dialog box and the one displayed if you open it from under the Message Queuing Triggers node is that now you don't have to fill in the queue details—it's already done for you.

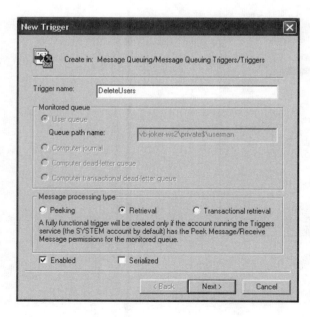

Figure 21-23. New Trigger dialog box

Give the trigger name by typing it in the Trigger name textbox; choose whether you want a serial trigger or nonserial trigger (see the "Trigger Types" section earlier in this chapter) by selecting or deselecting the Serialized option. Then select the message processing type to indicate whether you want the message removed from the queue (Retrieval or Transactional retrieval) when processing it, or not removed (Peeking). Click Next to associate one or more rules with the trigger. On the next page of the New Trigger dialog box you can associate an existing rule by selecting it on the Existing rules list, and clicking the Attach -> button to move it to the Attached rules list, as shown in Figure 21-24. You can add as many rules as you like, just make sure they don't contradict each other; otherwise, they will never trigger the rule action. Click Finish to end the trigger creation.

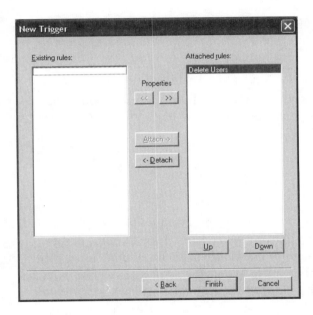

Figure 21-24. New Trigger rules dialog box

Testing a Trigger

Okay, so if you've followed the instructions up until now, you have the `DeleteUser` trigger associated with the local and private UserMan queue. The attached rule, Delete Users, will act on any incoming message in the UserMan queue with a body that contains the word "DeleteUser". If a message rule evaluates to true, the `DeleteRows` method of your `MSMQTrigger.CTrigger` component will be invoked by passing the label of the message as the only input parameter. The code to test the trigger can be seen in Listing 21-38.

Listing 21-38. Example Code That Triggers DeleteUser *Trigger*

```
1 Public Sub SendTriggerMessage()
2    Dim queUserMan As New MessageQueue(".\Private$\UserMan")
3    Dim msgUserMan As New Message()
4
5    ' Set up the formatter
6    queUserMan.Formatter = New XmlMessageFormatter( _
7       New Type() {GetType(String)})
8
9    ' Make sure the trigger acts on this message
10   msgUserMan.Body = "DeleteUser"
11   ' This is the invocation parameter
12   msgUserMan.Label = "Thomsen"
13   ' Send message to queue
14   queUserMan.Send(msgUserMan)
15 End Sub
```

If your trigger doesn't invoke the COM component or executable associated with the rule, please check the Application Log in the Event Viewer, as it will hold whatever error has occurred.

MSMQ 3.0 Feature Summary

I have touched upon some of the most exciting new features of MSMQ 3.0, but it includes more new functionality than is covered here. However, some of the functionality not shown here requires knowledge of ADSI and other tools. It's my hope and understanding that the **System.Messaging** namespace will be extended in the future to incorporate most if not all of the functionality in MSMQ 3.0, instead of just MSMQ 2.0 as it stands today. However, you'll also need to host your message queues on machines that can run MSMQ 3.0, which at the moment means Windows XP and a beta version of Windows .NET Server, if you want to use MSMQ 3.0 to the fullest extent.

Summary

This chapter introduced you to the concept of connectionless programming using message queues. I showed you how to create message queues from Server Explorer and the Computer Management MMC snap-in, and how to do it programmatically.

I discussed how you can locate message queues on the network; how message queues work with transactions; why you should use a message queue and not a database table; how the messages are ordered or sorted in a queue; and how you work with the various properties and methods of both the **MessageQueue** and **Message** classes.

You also saw how you can secure your messaging, and finally I gave you a brief introduction to MSMQ 3.0, which isn't natively supported by the .NET Framework, meaning you have to use it through COM Interop. I hope that the MSMQ 3.0 functionality will be incorporated in the next update of the .NET Framework classes, as it's a pain having to use it through COM Interop.

In the next chapter, you'll see how you can use the SQLXML 3.0 plug-in to work with your SQL Server 2000 data in XML format, including exposing the data using the HTTP protocol.

Part Nine

XML and SQL Server 2000

Using XML with SQL Server 2000

IN THIS CHAPTER, you'll learn the basics of using XML with SQL Server 2000, and you'll be introduced to the SQLXML 3.0 plug-in. This plug-in can be used to access SQL Server 2000 databases using HTTP,[1] once it's configured in Internet Information Services (IIS), and to manipulate SQL Server data using the SQLXML 3.0 Managed Classes, such as the **SqlXmlAdapter** class.

SQL Server and XML

Microsoft started adding built-in XML capabilities to its RDBMS flagship with the release of SQL Server 2000. Now you can have result sets returned as XML documents and access data in a SQL Server database using a combination of XML and an HTTP connection. I've already mentioned one of the new XML capabilities in Chapter 6, and in Listing 6-5 I showed you how the FOR XML clause can be used in a SELECT statement to make sure that the result set is formatted using XML. A few more keywords you can use in connection with the SELECT statement are shown in Table 22-1. Please note that the SELECT . . . FOR XML construct must always be used with any of the shown keywords. The Server Side and Client Side columns refer to whether the keyword can be used when executing the query on the server or the client.

> **NOTE** Because I feel it's important to understand some of the XML basics, you won't get to the actual VB .NET listings until later in this chapter. If you feel that you know enough about using XML with SQL Server, you might want to go straight to the "Inspecting the SQLXML 3.0 Managed Classes" section later in this chapter.

---

1. I'm using Internet Explorer 6.0 for the browser tests in this chapter, and I can't guarantee you'll get the same results with other browsers.

Table 22-1. SELECT . . . FOR XML Statement Keywords

Name	Description	Example	Client Side	Example	Example Output
AUTO	This XML mode keyword is used for returning the result set as a nested XML tree. Each table that is referenced in the SELECT statement returns at least one column as part of the result set is included in the XML output.	Yes	No	`SELECT * FROM tblUser FOR XML AUTO`	See Listing 22-1.
BINARY BASE64	This is the default format for binary data when AUTO is specified; thus, it is not needed. However, you need to specify this mode when you retrieve binary data using either EXPLICIT or RAW. This mode means that the binary data is encoded using the Base-64 format.	Yes	Yes	`SELECT * FROM tblUser FOR XML RAW, BINARY BASE64`	-
ELEMENTS	When you use the ELEMENTS keyword, the result set is returned as an XML document, similar to using just FOR XML AUTO. However, when ELEMENTS is also specified in the query, all the column values are also returned as elements, or rather as subelements of their respective table elements. This means that a column value is returned as a child element of a parent row, rather than as an attribute of the parent row.	Yes	Yes	`SELECT * FROM tblUser FOR XML AUTO, ELEMENTS`	See Listing 22-1.

Table 22-1. SELECT . . . FOR XML Statement Keywords (Continued)

Name	Description	Example	Client Side	Example	Example Output
EXPLICIT	The EXPLICIT keyword is used for letting the query writer (you, in most cases) control how the returned XML document should be shaped. I don't cover this topic in this chapter, but you can find out more in the SQLXML or SQL Server documentation. Here's a link on how to use EXPLICIT mode: `http://msdn.microsoft.com/library/default.asp?url=/library/en-us/xmlsql/ac_openxml_4y91.asp`.	Yes	Yes	-	-
NESTED	This XML mode keyword is used for formatting the result set on the client as a nested XML tree. Each table that is referenced in the SELECT statement returns at least one column as part of the result set is included in the XML output.	No	Yes	`SELECT * FROM tblUser FOR XML NESTED`	See Listing 22-1.
RAW	The RAW XML mode keyword is used for transforming each row in the result set into an XML element. This means that each row is output as an element with name "row."	Yes	Yes	`SELECT * FROM tblUser FOR XML RAW`	See Listing 22-2.
XMLDATA	The XMLDATA keyword option makes sure that an XML document schema is returned, but without a root element. The result set is then appended to the schema within the same namespace.	Yes	Yes	`SELECT * FROM tblUser FOR XML AUTO, XMLDATA`	See Listing 22-3.

Listing 22-1 demonstrates the use of some of the SELECT . . . FOR XML statement keywords.

Listing 22-1. SELECT . . . FOR XML [AUTO | NESTED], ELEMENTS Output

```
<?xml version="1.0" encoding="utf-8" ?>
- <UserMan>
-    <tblUser>
        <Id>1</Id>
        <FirstName>John</FirstName>
        <LastName>Doe</LastName>
        <LoginName>UserMan</LoginName>
        <Password>userman</Password>
     </tblUser>
-    <tblUser>
        <Id>2</Id>
        <LoginName>User1</LoginName>
        <Password>password</Password>
     </tblUser>
-    <tblUser>
        <Id>3</Id>
        <LoginName>User2</LoginName>
        <Password>password</Password>
     </tblUser>
-    <tblUser>
        <Id>4</Id>
        <LoginName>User3</LoginName>
        <Password>password</Password>
     </tblUser>
-    <tblUser>
        <Id>5</Id>
        <LoginName>User99</LoginName>
        <Password>password</Password>
     </tblUser>
  </UserMan>
```

Listing 22-1 shows you the output of the SELECT * FROM tblUser FOR XML AUTO, ELEMENTS or SELECT * FROM tblUser FOR XML NESTED, ELEMENTS query. Notice how all the columns are subelements of the table element, which are repeated for each row, and not attributes, as you can see in Listing 22-2.

 NOTE I won't be covering how to extract information from a database view in these sections, but basically it's done the very same way as I show you with tables.

Listing 22-2. SELECT . . . FOR XML RAW Output

```
<?xml version="1.0" encoding="utf-8" ?>
- <UserMan>
    <row Id="1" FirstName="John" LastName="Doe" LoginName="UserMan"
      Password="userman" />
    <row Id="2" LoginName="User1" Password="password" />
    <row Id="3" LoginName="User2" Password="password" />
    <row Id="4" LoginName="User3" Password="password" />
    <row Id="5" LoginName="User99" Password="password" />
  </UserMan>
```

In Listing 22-2 you can see how specifying the RAW mode creates elements for each row with the name of row, instead of tblUser, as browser output in Figure 22-9 later in this chapter. Please note that one of the row elements is too long to fit on one line. Listing 22-3 shows you how the output from an XMLDATA query looks.

Listing 22-3. SELECT . . . FOR XML AUTO, XMLDATA Output

```
<?xml version="1.0" encoding="utf-8" ?>
- <UserMan>
  - <Schema name="Schema1" xmlns="urn:schemas-microsoft-com:xml-data"
      xmlns:dt="urn:schemas-microsoft-com:datatypes">
    - <ElementType name="tblUser" content="empty" model="closed">
        <AttributeType name="Id" dt:type="i4" />
        <AttributeType name="ADName" dt:type="string" />
        <AttributeType name="ADSID" dt:type="string" />
        <AttributeType name="FirstName" dt:type="string" />
        <AttributeType name="LastName" dt:type="string" />
        <AttributeType name="LoginName" dt:type="string" />
        <AttributeType name="Password" dt:type="string" />
        <attribute type="Id" />
        <attribute type="ADName" />
        <attribute type="ADSID" />
        <attribute type="FirstName" />
        <attribute type="LastName" />
        <attribute type="LoginName" />
        <attribute type="Password" />
      </ElementType>
    </Schema>
    <tblUser xmlns="x-schema:#Schema1" Id="1" FirstName="John" LastName="Doe"
      LoginName="UserMan" Password="userman" />
    <tblUser xmlns="x-schema:#Schema1" Id="2" LoginName="User1"
      Password="password" />
```

```
        <tblUser xmlns="x-schema:#Schema1" Id="3" LoginName="User2"
          Password="password" />
        <tblUser xmlns="x-schema:#Schema1" Id="4" LoginName="User3"
          Password="password" />
        <tblUser xmlns="x-schema:#Schema1" Id="5" LoginName="User99"
          Password="password" />
      </UserMan>
```

Listing 22-3 shows you the output of the SELECT * FROM tblUser FOR XML AUTO, XMLDATA query. First you see the schema enclosed in the Schema tags, and after the schema you see the data in the result set, where each row is an element of the named schema.

There is certainly more to know about XML than this book can cover. If you need more information about XML, visit http://www.msdn.microsoft.com/library/default.asp?url=/nhp/Default.asp?contentid=28000438.

Using SQLXML 3.0

SQLXML 3.0 is a new plug-in for SQL Server that can be used to extend the XML capabilities in SQL Server 2000. As the version number 3.0 suggests, this is indeed a third release following the Web Release 1. I won't go into detail about what was included in the first two versions, but I will tell you about the features in SQLXML 3.0 that are related to the .NET Framework and HTTP support.

Installing SQLXML 3.0

You need to install the SQLXML 3.0 SP1[2] plug-in on a machine with at least the SQL Server client tools installed. In the scenario that I'm going to go through with you, I'm installing it on a machine with SQL Server 2000 installed and on my development machine, but as stated you can choose to install it on just your development machine as long as it has the SQL Server client tools installed. See your SQL Server documentation if you need to install the client tools. Basically, you're required to run the SQL Server Setup and choose what you want to install.

Another thing you need to have installed if you want to install HTTP support is IIS. This is the default on Windows 2000 Server and Windows .NET Server versions, but if you're installing on a workstation such as Windows 2000 Professional or Windows XP, you need to make sure that you have IIS installed.

---

2. You don't have to have the SQLXML 3.0 release version installed in order to install Service Pack 1 (SP1).

Anyway, you can download the SQLXML 3.0 SP1 plug-in from the MSDN Web site at this address: `http://msdn.microsoft.com/downloads/default.asp?URL=/` `downloads/sample.asp?url=/MSDN-FILES/027/001/824/msdncompositedoc.xml`.

Once you've downloaded the plug-in, you need to install it, which you do by running the SQLXML3_Q320833.EXE file. Double-click the file to start the setup. A complete installation doesn't take up that much space, so I chose to do a complete installation on both machines. A complete installation includes the following:

- ISAPI Extension and Configuration for SQLXML (HTTP support)

- SQLXML Bulk Load (COM object for loading XML data into SQL Server tables)

- SQLXML Managed Classes for the .NET Framework (that's us . . .)

- SQLXML SDK

- Microsoft XML Parser 4.0

- SQLXML Documentation

You can obviously choose to install any combination of the items in the preceding list, but you need to install the SQLXML Managed Classes and the XML Parser. This is the minimum requirement if you want to work with SQLXML from the .NET Framework. The ISAPI extension is for accessing SQL Server databases from a browser using HTTP, and it's necessary to reproduce the examples in this book. I don't cover the XML Parser or the Bulk Load feature[3] in this chapter.

 NOTE The default behavior of SQLXML 3.0 is to use the SQLXMLOLEDB provider for accessing SQL Server 2000. This provider is installed with SQLXML 3.0. However, the SQLXML 3.0 Managed Classes use the SQL Server .NET Data Provider for accessing SQL Server 2000. See Part Two of this book for more information on the SQL Server .NET Data Provider.

---

3.   You can find some information about this feature here: `http://msdn.microsoft.com/library/` `default.asp?url=/library/en-us/dnsql2k/html/sqlxml_BulkLoadOver.asp`.

Configuring the ISAPI Extension

You need to configure the ISAPI extension using the IIS Virtual Directory Management for SQLXML 3.0 MMC snap-in (see Figure 22-1) to gain access to data in your SQL Server databases using HTTP.

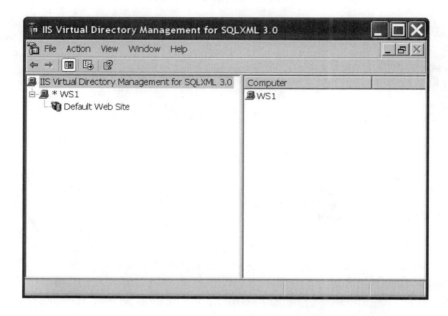

Figure 22-1. The IIS Virtual Directory Management for SQLXML 3.0 MMC snap-in

In Figure 22-1 you can see the IIS Virtual Directory Management for SQLXML 3.0 MMC snap-in opened on my development machine. If you install it on a machine on which you've also installed SQL Server, your MMC snap-in will look different. However, you'll always have the Default Web Site node. You can use the Configure IIS Support menu shortcut in the SQLXML 3.0 menu that SQLXML 3.0 Setup creates. Actually, there's a similar shortcut in the Microsoft SQL Server menu on the machine that hosts your SQL Server installation, but this is the one that shipped with SQL Server, meaning it's an older version. Here's what you need to do:

1. Expand the node for the machine on which you have installed SQLXML.

2. Select the Default Web Site node, right-click the node, and select New/Virtual Directory.

3. On the General tab, give the virtual directory a name (as in Figure 22-2), which must be used as part of the URL in a browser. Then assign a local path for the virtual directory (as in Figure 22-2). Please note that you must create the path manually if it doesn't already exist.

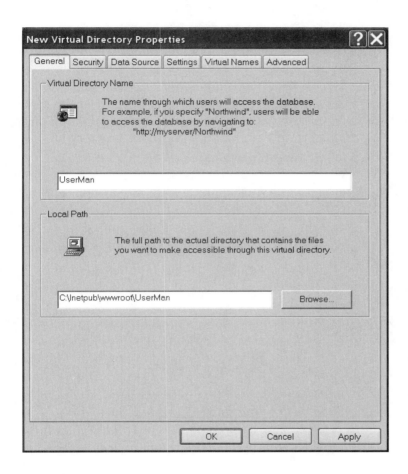

Figure 22-2. The General tab of the New Virtual Directory Properties dialog box

4. Click the Security tab. Here you'll enter the user credentials you want to use to connect to SQL Server (see Figure 22-3).

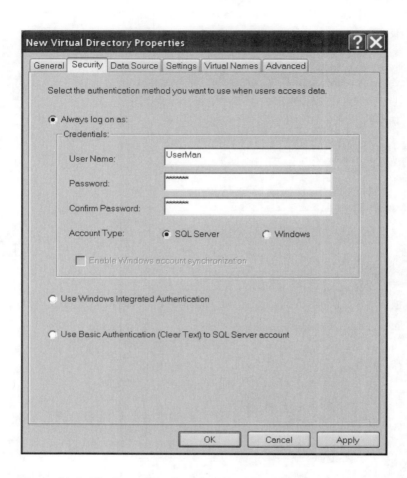

Figure 22-3. The Security tab of the New Virtual Directory Properties dialog box

5. Click the Data Source tab to indicate which SQL Server to access. You can also select which default database to use on the specified server (see Figure 22-4).

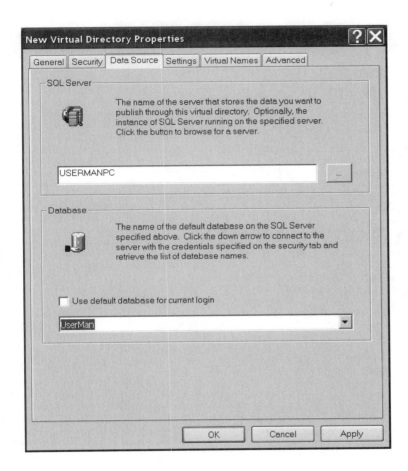

Figure 22-4. The Data Source tab of the New Virtual Directory Properties dialog box

6. On the Settings tab, you'll need to change one default setting (Figure 22-5):
Check the Allow sql= . . . or template= . . . URL queries check box.

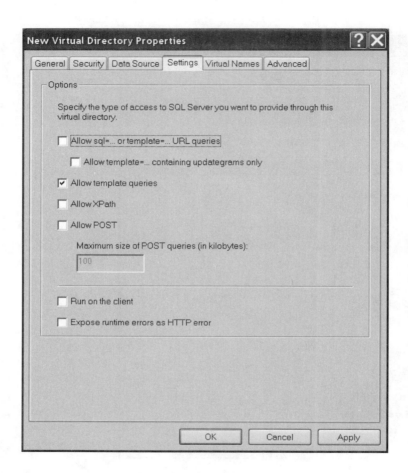

Figure 22-5. The Settings tab of the Virtual Directory Properties dialog box

In Figure 22-2, you can see General tab of the New Virtual Directory Properties dialog box. You need to give the virtual directory a name that can be used from an HTTP-capable application (a browser, for example) to access the content of the virtual directory. You also need to assign a local path where file content is stored.

In the Security tab of the New Virtual Directory Properties dialog box, shown in Figure 22-3, enter the user credentials you want to use to connect to SQL Server. You can use Windows Integrated Authentication, which means you need to log on as an existing user in Windows network; Basic Authentication, which means that the user needs to provide a user name and password (typically done in an HTTP form) that is sent as clear text (nonencrypted) to SQL Server for validation as a SQL Server login; or specify that you always want to use the same login, either Windows or SQL Server. The option you choose really depends on your setup, but I've chosen to always use the UserMan SQL Server login, as shown in Figure 22-3.

Figure 22-4 shows the Data Source tab of the New Virtual Directory Properties dialog box. This is where you specify which SQL Server to access and, optionally, which default database to use on the specified server. You'll need to type in the SQL Server you want to use for your virtual directory. You can also browse to the server by clicking the Browse button next to the textbox in the SQL Server frame. I've used USERMANPC, as shown in Figure 22-4, because I installed SQLXML on my development machine, which doesn't have SQL Server installed. You can also select a different default database if the supplied credentials on the Security tab give you a "wrong" default database. I recommend you use the Browse button for this purpose, because this way you ensure that the connection, security settings, database name, and so on are confirmed. The default database is the database that is used when you log on—don't change it. I have chosen the UserMan database as my default database.

There are other options that you can set, but the ones already shown are the only ones that aren't optional. However, for the purpose of the exercises later in this chapter, you need to change one default setting on the Settings tab, as shown in Figure 22-5. On the Settings tab, check the Allow sql=... or template=... URL queries check box for some of the queries later in this chapter.

Restarting the Virtual Directory Application

When you've made changes to your virtual directory, it's always a good idea to restart it to make sure that your changes are applied immediately. You can restart the virtual directory application by right-clicking the virtual directory in the IIS Virtual Directory Management for SQLXML 3.0 MMC snap-in. You can see the virtual directory selected in Figure 22-6. From the pop-up menu, click Restart Application and click Yes in the confirmation dialog box. Now a dialog box with either a success message or an error message is displayed. Click OK to close the message box.

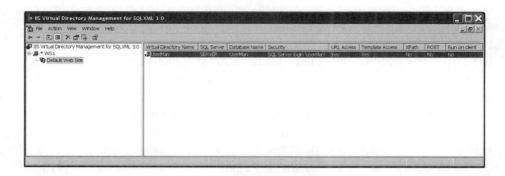

Figure 22-6. Virtual directory selected in the IIS Virtual Directory Management for SQLXML 3.0 MMC snap-in

When you restart the virtual directory application this way, the application is unloaded from memory and actually not restarted until the next time it's accessed.

Besides restarting your virtual directory application, you should close any browser windows you've been employing to query your SQL Server database using SQLXML 3.0.

Testing the ISAPI Extension

Once you've configured the ISAPI extension, you can test it using your browser. My first idea was to browse to the URL I specified during the ISAPI configuration, which is `http://localhost/userman`. Because I didn't specify a query to execute, which is really what this is all about, I get a standard HTTP 400 Bad Request error: "The page cannot be found", as shown in Figure 22-7.

Please see the following sections for information on how to specify queries from your browser.

Figure 22-7. Browsing to the new virtual directory

Executing a Direct Query from a Browser

Now let's see if you can actually execute a query directly from your browser. "Directly" in this case means without a template—just a simple query expressed in the address bar of your browser. The basic syntax is as follows:

```
http://servername/virtualdirectory?sql=
```

where `servername` is the name of the server you've installed SQLXML on, which is localhost in my case. `virtualdirectory` is the name you gave your virtual directory when you set up the virtual directory. (See Figure 22-2 earlier in this chapter.)

The `?sql=` bit is where the fun starts, because this is the actual query. Try this in your browser (don't worry about the lack of URL formatting—IIS and the ISAPI extension take care of it for you):

```
http:/servername/virtualdirectory?sql=SELECT * FROM tblUser FOR XML AUTO
```

If you've done as suggested when setting up the virtual directory, you should now have a browser window that looks similar to the one shown in Figure 22-8.

Figure 22-8. The XML page cannot be displayed

Figure 22-8 shows you what your browser window looks like when executing the query after making sure that URL queries are allowed.[4] The problem here is obviously that the returned XML has several root elements (tblUser). One way of fixing this is to execute this query:

```
http:/servername/virtualdirectory?sql=SELECT * FROM tblUser FOR XML AUTO&root=root
```

Now your browser window should look similar to Figure 22-9.

---

4. I assume that you have a clean system, or you might potentially get a different browser output.

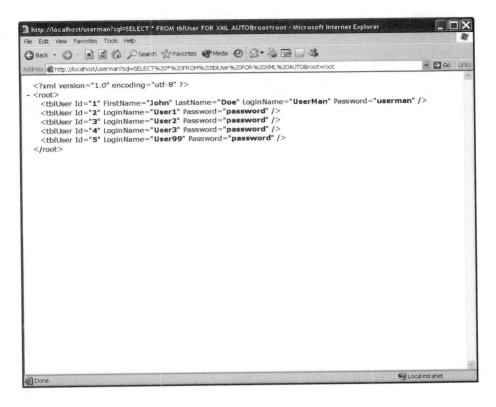

Figure 22-9. The tblUser table displayed as XML in a browser

The query used for producing the results shown in Figure 22-9 ensures that you have a root tag/node, or top-level element as it is called in Figure 22-8. Instead of root=root, you can use root=UserMan, or any other name than UserMan for that matter, as long as it doesn't contain spaces or special characters. This adds a root element by the name you specify.

You can also specify a template directly in the URL. The template in this case is a valid XML document that contains SQL statement(s). You can see the output of such a template query in Figure 22-10.

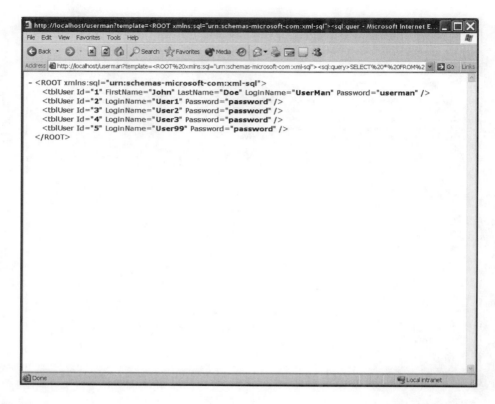

Figure 22-10. The tblUser table displayed as XML using a template directly in the URL

In Figure 22-10, you can see that the output from the template query is almost identical to the output shown in Figure 22-9. The full template statement used in Figure 22-10 looks like the one shown in Listing 22-4.

Listing 22-4. Template Query

```
<ROOT xmlns:sql="urn:schemas-microsoft-com:xml-sql">
   <sql:query>
      SELECT * FROM tblUser
      FOR XML AUTO
   </sql:query>
</ROOT>
```

The full template statement shown in Listing 22-4 has obviously been formatted to make it more readable. In your browser's address bar, it needs to be input as one line, with no carriage return or line feed characters.

Another way of querying the tables in your database is using XPath by first creating the dbobject virtual name. You do this by opening the IIS Virtual Directory Management for SQLXML 3.0 MMC snap-in and double-clicking your virtual directory. This brings up the properties dialog box for the virtual directory. Click the Virtual Names tab in the dialog box. The Virtual Names tab is shown in Figure 22-11.

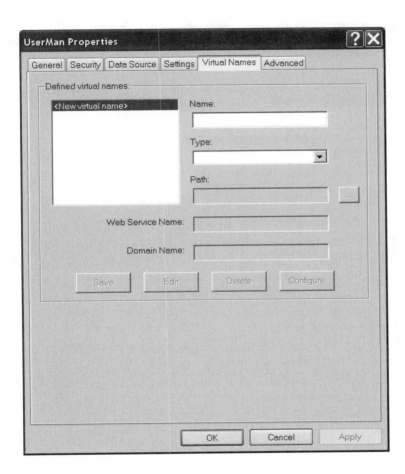

Figure 22-11. The Virtual Names tab of the Virtual Directory Properties dialog box

On the Virtual Names tab you need to create a virtual name for the **dbobject** type. You do this by selecting the New virtual name item on the list and typing in the name of your new **dbobject** type in the Name textbox of the Virtual Names tab.

In Figure 22-12, you can see that you need to select the **dbobject** item from the Type list. Click Save once you've done this to make sure your changes are saved before moving on. You also need to make sure that XPath queries are allowed by checking the Allow XPath check box on the Settings tab of the properties dialog box. Close the properties dialog box. Now you can try this direct database object query from your browser:

```
http://localhost/userman/DBObject/tblUser/@LoginName?root=UserMan
```

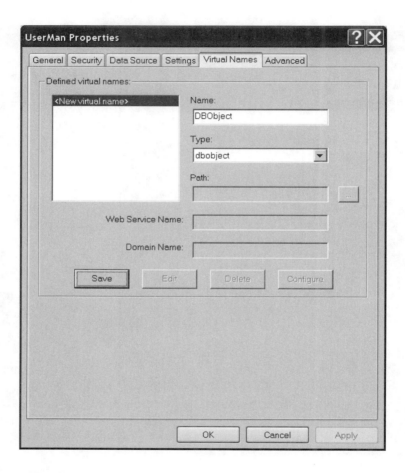

Figure 22-12. A new virtual name

 NOTE You can find a detailed description of XPath 1.0 at http://www.w3.org/TR/xpath, and a working draft for XPath 2.0 at http://www.w3.org/TR/xpath20.

If your browser doesn't display any output, you might have to restart the virtual directory application for the changes to be applied immediately. See the "Restarting the Virtual Directory Application" section earlier in this chapter. Otherwise, all the values from the LoginName column of the tblUser table are shown in your browser window as one long line of text without spaces to separate the various values. Actually, only nonnull values are displayed. You can use the DBObject virtual name for querying objects in your database, such as tables and views. Let's take a look at the previous query:

- *localhost:* This is the name of the Web server.

- *userman:* This is the name of your virtual directory.

- *DBObject:* This is the virtual name used for querying table objects directly using XPath.

- *tblUser:* This is the name of the table or view you want to query.

- *@LoginName:* This is the column name you want displayed.

- *?root=UserMan:* This specifies the name (UserMan) of the root element. This is required in SQLXML 3.0, whereas it wasn't in SQLXML 2.0.

All of the elements shown are required, but you can actually limit the output by specifying a valid value for any column in the table or view you query. For example, say you want to retrieve the LoginName for the user with an ID of 1 from the tblUser table. This is how your query should look:

```
http://localhost/userman/DBObject/tblUser[@Id=1]/@LoginName?root=UserMan
```

The optional predicate, which must be enclosed in brackets as shown, should be used when you only want a single value returned, because when you specify the predicate all values except for the first one are ignored.

Security Concern with Direct URL Queries

One problem with the direct query or template query approach is that it is a security concern. Basically, anyone can execute queries on your SQL Server, including action queries or non–row-returning queries. A better approach is to use templates directly, so for your own sake, please uncheck the Allow sql=... or template=... URL queries check box on the Settings tab of the Virtual Directory Properties dialog box and click OK. You might have to restart the virtual directory application for the changes to be applied immediately. See the "Restarting the Virtual Directory Application" section earlier in this chapter.

Executing a Query from the Browser Using File-Based Templates

Instead of executing queries and templates directly from a URL, it's much safer to provide some templates that users can execute. This way, you know exactly what kind of queries will be executed, because you can manage the templates. Before moving on, you need to make sure that the Allow template queries check box shown in Figure 22-5 is checked. Otherwise, you won't be allowed to execute file-based queries. You also need to define a virtual name for a template folder before you can execute any template from the folder. You do this by opening the IIS Virtual Directory Management for SQLXML 3.0 MMC snap-in and double-clicking your virtual directory. This brings up the properties dialog box for the virtual directory. Click the Virtual Names tab in the dialog box. (The Virtual Names tab is shown in Figure 22-11.)

On the Virtual Names tab you need to create a virtual name for the template folder. However, I recommend creating a subfolder for holding your templates first, because you can't create a new folder from this dialog box. Open Windows Explorer and create a subfolder in the UserMan folder with the name Templates. Basically, what you need to do is associate a virtual name with the new physical subfolder. You do this on the Virtual Names tab, where you select the New virtual name item on the list and type in the name of your new subfolder, Templates, in the Name textbox. You can see this in Figure 22-13.

In Figure 22-13 you can see that you also need to select the template item on the Type list and type in the new subfolder name or browse to the new subfolder. Click Save once you've done this and close the properties dialog box. Now try out the file-based template functionality. You can type the template shown in Listing 22-4 into any text editor, such as Notepad, or even an XML editor, and save it as the file AllUsers.xml in the physical folder that maps to your Templates virtual directory. Then you can test it from your browser, as shown in Figure 22-14. Well, you might need to change the URL slightly so it reads

```
http://localhost/userman/templates/allusers.xml
```

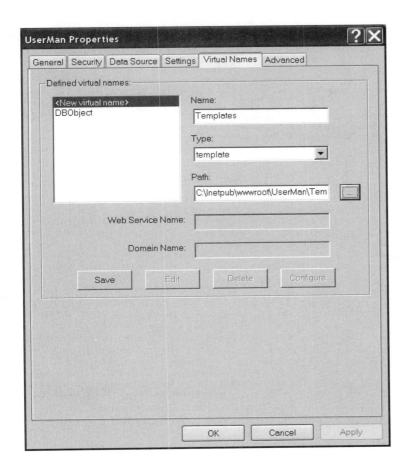

Figure 22-13. The new virtual template folder

This URL consists of the server name (localhost), the virtual directory (userman), the virtual template name (templates), and the name of a template (allusers.xml).

Does your browser window look like the one shown in Figure 22-14? If not, you might have to restart the virtual directory application. See the "Restarting the Virtual Directory Application" section earlier in this chapter.

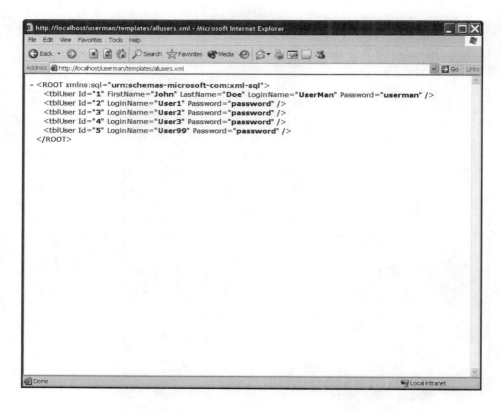

Figure 22-14. Successful output from executing a file-based template from a browser

As you can see from Figure 22-14, you simply need to add an XML document template, such as the AllUsers.xml one created earlier, and stick it in the Templates folder. Then your users can run the templates against your SQL Server data source.

Now, the template created earlier is fairly simple, but you can also create query templates that accept parameters, as shown in Listing 22-5.

Listing 22-5. Template Query with Parameters

```
<ROOT xmlns:sql="urn:schemas-microsoft-com:xml-sql">
  <sql:header>
    <sql:param name='LName'></sql:param>
  </sql:header>
  <sql:query>
    SELECT *
    FROM tblUser
    WHERE LastName = @LName
    FOR XML AUTO
  </sql:query>
</ROOT>
```

In Listing 22-5 I've created a query that accepts one parameter, LName. Parameters must be defined in the sql:header section of the template using a sql:param tag for each parameter. You can't specify the data type, and as such, all parameters are strings. SQL Server takes care of converting the passed parameter if it doesn't match the data type in the column being compared with the parameter. An XML error message is returned if the parameter is of a wrong data type.

Save the query in Listing 22-5 to a text file named Users.xml in the Templates folder, and run the following query from your browser:

```
http://localhost/userman/templates/users.xml?LName=Doe
```

Does your browser window now look like the one shown in Figure 22-15?

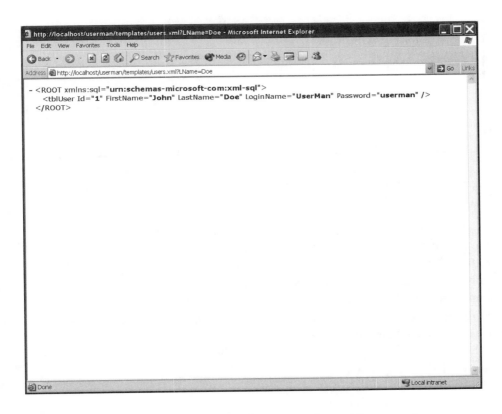

Figure 22-15. Successful browser output from a template with parameters

This is all very simple, because you specified that you want all users with a last name of Doe to be returned and that's that. What happens when you don't specify a value for LName? Run the query without specifying it, and your browser should now look like Figure 22-16.

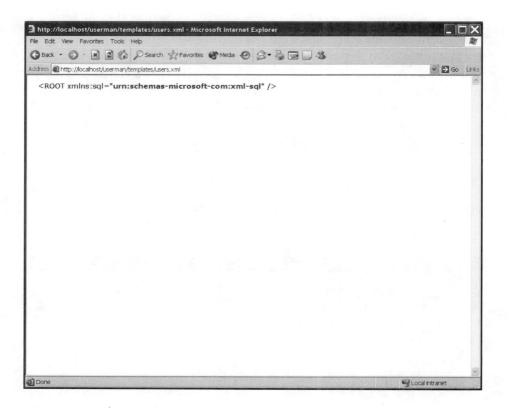

Figure 22-16. No rows returned from a template with blank parameter values

It's pretty evident what happens in Figure 22-16, isn't it? None of the rows in the tblUser table has a LastName of "" (empty string). If you were to add one row to the table with an empty string stored in the LastName column, you would have one row returned. However, you can specify a default value if the user running the template doesn't specify one. If you look at Line 3 in Listing 22-5, you'll notice that nothing has been typed in between the opening and closing sql:param tags. You can add a value here, such as Doe, which means that if the user doesn't specify a value in the URL, all users with a last name of Doe are returned. Change the third line of Listing 22-5 to this:

```
<sql:param name='LName'>Doe</sql:param>
```

So if you specify the following query in your browser, the output should look as in Figure 22-15:

```
http://localhost/userman/templates/users.xml
```

Executing a Stored Procedure from the Browser Using File-Based Templates

With the introduction of SQLXML 3.0, Microsoft has also made it possible to execute stored procedures from a browser, using templates. The UserMan database contains the uspGetUsers stored procedure, so let's try and create a template for executing it. Listing 22-6 shows the finished XML template.

Listing 22-6. A Stored Procedure XML Template

```
<ROOT xmlns:sql="urn:schemas-microsoft-com:xml-sql">
  <sql:query client-side-xml="1">
    EXEC uspGetUsers FOR XML NESTED
  </sql:query>
</ROOT>
```

The template in Listing 22-6 is pretty simple and it looks like the ones shown previously in this chapter. However, there are two differences:

- The `client-side-xml="1"` attribute setting, which dictates the XML formatting of the result set must be applied client-side. Please see the "Client-Side vs. Server-Side XML Formatting" section later in this chapter for more information on client-side vs. server-side XML formatting.

- The query is still T-SQL syntax, but instead of a SELECT query, it's now an EXEC statement followed by the name of the uspGetUsers stored procedure. Finally, I've added the FOR XML NESTED statement to the query.

Okay, so it's the query that's different, but not really any different from any T-SQL code executing a stored procedure. Well, there's the FOR XML NESTED statement appended to the standard T-SQL statement, but it goes without saying that you need this in order to return an XML-formatted result set. This is how you can execute the template from your browser (assuming you've saved Listing 22-6 in a file called uspGetUsers.xml in the \InetPub\wwwroot\UserMan\Templates folder):

```
http://localhost/userman/templates/uspGetUsers.xml
```

The output from the query is shown in Figure 22-17.

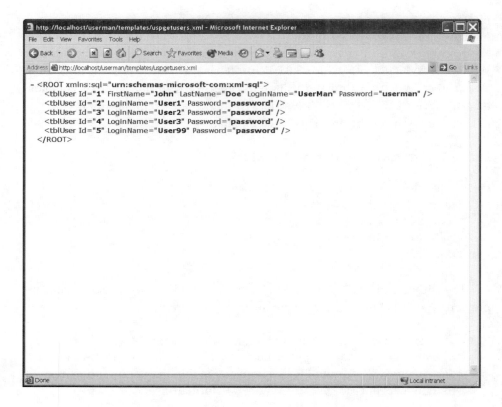

Figure 22-17. Output from the uspGetUsers Stored Procedure

The output shown is Figure 22-17 is no different from that in Figure 22-14 simply because beneath all the templates and stored procedure, it's really the same query that's being executed.

As you'll see from Table 22-2 later in this chapter, output from stored procedures can only be XML-formatted client-side output. This means that you can't leave out the **client-side-xml** attribute, or set the value to 0 to indicate server-side XML formatting. Also, you can't change the FOR XML NESTED statement to FOR XML AUTO to have SQL Server apply the formatting. If you do either of the two things mentioned, you'll get the output that is shown in Figure 22-18 in your browser from executing the template.

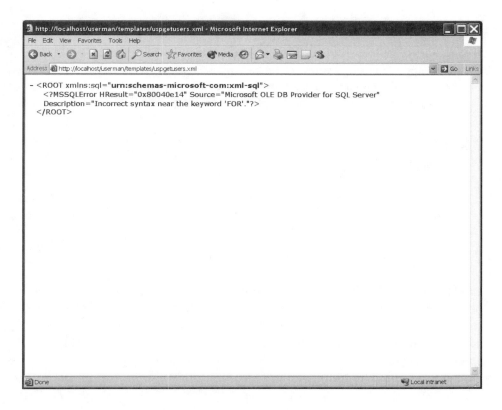

Figure 22-18. Output from the uspGetUsers.xml template when applying server-side XML formatting

As you can see from Figure 22-18, you get an error if you try to apply XML formatting to the output from a stored procedure at the server side. This is inconsistent with the behavior that occurs when running Listing 22-6. I'm not saying it's necessarily a bad thing, but it's hard to apply any logic to this inconsistent behavior.

NOTE   It would be handy if you can have the stored procedure apply the XML formatting by adding the FOR XML AUTO statement to a SELECT statement, and this is possible. You can still apply XML formatting to the client side, but you can also take out the FOR XML NESTED statement from the T-SQL statement and change the value for the **client-side-xml** attribute to 0.

Naming Security Issues

In this chapter I'm using names for the XML templates and virtual directories that resemble the database object they query, such as the uspGetUsers.xml template file that executes the uspGetUsers stored procedure. I've done this to make it easier for you to follow along, but it's really not a particularly good idea; it makes it possible for your users or, even worse, uninvited guests to guess the actual names of your database objects. So, visualize my finger pointing in the air while I state "Don't do it.. . ."

Client-Side vs. Server-Side XML Formatting

SQLXML 3.0 lets you specify where you want the formatting of your XML queries done; on the client side or on the server side. Normally, you consider using client-side vs. server-side processing as a result of performance, bandwidth, workload, and other criteria.[5] However, with SQLXML 3.0 there are other things to consider, namely the fact that certain functionality is only available on the client side or server side, as shown in Table 22-2.

Table 22-2. XML Functionality Availability

Functionality	Client-Side	Server-Side
GROUP BY clause	Yes	No
Aggregate functions (AVG, BINARY_CHECKSUM, CHECKSUM, CHECKSUM_AGG, COUNT, COUNT_BIG, GROUPING, MAX, MIN, SUM, STDEV, STDEVP, VAR, VARP)	Yes	No
Execute stored procedures	Yes	No
Query returning multiple result sets	No	Yes

So when you want to use the functionality specified in Table 22-2, make sure you specify the appropriate place to process your query, as discussed in the next section.

---

5. See the "Optimization Issues" section in Chapter 16 for a discussion of client-side vs. server-side processing.

Specifying Where to Format Your Query Result

Depending on how you execute your queries, there are different options for specifying where the XML formatting should occur. Please see the following sections for more information on the various ways of executing your query.

Direct Browser Queries Formatting Rules

In Table 22-1 shows that you can use the AUTO or NESTED keywords to indicate that a query should have XML formatting applied to the server side or client side. This indicates that you can execute direct queries from your browser and have the query decided where the XML formatting takes place. However, that isn't the case, because when you set a virtual directory, you can also specify where the XML formatting takes place. By default it takes place on the server side, but you can change that. Please see the "Internet Information Services Virtual Directory Formatting Settings" section later in this chapter for more information on how to do so.

This means that the following two queries will be submitted for processing and XML formatting on the server:

```
SELECT * FROM tblUser FOR XML AUTO
SELECT * FROM tblUser FOR XML NESTED
```

However, because SQL Server doesn't recognize the NESTED keyword, an error will occur. So if you want to execute the second query, you need to change the default behavior for the XML formatting location, as discussed in the "Internet Information Services Virtual Directory Formatting Settings" section later in this chapter.

Okay, so let's assume that you have set the default behavior for the XML formatting location to occur on the client side, and you run the two queries again.[6] Do you get an error on the first query, because it's supposed to have the XML formatting applied at the server? No you don't, and this is inconsistent with the behavior you get when you apply the formatting on the server side. The problem is how the SQLXMLOLEDB provider reads the query; if it detects the AUTO keyword, the query is sent for processing and XML formatting to the server, despite the default behavior for the XML formatting location. This issue has been raised with Microsoft, but I get the feeling that it's not an "issue," it's a feature.

---

6. It's a good idea to restart the virtual directory if you do make these kinds of changes.

Template Queries Formatting Rules

When you use templates for executing your XML queries from a browser,[7] you can specify the **client-side-xml** attribute as part of the **sql:query** node in your template with a value of 1 to indicate that the XML formatting must be done on the client side. So, if you want Listing 22-4 modified so that it applies the XML formatting on the client side instead of on the server side, your template must look like the one shown in Listing 22-7.

Listing 22-7. Template Query with Client-Side XML Formatting

```
<ROOT xmlns:sql="urn:schemas-microsoft-com:xml-sql">
   <sql:query client-side-xml="1">
      SELECT * FROM tblUser
      FOR XML AUTO
   </sql:query>
</ROOT>
```

In Listing 22-7, the value of 1 for the **client-side-xml** attribute of the **sql:query** node ensures that the XML formatting of the query result is done on the client side. If you set the value to 0, the formatting is done on the server side.

Are you with me this far? Good, but I also hear you ask why I use the AUTO keyword in the SELECT statement, because this keyword is supposed to be used with server-side formatting. You're absolutely right; you really should use the NESTED keyword instead of the AUTO keyword for applying the XML formatting on the client side. So, what's the deal then? Well, if you run the template in Listing 22-7 from your browser, the output is the same as in Figure 22-14, and if you change AUTO to NESTED you also get the same output. The SQLXMLOLEDB provider ignores the **client-side-xml="1"** attribute setting if you have the AUTO keyword in your query and requests that SQL Server apply the XML formatting. I think this is a problem, because this is inconsistent with the behavior you get when you set the value of the **client-side-xml** attribute to 0 and use the NESTED keyword in your query. In this situation you get an error as shown in Figure 22-19.

---

7. You can also use the SQLXMLOLEDB provider to XML template queries programmatically, but I only cover using the SQLXML 3.0 Managed Classes for this purpose.

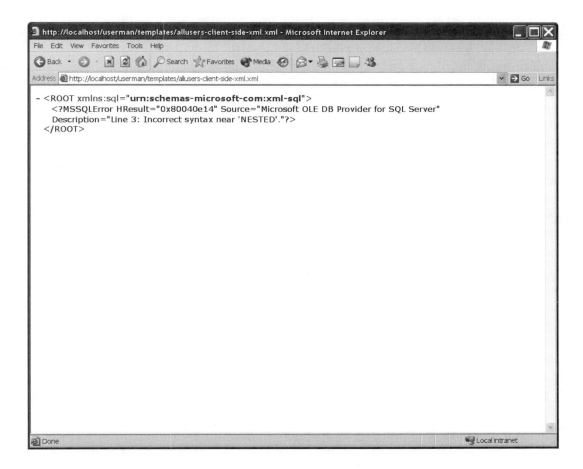

Figure 22-19. The NESTED keyword throws an exception

Because the query was passed for processing *and* XML formatting by SQL Server, and because SQL Server doesn't recognize the NESTED keyword, it only knows the AUTO keyword, so you get the error shown in Figure 22-19. My point is that if you get an error in this situation, you should also get an error when you use the AUTO keyword with the **client-side-xml="1"** attribute setting, but you don't.

If you don't specify the **client-side-xml** attribute, the IIS virtual directory formatting setting goes into effect, which I discuss in the next section, "Internet Information Services Virtual Directory Formatting Settings." If you do specify the **client-side-xml** attribute, it overrides the IIS virtual directory formatting setting.

Internet Information Services Virtual Directory Formatting Settings

In Figure 22-5 you can see the Settings tab of the New Virtual Directory Properties dialog box, and on this tab you have the Run on client check box. The default behavior is server-side XML formatting of the result set(s), so this check box is *not* selected by default. However, you only need to select it, click OK, and restart the virtual directory application[8] to change the XML formatting location to the client side. This setting can be overridden by explicitly specifying the XML formatting location in an XML query template.

SQLXML 3.0 Managed Classes

The SQLXML 3.0 Managed Classes are discussed in the "Inspecting the SQLXML 3.0 Managed Classes" section later in this chapter, but let's just take a quick look at how you specify client-side XML formatting for a result set.

The **SqlXmlCommand** class has a **ClientSideXml** property that sets or returns a **Boolean** value. You must this property to **True**, before executing your query.

Inspecting the SQLXML 3.0 Managed Classes

The SQLXML 3.0 plug-in comes with a set of managed classes that you can use from within the .NET Framework just like any other managed classes. The managed classes can be used to manipulate XML data on a SQL Server. Look at these managed classes as an extra option for manipulating data in SQL Server using XML and not as an alternative to the SQL Server .NET Data Provider. You should use the SQL Server .NET Data Provider, which is discussed in detail in Part Two, when you want to manipulate your SQL Server data using standard relational SQL queries. You should use the SQLXML 3.0 Managed Classes when you want to manipulate your SQL Server data using XML DiffGrams and UpdateGrams.

Basically, the difference between the SQLXML Managed Classes and the SQL Server .NET Data Provider is that the SQLXML Managed Classes can be used to manipulate nonrelational data, whereas the SQL Server .NET Data Provider can't. You can use the SQL Server .NET Data Provider with the XML FOR clause in your SELECT statement to extract data, but you can't execute XPath queries and templates as you can with the SQLXML Managed Classes.

---

8. See the "Restarting the Virtual Directory Application" section earlier in this chapter for information on how to restart the application.

The SQLXML 3.0 Managed Classes use the SQL Server OLE DB provider (SQLOLEDB) for connecting to SQL Server 2000. See Chapter 4 for more information. In order to use the SQLXML Managed Classes, you need to reference the **Microsoft.Data.SqlXml** namespace from your project. Needless to say, you need to install the SQLXML 3.0 plug-in first (see the "Installing SQLXML 3.0" section earlier in this chapter).

The SQLXML Managed Classes include the following classes:

- **SqlXmlParameter**

- **SqlXmlAdapter**

- **SqlXmlCommand**

As you can see by comparing these three classes with the number of classes in the SQL Server .NET Data Provider, SQLXML 3.0 has substantially fewer classes. However, the three classes in SQLXML 3.0 can perform most of the functionality in the SQL Server .NET Data Provider classes. You'll be introduced to the three SQLXML Managed Classes in the following sections. I make references to the equivalent SQL Server .NET Data Provider classes, and you can find detailed descriptions of these classes in Part Two of this book.

Looking at the SqlXmlParameter Class

The **SqlXmlParameter** class is a rather simple class that is used for specifying parameters with your SQL statements. Basically, this class can only be used in conjunction with the **SqlXmlCommand** class (discussed later in this chapter). An object of type **SqlXmlParameter** is instantiated using the **CreateParameter** method of the **SqlXmlCommand** class, like this:

```
Dim prmLastName As SqlXmlParameter = cmdUserMan.CreateParameter()
```

This class has no methods, but it does have two properties, as shown in Table 22-3.

*Table 22-3. **SqlParameter** Class Properties*

Name	Description	Example
Name	This is the name of the property, which must equal the column name you're supplying a value for. Actually, this is only true when you're using named parameters. If you specify your parameters with a question mark (?), you don't have to give your parameters a name, but instead you must make sure that you add the parameters by calling the **CreateParameter** method in the order the parameters appear in the query (counting from left to right).	prmLastName.Name = "LastName"
Value	This mandatory value is what you want to pass as the parameter. You don't have to specify the single quotes when the column you're querying is a string column; the parameter class takes care of it for you.	prmLastName.Value = "Doe" prmLastName.Value = "'Doe'"

Refer to Listings 22-18 and 22-19 in the "Looking at the SqlXmlCommand Class" section later in this chapter for some example code that shows you how to use the **SqlXmlParameter** class.

Looking at the SqlXmlAdapter Class

The **SqlXmlAdapter** class serves the same purpose as the **SqlDataAdapter** class, but it has no properties and only two noninherited methods. The two methods are **Fill** and **Update**, which I'm sure you recognize from the **SqlDataAdapter** class. See the "Retrieving SQL Server Data Using the SqlXmlAdapter Class" and "Updating SQL Server Data Using the SqlXmlAdapter Class" sections later in this chapter. The **SqlXmlAdapter** class can only work with the **DataSet** class for retrieving and updating data in your data source.

Another difference between the **SqlDataAdapter** and **SqlXmlAdapter** classes is the constructors for the class, as you'll see in the next section.

Instantiating a SqlXmlAdapter Object

The **SqlXmlAdapter** class can be instantiated in three different ways:

- Using a **SqlXmlCommand** class as the only argument. You must make sure that the **SqlXmlCommand** object (cmdUserMan) has been instantiated before you execute any of the methods of the **SqlXmlAdapter** class.

```
Dim dadUserMan As New SqlXmlAdapter(cmdUserMan)
```

- Using a command text string (strCommandText), a **SqlXmlCommandType** enum member, and a connection string (strConnectionString).

```
Dim dadUserMan As New SqlXmlAdapter(strCommandText, _
    SqlXmlCommandType.Sql, strConnectionString)
```

- Using a command stream (stmCommand), a **SqlXmlCommandType** enum member, and a connection string (strConnectionString).

```
Dim dadUserMan As New SqlXmlAdapter(stmCommand, _
    SqlXmlCommandType.Sql, strConnectionString)
```

It's beyond the scope of this book to work with streams, so I won't cover how to use a stream to instantiate a **SqlXmlAdapter** object, but besides that, here is a list of the various arguments:

- *cmdUserMan:* This must be an instantiated and initialized **SqlXmlCommand** object. See the "Looking at the SqlXmlCommand Class" section later in this chapter.

- *SqlXmlCommandType enum:* Use one of the following members: DiffGram, Sql (default), Template, TemplateFile, UpdateGram, or XPath. You'll see how to use these enum members later in this chapter.

- *strConnectionString:* Well, this one is pretty obvious, as it's really an OLE DB provider connection string. Please see the "ConnectionString Property" section in Chapter 5 for more information. Listing 22-8 shows you the one I use for the example code in the SQLXML 3.0 section.

Listing 22-8. A SQLXML 3.0 Connection String

```
1 Private Const PR_STR_CONNECTION_STRING As String = _
2    "Provider=SQLOLEDB;Data Source=USERMANPC;User Id=UserMan;" & _
3    "Password=userman;Initial Catalog=UserMan"
```

In Listing 22-8 you can see how I've set up the connection string to be used with the SQLXML 3.0 Managed Classes. Basically, it's just another OLE DB connection string.

Retrieving SQL Server Data Using the SqlXmlAdapter Class

There are two ways to retrieve data from your SQL Server and place it into your **DataSet** object: with or without a Command object. Listing 22-9 shows you how to do it both ways.

*Listing 22-9. Populating a **DataSet** Using the **SqlXmlAdapter***

```
1 Public Sub PopulateDataSetUsingSql()
2    ' Declare SELECT statement
3    Dim strSQL As String = "SELECT * FROM tblUser FOR XML AUTO, ELEMENTS"
4    ' Declare and instantiate DataSet
5    Dim dstUserMan As New DataSet("UserMan")
6    ' Declare, instantiate and initialize command
7    Dim cmdUser As New SqlXmlCommand(PR_STR_CONNECTION_STRING)
8    cmdUser.CommandText = strSQL
9
10   ' Declare and instantiate adapters
11   Dim dadUserMan1 As New SqlXmlAdapter(cmdUser)
12   Dim dadUserMan2 As New SqlXmlAdapter(strSQL, _
13      SqlXmlCommandType.Sql, PR_STR_CONNECTION_STRING)
14
15   ' Fill DataSet. Uncomment one of the lines below
16   ' and comment out the other to test either
17   dadUserMan1.Fill(dstUserMan)
18   'dadUserMan2.Fill(dstUserMan)
19 End Sub
```

In Listing 22-9 you can see how the two **SqlXmlAdapter**s, dadUserMan1 and dadUserMan2, are used to populate the dstUserMan **DataSet** object. If you notice the SELECT statement saved in the strSQL variable on Line 3, you'll see that I have specified , ELEMENTS as the last part of the SELECT statement. I've done this because otherwise the adapter will complain about too many root elements in the returned XML document. See Table 22-1 for an explanation of the ELEMENTS keyword. Remove the , ELEMENTS part of the statement and run the code to see an exception being thrown. Basically, what happens is that now all the rows returned are returned as elements, or rather subelements of the table element, which is then the root element.

If you leave out the ELEMENTS keyword in the SELECT statement, you can't use the dadUserMan2 DataAdapter (Line 18) for populating your **DataSet**, because there's no way of getting around the "missing" root element. However, when you use the dadUserMan1 adapter that is instantiated using a **SqlXmlCommand** object, you can actually set the **RootTag** property of the Command object and thus specify a root element to be used in the returned XML document. See Listing 22-10 for an example of this.

*Listing 22-10. Populating a DataSet Using the **SqlXmlAdapter** and **SqlXmlCommand** Classes*

```
1 Public Sub PopulateDataSetUsingSql2()
2   ' Declare SELECT statement
3   Dim strSQL As String = "SELECT * FROM tblUser FOR XML AUTO"
4   ' Declare and instantiate DataSet
5   Dim dstUserMan As New DataSet("UserMan")
6   ' Declare, instantiate and initialize command
7   Dim cmdUser As New SqlXmlCommand(PR_STR_CONNECTION_STRING)
8   cmdUser.CommandText = strSQL
9   ' You need to set the RootTag property, otherwise
10  ' there is no root tag and an exception
11  ' is thrown
12  cmdUser.RootTag = "UserMan"
13
14  ' Declare and instantiate adapter
15  Dim dadUserMan1 As New SqlXmlAdapter(cmdUser)
16
17  ' Fill DataSet
18  dadUserMan1.Fill(dstUserMan)
19 End Sub
```

In Listing 22-10, which is almost the same as the example code for the dadUserMan1 DataAdapter in Listing 22-8, I've used a SELECT statement (Line 3) without the ELEMENTS keyword, but instead used the **RootTag** property (Line 12) of the **SqlXmlCommand** class to specify the root element of the returned XML document.

So far you've seen how to use a straightforward SELECT statement with the XML-specific SQL Server 2000 keywords appended (FOR XML . . .). However, you have other options. One option is to use a template string instead of a SQL query string, as Listing 22-11 shows.

*Listing 22-11. Populating a **DataSet** Using the **SqlXmlAdapter** and a Template String*

```
1 Public Sub PopulateDataSetUsingStringTemplate()
2   ' Declare template
3   Dim strTemplate As String = _
4     "<ROOT xmlns:sql='urn:schemas-microsoft-com:xml-sql'>" & _
5     "<sql:query>" & "SELECT * FROM tblUser FOR XML AUTO" & _
6     "</sql:query>" & "</ROOT>"
7   ' Declare and instantiate DataSet
8   Dim dstUserMan As New DataSet("UserMan")
9
```

```
10    ' Declare and instantiate adapter
11    Dim dadUserMan As New SqlXmlAdapter(strTemplate, _
12      SqlXmlCommandType.Template, PR_STR_CONNECTION_STRING)
13
14    ' Fill DataSet
15    dadUserMan.Fill(dstUserMan)
16 End Sub
```

In Listing 22-11 the **SqlXmlAdapter** is instantiated with a template string (strTemplate) and the **Template** member of the **SqlXmlCommandType** enum (Line 12), which means that you execute an XML template in the form of a template string containing a SQL query instead of a SQL query.

If you look closer at the content of the strTemplate variable, you'll find that it's actually the same as the template query specified in Listing 22-4. The template in Listing 22-4 was used for executing from your browser's address bar, whereas Listing 22-11 shows you how to do the exact same thing using the SQLXML 3.0 Managed Classes. The output from Listing 22-4 is shown in Figure 22-9, and if you add the code in Listing 22-12 as Line 16 in Listing 22-9 and open the C:\ReturnedDocument.xml XML document, you can verify that it is the same output.

Listing 22-12. Writing an XML Document to Disk

```
dstUserMan.WriteXml("C:\ReturnedDocument.xml")
```

One thing you have to be careful about with the template string method is that the content of the strTemplate variable isn't checked, meaning you can have all sorts of invalid characters and so on in the string. The problem—or maybe it isn't a problem to you—is that no exception is thrown, so you have to spot this in a different way. One very simple way is to check the number of tables in the **DataSet** after you've executed the **Fill** method, like this:

```
MsgBox(dstUserMan.Tables.Count.ToString())
```

If the message box shows 0, then there's probably something wrong with your query template string, and if it shows 1, then it's probably working. I know this is simple, but it gives you an idea as to how to find out about possible problems: You check the content of your **DataSet**.

So far, so good, but you can also execute the same query (Listing 22-4) using a file-based template, just as you did from the browser (see Figure 22-14). Listing 22-13 shows you how to execute the file-based XML template from your code.

Listing 22-13. Executing a File-Based XML Template from Code

```
1 Public Sub PopulateDataSetUsingTemplateFile()
2    ' Declare template file
3    Dim strTemplateFile As String = "C:\DBPWVBNET\Chapter 22\" & _
4       "InetPub\wwwroot\UserMan\Templates\AllUsers.xml"
5    ' Declare output file
6    Dim strOutputFile As String = "C:\ReturnedDocument.xml"
7    ' Declare and instantiate DataSet
8    Dim dstUserMan As New DataSet("UserMan")
9
10   ' Declare and instantiate adapter
11   Dim dadUserMan As New SqlXmlAdapter(strTemplateFile, _
12      SqlXmlCommandType.TemplateFile, PR_STR_CONNECTION_STRING)
13
14   ' Fill DataSet
15   dadUserMan.Fill(dstUserMan)
16   ' Write xml document to disk
17   dstUserMan.WriteXml(strOutputFile)
18 End Sub
```

If you compare Listings 22-9, 22-10, and 22-13, you'll find that only real difference among them is that the very same XML template is input as either a string or a file, but the output is the same. If the template file you specify doesn't exist, a **FileNotFoundException** exception is thrown.

The template you executed in Listing 22-13 doesn't take any arguments, but you can execute the XML template shown in Listing 22-5 and get the same result as in Figure 22-15. However, if you replace the filename in Listing 22-13 with the name of the XML template with an argument (Users.xml), you'll have an empty XML document returned. It's empty, or rather, it doesn't have any elements but the ROOT one, because you didn't specify the LName argument (see Lines 3 and 8 of Listing 22-5). The problem is that you can't specify any arguments or parameters with the **SqlXmlAdapter** class. You need to use the **SqlXmlCommand** class for this.

NOTE   Arguments and parameters can't be used with the **SqlXmlAdapter** class; they can only be used with the **SqlXmlCommand** class.

Updating SQL Server Data Using the SqlXmlAdapter Class

If you think back to the **SqlDataAdapter** class introduced in Chapter 8, you'll remember that it's fairly easy to update your data source with changes from your **DataSet**. All you need to do is call the **Update** method of the **SqlDataAdapter** class, so this should be possible with the **SqlXmlAdapter** as well (see Listing 22-14).

*Listing 22-14. Updating the Data Source from a **DataSet***

```
 1 Public Sub UpdateDataSourceFromDataSet()
 2    ' Declare template file
 3    Dim strTemplateFile As String = "C:\DBPWVBNET\Chapter 22\" & _
 4        "InetPub\wwwroot\UserMan\Templates\AllUsers.xml"
 5    ' Declare and instantiate DataSet
 6    Dim dstUserMan As New DataSet("UserMan")
 7
 8    ' Declare and instantiate adapter
 9    Dim dadUserMan As New SqlXmlAdapter(strTemplateFile, _
10        SqlXmlCommandType.TemplateFile, _
11        PR_STR_CONNECTION_STRING)
12    ' Fill DataSet
13    dadUserMan.Fill(dstUserMan)
14    ' Update DataSet
15    dstUserMan.Tables("tblUser").Rows(0)("FirstName") = "Johnny"
16
17    ' Check for changes
18    If dstUserMan.HasChanges() Then
19      Try
20          ' Update data source
21          dadUserMan.Update(dstUserMan)
22      Catch objException As SqlXmlException
23          ' Start reading from beginning of stream
24          objException.ErrorStream.Position = 0
25          ' Read error message
26          Dim strError As String = New StreamReader( _
27              objException.ErrorStream).ReadToEnd()
28          ' Display error message
29          MsgBox(strError)
30      End Try
31    End If
32 End Sub
```

Basically, the example code in Listing 22-14 is the same as in Listing 22-13, except for Lines 14 through 31, where the **DataSet** is updated (the first row in the tblUser table has the FirstName column value set to "Johnny"), the changes are propagated back to the data source, and a possible exception is caught in the exception handler (Lines 22 through 30). The problem with Listing 22-14 is that it doesn't work, because as you can see if you run the example code, there's no mapping schema[9] for the DiffGram. Hmm—so the **SqlXmlAdapter** creates a DiffGram behind the scenes for updating the data source. I cover DiffGrams in the "Looking at the SqlXmlCommand Class" section later in this chapter.

Okay, so Listing 22-14 doesn't work, but can it be fixed? Yes and no. You can't assign a mapping schema to a **SqlXmlAdapter** object directly, only through a **SqlXmlCommand** object, and that's the whole secret; you need to use a **SqlXmlCommand** object to propagate changes back to the data source.

> **NOTE** If you want to use DiffGrams or UpdateGrams with the SQLXML 3.0 Managed Classes, you must use the **SqlXmlCommand** class because the **SqlXmlAdapter** class doesn't support this.

Looking at the SqlXmlCommand Class

The **SqlXmlCommand** class is the richest of the three SQLXML 3.0 Managed Classes because it exposes a number of methods and properties. I won't show you all of the methods and properties, but I will show you how to use most of them. Many of them will be used in various combinations in the example code listed in the following sections.

You can execute a simple row-returning query using the **SqlXmlCommand** class for populating a **DataSet** just as you can using the **SqlXmlAdapter** class (see Listings 22-9 and 22-10). However, the Command class can do much more than the DataAdapter class when it comes to executing queries. See the following sections for more information.

Instantiating a SqlXmlCommand Object

The **SqlXmlCommand** class is instantiated as follows:

```
Dim cmdUser As New SqlXmlCommand(PR_STR_CONNECTION_STRING)
```

This is the only way to instantiate a **SqlXmlCommand** object. You can see an example of this in Listings 22-9 and 22-10.

---

9. The mapping schema takes care of mapping the table schema in the **DataSet** with the table schema in the data source.

Executing a SQL Query

A row-returning query executed by the **SqlXmlCommand** class obviously needs to save the result of the query somewhere. You can see how you can use the Command class in conjunction with the **SqlXmlAdapter** class to save the return result to a **DataSet** in Listings 22-9 and 22-10, but you can also save it to an **XmlReader** class, as in Listing 22-15.

*Listing 22-15. Retrieving a Result Set in **XmlReader***

```
1 Public Sub PopulateXmlReader()
2    ' Declare XmlReader
3    Dim xrdUser As XmlReader
4    ' Declare SELECT statement
5    Dim strSQL As String = "SELECT * FROM tblUser FOR XML AUTO"
6    ' Declare, instantiate and initialize command
7    Dim cmdUser As New SqlXmlCommand(PR_STR_CONNECTION_STRING)
8    cmdUser.CommandText = strSQL
9    ' Retrieve result set in XmlReader
10   xrdUser = cmdUser.ExecuteXmlReader()
11 End Sub
```

In Listing 22-15 you can see how the SQL query declared on Line 5 is used for retrieving a result set from your data source by setting the **CommandText** property of the **SqlXmlCommand** class to the declared query string (Line 8). You don't have to specify the **CommandType** property, because the **SqlXmlCommandType.Sql** enum member is the default. Check out the "XmlReader" section in Chapter 7 for more information about the **XmlReader** class.

Besides saving the result set in an **XmlReader** class, you can save it to a stream, as shown in Listing 22-16. A *stream* is an abstraction of a sequence of bytes, where the abstraction can be a file or any other means of storing sequential data. There are two methods for saving to a stream: one for creating a new stream (**ExecuteStream**) and one for appending the results to an existing stream (**ExecuteToStream**).

Listing 22-16. Saving a Result Set to a Stream

```
1 Public Sub SaveCommandResultToStream()
2    Dim stmUser As Stream
3    Dim smwUser As StreamWriter
4    ' Declare SELECT statement
5    Dim strSQL As String = "SELECT * FROM tblUser FOR XML AUTO"
6    ' Declare, instantiate and initialize command
7    Dim cmdUser As New SqlXmlCommand(PR_STR_CONNECTION_STRING)
8    cmdUser.CommandText = strSQL
```

```
 9     ' You need to set the RootTag property,
10     ' otherwise there is no root tag/element
11     cmdUser.RootTag = "UserMan"
12
13     ' Execute command and save result set in stream
14     stmUser = cmdUser.ExecuteStream()
15     ' Read content of stream into stream reader
16     Dim smrUser As New StreamReader(stmUser)
17
18     ' Create new file to hold the result stream
19     smwUser = New StreamWriter("C:\Users.xml")
20     ' Write the result set to disk
21     smwUser.Write(smrUser.ReadToEnd())
22     ' Flush and close the stream writer
23     smwUser.Flush()
24     smwUser.Close()
25 End Sub
```

In Listing 22-16 I'm using the **ExecuteStream** method of the **SqlXmlCommand** class to save the result set to a stream. The stream is in memory, so I have also set up the example code so that the result set is read from the **Stream** object by a **StreamReader** object (Line 16) and finally written to disk by a **StreamWriter** object (Line 21). The output file, Users.xml, will look like Listing 22-2. You can also use the **Console** class to output the result set to the console, like this:

```
Console.WriteLine(smrUser.ReadToEnd())
```

You can obviously choose not to write the content to disk, but I have done so to enable you to actually see the result set. Using streams and readers, you can manipulate, display, and exchange your XML data in many different ways.

In cases where you have an existing stream of XML data, you might want to append another result set to the existing data. Listing 22-17 shows how to do this.

Listing 22-17. Appending a Result Set to a Stream

```
1 Public Sub AppendCommandResultToStream()
2     Dim stmUser As Stream
3     Dim smwUser As StreamWriter
4     ' Declare SELECT statement
5     Dim strSQL As String = "SELECT * FROM tblUser FOR XML AUTO"
6     ' Declare, instantiate and initialize command
7     Dim cmdUser As New SqlXmlCommand(PR_STR_CONNECTION_STRING)
8     cmdUser.CommandText = strSQL
```

```
 9    ' You need to set the RootTag property, otherwise
10    ' there is no root element to form a valid XML
11    ' document
12    cmdUser.RootTag = "UserMan"
13
14    ' Execute command and save result set in stream
15    stmUser = cmdUser.ExecuteStream()
16    ' Append new result set to existing stream
17    cmdUser.ExecuteToStream(stmUser)
18    ' Read content of stream into stream reader
19    Dim smrUser As New StreamReader(stmUser)
20
21    ' Create new file to hold the result stream
22    smwUser = New StreamWriter("C:\Users.xml")
23    ' Set the stream position to 0
24    stmUser.Position = 0
25    ' Write the result set to disk
26    smwUser.Write(smrUser.ReadToEnd())
27    ' Flush and close the stream writer
28    smwUser.Flush()
29    smwUser.Close()
30 End Sub
```

In Listing 22-17 I reuse the example code from Listing 22-16 and add the call to the **ExecuteToStream** method on Line 17. On Line 24 I make sure that the **Position** property of the **Stream** object (stmUser) is set to 0, because the **ReadToEnd** method reads from the current position in the stream. Basically, if you don't reposition the stream, you'll end up with an empty XML document (Users.xml), because the **ExecuteToStream** method positions the stream at the very end of the stream. As you can see from Listing 22-17, this is the same query I execute on Lines 15 and 17, which also means this is the same result set I add to the stream. If you run Listing 22-17 and open the resulting Users.xml XML document, you'll see that only one result set has been added to stream and then written to disk. Actually, this isn't quite true, because if you add a row to the tblUser table in the UserMan database in between the two calls, this row will also be added to the stream. This means that because the Id attribute of the tblUser element must be unique, the rows that already exist in the stream are rejected. If you look at Figure 22-20, you can see what I mean.

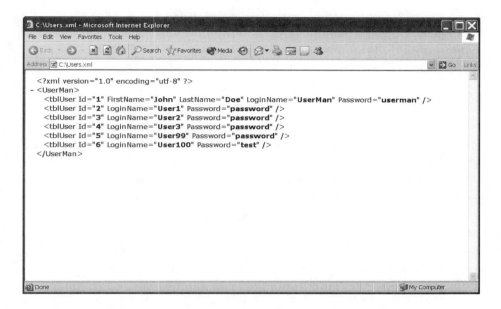

Figure 22-20. Output from Listing 22-15 with an extra row added between method calls

You can see that Figure 22-20 differs from Figure 22-9 by having one extra element—the element with an Id attribute of 6. This row was added to the tblUser table in between the calls to the **ExecuteStream** (Line 15) and the **ExecuteToStream** methods (Line 17).

In this section you saw how to execute standard SQL queries that don't take arguments or parameters. However, quite often you'll need to execute queries that do take parameters. Please see the following two sections, "Executing a SQL Query with Named Parameters" and "Executing a SQL Query with Positional Parameters," for more information on how to do this.

Executing a SQL Query with Named Parameters

SQL Server supports *named* parameters, meaning parameters that are referred to by name and not position. Listing 22-18 shows you an example of the code from Listing 22-16, in which a named parameter has been added to the query.

Listing 22-18. Executing a Query with Named Parameters

```
1 Public Sub ExecuteNamedParameterCommand()
2    Dim stmUser As Stream
3    Dim smwUser As StreamWriter
4    Dim prmLastName As SqlXmlParameter
5    ' Declare SELECT statement
6    Dim strSQL As String = "SELECT * FROM tblUser " & _
7        "WHERE LastName=LastName FOR XML AUTO"
8    ' Declare, instantiate and initialize command
9    Dim cmdUser As New SqlXmlCommand(PR_STR_CONNECTION_STRING)
10   cmdUser.CommandText = strSQL
11   ' You need to set the RootTag property, otherwise
12   ' there is no root element to form a valid XML
13   ' document
14   cmdUser.RootTag = "UserMan"
15   ' Add named parameter and set properties
16   prmLastName = cmdUser.CreateParameter()
17   prmLastName.Name = "LastName"
18   prmLastName.Value = "Doe"
19   ' Execute command and save result set in stream
20   stmUser = cmdUser.ExecuteStream()
21   ' Read content of stream into stream reader
22   Dim smrUser As New StreamReader(stmUser)
23
24   ' Create new file to hold the result stream
25   smwUser = New StreamWriter("C:\Users.xml")
26   ' Write the result set to disk
27   smwUser.Write(smrUser.ReadToEnd())
28   ' Flush and close the stream writer
29   smwUser.Flush()
30   smwUser.Close()
31 End Sub
```

In Listing 22-18 you can see how the query has been set up to accept a named parameter (Lines 6 and 7) and a named parameter is added to the **SqlXmlCommand** object using the **CreateParameter** method (Line 16). On Line 17 I set the name of the parameter, which must equal the name of column you're using the parameter on, and on Line 18 I tell the parameter to only retrieve rows for which the LastName column entry equals "Doe". The simple example in Listing 22-18 is the same as executing this query:

```
SELECT * FROM tblUser WHERE LastName='Doe' FOR XML AUTO"
```

NOTE It doesn't matter if you add single quotes to the **Value** property of the **SqlXmlParameter** class when the parameter is a string column, because the parameter class takes care of this.

Figure 22-21 shows you the resulting XML document from Listing 22-18 in a browser.

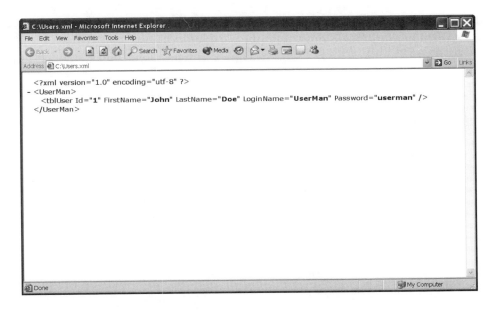

Figure 22-21. Output from Listing 22-18

NOTE If you don't supply a parameter—for example, if you comment out Lines 16 through 18 in Listing 22-18—all rows from the tblUser table will be returned. This is also true if you have more than one parameter and you only supply some of the parameters. The fact that all rows are returned when one or more parameter values are missing is in contrast to working with positional parameters (see Listing 22-19), where an exception is thrown if you don't supply the parameters.

Executing a SQL Query with Positional Parameters

Instead of using named parameters when executing a query, you can use *positional* parameters, meaning that the order in which they're added to the Command object must match the order in which they occur in the query, counting from left to right. For example, consider the following query:

```
SELECT * FROM tblUser
WHERE LastName=LastName AND FirstName=FirstName FOR XML AUTO"
```

In this query you must first add a parameter for the LastName column and then the FirstName column. If you do it the other way around, you won't find any matching rows (unless you reverse the parameter values as well). Anyway, Listing 22-19 shows you how to execute a query with positional parameters.

Listing 22-19. Executing a Query with Positional Parameters

```
1 Public Sub ExecutePositionalParameterCommand()
2    Dim stmUser As Stream
3    Dim smwUser As StreamWriter
4    Dim prmLastName, prmFirstName As SqlXmlParameter
5    ' Declare SELECT statement
6    Dim strSQL As String = "SELECT * FROM tblUser WHERE LastName=? " & _
7       "AND FirstName=? FOR XML AUTO"
8    ' Declare, instantiate and initialize command
9    Dim cmdUser As New SqlXmlCommand(PR_STR_CONNECTION_STRING)
10   cmdUser.CommandText = strSQL
11   ' You need to set the RootTag property, otherwise
12   ' there is no root element to form a valid XML
13   ' document
14   cmdUser.RootTag = "UserMan"
15   ' Add positional parameters and set value properties
16   prmLastName = cmdUser.CreateParameter()
17   prmLastName.Value = "Doe"
18   prmFirstName = cmdUser.CreateParameter()
19   prmFirstName.Value = "John"
20   ' Execute command and save result set in stream
21   stmUser = cmdUser.ExecuteStream()
22   ' Read content of stream into stream reader
23   Dim smrUser As New StreamReader(stmUser)
24
```

```
25    ' Create new file to hold the result stream
26    smwUser = New StreamWriter("C:\Users.xml")
27    ' Write the result set to disk
28    smwUser.Write(smrUser.ReadToEnd())
29    ' Flush and close the stream writer
30    smwUser.Flush()
31    smwUser.Close()
32 End Sub
```

In Listing 22-19, which produces the same output as Listing 22-18 (see Figure 22-21), I use positional parameters to specify the rows I want returned. I add the LastName parameter first and then the FirstName parameter, because they're specified in that particular order in the query (Lines 6 and 7). I then set only the **Value** property of the two Parameter objects, prmLastName and prmFirstName. Actually, it makes no difference whether or not you specify the **Name** property of the Parameter objects, as is done on Line 17 in Listing 22-18. You can even give the parameter a completely different name than that of the column you're querying; it's simply ignored when you use the question mark (?) to specify a parameter in the query. Personally, I prefer the named parameters approach because I find that it makes the code easier to read and, more important, it saves you the potential problem of an incorrect parameter sequence when your code is later changed.

 NOTE   If you don't supply the parameters specified—for example, if you comment out Lines 16 through 19 in Listing 22-19—a **COMException** exception is thrown. This isn't so when you work with named parameters (see Listing 22-18).

Executing XPath Queries

You can execute XPath queries in one of two ways: using a simple XPath query or executing against a mapping schema. I'll show you both ways.

A simple XPath query is executed as shown in Listing 22-20.

Listing 22-20. Executing a Simple XPath Query

```
1 Public Sub ExecuteXPathQuery()
2   Dim stmUser As Stream
3   Dim smwUser As StreamWriter
4   ' Declare, instantiate and initialize command
5   Dim cmdUser As New SqlXmlCommand(PR_STR_CONNECTION_STRING)
6   cmdUser.CommandText = "tblUser/@LoginName"
7   cmdUser.CommandType = SqlXmlCommandType.XPath
8   ' You need to set the RootTag property, otherwise
9   ' there is no root element to form a valid XML
10  ' document
11  cmdUser.RootTag = "UserMan"
12  ' Execute command and save result set in stream
13  stmUser = cmdUser.ExecuteStream()
14  ' Read content of stream into stream reader
15  Dim smrUser As New StreamReader(stmUser)
16
17  ' Create new file to hold the result stream
18  smwUser = New StreamWriter("C:\Users.xml")
19  ' Write the result set to disk
20  smwUser.Write(smrUser.ReadToEnd())
21  ' Flush and close the stream writer
22  smwUser.Flush()
23  smwUser.Close()
24 End Sub
```

In Listing 22-20 you can see how the **CommandType** property of the Command object is set to the **XPath** member of the **SqlXmlCommandType** enum (Line 7). Besides this, you need to set the **CommandText** property to the XPath query as is done in Line 6. The XPath query specified (tblUser/@LoginName) returns the non-null values from the LoginName column in the tblUser table. If this looks familiar to you, it's probably because you've read the paragraphs following Listing 22-4 in which I discussed executing XPath queries from a browser. The way you construct your simple XPath to be executed from code or the browser query is exactly the same.

Anyway, the output from Listing 22-20, which is the Users.xml XML document, can be displayed in a browser (see Figure 22-22).

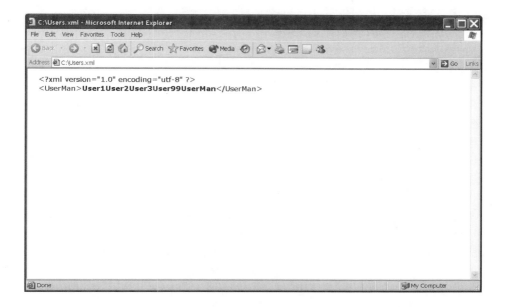

Figure 22-22. Output from Listing 22-20

In Figure 22-22 you can see the content of the Users.xml document, which is created when running the example code in Listing 22-20. There is no formatting of the XPath query output; as you can see from Figure 22-22, all column values are displayed as one long string, without spaces between the column values, within the UserMan root element.

If you need formatting of the returned XML document or values from more than one column returned, you must use a mapping schema, such as the one shown in Listing 22-21.

Listing 22-21. Mapping Schema for an XPath Query

```
1  <xsd:schema xmlns:xsd="http://www.w3.org/2001/XMLSchema"
2     xmlns:sql="urn:schemas-microsoft-com:mapping-schema">
3     <xsd:element name="Users" sql:relation="tblUser" >
4        <xsd:complexType>
5           <xsd:sequence>
6              <xsd:element name="FName"
7                 sql:field="FirstName"
8                 type="xsd:string" />
9              <xsd:element name="LName"
10                sql:field="LastName"
11                type="xsd:string" />
```

```
12            <xsd:element name="LogName"
13                sql:field="LoginName"
14                type="xsd:string" />
15            <xsd:element name="Pwd"
16                sql:field="Password"
17                type="xsd:string" />
18          </xsd:sequence>
19          <xsd:attribute name="Id" type="xsd:integer" />
20        </xsd:complexType>
21      </xsd:element>
22  </xsd:schema>
```

The mapping schema shown in Listing 22-21 defines an element named Users (Line 3) that you can query using XPath. This element has a relation to the tblUser table in the database. Then you have the definition of a complex type with the FirstName, LastName, LoginName, and Password columns in sequence. The columns, or rather elements, as they are in the XML document, will be returned in the XML document that is the output from an XPath query. Finally, you see the attribute definition on Line 19, which means that the value of the Id column in the table is added to each Users element as an attribute. This way, you have unique Users elements returned (see Figure 22-23 a little later). Listing 22-22 shows you how to output all the columns from the tblUser table, using the mapping schema shown in Listing 22-21, which has been saved to the file C:\Users.xsd.

Listing 22-22. Executing an XPath Query Against a Mapping Schema

```
1 Public Sub ExecuteXPathQueryUsingMappingSchema()
2    Dim stmUser As Stream
3    Dim smwUser As StreamWriter
4    ' Declare, instantiate and initialize command
5    Dim cmdUser As New SqlXmlCommand(PR_STR_CONNECTION_STRING)
6    cmdUser.CommandText = "Users"
7    cmdUser.CommandType = SqlXmlCommandType.XPath
8    cmdUser.SchemaPath = "C:\Users.xsd"
9    ' You need to set the RootTag property, otherwise
10   ' there is no root element to form a valid XML
11   ' document
12   cmdUser.RootTag = "UserMan"
13
14   ' Execute command and save result set in stream
15   stmUser = cmdUser.ExecuteStream()
16
```

```
17    ' Read content of stream into stream reader
18    Dim smrUser As New StreamReader(stmUser)
19
20    ' Create new file to hold the result stream
21    smwUser = New StreamWriter("C:\Users.xml")
22    ' Write the result set to disk
23    smwUser.Write(smrUser.ReadToEnd())
24    ' Flush and close the stream writer
25    smwUser.Flush()
26    smwUser.Close()
27 End Sub
```

The only difference between Listings 22-20 and 22-22 occurs in Line 6, where I have specified an XPath query (Listing 22-20) or an element that's mapped to a SQL Server table in a mapping schema (Listing 22-22), and the **SchemaPath** property, which has been set to the mapping schema file shown in Listing 22-21. You can see the output from running the example code in Listing 22-22 in Figure 22-23.

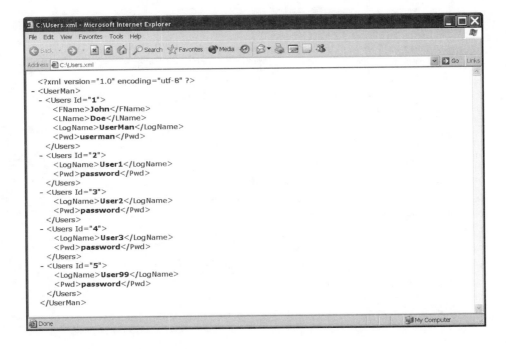

Figure 22-23. Output from Listing 22-22

Updating the Data Source Using the SqlXmlCommand Class

So far, you've seen how you can use the **SqlXmlCommand** class for querying the data source in various ways, but you can also use it to update the data source. There are a few different ways of doing this:

- Using the **ExecuteNonQuery** method

- Using a DiffGram

- Using an UpdateGram

The **ExecuteNonQuery** method is pretty straightforward. It works exactly like the method of the same name of the **SqlCommand** class, which you can find more information about in Chapter 6. Listing 22-23 shows you how to execute an action query or non–row-returning statement, such as a SQL DELETE, INSERT, or UPDATE statement.

Listing 22-23. Executing a Non–Row-Returning SQL Statement

```
 1 Public Sub ExecuteNonQuery()
 2    ' Declare, instantiate and initialize command
 3    Dim cmdUser As New SqlXmlCommand(PR_STR_CONNECTION_STRING)
 4    cmdUser.CommandText = "UPDATE tblUser " & _
 5       "SET FirstName='FirstName' WHERE FirstName ='John'"
 6
 7    Try
 8       ' Execute non query
 9       cmdUser.ExecuteNonQuery()
10    Catch objException As SqlXmlException
11       ' Start reading from beginning of stream
12       objException.ErrorStream.Position = 0
13       ' Read error message
14       Dim strError As String = New StreamReader( _
15          objException.ErrorStream).ReadToEnd()
16       ' Display error message
17       MsgBox(strError)
18    End Try
19 End Sub
```

Listing 22-23 updates the FirstName column of all rows in the tblUser table where the FirstName column holds the value "John" to the string "FirstName".

There isn't much magic to this as it's a simple SQL statement, but there's an important restriction on this way of executing non–row-returning SQL statements: The WHERE clause can only return 0 or 1 rows. If more rows are returned, a **COMException** exception is thrown. Try replacing Line 5 with this:

```
"SET FirstName='FirstName' WHERE FirstName IS NULL"
```

Because there is more than one row with a null value in the FirstName column, an exception is thrown; try running the example code.

However, the **ExecuteNonQuery** method can also be used to execute XML string templates and file-based XML templates.

Listing 22-24 shows you an XML template for updating your data source.

Listing 22-24. XML Template for Updating the Data Source

```
1 <ROOT xmlns:sql="urn:schemas-microsoft-com:xml-sql">
2   <sql:query>
3      UPDATE tblUser
4      SET FirstName='FirstName'
5      WHERE FirstName ='John'
6   </sql:query>
7 </ROOT>
```

The template in Listing 22-24 does the same thing as the SQL statement in Listing 22-23: It updates the tblUser table. Listing 22-25 shows you how to execute the template as a string template.

Listing 22-25. Executing a Non–Row-Returning String Template

```
1 Public Sub ExecuteNonQueryStringTemplate()
2    ' Declare, instantiate and initialize command
3    Dim cmdUser As New SqlXmlCommand(PR_STR_CONNECTION_STRING)
4    cmdUser.CommandText = _
5       "<ROOT xmlns:sql='urn:schemas-microsoft-com:xml-sql'>" & _
6       "<sql:query>" & _
7       "UPDATE tblUser " & _
8       "SET FirstName='FirstName' WHERE FirstName = 'John'" & _
9       "</sql:query>" & _
10      "</ROOT>"
11   cmdUser.CommandType = SqlXmlCommandType.Template
12
```

```
13    Try
14        ' Execute non query
15        cmdUser.ExecuteNonQuery()
16    Catch objException As SqlXmlException
17        ' Start reading from beginning of stream
18        objException.ErrorStream.Position = 0
19        ' Read error message
20        Dim strError As String = New StreamReader( _
21            objException.ErrorStream).ReadToEnd()
22        ' Display error message
23        MsgBox(strError)
24    End Try
25 End Sub
```

Listing 22-25 uses a string template for updating the data source, but you can also use a file-based template as in Listing 22-26, where the template shown in Listing 22-24 has been saved as a file named UpdateUsers.xml to C:\.

Listing 22-26. Executing a Non–Row-Returning Template

```
1 Public Sub ExecuteNonQueryTemplate()
2     ' Declare, instantiate and initialize command
3     Dim cmdUser As New SqlXmlCommand(PR_STR_CONNECTION_STRING)
4     cmdUser.CommandText = "C:\UpdateUsers.xml"
5     cmdUser.CommandType = SqlXmlCommandType.TemplateFile
6
7     Try
8         ' Execute non query
9         cmdUser.ExecuteNonQuery()
10    Catch objException As SqlXmlException
11        ' Start reading from beginning of stream
12        objException.ErrorStream.Position = 0
13        ' Read error message
14        Dim strError As String = New StreamReader( _
15            objException.ErrorStream).ReadToEnd()
16        ' Display error message
17        MsgBox(strError)
18    End Try
19 End Sub
```

Listings 22-25 and 22-26 are both used for executing a template that updates the data source. However, as stated earlier, you have two more options when you want to do this: DiffGrams and UpdateGrams.

DiffGrams were introduced with the .NET Framework for serializing **DataSet** objects for transporting over any network where the **DataSet** can be reconstructed from the information in the DiffGram. This means that DiffGrams are *not* specifically for use with SQL Server, although the coverage here is all about SQL Server usage. You can find more detailed information about DiffGrams at http://msdn.microsoft.com/library/default.asp?url=/library/en-us/cpguide/ html/cpcondiffgrams.asp.

In Listing 22-27 I show you how to create a DiffGram from a populated **DataSet** and then update your data source using the DiffGram.

Listing 22-27. Generating and Executing a DiffGram

```
1 Public Sub ExecuteDiffGram()
2     ' Declare template file
3     Dim strTemplate As String = "C:\AllUsers.xml"
4     ' Declare and instantiate DataSet
5     Dim dstUserMan As New DataSet("UserMan")
6
7     ' Declare and instantiate adapter
8     Dim dadUserMan As New SqlXmlAdapter(strTemplate, _
9        SqlXmlCommandType.TemplateFile, PR_STR_CONNECTION_STRING)
10
11    ' Fill DataSet
12    dadUserMan.Fill(dstUserMan)
13    ' Update DataSet
14    dstUserMan.Tables("tblUser").Rows(0)("FirstName") = "Johnny" ' Update
15    dstUserMan.Tables("tblUser").Rows(3).Delete()              ' Delete
16    dstUserMan.Tables("tblUser").Rows.Add(New Object(4) {Nothing, _
17       Nothing, Nothing, "NewLogin", "password"})             ' Insert
18    ' Save dataset as diffgram
19    dstUserMan.WriteXml("C:\Users-DiffGram.xml", XmlWriteMode.DiffGram)
20
21    ' Declare, instantiate and initialize command
22    Dim cmdUser As New SqlXmlCommand(PR_STR_CONNECTION_STRING)
23    cmdUser.CommandText = "C:\Users-DiffGram.xml"
24    cmdUser.CommandType = SqlXmlCommandType.TemplateFile
25    cmdUser.SchemaPath = "C:\Users-DiffGram.xsd"
26
```

```
27    Try
28        ' Execute non query
29        cmdUser.ExecuteNonQuery()
30    Catch objException As SqlXmlException
31        ' Start reading from beginning of stream
32        objException.ErrorStream.Position = 0
33        ' Read error message
34        Dim strError As String = New StreamReader( _
35            objException.ErrorStream).ReadToEnd()
36        ' Display error message
37        MsgBox(strError)
38    End Try
39 End Sub
```

In Listing 22-27 I populate the dstUserMan DataSet (Line 12) with the dadUserMan **SqlXmlAdapter** that uses the AllUsers.xml XML template file from Listing 22-4 saved to C:\. I then update, delete, and insert a row in the **DataSet** (Lines 14 through 17) and save the **DataSet** as a DiffGram in the file C:\Users-DiffGram.xml. Finally, the DiffGram file is used as a template for updating the data source (Lines 27 through 38). The DiffGram looks like Figure 22-24.

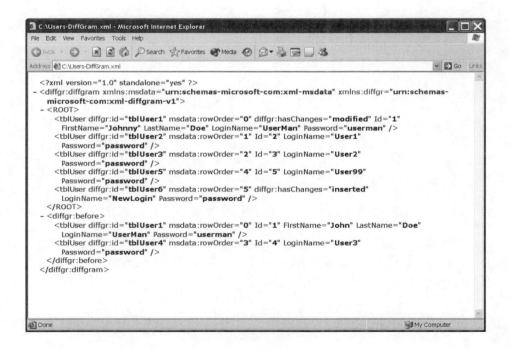

Figure 22-24. The DiffGram created in Listing 22-27

The real trick of Listing 22-27 is that without setting the **SchemaPath** property to an existing XML schema definition file (XSD) on Line 25, the update will do so, because there's no mapping between the DiffGram and the object in the data source. The Users-DiffGram.xsd file is shown in Listing 22-28.

Listing 22-28. XML Schema Definition File for Executing DiffGram

```xml
<xsd:schema xmlns:xsd="http://www.w3.org/2001/XMLSchema"
            xmlns:sql="urn:schemas-microsoft-com:mapping-schema">
  <xsd:element name="tblUser" sql:relation="tblUser" >
    <xsd:complexType>
      <xsd:sequence>
        <xsd:element name="UserId"
                     sql:field="Id"
                     sql:identity="ignore"
                     type="xsd:int" />
        <xsd:element name="FName"
                     sql:field="FirstName"
                     type="xsd:string" />
        <xsd:element name="LName"
                     sql:field="LastName"
                     type="xsd:string" />
        <xsd:element name="LogName"
                     sql:field="LoginName"
                     type="xsd:string" />
        <xsd:element name="Pwd"
                     sql:field="Password"
                     type="xsd:string" />
      </xsd:sequence>
    </xsd:complexType>
  </xsd:element>
</xsd:schema>
```

In Listing 22-27 I use the **DataSet** class to create a DiffGram, but you can just as well create a DiffGram manually instead of programmatically. You can use a DiffGram for any kind of update to the data in your data source and its XML, meaning it's in plain text format. This is very handy for communicating over the "wire" or the Internet, and especially through firewalls that generally don't allow binary objects to pass through.

A DiffGram is really a subset of an UpdateGram, which was introduced with the XML for Microsoft SQL Server 2000 Web Release 1,[10] the first version of SQLXML. I won't cover UpdateGrams in this chapter, but you can find more information here: `http://msdn.microsoft.com/library/default.asp?url=/library/en-us/sqlxml3/htm/updategram_5kkh.asp`.

Exception Handling with SQLXML 3.0 Managed Classes

As you've probably seen from some of the listings in this chapter, the exception handling process is different from the one introduced in previous chapters. I have a **Try . . . Catch . . . End Try** construct in listings where I know the code will possibly throw an exception. That's really the same as in other chapters, but it's the **Catch** block that's different. The **Catch** block is set up to catch all exceptions of type **SqlXmlException**, and that's pretty standard behavior too. However, if you try to read the error message as you'd normally do from the **SqlXmlException** instance as shown here, you always get a standard **COMException** error message:

```
1 Try
2    ' Do your stuff
3    ...
4 Catch objException As SqlXmlException
5    ' Display error message
6    MsgBox(objException.Message)
7 End Try
```

This exception handler will display the rather cryptic error message shown in Figure 22-25. The **COMException** exception is thrown by the SQLOLEDB provider, which is COM based.

Figure 22-25. Cryptic COMException error message

---

10. You can find more information about XML for Microsoft SQL Server 2000 Web Release 1 here: `http://msdn.microsoft.com/library/default.asp?url=/library/en-us/dnsql2k/html/updategrams.asp`.

As you can see from Figure 22-25, the error message is of little use. That's because the "real" error message has been sent back as a stream, and you can use the following example code to get a "proper" error message:

```
1 Try
2    ' Execute non query
3    cmdUser.ExecuteNonQuery()
4 Catch objException As SqlXmlException
5    ' Start reading from beginning of stream
6    objException.ErrorStream.Position = 0
7    ' Read error message
8    Dim strError As String = New StreamReader( _
9        objException.ErrorStream).ReadToEnd()
10   ' Display error message
11   MsgBox(strError)
12 End Try
```

This exception handler will display an error message like the one shown in Figure 22-26.

Figure 22-26. Helpful error message

The error message shown in Figure 22-26 is much more helpful than the one shown in Figure 22-25, so I suggest you always use the "helpful" exception handler when setting up **Try . . . Catch . . . End Try** constructs to deal with exceptions thrown by a SQLXML 3.0 Managed Class.

Using Web Services with SQLXML 3.0

One final thing I'll show you in this chapter is how you can expose your SQL Server 2000 stored procedures through Web services automatically created for you. In order to do this, you need to configure the SQLXML 3.0 ISAPI extension. Please see the "Configuring the ISAPI Extension" section earlier in this chapter for more information. After you've got the extension configured, follow the instructions below:

1. Open the IIS Virtual Directory Management for SQLXML 3.0 MMC snap-in.

2. Select the Virtual Names tab.

3. Select the <New virtual name> item on the list.

4. Type in **WebService** in the name textbox.

5. Select the soap item on the Type list.

6. Type in the path or browse to the \InetPub\wwwroot\UserMan folder.

7. Enter the domain name for your domain in the Domain Name textbox, or the name/IP address of the machine on which you want to host the Web service.

The Virtual Names tag should now resemble the one shown in Figure 22-27.

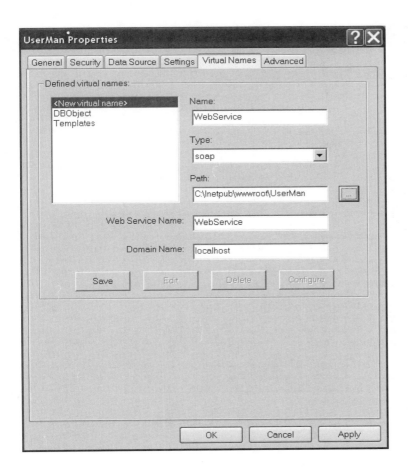

Figure 22-27. Setting up a SOAP virtual name

In Figure 22-27 you can see what your Virtual Name tab of the IIS Virtual Directory Management for SQLXML 3.0 MMC snap-in should look like before saving your changes. Please continue with the instructions below:

8. Click the Save button.

9. Click the Configure button, which brings up the Soap virtual name configuration dialog box as shown in Figure 22-28.

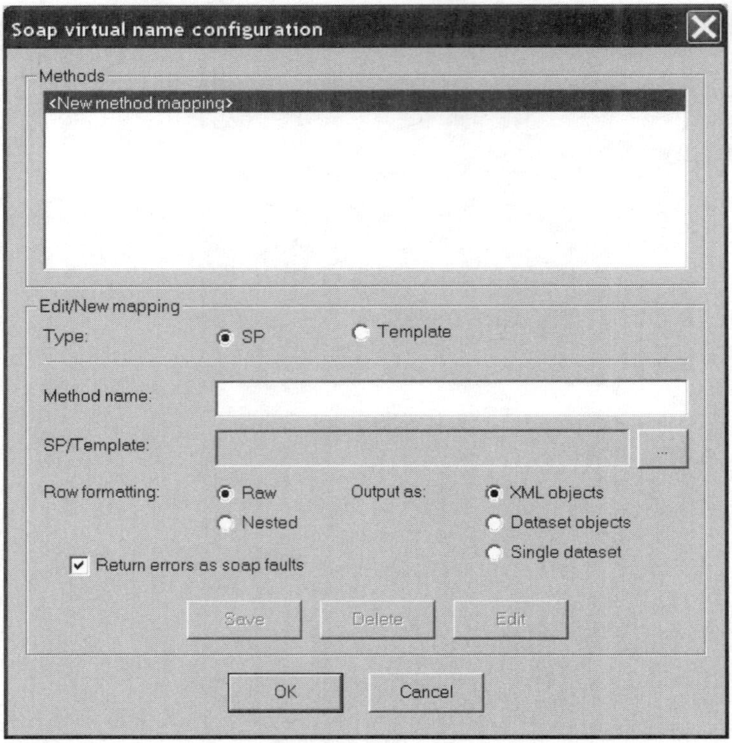

Figure 22-28. The Soap virtual name configuration dialog box

10. Select the SP Type option.

11. Click the button with the ellipsis next to the SP/Template textbox to bring up the SOAP stored procedure mapping dialog box as shown in Figure 22-29.

12. Select the uspGetUsers stored procedure on the list and click OK.

13. Select the Single dataset option, and click Save.

14. Click OK twice to close and save the new soap virtual name.

Now, if you've followed these instructions, a Web Services Description Language (WSDL) document is automatically created for you in the \Inetpub\wwwroot\UserMan folder. The name of the document is WebService.wsdl.

Figure 22-29. The SOAP stored procedure mapping dialog box

I won't be covering Web services in this book, as it is a topic that deserves an entire book itself. As a matter of fact, I'm currently coauthoring a book about XML Web services:

> *Building Web Services with Visual Basic .NET*, by Carsten Thomsen and Mark Dunn. To be published by Apress, March 2003. ISBN: 1-59059-007-4.

You can find more information about this book here:
http://www.apress.com/book/bookDisplay.html?bID=109.

Okay, I said I wasn't going to cover Web services in this book, but I'll obviously show you how to retrieve the **DataSet** returned by the Web service I just created. To do so, follow these instructions:

1. Open up or create a new project in VS .NET.[11]

2. Right-click the project file in Solution Explorer, and click the Add Web Reference menu item, which brings up the Add Web Reference dialog box.

---

11. You can see how it's done in the SQLXML 3.0 Project in the example code.

3. In the Address textbox type in the following text:
   http://localhost/userman/WebService?wsdl,[12] and press Enter.
   The Add Web Reference dialog box should now look like the one
   shown in Figure 22-30.

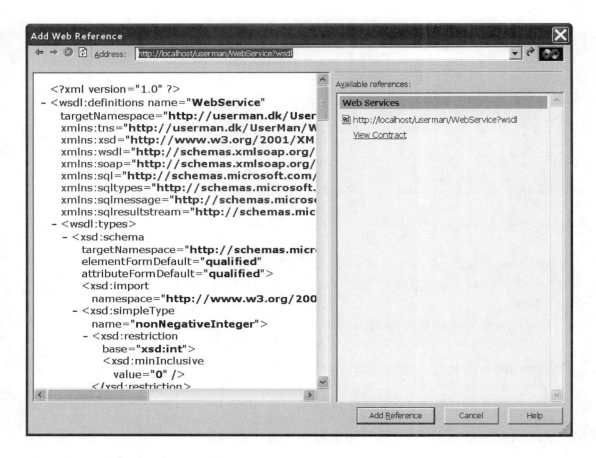

Figure 22-30. The Add Web Reference dialog box

4. Click the Add Reference button to add a reference to the Web service to
   your project.

---

12. Change localhost to the name of your server, if you didn't install SQLXML 3.0 and the Web
    Service on your local machine.

5. When you add a Web reference to your project, the default name is the name of the server where the Web service is located, localhost in this case. I don't know about you, but that's no good, as I need to reference it from code; to do so, I rename it SPWS, as shown in Figure 22-31.

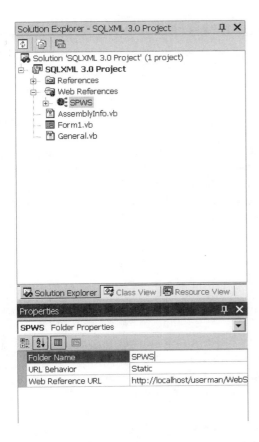

Figure 22-31. Renaming the localhost Web reference to SPWS

6. Add the code in Listing 22-29 to your project.

Listing 22-29. Calling the uspGetUsers Stored Procedure Web Service

```
 1 Private Sub btnExecuteWebServiceSP_Click(ByVal sender As System.Object, _
 2    ByVal e As System.EventArgs) Handles btnExecuteWebServiceSP.Click
 3    Dim dstUsers As DataSet
 4    Dim intReturn As Integer
 5
 6    ' Declare object as new SP Web Service
 7    Dim objWS As New SPWS.WebService()
 8
 9    ' Retrieve users from SP via Web Service
10    dstUsers = objWS.uspGetUsers(intReturn)
11 End Sub
```

In Listing 22-29 you can see how I have added code to the click event of a Windows Forms button. There's not much to explain about the code, except that through the objWS object I call the uspGetUsers stored procedure from the UserMan database on SQL Server, and I get all the users in the tblUser table returned in a **DataSet**. Please see Chapter 9 for more information on how to work with a **DataSet**. It doesn't come much easier than that!

Summary

This chapter showed you how to use the SQLXML 3.0 plug-in for accessing SQL Server databases using HTTP (typically in a browser), including configuring and testing the ISAPI extension. You also saw how to use the three SQLXML Managed Classes (**SqlXmlAdapter, SqlXmlCommand,** and **SqlXmlParameter**) from within the .NET Framework to manipulate data in SQL Server databases as XML.

You saw how to construct your exception handlers with the SQLXML 3.0 Managed Classes in order to get helpful error messages, and finally I showed you how to expose your SQL Server 2000 stored procedures as Web services.

The next chapter shows you how to wrap your data access in classes.

Part Ten

Data Wrappers

CHAPTER 23

Data Wrappers

Creating Classes (Wrappers) for Your Data Access

IN THIS CHAPTER I'll be going over how to wrap, or encapsulate, your data access in classes and components. You will see example code that covers some of the principles of Object Oriented Programming (OOP). *Wrapper* is generally a term used by programmers for the more proper term *class*. In the context of this book, a wrapper is a class. This chapter contains important information that I'll use in Chapter 26 to finish the UserMan example application. You'll also find hands-on exercises in this chapter that will take you through creating a database project, and adding scripts, queries, and command files.

Why Use Data Wrappers?

There are a number of reasons for using data wrappers and classes or components in general. Wrapping your data access in a class can prevent direct access to your data. You can set up permissions on the data so that it can be accessed only by an administrator or by your component. This gives you much better control over how the data is accessed and helps prevent potential tampering with your data.

Wrapping the data access in a component allows you to place the component where it is most appropriate in your network. By most appropriate, I mean the place on the network where the component is easy to access for the clients and easy for you to update, and the workload resulting from clients using the component is proficiently handled. Also, you need to consider security, and generally it's safer, although still a potential security risk, to place your components in a separate folder or virtual directory. This way your data, application, and components can be given different access restrictions, and thus those who have the rights to see your data won't have access to your components, unless specifically granted access. Obviously there's more to it than just placing a component in a different folder, but this can help you restrict direct access to your components. Programmatic access to your components can be and most often is a different matter altogether.

How and where you place your components obviously involves how you are distributing your application and what kind of application model you are using—client-server, n-tier, and so on.

Looking at Object Oriented Programming

In this section I'll cover some of the basic principles of OOP. This is only a short introduction, and if you are completely new to OOP, I suggest you do some reading, in order to fully exploit the potential of VB .NET. Suggested reading includes the following titles:

- *Moving to VB.NET: Strategies, Concepts, and Code,* by Dan Appleman. Apress, June 2001. ISBN: 1-893115-97-6.

- *Visual Basic .NET and the .NET Platform,* by Andrew Troelsen. Apress, October 2001. ISBN: 1-893115-26-7.

- *An Introduction to Object-Oriented Programming with Visual Basic .NET,* by Dan Clark. Apress, July 2002. ISBN: 1-59059-015-5.

- *Programming VB .NET: A Guide for Experienced Programmers,* by Gary Cornell. Apress, October 2001. ISBN: 1-893115-99-2. (Chapters 4, 5, and 6 in this book discuss OOP.)

More information about these titles can be found at http://www.apress.com.

I'll compare OOP to general programming guidelines and show you how you can apply OOP to the UserMan example application. This chapter is therefore a brief OOP introduction and lays the foundation for Chapter 26; the principles discussed in this chapter will be applied to the completion of the example application.

Okay, so let's have a look at the basic principles in OOP: polymorphism, inheritance, and encapsulation.

Polymorphism

Polymorphism, which is also called *many forms,* is the ability to call a particular method on an object instantiated from any class that is derived from a base class, without knowing which class the object was instantiated from.

Let me illustrate this using the standard **Object** class that is part of the .NET Framework base classes. All other classes in the Framework are derived from this class, and they all expose the **ToString** method. This method simply returns a **String** representation of the instantiated object. The idea is that you can always call the **ToString** method on an object to get the **String** representation without really knowing what subclass your object is derived from.

This means classes that inherit from another class should expose the same properties and methods as the base class, which makes it easy for a programmer to use standard methods and properties on any of your objects.

You can extend the inherited methods and properties if they can be overridden, which means that you don't have to expose the functionality of the base class. (Inheritance is discussed in the next section.)

My explanation is very simply put, but essentially this is what polymorphism is. See the "VB .NET Keywords Related to OOP" section later in this chapter for more information on how polymorphism is implemented in VB .NET.

Inheritance

Inheritance is the ability of a class to be derived from another class, or as the name inheritance suggests, inherit the characteristics of another class. You will encounter words such as *superclass* or *base class* to describe the class that is inherited from, and *subclass* or *derived class* for the class that inherits from another class.

There is support for two types of inheritance in VB .NET: *interface inheritance* and *implementation inheritance*. Interface inheritance is also called *has a . . .* inheritance, whereas implementation inheritance is often called *is a . . .* inheritance.

Interface Inheritance

An *interface* is a set of related public methods, properties, events, and indexers that the inheriting class must implement. An interface is a contract, so if you choose to implement an interface in your class, you are bound by the contract offered by the interface. This means you must implement all the methods and such specified in the interface. Please note that a class can implement any number of interfaces.

An interface doesn't include any implementation, which means that you cannot directly instantiate an interface. Instead, an interface must be implemented by a class, and it is this class you can instantiate. An interface is an abstract data type, and it provides for a very loose coupling between the interface and the classes that implement it. See Listing 23-1 for an example of how to implement interface inheritance.

NOTE It might be easier for you to see all the class files in the various projects in this chapter, and the classes and interfaces they contain, if you switch to Class View in Solution Explorer. To do so, press Ctrl+Shift+C or select the View ➤ Class View menu command.

Listing 23-1. Creating and Implementing an Interface

```
1 Public Interface IUserMan
2     Property TestProperty() As String
3     Sub TestMethod()
4 End Interface
5
6 Public Class CUserMan
7     Implements IUserMan
8
9     Private prstrUserName As String
10
11    Public Property UserName() As String _
12        Implements IUserMan.TestProperty
13        Get
14            UserName = prstrUserName
15        End Get
16
17        Set(ByVal vstrUserName As String)
18            prstrUserName = vstrUserName
19        End Set
20    End Property
21
22    Public Sub CalculateOnlineTime() _
23        Implements IUserMan.TestMethod
24    End Sub
25 End Class
26
27 Public Sub CreateUserManObject()
28    Dim objUserMan As New CUserMan()
29 End Sub
```

In Listing 23-1 I have created the IUserMan interface, which defines the TestProperty property and the TestMethod method. In the CUserMan class (Lines 6 through 25), I implement the IUserMan interface using the **Implements** statement on Line 7. As you can see from the code, it is necessary to implement public signatures (methods, properties, events, and indexers) in the class that implements the interface, but you are not required to keep the names of the signatures. See Lines 11 and 12, and 22 and 23, where I use the **Implements** keyword following a property and method declaration to indicate what signature in the interface is being implemented by the property and method.

I then create a procedure that generates an instance of the class that implements the interface (Lines 27 through 29). This is the ONLY way to instantiate an interface, so to speak.

Implementation Inheritance

Implementation inheritance should be used when you can use the *is a . . .* phrase to refer to a subclass or derived class. By this I mean that the subclass is a superclass or that the subclass is of the same type as the superclass. For example, say you have a superclass called CBird and subclasses called CHawk and CPigeon. It's obvious that the hawk and the pigeon are of type bird. That's what the *is a . . .* phrase indicates.

Implementation inheritance is especially great when a lot of functionality can be put into the base class, which in turn allows the derived classes to inherit this functionality without extending it. Not that you can't extend the code in the base class, but if you find you're extending most of the code from the base class, is implementation inheritance really what you need? Would interface inheritance not be better? Actually, it's not always so easy to make this choice. Keep the *is a . . .* phrase in mind when considering implementation inheritance. It might just make your decision a little bit easier.

The obvious advantage implementation inheritance has over interface inheritance is that you avoid potential duplication of code by placing all your standard code in the superclass.

Implementation inheritance results in tight coupling between the superclass and the subclass. See Listings 23-4 and 23-5 later in this chapter for examples of how implementation inheritance can be used.

Encapsulation

The term *encapsulation* has been used and abused over the years. You might get many different definitions if you ask different people about this OOP term. I'll try to give you a brief explanation of encapsulation, and how it's implemented and used in VB .NET.

Encapsulation, also called *information hiding,* is the ability to hide your code or implementation from the user of your class. This means that when you create your classes, you expose some public properties and methods, but your code decides how your private variables and such are manipulated. If you look at Listing 23-5 later in the chapter, you'll see I declare the private **String** variable prstrTest on Line 2; and because this variable is declared private, it cannot be accessed directly from a user of your class. Instead, I create the Test property, which provides access to the variable. I haven't actually implemented any checking of the value passed when setting the property, but this is generally the idea of encapsulation: no direct access to private members, only through exposed methods or properties for which you can validate the input. See Listing 23-2 for an example that validates the passed argument in the property **Set** procedure.

*Listing 23-2. Validating the Argument of a Property **Set** Procedure*

```
1 Set(ByVal vstrTest As String)
2     ' Check if the string contains any invalid chars
3     If InStr(vstrTest, "@") = 0 Then
4         prstrTest = vstrTest
5     End If
6 End Set
```

VB .NET Keywords Related to OOP

In VB .NET, a few keywords are related to OOP, either directly or indirectly. Table 23-1 lists these keywords.

Table 23-1. OOP-Related Keywords in VB .NET

Keyword	Definition
Implements	The **Implements** keyword is used for specifying that a class, method, property, event, or indexer implements the corresponding feature in an interface. See Listing 23-1 earlier in this chapter for an example that uses the **Implements** keyword.
Inherits	This keyword is used for inheriting from another class, called the superclass or base class. See Listing 23-4 later in this chapter for an example.
Interface	The **Interface** keyword is used for specifying an interface. See Listing 23-1 earlier for an example that uses the **Implements** keyword.
MustInherit	Any class that is marked with **MustInherit** can only act as a base class or an abstract class, and it cannot be instantiated. If you try to instantiate such a class using the **New** operator, a compile-time exception is thrown. **MustInherit** cannot be used for declaring methods or properties in a class. See Listing 23-3 later in this chapter to see an example of how not to use this method and Listing 23-4 for an example that shows the right way.

Table 23-1. OOP-Related Keywords in VB .NET (Continued)

Keyword	Definition
MustOverride	A property or method marked with this keyword *must* be overridden in a derived class. If you only want to give the programmer deriving your class the option of overriding the method or property, you must use the **Overridable** keyword in your declaration.
NotOverridable	If you mark a property or method with this keyword, you're explicitly telling the deriving class that the method or property cannot be overridden. You don't actually have to specify this for procedures that don't override a procedure in base class, because this is the default behavior. However, it does make your code more readable.
Overloads	The **Overloads** statement is for declaring several procedures with the same name within the same class. The parameter list is the only difference between the procedures. The compiler then makes the choice when your code calls the procedure, depending on the supplied arguments.
Overridable	A property or method marked with this keyword can be overridden in a derived class. It does not mean you have to override it, however. You don't actually have to specify this for procedures that override a procedure in base class, because this is the default behavior. However, it does make your code more readable. If you want to make sure it is overridden in a derived class, you must use the **MustOverride** keyword in your declaration. See Listing 23-5 later in this chapter for how to override a property in a derived class.
Overrides	The method or property marked with this keyword overrides the method or property in the base class with the same name. You should always use this keyword when overriding a method or property declared in the base class. See Listing 23-5 later in this chapter for how to override a property in a derived class.
Shared	When a property or method is marked with the keyword **Shared**, the property or method can be accessed without first instantiating an object of the class in which the property or method is contained. There's more to the **Shared** keyword, but in connection with OOP this is an important feature. Please see your documentation for more information on **Shared**.

Listing 23-3 shows an example of how *not* to use the **MustInherit** method listed in Table 23-1.

*Listing 23-3. A **MustInherit** Class That Can't Be Instantiated*

```
1 Public MustInherit Class CMustInherit
2    Private prstrTest As String
3
4    Public Property Test() As String
5       Get
6          Test = prstrTest
7       End Get
8
9       Set(ByVal vstrTest As String)
10          prstrTest = vstrTest
11       End Set
12    End Property
13 End Class
14
15 Public Sub InstantiateMustInheritClass()
16    'Dim objMustInherit As New CMustInherit()
17 End Sub
```

In Listing 23-3 the CMustInherit class has been declared with the **MustInherit** keyword, which means that an instance of the class can only be instantiated if it's inherited by another class. This means Line 16 will throw an exception at compile time because the syntax is wrong.

However, if you do as in Listing 23-4, where I wrap the CMustInherit class in the CWrapper class, you can inherit from and instantiate the CWrapper class as shown on Line 7.

*Listing 23-4. A **MustInherit** Class That Can Be Instantiated*

```
1 Public Class CWrapper
2    Inherits CMustInherit
3
4 End Class
5
6 Public Sub InstantiateMustInheritClassWrapper()
7     Dim objMustInherit As New CWrapper()
8 End Sub
```

Listing 23-5 shows you how to override a property in a derived class.

Listing 23-5. Overriding a Property in a Derived Class

```
1 Public Class COverridable
2     Private prstrTest As String
3
4     Public Overridable Property Test() As String
5        Get
6           Test = prstrTest
7        End Get
8
9        Set(ByVal vstrTest As String)
10          prstrTest = vstrTest
11       End Set
12    End Property
13 End Class
14
15 Public Class CWrapper1
16    Inherits COverridable
17
18    Private prstrTest As String
19
20    Public Overrides Property Test() As String
21       Get
22          Test = prstrTest & "Overridden"
23       End Get
24
25       Set(ByVal vstrTest As String)
26          prstrTest = vstrTest
27       End Set
28    End Property
29 End Class
```

In Listing 23-5 two classes have been declared: CVirtual and CWrapper. CVirtual is the base class from which CWrapper inherits. On Line 4, the Test property is declared as overridable, and in the derived class on Line 20 this property has indeed been overridden using the **Overrides** keyword. The **Overrides** keyword is always necessary when you're overriding a method or property—it doesn't matter if the property or method is declared using either the **MustOverride** or **Overridable** keyword.

Wrapping a Database

Now that some of the initial details are out of the way, let's take a look at what to wrap and how in a database. If you've familiarized yourself with the database concepts in Chapter 2, you'll be well off when I walk you through the analysis and design stage. Basically, wrapping your database access is like grouping your data in related tables. Actually, since you've already broken down your data into tables, you've more or less found a way of defining your classes and wrappers.

Having a class for each table in your database is often the most satisfying solution when it comes to maintenance as well as the users of your classes and/or components. Now that I mention components, I also have to add that one class doesn't necessarily constitute one component. Quite often, you'll have more than one class in your component, but that depends on how you decide to distribute your business and data services.

Okay, so what needs to happen here? Classes and possibly components that hold the classes first need to be created. Since this book is strictly about data manipulation, I won't be covering business services, only data services. If you look at the schema for the UserMan database (see Figure 2-10 in Chapter 2), you'll see the following tables: tblLog, tblRights, tblUser, and tblUserRights.

To follow my own advice, I need to create a class for each of these tables; for the purpose of showing you the what and how, I'm going to create the CUser class.

Creating the CUser Class

The tblUser table has the following columns: Id, ADName, ADSID, FirstName, LastName, LoginName, and Password.

What I need to do now is find out what columns I'll have to expose from the class, and if the column is exposed, whether it will feature read-write, read-only, or write-only access. See Table 23-2 for a list of columns, data types, and access types.

Now, if you look at Table 23-2, there are a couple of columns for which the access type can be discussed in further detail. ADName and ADSID can change depending on the AD connected, but why do I want the user of the class to be able to do this? First of all, I need to make sure that it's possible to set these values. Who's allowed to do it will be taken care of from the application.

Table 23-2. The tblUser Columns

Column Name	Data Type	Nullable	Access Type	Description
Id	int	No	Read-only	This is the ID used for looking up values in related tables. This is an IDENTITY column, so you'll never have to set the value for it.
ADName	varchar	Yes	Read-write	This is the Active Directory name for the user, if he or she is a member of the Active Directory.
ADSID	varchar	Yes	Read-write	This is the Active Directory security identifier (SID) for the user, if he or she is a member of the Active Directory.
FirstName	varchar	Yes	Read-write	This is the user's first, or given, name.
LastName	varchar	Yes	Read-write	This is the user's last name, or surname.
LoginName	varchar	No	Read-write	This is the user's login name, which he or she must use in conjunction with the password when logging onto the system.
Password	varchar	No	Read-write	This is the user's password, which he or she must use in conjunction with the login name when logging onto the system.

Next, a new Class Library project needs to be created and a new class added to it that holds the methods, properties, and so on of the CUser class.

Exercise

Create a new Class Library project called **UserMan** and rename the existing class (Class1) **CUser**. Open the CUser class, if it's not already open, and change the class name to **CUser** as well.

It's time to add private variables, methods, and properties that can handle access to the database table. For all the columns, it's best to create properties, because all they do is read or write a value. Before creating the properties, it's a good idea to create private variables that hold the values in order to avoid having to access the database every time a variable is read. See Listing 23-6 for some example code that creates private variables to hold the user values from the database table.

Exercise

Add a private variable to the CUser class for every column in the tblUser table. See Listing 23-6 for an example.

Listing 23-6. Creating Private Variables to Hold the User Values

```
1 Private prlngId As Long
2 Private prstrADName As String
3 Private prstrADSID As String
4 Private prstrFirstName As String
5 Private prstrLastName As String
6 Private prstrLoginName As String
7 Private prstrPassword As String
```

Listing 23-6 is simply a list of private variables that correspond directly to the columns in the tblUser table. Now properties need to be added to set and retrieve the values from the variables. See Listing 23-7 for an example of the **Id** property.

*Listing 23-7. The Read-Only **Id** Property*

```
1 Public ReadOnly Property Id() As Long
2     Get
3         Id = prlngId
4     End Get
5 End Property
```

Exercise

Add properties for all the columns in the tblUser table to the CUser class. See Listings 23-7 and 23-8 for examples.

*Listing 23-8. The Read-Write **ADName** Property*

```
1 Public Property ADName() As String
2    Get
3       ADName = prstrADName
4    End Get
5
6    Set(ByVal vstrADName As String)
7       prstrADName = vstrADName
8    End Set
9 End Property
```

Listing 23-8 shows you how the ADName column in the database table can be accessed using a property. Actually this is not quite true, because only a private variable is being accessed. However, the code for accessing the database table and Active Directory will be added in Chapter 26.

All the properties of data type **String** can be set to a maximum length in the database, so it's a good idea to add a check if the passed string is shorter than or equal to this length. This also means that you need to hold the maximum length values in private variables, as in Listing 23-9.

Exercise

Add a private variable to the CUser class for every column in the tblUser table that has a maximum length. See Listing 23-9 for an example.

Listing 23-9. Creating Private Variables to Hold the Maximum Length of Table Columns

```
1 ' User table column max lengths
2 Private printADNameMaxLen As Integer
3 Private printADSIDMaxLen As Integer
4 Private printFirstNameMaxLen As Integer
5 Private printLastNameMaxLen As Integer
6 Private printLoginNameMaxLen As Integer
7 Private printPasswordMaxLen As Integer
```

The length check for the property **Set** procedures now needs to be created. This can be done as shown in Listing 23-10.

Exercise

Add a check of the length of the passed argument in the property **Set** procedures. Keep in mind only those procedures set a variable that corresponds to a column in the database table with a maximum length. See Listing 23-10 for example code.

*Listing 23-10. Creating Maximum Length Checks of Property **Set** Arguments*

```
1 Set(ByVal vstrADName As String)
2    If vstrADName.Length <= printADNameMaxLen Then
3        prstrADName = vstrADName
4    Else
5        prstrADName = vstrADName.Substring(0, printADNameMaxLen)
6    End If
7 End Set
```

In Listing 23-10, I check if the length of the passed argument is shorter than or equal to the maximum length of the table column by comparing the length with the value of the private variable printADNameMaxLen. If it is shorter, the value is stored, and if not, the first printADNameMaxLen number of characters from the vstrADName string is stored. I suppose you could throw an exception here, but is it really that bad to pass a string with too many characters? The reason I need to perform this check is that if I try to pass a string that is too long to the database, an exception will be thrown. All right, this check can certainly be done in different ways, and I'm sure you know one or two other ways you might normally use, but this is merely to demonstrate how you can build up your properties.

Exercise

Add a check on the LoginName property to make sure that the login name doesn't contain any spaces. See Listing 23-11 for example code.

Listing 23-11. Checking for Spaces When Setting LoginName

```
1 Public Property LoginName() As String
2    Get
3        LoginName = prstrLoginName
4    End Get
5
```

```
 6    Set(ByVal vstrLoginName As String)
 7       ' Check if the string contains any spaces
 8       If vstrLoginName.IndexOf(" ") = -1 Then
 9          If vstrLoginName.Length <= printLoginNameMaxLen Then
10             prstrLoginName = vstrLoginName
11          Else
12             prstrLoginName = vstrLoginName.Substring(0, printLoginNameMaxLen)
13          End If
14       End If
15    End Set
16 End Property
```

In Listing 23-11 I use the **IndexOf** method of the **String** class to check the passed value for spaces in the LoginName property. You can choose to ignore spaces contained in the LoginName, but that just isn't a very elegant solution. See the "Adding Events" section later in this chapter for ideas on how to handle cases where the LoginName does contain spaces.

Adding a Constructor and a Destructor

You need a constructor and a destructor in any class you create to instantiate and destroy your class. However, when you base your class on the standard **Object** class, which ultimately all classes created with the .NET Framework do, you don't have to create the procedures yourself; it's all done for you behind the scenes. If you look at the CUser class that you created earlier, the constructor isn't shown in your code. Listing 23-12 presents the default class constructor.

Listing 23-12. The Default Class Constructor

```
1 Public Sub New()
2    MyBase.New()
3 End Sub
```

Listing 23-12 shows you the default constructor, and although it isn't shown in your code by default, when creating a new class, it's still there behind there scenes. Please note the call to **MyBase.New** on Line 2. This is a call to the base class' constructor, which in our case is the **Object** class. The VB .NET runtime implicitly calls the constructor of the base class, so unless it's overloaded, and there's no accessible overload that accepts no parameters, you don't have to call it explicitly from your code. In the constructor, you'd normally place calls to constructors of other objects that you need to work with in an instance of your class, and other method or function calls that are needed to run a class instance.

NOTE Now, in OOP you have the terms *constructor* and *destructor*. I have discussed the constructor, so now I need to discuss the destructor. However, in managed code you use garbage collection, which takes care of destroying your class instances. This means that referring to destructors in managed code isn't correct, technically speaking, but in keeping with OOP terminology, I'll use the word *destructor* in this chapter.

The destructor isn't created for you in your code either, and in many cases, it isn't needed. In VB .NET, you have two destructors, so to speak: the **Finalize** and **Dispose** methods. The **Finalize** method is protected and can't be called from outside the class in which it's implemented. Like most other destructors, **Finalize** is automatically called when a class instance is destroyed. Because of the garbage collection used in the .NET Framework, you can't rely on the **Finalize** method being called as soon as the object is destroyed. It won't happen until the garbage collector detects your object and determines whether it's orphaned or no longer referenced from anywhere. Therefore, the **Finalize** method is used for placing housekeeping that must be run before the object is destroyed, such as persisting the object's state. However, make sure you only implement a **Finalize** method if it's really needed, because there's a slight overhead in terms of performance when you implement it. Personally, I think it's rarely needed. If you do need one, you can create it as shown in Listing 23-13.

Listing 23-13. The Default Class Destructor

```
1 Protected Overrides Sub Finalize()
2     ' Do your housekeeping here
3     ' ...
4     ' Call the base class' destructor
5     MyBase.Finalize()
6 End Sub
```

Okay, so the **Finalize** method is protected and can only be called from a driving class or from within the class itself. What do you do then if you have an instance of the class in your code that you want to destroy explicitly? You call the **Dispose** method from your code to explicitly destroy it. Please note that the **Dispose** method isn't called automatically; it's up to the consumers of a class to call it. There's one small problem, however. Your class must explicitly implement the **IDisposible** interface, which has exactly one method, the **Dispose** method. Listing 23-14 shows you how to implement the **IDisposible** interface.

*Listing 23-14. The **Dispose** Destructor*

```
1 Implements IDisposable
2
3 Public Overloads Sub Dispose() Implements IDisposable.Dispose
4    ' Do your unmanaged housekeeping here
5    ' ...
6 End Sub
```

As you can see from Listing 23-14, the **Dispose** method is the destructor in which you should place the housekeeping of all your unmanaged code, such as COM objects. Please note that it's up to you to make sure that it's safe to call the **Dispose** method more than once. I suggest you use a **Boolean** variable to keep track of this. Another thing you need to do is to add a call to the **Shared SupressFinalize** method of the **GC** class. Otherwise **Finalize** will eventually be called as well, possibly creating problems because the code in the **Finalize** and **Dispose** methods overlap.

One reason for adding code to the constructor and destructor of your class is you need to create objects that must be kept alive for the duration of your class. One such object can be a connection to your database. I'm not telling you to implement code this way, but I'm trying to give you an idea of what you can use constructors and destructors for. Another purpose is to read some initialization values from a file or perhaps the Windows Registry, or when you want to pass one or more values to the class for initialization (see from Line 14 on in Listing 23-15). I'm sure you get the idea: Put code in the constructor that needs to run before an instance of your class is fully instantiated and make sure you close and destroy any files and/or object references you've been using in the destructor. One reason to do this is to close or destroy a connection to your database, if you're not doing this elsewhere; you need to explicitly close an open connection in order for it to be returned to the connection pool, and to make sure the connection isn't kept alive and thus run the risk of causing memory leaks. The connection might be kept alive because the garbage collector doesn't destroy it, even if there are no references to it! See the "Pooling Connections" section in Chapter 5 for more information.

Adding Events

Sometimes it's preferable to use events rather than to raise exceptions for minor errors in your classes. Events are messages sent to an instance of a class in response to a certain action or actions. In Listing 23-11 you check the value passed to the LoginName property **Set**, but you don't do anything if the value contains spaces. You can choose to ignore any spaces, but that's really no good. You can also raise an exception using the **Throw** statement, perhaps even your custom exception. See the "Creating Your Own Exception" and "Throwing a Structured Exception" sections in Chapter 14 for more information on creating exception classes and throwing exceptions.

Your third option is to create and raise events in your class, as follows:

1. Create an event class that defines the data for the event (see Listing 23-15).

2. Declare an event delegate (see Listing 23-16 later in this chapter).

3. Declare an event (see Listing 23-17 later in this chapter).

Well, you don't have to follow every step in these instructions, because you don't really have to create an event class, but see the documentation if you need more information on events and delegates, or even better, check out the books I mentioned at the beginning of this chapter.

Listing 23-15. An Error Event Class

```
1 Public Class CErrorEventArgs
2    Inherits EventArgs
3
4    Public Enum ErrorStatusEnum As Integer
5       NoError = 0
6       ServerDown = 1
7       TimeOut = 2
8       InvalidLoginName = 3
9    End Enum
10
11   Private printErrorStatus As ErrorStatusEnum = ErrorStatusEnum.NoError
12   Private prstrErrorMessage As String
13
14   ' Class constructor
15   Public Sub New(ByVal enuErrorStatus As ErrorStatusEnum)
16      ' Save the error status
17      printErrorStatus = enuErrorStatus
18
19      ' Set the error message
20      Select Case printErrorStatus
21         Case ErrorStatusEnum.NoError
22            prstrErrorMessage = "No error"
23         Case ErrorStatusEnum.InvalidLoginName
24            prstrErrorMessage = _
25               "There are invalid characters in the LoginName!"
```

```
26          Case ErrorStatusEnum.ServerDown
27            prstrErrorMessage = _
28               "The database server is currently unavailable!"
29          Case ErrorStatusEnum.TimeOut
30            prstrErrorMessage = _
31               "A timeout connecting to the server has occurred!"
32          Case Else
33            prstrErrorMessage = "Unknown error!"
34       End Select
35    End Sub
36
37    ' Returns the error status
38    Public ReadOnly Property Status() As ErrorStatusEnum
39       Get
40          Return printErrorStatus
41       End Get
42    End Property
43
44    ' Returns the error message
45    Public ReadOnly Property Message() As String
46       Get
47          Return prstrErrorMessage
48       End Get
49    End Property
50 End Class
```

In Listing 23-15 I create the CErrorEventArgs class that is used for defining event data, or rather error data in this case. First, I create a public enum (ErrorStatusEnum) on Lines 4 through 9, which is used for instantiating the class. This enum's purpose is to hold all the possible error numbers you can think of, but I've supplied a few for you to see. The **InvalidLoginName** member is the one I show in detail. I also create two private variables, printErrorStatus and prstrErrorMessage, on Lines 11 and 12 that hold the internal values for the two read-only properties **Status** (Lines 38 through 42) and **Message** (Lines 45 through 49). The constructor (Lines 15 through 35) takes one argument, a member of the **ErrorStatusEnum** enum. In the constructor, the passed value is saved and the message text is determined from the error status in the **Select Case** construct on Lines 20 through 34.

NOTE It's generally a good idea to use enums for passing arguments to methods and properties if possible. You can only use integer values in enums, and enums are really only good in situations where you know a variable or the like can only hold a certain subrange of values, such as 1 to 25. Using enums helps you eliminate possible errors in passed argument values, because when an argument is specified as being type enum (Line 15), you can only pass a member of that enum.

In Listing 23-16 I declare the ErrorEventHandler delegate, which is to be used for hooking up error events in the CUser class.

Listing 23-16. Declaring an Event Delegate

```
1 ' Declare delegate for hooking up error notifications
2 Public Delegate Sub ErrorEventHandler(ByVal sender As Object, _
3    ByVal e As CErrorEventArgs)
```

In the CUser class, you now need to declare the event, as shown in Listing 23-17.

Listing 23-17. Declaring the Event and the Method Raising the Event

```
1 Public Event OnError(ByVal sender As Object, _
2    ByVal e As CErrorEventArgs)
```

All you need to do now is to hook the event with a method with the same signature as the event delegate shown in Listing 23-16. Listing 23-18 shows you a very simple method that displays the value of the Message property in a message box.

Listing 23-18. Method That Receives the Event

```
1 Public Sub ErrorEvent(ByVal sender As Object, _
2    ByVal e As UserMan.CErrorEventArgs)
3    MsgBox(e.Message)
4 End Sub
```

Listing 23-18 shows the ErrorEvent procedure that has the same signature as the event delegate. Now you need to hook up the OnError event of the CUser class to the ErrorEvent procedure in Listing 23-18. You can see how in Listing 23-19.

Listing 23-19. Hook Up the Event Receiver to the Event

```
1 ' Declare user object
2 Dim objUser As New UserMan.CUser()
3
4 ' Hook the event up to a method
5 AddHandler objUser.OnError, AddressOf ErrorEvent
6
7 ' Set the LoginName with spaces
8 objUser.LoginName = "dfhg ljlkj"
```

In Listing 23-19, I declare the objUser object as being type CUser, and I then hook up the OnError event of the CUser class to the ErrorEvent procedure shown in Listing 23-18. Line 8 is where I want to trigger the event by setting the LoginName property to an invalid value.

If you've followed along up to this point, your CUser class can now throw errors using the protected OnError method shown in Listing 23-17. I show you the modification to the LoginName **Set** property in Listing 23-20. You can see the original example code in Listing 23-11.

Listing 23-20. Trigger Invalid LoginName *Error Event*

```
11          Else
12              ' Instantiates the event source
13              Dim objErrorEvent As New _
14                CErrorEventArgs( _
15                    CErrorEventArgs.ErrorStatusEnum.InvalidLoginName)
16              ' Triggers the error event
17              RaiseEvent OnError(Me, objErrorEvent)
18          End If
```

Listing 23-20 shows you how you can modify the LoginName **Set** property procedure of the CUser class when checking for invalid characters in the passed LoginName value. First, you create an instance of the CErrorEventArgs class with the error event you want to trigger (ErrorStatusEnum.InvalidLoginName), and then you trigger the event by executing the **RaiseEvent** statement and passing the OnError event, the class instance in which the code resides, and your instance of the CErrorEventArgs class. I'm sure you can see how the error event can easily be used in other parts of the user class. Check out the example code available on the Apress Web site to see the full event example shown in the previous listings.

The CUser class isn't finished yet—a lot more code needs to be added to it, such as data-aware classes (for example, connections and commands), but I'm sure you get the idea of how to create wrappers for all your data access. I'll give you more ideas and hints in Chapter 26, when I finish the UserMan example application.

Summary

This chapter took you on a short journey through OOP and how to apply OOP to your data access code. The three main concepts of OOP were discussed: polymorphism, inheritance, and encapsulation. With regards to inheritance, I briefly outlined the differences between interface and implementation inheritance.

I also went over how to wrap your data access code in classes, in the context of creating a class for accessing the tblUser database table in the UserMan example application, and introduced you to constructors, destructors, events, and delegates. This work will be finished in Chapter 26.

The next chapter covers creating and using data-bound controls in Windows Forms.

Part Eleven

Data-Bound Controls

CHAPTER 24

Windows Data-Bound Controls

Creating and Working with Windows Data-Bound Controls

IN THIS CHAPTER I'll discuss data-bound controls and Windows data-bound controls in particular. I'll touch upon the subject of why they are so popular with some developers and extremely unpopular with others. I'll explore how to use some of the Windows data-bound controls that come with Visual Studio .NET. I'll also show you how to create your own Windows data-bound controls. Keep an eye out for the hands-on exercises that appear throughout this chapter.

This chapter is by no means an exhaustive reference to working with Windows data-bound controls. However, here you'll see the very basics of working with Windows data-bound controls.

Data-Bound Controls vs. Manual Data Hooking

A *data-bound control,* such as a list box, a grid, or a textbox, is a control that has a connection to a data source. In most cases the connection is filtered so that the control only sees one field of the current row from the data source. This means the developer doesn't have to take care of updating the control when the underlying data changes or updating the data source when user input has changed the data in the control. Data-bound controls are there to make your life as a developer easier.

Manual data hooking is an alternative to data-bound controls that has always been around. *Manual data hooking* describes the process by which you as a developer retrieve values from a data source and display them in one or more UI controls. However, when Visual Basic[1] started shipping with controls that were data bound,

---

1. Visual Basic 3.0 was the first major programming language to introduce data-bound controls.

the developer community suddenly had an extra tool to use for displaying and manipulating data.

I think that data-bound controls are a great idea, because they save you from having to develop lots of code that otherwise takes care of the manual data hooking. With manual data hooking you have full control over how the data is handled, whereas data-bound controls often severely limit your ability to intervene and manipulate the data before being displayed or before being written back to the data source. This has been an annoying extra "feature" of data-bound controls for a long time, and I bet you know someone who tells you *not* to use data-bound controls because of this drawback. I've been using data-bound controls mainly for display purposes or read-only data, because then I don't have to worry about problems with updating the data source once the user changes the displayed data.

Traditionally, all data-bound controls were bound to a single data control that took care of the binding to the data source, as shown in Figure 24-1.

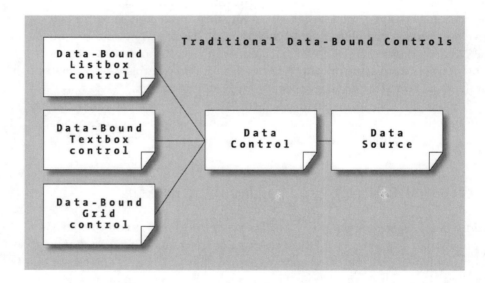

Figure 24-1. Traditional data-bound controls

In Figure 24-1 notice how the data control takes care of the communication between the data source and the data-bound controls. This effectively means that you as a programmer don't have control over the way data is transferred from the data source to the bound controls and back again. The data control encapsulates all this for you, but it leaves you with very few options regarding how the data source is updated.

Different Controls for Different UIs

Visual Studio .NET supports several UIs, and they each require different controls. The Web and Windows are two of the UIs that VS .NET supports. For example, if you look at the Toolbox in the IDE, you can see different tabs of controls for different purposes. If you display the Toolbox in your IDE and look at the Windows Forms tab and the Web Forms tab, many of the controls are named the same. This doesn't mean they're the same controls—on the contrary, they aren't. However, they do serve a similar purpose. Read this chapter about Windows data-bound controls and Chapter 25 about Web data-bound controls to find out more about the important distinctions.

Using Data-Bound Controls with Windows Forms

Data binding in Windows Forms requires a data provider and a data consumer. The data provider is not just a so-called traditional data source, such as a database table. In fact, data binding on Windows Forms can be much more than that. It can involve a collection or an array and any of the data structures from ADO.NET. These data structures include the DataReader and **DataSet** classes. I'll cover data binding with the ADO.NET data structures in this section.

 NOTE   See Chapters 7 and 9 for more information on the DataReader and **DataSet** data structures.

All Windows Forms have a **BindingContext** object. When you bind a control on a Windows Form to a data structure, this control will have an associated **CurrencyManager** object. The **CurrencyManager** object handles the communication with the data structure and is responsible for keeping the data-bound controls synchronized. All controls bound to a currency manager display data from the same row at the same time, and one Windows Form can have more than one currency manager. This happens when the Windows Form has more than one data source, because the form maintains one currency manager for each data source associated with the form.

Another important aspect of the currency manager is its ability to know the current position in the data source. You can read the position using the **Position** property of the **CurrencyManager** class. This is especially useful with ADO.NET data structures, such as the **DataTable** class, because they don't provide cursor functionality—that is, you can't retrieve a cursor or pointer to the current row.

However, this can be achieved with the currency manager. You'll see how the **CurrencyManager** object is used in the "Looking at the Code Created by the Data Form Wizard" section later in this chapter.

Examining the Binding Context

The *binding context* keeps track of all the currency managers on a Windows Form. Even if there aren't any currency managers and data sources, your Windows Form will always have a **BindingContext** object associated with it. As a matter of fact, this is true for all classes derived from the **Control** class, which is also part of the **System.Windows.Forms** namespace.

It's the binding context with which the data-bound control communicates. The binding context talks to the currency manager, which in turn talks to the data source, as shown in Figure 24-2. I'll show you how the **BindingContext** object is used in code in the "Looking at the Code Created by the Data Form Wizard" section later in this chapter.

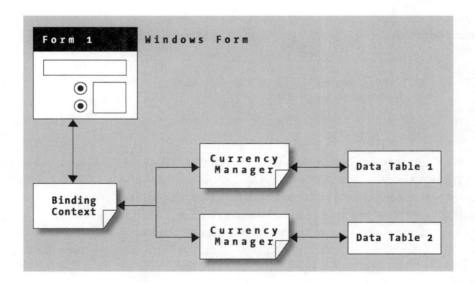

Figure 24-2. How data-bound controls communicate with the data source

Creating a Form Using the Data Form Wizard

Instead of doing all the hard work yourself, you can let the Data Form Wizard create your form with one or more data-bound controls. I'll take you through this process, because it will help you understand how controls are bound to data in Windows Forms. Here's how to create a new form:

1. Add a new item to your project and make sure you select the Data Form Wizard template. You can do this by right-clicking your project in Solution Explorer and clicking the Add ➤ Add New Item menu item.

2. Give the new form a name. This brings up the Data Form Wizard. Click Next.

3. The Choose the dataset you want to use dialog box appears (see Figure 24-3). Select the Create a new dataset named option if you want to create a new **DataSet**, and type the name of the **DataSet** in the textbox. Or select the Use the following dataset option and choose an existing **DataSet** from the drop-down list box. (This option is only available if you already have a **DataSet** in your project.) Click Next.

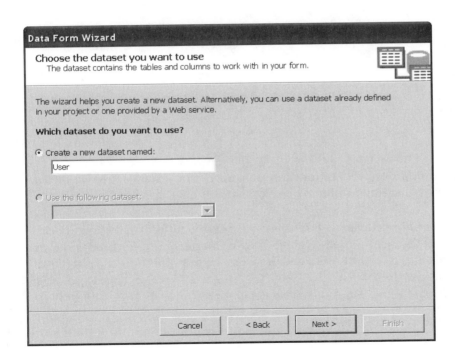

*Figure 24-3. Choosing a **DataSet** in the Data Form Wizard*

4. The Choose a data connection dialog box appears (see Figure 24-4). Select the desired database connection in the Which connection should the wizard use? drop-down list box. Click Next. You might be prompted for a password depending on how the connection has been set up.

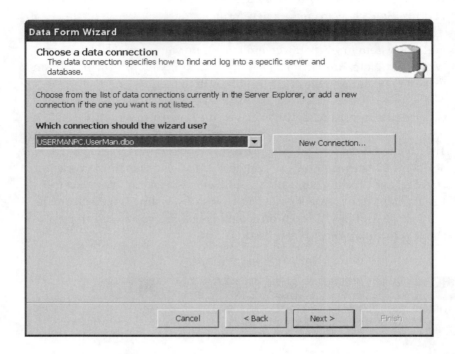

Figure 24-4. Choosing a connection in the Data Form Wizard

5. The Choose tables or views dialog box appears (see Figure 24-5). Select the desired tables and/or views from the Available item(s) tree view. Click the right arrow button to make your selections. Click Next.

6. The Choose tables and columns to display on the form dialog box appears (see Figure 24-6). Select a table from the Master or single table drop-down list box. If you only want data from one table in your form, this is all you need to do. If you want to create a master detail form, you must also select a table in the Detail table drop-down list box.

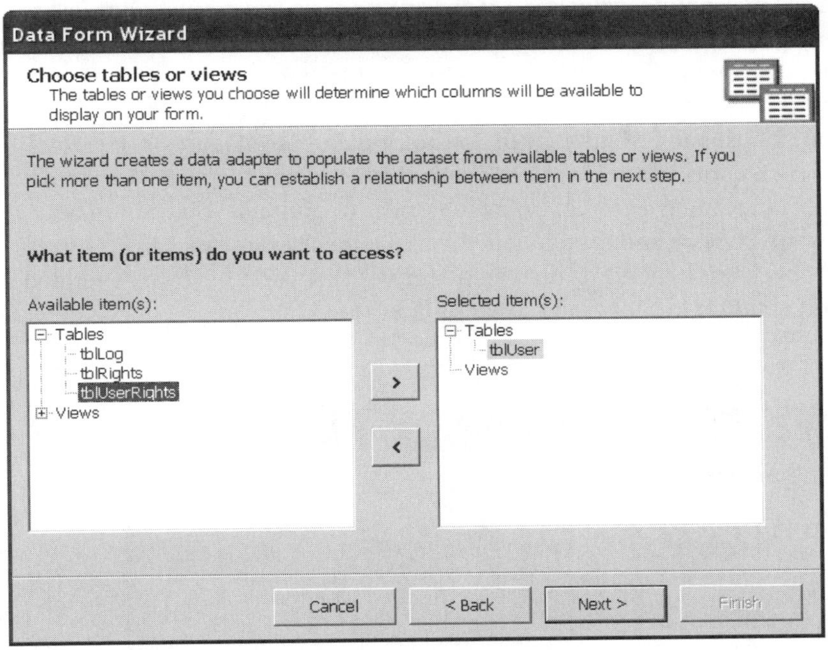

Figure 24-5. *Choosing tables and views in the Data Form Wizard*

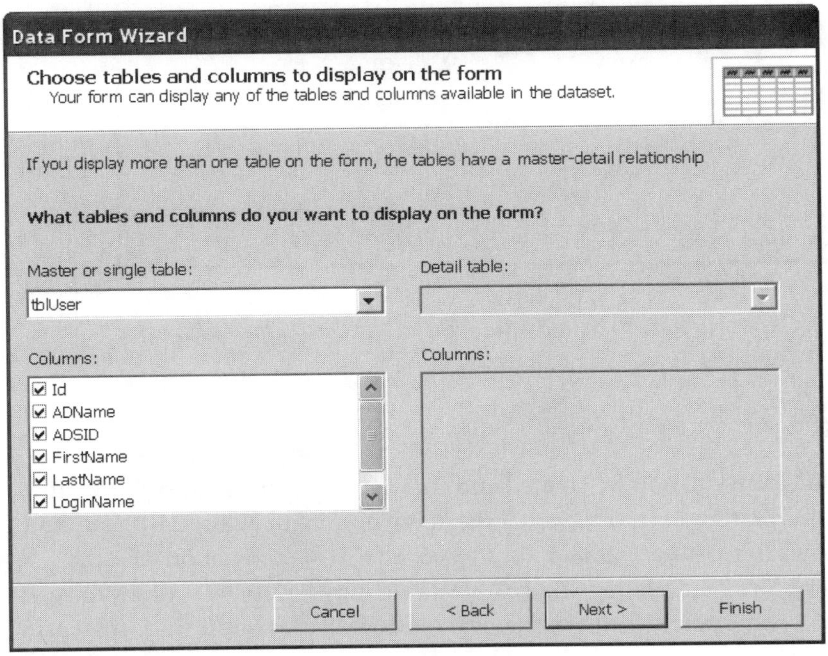

Figure 24-6. *Choosing tables and columns in the Data Form Wizard*

7. Check the columns you want displayed on your form in the Columns list boxes. (The right-hand Columns list box will be activated only if you selected a table from the Detail table drop-down list.) Click Next.

8. The Choose the display style dialog box appears (see Figure 24-7). Select the All records in a grid option if you want your data displayed in a grid. Select the Single record in individual controls option if you want to be able to navigate and manipulate the data. Check or uncheck the Cancel All check box depending on whether or not you want the form generated with a button to cancel all changes made.

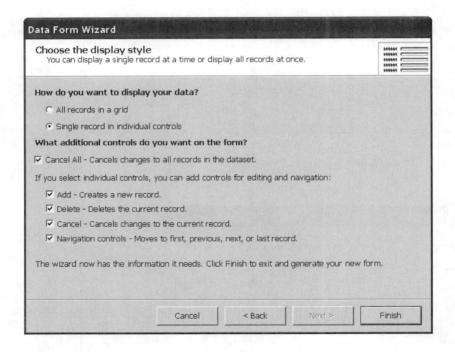

Figure 24-7. Choosing how to display the data in the Data Form Wizard

9. Click Finish.

The data form will now be created and shown in the IDE. If you followed the figures when creating your form, you'll see at the bottom of Figure 24-8 that the wizard creates the objUser **DataSet**, the OleDbConnection1 connection, and the OleDbDataAdapter1 DataAdapter. These objects are only for use by the new form. If you open the code behind file (.vb), you will see how all the code is there for you to manipulate. You can change it to your liking, because it's all there. This is definitely different from the way it was done in versions of Visual Basic[2] prior to VB .NET. You can see how the wizard has created all the OLE DB .NET Data Provider data objects, such as the insert, update, delete, and select commands, and the DataAdapter and Connection objects.

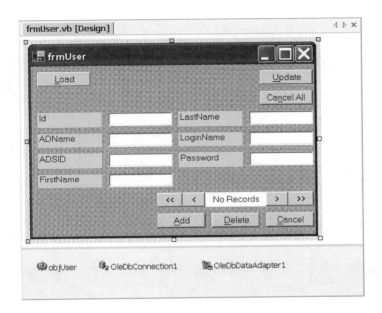

Figure 24-8. A form created by the Data Form Wizard

 NOTE   See Chapter 8 for a discussion of DataAdapters.

   The wizard also creates a strongly typed XML **DataSet** file (.xsd). Another file it creates that is not normally shown in Solution Explorer is the class file, which encapsulates or wraps the data access. This file has the same name as the **DataSet** file (.xsd), but with a .vb extension. This file should appears in the folder you've selected to save your project in, or you can click the Show All Files button in Solution Explorer to see it. This button is located at the very top of the Solution Explorer window, as shown in Figure 24-9.

---

2.   I keep referring to previous versions of VB because many Windows developers have used VB either professionally or as a prototyping tool, where data-bound controls have been used extensively.

Figure 24-9. The Show All Files button in the Solution Explorer window

Exercise

1. Create a new connection to the UserMan database from Server Explorer if you don't already have one.

2. Add a new form using the Data Form Wizard and name the form **frmUser**.

3. Create a new **DataSet** called **User** in the wizard dialog box.

4. Select the UserMan database connection and add the tblUser table.

5. Display the data as a single record in individual controls.

The new form should look like the form shown in Figure 24-8.

One thing you might have noticed is that the wizard always uses the OLE DB .NET Data Provider. This is also true when you connect to a SQL Server, which is obviously not ideal if you want to work exclusively with SQL Server 7.0 or later. You can, if you're the adventurous type, do a search and replace in your code of the OLE DB .NET Data Provider classes and types, but only if you feel comfortable with the **System.Data.OleDb** and **System.Data.SqlClient** namespaces. This process is not straightforward and although I've done it once or twice, it takes a while. Mind you, once you start, you won't get the code running until you've completed the replacement. Start with replacing *OleDb* with *Sql* and you're on your way.

Looking at the Code Created by the Data Form Wizard

I'll now go through the code created by the Data Form Wizard, and if you want to follow along, I suggest you open the project in which you created the frmUser form from the previous exercise. If you didn't perform the exercise, now would be a good time to do so, as I'll cover how the **CurrencyManager** and **BindingContext** objects are used in code.

If you open the frmUser form in the Code Editor, not in Design view, you'll see several hundred lines of code. Just think about that for a minute—how long do you think it will take you to type this in yourself? What I'm getting at here is that even if the code generated by the Data Form Wizard often needs to be adjusted slightly, it will save you a lot of time compared to typing it all in yourself.

If you're following along, scroll down the code until you reach the **New** constructor and the **Dispose** method. To get a better look at the code in the Code Editor, expand the Windows Forms Designer–generated code region by clicking the plus sign (+) next to the line number where you see the text "Windows Forms Designer generated code" (approximately Line 4). This is similar to what you would do in Windows Explorer when you go file hunting. If the code region is already expanded, a minus sign (–) is shown, and you'll see the text "#region Windows Form Designer generated code".

Notice that just after the constructor and **Dispose** methods, the wizard has put the declaration of all the objects used by the form. This includes the data objects, such as the DataAdapter, Connection, and Command objects, as well as all the buttons and labels shown on the form. All these objects and controls are declared so that the objects are only accessible to the form class itself and other classes and so on within the same project.

One declaration I want you to look closer at is the objUser object. This object is of type `<ProjectName>`.User, where *ProjectName* is the name of your project and User is the class. Can't recall creating this class? Don't worry, that's because the wizard did. Right-click the class and select Go To Definition from the pop-up menu. This brings up the User class in the Code Editor window. This class is derived from the **DataSet** class in the **System.Data** namespace, which basically means this class is the disconnected part of the data source you will be binding to. The User class is located in the User.vb[3] file, which also holds the following classes:

---

3. You can't by default see this file in Solution Explorer, but see Figure 24-9 for information on how to have this file displayed.

- *tblUserDataTable:* Derived from **System.Data.DataTable**. Implements public properties such as **Count** and **Item**. The class also holds procedures for manipulating rows in the table and an enumerator.

- *tblUserRow:* Derived from **System.Data.DataRow**. Implements properties for getting and setting column values in rows in the tblUser table, a constructor, **Boolean** functions to check for **Null** values in columns, and functions to set the column values to **Null**.

- *tblUserRowChangeEvent:* Derived from **System.EventArgs**. This class is the base class for event data, which means this class is used for controlling events in connection with data manipulation in the tblUser table through the User class.

Okay, now back in the frmUser.vb file: In the **InitializeComponent** procedure, all the objects are instantiated and initialized. Please take a look at the **ConnectionString** property of the connection—it includes a hard-coded workstation ID. Do feel free to take it out if it bothers you.

Outside the Windows Forms Designer–generated code region, you have all the private procedures for the **Click** events of the buttons on the form; a procedure for updating the current row position label; **Sub** procedures for updating, loading, or filling the **DataSet**; and finally, a procedure for updating the data source.

You should really take a long and close look at these files and classes, because there is loads of information in them. If you do a search in the frmUser.vb file for the **BindingContext** object, you'll see what operations it actually performs with regard to manipulating the data.

Binding a Windows Form Control to a Data Source

Any Windows Form control that is derived from the **Control** class, which is a member of the **System.Windows.Forms** namespace, can be bound to any property of an object and thus a data source. If you go back to the code generated by the Data Form Wizard earlier in this chapter, you can search the code and find how the **DataBindings** property of all the buttons on the form is being used to bind to the objUser object mentioned in the previous section. The **DataBindings** property returns a **ControlBindingsCollection**, and this collection has an **Add** method, which you can see used in the generated code to add a **Binding** object. This **Binding** object is the real trick of the data binding. It is created by the **Add** method of the **ControlBindingsCollection**, and it specifies how a certain control property is bound to a certain member of a data source. The following example code is taken from the code generated by the Data Form Wizard:

```
Me.editId.DataBindings.Add(New _
    System.Windows.Forms.Binding("Text", Me.objUser, "tblUser.Id"))
```

The `editId` item is a **TextBox** control, but as stated previously, you can bind data to any control derived from the **Control** class. In the example, the textbox is bound to the Id column of the tblUser table (data member) from the `objUser` object (data source). The first argument, which reads "Text", specifies that it is the **Text** property of the `editId` **TextBox** control bound to the Id column.

Using the BindingContext Object

The **BindingContext** object can be associated with a Windows Form, and when it is, it's a global object, meaning you don't have to instantiate it. If you do a search, you'll see many instances of **Me.BindingContext** in the code, which indicates the **BindingContext** object is indeed associated with, or rather a part of, the current Windows Form object. The noninherited, public property and method of the **BindingContext** class are shown in Table 24-1.

*Table 24-1. Public Property and Method of the **BindingContext** Class*

Name	Property/Method	Description
Item	Property	This overloaded, read-only property returns the **BindingManagerBase** object associated with the data source.
Contains()	Method	This overloaded method returns a **Boolean** value indicating if the **BindingContext** object contains the specified **BindingManagerBase**.

As you can see from Table 24-1, there just aren't that many public properties and methods to use, but this is not really a problem. Remember that the **BindingContext** object holds a **CurrencyManager** object for each data source on the form. This means you don't really have to manipulate the **BindingContext** object at all, but you have to use this object's **Item** property to get to the **CurrencyManager** objects and/or the **Contains** method to check if a specific **CurrencyManager** exists. Does this make sense to you? It probably would have if I hadn't used two terms for virtually the same thing: **CurrencyManager** and **BindingManagerBase**.

The **BindingManagerBase** class is abstract, meaning it must be derived or inherited before you can use it. Yes, you guessed it: The **CurrencyManager** class does indeed inherit from the **BindingManagerBase** class. So for the purpose of discussing data-bound controls on Windows Forms, these two classes are more or less the same.

Okay, so before continuing on with the **CurrencyManager** class, let me explain how to get to it using the **BindingContext** object. In the case of the source code created by the Data Form Wizard, I'll use **Me.BindingContext** to refer to the **BindingContext** object of the frmUser form. Listings 24-1 and 24-2 show you two different ways of accessing the currency manager.

*Listing 24-1. Saving a Reference to **CurrencyManager***

```
Dim objCurrencyManager As CurrencyManager
objCurrencyManager = Me.BindingContext(objUser, "tblUser")
```

*Listing 24-2. Accessing the **Count** Property of **CurrencyManager** Through the Binding Context*

```
Me.BindingContext(objUser, "tblUser").Count
```

As you can see from Listings 24-1 and 24-2, you can choose to either reference the currency manager through the **BindingContext** object (as shown in Listing 24-2) or save a reference to it and use it directly (as shown in Listing 24-1). The method you choose doesn't really make a difference—it's a matter of preference. One thing to notice about the **CurrencyManager** class is that it doesn't have a constructor, so you can only instantiate an object of data type **CurrencyManager** using the indexer of a **BindingContext** object.

Using the CurrencyManager Object

Now look at the **CurrencyManager** class, because that's the juicy one—the one with all the properties and methods you'll be using extensively in your code when you create data-bound controls. Table 24-2 lists all the noninherited, public properties of the currency manager, and Table 24-3 shows you all the noninherited, public methods.

As Tables 24-2 and 24-3 indicate, the **CurrencyManager** class has methods and properties for performing just about any action on the data source.

*Table 24-2. Properties of the **CurrencyManager** Class*

Property Name	Description
Bindings	This read-only property returns a **BindingsCollection** object that holds all the **Bindings** objects being managed by **CurrencyManager**.
Count	The **Count** property, which is read-only, returns an **Integer** value that indicates the number of rows managed by **CurrencyManager**.
Current	This property returns the current object. Because the returned object is of data type **Object**, you need to cast it to the same data type as the data type contained by the data source before you can use it.
List	This property returns the list for **CurrencyManager** and the data type is an **IList** object. Basically, this means that you can cast it to any data type that implements the **IList** interface.
Position	The **Position** property retrieves or sets the current position in the data source or rather underlying list. The value is 0 based and of data type **Integer**.

*Table 24-3. Important Methods of the **CurrencyManager** Class*

Method Name	Description	Example
AddNew()	The **AddNew** method adds a new item to the underlying list. In the case of a **DataTable**, the new item is a **DataRow**.	`Me.BindingContext(objUser, "tblUser").AddNew()` (taken from the code generated by the Data Form Wizard)
CancelCurrentEdit()	This method cancels the current edit operation. The data is *not* saved in its current condition. Data is reverted back to the condition it was in when you started the edit operation. If you need to end the edit operation and save any changes, you should use the **EndCurrentEdit** method for this purpose instead.	`Me.BindingContext(objUser, "tblUser").CancelCurrentEdit()` (taken from the code generated by the Data Form Wizard)
EndCurrentEdit()	The **EndCurrentEdit** method is used for ending the current edit operation. The data is saved in its current condition, so this does *not* cancel the edits. Use the **CancelCurrentEdit** method for this purpose instead.	`Me.BindingContext(objUser, "tblUser").EndCurrentEdit()` (taken from the code generated by the Data Form Wizard)

*Table 24-3. Important Methods of the **CurrencyManager** Class (Continued)*

Method Name	Description	Example
Refresh()	The **Refresh** method refreshes, or rather repopulates, the bound controls. This method is for use with data sources that do not support change notification, such as an array. **DataSet**s and **DataTable**s do support change notification, meaning this method is not needed with objects of these data types.	`Me.BindingContext(objUser, "tblUser").Refresh()`
RemoveAt(int intIndex)	This method deletes the item at the specified index position.	`Me.BindingContext(objUser, "tblUser").RemoveAt(0)`
ResumeBinding()	This method and the **SuspendBinding** method are used for temporarily suspending the data binding. You should use these two methods if you want to let a user perform several edits without validating these edits until binding is resumed. This method resumes suspended binding.	`Me.BindingContext(objUser, "tblUser").ResumeBinding()`
SuspendBinding()	This method and the **ResumeBinding** method are used for temporarily suspending the data binding. You should use these two methods if you want to let a user perform several edits without validating these edits until binding is resumed. This method suspends binding.	`Me.BindingContext(objUser, "tblUser").SuspendBinding()`

Retrieving the Number of Rows in the Data Source

Occasionally it is desirable to retrieve the number of rows in the data source to which the controls are bound for display purposes, such as to show that the current row is number *n* of the actual number of rows. This can be easily achieved using the **Count** property of the **CurrencyManager** class, as follows:

```
MsgBox("This is row number " & (Me.BindingContext(objUser, _
    "tblUser").Position + 1).ToString() & " of " & Me.BindingContext(objUser, _
    "tblUser").Count.ToString() & " rows.")
```

This code obviously uses both the **Position** and **Count** properties to display the current row position and the number of rows. Because the **Position** property is 0 based, I've added the value 1 to this property at display time. This is done to make sure that the current position is 1 based as it is with the **Count** property.

Retrieving the Current Row of a Data Source

Sometimes you need to manipulate the content of the current row in the data source. You can do this using the **Current** property of the **CurrencyManager** class. However, this property returns a value of data **Object**, which means you have to cast this value to the same data type used by the data source. When the data source is accessed through a **DataSet**, **DataTable**, or **DataViewManager** object, you're actually binding to a **DataView** object. In this situation, you have to convert the returned object to a **DataRowView** object.

```
Dim drwCurrent As DataRowView = _
    CType(Me.BindingContext(objUser, "tblUser").Current, DataRowView)
```

In the example code, drwCurrent now holds the current row in the data source.

Retrieving and Setting the Current Position in a Data Source

You can retrieve and set the current position in the data source using the **Position** property of the **CurrencyManager** class. See the section "Retrieving the Number of Rows in the Data Source" earlier in this chapter for example code of how to read the **Position** property.

However, retrieving the current position in the data source is not the only thing you can do with the **Position** property—you can also set the position. That's right; you can use the **Position** property to move around the data source. Best of all, it's extremely easy to do so, as this example demonstrates:

```
Me.BindingContext(objUser, "tblUser").Position = 3
```

This code makes the fourth row the current one (the **Position** property is 0 based). Table 24-4 shows you how to make specific rows current.

Table 24-4. Navigating to Specific Rows in the Data Source in a Bound Control

Position	Example
First row	`Me.BindingContext(objUser, "tblUser").Position = 0`
Last row	`Me.BindingContext(objUser, "tblUser").Position =` `Me.BindingContext(objUser, "tblUser").Count - 1`
Next row	`Me.BindingContext(objUser, "tblUser").Position += 1`
Previous row	`Me.BindingContext(objUser, "tblUser").Position -= 1`

In connection with moving around the data source, you need to check the validity of the move before you actually perform it.[4]

So if you want to move to the previous row, make sure you are not at position 0, which is the first row. Check it like this:

```
If Not Me.BindingContext(objUser, "tblUser").Position = 0 Then
```

If you want to move to the next row, check if you're currently at the last row, as follows:

```
If Not Me.BindingContext(objUser, "tblUser").Position = _
    Me.BindingContext(objUser, "tblUser").Count - 1) Then
```

Controlling Validation of Edit Operations

When you edit the data in the data source, the **CurrentChanged** and **ItemChanged** events are triggered. This is good, because you can respond to these events and perform whatever actions you need to in your application. However, sometimes it is *not* desirable to have events fired. If you're doing a bulk update, it's better to respond to these events after the update has been applied. You can do this using the **SuspendBinding** and the **ResumeBinding** methods. These methods are used for temporarily suspending the data binding. See Listing 24-3 for an example of how to suspend and resume data binding.

---

4. Actually, this isn't truly necessary, because **CurrencyManager** handles takes and simply ignores requests to move to a nonexistent row. However, I feel its good programming practice to do so.

Listing 24-3. Suspend and Resume Data Binding

```
1 ' Suspend data binding
2 Me.BindingContext(objUser, "tblUser").SuspendBinding()
3 ' Perform bulk edits
4 …
5 ' Resume data binding
6 Me.BindingContext(objUser, "tblUser").ResumeBinding()
```

Listing 24-3 shows you how to first suspend the data binding before performing your bulk edits and then finally resume the data binding. No events are triggered between Lines 2 and 6.

Creating Your Own Data-Bound Windows Form Control

As I've already shown, it's fairly easy to create a data-bound Windows Form control. I suggest you always use the Data Form Wizard for this purpose if you're creating a control with a form-like UI. Even if it means you have to change some of the wizard-generated code afterward, it'll nearly always be quicker and easier to use this approach.

Obviously, when you're using a form-like approach, you'll be creating a component with a UI—and that won't do in some cases, such as when you really just need a control for your existing forms. This is when you need to create a Windows user control. You can do so in any Windows project by following these simple steps:

1. Create a new or use an existing Windows Control Library project. This will create a User Control template with the default name of UserControl1. You can optionally change this name to reflect the data the user control displays.

2. Open the user control in design mode.

3. Drag the required Windows Form controls from the Toolbox onto the Windows user control when it's in design mode.

4. Create a class like the objUser class in the wizard-generated code that is the data source. Optionally you can drag a database table directly from Server Explorer onto a form. This will create a Connection and DataAdapter object. Then right-click the DataAdapter in design mode and click the Generate DataSet menu item. This will create a strongly typed **DataSet** you can use as the data source for binding the controls in your user control. See Figure 24-10.

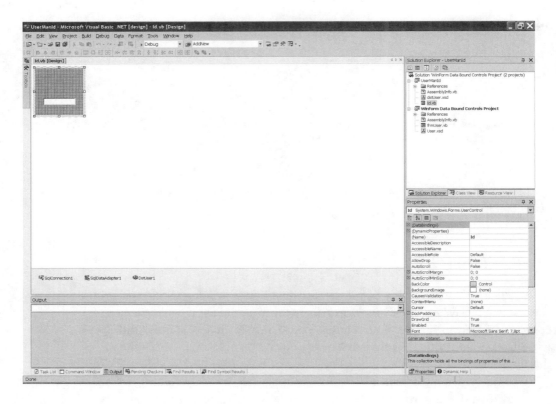

Figure 24-10. A Windows Control Library project with custom control open in design mode

5. Bind one or more properties of each of the Windows Form controls you have placed on the Windows user control to a property of the data source class.

That's all there is to it! Okay, this is really simple, and there's certainly more you have to do when you want to create fancy-looking user controls with edit facilities. However, to create a user control that simply displays the first row in a table, this really is all there is to it.

Exercise

Create a new user control and name it UserManId. Add a **TextBox** control to the user control and bind it to the Id column of the tblUser table. You can find an example of how to do this in the accompanying example code for this chapter on the Apress Web site.

Adding Your Own Data-Bound Windows Form Control to the Toolbox

When you have created your Windows Control Library and finished coding one or more user controls in the project, you can simply drag the user controls to the Toolbox to add them to it, as shown in Figure 24-11.

Figure 24-11. A Windows custom control as part of the Windows Form tab of the Toolbox

Figure 24-11 shows that the Id Windows custom control created in the previous exercise has been added to the Windows Form tab of the Toolbox.

Summary

In this chapter I explained what data-bound controls are and how you use them in Windows Forms. I showed you the **CurrencyManager** and **BindingContext** classes in regard to data binding in Windows Forms and demonstrated how they're used for data binding. I also discussed the **DataBindings** property of the Windows Form control derived from the **Control** class and showed you how to manually bind a Windows Form control to a data source.

In the next chapter I'll show you how data binding works in Web Forms, including state management, and how you can create your own Web custom control.

CHAPTER 25

Web Data-Bound Controls

Creating and Working with Web Data-Bound Controls

IN THIS CHAPTER I'll discuss Web data-bound controls in particular. If you need an overview of data-bound controls in general, please refer to the opening sections of Chapter 24.

This chapter is by no means an exhaustive reference to working with Web data-bound controls. However, here you'll see the very basics of working with Web data-bound controls.

Using Data-Bound Controls with Web Forms

Data binding your Web controls is quite different behind the scenes from how it works in Windows Forms. It's especially different because the data-binding architecture for Web Forms doesn't support automatic updates. This doesn't mean that it isn't possible to update your data source with changes from your Web UI, but it does take a little more work.

If you want to create Web Forms with updateable data,[1] it ultimately comes down to how you maintain the state of your data when the Web Form is refreshed, causing a server roundtrip. See the "Maintaining State" section later in this chapter. Another decision you need to make is how the underlying data is kept, meaning where it's stored. Is the data in a **DataSet** or a DataReader? Please see the "Choosing the Right Data Storage" section later in this chapter for more information on what data storage you should choose.

---

1. If you just want read-only data, you don't really have a problem, because data is retrieved every time the Web Form is refreshed.

Binding ASP.NET Server Controls to a Data Source

All controls inherited from the **Control** class in the **System.Web.UI** namespace
have a **DataBind** method that can bind the control to a data source when called. In
order for the data binding to work in single-value server controls,[2] you must set
one or more properties of the control. Basically, any property of the control can be
set, although most of the time you'll probably set the **Text** property, which is the
property that generally gets displayed. If you have a **TextBox** control on a Web
Form and you want to set the property at design time, you need to select the control
on the Web Form in Design view and open the Properties window (press F4) if it's not
already open. Then you need to click the button with the ellipsis in the (DataBindings)
field in the Properties window, as indicated by the mouse cursor in Figure 25-1.

Figure 25-1. The (DataBindings) field in the Properties window

---

2. Nonsingle value controls such as **DataGrid**, which is covered in the next section, require a
   special form of data binding.

If you click the button indicated in Figure 25-1, the DataBindings dialog box appears. In this dialog box you must select the property you want to bind from the Bindable Properties list, and select either the Simple binding or Custom binding expression option button.

NOTE   You haven't actually created a typed **DataSet** yet, although I'm referring to one as the data source in the coming section. However, this is just an intro as to how you can simply bind your Web controls. Bear with me, and you'll get to the code in the "Creating a Form Using the Data Form Wizard" section later in this chapter. You can find more information on typed **DataSet**s in Chapter 13. Actually, if you read Chapter 24, which is about Windows data-bound controls, you'll know the score.

Figure 25-2 shows you how I've opted for setting the **Text** property of the txtFirstName **TextBox** control. You can also see from Figure 25-2 that I've chosen the Simple binding option and selected to bind to the FirstName column of the DstUser1 typed **DataSet**. The Simple binding tree view lists all typed **DataSet**s in your project as well as any data controls you've dragged onto the Web Form in Design view, such as Connection, DataAdapter, and **DataView** objects. Another thing Figure 25-2 shows is that I'm binding to the FirstName column of the first row (0) of the **DataView** (accessed through the **DefaultView** property) of the **DataTable** (accessed through the **Tables** collection property) of the DstUser1 **DataSet**. This isn't necessarily the way you'd normally access a value in a column in a **DataTable** in your **DataSet**, because quite often you would use the **DataTable** directly and not the **DefaultView** property. Anyway, this was just to show you that you're actually binding to the column values of the **DataTable**, even if it's not done directly.

As I'm sure you've noticed, there's no **DataBinding** property of the **Control** class or any classes derived from it, which is why you can freely choose any other property to be bound to the data source. All there is to do now is to call the **DataBind** method of the **TextBox** control and the control is data bound. You decide if you want to place that call in the **Page_Load** event procedure or any procedure for that matter, as long as it's called after the Web Form page initialization (**OnInit** procedure).

NOTE The **DataBind** method of the **Control** class also calls the method of the same name on all child controls. This means that if you call this method on the Web Form itself (accessed through the **Me** object), the **DataBind** method will also be called on all controls on the Web Form derived from the **Control** class.

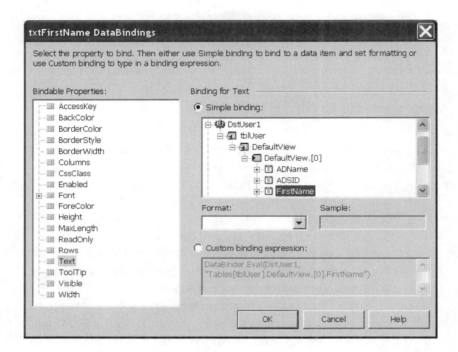

Figure 25-2. The DataBindings dialog box

Maintaining State

The problem with any data binding in ASP.NET is maintaining the state. Web Forms, and ultimately the ASP.NET page framework, generally communicate with the client, such as a browser, using the Hypertext Transfer Protocol (HTTP). The problem concerning data binding with the HTTP protocol is that it is stateless. This means state information is lost every time the page or your Web Form is refreshed, including the data to which your controls are bound. The Web Form is refreshed when the user of the client requests new or more information from the server, such as when a user clicks the Send button in a browser after filling in his or her personal details.

The problem in this scenario is that the user might have entered some invalid data or even left out some required data. Your Web Form would then need to inform the user about the error and at the same time redisplay the form with the entered information.[3] Because the information is lost when the Web Form is refreshed, you need to handle this yourself, meaning you have to save the information elsewhere.

How to save this information is not exactly difficult, but choosing the right way of doing so can be a tricky task, because there are several options available to you:

- You can save the information in the Web Form's **ViewState** property. This means storing the information on the client.

- You can store information in the **Session** and **Application** objects. These objects are probably familiar to you if you've been developing Web sites using Visual InterDev. (I don't cover these objects in this book, but you can find plenty of information about them in the Visual Studio .NET MSDN Library.) This means storing the information on the server.

The option you should choose really depends on your circumstances. I can make one simple recommendation: Try out the different options if and when performance is an issue. "Testing" is the key word here.

Recall that a Web Form loses its state when it's being refreshed, but this isn't too difficult to handle, because the current properties of the page (Web Form), the page itself, and the base properties of the server controls and their state are automatically saved between roundtrips. All you need to worry about is when you have information that is *not* part of the mentioned controls and/or properties, such as private variables and contents of standard HTML elements.

Choosing the Right Data Storage

When you set out to design your Web Forms with data-bound controls, you need to decide where to store your data and, ultimately, how the data is retrieved from your data source. In terms of ADO.NET, which is what this book is about, there are two options:

- DataReader, Command, and Connection objects

- **DataSet**, DataAdapter, Command, and Connection objects

---

3. In many cases you can use some of the server validation controls, which will save you the Web server roundtrip because they're output as client-side script. As such, simple validation, such as required fields, won't need a Web server roundtrip to be validated. However, there are other cases where some or all of the Web Form input needs to be checked against your business rules, and this must be done dynamically, meaning it must be tested against the current content of your DBMS, and that requires a Web server roundtrip.

The Connection, Command, DataReader, and the DataAdapter classes are explained in detail in Chapters 5, 6, 7, and 8, and the **DataSet** class is explained in Chapter 9.

Option 1, which is a connected scenario,[4] is hardly ever the right choice for a Web application, because keeping a connection from your Web Forms to your data source alive isn't very scalable and certainly requires a lot of resources, and the more resources the more pages (Web Forms) your application serves concurrently. Another thing is that the DataReader class is read-only, meaning you can't really use it for updateable data Web Forms.[5]

Option 2 uses the DataAdapter, Connection, and Command classes for retrieving data from and updating the data in the data source, and the **DataSet** as a local cache of the data in the data source. This is the approach the Data Form Wizard uses when you create your data-bound Web Forms with it. See the "Creating a Form Using the Data Form Wizard" section later in this chapter for more information on how to use the Data Form Wizard and learn from the code generated by it.

My recommendation is that if you want updateable, data-bound Web Forms, go with Option 2.

Data Storage State

If you've decided to go for working with a **DataSet** object as the data storage in your updateable, data-bound Web Form, you'll also need to decide on how to save the state of the **DataSet** between server roundtrips, if at all. As I see it, you have two options:

1. Re-create the **DataSet** every time the Web Form is loaded.

2. Save the state using one of the options discussed in the "Maintaining State" section earlier in this chapter.

If you decide to go with Option 1, you need to make sure that any changes to the **DataSet** are propagated back to the data source every time the Web Form is unloaded. This might involve a lot of data traveling across the network, because you have the data coming from the data source every time the Web Form is created, and then you possibly have data traveling the other way when the Web Form is

---

4. The Connection object must be kept open for as long as you read from the DataReader, effectively ruling out the use of this data class combination. You can, of course, loop through all the rows in the DataReader and add them to a **DataGrid** or a different set of controls, but isn't that just manual data hooking, as discussed in the "Data-Bound Controls vs. Manual Data Hooking" section Chapter 24?

5. You can, of course, create your own workaround, effectively overcoming the read-only disadvantage of the DataReader class, but why bother when there are other, easier options, such as using the **DataSet** class?

unloaded (if any data has been changed). This will require more processing from your data source as well.

The previously mentioned issues might not be problematic at all depending on your setup. How much data is sent from the server/data source for every Web Form creation, how loaded is your data source, and how many concurrent users do you expect?

Option 2 doesn't require as much data to travel across the network as frequently as Option 1, but now you need to consider where to store the data between roundtrips: on the server or on the client? If you store it on the server, you'll still need the data to travel across the network every time the Web Form is created, but you won't be burdening your data source. However, you risk the data in the **DataSet** being out-dated, and you'll have to solve potential problems when you try to update the data source. If you store it on the client, you'll also avoid having the data travel across the network every time the Web Form is created, but this requires saving your data in the Web Form's view state or a hidden field.[6] This means that it becomes part of the HTML that the client browser needs to parse, and if it's a large amount of data, the Web Form might take quite a while to load.

Whichever option you choose, make sure you've considered everything care-fully and you understand the implications your choice will have for your application and the client using it. Another thing to do is try out more than one option and perform some benchmarking on network load, Web Form loading time, data source load, and so on.

Creating a Form Using the Data Form Wizard

Instead of doing all the hard work yourself (doing the data binding manually), let the Data Form Wizard create your Web Form with one or more data-bound controls for you as you would with a Windows Form. This wizard does more or less the same thing, but it will only let you create read-only Web Forms. This means you have to take care of creating updateable pages yourself. I'll take you through this process, because it will help you understand how controls are bound to data in Web Forms. Here's how to create a new form:

1. Add a new item to your project and make sure you select the Data Form Wizard template. You can do this by right-clicking your project in the Solution Explorer and clicking the Add ➤ Add New Item menu item.

2. Give the new form a name. This brings up the Data Form Wizard. Click Next.

---

6. View state is actually implemented as a hidden form field as well.

3. The Choose the dataset you want to use dialog box appears (see Figure 25-3). Select the Create a new dataset named option if you want to create a new **DataSet**, and type the name of the **DataSet** in the textbox. Or select the Use the following dataset option and choose an existing **DataSet** from the drop-down list box. (This option is only available if you already have a typed **DataSet** in your project.) Click Next.

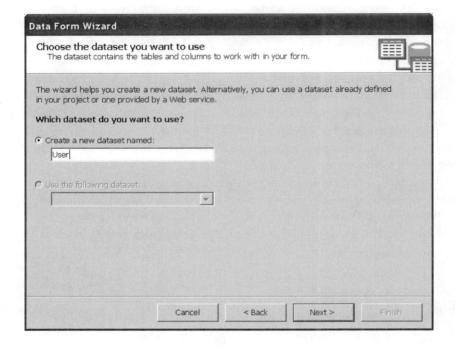

*Figure 25-3. Choosing a **DataSet** in the Data Form Wizard*

4. The Choose a data connection dialog box appears (see Figure 25-4). Select the desired database connection in the Which connection should the wizard use? drop-down list box. Click Next. You might be prompted for a password depending on how the connection has been set up.

5. The Choose tables or views dialog box appears (see Figure 25-5). Select the desired tables and/or views from the Available item(s) tree view. Click the right arrow button to make your selections. Click Next.

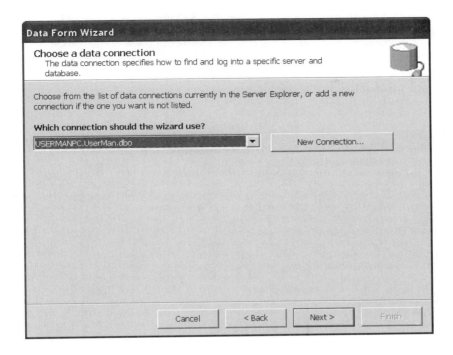

Figure 25-4. Choosing a connection in the Data Form Wizard

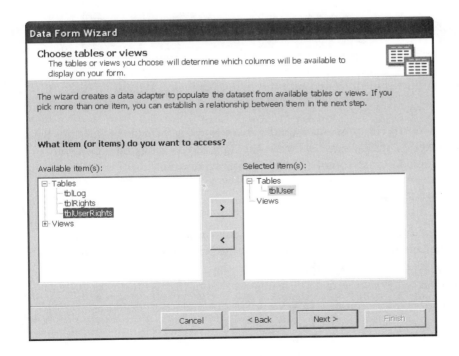

Figure 25-5. Choosing tables and views in the Data Form Wizard

6. The Choose tables and columns to display on the form dialog box appears (see Figure 25-6). Select a table from the Master or single table drop-down list box. If you only want data from one table in your form, this is all you need to do. If you want to create a master detail form, you must also select a table in the Detail table drop-down list box.

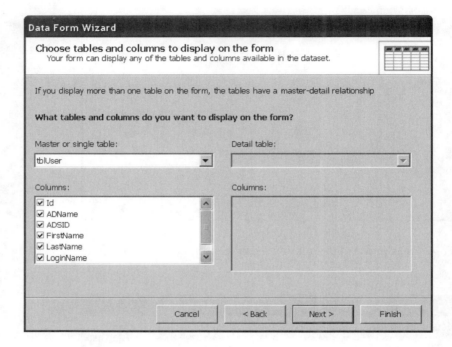

Figure 25-6. Choosing tables and columns in the Data Form Wizard

7. Check the columns you want displayed on your form in the Columns list boxes. (The Columns list box on the right will be activated only if you selected a table from the Detail table drop-down list.)

8. Click Finish.

The data form will now be created and shown in the IDE. If you followed the figures when creating your form, you'll see at the bottom of Figure 25-7 that the wizard creates the objUser **DataSet**, the OleDbConnection1 connection, and the OleDbDataAdapter1 DataAdapter. These objects are only for use by the new form.

If you open the code behind file (.vb), you will see how all the code is at your mercy. You can change it to your liking, because it's all there. This is definitely different from the way it was done in versions of Visual Basic[7] prior to VB .NET. Notice how the wizard has created all the OLE DB .NET Data Provider data objects, such as the insert, update, delete, and select commands, and the DataAdapter and Connection objects.

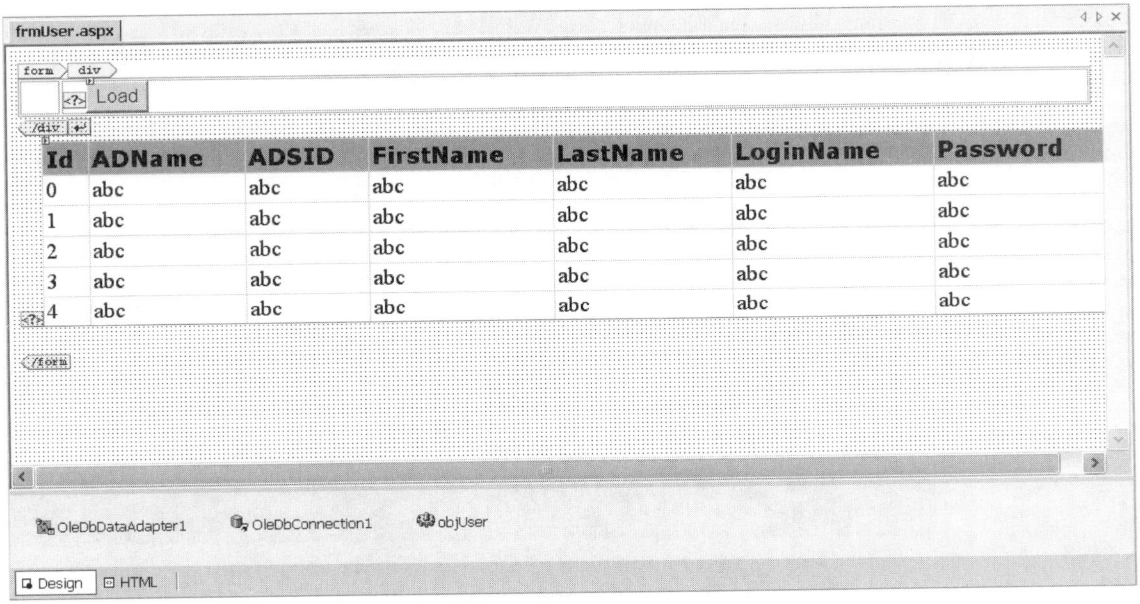

Figure 25-7. A form created by the Data Form Wizard

The wizard also creates a strongly typed XML **DataSet** file (.xsd). Another file it creates that is not normally shown in the Solution Explorer is the class file, which encapsulates or wraps the data access. This file has the same name as the **DataSet** file (.xsd), but with a .vb extension. You can see this file in the folder you've selected to save your project in, or you can click the Show All Files button in the Solution Explorer. This button is located at the very top of the Solution Explorer window, as shown in Figure 25-8.

---

7. I keep referring to previous versions of VB because many Windows developers have used VB either professionally or as a prototyping tool, where data-bound controls have been used extensively.

Figure 25-8. The Show All Files button in the Solution Explorer window

Exercise

1. Create a new connection to the UserMan database from the Server Explorer if you don't already have one.

2. Add a new form using the Data Form Wizard and name the form **frmUser**.

3. Create a new **DataSet** called **User** in the wizard dialog box.

4. Select the UserMan database connection and add the tblUser table.

5. Display the data as a single record in individual controls.

The new form should look like the form shown in Figure 25-7.

One thing you might have noticed is that the wizard always uses the OLE DB .NET Data Provider. This is also true when you connect to a SQL Server, which is obviously not ideal if you want to work exclusively with SQL Server 7.0 or later.

Anyway, try running the project after the wizard finishes to see how nicely it displays your data as read-only in a data grid. You'll see that a typed **DataSet** has been generated and referenced from code. There are two **Public** procedures that the Data Form Wizard creates: the FillDataSet and LoadDataSet procedures. I won't show them here, as you can simply take a look at the code in the WebFormsDataBoundControls project or have the Data Form Wizard create a new data-bound Web Form for you. The **LoadDataSet** procedure, which calls the **FillDataSet** procedure, is being called from the buttonLoad_Click event procedure. This also means that the Web Form, as it has been generated by the Data Form Wizard, doesn't display any data when it loads. You need to click the Load button on the Web Form and then the "magic" starts.

Making the Web Form Updateable

Now that you have your data-bound Web Form, it would be nice if it were updateable as well, don't you think? Well, I had to decide whether or not I wanted to re-create the **DataSet** every time the Web Form loads or if I wanted to save the state of the **DataSet** between roundtrips, and I decided that with the amount of data that I'm transferring across the network and the number of expected users (no more than 100), I'd go with the notion of re-creating the **DataSet** every time the Web Form loads. This also means that I need to make sure that any changes to the data on the client are propagated back to the data source every time the Web Form is unloaded, or every time a row is updated, or simply when the user clicks an Update button.

Here's what I need to do:

- *Make the **DataGrid** control updateable.* This can be done by selecting the grid on the Web Form in Design view, right-clicking, and selecting the Property builder command from the pop-up menu. This brings up Properties dialog box. Click the Columns button on the left; expand the Button Column node in the Available columns tree view; select the Edit, Update, Cancel node; and click the Add (>) button next to the tree view as shown in Figure 25-9 a little later. This adds the Edit, Update, and Cancel buttons (or rather, links) to the **DataGrid**. Click OK.

- *Add code to the Edit, Update, and Cancel events of the **DataGrid**.* Switch to Code view and insert code in the **CancelCommand**, **EditCommand**, and **UpdateCommand** event procedures You can see the code in Listings 25-1, 25-2, and 25-3 later in this chapter.

- *Remove the Load button from the Web Form and move the associated code to the **Page_Load** procedure.* This way the data is automatically retrieved and displayed when the Web Form is loaded. The **Page_Load** event procedure should then look like Listing 25-4 later in this chapter.

Figure 25-9 illustrates how you can use the **DataGrid** Properties dialog box to add Edit, Update, and Cancel buttons or links to a **DataGrid** control.

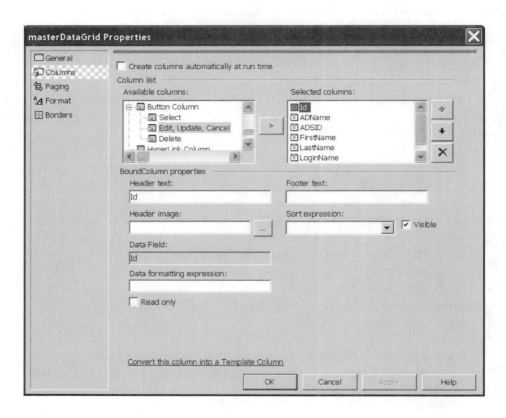

*Figure 25-9. The **DataGrid** Properties dialog box*

Listing 25-1 shows the **DataGrid EditCommand** event procedure.

*Listing 25-1. **DataGrid EditCommand** Event Procedure*

```
1 Private Sub masterDataGrid_EditCommand(ByVal source As Object, _
2    ByVal e As System.Web.UI.WebControls.DataGridCommandEventArgs) _
3    Handles masterDataGrid.EditCommand
4    masterDataGrid.EditItemIndex = e.Item.ItemIndex
5    masterDataGrid.DataBind()
6 End Sub
```

In Listing 25-1 you can see the code needed to start editing a row in the **DataGrid** control. On Line 4 the **EditItemIndex** property is set to the value of the row you clicked the Edit link on (see Figure 25-10), and on Line 5 the **DataBind** method is called, which means that the **DataGrid** control rebinds to the data source and notices the new value of the **EditItemIndex**. This also means that when the Web Form has been reloaded in the browser it looks like Figure 25-11.

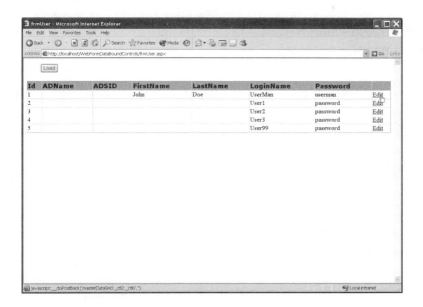

Figure 25-10. The Data Form Wizard–generated Web Form in read-only mode

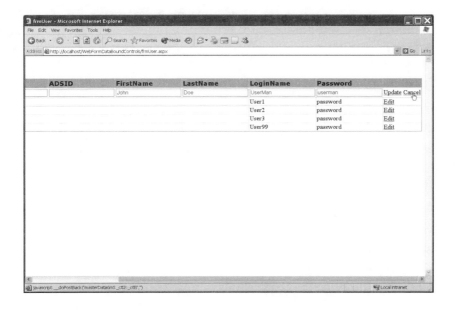

Figure 25-11. The Data Form Wizard-generated Web Form in edit mode

In Figure 25-10 notice the Edit link has been added to the **DataGrid**, making it possible to enter edit mode.

Listing 25-2 shows you how edit mode is canceled by setting the **EditItemIndex** property to –1 and rebinding to the data source. Edit mode can be canceled by the user clicking the Cancel link, as shown in Figure 25-11. In Figure 25-11, the Web Form is in edit mode, meaning the Cancel and Update links have been added to the row that is currently being edited.

*Listing 25-2. **DataGrid CancelCommand** Event Procedure*

```
1 Private Sub masterDataGrid_CancelCommand(ByVal source As Object, _
2    ByVal e As System.Web.UI.WebControls.DataGridCommandEventArgs) _
3    Handles masterDataGrid.CancelCommand
4    masterDataGrid.EditItemIndex = -1
5    masterDataGrid.DataBind()
6 End Sub
```

In Listing 25-3 you can see the code needed to update the data source with the new values in the row being edited. The **UpdateCommand** procedure is invoked by clicking the Update link, which is displayed when the Web Form is in edit mode, as shown in Figure 25-11.

*Listing 25-3. **DataGrid UpdateCommand** Event Procedure*

```
1 Private Sub masterDataGrid_UpdateCommand(ByVal source As Object, _
2    ByVal e As System.Web.UI.WebControls.DataGridCommandEventArgs) _
3    Handles masterDataGrid.UpdateCommand
4    Dim drwUser As User.tblUserRow
5    Dim txtEdit As TextBox
6    Dim intKey As Integer
7
8    ' Save the key field of edited row
9    intKey = CInt(masterDataGrid.DataKeys(e.Item.ItemIndex))
10
11   ' Locate the row in the DataSet that has been edited
12   ' by using the saved key as an argument for the FindById
13   ' procedure
14   drwUser = objUser.tblUser.FindById(intKey)
15
16   ' Update the DataSet with the changed values, through
17   ' the located data row
18   txtEdit = CType(e.Item.Cells(1).Controls(0), TextBox)
19   drwUser.ADName = txtEdit.Text
```

```
20    txtEdit = CType(e.Item.Cells(2).Controls(0), TextBox)
21    drwUser.ADSID = txtEdit.Text
22    txtEdit = CType(e.Item.Cells(3).Controls(0), TextBox)
23    drwUser.FirstName = txtEdit.Text
24    txtEdit = CType(e.Item.Cells(4).Controls(0), TextBox)
25    drwUser.LastName = txtEdit.Text
26    txtEdit = CType(e.Item.Cells(5).Controls(0), TextBox)
27    drwUser.LoginName = txtEdit.Text
28    txtEdit = CType(e.Item.Cells(6).Controls(0), TextBox)
29    drwUser.Password = txtEdit.Text
30
31    ' Update the data source
32    OleDbDataAdapter1.Update(objUser)
33
34    ' Take the DataGrid out of editing mode and rebind
35    masterDataGrid.EditItemIndex = -1
36    masterDataGrid.DataBind()
37 End Sub
```

Listing 25-3 has a lot of "manual" code for updating the data source, but that's the way it works.

Listing 25-4 shows the code the Data Form Wizard generated and placed in the **Click** event procedure of the Load button has been moved to the **Page_Load** event procedure. This means that the **DataGrid** control is populated when the form loads instead of when the Load button is clicked.

*Listing 25-4. Web Form **Page_Load** Event Procedure*

```
1 Private Sub Page_Load(ByVal sender As System.Object, _
2     ByVal e As System.EventArgs) Handles MyBase.Load
3   Try
4       Me.LoadDataSet()
5       Me.masterDataGrid.SelectedIndex = -1
6       Me.masterDataGrid.DataBind()
7   Catch eLoad As System.Exception
8       Me.Response.Write(eLoad.Message)
9   End Try
10 End Sub
```

The WebFormDataBoundControls project, which you can find in the accompanying example code on the Apress Web site, has been created using the Data Form Wizard and then customized according to the previous list.

Creating Your Own Data-Bound Web Form Control

Because the Data Form Wizard for Web Forms always creates read-only forms with a **DataGrid** control, it can be a lot of work making it updateable and/or using separate controls instead of the data grid. However, the initial code to build upon is there and it's easier to extend the wizard-generated code than to do it all by hand.

When you're using a form-like approach as suggested in the preceding section, you will be creating a page UI, and that won't do in some cases. Sometimes you need a control that can be dragged from the Toolbox onto a Web Form. In those instances, you need to create a Web user control. You can create a Web user control in any Web project by adding a new item to your project. When the Add New Item dialog box appears, you select the Web User Control template, give the user control a name, and click OK. Here is what else you need to do:

1. Drag the required Web Form controls from the Toolbox onto the Web user control when it's in design mode.

2. Create a **DataSet** for binding the controls to. To do so, drag the table you want as your **DataSet** from the Server Explorer onto the Web user control. This creates a new Connection and a new DataAdapter object, as shown in Figure 25-12. These objects are set to point at the data source you dragged from the Server Explorer, meaning you don't have to initialize them.

3. Create a **DataSet** from the DataAdapter object. Select the SqlDataAdapter1 object and right-click it. Then select Generate Dataset from the pop-up menu.

4. In the Generate Dataset dialog box (shown in Figure 25-13), specify that you want to create a new **DataSet** by selecting New and then giving the **DataSet** a name in the text field next to the New option. Click OK.

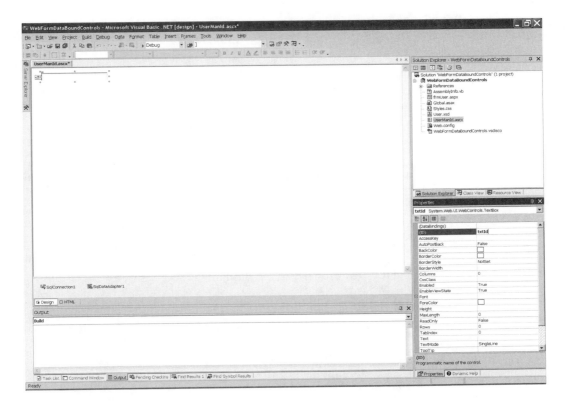

Figure 25-12. A Web user control in design mode with data objects

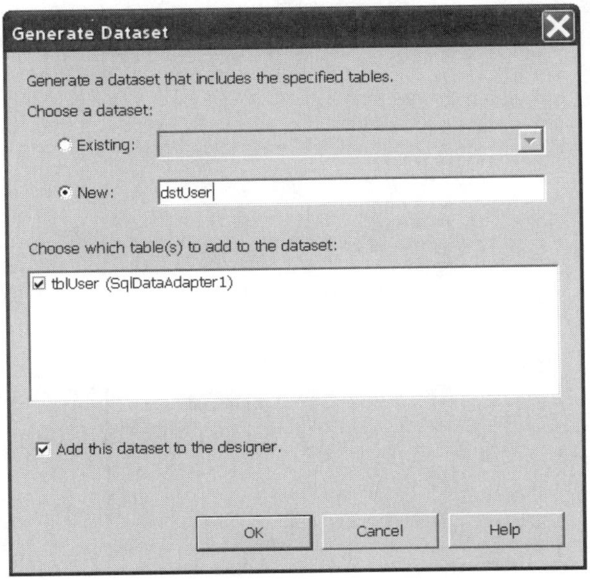

Figure 25-13. The Generate Dataset dialog box

5. The **DataSet**, DstUser1 in this example, is now visually added to the data design view next to the data adapter object.

6. Bind one or more properties of each of the Web Form controls you have placed on the Web user control to a property of the data source class. Do so by following these steps:

   a. Select the Web user control in design mode.

   b. Select the Properties window and place the cursor in the DataBindings textbox.

   c. Click the button with the ellipsis (. . .) next to the textbox. This brings up the DataBindings dialog box.

   d. Select the **Text** property in the Bindable Properties tree view.

   e. Check the Simple binding radio button and expand the DstUser1 **DataSet** in the tree view below the Simple binding radio button.

   f. Keep expanding the nodes so you can select the Id column of the tblUser table from the **DataSet**, as shown in Figure 25-14. Click OK.

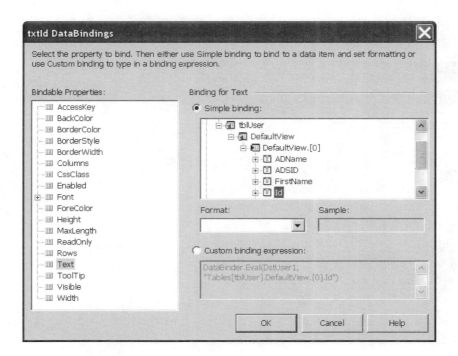

Figure 25-14. The DataBindings dialog box

7. Place the code from Listing 25-5 in the **Page_Load** subprocedure in the code for the Web user control.

Listing 25-5. Finishing the Data Binding in a Web User Control

```
' Open connection
SqlConnection1.Open()
' Fill DataSet
SqlDataAdapter1.Fill(DstUser1, "tblUser")
' Bind controls to data source
txtId.DataBind()
```

The example in Listing 25-5 is pretty simple, but this really is all you need if you perform the other steps. You now have a data-bound user control you can use on any Web page.

The question is if you really want to do it this way. You may have other considerations: do you really want to open a connection for just one control, what about closing the connection, and so forth. You know the drill—the example code is simply to show how easily it can be done. How you finish the user control is entirely up to you.

Exercise

Create a new user control and name it **UserManId**. Add a **TextBox** control to the user control and bind it to the Id column of the tblUser table. You can find an example of how this is done in the accompanying example code on the Apress Web site.

Summary

In this chapter I explained how data binding works in Web Forms, including state management, and how you can create your own Web custom control.

In the next chapter I'll finish the UserMan example application that I've been referring to throughout the book, and I'll give you some ideas and tips on how to take the example further if you want build your own application based on the UserMan application.

Part Twelve

Example Application

CHAPTER 26

UserMan

Finishing the Example Application

IN THIS CHAPTER, I finish the UserMan example application that you've built upon throughout this book, assuming you've followed the exercises along the way. I also give you some ideas as to how to take it further, if you feel the application can be the building block that you need for your very own .NET application.

The example application created throughout the book is all about implementing a user administration system that works with user information extracted from Active Directory, the directory system in Windows 2000 and later versions.

Identifying the UserMan Information

Let me state all the particulars about what the UserMan application should do, how it should do it, and so on. UserMan is a user management system that performs the following tasks:

- Logging on and off from the system (checking the tblUser table)

- Adding, editing, and deleting a user (tblUser table)

- Updating and checking a user's permissions (tblUserRights table)

- Logging all user activity (tblLog table)

- Adding, updating, and deleting user rights or permissions (tblRights table)

These are the duties of the UserMan application as I've written it, but it obviously needs more than this to be considered for any sort of deployment in an organization.

Discovering the Objects

This section covers the items in the UserMan application that you can identify as actual objects.

Database Objects

The database has already been written and it consists of the following tables:

- tblUser

- tblUserRights

- tblRights

- tblLog

The database schema for the UserMan database is shown in Figure 26-1.

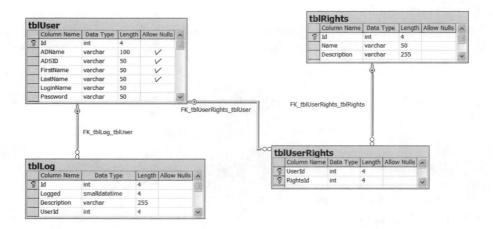

Figure 26-1. UserMan database schema

Keeping the guidelines from Chapter 23 in mind, your next step in developing this application is figuring out how to wrap the access to these tables in one or more classes. Actually, this is fairly easy, because it almost always makes sense to wrap each table in a class. I've had to wrap more than one table in the same class for other applications, but in most cases I've wrapped one table per class. The tables in the UserMan database are clearly defined, and although they're related, they should be accessed individually for adding, updating, and deleting rows. So you need four classes for the relational database:

- CUser

- CUserRights

- CRights

- CLog

Finishing the CUser Class

You started creating the CUser class in Chapter 23, so let's finish this particular class now. The rest of the classes look quite alike, and they can be found in the downloads section on the Apress site (http://www.apress.com) or at the UserMan site[1] (http://www.userman.dk). First you need to add some database connectivity. Listing 26-1 shows you the private constants and variables needed.

Listing 26-1. Private Database Constants and Variables for the CUser *Class*

```
1 ' Database constants
2 Private Const PR_STR_CONNECTION As String = "Data Source=USERMANPC;" & _
3   "User ID=UserMan;Password=userman;Initial Catalog=UserMan"
4 Private Const PR_STR_SQL_TABLE_NAME As String = "tblUser"
5
6 Private Const PR_STR_SQL_FIELD_ID_NAME As String = "Id"
7 Private Const PR_STR_SQL_FIELD_FIRST_NAME As String = "FirstName"
8 Private Const PR_STR_SQL_FIELD_LAST_NAME As String = "LastName"
9 Private Const PR_STR_SQL_FIELD_LOGIN_NAME As String = "LoginName"
10 Private Const PR_STR_SQL_FIELD_PASSWORD_NAME As String = "Password"
11 Private Const PR_STR_SQL_FIELD_ADSID_NAME As String = "ADSID"
12 Private Const PR_STR_SQL_FIELD_ADNAME_NAME As String = "ADName"
13
14 Private Const PR_STR_SQL_USER_SELECT As String = "SELECT * FROM " & _
15     PR_STR_SQL_TABLE_NAME
```

---

1.   Don't forget to have the book by your side when you log on to the UserMan site, because you're required to enter a word from a page in the book to gain access.

```
16 Private Const PR_STR_SQL_USER_DELETE As String = "DELETE FROM " & _
17  PR_STR_SQL_TABLE_NAME & " WHERE " & PR_STR_SQL_FIELD_ID_NAME & "=@" & _
18  PR_STR_SQL_FIELD_ID_NAME
19 Private Const PR_STR_SQL_USER_INSERT As String = "INSERT INTO " & _
20    PR_STR_SQL_TABLE_NAME & "(" & PR_STR_SQL_FIELD_FIRST_NAME & ", " & _
21    PR_STR_SQL_FIELD_LAST_NAME & ", " & PR_STR_SQL_FIELD_LOGIN_NAME & _
22    ", " & PR_STR_SQL_FIELD_PASSWORD_NAME & ") VALUES(@" & _
23    PR_STR_SQL_FIELD_FIRST_NAME & ", @" & PR_STR_SQL_FIELD_LAST_NAME & _
24    ", @" & PR_STR_SQL_FIELD_LOGIN_NAME & ", @" & _
25    PR_STR_SQL_FIELD_PASSWORD_NAME & ")"
26 Private Const PR_STR_SQL_USER_UPDATE As String = "UPDATE " & _
27  PR_STR_SQL_TABLE_NAME & " SET " & PR_STR_SQL_FIELD_FIRST_NAME & "=@" & _
28  PR_STR_SQL_FIELD_FIRST_NAME & ", " & PR_STR_SQL_FIELD_LAST_NAME & "=@" & _
29  PR_STR_SQL_FIELD_LAST_NAME & ", " & PR_STR_SQL_FIELD_LOGIN_NAME & "=@" & _
30  PR_STR_SQL_FIELD_LOGIN_NAME & ", " & PR_STR_SQL_FIELD_PASSWORD_NAME & _
31  "=@" & PR_STR_SQL_FIELD_PASSWORD_NAME & " WHERE " & _
32  PR_STR_SQL_FIELD_ID_NAME & "=@" & PR_STR_SQL_FIELD_ID_NAME
33 Private Const PR_STR_SQL_TABLE_USER_FIELD_ID As String = "Id"
34
35 ' Database variables
36 Private Shared prshcnnUserMan As SqlConnection
37 Private prdadUserMan As SqlDataAdapter
38 Private prdstUserMan As DataSet
39
40 ' For direct user table manipulation
41 Private prcmmUser As SqlCommand
42 ' The Command objects for the DataSet manipulation
43 Private prcmmUserSelect, prcmmUserDelete, prcmmUserInsert, _
44    prcmmUserUpdate As SqlCommand
45 ' Parameter objects for the DataSet manipulation
46 Private prprmSQLDelete, prprmSQLUpdate, prprmSQLInsert As SqlParameter
47
48 ' User table column values
49 Private prlngId As Long = 0
50 Private prstrADName As String
51 Private prstrADSID As String
52 Private prstrFirstName As String
53 Private prstrLastName As String
54 Private prstrLoginName As String
55 Private prstrPassword As String
56
57 ' User table column max lengths
58 Private printADNameMaxLen As Integer
59 Private printADSIDMaxLen As Integer
```

```
60 Private printFirstNameMaxLen As Integer
61 Private printLastNameMaxLen As Integer
62 Private printLoginNameMaxLen As Integer
63 Private printPasswordMaxLen As Integer
64
65 ' For logging user activity
66 Private probjLog As New CLog()
```

Listing 26-1 includes a few private constants, one for the connection string (PR_STR_CONNECTION), one for the table name (PR_STR_SQL_TABLE_NAME), some for the field names in the table, and the command strings for selecting, inserting, updating, and deleting rows from the user table (PR_STR_SQL_USER_ . . .). There are also a few database objects, such as the Connection object (prshcnnUserMan), the DataAdapter object (prdadUserMan), the **DataSet** object (prdstUserMan), and so on. Line 66 creates an instance of the CLog class (probjLog) that is used for logging all user activity. Please see the accompanying example code on the Apress Web site for the CLog class.

I'm sure you've already taken a closer look at the way I create my constants and you either hate it or like it. The fact is that it has taken me awhile to get used to this approach, but it does save me a lot of hassle when I change various names, such as table or column names, because I only have to make updates in one place. Feel free to think what you like.

 NOTE If you need more information on any of the objects mentioned previously, I suggest you read Part Two and Part Three of this book.

I have also added the private variables from Chapter 23 for storing the table column values and the maximum column lengths. Regarding the column length variables, well, you need to set them, and that's what is shown in Listing 26-2.

Listing 26-2. Setting the Maximum Column Length Variables

```
1 Private Sub prSetColumnMaxLength()
2    Const STR_COLUMN_SIZE As String = "ColumnSize"
3
4    Dim drdSchema As SqlDataReader
5    Dim dtbSchema As DataTable
6    Dim cmmUserSchema = New SqlCommand()
7
```

```
8    cmmUserSchema.CommandType = CommandType.Text
9    cmmUserSchema.Connection = prshcnnUserMan
10   cmmUserSchema.CommandText = "SELECT * FROM " & PR_STR_SQL_TABLE_NAME
11
12   ' Return DataReader
13   drdSchema = cmmUserSchema.ExecuteReader()
14
15   ' Read schema from source table
16   dtbSchema = drdSchema.GetSchemaTable()
17
18   ' Save the maxlength values
19   printFirstNameMaxLen = CInt(dtbSchema.Rows(3)(STR_COLUMN_SIZE))
20   printLastNameMaxLen = CInt(dtbSchema.Rows(4)(STR_COLUMN_SIZE))
21   printLoginNameMaxLen = CInt(dtbSchema.Rows(5)(STR_COLUMN_SIZE))
22   printPasswordMaxLen = CInt(dtbSchema.Rows(6)(STR_COLUMN_SIZE))
23
24   ' Close DataReader
25   drdSchema.Close()
26 End Sub
```

In Listing 26-2 I use the **GetSchemaTable** method of the DataReader class to retrieve information about all the columns from the tblUser table in a **DataTable** object. Once this method has been called (Line 16), you can save the maximum column length for those columns it applies to[2] by retrieving the value of the **ColumnSize** column (Lines 19 through 22). When you use the **GetSchemaTable** method, each column of a row in the DataReader object is returned as one row with information about the column. This means that Rows(3) (Line 19) refers to the fourth column of the tblUser table, which is the FirstName column (you can see the database schema in Figure 26-1).

Making the Connection Object Shared

If you look at the Connection object on Line 35 in Listing 26-1, you will see that I have declared it using the **Shared** access modifier. I have done this so the Connection object will be shared amongst all instances of the CUser class—that is, they will all use the same single connection. Also, this keeps the Connection object alive until the last instance of the class has been destroyed. Is this good or bad? Well, you be the judge. Just make sure you think about such issues as scalability, performance, and the overall number of users when you decide to change the declaration or leave it for that matter. Another thing you should notice is that when you use a DataReader object on a Connection object, the Connection object

---

2. This is generally columns of any string data type, such as varchar in SQL Server.

will not be able to serve other data classes. How does this make you feel about Listing 26-2?[3]

 NOTE Programming is an art on its own, and it's up to you to make the most of your application. What is good for one application might be extremely bad for another. This book has given you some things to consider when you design and implement your application, if nothing else.

If you've been adding these private variables and constants to your CUser class, I am sure you've found out that **SqlConnection**, **SqlCommand**, and other such data types aren't being recognized. To rectify this, you need to import the **System.Data.SqlClient** namespace by adding the following as the very first line of code in your CUser class:

```
Imports System.Data.SqlClient
```

Opening the Database Connection

If you've added all the database variables needed for accessing the UserMan database, the next step is to set up the code shown in Listing 26-3, which establishes the database connection.

Listing 26-3. Connecting to the Database

```
1 Private Sub prOpenDatabaseConnection()
2    Try
3        ' Check if the connection has already been instantiated
4        If prshcnnUserMan Is Nothing Then
5            ' Instantiate the connection
6            prshcnnUserMan = New SqlConnection(PR_STR_CONNECTION)
7            ' Check if the connection is closed
8            If (prshcnnUserMan.State = ConnectionState.Closed) Then
9                ' Open the connection
10               prshcnnUserMan.Open()
11               ' Log activity if the user has already been logged on
12               If prlngId > 0 Then
```

---

3. There's no correct answer to this, but do consider this when designing your application. If the prSetColumnMaxLength procedure is called when the CUser class is instantiated, does it really matter then?

```
13              probjLog.Logged = DateTime.Now
14              probjLog.Description = "Database connection opened."
15              probjLog.UserId = prlngId
16              probjLog.AddLogEntry()
17            End If
18          End If
19        End If
20    Catch objSqlException As SqlException
21      ' A Connection low-level exception was thrown. Add a description and
22      ' re-throw the exception to the caller of this class
23     Throw New Exception("The connection to the UserMan database " & _
24        "could not be established, due to a connection low-level error", _
25        objSqlException)
26    Catch objE As Exception
27      ' Any other exception thrown is handled here
28      Throw New Exception("The connection to the UserMan database " & _
29          "could not be established.", objE)
30    End Try
31 End Sub
```

In Listing 26-3 I open the connection in the private prOpenDatabaseConnection procedure. I have chosen to make the procedure private because clients don't need to perform this operation. It should be handled when you instantiate the class (see Listing 26-4 in the next section). I make sure that the connection hasn't been instantiated before I do so, and that it's closed before I try to open it. If it isn't closed when I open it, an exception is thrown. If an exception occurs, I throw a new exception with a message detailing what went on, and then I add the current exception to the **InnerException** property of the new exception. This way the caller of this class can see the original exception thrown and my error message as well.

Instantiating Your Class

Any initialization of variables and such that isn't handled by an initializer should be placed in the constructor, as shown in Listing 26-4.

Listing 26-4. Opening the Database Connection at Class Instantiation

```
1 Public Sub New()
2    MyBase.New()
3    ' Open the database connection
4    prOpenDatabaseConnection()
5 End Sub
```

Listing 26-4 shows you how to make sure that the database connection is open and ready for use after the client has instantiated the class. Placing a call to the custom prOpenDatabaseConnection procedure in the constructor does this.

Closing the Database Connection

Just as you need to open your database connection, it must also be closed again to preserve connection resources, and ensure no memory leaks occur. Listing 26-5 shows you how to do this.

Listing 26-5. Closing the Database Connection

```
1 Private Sub prCloseDatabaseConnection()
2    Try
3        ' Close the connection
4        prshcnnUserMan.Close()
5        ' Log activity if the user has already been logged on
6        If prlngId > 0 Then
7            probjLog.Logged = DateTime.Now
8            probjLog.Description = "Database connection closed."
9            probjLog.UserId = prlngId
10           probjLog.AddLogEntry()
11       End If
12   Catch objE As Exception
13       Throw New Exception("The connection to the UserMan database " & _
14           "could not be closed properly.", objE)
15   End Try
16 End Sub
```

Listing 26-5 closes the database connection using the **Close** method of the Connection class. This method isn't really known for throwing that many exceptions, so the exception handler might be overkill. You be the judge, and take it out if it bothers you.

As you can see, I have also chosen to make this procedure private, as is the case with the prOpenDatabaseConnection procedure. I have done this for the same reason: The client shouldn't be able to call this method—it should be done automatically by your code when the class is disposed of.

Disposing of Your Class

When your class is disposed of, you must make sure that your connection is closed. Placing a call to a procedure that performs the closing of the connection in the class' destructor does this (see Listing 26-6).

Listing 26-6. Disposing of a Class

```
1 Protected Overrides Sub Finalize()
2    ' Do your housekeeping here
3    prCloseDatabaseConnection()
4    ' Call the base class' destructor
5    MyBase.Finalize()
6 End Sub
7
8 Public Overloads Sub Dispose() Implements IDisposable.Dispose
9    ' Do your housekeeping here
10   prCloseDatabaseConnection()
11   ' Now you need to make sure the Finalize method isn't
12   ' called as well, because you've already done
13   ' the housekeeping
14   GC.SuppressFinalize(Me)
15   ' Always call this method on the base class,
16   ' if it implements one
17   'MyBase.Dispose()
18 End Sub
```

In Listing 26-6 I close the database connection from within the class finalizer and **Dispose** method. Please see Chapter 23 for more information on these procedures. You need to close the database connection explicitly; otherwise it will stay open and not be returned to the pool.

NOTE   Chapter 5 tells you more about connections and connection pools.

Instantiating the Command Objects

The Command objects used by the DataAdapter for manipulating the data source and the generic Command object need to be instantiated, as demonstrated in Listing 26-7.

Listing 26-7. Instantiating the Command Objects

```
1 Private Sub prInstantiateCommands()
2    ' Instantiate the DataSet Command objects
3    prcmmUserSelect = New SqlCommand(PR_STR_SQL_USER_SELECT, prshcnnUserMan)
4    prcmmUserDelete = New SqlCommand(PR_STR_SQL_USER_DELETE, prshcnnUserMan)
5    prcmmUserInsert = New SqlCommand(PR_STR_SQL_USER_INSERT, prshcnnUserMan)
6    prcmmUserUpdate = New SqlCommand(PR_STR_SQL_USER_UPDATE, prshcnnUserMan)
7    ' Instantiate and initialize generic Command object
8    prcmmUser = New SqlCommand()
9    prcmmUser.Connection = prshcnnUserMan
10 End Sub
```

In Listing 26-7 I instantiate the Command objects used by the DataAdapter for selecting, adding, updating, and deleting rows in the data source. I then instantiate the generic Command object that can be used directly on the data source so that, for example, I can retrieve only certain columns from a table in a DataReader using the Command object's **ExecuteReader** method. I haven't specified any command text as this can be done when the command is executed, but I do specify the shared connection as the command's connection, because this is the connection I will use for all queries through this command. The prInstantiateCommands procedure should be added to the constructor in Listing 26-4 after the call to open the database connection.

Instantiating the DataSet Object

In line with most other objects, **DataSet** objects need to be instantiated as well before you can use them. Listing 26-8 shows you how to do this.

*Listing 26-8. Instantiating the **DataSet***

```
1 Private Sub prInstantiateDataSet()
2    prdstUserMan = New DataSet()
3 End Sub
```

As you can see from Listing 26-8, there isn't much code in the prInstantiateDataSet procedure. You don't really need any more code and as such you can consider taking the single line of code out of the procedure and placing it where you would normally place a call to the procedure. In any case, the instantiation code should be placed in the class constructor.

Instantiating and Initializing the DataAdapter

I just showed you how to instantiate the **DataSet**, but the **DataSet** needs to be populated from the data source, and this must be done using the DataAdapter. So, let's go ahead and instantiate and initialize the DataAdapter as shown in Listing 26-9.

Listing 26-9. Instantiating and Initializing the DataAdapter

```
1 Private Sub prInstantiateAndInitializeDataAdapter()
2    prdadUserMan = New SqlDataAdapter()
3    prdadUserMan.SelectCommand = prcmmUserSelect
4    prdadUserMan.InsertCommand = prcmmUserInsert
5    prdadUserMan.DeleteCommand = prcmmUserDelete
6    prdadUserMan.UpdateCommand = prcmmUserUpdate
7 End Sub
```

In Listing 26-9 I instantiate the DataAdapter and initialize the command properties by setting them to the already instantiated Command objects. You should add a call to the prInstantiateAndInitializeDataAdapter procedure to the class constructor.

Adding Command Object Parameters

Chapter 6 shows you how to add parameters to your Command objects so that the DataAdapter knows exactly how to query your data source. Listing 26-10 shows you how to perform this task for UserMan.

Listing 26-10. Adding Command Object Parameters

```
1 Private Sub prAddCommandObjectParameters()
2    ' Add delete command parameters
3    prprmSQLDelete = prdadUserMan.DeleteCommand.Parameters.Add("@" & _
4       PR_STR_SQL_FIELD_ID_NAME, SqlDbType.Int, 0, PR_STR_SQL_FIELD_ID_NAME)
5    prprmSQLDelete.Direction = ParameterDirection.Input
6    prprmSQLDelete.SourceVersion = DataRowVersion.Original
7
8    ' Add update command parameters
9    prcmmUserUpdate.Parameters.Add("@" + PR_STR_SQL_FIELD_FIRST_NAME, _
10      SqlDbType.VarChar, 50, PR_STR_SQL_FIELD_FIRST_NAME)
11   prcmmUserUpdate.Parameters.Add("@" + PR_STR_SQL_FIELD_LAST_NAME, _
12      SqlDbType.VarChar, 50, PR_STR_SQL_FIELD_LAST_NAME)
13   prcmmUserUpdate.Parameters.Add("@" + PR_STR_SQL_FIELD_LOGIN_NAME, _
14      SqlDbType.VarChar, 50, PR_STR_SQL_FIELD_LOGIN_NAME)
15   prcmmUserUpdate.Parameters.Add("@" + PR_STR_SQL_FIELD_PASSWORD_NAME, _
16      SqlDbType.VarChar, 50, PR_STR_SQL_FIELD_PASSWORD_NAME)
17   prprmSQLUpdate = prdadUserMan.UpdateCommand.Parameters.Add("@" & _
18      PR_STR_SQL_FIELD_ID_NAME, SqlDbType.Int, 0, PR_STR_SQL_FIELD_ID_NAME)
19   prprmSQLUpdate.Direction = ParameterDirection.Input
20   prprmSQLUpdate.SourceVersion = DataRowVersion.Original
21
22   ' Add insert command parameters
23   prcmmUserInsert.Parameters.Add(PR_STR_SQL_FIELD_FIRST_NAME, _
24      SqlDbType.VarChar, 50, PR_STR_SQL_FIELD_FIRST_NAME)
25   prcmmUserInsert.Parameters.Add("@" + PR_STR_SQL_FIELD_LAST_NAME, _
26      SqlDbType.VarChar, 50, PR_STR_SQL_FIELD_LAST_NAME)
27   prcmmUserInsert.Parameters.Add("@" + PR_STR_SQL_FIELD_LOGIN_NAME, _
28      SqlDbType.VarChar, 50, PR_STR_SQL_FIELD_LOGIN_NAME)
29   prcmmUserInsert.Parameters.Add("@" + PR_STR_SQL_FIELD_PASSWORD_NAME, _
30      SqlDbType.VarChar, 50, PR_STR_SQL_FIELD_PASSWORD_NAME)
31 End Sub
```

In Listing 26-10 I add the parameters needed by the DataAdapter
for manipulating the data source to the Command objects. The call to the
`prAddCommandObjectParameters` procedure should be added to the class constructor
in Listing 26-4.

Filling the DataSet

Now that everything has been set up, all you need to do is fill the **DataSet** with data from the data source. See Listing 26-11 for example code that accomplishes this task.

*Listing 26-11. Populating the **DataSet** with Data from the Data Source*

```
1 Private Sub prPopulateDataSet()
2    Try
3        prdadUserMan.Fill(prdstUserMan, PR_STR_SQL_TABLE_NAME)
4    Catch objSystemException As SystemException
5        Throw New Exception("The DataSet could not be populated, " & _
6            "because the source table was invalid.", objSystemException)
7    Catch objE As Exception
8        Throw New Exception("The DataSet could not be populated.", objE)
9    End Try
10 End Sub
```

Listing 26-11 is pretty simple—I try to fill the **DataSet** with data from the tblUser table in the data source. If an exception is thrown, I rethrow it with the original exception. This method should also be added to the class constructor.

Hooking Up the Public Properties to the DataSet

Now that the **DataSet** has been populated, the public properties can be hooked up to the **DataSet**. All the properties read and set private variables, so you need to read the values from the populated **DataSet** and save them in the corresponding private variables, as demonstrated in Listing 26-12.

*Listing 26-12. Saving the **DataSet** Values*

```
1 Private Sub prSaveDataSetValues()
2    ' Save user id
3    prlngId = CLng(prdstUserMan.Tables(PR_STR_SQL_TABLE_NAME).Rows(0) _
4        (PR_STR_SQL_FIELD_ID_NAME))
5    ' Check if ADName is Null
6    If prdstUserMan.Tables(PR_STR_SQL_TABLE_NAME).Rows(0). _
7        IsNull(PR_STR_SQL_FIELD_ADNAME_NAME) Then
8        prstrADName = ""
9    Else
10       prstrADName = prdstUserMan.Tables(PR_STR_SQL_TABLE_NAME).Rows(0) _
11           (PR_STR_SQL_FIELD_ADNAME_NAME).ToString()
12    End If
```

```
13    ' Check if ADSID is Null
14    If prdstUserMan.Tables(PR_STR_SQL_TABLE_NAME).Rows(0). _
15      IsNull(PR_STR_SQL_FIELD_ADSID_NAME) Then
16      prstrADSID = ""
17    Else
18      prstrADSID = prdstUserMan.Tables(PR_STR_SQL_TABLE_NAME).Rows(0) _
19        (PR_STR_SQL_FIELD_ADSID_NAME).ToString()
20    End If
21    ' Check if first name is Null
22    If prdstUserMan.Tables(PR_STR_SQL_TABLE_NAME).Rows(0). _
23      IsNull(PR_STR_SQL_FIELD_FIRST_NAME) Then
24      prstrFirstName = ""
25    Else
26      prstrFirstName = prdstUserMan.Tables(PR_STR_SQL_TABLE_NAME).Rows(0) _
27        (PR_STR_SQL_FIELD_FIRST_NAME).ToString()
28    End If
29    ' Check if last name is Null
30    If prdstUserMan.Tables(PR_STR_SQL_TABLE_NAME).Rows(0). _
31      IsNull(PR_STR_SQL_FIELD_LAST_NAME) Then
32      prstrLastName = ""
33    Else
34      prstrLastName = prdstUserMan.Tables(PR_STR_SQL_TABLE_NAME).Rows(0) _
35        (PR_STR_SQL_FIELD_LAST_NAME).ToString()
36    End If
37    ' Check if login name is Null
38    If prdstUserMan.Tables(PR_STR_SQL_TABLE_NAME).Rows(0). _
39      IsNull(PR_STR_SQL_FIELD_LOGIN_NAME) Then
40      prstrLoginName = ""
41    Else
42      prstrLoginName = prdstUserMan.Tables(PR_STR_SQL_TABLE_NAME).Rows(0) _
43        (PR_STR_SQL_FIELD_LOGIN_NAME).ToString()
44    End If
45    ' Check if password is Null
46    If prdstUserMan.Tables(PR_STR_SQL_TABLE_NAME).Rows(0). _
47      IsNull(PR_STR_SQL_FIELD_PASSWORD_NAME) Then
48      prstrPassword = ""
49    Else
50      prstrPassword = prdstUserMan.Tables(PR_STR_SQL_TABLE_NAME).Rows(0) _
51        (PR_STR_SQL_FIELD_PASSWORD_NAME).ToString()
52    End If
53 End Sub
```

In Listing 26-12 I simply read the values from the **DataSet** and save them in the corresponding private variables. Please note that I read from the very first row in the **DataSet**. I do this in order to facilitate sorting and filtering, which can be added later on. I've added a check for null values for the columns in the database that allow storing null values.

Specifying the Parent Class

I don't know if you are wondering about what class your CUser class is derived from. If you've followed along with the example, you haven't actually told the compiler to inherit from another class. For the purposes of the UserMan application, you don't have to, because you want to inherit from the **Object** class, which is done implicitly. This means you don't have to add the Inherits Object statement to your class declaration. However, if there is a different class you want to inherit from, you need to add the statement on the line following the class declaration, like this:

```
Public Class CUser
    Inherits Object
```

CROSS-REFERENCE   I discuss these issues in Chapter 23, where you started creating the CUser class.

What Else Is Needed?

Obviously the CUser class isn't finished yet, although you've added a lot of code to it. What you need now is to add code to allow filtering and sorting of the rows in the **DataSet**, and, more importantly, code for updating the data source.

NOTE   I have already added this code and a few other procedures to the CUser class, which can be found in the downloads section on the Apress Web site (http://www.apress.com).

Active Directory Object

You need an object for reading the values for the ADSID and ADName columns in the tblUser table. Listing 26-13 shows example code for this purpose.

Listing 26-13. The Active Directory Class

```
 1 Imports System.Data.OleDb
 2 Imports System.Runtime.InteropServices
 3
 4 Public Class CActiveDirectory
 5    Implements IDisposable
 6
 7    Private Const PR_STR_CONNECTION_STRING As String = _
 8       "Provider=ADsDSOObject;User Id=UserMan;Password=userman;"
 9    Private prstrADName As String
10    Private prstrADSID As String
11    Private prstrUserName As String
12
13    Sub New(ByVal UserName As String)
14       prstrUserName = UserName
15       prOpenConnection()
16    End Sub
17
18    Protected Overrides Sub Finalize()
19       ' Do your housekeeping here
20       prCloseConnection()
21       ' Call the base class' destructor
22      MyBase.Finalize()
23     End Sub
24
25     Public Overloads Sub Dispose() Implements IDisposable.Dispose
26        ' Do your housekeeping here
27        prCloseConnection()
28       ' Now you need to make sure the Finalize method isn't
29       ' called as well, because you've already done
30       ' the housekeeping
31       GC.SuppressFinalize(Me)
32       ' Always call this method on the base class,
33       ' if it implements one
34       'MyBase.Dispose()
35    End Sub
36
37    ' Database objects
38    Private prcnnAD As OleDbConnection
39    Private prcmmAD As OleDbCommand
40    Private prdrdAD As OleDbDataReader
41
```

```
42    Private Sub prOpenConnection()
43       ' Instantiate and open connection
44       prcnnAD = New OleDbConnection(PR_STR_CONNECTION_STRING)
45       prcnnAD.Open()
46       prRetrieveUserInformation()
47    End Sub
48
49    Private Sub prCloseConnection()
50       ' Close connection
51       prcnnAD.Close()
52    End Sub
53
54    Private Sub prRetrieveUserInformation()
55       Dim arrbytSID() As Byte
56
57       Try
58          ' Instantiate command
59          prcmmAD = New OleDbCommand("SELECT objectSid, " & _
60             "samAccountName FROM 'LDAP://dotnetservices.biz' " & _
61             "WHERE objectCategory='person' AND " & _
62             "objectClass='user' AND cn='" & prstrUserName & "'", prcnnAD)
63          ' Retrieve user info in DataReader
64          prdrdAD = prcmmAD.ExecuteReader()
65          ' Move to the first row
66          If prdrdAD.Read() Then
67             ' Save SAM account name (pre-Windows 2000)
68             prstrADName = prdrdAD("samAccountName").ToString()
69             ' Save human readable SID
70             prstrADSID = prConvertSID2SDDL(prdrdAD("objectSid"))
71          End If
72       Catch objE As Exception
73          Throw New Exception("An error occurred trying to retrieve " & _
74             "the user information from Active Directory.", objE)
75       End Try
76    End Sub
77
78    Public ReadOnly Property ADName() As String
79       Get
80          Return prstrADName
81       End Get
82    End Property
83
```

```
84    Public ReadOnly Property ADSID() As String
85       Get
86          Return prstrADSID
87       End Get
88    End Property
89 End Class
```

As you can see from Listing 26-13, I have used the OLE DB .NET Data Provider for retrieving the user information from AD. This provider is read-only when used with Active Directory, but this is okay because I only want to retrieve information.

CROSS-REFERENCE   You can find more information about Active Directory access in Chapter 19.

NOTE   A finished CActiveDirectory class can be found in the downloads section on the Apress Web site (http://www.apress.com) or at the UserMan site[4] (http://www.userman.dk).

The constructor (Lines 13 through 16) for the CActiveDirectory class takes the login name of a user as the only argument, and this name is used for searching Active Directory for the samAccountName and the SID. This means that the CActiveDirectory class can be called from any client, such as the CUser class shown in Listing 26-14.

Listing 26-14. Calling the Active Directory Class

```
1 Public Sub GetADUserInfo()
2    probjActiveDirectory = New CActiveDirectory(prstrLoginName)
3    prstrADName = probjActiveDirectory.ADName
4    prstrADSID = probjActiveDirectory.ADSID
5 End Sub
```

---

4. Don't forget to have the book by your side when you log on to the UserMan site, because you're required to enter a word from a page in the book to gain access.

Other Objects

You need to create more classes than the ones you've already created, because you haven't finished wrapping all your data access. Here are some suggestions:

- Message queuing

- Data-bound controls

Wrapping Classes as Components

When you are done creating all your classes, you need to decide if one or more of them need to be wrapped as a component for deployment on a server. In most cases, it's a matter of which architecture your application has that determines if a class is wrapped in a component.

Creating the Client

At this point, the database has been put together and I've shown you how to create wrapper classes for some of the data-related access that I have covered in this book. So what is needed now is the client application, a Windows client based on a Windows Form. There isn't much in creating the Windows client that has anything to do with accessing the data in the UserMan application. I have therefore decided to leave out any example code from the Windows client in this chapter. However, you can find a finished sample of the UserMan Windows client in the downloads section on the Apress Web site (http://www.apress.com) or at the UserMan site[5] (http://www.userman.dk). The code holds plenty of comments that make it easier for you to read.

Tips and Ideas

In this section I give you some tips and ideas for further developing the UserMan application so that you can perhaps use it for your own purposes. I have grouped the suggestions so that they are easier for you to go through.

---

5. Don't forget to have the book by your side when you log on to the UserMan site, because you're required to enter a word from a page in the book to gain access.

Database Suggestions

In this section you will find all the suggestions that are related to database improvements and/or enhancements.

Password Column in User Table

As you've probably noticed, the Password column in the tblUser table is a varchar(50) column that anyone with read access to the table can read. This means the password of any user, including the administrator's (UserMan), can be read by a user with read access. This is obviously not the way it should be. Several third-party vendors produce encryption components, but at the time of this writing, I haven't seen any for the .NET Framework. However, when you read this there probably will be one, or you could use a COM component though COM Interop (COM Interop is covered in Appendix B in brief). You can also choose to use the encryption features of the **System.Security.Cryptography** namespace.

Another option is to create your own password encryption scheme. If you feel access to your network is fairly secure, a handy little routine of your own might be all that's needed.

Log to the Event Log

Instead of logging to the tblLog table in the UserMan database, you could log events in the Windows NT Event Log. This will make your events available to all users able to read the Event Log on your network. Check out the **EventLog** class in the **System.Diagnostics** namespace for more information on how to read from and write to the Event Log.

Pass the Connection Object to the Various Classes

Instead of having a connection in each of your classes, you should consider passing an open connection to them for their use. This way you can share a connection between the classes. Again, this depends on how you've created your application, how it's been deployed, and the amount of traffic you expect on a single connection.

One last thing to consider if you want to implement this enhancement is whether any DataReader you include will use the connection exclusively while it's open. So with DataReaders this is obviously not an option, unless you choose to have a general connection for your **DataSet** objects and one or more others for your DataReader objects.

Create Stored Procedures for Accessing Your Database Tables

As the classes are currently implemented, they access the data directly. However, you can change the implementation of the classes to use stored procedures instead. You might not want to do this until you see how performance is and determine whether it could be improved by using stored procedures instead. One of the really good things about using classes for database access in your application is you can change the implementation of your classes as long as you leave the interface intact, and the client applications won't detect that anything has changed.

Set Up Triggers to Enforce Business Rules

In Chapter 18, I showed you how to implement simple triggers, such as enforcing the inclusion of both a first name and a last name for a user, if you supply either. This is just one of many simple tasks that you can let a trigger handle for you instead of placing this functionality in your classes or, even worse, in your client code.

Set Up Database Security

I haven't done anything to implement security on the database level, meaning that more or less anyone with access to your network and DBMS can access your UserMan database. I suggest one of the first things you do is add some sort of security if you haven't already done so. Ask your system administrator or read the documentation that comes with your DBMS for more information on how to implement security at the database level.

Use Constants for Table and Column Names

Replace all hard-coded table and column names such as tblUser and Id with constants as shown in Listing 26-1. It makes your code easier to update and maintain, and I personally think it makes your code easier to read, although you should feel free to disagree on this one.

Use Local Transactions

It's always a good thing to use transactions with any operations that write to a database. This hasn't been implemented in the classes for UserMan, and I strongly suggest you consider adding local transaction support.

CROSS-REFERENCE   Chapter 5 discusses local transactions, which are transactions that are explicitly started and ended using the Connection object.

General Suggestions

This section contains ideas and suggestions that don't really fit in elsewhere.

Let Active Directory Validate Users

Instead of having your own validation routine, why not let Active Directory perform one for you? This of course means that all users of your application need to be stored in Active Directory. Simply extend the Active Directory class to allow writing as well as reading.

Use Web Services to Expose Some Functionality

You could expose some of the application functionality from one or more Web services. I won't be going into detail about Web Services in this book, but basically you use Web services as methods of a Web server to expose certain functionality across the Internet, intranet, or indeed any network using Simple Object Access Protocol (SOAP) over HTTP. This guarantees that you can use this functionality through a firewall.

NOTE   I'm currently writing a book with my coauthor Mark Dunn about XML Web Services, called *Building Web Services with Visual Basic .NET* (ISBN: 1-59059-007-4), to be published by Apress, and it will be available March 2003. Look here for more information:
http://www.apress.com/book/bookDisplay.html?bID=109.

Exception Handling

The two client applications have very little exception handling, and this is obviously not good. Go through the code and place exception handlers where you feel it's necessary. Looking over the various classes for places to add exception handling is probably not a bad idea either!

Use Automatic Transactions

All .NET Framework classes can be part of an automatic transaction. This means you can roll back or commit changes made in classes just as you can with database operations. All you have to do is make your class transactional. See the documentation for more information on how to do this.

Summary

This chapter finished the example application that the rest of the chapters in this book have been built upon. I showed you how to use some of the data-related tools and/or methods, such as Active Directory access and SQL Server access, introduced in earlier chapters, to build and finish the sample application.

I went on to give you some ideas and tips on how to take the sample application further and customize it for your own use.

Here we are at the end of the last chapter of this book. I sincerely hope you've enjoyed reading it as much as I have enjoyed writing it. I would love to hear from you if you have any queries and/or suggestions regarding this book. You can reach me at carstent@dotnetservices.biz. I am also interested in hearing from you if you have any improvements to the example application that you want to share with other readers. If so, please take a look here: http://www.userman.dk.

Appendixes

Cursors and Locking

IN THIS APPENDIX I'll show you database cursors and how they work in different scenarios. This means that I'll cover cursor location and the various cursor types. Keep in mind that the cursor sections in this appendix comprise a short, but broad discussion of cursors, and how they relate to classic ADO and ADO.NET.

The second part of this appendix covers server-side locking of data, or rather concurrency issues in a distributed application setup, with regard to ADO.NET. This means that you get to see how you can effectively lock the data at the data source, ensuring that no one overwrites your data, while you have the data opened; you also get to see how you can handle concurrency issues that occur when you try to update some data at the data source, when they've changed in between the time you read the data and the time you try to update them.

Looking at Cursors

A *cursor* is merely a pointer to a specific row in a result set. This means you have a means of navigating through a result set and working with a specific row—the row the cursor is pointing at. However, a cursor doesn't order the rows in a result set in any way; this is done by your query statement. Depending on the data class used, the cursor is generally positioned at the first row or just before the first row (see Figure A-1 later in this appendix) in the result set, when you open it.

> **NOTE** I realize that if database cursors are new to you, you might possibly be confused about the cursor being used to describe a specific point on a display device. However, although the cursor used with display devices, such as a standard monitor, has nothing to do with a database cursor, both types of cursor do in fact perform the same function: They point to a specific place at a given time, and can be moved around the given context.

In ADO and ADO.NET a result set is usually represented as a data class such as the ADO **Recordset** object or the ADO.NET DataReader or **DataTable** classes. In ADO you have a lot of choices for how to deal and work with cursors, whereas your options in ADO.NET are quite limited, meaning you don't have support for server-side cursors (see the "Server-Side Cursors" section later in this appendix). This is because of the disconnected architecture of ADO.NET and its data source independence.

Having unintentionally implied that ADO is better than ADO.NET when it comes to cursors, I also have to add to the equation that any row in the **DataTable** class in ADO.NET can be accessed using an indexer. This means that you can access any row without moving the cursor to that specific row; you simply specify the zero-based index for the wanted row, and you have access to the data contained in that particular row.

Many professional developers generally don't work with cursors, even if the tools they use give them the option to do so. It's considered bad programming practice to use cursors by many, but personally I can see it both ways.

Anyway, cursors are generally categorized by their characteristics: location and type.

Cursor Location

In regard to location, cursors come in two different flavors: client-side cursors and server-side cursors. As the names imply, they refer to pointers to data on either the client side or the server side. There are advantages and disadvantages to both types, as discussed in the following sections.

Client-Side Cursors

Client-side cursors, or local cursors, are used for navigating in a result set located locally, or on the client.[1] This means that all the rows you select in your query and so forth will have to be transferred to the client in one form or another. Depending on the number of rows, this can be costly in terms of network traffic and storage space on the client. Storage space can be memory as well as disk space, depending on the cursor type and/or available memory on the client. Client-side cursors, which I cover in the "Cursor Types" section later in this appendix, are static.

Server-Side Cursors

Server-side cursors, or remote cursors, are used for navigating in a result set located remotely, or on the server. ADO.NET doesn't currently have intrinsic

---

1. I specifically specify "on the client," because you might have a component running in the middle-tier.

support for the use of server-side cursors (except for the DataReader class), so your only choice here is ADO. The reason may be that the various data sources differ a lot in the way they're implemented. This means it's extremely difficult to expose server-side cursors (and other server-side functionality) in a way that hides the complexity that goes into dealing with many different data sources. What you want is for the server-side cursor to behave and operate the same way, whatever data source you are accessing!

I'm sure there'll be some server-side functionality in later versions, however. Having said that, note that the DataReader class uses a server-side cursor. Mind you, you can't really control the DataReader class—you can only move forward one row at a time—so what you would normally expect from server-side cursor functionality is not exactly what you get from the DataReader class.

ADO.NET only uses client-side cursors (except for the DataReader class), whereas you can specify your cursor location preference with ADO. So to cut a long story short, if you need the functionality of server-side cursors, ADO is currently your only choice! Actually, if you are after server-side processing, then look into using stored procedures and triggers, which are discussed in Part Six.

Cursor Types

There are numerous cursor types. The following sections briefly describe the ones you can use in ADO and ADO.NET, which are listed here:

- Forward-only cursors
- Static cursors
- Dynamic cursors
- Keyset cursors

Forward-Only Cursors

This cursor type requires the least amount of overhead. As the name suggests, you can only move forward one row at a time in a result set with this kind of cursor. Well, this is not entirely true—you can close the data class holding the result set and then reopen it to move the cursor to the first row or BOF (short for Beginning-Of-File), which is just before the first row (see Figure A-1).

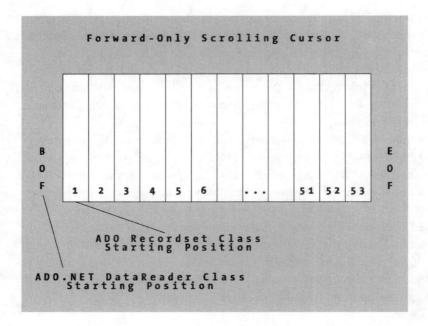

Figure A-1. BOF (Beginning-Of-File)

A forward-only cursor is dynamic by default, meaning that when a row is accessed it's read from the data source, so that changes that have been committed to the row after the result set was generated will be seen. This, however, is NOT the case with the ADO.NET DataReader class. Changes to the underlying rows in an open DataReader object can't be seen!

This cursor type is the only one used by the ADO.NET DataReader class, and it's one of four cursor types used by the ADO **Recordset** class.

Static Cursors

A static cursor is exactly what the name says, static! Well, let's get one thing straight: It's the **DataSet** that is static, not the cursor, which means that the content of a result set is static (that is, the content of the result set will not change after you have opened it). Changes made to the result set after it's opened will not be detected, although changes made by the static cursor itself generally are detected and reflected in the result set, depending on the implementation.

Unlike a forward-only cursor, the static cursor has the ability to scroll both forward and backward. This cursor is one of four cursor types used by the ADO **Recordset** class.

Dynamic Cursors

The dynamic cursor is very good for dealing with concurrency issues, because it detects all changes made to the result set after the cursor is open. The dynamic cursor can of course scroll both forward and backward. The dynamic cursor has the most overhead of the four cursor types described and as such it can prove costly to use, especially in situations where one of the other cursor types can be used instead.

This cursor is one of four cursor types used by the ADO **Recordset** class.

Keyset Cursors

The keyset cursor can be thought of as a cross between a static cursor and a dynamic cursor, because it has functionality that is unique to one or the other. Changes to values in data columns are detected. Insertions made by the cursor will be appended to the result set, whereas insertions made by others will only be visible if the cursor is closed and opened again. Deletions are a completely different ball game when you have a keyset cursor. Deletions made by other cursors can be detected, but deletions made by the keyset cursor itself can't be detected.

This cursor is one of four cursor types used by the ADO **Recordset** class.

Examining Data Source Locking

When you update the data source with changes from your **DataSet** and **DataTable** objects, it's important to know what happens at the data source. It's important because the data you have in your **DataSet** or **DataTable** might not be up to date, meaning that someone else may have changed the data after you retrieved it from the data source. This can be a problem, especially with a disconnected architecture like ADO.NET's, because there's no standard way of locking the rows at the data source that you're manipulating in your **DataSet**. In classic ADO, depending on your data source, you can specify various types and levels of locking, because ADO has a connected architecture. This isn't the case with ADO.NET, which means that ADO.NET uses what is referred to as *optimistic locking*.

Two kinds of general locking are available, pessimistic locking and optimistic locking, and both of them described in the coming sections. However, it's always a good idea to minimize the extent of the locking at the data source, because it will cause problems when more than one client or a server process wants to update the data at the same time. On the other hand, it can also be a problem if no locking is applied and one client updates some data, which is later overwritten by another client (a typical optimistic locking scenario).

There are no hard and fast rules for how and when you should apply locking at the data source, because it really depends on the application architecture, the number of clients, the update frequency, and so on. So, it's generally up to you as a developer to make the most of what your DBMS and database administrator presents you with in terms of access and locking capabilities, and to provide your users with a minimum of problems in terms of performance, lost or overwritten data, and denied data access caused by locked rows.

Pessimistic Locking

Pessimistic locking, or *pessimistic concurrency,*[2] is a locking type that locks a section of the table at the data source when you request the data,[3] effectively denying changes from all other clients, until you've released the locking. The lock is generally put in place when you retrieve the data and released when you disconnect from the data source or release the data you've retrieved. Pessimistic locking can be a good option in environments with a high contention for the data, meaning the data is manipulated frequently and by a large number of clients. However, if a client locks data for more than just a short period, it will most certainly cause problems for other clients that need to access and update the same data.

Although pessimistic locking can't be achieved directly with ADO.NET, you can apply it to your application using transactions. I won't be going into how to use transactions here as it's covered in Chapter 5, but what you need to do is to look at how you can use the **IsolationLevel** enum with transactions to achieve some kind of locking at the data source. See Listing A-1 for an example on how to do this.

Listing A-1. Using Transactions to Lock Data at Data Source

```
1 Public Sub LockDataSourceRowsUsingTransactions()
2    Const STR_SQL_USER_SELECT As String = "SELECT * FROM tblUser"
3
4    Dim cnnLocked, cnnUnlocked As SqlConnection
5    Dim dadLocked, dadUnlocked As SqlDataAdapter
6    Dim traUserMan As SqlTransaction
7    Dim cmdSelectUsers As SqlCommand
8    Dim dstLocked As New DataSet("Locked DataSet")
```

---

2. Locking really isn't the same as concurrency, but we all have different ideas about concepts such as concurrency. Anyway, although locking is related to concurrency, concurrency is really the requirement for access to data for any reason, meaning it refers as much to reads as to writes.

3. With most kinds of pessimistic concurrency, you have the option of specifying that you only want read-only data returned, which means no locks will be applied at the data source.

```
 9      Dim dstUnlocked As New DataSet("Unlocked DataSet")
10
11      ' Instantiate and open the connections
12      cnnLocked = New SqlConnection(STR_CONNECTION_STRING)
13      cnnLocked.Open()
14      cnnUnlocked = New SqlConnection(STR_CONNECTION_STRING)
15      cnnUnlocked.Open()
16      ' Begin transaction
17      traUserMan = cnnLocked.BeginTransaction(IsolationLevel.Serializable)
18      ' Set up select command
19      cmdSelectUsers = New SqlCommand(STR_SQL_USER_SELECT, cnnLocked, _
20        traUserMan)
21
22      ' Instantiate and initialize data adapters
23      dadLocked = New SqlDataAdapter(STR_SQL_USER_SELECT, cnnLocked)
24      dadLocked.SelectCommand = cmdSelectUsers
25      dadUnlocked = New SqlDataAdapter(STR_SQL_USER_SELECT, cnnUnlocked)
26      ' Declare and instantiate command builders
27      Dim cmbUser1 As New SqlCommandBuilder(dadLocked)
28      Dim cmbUser2 As New SqlCommandBuilder(dadUnlocked)
29
30      ' Populate the DataSets
31      dadLocked.Fill(dstLocked, "tblUser")
32      dadUnlocked.Fill(dstUnlocked, "tblUser")
33
34      ' Update an existing row in unlocked DataSet
35      dstUnlocked.Tables("tblUser").Rows(2)("FirstName") = "FirstName"
36
37      Try
38         ' Update the unlocked data source
39        dadUnlocked.Update(dstUnlocked, "tblUser")
40         ' Commit transaction
41        traUserMan.Commit()
42      Catch objE As SqlException
43         ' Roll back transaction
44        traUserMan.Rollback()
45        MessageBox.Show(objE.Message)
46      Finally
47         ' Close connections
48        cnnLocked.Close()
49        cnnUnlocked.Close()
50      End Try
51 End Sub
```

In Listing A-1 I set up and use two **SqlDataAdapter** objects, two **SqlConnection** objects, two **DataSet** objects, two **SqlCommandBuilder** objects, one **SqlCommand** object, and one **SqlTransaction** object. Except for the traUserMan Transaction object, which is instantiated and started by calling the **BeginTransaction** method of the cnnLocked connection object on Line 17, the two DataAdapters do the same. However, the Transaction object makes the difference by specifying the **Serializable** isolation level enum member, which means that all rows in the dadLocked **DataSet** will be locked at the data source. Because the two DataAdapters work on the same data (they're populated on Lines 31 and 32), the update of the data source with changes made to the dstUnlocked **DataSet**, which occurs on Line 39, will fail. The lock placed at the data source results in a time-out exception when you call the **Update** method on the **dadUnlocked** data adapter. The lock doesn't prevent any other client from reading the same data, only updating and deleting them. See Chapter 5 for more information on the Transaction class and the **IsolationLevel** enum.

 NOTE   This method works with all three .NET Data Providers described in this book (SQL Server .NET Data Provider, OLE DB .NET Data Provider, and ODBC .NET Data Provider), provided the underlying data source supports transactions and row locking! This effectively rules out Microsoft Access and MySQL 3.23.51.

Optimistic Locking

Optimistic locking, or *optimistic concurrency*,[4] isn't really a locking concept, because no locking is applied. When you extract the data from the data source and into your **DataSet**, that same data can be modified at the data source by any other client with the right permissions. If this happens and you later update the same data, you're effectively overwriting the changes made to the data between the time you retrieved the data and the time you update it; *last in wins*. Optimistic locking can help you prevent this and should generally be used when your application has a disconnected architecture, like when accessing data over the Internet or any other WAN, and when you want a scalable solution that doesn't lock data at the data source.

ADO.NET uses or rather can use optimistic concurrency, meaning that it's up to you as a programmer to apply optimistic locking to avoid the last-in-wins

---

4.   Locking really isn't the same as concurrency, but we all have different ideas about concepts such as concurrency. Anyway, although locking is related to concurrency, it's really the requirement for access to data for any reason, meaning it refers as much to reads as to writes.

problem. ADO.NET gives you the "tools" to write your application logic to handle problems that optimistic locking can cause. Let's say that you retrieve data from your data source and save it in your **DataSet**, and then you change the data in the **DataSet**, while someone else changes the original data at the data source. If you then try to update the data source with the changes from your **DataSet**, a concurrency violation occurs and the **DBConcurrencyException** exception is thrown.

NOTE A concurrency violation only occurs if changes are made to the same row, meaning that you can have two clients update different rows without a **DBConcurrencyException** being thrown. However, the **DBConcurrencyException** exception is thrown if you update different columns in the same row.

Listing A-2 shows you how to trigger and catch a concurrency violation.

Listing A-2. Triggering and Catching Concurrency Violation

```
1 Public Sub TriggerConcurrencyViolation()
2    Const STR_SQL_USER_SELECT As String = "SELECT * FROM tblUser"
3
4    Dim cnnUser1, cnnUser2 As SqlConnection
5    Dim dadUser1, dadUser2 As SqlDataAdapter
6    Dim dstUser1 As New DataSet("User1 DataSet")
7    Dim dstUser2 As New DataSet("User2 DataSet")
8
9    ' Instantiate and open the connections
10   cnnUser1 = New SqlConnection(STR_CONNECTION_STRING)
11   cnnUser1.Open()
12   cnnUser2 = New SqlConnection(STR_CONNECTION_STRING)
13   cnnUser2.Open()
14
15   ' Instantiate and initialize data adapters
16   dadUser1 = New SqlDataAdapter(STR_SQL_USER_SELECT, cnnUser1)
17   dadUser2 = New SqlDataAdapter(STR_SQL_USER_SELECT, cnnUser2)
18   Dim cmbUser1 As New SqlCommandBuilder(dadUser1)
19   Dim cmbUser2 As New SqlCommandBuilder(dadUser2)
20
21   ' Populate the DataSets
22   dadUser1.Fill(dstUser1, "tblUser")
23   dadUser2.Fill(dstUser2, "tblUser")
24
```

```
25     ' Update an existing row in first DataSet
26     dstUser1.Tables("tblUser").Rows(2)("FirstName") = "FirstName"
27     ' Update the data source with changes to the first DataSet
28     dadUser1.Update(dstUser1, "tblUser")
29     ' Update an existing row in second DataSet
30     dstUser2.Tables("tblUser").Rows(2)("ADName") = "ADName"
31
32     Try
33         ' Update the data source with changes to the second DataSet
34         dadUser2.Update(dstUser2, "tblUser")
35
36     Catch objE As DBConcurrencyException
37         MessageBox.Show(objE.Message)
38     Finally
39         ' Close connections
40         cnnUser1.Close()
41         cnnUser2.Close()
42     End Try
43 End Sub
```

In Listing A-2 I set up two DataAdapters (Lines 16 through 19) that populate two **DataSet**s (Lines 22 through 23) with the same data from the very same data source. Then I change the FirstName column of the third row of the tblUser table in the first **DataSet** (Line 26), and propagate the change back to the data source (Line 28). Then I make a change to the ADName column of the third row of the second **DataSet** and try to update the data source. Because there has been a change to the original data that you're now trying to update, a concurrency violation occurs. What happens is that the DataAdapter looks at the original column values in a row (**DataRowVersion.Original**) and compares it with the row that it tries to update at the data source. If any of the column values at the data source are different from the original column values in the **DataSet**, the concurrency violation occurs. Now, as you can see from Listing A-2, I'm using two **SqlCommandBuilder** objects (Lines 18 and 19) to automatically generate the insert, update, and delete statements. It's actually these statements that take care of generating a **DBConcurrencyException** exception. If you look at the auto-generated code for the update statement, which is the only one needed in the example, you can see how much the CommandBuilder class does for you (the listing has been edited to make it appear "nicer," meaning extra spaces have been taken out, and so on):

```
"UPDATE tblUser SET FirstName = @p1 WHERE ((Id = @p2) AND ((ADName IS NULL AND
@p3 IS NULL) OR (ADName = @p4)) AND ((ADSID IS NULL AND @p5 IS NULL) OR
(ADSID = @p6)) AND ((FirstName IS NULL AND @p7 IS NULL) OR (FirstName = @p8))
AND ((LastName IS NULL AND @p9 IS NULL) OR (LastName = @p10)) AND (
(LoginName IS NULL AND @p11 IS NULL) OR (LoginName = @p12)) AND
((Password IS NULL AND @p13 IS NULL) OR (Password = @p14)) )"
```

As you can see, the update statement tries to update all the columns, if new values have been set in the row using the SET clause, but it's the WHERE clause that's the important one here. Basically, the WHERE clause makes sure that you only update the row in the data source, if it hasn't been deleted (the NULL check, like ADName IS NULL AND @p8 IS NULL) and if *all* original values are present. The current values in the data source are matched with the original values in the row (ADName=@p4), which means that the **SqlDataAdapter** uses the column values **DataRowVersion.Original** as the parameter (@p4) for the matching. You need to keep this in mind if you construct your own SQL statements, instead of using the CommandBuilder class, which you definitely will be doing when the **DataTables** in your **DataSet** are made up of two or more joined tables from the data source.[5]

If you don't want to handle concurrency violations, you can apply the last-in-wins way of working with your application, like in Listing A-3.

Listing A-3. Ignoring Concurrency Violations

```
1  Public Sub IgnoreConcurrencyViolations()
2     Const STR_SQL_USER_SELECT As String = "SELECT * FROM tblUser"
3     Const STR_SQL_USER_UPDATE As String = "UPDATE tblUser SET " & _
4        "ADName=@ADName, ADSID=@ADSID, FirstName=@FirstName, " & _
5        "LastName=@LastName, LoginName=@LoginName, Password=@Password " & _
6        "WHERE Id=@Id"
7
8     Dim cmmUserUpdate1, cmmUserUpdate2 As SqlCommand
9     Dim prmSQLUpdate As SqlParameter
10
11    Dim cnnUser1 As SqlConnection
12    Dim dadUser1, dadUser2 As SqlDataAdapter
13    Dim dstUser1 As New DataSet("User DataSet1")
14    Dim dstUser2 As New DataSet("User DataSet2")
```

---

5. The CommandBuilder class can only be used when dealing with **DataTables** that are based on single tables in the data source. See Chapter 8 for more information the CommandBuilder class.

```vb
15    ' Instantiate and open the connection
16    cnnUser1 = New SqlConnection(STR_CONNECTION_STRING)
17    cnnUser1.Open()
18
19    ' Instantiate the update commands
20    cmmUserUpdate1 = New SqlCommand(STR_SQL_USER_UPDATE, cnnUser1)
21    cmmUserUpdate2 = New SqlCommand(STR_SQL_USER_UPDATE, cnnUser1)
22
23    ' Instantiate and initialize data adapters
24    dadUser1 = New SqlDataAdapter(STR_SQL_USER_SELECT, cnnUser1)
25    dadUser2 = New SqlDataAdapter(STR_SQL_USER_SELECT, cnnUser1)
26
27    ' Set data adapters update command property
28    dadUser1.UpdateCommand = cmmUserUpdate1
29    dadUser2.UpdateCommand = cmmUserUpdate2
30
31    ' Add Update command parameters
32    cmmUserUpdate1.Parameters.Add("@ADName", SqlDbType.VarChar, 100, _
33        cnnLocked, "ADName")
34    cmmUserUpdate1.Parameters.Add("@ADSID", SqlDbType.VarChar, 50, "ADSID")
35    cmmUserUpdate1.Parameters.Add("@FirstName", SqlDbType.VarChar, 50, _
36        "FirstName")
37    cmmUserUpdate1.Parameters.Add("@LastName", SqlDbType.VarChar, 50, _
38        "LastName")
39    cmmUserUpdate1.Parameters.Add("@LoginName", SqlDbType.VarChar, 50, _
40        "LoginName")
41    cmmUserUpdate1.Parameters.Add("@Password", SqlDbType.VarChar, 50, _
42        "Password")
43
44    prmSQLUpdate = dadUser1.UpdateCommand.Parameters.Add("@Id",
45        SqlDbType.Int, 4, "Id")
46    prmSQLUpdate.Direction = ParameterDirection.Input
47    prmSQLUpdate.SourceVersion = DataRowVersion.Original
48
49    cmmUserUpdate2.Parameters.Add("@ADName", SqlDbType.VarChar, 100, _
50        "ADName")
51    cmmUserUpdate2.Parameters.Add("@ADSID", SqlDbType.VarChar, 50, "ADSID")
52    cmmUserUpdate2.Parameters.Add("@FirstName", SqlDbType.VarChar, 50, _
53        "FirstName")
54    cmmUserUpdate2.Parameters.Add("@LastName", SqlDbType.VarChar, 50, _
55        "LastName")
```

```
56   cmmUserUpdate2.Parameters.Add("@LoginName", SqlDbType.VarChar, 50, _
57      "LoginName")
58   cmmUserUpdate2.Parameters.Add("@Password", SqlDbType.VarChar, 50, _
59      "Password")
60
61   prmSQLUpdate = dadUser2.UpdateCommand.Parameters.Add("@Id", _
62      SqlDbType.Int, 4, "Id")
63   prmSQLUpdate.Direction = ParameterDirection.Input
64   prmSQLUpdate.SourceVersion = DataRowVersion.Original
65
66   ' Populate the DataSets
67   dadUser1.Fill(dstUser1, "tblUser")
68   dadUser2.Fill(dstUser2, "tblUser")
69
70   ' Update an existing row in first DataSet
71   dstUser1.Tables("tblUser").Rows(2)("FirstName") = "FirstName"
72   ' Update the data source with changes to the first DataSet
73   dadUser1.Update(dstUser1, "tblUser")
74   ' Update an existing row in second DataSet
75   dstUser2.Tables("tblUser").Rows(2)("FirstName") = "FName"
76   ' Update the data source with changes to the second DataSet
77   dadUser2.Update(dstUser2, "tblUser")
78 End Sub
```

In Listing A-3 I build the update statement manually on Lines 3 through 6, and it's quite different from the one created by the CommandBuilder class in Listing A-2. I'm not creating the insert and update statements as they're not needed by the example code, because it only updates a row. Anyway, the real difference between Listings A-2 and A-3 is in Lines 27 through 64, which is the manual setup of the update statement, including instantiation of the command classes and parameters needed for the update. If you run the example code in Listing A-3, no exceptions will be thrown and the value of the FirstName column will be *FName*, because as far as the second DataAdapter (dadUser2) is concerned, the row in the data source hasn't been changed since the rows were retrieved on Line 68. When dadUser2 matches the rows in the dstUser2 **DataSet**, it only compares the Id column, which will always be the same, because this is the primary key. Well, if some donkey has deleted the row before you get to call the **Update** method on Line 77, a **SqlException** exception is thrown. You can add an exception handler to catch this kind of exception, should you want to use the last-in-wins method in your application.

However, should you choose to handle concurrency violations, rather than ignoring them, you can do this using an exception handler, as shown in Listing A-4.

Listing A-4. Handling Concurrency Violations

```
1  Public Sub HandleConcurrencyViolations()
2     Const STR_SQL_USER_SELECT As String = "SELECT * FROM tblUser"
3
4     Dim cnnUser1 As SqlConnection
5     Dim dadUser1, dadUser2 As SqlDataAdapter
6     Dim dstUser1 = New DataSet("User DataSet1")
7     Dim dstUser2 = New DataSet("User DataSet2")
8
9     ' Instantiate and open the connection
10    cnnUser1 = New SqlConnection(STR_CONNECTION_STRING)
11    cnnUser1.Open()
12
13    ' Instantiate and initialize data adapters
14    dadUser1 = New SqlDataAdapter(STR_SQL_USER_SELECT, cnnUser1)
15    dadUser2 = New SqlDataAdapter(STR_SQL_USER_SELECT, cnnUser1)
16    ' Declare and instantiate command builder
17    Dim cmbUser1 As New SqlCommandBuilder(dadUser1)
18    Dim cmbUser2 As New SqlCommandBuilder(dadUser2)
19
20    ' Populate the DataSets
21    dadUser1.Fill(dstUser1, "tblUser")
22    dadUser2.Fill(dstUser2, "tblUser")
23
24    ' Update an existing row in first DataSet
25    dstUser1.Tables("tblUser").Rows(2)("FirstName") = "FirstName"
26    ' Update the data source with changes to the first DataSet
27    dadUser1.Update(dstUser1, "tblUser")
28    ' Update an existing row in second DataSet
29    dstUser2.Tables("tblUser").Rows(2)("FirstName") = "FName"
30
31    Try
32       ' Update the data source with changes to the second DataSet
33       dadUser2.Update(dstUser2, "tblUser")
34    Catch objE As DBConcurrencyException
35       Dim objResult As MsgBoxResult
36       Dim strCurrentDataSourceFirstName As String
37       ' Instantiate command to find the current data source value
38       Dim cmdCurrentDataSourceValue As New _
39          SqlCommand("SELECT FirstName FROM tblUser WHERE Id=" & _
40          objE.Row("Id", DataRowVersion.Original).ToString(), cnnUser1)
41
```

```
42      ' Find current value in data source
43      strCurrentDataSourceFirstName = _
44          CStr(cmdCurrentDataSourceValue.ExecuteScalar())
45
46      ' Prompt the user about which value to save
47      objResult = MsgBox("A concurrency violation exception was thrown" & _
48          "when updating the source. " & _
49          "These are the values for the column in error:\n\n" & _
50          "Original DataSet Value: " & objE.Row("FirstName", _
51          DataRowVersion.Original).ToString() & ControlChars.CrLf & _
52          "Current Data Source Value: " & strCurrentDataSourceFirstName & _
53          ControlChars.CrLf & "Current DataSet Value: " & _
54          objE.Row("FirstName", DataRowVersion.Current).ToString() & _
55          ControlChars.CrLf & _
56          "Do you want to overwrite the current data source value?", _
57          MsgBoxStyle.Question Or MsgBoxStyle.YesNo, _
58          "Concurrency Violation")
59      ' Does the user want to overwrite the current data source value?
60      If objResult = MsgBoxResult.Yes Then
61          ' Merge the content of the data source with the DataSet in error
62          dstUser2.Merge(dstUser1, True)
63          dadUser2.Update(dstUser2, "tblUser")
64      End If
65    Finally
66      ' Close connection
67      cnnUser1.Close()
68    End Try
69 End Sub
```

Now, the example code in Listing A-4 takes care of concurrency violations and leaves it up to the user whether the new value should be overwritten. The trick to overwriting the current values in the data source with the current values in the **DataSet**, despite the fact that the original values in the **DataSet** doesn't match the current data source values, can be found on Line 62; I merge the values from the first **DataSet** into the second **DataSet**, preserving the changes I've made. In this case it means that the original value of the changed FirstName column in the second **DataSet** is set to the current value of the same column in the equivalent row in the first **DataSet**, which is in fact the same as the current value in the data source, unless another user has changed it again . . .

The example code in Listing A-4 isn't fully finished, as it only looks at the one column I know has been tampered with, but I'm sure you now know how to create code that handles concurrency on a more general level, meaning violations in all columns are handled.

Anyway, this isn't the only way to deal with concurrency violations—there are many other ways, and one other way is to make use of unique values across your database. The unique values, one column per table row, are then updated automatically every time a row is changed. The value can be a date and time, but as long as it's unique and changes can be detected, it doesn't matter what kind of a value it is. What you do then is to match the current value of this column at the data source with the original value in your row in the **DataSet**, before you update the row in the data source. SQL Server has a data type that automatically implements this for you: the **timestamp** data type. The unique value approach is really much the same technique as Listing A-4 uses, but to some extent it's simpler and yet not quite as flexible. In Listing A-4 you're in charge of how many columns you want to check for changes[6] before the concurrency violation is thrown, whereas the timestamp method is based on the entire row.

In Listing A-4 I've used the automatic approach with the DataAdapters with regard to building the insert, update, and delete statements. However, if you want to do it the manual way, like in Listing A-3, all you need to do is to change the STR_SQL_USER_UPDATE constant to this:

```
Const STR_SQL_USER_UPDATE As String = "UPDATE tblUser SET ADName=@ADName," & _
    "ADSID=@ADSID, FirstName=@FirstName, LastName=@LastName, " & _
    "LoginName=@LoginName, Password=@Password WHERE ((Id=@Id) AND " & _
    "((ADName IS NULL AND @ADName IS NULL) OR (ADName=@ADName)) AND ((" & _
    "ADSID IS NULL AND @ADSID IS NULL) OR (ADSID=@ADSID)) AND ((FirstName" & _
    " IS NULL AND @FirstName IS NULL) OR (FirstName=@FirstName)) AND " & _
    "((LastName IS NULL AND @LastName IS NULL) OR (LastName=@LastName)) " & _
    "AND ((LoginName IS NULL AND @LoginName IS NULL) OR (LoginName=" & _
    "@LoginName)) AND ((Password IS NULL AND @Password IS NULL) OR " & _
    "(Password=@Password)))"
```

---

6. You can edit the example code to ignore changes to one or more columns when matching the original row values with the current data source values, meaning that changes to the ADSID and ADName columns might be unimportant, for instance.

Summary

In this appendix I discussed cursors and locking. The following ground was covered:

- Cursor location (server side and client side)

- Cursor type (forward-only, static, dynamic, and keyset)

- Locking types (pessimistic and optimistic)

- Pessimistic concurrency and how to implement it with transactional locking of data at the data source

- Optimistic concurrency and how to respond to concurrency violations

- Last-in-wins, which happens when you ignore concurrency violations

The next appendix covers classic ADO and COM Interop in general.

APPENDIX B

Using Classic ADO
and COM Interop

IN THIS APPENDIX I'll introduce you to classic ADO and COM Interop. Well, this isn't entirely true, as I won't be covering classic ADO as such. However, classic ADO is COM based, and thus you need to access it from your .NET applications through something called COM Interop.[1] So, this rather short appendix is an overview of the inner workings of COM Interop and how you use it to work with classic ADO in your .NET applications.

Understanding and Using COM Interop

Because previous versions of ADO are built as COM components, you need to use COM Interop to interact with ADO. COM Interop provides a way of interfacing with COM components in order to use them, and vice versa for that matter. I will only be discussing the COM-to-.NET usage in this section.

You need to use COM Interop whenever you want to access a COM component. There is much more to COM Interop than I am going to cover in this section, so if you need some more information, I suggest you check out these books:

- *Moving to VB.NET: Strategies, Concepts and Code,* by Dan Appleman. Apress, June 2001. ISBN 1-893115-97-6.

- *In Search of the Lost Win32 API: .NET Framework Solutions,* by John Paul Mueller. Sybex, October 2002. ISBN 078214134X.

- *COM and .NET Interoperability,* by Andrew Troelsen. Apress, April 2002. ISBN 1-59059-011-2.

There are several ways of using COM components from within the .NET Framework. They all involve exposing a COM component to the world of managed code. The CLR expects all types to be defined as metadata in an assembly. This goes for COM types as well. So the job at hand is to convert your COM types to

---

1. Interop is short for interoperability.

metadata, or rather generate metadata for your COM types. This metadata is really an assembly called the *Runtime Callable Wrapper* (RCW). The .NET application uses the RCW, which exposes the COM classes, method, and properties contained in the COM DLL to the .NET application. The RCW takes care of the communication between the .NET application and the COM DLL.

I will show you the two easy ways of generating the metadata, and I suggest that you pick either method for use with classic ADO. The first involves running the command line Type Library Importer, TlbImp.exe, on the COM component to generate metadata in an assembly. Please note that the component must contain a type library. If it doesn't, then there's probably a separate type library file for importing (*.tlb). Any client that writes managed code can use the resulting assembly. Say you want to import the ADO 2.7 library, which is usually located in the Program Files\Files\System\Ado folder. You need to do this if you want to run the example code in Listing 9-3 in Chapter 9. To do so, you would open a command prompt, go to the Ado folder, and then execute the following command: \Program Files\Microsoft Visual Studio .NET\FrameworkSDK\Bin\ TlbImp msado26.tlb. Replace the path to match your setup. I know the filename looks as if it's ado version 2.6, but MS has chosen to name the file like this. It's probably because version 2.7 is really only a minor upgrade, which was originally intended to be a service pack. Anyway, the output from running the TlbImp.exe file is the ADODB.DLL assembly, which holds the ADODB namespace. (Surely this must look familiar to you. . .). Adding a reference to your project can reference this assembly. See the next option for generating metadata. If you need to see all the command options available to you, just run TlbImp.exe with no arguments from the command line. The options will then be displayed.

The second way to generate the metadata involves adding a reference to the COM components in your project, as shown in Figure B-1. This way the IDE generates the metadata for you. You can access the Add Reference dialog box by clicking the Add Reference command in the Project menu.

You can use either of these two methods to access any COM types, and as such all of your COM components can still be part of your applications. Mind you, it's advisable to port all of these components to .NET classes, because there's overhead when using COM Interop. Once you have added a reference to a COM component in your project, you can use the Object Browser to see all the types.

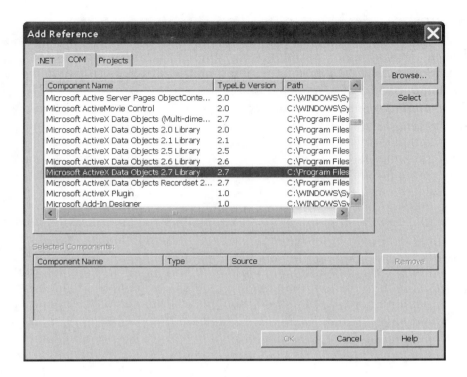

Figure B-1. The Add Reference dialog box

Okay, now that I have suggested you do all this, I might as well reveal that it isn't really necessary. It's not necessary because Microsoft has decided to include some Primary Interop Assemblies with VS .NET. Guess what, ADO is one of them. This means a .NET Framework wrapper already exists for the ADO COM libraries. So all you really have to do is add a reference to this wrapper. You can access the Add Reference dialog box by clicking the Add Reference command in the Project menu. In the Add Reference dialog box the wrapper assembly can be found on the .NET tab with the component name adodb. Select it from the list, click Select, and then click OK. Now the RCW has been added to your project.

The Primary Interop Assemblies can be found in the \Program Files\ Microsoft.NET\Primary Interop Assemblies folder. If you place your RCWs in this folder, they are automatically added to the .NET tab in the Add Reference dialog box.

Summary

In this short appendix I gave you an overview of how the COM-based classic ADO can be used from your .NET applications through COM Interop. I also gave you a quick rundown of how COM Interop works.

In the next appendix, you can find tables of properties, methods, and events for the connected layer of ADO.NET.

Connected Layer Properties, Methods, and Events

THIS APPENDIX IS FOR referencing the properties, methods, and events of the various classes of the ADO.NET connected layer, which is covered in Part Two of the book. The classes are listed in the order they're covered in the chapters in Part Two.

Connection Class

In this section you'll find the properties, methods, and events of the three Connection classes, **OdbcConnection**, **OleDbConnection**, and **SqlConnection**. For some of the properties, methods, and events, like the Connection properties, you'll find separate tables for each of the Connection classes, whereas other tables hold properties, methods, or events for all of the Connection classes, and specifically states if one of the mentioned properties, methods, or events are specific to one or more of the Connection classes.

Table C-1 lists the **ConnectionString** Property Values, followed by Table C-2, which describes the **OdbcConnection** class properties.

Table C-1. **ConnectionString** *Property Values*

Value Name	Default Value	Required
Addr *Address*	-	Yes
Application Name	The name of the application or the name of the .NET Data Provider if an application isn't provided	No
AttachDBFilename	-	No
Connect Timeout *Connection Timeout*	15	No

Description	Example	Provider Specific
The name, such as a NETBIOS name or network address, like an IP address, of a SQL Server to which you want to connect.	`Addr='USERMANPC'` `Address='10.0.0.1'`	Yes (works with the **SqlConnection** class and the SQLOLEDB provider with the **OleDbConnection** class)
The name of your application.	`Application Name='UserMan'`	Yes (works with the **SqlConnection** class and the SQLOLEDB provider with the **OleDbConnection** class)
The name of the primary database file to attach. The name of the attachable database includes the full path. This value is typically used with file-based databases such as Microsoft Access.	`AttachDBFileName='C:\Program Files\UserMan\Data\UserMan.mdb'`	No
The number of seconds to wait when connecting to a database before terminating the connection attempt. An **InvalidOperationException** exception is thrown if a time-out occurs.	`Connection Timeout=15` `Connect Timeout=15`	Yes (works with the **SqlConnection** class only)

*Table C-1. **ConnectionString** Property Values (Continued)*

Value Name	Default Value	Required
Connection Lifetime	0	No

Description	Example	Provider Specific
You can use this value to specify when the connection should be destroyed. This value is only relevant with regards to connection pooling, and as such the value (in seconds) specifies the acceptable time span compared to the time created and the time the connection is returned to the connection pool. In other words, this means the total number of seconds the connection has been alive (time of returning to pool minus time of creation) is compared to this value. If the **Connection Lifetime** value is less than the number of seconds the connection has been alive, then the connection is destroyed. This value is very useful in load-balancing situations, because if you set the **Connection Lifetime** to a low value, then it's more often the than not destroyed upon returning to the connection pool. This means that when the connection is re-created, it might be created on a different server, depending on the load on the servers. How low you set the value is a matter of the number of servers participating in the load-balancing scheme and how loaded they really are. In the end these kind of things are really a matter of experience and testing.	`Connection Lifetime=10`	Yes (works with the **SqlConnection** class and the SQLOLEDB provider with the **OleDbConnection** class)

*Table C-1. **ConnectionString** Property Values (Continued)*

Value Name	Default Value	Required
Connection Reset	'true'	No
Current Language	-	No
Database	-	Yes
DATABASE	"" (empty **String**)	Yes (when used with DBMS-based data sources)
Data Source	-	Yes

Description	Example	Provider Specific
This value determines if the connection is reset when it's destroyed, or rather removed from the connection pool. If you set this value to 'false', you can avoid an extra round-trip to the server when you require the connection. You should be aware that the connection has not been reset, so the connection will keep whatever values you have set before it was returned to the connection pool. Generally, you should keep the default setting, but in cases where you know that none of the connection settings have been tampered with, it might save you the valuable time needed to create the connection. If you only have one or perhaps a few connections open at any given time, this setting isn't going to improve noticeably your performance. However, if you open a new connection in every procedure and have many of these procedures executed at the same time in several applications, and you know that the connection settings aren't changed while the connection is open, then it's probably valuable to set this value to 'false'.	Connection Reset='false'	Yes (works with the **SqlConnection** class and the SQLOLEDB provider with the **OleDbConnection** class)
This is the SQL Server Language record name. Check your SQL Server documentation for a list of supported names. An exception is thrown if a nonsupported language is specified.	Current Language='English'	Yes (works with the **SqlConnection** class and the SQLOLEDB provider with the **OleDbConnection** class)
The name of your database.	Database='UserMan'	Yes (works with the **SqlConnection** class and the SQLOLEDB provider with the **OleDbConnection** class)
The name of your database. This value name is used with DBMS-based databases like SQL Server and Oracle.	DATABASE=UserMan	Yes (works with the **OdbcConnection** class)
Basically the same as **Addr** or **Address**, but it also works with an Microsoft Access JET database.	Data Source='C:\Program Files\UserMan\Data\UserMan.mdb' Data Source='USERMANPC'	No

Table C-1. **ConnectionString** Property Values (Continued)

Value Name	Default Value	Required
DBALIAS	"" (empty **String**)	Yes
DBQ	"" (empty **String**)	Yes (when used with file-based data sources)
DRIVER	-	Yes
DSN	"" (empty **String**)	No
Enlist	'true'	No
FIL	"" (empty **String**)	Yes (when used with file-based data sources)

Description	Example	Provider Specific
The alias of your database, which is often the same as your database name. This value name is only used with IBM DB2 databases, and if you've set up the IBM DB2 Client tools correctly, this value name is the equivalent of the generic **SERVER** and **DATABASE**, or the **DSN** value name.	DBALIAS=UserMan	Yes (works with the **OdbcConnection** class, using the {IBM DB2 ODBC DRIVER} driver.)
The database filename, including the full file system path. This value name is used with file-based databases like dBase and Microsoft Access.	DBQ=C:\UserMan.mdb	Yes (works with the **OdbcConnection** class)
The name of the ODBC driver enclosed in curly brackets, {}.	Driver={SQL Server}	Yes (works with the **OdbcConnection** class)
You can use the Data Source Name (DSN), which exists on the local machine, to specify the name of an ODBC data source. You can use a DSN instead of specifying DRIVER, UID, PWD, and other value names. A DSN can be user, system, or file based, which means that it's available to the current user, all users on the local machine, or anyone who can access the file that contains the DSN information. The file-based DSN is obviously a good option if you want to distribute it to other machines. You can see more in the ODBC Data Source Administrator that is installed on your machine (usually located under Programs ➤ Administrative Tools in the Start menu, but can often be accessed from the Control Panel as well). This application is used for creating, modifying, and deleting DSNs.	DSN=UserMan	Yes (works with the **OdbcConnection** class only)
Enlists the connection in the thread's current transaction when set to 'true'.	Enlist='false'	Yes (works with the **SqlConnection** class only)
This value name is used for specifying the file type when accessing a file-based data source, such as Excel and Microsoft Access.	FIL=Excel 7.0	Yes (works with the **OdbcConnection** class)

Table C-1. **ConnectionString** *Property Values (Continued)*

Value Name	Default Value	Required
File Name	-	No
Initial Catalog (the same as *Database*)	-	-
Initial File Name (the same as *AttachDBFilename*)	-	-
Integrated Security	'false'	No
Max Pool Size	100	No
Min Pool Size	0	No

Description	Example	Provider Specific
For use with a Microsoft Data Link File (UDL).	`File Name='Test.udl'`	Yes (works with the **OleDbConnection** class only)
-	-	-
-	-	-
Specifies if the connection should be secure. The possible values are 'true', 'yes', and 'sspi', which all specify a secure connection, and the default value 'false' and 'no', which obviously specify a nonsecure connection.	`Integrated Security='true'`	Yes (works with the **SqlConnection** class)
Specifies the maximum number of connections in the connection pool. This number must be greater than or equal to **Min Pool Size**, or an exception is thrown. Setting **Min Pool Size** and **Max Pool Size** to the same value tends to reduce memory fragmentation, and in some cases this can help reduce the number of errors that SQL Server experiences.	`Max Pool Size=200`	Yes (works with the **SqlConnection** class and the SQLOLEDB provider with the **OleDbConnection** class)
Specifies the minimum number of connections in the connection pool. This number must be less than or equal to **Max Pool Size**, or an exception is thrown. Please be aware of the default value for **Max Pool Size**, meaning that if you don't specify **Max Pool Size**, which has a default value of 100, and you set the **Min Pool Size** to 101, an exception will be thrown. Setting **Min Pool Size** and **Max Pool Size** to the same value tends to reduce memory fragmentation, and in some cases this can help reduce the number of errors that SQL Server experiences.	`Min Pool Size=10`	Yes (works with the **SqlConnection** class and the SQLOLEDB provider with the **OleDbConnection** class)

Table C-1. **ConnectionString** *Property Values (Continued)*

Value Name	Default Value	Required
Net *Network Library*	'dbmssocn'	No
Network Address (the same as **Addr** or **Address**)	-	-
Packet Size	8192	No
Password *Pwd*	-	Yes, if your database has been secured
PWD	"" (empty **String**)	Yes
Persist Security Info	'false'	No

Description	Example	Provider Specific
The network library used for connecting to SQL Server. Possible values are 'dbmssocn' (TCP/IP), 'dbnmpntw' (Named Pipes), 'dbmsrpcn' (Multiprotocol), 'dbmsvinn' (Banyan Vines), 'dbmsadsn' (Apple Talk), 'dbmsgnet' (VIA), 'dbmsipcn' (Shared Memory), and 'dbmsspxn' (IPX/SPX). Please note that the corresponding library file (DLL) must be installed on both the system you connect to and the system from which you connect.	Net='dbnmpntw'	Yes (works with **SqlConnection** class and the SQLOLEDB provider with the class **OleDbConnection**)
-	-	-
The packet size specified in bytes for communicating with your data source across the network. This value must be in the range 512 to 32767. An exception is thrown if not. However, it's best to keep your packet sizes in numbers that has been raised to the power of 2, which means 512, 1024, 2048, 4096, 8192, and 16384, because the network then won't have to pad your packets up to the nearest mentioned number with zeros.	Packet Size='512'	Yes (works with the **SqlConnection** class and the SQLOLEDB provider with the **OleDbConnection** class)
The password that corresponds to the User ID.	Password='userman' Pwd='userman'	No
The password that corresponds to the specified UID. You can also use **Password**, but you need to use these value names in pairs, meaning that if you use **Password**, you must also use **User ID**; if you use **PWD**, you must also use **UID**.	PWD='userman'	Yes (works with the **OdbcConnection** class)
Helps you keep sensitive information like passwords safe. The possible values are 'true' and 'yes', which don't keep your sensitive information safe, and 'false' and 'no', which obviously do keep it safe.	Persist Security Info='true'	No

Table C-1. **ConnectionString** *Property Values (Continued)*

Value Name	Default Value	Required
Pooling	'true'	No
Provider	-	Yes
Server (the same as **Addr** or **Address**)	-	-
SERVER	"" (empty **String**)	Yes (when used with DBMS-based data sources)
Trusted_Connection (the same as **Integrated Security**)	-	-
UID	"" (empty **String**)	Yes
User ID	-	Yes, if your database has been secured
Workstation ID	The name of the client computer or the computer from which you are connecting	No

Description	Example	Provider Specific
The Connection object is taken from the appropriate pool if the value is set to 'true'. If there are no available Connection objects in the pool, a new one is created and added to the pool.	Pooling='false'	Yes (works with the **SqlConnection** class only)
Specifies the name of the OLE DB provider you want to use for accessing your data source. You can specify a version independent ProgID (SQLOLEDB) or a ProgID with version specification (SQLOLEDB.1). The ProgIDs are saved in the Registry database.	Provider=SQLOLEDB Provider=MSDAORA Provider=Microsoft.Jet.OLEDB.4.0	Yes (works with the **OleDbConnection** class only)
-	-	-
The server you want to connect to.	SERVER=USERMAN	Yes (works with the **OdbcConnection** class)
-	-	-
The user ID you wish to connect with.	UID=UserMan	Yes (works with the **OdbcConnection** class)
The User ID you wish to connect with.	User ID='UserMan'	No
The name of the client computer or the computer from which you are connecting.	Workstation ID='USERMANPC'	No

Table C-2. **OdbcConnection** *Class Properties*

Property Name	Default Value	ConnectionString Equivalent	Description	Read	Write
ConnectionTimeout	15	There's no equivalent **ConnectionString** value.	The number of seconds to wait when connecting to a database before terminating the connection attempt. An exception is thrown if a time-out occurs. Setting this value to 0 means that the Connection class will wait indefinitely for a connection, and you should generally avoid this as it can potentially lead to deadlocks and/or wasted resources.	Yes	Yes
Database	"" (empty **String**)	**DATABASE**	-	Yes	No
DataSource	"" (empty **String**)	There's no equivalent **ConnectionString** value.	This property retrieves the filename and location of the data source.	Yes	No
Driver	-	There's no equivalent **ConnectionString** value.	Returns the name of the ODBC driver, which is usually the name of the driver DLL.	Yes	No
ServerVersion	-	There's no equivalent **ConnectionString** value.	This property receives a string from the DBMS containing the version number. If the **State** property equals **Closed** when you read this |property, the **InvalidOperationException** exception is thrown. An empty **String** is returned if the ODBC driver doesn't support this property.	Yes	No

Table C-2. **OdbcConnection** *Class Properties (Continued)*

Property Name	Default Value	ConnectionString Equivalent	Description	Read	Write
State	**Closed**	There's no equivalent **ConnectionString** value.	This property gets the current state of the connection; possible values are **Closed** and **Open**. These values are taken from the enum **ConnectionState** , which is part of the **System.Data** namespace.	Yes	No

In Table C-3 you can find a list of the **OleDbConnection** class properties, but please note that the Description column is empty, or rather holds a single dash (-), if the property covered in the row has a **ConnectionString** property equivalent. This means that you can read the description in Table C-1 instead. Likewise, Table C-4 lists the **SqlConnection** class properties.

Table C-3. **OleDbConnection** *Class Properties*

Property Name	Default Value	ConnectionString Equivalent	Description	Read	Write
ConnectionTimeout	15	**Connection Timeout**	-	Yes	No
Database	-	**Database** or **Initial Catalog**	-	Yes	No
DataSource	-	**Addr** or **Address**	-	Yes	No
Provider	-	**Provider**	-	Yes	No
ServerVersion	-	There's no equivalent **ConnectionString** value.	This property receives a string from the DBMS containing the version number. If the **State** property equals **Closed**, when you read this property, the exception **InvalidOperationException** is thrown. An empty **String** is returned if the OLE DB Provider doesn't support this property.	Yes	No

Table C-3. **OleDbConnection** *Class Properties (Continued)*

Property Name	Default Value	ConnectionString Equivalent	Description	Read	Write
State	**Closed**	There's no equivalent **ConnectionString** value.	This property gets the current state of the connection; possible values are **Closed** and **Open**. These values are taken from the **ConnectionState** enum, which is part of the **System.Data** namespace.	Yes	No

Table C-4. **SqlConnection** *Class Properties*

Property Name	Default Value	ConnectionString Equivalent	Description	Read	Write
ConnectionTimeout	15	**Connection Timeout**	-	Yes	No
Database	"" (empty String)	**Database** or **Initial Catalog**	-	Yes	No
DataSource	"" (empty String)	**Addr** or **Address**	-	Yes	No
PacketSize	8192	**Packet Size**	This property retrieves the packet size for communicating with your data source across the network. The value returned is specified in bytes.	Yes	No

*Table C-4. **SqlConnection** Class Properties (Continued)*

Property Name	Default Value	ConnectionString Equivalent	Description	Read	Write
ServerVersion	"" (empty **String**)	There's no equivalent **ConnectionString** value.	This property receives a string from SQL Server containing the version of the current SQL Server. If the **State** property equals **Closed**, when you read this property, the **InvalidOperationException** exception is thrown.	Yes	No
State	**Closed**	There's no equivalent **ConnectionString** value.	This property gets the current state of the connection; possible values are **Open** and **Closed**. These values are taken from the **ConnectionState** enum, which is part of the **System.Data** namespace.	Yes	No
WorkstationId	The name of the client computer or an empty string.	**Workstation ID**	This property returns a **String** identifying the database client.	Yes	No

Public class methods for **OdbcConnection**, **OleDbConnection**, and **SqlConnection** appear in Tables C-5, C-6, and C-7, respectively.

Table C-5. **OdbcConnection** *Class Methods*

Method Name	Description	Return Value	Overloaded
BeginTransaction()	Begins a transaction on the Connection object. This method is overloaded, so see "Transactions" in Chapter 5 for more information.	The instantiated **OdbcTransaction** object	Yes
ChangeDatabase(ByVal strDatabase As String)	This method, which can't be overridden, changes the database for the connection to the database passed in the strDatabase variable. The connection must be open or else an exception **InvalidOperationException** is thrown.	-	No
Close()	This method takes no arguments, and it simply closes an open connection. Any pending transactions are rolled back when you call this method.	-	No
CreateCommand()	This method creates an **OdbcCommand**. The **OdbcCommand** object is associated with the Connection object.	The instantiated **OdbcCommand** object	No
Equals()	This method, which is inherited from the **Object** class, can be used to determine if two connections are the same.	Data type **Boolean**	Yes
GetHashCode()	This method, which is inherited from the **Object** class, returns the hash code for the connection. The hash code is a number that corresponds to the value of the connection.	Data type **Integer**	No

*Table C-5. **OdbcConnection** Class Methods (Continued)*

Method Name	Description	Return Value	Overloaded
GetType()	This method, which is inherited from the **Object** class, returns the object type, or rather the metadata associated with the class that an object is inherited from. If you need the class name, you can get it using `cnnUserMan.GetType.ToString`.	Data type **Type**	No
Open()	This method, which can't be overridden, is used for opening the connection to the data source with the current property settings. Different exceptions can be thrown under various circumstances (see the "Connection Class Exceptions" section in Chapter 5 for details.)	-	No
ReleaseObjectPool()	This method is used for indicating that the connection pool can be cleared when the last underlying ODBC driver is released.	-	No
ToString()	This method, which is inherited from the **Object** class, returns a string representation of the connection. If you call the method using `MessageBox.Show(cnnUserMan.ToString())`, the message box displayed should contain the text "System.Data.OleDb.OdbcConnection". This is the name of the object (**OdbcConnection**) including the namespace in which it's contained (**Microsoft.Data.Odbc**).	Data type **String**	No

Table C-6. **OleDbConnection** *Class Methods*

Method Name	Description	Return Value	Overloaded
BeginTransaction()	Begins a transaction on the Connection object. This method is overloaded, so see "Transactions" in Chapter 5 for more information.	The instantiated **OleDbTransaction** object	Yes
ChangeDatabase(ByVal strDatabase As String)	This method, which can't be overridden, changes the database for the connection to the database passed in the `strDatabase` variable. The connection must be open or else an **InvalidOperationException** exception is thrown.	-	No
Close()	This method takes no arguments, and it simply closes an open connection. Any pending transactions are rolled back when you call this method.	-	No
CreateCommand()	This method creates an **OleDbCommand**. The **OleDbCommand** object is associated with the Connection object.	The instantiated **OleDbCommand** object	No
Equals()	This method, which is inherited from the **Object** class, can be used to determine if two connections are the same.	Data type **Boolean**	Yes
GetOleDbSchemaTable (ByVal guiSchema As Guid, ByVal objRestrictions() As Object)	This method is used for retrieving the schema table for the `guiSchema` after applying `objRestrictions`. You can use this method to return a list of tables in the current database and other schema information.	Data type **DataTable**	No

*Table C-6. **OleDbConnection** Class Methods (Continued)*

Method Name	Description	Return Value	Overloaded
GetType()	This method, which is inherited from the **Object** class, returns the object type, or rather the metadata associated with the class that an object is inherited from. If you need the class name, you can get it using `cnnUserMan.GetType.ToString`.	Data type **Type**	No
Open()	This method, which can't be overridden, is used for opening the connection to the data source with the current property settings. Different exceptions can be thrown under various circumstances (see the "Connection Class Exceptions" section in Chapter 5 for details.)	-	No
ReleaseObjectPool()	This method is used for indicating that the connection pool can be cleared when the last underlying OLE DB provider is released.	-	No
ToString()	This method, which is inherited from the **Object** class, returns a string representation of the connection. If you call the method using `MessageBox.Show(cnnUserMan.ToString())`, the message box displayed should contain the text "System.Data.OleDb.OleDbConnection". This is the name of the object (**OleDbConnection**) including the namespace in which it's contained (**System.Data.OleDb**).	Data type **String**	No

*Table C-7. **SqlConnection** Class Methods*

Method Name	Description	Return Value	Overloaded
BeginTransaction()	Begins a transaction on the Connection object. This method is overloaded, so see the "Transactions" section in Chapter 5 for more information.	The instantiated **SqlTransaction** object	Yes
ChangeDatabase(ByVal strDatabase As String)	This method, which can't be overridden, changes the database for the connection to the database passed in the strDatabase argument. The connection must be open or else an **InvalidOperationException** exception is thrown.	-	No
Close()	This method takes no arguments, and it simply closes an open connection. Any pending transactions are rolled back when you call this method.	-	No
CreateCommand()	This method creates a **SqlCommand** object. The **SqlCommand** object is associated with the Connection object, meaning the **SqlCommand** object's connection is the one you use call this method on.	The instantiated **SqlCommand** object	No
Equals()	This method, which is inherited from the **Object** class, can be used to determine if two connections are the same.	Data type **Boolean**	Yes

*Table C-7. **SqlConnection** Class Methods (Continued)*

Method Name	Description	Return Value	Overloaded
GetHashCode()	This method, which is inherited from the **Object** class, returns the hash code for the connection.	Data type **Integer**	No
GetType()	This method, which is inherited from the **Object** class, returns the object type, or rather the metadata associated with the class from which an object is inherited. If you need the class name, you can get it using `cnnUserMan.GetType.ToString`.	Data type **Type**	No
Open()	This method, which can't be overridden, is used for opening the connection to the data source with the current property settings. Different exceptions can be thrown under various circumstances (see the "Connection Class Exceptions" section in Chapter 5.)	-	No
ToString()	This method, which is inherited from the **Object** class, returns a string representation of the connection. If you call the method using `Message-Box.Show(cnnUserMan.ToString())`, the message box displayed should contain the text "System.Data.SqlClient.SqlConnection". This is the name of the object (**SqlConnection**) including the namespace in which it's contained (**System.Data.SqlClient**).	Data type **String**	No

All three Connection classes expose the same events, and these noninherited events are listed in Table C-8.

Table C-8. Connection Class Events

Event Name	Description
InfoMessage	This event is triggered when the provider, driver, or data source sends a warning or an informational message. Basically, this event is triggered if the provider, driver, or data source needs to inform the connecting application about any nonserious event, or anything else besides errors. See the "Handling Provider, Driver, and Data Source Messages" section in Chapter 5 for some example code that handles this event. In the case of SQL Server, this event is triggered when SQL server raises a message with a severity of 10 or less. Serious problems at your data source, provider, or driver trigger an exception that you must catch in an exception handler (see Chapter 14 for more information about exception handling). In the case of SQL Server, exceptions are thrown when messages with a severity between 11 and 20 (both inclusive) are raised. So, to catch all kinds of messages from the provider, driver, and data source, you really need to handle the **InfoMessage** event, as well as set up an exception handler. In the case of SQL Server, when a message with a severity of 21 through 25 is raised, the connection is closed. However, this doesn't trigger the **InfoMessage** event, nor does it throw an exception, but you can catch this error in the **StateChange** event.
StateChange	This event is triggered immediately, when the state of your connection changes—that is, when your connection goes from open to closed and vice versa. The procedure that handles the event is passed an argument of type **StateChangeEventArgs**, which holds two properties that can tell you the current state and the original state. This means that you know whether the connection was being closed or opened. See the "Handling Connection State Changes" section in Chapter 5 to see how to handle state change events.

Table C-9 shows you all the members of the **ConnectionState** enum, but currently only the **Closed** and **Open** members are supported.

*Table C-9. Members of the **ConnectionState** Enum*

Name	Description
Closed	The connection is closed.
Open	The connection is open.
Connecting	The connection is currently connecting to the data source.
Executing	The connection is executing a command.
Fetching	The connection is retrieving data from the data source.
Broken	The connection can't be used as the connection is in error. This usually occurs if the network fails. The only valid method in this state is **Close**, and all properties are read-only.

Tables C-10, C-11, and C-12 show the various versions of the **BeginTransaction** method, which is overloaded.

*Table C-10. Overloads of the **BeginTransaction** Method of the **OdbcConnection** Class*

Call	Description
BeginTransaction()	This version takes no arguments, and you should use it when you want to use the default isolation level.
BeginTransaction(ByVal enuIsolationLevel As IsolationLevel)	Takes the transaction's isolation level as the only argument. You should use this version of the method when you want to specify the isolation level. Refer to Listing 5-14 in Chapter 5 for an example, but replace **SqlConnection** and **SqlTransaction** in the example with **OdbcConnection** and **OdbcTransaction**. Refer to Table C-13 for more information on the isolation level.

*Table C-11. Overloads of the **BeginTransaction** Method of the **OleDbConnection** Class*

Call	Description
BeginTransaction()	This version takes no arguments, and you should use it when you are not nesting your transactions and you want to use the default isolation level.
BeginTransaction(ByVal enuIsolationLevel As IsolationLevel)	Takes the transaction's isolation level as the only argument. You should use this version of the method when you want to specify the isolation level. Refer to Listing 5-14 in Chapter 5 for an example, but replace **SqlConnection** and **SqlTransaction** in the example with **OleDbConnection** and **OleDbTransaction**. Refer to Table C-13 for more information on the isolation level.

*Table C-12. Overloads of the **BeginTransaction** Method of the **SqlConnection** Class*

Call	Description
BeginTransaction()	This version takes no arguments, and you should use it when you are not nesting your transactions and you want to use the default isolation level.
BeginTransaction(ByVal enuIsolationLevel As IsolationLevel)	Takes the transaction's isolation level as the only argument. You should use this version of the method when you want to specify the isolation level. Refer to Listing 5-14 in Chapter 5 for an example, and Table C-13 for more information on the isolation level.
BeginTransaction(ByVal strName As String)	Takes the name of the transaction as the only argument. You should use this version of the method when you want to nest your transactions and thus name those for easier identification (see Listing 5-10 in Chapter 5). Please note that strName can't contain spaces and has to start with a letter or one of the following characters: # (pound sign), _ (underscore). Subsequent characters may also be numeric (0–9).

*Table C-12. Overloads of the **BeginTransaction** Method of the **SqlConnection** Class (Continued)*

Call	Description
BeginTransaction(IsolationLevel enuIsolationLevel string strName)	Takes the transactions isolation level and the name of the transaction as arguments. You should use this version of the method when you want to specify the isolation level and you want to nest your transactions and thus name those for easier identification (see Listing 5-11). Please note that strName can't contain spaces and has to start with a letter or one of the following characters: # (pound sign), _ (underscore). Subsequent characters may also be numeric (0–9).

Table C-13 shows the various members of the **IsolationLevel** enum, which is used for specifying the isolation level for a transaction.

*Table C-13. Members of the **IsolationLevel** Enum*

Name	Description
Chaos	You can't overwrite pending changes from more highly isolated transactions.
ReadCommitted	Although the shared locks will be held until the end of the read, thus avoiding dirty reads, the data can be changed before the transaction ends. This can result in phantom data or nonrepeatable reads. This means the data you read isn't guaranteed to be the same the next time you perform the same read request.
ReadUncommitted	Dirty reads are possible, because no shared locks are in effect and any exclusive locks won't be honored.
RepeatableRead	All data that is part of the query will be locked so that other users can't update the data. This will prevent nonrepeatable reads, but phantom rows are still possible.
Serializable	The **DataSet** is locked using a range lock, and this prevents other users from updating or inserting rows in the **DataSet** until the transaction ends (see "Using the DataSet Class" in Chapter 9).
Unspecified	The isolation level can't be determined, because a different isolation level than the one specified is being used.

Transaction Class

In this section you'll find the properties, and methods of the three Transaction classes, **OdbcTransaction**, **OleDbTransaction**, and **SqlTransaction**, in Tables C-14 and C-15, respectively.

Table C-14. Transaction Class Properties

Property Name	Description	Read	Write
Connection	Retrieves the Connection object that is associated with the transaction. **Nothing** is returned if the transaction is invalid.	Yes	No
IsolationLevel	Specifies the level of isolation for the transaction (see Table C-13). The specified isolation level applies to the entire transaction, because parallel transactions aren't supported. See "Determining the Isolation Level of a Running Transaction" and "Examining the Isolation Level" in Chapter 5 for more details.	Yes	No

Table C-15. Transaction Class Methods

Method Name	Description	Return Value	Overloaded
Begin()	(**OleDbTransaction** only) Begins a new transaction, nested within the Transaction object you execute the **Begin** method on. See the "Nesting Transactions with OleDbTransaction" section in Chapter 5 for more information.	**OleDbTransaction** object	Yes
Commit()	This method commits the current database transaction. See the "Committing a Manual Transaction" section in Chapter 5 for more information.	-	No
Rollback()	Rolls back the pending changes, so they aren't applied to the database. See the "Aborting a Manual Transaction" section in Chapter 5 for more information.	-	Yes

Table C-15. Transaction Class Methods (Continued)

Method Name	Description	Return Value	Overloaded
Save()	(**SqlTransaction** only) Saves a reference point, which you can roll back to using the **Rollback** method. See the "Nesting Transactions and Using Transaction Save Points with SqlTransaction" section in Chapter 5 for more information.		No

Exception and Error Classes

In this section you'll find the properties, and methods of the Error and Exception classes for the three covered .NET Data Providers, SQL Server .NET Data Provider, OLE DB .NET Data Provider, and ODBC .NET Data Provider.

All the properties in Table C-16, which belong to the **OdbcError** class, are read-only. As is the case with the **OleDbError** class properties in Table C-19, they don't look all that different from the ones in the ADO errors collection, do they?

*Table C-16. **OdbcError** Class Properties*

Property Name	Description
Message	Returns a description of the error as a variable of data type **String**.
NativeError	Returns the database-specific error information as a variable of data type **Integer**.
Source	Returns the name of the driver in which the exception occurred or was generated by as a variable of data type **String**.
SQLState	Returns the ANSI SQL standard error code as a variable of data type **String**. This error code is always five characters long.

The **OdbcException** class properties and methods appear in Tables C-17 and C-18, respectively.

*Table C-17. **OdbcException** Class Properties*

Property Name	Accessibility	Description	Return Value	Read	Write
Errors	**Public**	This is actually a collection of the **OdbcError** class. See the "Examining the OdbcError Class" section in Chapter 5 for more information.	Data type **OdbcErrorCollection**	Yes	No
HelpLink	**Public**	This property, which is inherited from the **Exception** class, returns or sets the URN or URL that points to a HTML help file.	Data type **String**	Yes	Yes
HResult	**Protected**	This property, which is inherited from the **Exception** class, returns or sets the HRESULT for an exception.	Data type **Integer**	Yes	Yes
InnerException	**Public**	This property, which is inherited from the **Exception** class, returns a reference to the inner exception. This property generally holds the previously occurring exception or the exception that caused the current exception.	Data type **Exception**	Yes	No

Table C-17. **OdbcException** Class Properties (Continued)

Property Name	Accessibility	Description	Return Value	Read	Write
Message	Public	This property is overridden, so you might want to check out the **Message** property of the **OdbcError**, class if you want a particular error message. If you use this property, the error messages of all the **OdbcError** objects in the **OdbcErrorCollection** (returned with the **Errors** property) are returned as one long string, separated by a carriage return.	Data type **String**	Yes	No
Source	Public	Returns the name of the provider in which the first error contained as an **OdbcError** object in the **OdbcErrorCollection** (returned with the **Errors** property), occurred or was generated by.	Data type **String**	Yes	No
StackTrace	Public	This property, which is inherited from the **Exception** class, returns the stack trace, meaning the call stack, in descending order. You can use the call stack to identify the location in your code where the error occurred.	Data type **String**	Yes	No
TargetSite	Public	This property, which is inherited from the **Exception** class, returns the method that threw the exception. Check out general error handling in Chapter 14 for more information about the **MethodBase** object.	Data type **MethodBase**	Yes	No

Table C-18. **OdbcException** *Class Methods*

Method Name	Accessibility	Description	Return Value
GetBaseException()	**Public**	This method, which is inherited from the **Exception** class, returns the original exception thrown. It's useful in cases where one exception has triggered another and so forth. The reference returned will point to the current exception if this is the only exception thrown.	Data type **Exception**
ToString()	**Public**	This method, which is inherited from the **Exception** class, returns the fully qualified exception name of the **OdbcException** class. The error message (**Message** property), the inner exception name (**InnerException** property), and the stack trace (**StackTrace** property), might also be returned.	Data type **String**

All the properties in Table C-19, which belong to the **OleDbError** class, are read-only. As is the case with the **OdbcError** class properties in Listing C-16, they don't look all that different from the ones in the ADO errors collection, do they?

Table C-19. **OleDbError** *Class Properties*

Property Name	Description
Message	Returns a description of the error as a variable of data type **String**.
NativeError	Returns the database-specific error information as a variable of data type **Integer**.
Source	Returns the name of the provider in which the exception occurred or was generated from as a variable of data type **String**.
SQLState	Returns the ANSI SQL standard error code as a variable of data type **String**. This error code is always five characters long.

The **OleDbException** class properties and methods appear in Tables C-20 and C-21, respectively.

*Table C-20. **OleDbException** Class Properties*

Property Name	Accessibility	Description	Return Value	Read	Write
ErrorCode	**Public**	This property returns the error identification number for the error. The identification number is an HRESULT.	Data type **Integer**	Yes	No
Errors	**Public**	This is actually a collection of the **OleDbError** class. See the "Examining the OleDbError Class" section in Chapter 5 for more information.	Data type **OleDbError-Collection**	Yes	No
HelpLink	**Public**	This property, which is inherited from the **Exception** class, returns or sets the URN or URL that points to an HTML help file.	Data type **String**	Yes	Yes
HResult	**Protected**	This property, which is inherited from the **Exception** class, returns or sets the HRESULT for an exception.	Data type **Integer**	Yes	Yes
InnerException	**Public**	This property, which is inherited from the **Exception** class, returns a reference to the inner exception. This property generally holds the previously occurring exception or the exception that caused the current exception.	Data type **Exception**	Yes	No
Message	**Public**	This property is overridden, so you might want to check out the **Message** property of the **OleDbError** class if you want a particular error message. If you use this property, the error messages of all the **OleDbError** objects in the **OleDbErrorCollection** (returned with the **Errors** property) are returned as one long string, separated by a carriage return.	Data type **String**	Yes	No

Table C-20. **OleDbException** *Class Properties (Continued)*

Property Name	Accessibility	Description	Return Value	Read	Write
Source	**Public**	Returns the name of the provider in which the first error contained as an **OleDbError** object in the **OleDbErrorCollection** (returned with the **Errors** property) occurred or was generated by.	Data type **String**	Yes	No
StackTrace	**Public**	This property, which is inherited from the **Exception** class, returns the stack trace, meaning the call stack, in descending order. You can use the call stack to identify the location in your code where the error occurred.	Data type **String**	Yes	No
TargetSite	**Public**	This property, which is inherited from the **Exception** class, returns the method that threw the exception. Check out general error handling in Chapter 14 for more information about the **MethodBase** object.	Data type **MethodBase**	Yes	No

Table C-21. **OleDbException** *Class Methods*

Method Name	Accessibility	Description	Return Value
GetBaseException()	**Public**	This method, which is inherited from the **Exception** class, returns the original exception thrown. It's useful in cases where one exception has triggered another and so forth. The reference returned will point to the current exception if this is the only exception thrown.	Data type **Exception**
ToString()	**Public**	This method, which is inherited from the **Exception** class, can be used to return the fully qualified exception name. The error message (**Message** property), the inner exception name (**InnerException** property), and the stack trace (**StackTrace** property) might also be returned.	Data type **String**

As with the **OdbcError** and **OleDbError** classes, all the properties for the
SqlError class, which are listed in Table C-22, are read-only. The **SqlError** class
properties are somewhat different from the ones in the **OdbcError** and **OleDbError**
classes, however. This comes from the fact that the SQL Server .NET Data Provider
has been tailor-made for use with SQL Server, whereas the ODBC .NET Data
Provider and the OLE DB .NET Data Provider are generic data providers for use
with a number of different data sources.

*Table C-22. **SqlError** Class Properties*

Property Name	Description
Class	Returns the level of severity for the warning or error that occurred. The return value is of data type **Byte**, and the valid range is 1–25, corresponding to the SQL Server error severity range.
LineNumber	Returns the line number where the error occurred in a stored procedure or batch of T-SQL statements, as data type **Integer**.
Message	Returns a description of the error as a variable of data type **String**.
Number	Returns the number that uniquely identifies the type of error that occurred, as a variable of data type **Integer**.
Procedure	Returns the name of the stored procedure in which the error occurred. This property can also return the name of the RPC call that generated the error. The returned value is of data type **String**.
Server	Returns the name of the SQL Server in which context the error occurred as data type **String**.
Source	Returns the name of the provider in which the error occurred or was generated by as data type **String**.
State	Returns the SQL Server error code if any, as a variable of data type **Byte**.

The **SqlException** class properties and methods appear in Tables C-23 and
C-24, respectively.

Command Class

Tables C-25, C-26, and C-27 list all the public, noninherited Command class properties in alphabetical order and show the equivalent Command class constructor
argument (see the "The Overloaded Command Constructor" section in Chapter 6).

*Table C-23. **SqlException** Class Properties*

Property Name	Accessibility	Description
Class	**Public**	Returns the level of severity for the first warning or error contained as a **SqlError** object in the **SqlErrorCollection** (returned with the **Errors** property). The return value has a valid range of 1–25, corresponding to the SQL Server error severity range.
Errors	**Public**	This is actually a collection of the **SqlError** class. See the "Examining the SqlError Class" section in Chapter 5 for more information.
HelpLink	**Public**	This property, which is inherited from the **Exception** class, returns or sets the URN or URL that points to a HTML help file.
HResult	**Protected**	This property, which is inherited from the **Exception** class, returns or sets the HRESULT for an exception.
InnerException	**Public**	This property, which is inherited from the **Exception** class, returns a reference to the inner exception. This property generally holds the previously occurring exception or the exception that caused the current exception.
LineNumber	**Public**	Returns the line number where the first error contained as a **SqlError** object in the **SqlErrorCollection** (returned with the **Errors** property) occurred in a stored procedure or batch of T-SQL statements.
Message	**Public**	This property is overridden, so you might want to check out the **Message** property of the **SqlError** class if you want a particular error message. If you use this property, the error messages of all the **SqlError** objects in the **SqlErrorCollection** (returned with the **Errors** property) are returned as one long string, separated by a carriage return.
Number	**Public**	Returns the number that uniquely identifies the type of error that occurred for the error contained as a **SqlError** object in the **SqlErrorCollection** (returned with the **Errors** property).
Procedure	**Public**	Returns the name of the stored procedure in which the first error contained as a **SqlError** object in the **SqlErrorCollection** (returned with the **Errors** property) occurred. This property can also return the name of the RPC call that generated the error.

Return Value	Read	Write
Data type **Byte**	Yes	No
Data type **SqlErrorCollection**	Yes	No
Data type **String**	Yes	Yes
Data Type **Integer**	Yes	Yes
Data type **Exception**	Yes	No
Data type **Integer**	Yes	No
Data type **String**	Yes	No
Data type **Integer**	Yes	No
Data type **String**	Yes	No

Table C-23. SqlException Class Properties (Continued)

Property Name	Accessibility	Description
Source	**Public**	Returns the name of the provider in which the first error contained as a **SqlError** object in the **SqlErrorCollection** (returned with the **Errors** property) occurred or was generated by.
Server	**Public**	Returns the name of the SQL Server in which context the first error contained as a **SqlError** object in the **SqlErrorCollection** (returned with the **Errors** property) occurred.
StackTrace	**Public**	This property, which is inherited from the **Exception** class, returns the stack trace, meaning the call stack, in descending order. You can use the call stack to identify the location in your code where the error occurred.
TargetSite	**Public**	This property, which is inherited from the **Exception** class, returns the method that threw the exception. Check out general error handling in Chapter 14 for more information about the **Method-Base** object.

Table C-24. SqlException Class Methods

Method Name	Accessibility	Description	Return Value
GetBaseException()	Public	This method, which is inherited from the **Exception** class, returns the original exception thrown. It's useful in cases where one exception has triggered another. The reference returned will point to the current exception if this is the only exception thrown.	Data type **Exception**
ToString()	Public	This method, which is inherited from the **Exception** class, returns the fully qualified exception name of the **SqlException** class. The error message (**Message** property), the inner exception name (**InnerException** property), and the stack trace (**StackTrace** property) might also be returned.	Data type **String**

*Table C-23. **SqlException** Class Properties (Continued)*

Return Value	Read	Write
Data type **String**.	Yes	No
Data type **String**	Yes	No
Data type **String**	Yes	No
Data type **MethodBase**	Yes	No

Command Class

Tables C-25, C-26, and C-27 list all the public, noninherited Command class properties in alphabetical order and show the equivalent Command class constructor argument (see the "The Overloaded Command Constructor" section in Chapter 6).

NOTE Documentation for ODBC standard escape sequences can be found in the documentation for your ODBC driver or at these addresses: http://msdn.microsoft.com/library/default.asp?url=/library/en-us/odbc/htm/odbcescape_sequences_in_odbc.asp and http://msdn.microsoft.com/library/default.asp?url=/library/en-us/odbc/htm/odbcodbc_escape_sequences.asp

Table C-25. **OdbcCommand** *Class Properties*

Property Name	Description
CommandText	This is the query text or the name of a stored procedure to execute. You need to set this property to the name of a stored procedure when the **CommandType** property is set to **CommandType.StoredProcedure**. However, the property must be set using standard ODBC escape sequences for stored procedures (see the note later in this section for more information). You can only set this property when the connection is open and available, which means that the connection can't be executing or retrieving rows when you set the property. Because the ODBC .NET Data Provider doesn't support named parameters, the parameters must be indicated by a question mark (?) to show where the parameter values are supposed to go in the SQL statement.
CommandTimeout	This is the number of seconds to wait for the command to execute. If the command has not been executed within this period, an exception is thrown. Set the value of this property to 0 if you don't want a time limit.
CommandType	This property determines how the **CommandText** property is interpreted. It must be set to one of the members of the **CommandType** enum. See Table C-29 for more information.
Connection	This is the connection to the data source. You can only set this property when the current connection is either closed or open and available, which means that the connection can't be executing or retrieving rows when you set the property. See more about connections in Chapter 5.
DesignTimeVisible	Used to indicate if the Command object should be visible in a custom user interface control.
Parameters	Retrieves the **OdbcParameterCollection**, which holds the parameters for the **CommandText** property. Because the ODBC .NET Data Provider doesn't support named parameters, the parameters must be added to this collection in the order in which the question marks (?) appear in the SQL statement in the **CommandText** property. See the **CreateParameter** method in Table C-28 later in this appendix for information on how to add parameters to this collection.
Transaction	This property is used for retrieving or setting the transaction the command is executing within, if any. Please note that the Transaction object must be connected to the same Connection object as the Command object. This property can only be set if it hasn't been set previously, or if the command isn't executing when you set the property.
UpdatedRowSource	Gets or sets whether—and if so how—the command results are applied to the row source after the command has been executed. This property needs to be set to one of the **UpdateRowSource** enum values. See Table C-30 for more information.

Command Constructor Equivalent	Default Value	Read	Write
strSQL	"" (empty string)	Yes	Yes
-	30	Yes	Yes
-	**CommandType.Text**	Yes	Yes
cnnUserMan	**Nothing**	Yes	Yes
-	**False**	Yes	Yes
-	An empty collection	Yes	No
traUserMan	**Nothing**	Yes	Yes
-	**Both** (**None** if the command is automatically generated by a **OdbcCommandBuilder** object)	Yes	Yes

Table C-26. **OleDbCommand** *Class Properties*

Property Name	Description
CommandText	The query text or the name of a stored procedure to execute. When you set this property to the same value as the current value, the assignment is left out. You need to set this property to the name of a stored procedure when the **CommandType** property is set to **CommandType.StoredProcedure**. You can only set this property when the connection is open and available, which means that the connection can't be executing or retrieving rows when you set this property. Because the OLE DB .NET Data Provider doesn't support named parameters, the parameters must be indicated by a question mark (?) to show where the parameter values are supposed to go in the SQL statement.
CommandTimeout	This is the number of seconds to wait for the command to execute. If the command has not been executed within this period, an exception is thrown. Set the value of this property to 0 if you don't want a time limit.
CommandType	This property determines how the **CommandText** property is interpreted. It must be set to one of the members of the **CommandType** enum. See Table C-29 for more information.
Connection	This is the connection to the data source. You can only set this property when the current connection is either closed or open and available, which means that the connection can't be executing or retrieving rows when you set the property. See more about connections in Chapter 5.
DesignTimeVisible	Used to indicate if the Command object should be visible in a custom user interface control.
Parameters	Retrieves the **OleDbParameterCollection**, which holds the parameters for the **CommandText** property. Because the OLE DB .NET Data Provider doesn't support named parameters, the parameters must be added to this collection in the order in which the question marks (?) appear in the SQL statement in the **CommandText** property. See the **CreateParameter** method in Table C-28 later in this appendix for information on how to add parameters to this collection.
Transaction	This property is used for retrieving or setting the transaction the command is executing within, if any. Please note that the Transaction object must be connected to the same Connection object as the Command object. This property can only be set if it hasn't been set previously, or if the command isn't executing when you set the property.
UpdatedRowSource	Gets or sets whether—and if so how—the command results are applied to the row source after the command has been executed. This property needs to be set to one of the **UpdateRowSource** enum values. See Table C-30 for more information.

Command Constructor Equivalent	Default Value	Read	Write
strSQL	"" (empty string)	Yes	Yes
-	30	Yes	Yes
-	**Text**	Yes	Yes
cnnUserMan	**Nothing**	Yes	Yes
-	**False**	Yes	Yes
-	An empty collection	Yes	No
traUserMan	**Nothing**	Yes	Yes
-	**Both** (**None** if the command is automatically generated by a **OleDbCommandBuilder** object)	Yes	Yes

*Table C-27. **SqlCommand** Class Properties*

Property Name	Description
CommandText	The T-SQL query text or the name of a stored procedure to execute. When you set this property to the same value as the current one, the assignment is left out. You need to set this property to the name of a stored procedure when the **CommandType** property is set to **CommandType.StoredProcedure**. You can only set this property when the connection is open and available, which means that the connection can't be executing or retrieving rows when you set this property. Because the SQL Server .NET Data Provider only supports named parameters, you can't use the question mark (?) to specify where the parameter values are supposed to go in the SQL statement.
CommandTimeout	This is the number of seconds to wait for the command to execute. If the command has not been executed within this period, an exception is thrown. Set the value of this property to 0 if you don't want a time limit.
CommandType	This property determines how the **CommandText** property is interpreted. It must be set to one of the members of the **CommandType** enum. See Table C-29 for more information.
Connection	This is the connection to the data source. You can only set this property when the current connection is either closed or open and available, which means that the connection can't be executing or retrieving rows when you set the property. See more about connections in Chapter 5.
DesignTimeVisible	Used to indicate if the Command object should be visible in a custom user interface control.
Parameters	Retrieves the **SqlParameterCollection**, which holds the parameters for the **CommandText** property. Because the SQL Server .NET Data Provider only supports named parameters, you can add the parameters to this collection in any order. See the **CreateParameter** method in Table C-28 later in this appendix for information on how to add parameters to this collection.
Transaction	This property is used for retrieving or setting the transaction the command is executing within, if any. Please note that the Transaction object must be connected to the same Connection object as the Command object. This property can only be set if it hasn't been set previously, or if the command isn't executing when you set the property.
UpdatedRowSource	Gets or sets whether—and if so how—the command results are applied to the row source after the command has been executed. This property needs to be set to one of the **UpdateRowSource** enum values. See Table C-30 for more information.

Command Constructor Equivalent	Default Value	Read	Write
strSQL	"" (empty string)	Yes	Yes
-	30	Yes	Yes
-	**Text**	Yes	Yes
cnnUserMan	**Nothing**	Yes	Yes
-	**False**	Yes	Yes
-	An empty collection	Yes	No
traUserMan	**Nothing**	Yes	Yes
-	**Both** (**None** if the command is automatically generated by a **OleDbCommandBuilder** object)	Yes	Yes

Table C-28 lists all the public, noninherited class methods for the three Command classes, **OdbcCommand**, **OleDbCommand**, and **SqlCommand**, in alphabetical order.

Table C-28. Command Class Methods

Method Name	Description
Cancel()	Cancels the executing command if there is one. Otherwise, nothing happens. Please note that no exception is thrown if the executing command can't be cancelled.
CreateParameter()	This method can be used to create and instantiate an **OdbcParameter**, an **OleDbParameter**, or a **SqlParameter** object. This is the equivalent of instantiating an **OdbcParameter** object using `prmTest = New OdbcParameter()`, or an **OleDbParameter** object using `prmTest = New OleDbParameter()`, or a **SqlParameter** object using `prmTest = New SqlParameter()`. You can add parameters to the parameters collection using the **Add** method of the collection. The parameters collection can be retrieved using the **Parameters** property.
ExecuteNonQuery()	Executes the query specified in the **CommandText** property. The number of rows affected is returned. Even if the **CommandText** property contains a row-returning statement, no rows will be returned. The value -1 is returned if you specify a row-returning statement as command text. This is also true if you specify any other statement that doesn't affect the rows in the data source. If you've specified output parameters with your Command object, these will be populated and returned to you, even if no rows are returned.

Table C-28. Command Class Methods (Continued)

Method Name	Description
ExecuteReader()	Executes the query specified in the **CommandText** property. The returned object is a forward-only, read-only data object of type **SqlDataReader**, **OdbcDataReader**, or **OleDbDataReader**. This method is used when you execute a row-returning command, such as a SQL SELECT statement. Although it's possible to execute a non–row-returning command using this method, it's recommended that you use the **ExecuteNonQuery** method for that purpose. The reason for this is that even though the query doesn't return rows, the method still tries to build and return a forward-only data object. This method is overloaded (see the "Executing a Command" section in Chapter 6).
ExecuteScalar()	This method is for retrieving a single value, such as an aggregate value like COUNT(*). There's less overhead and coding involved in using this method than in using the **ExecuteReader** method (see the "Executing a Command" section in Chapter 6). Basically, only the first column of the first row is returned. This means that if the query returns several rows and columns, they'll be ignored.
ExecuteXmlReader()	This method is for retrieving a result set as XML (see the "Executing a Command" section in Chapter 6). This is a **SqlCommand** class method only. An **XmlReader** holding the retrieved data is returned.
Prepare()	This method is used for compiling (preparing) the command. You can use this method when the **CommandType** property is set to **Text** or **StoredProcedure**. If, however, the **CommandType** property is set to **TableDirect**, nothing happens. You can use this command to speed up execution once you call one of the execute commands, especially if your command has any parameters. The method takes no arguments, and it's simply called like this: `cmmUserMan.Prepare()`.
ResetCommandTimeout()	Resets the **CommandTimeout** property to the default value, which is 30. There's no difference in explicitly setting the **CommandTimeout** property to 30 and calling this method. However, I feel that it makes your code more readable if you use this method, because the name of the method says it all. The method takes no arguments, and it's called like this: `cmmUserMan.ResetCommandTimeout()`.

Table C-29 lists the **CommandType** enum members, and Table C-30 lists the **UpdateRowSource** enum members.

*Table C-29. **CommandType** Enum Members*

Member Name	Description
StoredProcedure	The **CommandText** property must hold the name of a stored procedure. If you're using the ODBC .NET Data Provider, you might have to specify it using standard ODBC escape sequences. See the note just before Table C-26.
TableDirect	If you set the **CommandType** property to **TableDirect**, you must also set the **CommandText** to the name of the table you want to access. You can actually access more than one table if you specify all the tables you want to access, each separated by a comma. All the rows of the named table(s) are returned when you execute the command. If more tables were specified, they're returned as a joined table. The Microsoft.Jet.OLEDB.4.0 and earlier OLE DB provider doesn't support retrieving rows from more than one table at a time. The **TableDirect** enum member isn't supported by the ODBC .NET Data Provider or the SQL Server .NET Data Provider.
Text	The **CommandText** property is interpreted as a query like a SELECT statement, and so on. Please note that the ODBC .NET Data Provider and OLE DB .NET Data Provider don't support named parameters, which means that you must specify arguments using the question mark (?). You can only set this property when the connection is open and available, which means that the connection can't be executing or fetching rows when you set the property.

*Table C-30. **UpdateRowSource** Enum Members*

Member Name	Description
Both	The sum of the **FirstReturnedRecord** and **OutputParameters** values.
FirstReturnedRecord	Only data in the first returned record/row is mapped to the changed row in the **DataSet**.
None	Returned parameters and/ rows will be ignored.
OutputParameters	Only the output parameters are mapped to the changed row in the **DataSet**.

Parameter Class

In Table C-31, you can see all the public properties of the three Parameter classes, **OdbcParameter**, **OleDbParameter**, and **SqlParameter**. The properties are the same for all three classes, unless otherwise specified.

Table C-31. Parameter Class Properties

Property Name	Description	Default Value
DbType	Retrieves or sets the data type of the parameter. This property is directly linked to the **OdbcType**, **OleDbType**, or **SqlDbType** property, depending on which Parameter class you use. This means that if you set this property, the other linked property is updated with the corresponding data type, and vice versa. This property must be set to one of the **DbType** enum members. The **Object** data type isn't supported by the ODBC .NET Data Provider.	**String**
Direction	This property retrieves or sets a value indicating the type of parameter: input, output, input and output, or a stored procedure return value. You must set this property to a member of the **ParameterDirection** enum (see Table C-32).	**Input**
IsNullable	The **IsNullable** property, which holds a **Boolean** value, determines if the parameter can hold a null value (**Nothing**).	**False**
OdbcType	(**OdbcParameter** only) This property retrieves or sets the ODBC specific data type of the parameter. You must set this property to a member of the **OdbcType** enum. This property is directly linked to the **DbType** property, meaning that if you set this property, the **DbType** property is updated with the corresponding data type, and vice versa.	**NChar**
OleDbType	(**OleDbParameter** only) This property retrieves or sets the OLE DB–specific data type of the parameter. You must set this property to a member of the **OleDbType** enum. This property is directly linked to the **DbType** property, meaning that if you set this property, the **DbType** property is updated with the corresponding data type, and vice versa.	**VarWChar**

Table C-31. Parameter Class Properties (Continued)

Property Name	Description	Default Value
Offset	(**SqlParameter** only) The **Offset** property retrieves or sets the offset to the **Value** property. This property is ignored for data types other than binary data and strings. This property holds the number of bytes (binary data) or the number of characters (string data), excluding a possible terminating character.	0
ParameterName	(**OdbcParameter** and **OleDbParameter** only) This property retrieves or sets the name of the **OdbcParameter** or **OleDbParameter** instance. Because the ODBC .NET Data Provider and the OLE DB .NET Data Provider don't support named parameters, it's not required that you give your parameters a name. Personally, I feel that it does make your code easier to read if you do. Parameter names are ignored when the actual parameter binding takes place.	"" (an empty **String**)
ParameterName	(**SqlParameter** only) This property retrieves or sets the name of the **SqlParameter**. All parameters must have a name that corresponds to the name used in the SQL statement. The name of a parameter must be specified using the @ character followed by the name. The name cannot contain spaces.	"" (an empty **String**)
Precision	The **Precision** property retrieves or sets the maximum number of digits used to represent the **Value** property. In this case, the maximum number of digits actually refers to the total number of digits in a number, meaning both the digits to the left and the right of the decimal point. The value 1234.567 has a precision of 7.	0
Scale	The Scale property, which is used for noninteger numbers, retrieves or sets the number of decimal places to which **Value** is resolved. This means the number of digits to the right of the decimal point. Therefore, the value 1234.123 has a scale of 3.	0

Table C-31. Parameter Class Properties (Continued)

Property Name	Description	Default Value
Size	The **Size** property retrieves or sets the maximum byte (ANSI string and nonstring data types) or character (Unicode strings) size for the data in the column. If you set this property to a value less than the actual number of characters in the **Value** property for an input parameter, only the number of characters specified with the **Size** property is used when the parameter binding is performed. So if you set the **Size** property to *3* and the **Value** property to *John*, only *Joh* will be used as the input value for the parameter. It's the same story for an output parameter, if **Size** is less than the number of bytes or characters to be returned, the byte array or string will be truncated to fit into the output parameter.	The actual size of the parameter, meaning 4 if you set the **Value** property of an input parameter to *John*.
SourceColumn	This property retrieves or sets the name of the source column, meaning that you can use this property to specify what column holds the value of the parameter. This means that you don't explicitly have to set the **Value** property. For input parameters, the value is retrieved from the **DataTable** object, and for output parameters, it's retrieved from the data source.	"" (an empty **String**)
SourceVersion	The **SourceVersion** property is used for retrieving or setting which version of data row to use. You must set this property to one of the members of the **DataRowVersion** enum.	**Current**
SqlDbType	(**SqlParameter** only) This property retrieves or sets the SQL Server–specific data type of the parameter. You must set this property to a member of the **SqlDbType** enum. This property is directly linked to the **DbType** property, meaning that if you set this property, the **DbType** property is updated with the corresponding data type, and vice versa.	**NVarChar**
Value	This property retrieves or sets the value of the parameter. For input parameters, you must populate this property, before adding the parameter to the parameters collection. For output parameters, you can read the value after the last row has been read from the data source, meaning after the command has finished executing. If you're populating a DataReader, you must also close the DataReader before you can retrieve the output value from this property. See more about DataReader objects in Chapter 7.	**Nothing**

Table C-32 lists the **ParameterDirection** enum members, followed by the **CommandBehavior** enum members in Table C-33.

*Table C-32. **ParameterDirection** Enum Members*

Member Name	Description
Input	This member specifies an input-only parameter, meaning this parameter will not be changed during execution.
InputOutput	The parameter can hold both input and output values.
Output	If you use this member, you specify that your parameter is an output-only parameter.
ReturnValue	This member specifies that the parameter holds a return value from executing a stored procedure, stored function, built-in function, or even a user-defined function.

*Table C-33. **CommandBehavior** Enum Members*

Member Name	Description
CloseConnection	You should use this member with the **ExecuteReader** method when you want the associated Connection object to be closed once you close the DataReader object.
Default	As the name suggests, this is the default value, which is assumed if you don't specify a member of the **CommandBehavior** enum. This member means that it's possible to have multiple results returned, and the query may affect the state of the database.
KeyInfo	Use this member when you want column and primary key information returned, as well as the rows returned by the SQL statement. No locking is applied at the data source when you use this member with the **ExecuteReader** method. If you only need general column information, you should use the **SchemaOnly** member. You still need to use the **GetSchemaTable** method of the DataReader class after retrieving the column information to put the information into a **DataTable**. When you use the **KeyInfo** member with the SQL Server .NET Data Provider, a FOR BROWSE clause is appended to the SQL statement. You need to be aware of this, because it might interference with the use of SET FMTONLY ON statements, which returns metadata only to the client. Please see your SQL Server Books Online for more information about the two statements.

*Table C-33. **CommandBehavior** Enum Members (Continued)*

Member Name	Description
SchemaOnly	Use this member when you only want column information returned. The database state isn't affected when you use this member with the **ExecuteReader** method. If you need primary key information as well as the general column information, you need to use the **KeyInfo** member. You still need to use the **GetSchemaTable** method of the DataReader class after retrieving the column information, to put the information into a **DataTable**. This actually means that you can extract the column information or metadata information without using the **SchemaOnly** member with the **ExecuteReader** method of the Command class. So why use this member? Well, you should use it in cases where you only need the column information returned, and not all the rows that the SQL statement will return. It saves you the overhead of having the data source extract the rows.
SequentialAccess	**SequentialAccess** is used for loading one column at a time, in a sequential manner, just as the rows in a DataReader are read one at a time. In other words, **SequentialAccess** makes the DataReader load the data as a stream. One thing to keep in mind though, is that while it provides sequential access to the columns, you don't actually have to read them one by one. This means that you can read the content of column 3, without reading columns 0, 1, and 2. However, once you've read column 3, you can't access columns 0, 1, and 2. It works much the same way as with reading rows. This member is particularly useful for working with columns of data type Binary Large Object (BLOB), because only one column is ever in memory at a time. You should generally use this member when you use the **GetBytes** and **GetChars** methods of the DataReader class to retrieve the content of a single field.
SingleResult	When you use this member with the **ExecuteReader** method, only one result set is returned in the DataReader. This is also true if you've specified a batch of SQL statements for the **CommandText** property of the Command object; only the first result is ever returned.
SingleRow	You should use this member to return a single row only, if any, depending on your SQL statement. The database state may be affected when using this member. It's obvious that you can use this member to optimize performance by only having one row returned, but it's optional for the .NET Data Providers to optimize the performance of the command. If your SQL statement returns more than one row, only the first row is returned in the DataReader object. Please note that if you have multiple results returned, each of these results will have exactly one row.

DataReader Class

In this section you'll find the properties and methods of the DataReader class. They're the same for all of the three covered .NET Data Providers, SQL Server .NET Data Provider, OLE DB .NET Data Provider, and ODBC .NET Data Provider, unless otherwise stated

The DataReader class has the properties shown in ascending order in Table C-34.

Table C-34. DataReader Class Properties

Name	Description
Depth	This read-only property is use with hierarchical result sets, such as XML data. The return value indicates how far down a node you currently are or the depth of the current element in the stack of XML elements. This isn't supported by the SQL Server .NET Data Provider, which means it will always return 0, because this is the depth value for the outermost table.
FieldCount	This read-only property returns the number of columns in the current row and 0 if the DataReader isn't positioned at a valid row, like when the DataReader has been instantiated and you haven't called the **Read** method yet. The **NotSupportedException** exception is thrown if the DataReader isn't connected to a data source.
IsClosed	This property, which is read-only, indicates if the DataReader is closed. **True** is returned if the DataReader is closed and **False** if not. It goes without saying, but this property can be called when the DataReader is closed.
Item	The **Item** property, which is read-only, retrieves the value of the specified column in its native format. The column is specified with the column ordinal (zero-based), drdUser.Item(3), or using the column name, drdUser.Item(FirstName). This property is the default property, which means you can leave it out, like this: drdUser(3) or drdUser("FirstName").
RecordsAffected	This read-only property retrieves the number of records that was affected (inserted, updated, or deleted) by the command. Although you can read this property when the DataReader is open, it won't be set until you have read all the rows and closed the DataReader. -1 is returned if the executed command was a row-returning statement, like a SELECT statement. 0 is returned if no rows were affected by the command. If the command holds multiple SQL statements, the number of rows affected by all statements is returned.

Table C-35 lists the noninherited and public methods of the DataReader class in alphabetical order. Please note that all the methods in Table C-35 marked with an asterisk (*) require that the data contained in the specified column be of the same type as the method indicates. This means that the **GetBoolean** method must be used for returning a **Boolean** value from the column.

All the GetSql methods such as **GetSqlBinary**, which are relevant to the **SqlDataReader** class only, belong to the **System.Data.SqlTypes** namespace. Most of these methods have corresponding methods that work with all the DataReader classes. They work with the same data types in the data source (SQL Server), but the data type returned is different. So which method you should pick when working with SQL Server as your data source really depends on the data types you want to work with in your application: Do you want native SQL Server data types or do you want .NET Framework data types? Well, it's not that simple—it's also a matter of performance. If you choose to work with .NET Framework data types, an implicit data type conversion is performed behind the scenes, and any conversion takes time. The performance issue might not be enough for you to notice, but depending on the number of reads you do, it might be something you need to consider. Also, using the native SQL Server data types will prevent possible type conversion errors, such as loss of precision for floating-point numbers.

Table C-35. DataReader Class Methods

Name	Description
Close()	Closes the DataReader. You must call this method before you can use the connection for any other purpose, because the DataReader keeps the connection busy as long as it's open.
*GetBoolean(ByVal intOrdinal As Integer)	Returns the **Boolean** value of the specified column intOrdinal. The corresponding SQL Server data type is **bit**.
*GetByte(ByVal intOrdinal As Integer)	Returns the value of the specified column intOrdinal as a **Byte**. The corresponding SQL Server data type is **tinyint**.
*GetBytes(ByVal intOrdinal As Integer, ByVal lngDataIndex As Long, ByVal arrbytBuffer() As Byte, ByVal intBufferIndex As Integer, ByVal intLength As Integer)	Returns the value of the specified column intOrdinal as an array of **Byte**s in the arrbytBuffer argument. The length of the specified column is returned as the result of the method call. intLength specifies the maximum number of bytes to copy into the byte array. intBufferIndex is the starting point in the buffer. When the bytes are copied into the buffer, they're placed starting from the intBufferIndex point. The bytes are copied from the data source starting from the lngDataIndex point. You can use this method when you need to read large images from the database and the method largely corresponds to the **GetChunk** method in ADO. The corresponding SQL Server data types are **binary**, **image**, and **varbinary**.
*GetChar(ByVal intOrdinal As Integer)	Returns the value of the specified column (intOrdinal) as a **Char**. The corresponding SQL Server data type is **char**.

Example

```
drdTest.Close()
```

```
Dim blnTest As Boolean = drdTest.GetBoolean(0)
```

```
Dim bytTest As Byte = drdTest.GetByte(0)
```

```
Dim lngNumBytes As Long = drdSql.GetBytes(1, 0, Nothing, 0, Integer.MaxValue)
Dim arrbytImage(lngNumBytes) As Byte
drdSql.GetBytes(1, 0, arrbytImage, 0, CInt(lngNumBytes))
```

The example reads an image from column 1 in the current row of the DataReader. The image is saved in the arrbytImage **Byte** array. The first line retrieves the size of the image (passing **Nothing** for the arrbytBuffer argument), which is then used for sizing the array on the second line, and finally the third line retrieves the image.

```
chrTest = drdTest.GetChar(0)
```

Table C-35. DataReader Class Methods (Continued)

Name	Description
GetChars(ByVal intOrdinal As Integer, ByVal lngDataIndex As Long, ByVal arrchrBuffer() As Char, ByVal intBufferIndex As Integer, ByVal intLength As Integer)	Returns the value of the specified column (intOrdinal) as an array of **Char**s in the arrchrBuffer argument. The length of the specified column is returned as the result of the method call. intLength specifies the maximum number of characters to copy into the character array. intBufferIndex is the starting point in the buffer. When the characters are copied into the buffer, they're placed starting from the intBufferIndex point. The characters are copied from the data source starting from the lngDataIndex point. The corresponding SQL Server data types are **char**, **nchar**, **ntext**, **nvarchar**, **text**, and **varchar**.
GetDataTypeName(ByVal intOrdinal As Integer)	Returns the name of the data type used by the data source for the specified column.
GetDateTime(ByVal intOrdinal As Integer)	Returns the **DateTime** value stored in the column specified by intOrdinal. The corresponding SQL Server data types are **datetime** and **smalldatetime**. The **DateTime** data type indicates values between January 1, 0001, and December 31, 9999 (Common Era).
GetDecimal(ByVal intOrdinal As Integer)	Returns the **Decimal** value stored in the column specified by intOrdinal. The corresponding SQL Server data types are **decimal**, **money**, **numeric**, and **smallmoney**.
GetDouble(ByVal intOrdinal As Integer)	Returns the **Double** value stored in the column specified by intOrdinal. The corresponding SQL Server data type is **float**.
GetFieldType(ByVal intOrdinal As Integer)	Returns the data type of the column specified by intOrdinal. The returned object is of type **Type**.
GetFloat(ByVal intOrdinal As Integer)	Returns the single precision floating-point number stored in the column specified by intOrdinal. The returned object is of data type **Float**. The corresponding SQL Server data type is **real**.
GetGuid(ByVal intOrdinal As Integer)	Returns the globally unique identifier stored in the column specified by intOrdinal. The returned object is of data type **Guid**. The corresponding SQL Server data type is **uniqueidentifier**.

Example

```
Dim lngNumChars As Long = drdSql.GetChars(1, 0, Nothing, 0, Integer.MaxValue)
Dim arrchrTest(lngNumChars) As Char
drdSql.GetChars(1, 0, arrchrTest, 0, CInt(lngNumChars))
```

```
Dim strDataType As String = drdTest.GetDataTypeName(0)
```

```
Dim dtmTest As DateTime = drdTest.GetDateTime(0)
```

```
Dim decTest As Decimal = drdTest.GetDecimal(0)
```

```
Dim dblTest As Double = drdTest.GetDouble(0)
```

```
Dim typTest As Type = drdTest.GetFieldType(0)
```

```
fltTest = drdTest.GetFloat(0)
```

```
Dim guiTest As Guid = drdTest.GetGuid(0)
```

Table C-35. DataReader Class Methods (Continued)

Name	Description
GetInt16(ByVal intOrdinal As Integer)	Returns the 16-bit signed integer stored in the column specified by intOrdinal. The returned object is of data type **Short**. The corresponding SQL Server data type is **smallint**.
GetInt32(ByVal intOrdinal As Integer)	Returns the 32-bit signed integer stored in the column specified by intOrdinal. The returned object is of data type **Integer**. The corresponding SQL Server data type is **int**.
GetInt64(ByVal intOrdinal As Integer)	Returns the 64-bit signed integer stored in the column specified by intOrdinal. The returned object is of data type **Long**. The corresponding SQL Server data type is **bigint**.
GetName(ByVal intOrdinal As Integer)	Returns the name of the column specified by intOrdinal. The returned object is of data type **String**. This method is the reverse of **GetOrdinal**.
GetOrdinal(ByVal strName As String)	Returns the ordinal for the column specified by strName. The returned object is of data type **Integer**. This method is the reverse of **GetName**.
GetSchemaTable()	This method returns a **DataTable** object that describes the metadata for the columns in the DataReader. The metadata includes column name, size, ordinal, and key information. See Table C-33 for a list of **CommandBehavior** enum members that affect the information returned in a DataReader object when you call the **ExecuteReader** method of the Command class.
GetSqlBinary(ByVal intOrdinal As Integer)	(**SqlDataReader** only) Returns the variable-length binary data stream stored in the column specified by intOrdinal. The returned object is of data type **SqlBinary**. The corresponding SQL Server data types are **binary** and **image**.

Example

```
Dim shrTest As Short = drdTest.GetInt16(0)
```

```
Dim intTest As Integer = drdTest.GetInt32(0)
```

```
Dim lngTest As Long = drdTest.GetInt64(0)
```

```
Dim strTest As String = drdTest.GetName(0)
```

```
Dim intTest As Integer = drdTest.GetOrdinal(0)
```

```
Dim dtbSchema As New DataTable() = drdTest.GetSchemaTable()
```

```
Dim sbnTest As SqlBinary = drdTest.GetSqlBinary(0)
```

Table C-35. DataReader Class Methods (Continued)

Name	Description
GetSqlBoolean(ByVal intOrdinal As Integer)	(**SqlDataReader** only) Returns the value stored in the column specified by `intOrdinal`. The returned object is of data type **SqlBoolean**, which is a value of 0 or 1. Nonzero values are interpreted as 1. The corresponding SQL Server data type is **bit**. Although this method works with the same SQL Server data type as the **GetBoolean** method, the return value is different.
GetSqlByte(ByVal intOrdinal As Integer)	(**SqlDataReader** only) Returns the 8-bit unsigned integer stored in the column specified by `intOrdinal`. The returned object is of data type **SqlByte**. The corresponding SQL Server data type is **tinyint**.
GetSqlDateTime(ByVal intOrdinal As Integer)	(**SqlDataReader** only) Returns the date and time value stored in the column specified by `intOrdinal`. The returned object is of data type **SqlDateTime**. The corresponding SQL Server data types are **datetime** and **smalldatetime**. The **SqlDateTime** data type indicates values between January 1, 1753, and December 31, 9999.
GetSqlDecimal(ByVal intOrdinal As Integer)	(**SqlDataReader** only) Returns the **SqlDecimal** value stored in the column specified by `intOrdinal`.
GetSqlDouble(ByVal intOrdinal As Integer)	(**SqlDataReader** only) Returns the **SqlDouble** value stored in the column specified by `intOrdinal`. The corresponding SQL Server data type is **float**.
GetSqlGuid(ByVal intOrdinal As Integer)	(**SqlDataReader** only) Returns the globally unique identifier stored in the column specified by `intOrdinal`. The returned object is of data type **SqlGuid**. The corresponding SQL Server data type is **uniqueidentifier**.
GetSqlInt16(ByVal intOrdinal As Integer)	(**SqlDataReader** only) Returns the 16-bit signed integer stored in the column specified by `intOrdinal`. The returned object is of data type **SqlInt16**. The corresponding SQL Server data type is **smallint**.
GetSqlInt32(ByVal intOrdinal As Integer)	(**SqlDataReader** only) Returns the 32-bit signed integer stored in the column specified by `intOrdinal`. The returned object is of data type **SqlInt32**. The corresponding SQL Server data type is **int**.

Example

```
Dim sbtTest As SqlBoolean = drdTest.GetSqlBit(0)
```

```
Dim sbyTest As SqlByte = drdTest.GetSqlByte(0)
```

```
Dim sdtTest As SqlDateTime = drdTest.GetSqlDateTime(0)
```

```
Dim sdcTest As SqlDecimal = drdTest.GetSqlDecimal(0)
```

```
Dim sdbTest As SqlDouble = drdTest.GetSqlDouble(0)
```

```
Dim sguTest As SqlGuid = drdTest.GetSqlGuid(0)
```

```
Dim s16Test As SqlInt16 = drdTest.GetSqlInt16(0)
```

```
Dim s32Test As SqlInt32 = drdTest.GetSqlInt32(0)
```

Table C-35. DataReader Class Methods (Continued)

Name	Description
*GetSqlInt64(ByVal intOrdinal As Integer)	(**SqlDataReader** only) Returns the 64-bit signed integer stored in the column specified by intOrdinal. The returned object is of data type **SqlInt64**. The corresponding SQL Server data type is **bigint**.
*GetSqlMoney(ByVal intOrdinal As Integer)	(**SqlDataReader** only) Returns the **SqlMoney** value stored in the column specified by intOrdinal. The corresponding SQL Server data types are **money** and **smallmoney**.
*GetSqlSingle(ByVal intOrdinal As Integer)	(**SqlDataReader** only) Returns the **SqlSingle** value stored in the column specified by intOrdinal. The corresponding SQL Server data type is **real**.
*GetSqlString(ByVal intOrdinal As Integer)	(**SqlDataReader** only) Returns the **SqlString** value stored in the column specified by intOrdinal. The corresponding SQL Server data types are **char**, **nchar**, **ntext**, **nvarchar**, **text**, and **varchar**.
GetSqlValue(ByVal intOrdinal As Integer)	(**SqlDataReader** only) Returns an object that represents the underlying data type (**SqlDbType**) specified by intOrdinal. The returned object is of data type **Object**. You can use **GetType**, **ToString**, and other methods on the returned object to get the information wanted.
GetSqlValues(ByVal arrobjValues() As Object)	(**SqlDataReader** only) Returns all the attribute fields for the columns in the current row in the arrobjValues array. The array supplied can have fewer or more elements than there are columns in the current row. Only the number of elements in the array is copied from the current row if there are fewer elements in the array. The returned **Integer** is the number of objects in the array.
*GetString(ByVal intOrdinal As Integer)	Returns the **String** value stored in the column specified by intOrdinal. The corresponding SQL Server data types are **char**, **nchar**, **ntext**, **nvarchar**, **text**, and **varchar**.
*GetTimeSpan(ByVal intOrdinal As Integer)	(**OleDbDataReader** class only) Returns the **TimeSpan** value stored in the column specified by intOrdinal.

Example

```
Dim s64Test As SqlInt64 = drdTest.GetSqlInt64(0)
```

```
Dim smoTest As SqlMoney = drdTest.GetSqlMoney(0)
```

```
Dim ssgTest As SqlSingle = drdTest.GetSqlSingle(0)
```

```
Dim sstTest As SqlString = drdTest.GetSqlString(0)
```

```
Dim objTest As Object = drdTest.GetSqlValue(0)
```

```
Dim arrobjValues(Integer.MaxValue) As Byte
Dim intNumFields As Integer = drdTest.GetSqlValues(arrobjValues)
```

```
Dim strTest As String = drdTest.GetString(0)
```

```
Dim tmsTest As TimeSpan = drdTest.GetTimeSpan(0)
```

Table C-35. DataReader Class Methods (Continued)

Name	Description
GetValue(ByVal intOrdinal As Integer)	Returns the value stored in the column specified by intOrdinal as a variable of data type **Object**. The value returned is in native .NET format. Null values are returned as **DBNull**.
GetValues(ByVal arrobjValues() As Object)	Returns all the attribute column values for the current row in the arrobjValues array. The array supplied can have fewer or more elements than there are columns in the current row. Only the number of elements in the array is copied from the current row if there are fewer elements in the array. The returned **Integer** is the number of objects in the array.
IsDBNull(ByVal intOrdinal As Integer)	This method returns **True** if the column specified by intOrdinal is equal to **DBNull**, otherwise it returns **False**. **DBNull** means that the column does not hold a known value or a null value.
NextResult()	This method positions the DataReader at the next result in the result set returned by the command. This method has no effect if the command query does not contain a batch of row-returning SQL statements or if the current result is the last in the result set. **True** is returned if there are more results and **False** otherwise. The DataReader is positioned at the first result by default when instantiated.
Read()	This method positions the DataReader at the next row. Please note that you must call this method after the DataReader has been instantiated before you can access any of the data in the DataReader. This is because the DataReader, unlike the **Recordset** object in ADO, isn't positioned at the first row by default. **True** is returned if the DataReader is positioned at the next row and **False** if not.

Example

```
Dim objTest As Object = drdTest.GetValue(0)
```

```
Dim arrobjValues(Integer.MaxValue) As Object
Dim intNumFields As Integer = drdTest.GetValues(arrobjValues)
```

```
If drdTest.IsDBNull(0) Then
```

```
If drdTest.NextResult() Then
```

```
If drdTest.Read() Then
```

XmlReader Class

In this section you'll find the properties and methods of the **XmlReader** class, and the two supporting enums, **ReadState** and **XmlSpace**.

The **XmlReader** class has the properties, shown in alphabetical order, in Table C-36.

*Table C-36. **XmlReader** Class Properties*

Name	Description
AttributeCount	Returns the number of attributes, including default ones, on the current node. Only the **Element**, **DocumentType**, and **XmlDeclaration** type nodes have attributes, which means that this property is only relevant to these types of nodes. If you've used the **ExecuteXmlReader** method of the **SqlCommand** class, then the **AttributeCount** property will return the number of nonnull values in the current row. This property is abstract and read-only.
BaseURI	Returns the base URI of the current node. An empty string is returned if there's no base URI. You can use this property to tell you exactly where a specific node in a networked XML document comes from. This is handy, because networked XML documents are often comprised of many smaller parts of XML data and/or schema. This property is read-only and must be overridden, and it has no real meaning if your **XmlReader** has been returned by the **ExecuteXmlReader** method of the **SqlCommand** class.
CanResolveEntity	This property is overridable and read-only, and it returns a value that indicates if the reader can parse and resolve entities. **False** is always returned for instances of the **XmlReader** class that don't support DTD information. You should call this property to see if your **XmlReader** can resolve an entity before calling the **ResolveEntity** method, as it will throw an exception if can't.
Depth	The return value indicates how far down a node you currently are or the depth of the current node in the stack of XML elements. This property is read-only, and must be overridden in a derived class.
EOF	This property, which is read-only and must be overridden in a derived class, returns a **Boolean** value that indicates if the **XmlReader** is positioned at the end of the stream.
HasAttributes	This property, which is read-only, returns a **Boolean** value that indicates if the current node has any attributes.
HasValue	This read-only property, which must be overridden in a derived class, returns a **Boolean** value that indicates if the current node can hold a value. The value is of property type **Value**.

*Table C-36. **XmlReader** Class Properties (Continued)*

Name	Description
IsDefault	This property, which is read-only and must be overridden in a derived class, returns a **Boolean** value that indicates if the current node is an attribute node with a value generated from a default value, which is defined in a schema or DTD, or if it has been explicitly set. You should only use this property with an attribute node.
IsEmptyElement	This property, which is read-only and must be overridden in a derived class, returns a **Boolean** value that indicates if the current node is an empty element. An empty element can be defined like this: <DataElement/>, meaning the start and end tags are expressed in one tag, using the forward slash as the last character in the tag.
Item	This overloaded and read-only property, which must be overridden in a derived class, returns the value of the specified attribute of the current node. **String.Empty** is returned if the attribute isn't found. You can pass the index of the attribute (**Integer**), the name of the attribute (**String**), or the local name and the namespace URI. The reader is *not* repositioned when accessing this property.
LocalName	This property, which is read-only and must be overridden in a derived class, returns the name of the current node without the namespace prefix. An empty **String** is returned for node types that do not have a name. If you have used the **ExecuteXmlReader** method of a command class, then the **LocalName** property will return the name of the table.
Name	This property, which is read-only and must be overridden in a derived class, returns the qualified name of the current node or the name with the namespace prefix. If the node doesn't have a name, **String.Empty** is returned.
NameSpaceURI	This property, which is read-only and must be overridden in a derived class, returns the namespace URI for the current node. Note that this property is only relevant to **Element** and **Attribute** nodes, and an empty string is returned if no namespace URI exists.
NameTable	This property, which is read-only and must be overridden in a derived class, returns the **XmlNameTable** object associated with the implementation.
NodeType	This read-only property, which must be overridden in a derived class, returns the type for the current node. The data type returned is **XmlNodeType**.
Prefix	This read-only property, which must be overridden in a derived class, returns the namespace prefix for the current node.

*Table C-36. **XmlReader** Class Properties (Continued)*

Name	Description
QuoteChar	This property returns the quotation mark used for enclosing values of attribute nodes. This property is read-only and must be overridden in a derived class, and it returns either a single quotation mark (') or a double quotation mark ("). The property only applies to attribute nodes and the return value is of data type **Char**.
ReadState	This property returns the read state of the stream. It's read-only and must be overridden in a derived class, and it returns a member of the **ReadState** enum (see Table C-37).
Value	This read-only property, which must be overridden in a derived class, returns the text value of the current node. If the current node does not have a value to return, **String.Empty** is returned.
XmlLang	This read-only property, which must be overridden in a derived class, returns the **xml:lang** scope currently being used, retrieved from the root node. Please note that this property value is also part of the **XmlNameTable** returned from the **NameTable** property.
XmlSpace	This read-only property, which must be overridden in a derived class, returns the **xml:space** scope currently being used. The value returned is a member of the **XmlSpace** enum (see Table C-38).

Table C-37 lists the **ReadState** enum members, and Table C-38 lists the **XmlSpace** enum members.

*Table C-37. **ReadState** Enum Members*

Name	Description
Closed	The Close method has been executed on the **XmlReader**.
EndOfFile	The end of the stream has been reached (successfully).
Error	An error has occurred. This means that **XmlReader** can't continue reading the stream.
Initial	You have not called the **Read** method yet, so the reader is at its initial position.
Interactive	A read operation is currently in progress, but you can still call other methods on the reader.

*Table C-38. **XmlSpace** Enum Members*

Name	Description
Default	The **xml:space** scope is **default**.
None	There's no **xml:space** scope.
Preserve	The xml:space scope is **preserve**.

Table C-39 lists the noninherited and public methods of the **XmlReader** class in alphabetical order.

Table C-39. **XmlReader** *Class Methods*

Name	Description
Close()	This abstract method resets all properties, releases any resources held, and changes the **ReadState** property to **Closed**. No exception is thrown if the **XmlReader** is already closed.
GetAttribute()	This overloaded method, which must be overridden in a derived class, returns the value of an attribute. See the example code, which returns the LoginName for the current node or row in the tblUser table. The reader has been instantiated elsewhere with the **ExecuteXmlReader** method of the Command class.
IsName(ByVal strName As String)	This **Shared** method returns a **Boolean** value indicating if strName is a valid XML name, checked against the W3C XML 1.0 recommendation.
IsNameToken(ByVal strNameToken As String)	The **IsNameToken** method is **Shared** and returns a **Boolean** value indicating if strNameToken is a valid XML name token, checked against the W3C XML 1.0 recommendation.
IsStartElement()	This overloaded method returns a **Boolean** value indicating if the current content node is a start tag or an empty element tag.
LookupNamespace(ByVal strPrefix As String)	This method, which must be overridden in a derived class, resolves strPrefix in the current elements scope and returns the namespace URI for the strPrefix. If a matching prefix can't be found, **Nothing** is returned.
MoveToAttribute()	This overloaded method, which must be overridden in a derived class, moves to the attribute matching the passed argument(s). If your **XmlReader** has been returned by the **ExecuteXmlReader** method of a Command class, this method can be used to move between the columns in the current row.
MoveToContent()	This overridable method checks if the current node is a content node, and skips to the next content node, or EOF if no content node is found. If the current node is an attribute node, then the reader's position is moved back to the element that owns the attribute node.

Example

```
xrdTest.Close()
```

```
xrdTest.GetAttribute(3)
xrdTest.GetAttribute("LoginName")
```

```
Dim blnValidName As Boolean = xrdTest.IsName("XML Name")
```

```
Dim blnValidNameToken As Boolean = xrdTest.IsNameToken("XML Name Token")
```

```
If xrdTest.IsStartElement() Then
```

```
Dim strNamespaceURI As String = xrdTest.LookupNamespace("MyNameSpace")
```

```
xrdTest.MoveToAttribute(0)
Dim blnAttributeFound As Boolean = xrdTest.MoveToAttribute("LoginName")
```

```
xrdTest.MoveToContent()
```

Table C-39. **XmlReader** *Class Methods (Continued)*

Name	Description
MoveToElement()	This method, which must be overridden in a derived class, moves to the element in which the current attribute node exists. A **Boolean** value is returned based on whether the current attribute is owned by an element. If your **XmlReader** has been returned by the **ExecuteXmlReader** method of a command class, this method can be used in conjunction with the **MoveToAttribute** method to move to a specific attribute/column and then back to the element or row that owns the attribute or column. A **Boolean** value is returned indicating if the move was successful, which also means that the reader's position isn't changed if **False** is returned.
MoveToFirstAttribute()	This method, which must be overridden in a derived class, moves to the first attribute in an element. If your **XmlReader** has been returned by the **ExecuteXmlReader** method of a command class, this method can be used to move to the first column in the current row. A **Boolean** value is returned indicating if the move was successful, which also means that the reader's position isn't changed if **False** is returned.
MoveToNextAttribute()	This method, which must be overridden in a derived class, moves to the next attribute in an element. If your **XmlReader** has been returned by the **ExecuteXmlReader** method of a command class, this method can be used to move to the next column in the current row. A **Boolean** value is returned indicating if there is a next node and thus the move succeeded, which also means that the reader's position isn't changed if **False** is returned.
Read()	Reads the next node in the stream. This method, which must be overridden in a derived class, must be called before any other properties or methods can be called. Actually, this isn't quite true, as the initial value can be returned from some properties if the reader has not yet been positioned at the first row or element. A **Boolean** value is returned indicating if the reader's position was moved to the next element or row.
ReadAttributeValue()	This method that must be overridden in a derived class, parses the attribute value into **Text**, **EndEntity**, or **EntityReference** nodes. A **Boolean** value is returned indicating if there are any nodes to return.
ReadElementString()	This overridable and overloaded method is used for reading simple text-only elements.

Example

```
Dim blnAttributePos As Boolean = xrdTest.MoveToElement()
```

```
Dim blnFirstAttributeFound As Boolean = xrdTest.MoveToFirstAttribute()
```

```
Dim blnNextAttributeFound As Boolean = xrdTest.MoveToNextAttribute()
```

```
blnRead = xrdTest.Read()
```

```
blnRead = xrdTest.ReadAttributeValue()
```

```
Dim strTextElement As String = xrdTest.ReadElementString()
Dim strTextElement As String = xrdTest.ReadElementString("ElementName")
```

*Table C-39. **XmlReader** Class Methods (Continued)*

Name	Description
ReadEndElement()	This overridable method is for checking if the current node is an end tag. If the current node is an end tag, the reader position is advanced to the next node.
ReadInnerXml()	This method, which must be overridden in a derived class, returns all the content of the current node as a string. The returned string includes markup text.
ReadOuterXml()	This method, which must be overridden in a derived class, returns all the content of the current node and all the children nodes as a string. The returned string includes markup text. If your **XmlReader** has been returned by the **ExecuteXmlReader** method of a command class, this method will return the current row as an XML node. Please note that only nonnull columns will be returned as attributes.
ReadStartElement()	This overridable and overloaded method is for checking if the current node is an element. If the current node is an element, the reader position is advanced to the next node.
ReadString()	This method, which must be overridden in a derived class, is for reading the contents of an element or text node and returning it as a **String**.
ResolveEntity()	This method, which must be overridden in a derived class, is for use with **EntityReferences** nodes. It resolves the entity reference for this type of node.
Skip()	Skips the current element or moves to the next element. Depending on where the reader is positioned, the **Skip** method can perform the same function as the **Read** method. This happens when the reader is positioned on a leaf node. Please note that this method checks for well-formed XML.

Example

```
xrdTest.ReadEndElement()
```

```
Dim strContent As String = xrdTest.ReadInnerXml()
```

```
Dim strContent As String = xrdTest.ReadOuterXml()
```

```
xrdTest.ReadStartElement()
xrdTest.ReadStartElement("ElementName")
```

```
Dim strElement As String = xrdTest.ReadString()
```

```
xrdTest.ResolveEntity()
```

```
xrdTest.Skip()
```

DataAdapter Class

In this section you'll find the properties, methods, and events of the DataAdapter class, and the four supporting enums, **MissingMappingAction**, **MissingSchemaAction**, **DataRowVersion**, and **SchemaType**.

The DataAdapter class has the properties shown in Table C-40 in alphabetical order. Please note that only the public, noninherited properties are shown. Actually, this isn't entirely true, because only properties that are inherited from base classes like **Object** are left out. This means that properties inherited from the DataAdapter class are shown. The properties listed are the same for the three DataAdapter classes: **OdbcDataAdapter**, **OleDbDataAdapter**, and **SqlDataAdapter**.

Table C-40. DataAdapter Class Properties

Name	Description
AcceptChangesDuringFill	This read-write property returns or sets a **Boolean** value indicating if the **AcceptChanges** method is called on the **DataRow** class after it has been added to a **DataTable**. The default value is **True**. If you set this property to **False**, new rows added to the **DataTable** during the **Fill** operation will be marked as inserted.
ContinueUpdateOnError	This property returns or sets a **Boolean** value that indicates if the update should continue if an error is encountered during a row update. Otherwise, an exception is thrown. The default is **False**. If you set this property to **True**, the row in which the error is encountered is skipped, the error information "logged" to the **RowError** property of the **DataRow** in question, and the remaining rows updated.
DeleteCommand	This read-write property returns or sets the SQL statement through a Command object, which will be used when rows are deleted from the data source. When you call the **Update** method on the DataAdapter, the rows in the data source that match the deleted rows in the **DataSet** are deleted. This property can be automatically generated by an associated CommandBuilder object if the **DataTable** in the **DataSet** you're trying to update is based on a single table, and the column(s) making up the primary key is part of the rows selected with the Command object associated with the **SelectCommand** property.

Table C-40. DataAdapter Class Properties (Continued)

Name	Description
InsertCommand	This read-write property returns or sets the SQL statement through a Command object, which will be used when rows are inserted into the data source. When you call the **Update** method on the DataAdapter, the inserted rows in the **DataSet** are inserted in the data source. This property can be automatically generated by an associated CommandBuilder object if the **DataTable** in the **DataSet** you're trying to update is based on a single table, and the column(s) making up the primary key is part of the rows selected with the Command object associated with the **SelectCommand** property.
MissingMappingAction	This read-write property returns or sets a value that indicates if unmapped source tables or source columns should be parsed with their source names, or if an exception should be thrown. This means that this property decides which action to take when there's no mapping for a source table or source column in the **DataSet**. The valid values are all the members of the **MissingMappingAction** enum, which you can see in Table C-41.
MissingSchemaAction	This read-write property returns or sets a value that indicates if missing source tables or columns and relationships should be added to the schema in the **DataSet** if they should be ignored, or if an exception should be thrown. This means that this property decides which action to take when a table, column, and/or relationship in the data source is missing from the **DataSet**. The valid values are all the members of the **MissingSchemaAction** enum, which you can see in Table C-42.
SelectCommand	This read-write property returns or sets the SQL statement that will be used when rows are selected/retrieved from the data source using the **Fill** command of the DataAdapter. This property must always be set, directly or indirectly, although it's okay if the SELECT statement doesn't return any rows. In such a case, no tables are added to the **DataSet**, but no exception is thrown.
TableMappings	This read-only property returns a value that indicates how a table in the data source should be mapped to a table in the **DataSet**. The returned value is a collection of **DataTableMapping** objects. The default value is an empty collection.

Table C-40. DataAdapter Class Properties (Continued)

Name	Description
UpdateCommand	This read-write property returns or sets the SQL statement that will be used when rows are updated in the data source. When you call the **Update** method on the DataAdapter, the rows in the data source that match the updated rows in the **DataSet** are updated. This property can be automatically generated by an associated CommandBuilder object if the **DataTable** in the **DataSet** you're trying to update is based on a single table, and the column(s) making up the primary key is part of the rows selected with the Command object associated with the **SelectCommand** property.

Table C-41 shows the **MissingMappingAction** enum members, and Table C-42 shows the **MissingSchemaAction** enum members.

*Table C-41. **MissingMappingAction** Enum Members*

Member name	Description
Error	If you use this member, a **SystemException** exception is generated when a source table or column mapping is missing.
Ignore	This member ignores a missing mapping for the source table or column. This means that **Nothing** is returned in its place.
Passthrough	When using this member, the source table or column is created and added to the **DataSet** using the original name from the data source.

*Table C-42. **MissingSchemaAction** Enum Members*

Member name	Description
Add	This member makes sure the missing source columns are added to the **DataSet**.
AddWithKey	This member makes sure the missing source columns, including primary key information, are added to the **DataSet**.
Error	If you use this member, a **SystemException** exception is generated when a source table or column is missing from the **DataSet**.
Ignore	Using this member means ignoring extra columns.

Table C-43 lists the noninherited and public methods of the DataAdapter class in alphabetical order. The methods listed are the same for the three DataAdapter classes, **OdbcDataAdapter**, **OleDbDataAdapter**, and **SqlDataAdapter**, unless otherwise stated.

Table C-43. DataAdapter Class Methods

Name	Description	Example
Fill()	(**SqlDataAdapter** and **OdbcDataAdapter** only) The **Fill** method is overloaded and inherited from the **DbDataAdapter** class. The method is used for adding and/or updating rows in a **DataSet** or **DataTable**. This means you will have a copy of the requested data in the data source in your **DataSet** or **DataTable**.	See the "Populating Your DataSet Using the DataAdapter" section in Chapter 9 for some examples.
Fill()	(**OleDbDataAdapter** only) The **Fill** method is overloaded, and some of the overloaded versions of the method are inherited from the **DbDataAdapter** class. The method is used for adding and/or updating rows in the **DataSet** or **DataTable** based on the rows in an ADO **Recordset** object, ADO **Record** object, or from your data source.	See the "Populating Your DataSet Using the DataAdapter" section in Chapter 9 for some examples.
FillSchema()	The **FillSchema** method is overloaded and inherited from the **DbDataAdapter** class. The method is used for adding a **DataTable** object to a **DataSet**. The schema of this **DataTable** object is configured to match that of the table in the data source, based on the arguments passed.	See the "Retrieving the Schema from Data Source" section in Chapter 8 for some examples.

Table C-43. *DataAdapter Class Methods (Continued)*

Name	Description	Example
GetFillParameters()	The **GetFillParameters** method is inherited from the **DbDataAdapter** class. The method retrieves all the parameters that are used when the SQL SELECT statement is executed by calling the **Fill** method of the DataAdapter class. The returned value should be stored in an array of **IDataParameter** objects.	`Dim arrprmSelect() As OdbcDataParameter = dadUser.GetFillParameters()` `Dim arrprmSelect() As OleDbDataParameter = dadUser.GetFillParameters()` `Dim arrprmSelect() As SqlDataParameter = dadUser.GetFillParameters()`
Update()	The **Update** method is overloaded and inherited from the **DbDataAdapter** class. The method is used for updating the data source with the changes from the **DataSet**. This means the Comm and object associated with the **Insert-Command**, **UpdateCommand**, and **DeleteCommand** properties will be executed for each inserted, modified, and deleted row respectively.	See "Updating Your Data Source Using the DataAdapter" in Chapter 9 for some examples.

Table C-44 lists the **DataRowVersion** enum members.

Table C-44. **DataRowVersion** *Enum Members*

Member name	Description
Current	Using this member, you can specify that the row contains current values. When used with Parameter objects, it means that the current value of a particular column is used as the value for the parameter.
Default	You use this member when you want to use the default column values, which are specified by the data source or the **DataSet/DataTable** schema.
Original	This member specifies that the row contains its original values. When used with Parameter objects, it means that the original value of a particular column is used as the value for the parameter.
Proposed	This member indicates that the row contains proposed values, meaning values that haven't yet been saved to the **DataRow** object, making them current values. This member is for when you use the **BeginEdit**, **CancelEdit**, and **EndEdit** methods of the **DataRow** class. This member isn't for use with Parameter objects.

Table C-45 lists the noninherited and public events of the DataAdapter class in ascending order. The events listed are the same for the three DataAdapter classes: **OdbcDataAdapter**, **OleDbDataAdapter**, and **SqlDataAdapter**.

Table C-45. DataAdapter Class Events

Name	Description	Example
FillError	The **FillError** event is inherited from the **DbDataAdapter** class. It's triggered whenever an error occurs during a fill operation, meaning when you populate or refresh your **DataSet** or **DataTable** with the **Fill** method. Basically, you can use this event to respond to errors during a fill operation and decide whether the operation should continue.	See the "Handling Fill Operation Errors" section in Chapter 8 for an example.
RowUpdated	This event is triggered after a command has been executed against your data source. You can use this event to inspect possible errors that don't throw an exception, the status of the update command, the **DataRow** with the values that has been used for updating the data source, and other properties. This event is called for every row you change in your **DataSet** or **DataTable** when you call the **Update** method, and you can use it in conjunction with the **RowUpdating** event to "supervise" an update operation.	See the "Handling Row Updates" section in Chapter 8 for an example.
RowUpdating	This event is triggered before a command is executed against your data source. You can use this event to inspect possible errors that don't throw an exception, the status of the update command, the **DataRow** with the values that will be used for updating the data source and other properties. This event is called for every row you change in your **DataSet** or **DataTable** when you call the **Update** method, and you can use it in conjunction with the **RowUpdated** event to "supervise" an update operation.	See the "Handling Row Updates" section in Chapter 8 for an example.

Table C-46 presents the **SchemaType** enum members.

Table C-46. SchemaType Enum Members

Member name	Description
Mapped	Specifying this member applies an existing table schema to the schema retrieved from the data source. This means that the combined schema is used for configuring the **DataTable**.
Source	This member ignores any existing schema in a **DataTable**, which means that the **DataTable** is configured using the schema retrieved from the data source.

Summary

In this appendix, you saw the public, noninherited properties, methods, and events of the various classes of the ADO.NET connected layer. The following classes and enums were shown:

- **OdbcConnection, OleDbConnection**, and **SqlConnection**

- **ConnectionState**

- **OdbcTransaction, OleDbTransaction**, and **SqlTransaction**

- **OdbcError, OdbcError**, and **SqlError**

- **OdbcException, OdbcException**, and **SqlException**

- **OdbcCommand, OleDbCommand**, and **SqlCommand**

- **CommandType**

- **UpdateRowSource**

- **OdbcParameter, OleDbParameter**, and **SqlParameter**

- **ParameterDirection**

- **CommandBehavior**

- **OdbcDataReader, OleDbDataReader, SqlDataReader**, and **XmlReader**

- **ReadState**

- **XmlSpace**

- **OdbcDataAdapter, OleDbDataAdapter**, and **SqlDataAdapter**

- **MissingMappingAction**

- **MissingSchemaAction**

- **OdbcCommandBuilder, OleDbCommandBuilder**, and **SqlCommandBuilder**

- **DataRowVersion**

- **SchemaType**

In Appendix D, which is next, you can find a reference for the properties, methods, and events of the various classes of the ADO.NET disconnected layer.

APPENDIX D

Disconnected Layer Properties, Methods, and Events

THIS APPENDIX IS FOR referencing the properties, methods, and events of the various classes of the ADO.NET disconnected layer, which is covered in Part Three of the book. The classes are listed in the order they're covered in the chapters in Part Three.

DataSet Class

The **DataSet** class has the properties shown in Table D-1 in alphabetical order. Please note that only the public, noninherited properties are shown. Likewise, Table D-2 lists the noninherited and public methods of this class in alphabetical order.

*Table D-1. **DataSet** Class Properties*

Property Name	Description
CaseSensitive	This read-write property determines if string comparisons in the **DataTable** objects, contained in the **Tables** collection property, are case sensitive. This property also affects how filter, sort, and search operations are performed. When you set this property, you also by default set the same property of all the **DataTable** objects in the **Tables** collection. This doesn't mean that it's forced upon the **DataTable** objects, because if you explicitly set this property of a **DataTable** in the **Tables** collection, either before or after you set the property on the containing **DataSet**, the value for the property in that **DataTable** will not be changed.
DataSetName	Returns or sets the name of the **DataSet**. The name is for the developers use only; it's not used by the **DataSet**, meaning that it's there for you to use if you want an easy way of telling **DataSet** objects apart. This is particularly important when you persist your **DataSet** to an XML file, because the name is used as the root node in the XML file. This property can also be set when instantiating the **DataSet** by supplying the name as the only argument.
DefaultViewManager	This read-only property returns a view of the data in the **DataSet**. This view can be filtered or sorted, and you can search and navigate through it. Instead of setting up a view on each of the **DataTable**'s in the **DataSet** separately, you can use the **DataViewManager** object returned by the **DefaultViewManager** property to create your custom view of all or just a portion of the data in the **DataSet**.
EnforceConstraints	This property value determines if the constraint rules are enforced when an update operation is executed. The **ConstraintException** exception is thrown if one or more constraints can't be enforced. The constraints are saved in the **ConstraintCollection** collection (retrieved with the **Constraints** property) of each **DataTable** object in the **DataSet**.
ExtendedProperties	Returns the collection of custom properties or custom user information. The returned data type is a **PropertyCollection** class. You can add information to the property collection by using the **Add** method of this collection.
HasErrors	Returns a **Boolean** value indicating if there are any errors in the rows in the **DataTable** objects contained in the **Tables** collection of the **DataSet**. You can use this property before checking any of the individual tables that also have a **HasErrors** property, meaning if the **HasErrors** property of the **DataSet** object returns **False**, there's no need to check the individual **DataTable** objects contained in the **Tables** collection of the **DataSet**.

Default Value	Example
False	`dstUserMan.CaseSensitive = False`
NewDataSet	Listing 9-2
The returned value is of data type **DataViewManager**.	-
True	`dstUserMan.EnforceConstraints = True`
-	`dstUserMan.ExtendedProperties.Add("New Property", "New Property Value")`
-	Listings 9-9 and 9-10

*Table D-1. **DataSet** Class Properties (Continued)*

Property Name	Description
Locale	This read-write property holds the locale information that is used for comparing strings in a table. The value is of data type **CultureInfo**. When you set this property, you also set the same property of all **DataTable** objects in the **Tables** collection. This doesn't mean that it's forced upon the **DataTable** objects, because if you explicitly set this property of a **DataTable** in the **Tables** collection before or after you set the property on the **DataSet**, the value for the property in the **DataTable** will not be changed.
Namespace	This read-write property holds the namespace for the **DataSet**. It's used when you read an XML document into the **DataSet** or when you write an XML document from the **DataSet** using one of these methods: **ReadXml**, **ReadXmlSchema**, **WriteXml**, or **WriteXmlSchema**. The namespace is used for scoping the XML elements and attributes in the **DataSet**. When you set this property, you also set the same property of all **DataTable** objects in the **Tables** collection. This doesn't mean that it's forced upon the **DataTable** objects, because if you explicitly set this property of a **DataTable** in the **Tables** collection before or after you set the property on the **DataSet**, the value for the property in the **DataTable** won't be changed.
Prefix	This read-write property holds the namespace prefix for the **DataSet**. The prefix is used in an XML document for identifying which elements belongs to the namespace of the **DataSet** object. The namespace is set with the **Namespace** property.
Relations	Returns the collection of relations from the **DataSet**. This collection allows navigation between related tables (parent to child table[s], or vice versa). The returned value is of data type **DataRelationCollection**, and it holds objects of data type **DataRelation**. **Nothing** is returned if no data relations exist. The **DataRelationCollection** allows you to navigate between related parent and child **DataTable** objects.
Tables	Returns the collection of **DataTable** objects contained in the **DataSet**. The returned value is of data type **DataTableCollection**, which holds objects of data type **DataTable**. **Nothing** is returned if no **DataTables** exist. **DataTable** objects are automatically added to this collection when you use the **Fill** method of the DataAdapter to populate a **DataSet**. You can also use the **Add** method of the **DataTableCollection** class to add tables, and the **Remove** method to remove tables form the collection.

Default Value	Example
Nothing	-
"" (empty **String**)	-
"" (empty **String**)	-
Nothing	-
Nothing	-

*Table D-2. **DataSet** Class Methods*

Method Name	Description	Example
AcceptChanges()	This method accepts or commits all the changes that have been made to the **DataSet** since the last time the method was called or since the **DataSet** was loaded. Be aware that this method will call the **AcceptChanges** method on *all* tables in the **Tables** collection, which in turn calls the **AcceptChanges** method on all **DataRow** objects in the **Rows** collection of each **DataTable**. So, if you need to only accept changes to a specific table, then call the **AcceptChanges** method on that particular table. If any **DataRow** object, found in the **Rows** collection of the **DataTable** contained in the **DataSet**'s **Tables** collection, is still in edit mode, the edit mode will be ended successfully, and the changes made accepted.	Listings 9-9 and 9-10
Clear()	This method clears the **DataSet** for data, which means that all rows are being removed from all tables in the **Tables** collection. This method does *not* clear the data structure, only the data itself.	dstUser.Clear()
Clone()	The **Clone** method is for cloning or copying the data structure of the **DataSet**. This does *not* include the data itself, but only the tables, schemas, relations, and constraints. If you need to copy the data as well, you need to use the **Copy** method.	dstClone = stUser.Clone()
Copy()	The **Copy** method is for cloning the data structure of the **DataSet** and copying the data from the **DataSet** into the new **DataSet**. If you only need to clone the data structure, you need to use the **Clone** method.	dstCopy = stUser.Copy()

*Table D-2. **DataSet** Class Methods (Continued)*

Method Name	Description	Example
GetChanges()	This overloaded method is used for retrieving a copy of the **DataSet** that contains all the changes that have been made since the last time the **AcceptChanges** method was called or since the **DataSet** was loaded. You can use the method without an argument, or you can indicate what kind of changes you want returned in the **DataSet** by specifying a member of the **DataRowState** enum (see Table D-3).	Listings 9-9 and 9-10
GetXml()	The **GetXml** method returns the data in the **DataSet** as XML data in a **String** variable. If you need to write to a file, use the **WriteXml** method. You really should use the **GetXml** method to retrieve the data contained in a **DataSet** in a **String** variable that you can manipulate. If you later need to persist the modified data, you can use the **WriteXml** method.	`strXMLData = dstUser.GetXml()`
GetXmlSchema()	The **GetXmlSchema** method returns the XSD schema for data in the **DataSet** in a **String** variable. If you need to write the schema to a file, use the **WriteXmlSchema** method.	`strXMLSchema = dstUser.GetXmlSchema()`
HasChanges()	This method can be used to detect if there are any changes to the data in the **DataSet**. The method is overloaded, and one version takes a member of the **DataRowState** enum as an argument. This way you can specify whether you only want to detect a specific change, such as added rows. A **Boolean** value indicating if there are any changes is returned.	Listings 9-9 and 9-10
InferXmlSchema()	This overloaded method infers or copies the XML schema from an **XmlReader**, a **Stream**, a **TextReader**, or a file into the **DataSet**.	`dstUser.InferXmlSchema(xrdUser, arrstrURIExclude)`

*Table D-2. **DataSet** Class Methods (Continued)*

Method Name	Description	Example
Merge()	The **Merge** method is overloaded and is used for merging the **DataSet** with other data, in the form of an array of **DataRow** objects, into another **DataSet**, or with a **DataTable**.	Listings 9-4, 9-5, and 9-6

ReadXml()	This overloaded method is for reading XML schema and data into the **DataSet**. The XML schema and data is read from a **Stream,** a file, a **TextReader,** or an **XmlReader,** with or without specifying how the XML schema should be read, using a member of the **XmlReadMode** enum (see Table D-4). The mode used to read the data is returned as a member of the **XmlReadMode** enum. If you only want to read the XML schema, you can use the **ReadXmlSchema** method.	`Dim intReadMode = dstUser.ReadXml(xrdUser)`
		 `Dim intReadMode = dstUser.ReadXml(xrdUser, XmlReadMode.Auto)`
		 `Dim intReadMode = dstUser.ReadXml (stmUser)`
		 `Dim intReadMode = dstUser.ReadXml (stmUser, XmlReadMode.DiffGram)`
		 `Dim intReadMode = dstUser.ReadXml (strXMLFile)`
		 `Dim intReadMode = dstUser.ReadXml (strXMLFile, XmlReadMode.Fragment)`
		 `Dim intReadMode = dstUser.ReadXml (trdUser)`
		 `Dim intReadMode = dstUser.ReadXml (trdUser, XmlReadMode.Auto)`

ReadXmlSchema()	This overloaded method is for reading XML schema into the **DataSet**. The XML schema is read from an **XmlReader**, a **Stream**, a file, or a **TextReader**, with or without specifying how the XML schema should be read, using a member of the **XmlReadMode** enum (see Table D-4). If you want to read the XML schema and the data, you can use the **ReadXml** method.	`dstUser.ReadXmlSchema(xrdUser)`
		 `dstUser.ReadXmlSchema(stmUser)`
		 `dstUser.ReadXmlSchema(strXMLFile)`
		 `dstUser.ReadXmlSchema(trdUser)`

*Table D-2. **DataSet** Class Methods (Continued)*

Method Name	Description	Example
RejectChanges()	This method rejects or rolls back the changes made to the **DataSet** since the last time the **AcceptChanges** method was called or since the **DataSet** was loaded. Be aware that this method will call the **RejectChanges** method on *all* tables in the **Tables** collection, which in turn calls the **RejectChanges** method on all **DataRow** objects in the **Rows** collection of each **DataTable**. So if you need to reject changes only to a specific table, then call the **RejectChanges** method on this table.	Listings 9-9 and 9-10
Reset()	This overridable method resets the **DataSet** to its original state, meaning the state it had after instantiation.	`dstUser.Reset()`

WriteXml()	This overloaded method is for writing XML schema and data from the **DataSet**. The XML schema and data is written to an **XmlWriter**, a **Stream**, a file, or a **TextWriter**, with or without specifying how the XML schema should be written, using a member of the **XmlWriteMode** enum (see Table D-5). If you want to write only the XML schema, you can use the **WriteXmlSchema** method.	`dstUser.WriteXml(xwrUser)`
		`dstUser.WriteXml(xwrUser,`
		`XmlWriteMode.DiffGram)`
		`dstUser.WriteXml(stmUser)`
		`dstUser.WriteXml(stmUser,`
		`XmlWriteMode.DiffGram)`
		`dstUser.WriteXml(strXMLFile)`
		`dstUser.WriteXml(strXMLFile,`
		`XmlWriteMode.IgnoreSchema)`
		`dstUser.WriteXml(twrUser)`
		`dstUser.WriteXml(twrUser,`
		`XmlWriteMode.WriteSchema)`

WriteXmlSchema()	This overloaded method is for writing the XML schema from the **DataSet**. The XML schema is written to an **XmlWriter**, a **Stream**, a file, or a **TextWriter**. If you want to write the XML schema and the data, you can use the **WriteXml** method.	`dstUser.WriteXmlSchema(xrdUser)`
		`dstUser.WriteXmlSchema(stmUser)`
		`dstUser.WriteXmlSchema(strXML-`
		`File)`
		`dstUser.WriteXmlSchema(trdUser)`

In Tables D-3, D-4, and D-5, you'll find listings of the enum members for **DataRowState**, **XmlReadMode**, and **XmlWriteMode**, respectively.

*Table D-3. **DataRowState** Enum Members*

Member Name	Description
Added	This member specifies that the row has been added to a **DataRowCollection**, and the **AcceptChanges** method has not yet been called. If you use this member with the **GetChanges** method, all inserted rows are returned in a **DataSet**.
Deleted	A row marked with the **Deleted** member has been deleted using the **Delete** method of the **DataRow**. If you use this member with the **GetChanges** method, all deleted rows are returned in a **DataSet**.
Detached	The row has been created, but is not yet part of a **DataRowCollection** collection class. This state is set when a row is created, before it is added to a **DataRowCollection**. This state is also used if a row is removed from a collection. This member is not to be used with the **GetChanges** method.
Modified	A **DataRow** marked with this member has been modified, and **AcceptChanges** has not yet been called. If you use this member with the **GetChanges** method, all modified rows are returned in a **DataSet**.
Unchanged	If a row is marked with this member, it has not been changed since **AcceptChanges** was last called or since the **DataTable** was created.

*Table D-4. **XmlReadMode** Enum Members*

Member Name	Description
Auto	This is the default member, and it automatically resets the **XmlReadMode** property, based on the data and schema (if any) it reads, and/or the current **DataSet** schema (if any). Please see the various members for an appropriate description: If the data read is a DiffGram, **XmlReadMode** is set to **DiffGram**. If your **DataSet** already has a schema, or the document to read contains an inline schema, **XmlReadMode** is set to **ReadSchema**. If your **DataSet** doesn't have a schema, and the document to read doesn't contain an inline schema, **XmlReadMode** is set to **InferSchema**.
DiffGram	This member makes the **ReadXml** method read the XML data as a DiffGram. This means changes from the DiffGram are applied to the **DataSet**. This is almost identical to a merge operation using one of the **Merge** method overloads, which means that the **RowState** values are preserved (see Table D-3 for possible values). Generally, you should only use DiffGram output from the **WriteXml** method as input to the **ReadXml** method. An exception is thrown and the operation fails, if the destination **DataSet** doesn't have the same schema as the **DataSet** on which you called the **WriteXml** method.
Fragment	With this member, you can read XML documents, like those generated by SQL Server with an FOR XML style query. The default namespace is read as the inline schema when using this member with the **ReadXml** method.
IgnoreSchema	The **ReadXml** method ignores the inline schema (if any) when you use this member, and the data is inserted into the **DataSet** using the existing schema. Data that doesn't match the existing **DataSet** schema is discarded. **IgnoreSchema** has the exact same functionality as **DiffGram** when the data you're trying to read is a DiffGram.

Table D-4. **XmlReadMode** *Enum Members (Continued)*

Member Name	Description
InferSchema	The **ReadXml** method ignores the inline schema (if any) when you use this member, and the schema from the data being read is inferred, and the data loaded. If the destination **DataSet** already has a schema, this schema will be extended with new tables and/or columns added to existing tables. An exception is thrown if the inferred table already exists, but with a different namespace, or if any of the inferred columns conflict with existing columns.
ReadSchema	The **ReadXml** method reads the inline schema (if any), and loads the data. If the destination **DataSet** already has a schema, this schema will be extended with new tables. However, an exception is thrown if any of the tables in the inline schema already exist in the **DataSet**. This is different from the **InferSchema** member, which also adds columns to existing tables.

Table D-5. **XmlWriteMode** *Enum Members*

Member Name	Description
DiffGram	If you use this member, your **DataSet** is written as a DiffGram. This includes original and current values. If you only need original or current values in your DiffGram, make sure you call the **GetChanges** method with the right **DataRowState** enum member before you call the **WriteXml** method.
IgnoreSchema	This member makes sure that the current content of your **DataSet** is written as XML data, but without an XSD schema. This also means that if no data has been loaded in the **DataSet**, nothing is written.
WriteSchema	This is the default member, and it makes sure that the current content of your **DataSet** is written as XML data, including the relational data structure as an inline XSD schema (if a schema already exists in the **DataSet**). Only the inline schema is written if your **DataSet** has a schema, but no data.

Table D-6 lists the public versions of the **Fill** method.

Table D-6. The Various Versions of the Overloaded **Fill** *Method (DataAdapter)*

Example Code	Description
Dim intNumRows As Integer = dadUserMan.Fill(dstUser)	This version of the method populates the dstUser **DataSet** and saves the number of rows returned in intNumRows. Because you haven't specified the table name anywhere, the new **DataTable** in the **Tables** collection is named "Table". You can check the table name using a statement similar to the following: `MessageBox.Show(dstUserMan.Tables(0).TableName.ToString)`. You can change the table name by setting the **TableName** property of the **DataTable** object to the new name.
Dim intNumRows As Integer dadUserMan.Fill(dstUser, "tblUser")	This version of the method populates the dstUser **DataSet** and returns the number of rows returned in intNumRows. Because you have specified the source table name, the new **DataTable** in the **Tables** collection of the **DataSet** is called "tblUser" (like in the UserMan data source). You can check the table name using a statement similar to the following: `MessageBox.Show(dstUserMan.Tables(0).TableName.ToString)`.
Dim intNumRows As Integer dadUserMan.Fill(dstUser, 0, 2, "tblUser")	This version of the method populates the dstUser **DataSet** and returns the number of rows returned in intNumRows. Because you have specified the source table name, the new **DataTable** in the **Tables** collection in the **DataSet** is called "tblUser", like in the UserMan data source. The 0, which is the starting index, indicates that the population should start at the row with index 0, which is the first row. The 2, which is the ending index, forces a maximum of two rows to be returned. This method should be used if you don't want all the rows, specified in the SELECT statement, returned. You can check the number of rows returned in the intNumRows variable.

*Table D-6. The Various Versions of the Overloaded **Fill** Method (DataAdapter) (Continued)*

Example Code	Description
Dim intNumRows As Integer *dadUserMan.Fill(dtbUser)*	This version of the method populates a **DataTable** and not a **DataSet**, unlike most of the other overloads. The number of rows returned is saved in `intNumRows`. Because you haven't specified the source table name, the **DataTable** doesn't have a name. You can prevent this by giving the **DataTable** a name when you instantiate it, using a statement like `dtbUser = New DataTable("tblUser")`, or you can do it after you instantiate the **DataTable**. This is done by setting the **TableName** property.
Dim intNumRows As Integer *dadUserMan.Fill(dtbUser, rstADO)*	(**OleDbDataAdapter** only) This version of the method populates a **DataTable** and not a **DataSet**, unlike most of the other overloads. The number of rows returned is saved in `intNumRows`. The rows from the ADO **Recordset** object are copied to the **DataTable**. You can also specify an ADO **Record** object in case of the `rstADO` **Recordset** object.
Dim intNumRows As Integer *dadUserMan.Fill(dstUser, rstADO, "tblUser")*	(**OleDbDataAdapter** only) This version of the method populates the `dstUser` **DataSet** and returns the number of rows returned in `intNumRows`. Because you have specified the source table name, the new **DataTable** in the **Tables** collection in the **DataSet** is called "tblUser". The rows from the ADO **Recordset** object are copied to the **DataTable**. You can also specify an ADO **Record** object in the case of the `rstADO` **Recordset** object.

Table D-7 shows the enum members for **MissingSchemaAction**.

*Table D-7. **MissingSchemaAction** Enum Members*

Member Name	Description
Add	This member, which is the default member, makes sure that columns missing from the destination **DataSet** schema are added to the schema.
AddWithKey	This member makes sure that columns missing from the destination **DataSet** schema are added to the schema, including primary key information.
Error	This member makes sure a **SystemException** exception is thrown if one or more columns are missing from the destination **DataSet** schema.
Ignore	When using this member, columns missing from the destination **DataSet** schema are ignored.

DataTable Class

The **DataTable** class has the properties shown in alphabetical order in Table D-8. Please note that only the public, noninherited properties are shown. Similarly, Table D-9 lists the noninherited and public methods of the **DataTable** class, and Table D-10 lists the noninherited and public events of the **DataTable** class, all in alphabetical order.

*Table D-8. **DataTable** Class Properties*

Property Name	Description
CaseSensitive	This property indicates if a string comparison in the table is case sensitive. A **Boolean** value is set or returned. If the **DataTable** is part of a **DataSet**, this property is set to the value of the **DataSet**'s **CaseSensitive** property. However, if the **DataTable** has been created programmatically, this property is set to **False** by default. This can lead to confusion when working with **DataTable** objects, as the default value is inconsistent, depending on how the **DataTable** is created.
ChildRelations	The **ChildRelations** property returns a collection of child relations for the **DataTable**. This property is read-only, and the data type returned is **DataRelationCollection**. If no relations exist, **Nothing** is returned.
Columns	This property returns the **DataColumnCollection** collection of columns that makes up the **DataTable**. This property is read-only. **Nothing** is returned if no columns exist.
Constraints	The **Constraints** property returns the collection of constraints belonging to the **DataTable**. This property is read-only, and the data type returned is **ConstraintCollection**. If no constraints exist, **Nothing** is returned.
DataSet	This read-only property returns the **DataSet** to which the table belongs. This means the returned object is of data type **DataSet**.
DefaultView	This read-only property returns a **DataView** object that is a customized view of the table. The returned **DataView** can be used for filtering, sorting, and searching a **DataTable**. See the "Using the DataView Class" section in Chapter 10 for more information on the **DataView** class.
DisplayExpression	The **DisplayExpression** property returns or sets an expression, which returns a value that is used to represent the table in the UI. This property can be used to dynamically create text based on the current data.
ExtendedProperties	This read-only property returns a **PropertyCollection** collection of customized user information. You can use the **Add** method of this property to add custom information to a **DataTable**, like this: `dtbUser.ExtendedProperties.Add("New Property", "New Property Value")`
HasErrors	This read-only property returns a **Boolean** value indicating if any errors exist in any of the rows in the **DataTable**.

*Table D-8. **DataTable** Class Properties (Continued)*

Property Name	Description
Locale	The **Locale** property returns or sets the **CultureInfo** object. This object provides the locale information that is used for comparing strings in the **DataTable**. This means you can specify the locale that matches the data contained in the **DataTable** and thus make sure specific characters are sorted correctly and string comparisons are performed according to the rules of the locale. By default, this property is set to the value of the **DataSet**'s **Locale** property. However, if the **DataTable** doesn't belong to a **DataSet**, this property is set to the current culture of the system. This is something you need to keep in mind when working with data presented in different cultures. For consistency reasons, might it have been better if this property was always set to the culture of the system?
MinimumCapacity	This property returns or sets the initial starting size for the **DataTable**. The property is of data type **Integer** and the default value is 25. The value specifies the number of rows that the **DataTable** will be able to hold initially before creating extra resources to accommodate more rows. You should set this property when performance is critical, because it's faster to allocate the resources before you start populating the **DataTable**. So set the property to the smallest value appropriate for the number of rows returned when performance is critical.
Namespace	The Namespace property returns or sets the namespace used for XML representation of the data in the DataTable.
ParentRelations	The **ParentRelations** property enables navigation between related parent/child **DataTable**s by returning a collection of parent relations for the **DataTable** as a **DataRelationCollection** object. This property is read-only. **Nothing** is returned if no parent relations exist.
Prefix	This read-write property holds the namespace prefix for the **DataTable**. The namespace prefix is used when the **DataTable** is represented as XML. The data type for this property is **String**.
PrimaryKey	The **PrimaryKey** property is read-write enabled, and it returns or sets an array of **DataColumn** objects that are the primary keys for the **DataTable**. A **DataException** exception is thrown if you try to set a column that is already a foreign key.
Rows	This read-only property returns the **DataRowCollection** object that holds all the **DataRow** objects making up the data in this **DataTable**. **Nothing** is returned if there are no rows in the table.
TableName	This read-write property holds the name for the DataTable. The name property is used when the table is looked up in the Tables collection of the DataSet. The data type for this property is String, and the default value is an empty string ("").

Table D-9. **DataTable** *Class Methods*

Method Name	Description
AcceptChanges()	This method accepts or commits all the changes that have been made to the **DataTable** since the last time the method was called or since the **DataTable** was loaded. Because this method changes the row state of all changed rows in the **DataTable**, you shouldn't call this method until after you attempt to call the **Update** method on the DataAdapter. If **AcceptChanges** is called before you update the **DataSet**, no changes will be propagated back to the **DataSet**, because the **RowState** property of the changed rows will be changed back to **Unchanged**, meaning they won't appear to have been changed. When you call this method, rows marked as **Deleted** will be removed from the **DataTable**, whereas rows marked as **Added** or **Modified** will be marked as **Unchanged**.
BeginLoadData()	The **BeginLoadData** method is used in conjunction with the **EndLoadData** method. This method turns off index maintenance, constraints, and notifications while loading the data with the **LoadDataRow** method.
Clear()	This method clears all rows from the **DataTable**. If any of the rows has child rows in other **DataTable**s with which the current **DataTable** has an enforced relationship,[a] an exception is thrown, unless the relationship specifies a cascading delete.
Clone()	The **Clone** method is for cloning or copying the data structure of the **DataTable**. This does *not* include the data itself, only the schemas, relations, and constraints. If you need to copy the data as well, you have to use the **Copy** method.
Compute(ByVal strExpression As String, ByVal strFilter As String)	The **Compute** method computes strExpression on the current rows that pass the strFilter criteria. Please note that the strExpression expression must contain an aggregate function, such as **SUM** or **COUNT**.
Copy()	The **Copy** method is for cloning the data structure of a **DataTable** and copying the data from that **DataTable** into the new **DataTable**. If you only need to clone the data structure, you should use the **Clone** method.
EndLoadData()	The **EndLoadData** method turns back on index maintenance, constraints, and notifications after it has been turned off with the **BeginLoadData** method. Use the **EndLoadData** and **BeginLoadData** methods when loading the data with the **LoadDataRow** method.

Example

```
dtbUser.AcceptChanges()
```

```
dtbUser.BeginLoadData()
```

```
dtbUser.Clear()
```

```
Dim dtbClone As DataTable = dtbUser.Clone()
```

```
Dim objCompute As Object = dtbUser.Compute("COUNT(FirstName)", "LastName IS NOT NULL")
```

```
Dim dtbCopy As DataTable = dtbUser.Copy()
```

```
dtbUser.EndLoadData()
```

Table D-9. **DataTable** *Class Methods (Continued)*

Method Name	Description
GetChanges()	This overloaded method is used for retrieving a copy of the **DataTable** that contains all the changes that have been made since the last time the **AcceptChanges** method was called or since the **DataTable** was loaded. You can use the method without arguments or you can indicate what kind of changes you want returned in the **DataTable** by specifying a member of the **DataRowState** enum (see Table D-3).
GetErrors()	The **GetErrors** method returns an array of **DataRow** objects. The array includes all rows in the **DataTable** that contain errors. Generally, you should always call this method, and make sure you fix all errors, before calling the **Update** method on the DataAdapter
ImportRow(ByVal drwImport As DataRow)	The **ImportRow** method copies a **DataRow** object into a **DataTable**. The copy includes original and current values, errors, and **DataRowState** values. In short, everything from the **DataRow** object is copied across, in contrast to the **NewRow** method, which uses the schema, including default values, of the **DataTable**.
LoadDataRow(ByVal arrobjValues() As Object, ByVal blnAcceptChanges As Boolean)	The **LoadDataRow** method finds a specific row using the values in the arrobjValues array. The values in the array are used to compare with primary key column(s) in the **DataTable**. If a matching row is found, it's updated. Otherwise, a new row is created using the arrobjValues values.
NewRow()	The **NewRow** method creates a new **DataRow** object with the same schema as the **DataTable**. Th row isn't added to the schema of the **DataTable**; you need to call the **Add** method of the **DataRowCollection**, which you can access through the **Rows** property of the **DataTable**.
RejectChanges()	This method rejects or rolls back the changes made to the **DataTable** since the last time the **AcceptChanges** method was called or since the **DataTable** was loaded. This means that any row that's in edit mode when the method is called is cancelled. When you call this method, rows marked as **Added** will be removed from the **DataTable**, whereas rows marked as **Deleted** or **Modified** will be marked as with their original row state.
Reset()	This overridable method resets the **DataTable** to its original state.
Select()	The **Select** method is overloaded and is used for retrieving an array of **DataRow** objects. The returned data rows are ordered after the primary key. If no primary key exists, the rows are returned ordered the way they were originally added to the **DataTable**. Actually, this is only true if you use one of the overloaded versions that don't take the sort order as an argument.

a. Constraints, such as foreign keys, are enforced when the **EnforceConstraints** property is set to **True**, which is the default.

Example

```
Dim dtbChanges As DataTable = dtbUser.GetChanges()
Dim dtbAdded As DataTable = dtbUser.GetChanges(DataRowState.Added)
```

```
Dim arrdrwErrors() As DataRow = dtbUser.GetErrors()
```

```
dtbUser.ImportRow(drwImport)
```

```
Dim drwLoad As DataTable = dtbUser.LoadDataRow(arrobjValues, False)
```

```
Dim drwNew As DataRow = dtbUser.NewRow()
```

```
dtbUser.RejectChanges()
```

```
dtbUser.Reset()
```

```
Dim arrdrwAllDataRows() As DataRow = dtbUser.Select()
Dim arrdrwFirstNameUnsortedDataRows As DataRow = dtbUser.Select("FirstName = 'John'")
Dim arrdrwFirstNameSortedDataRows As DataRow = dtbUser.Select("FirstName = 'John'", "LastName ASC")
Dim arrdrwFirstNameSortedOriginalDataRows As DataRow = dtbUser.Select("FirstName = 'John'",
"LastName ASC", DataViewRowState.OriginalRows)
```

Table D-10. **DataTable** *Class Events*

Event Name	Description	Example
ColumnChanged	This event occurs *after* a **DataColumn** value has been changed.	See the "Handling Column Changes" section in Chapter 10.
ColumnChanging	The **ColumnChanging** event occurs *when* a **DataColumn** value is being changed.	See the "Handling Column Changes" section in Chapter 10.
RowChanged	This event occurs *after* a **DataRow** in the **DataTable** has been changed.	See the "Handling Row Changes" section in Chapter 10.
RowChanging	The **RowChanging** event occurs *when* a **DataRow** in the **DataTable** is being changed.	See the "Handling Row Changes" section in Chapter 10.
RowDeleted	This event occurs *after* a **DataRow** in the **DataTable** has been deleted.	See the "Handling Row Deletions" section in Chapter 10.
RowDeleting	The **RowDeleting** event occurs *when* a **DataRow** in the **DataTable** is being deleted.	See the "Handling Row Deletions" section in Chapter 10.

Table D-11 presents the enum members of the **DataViewRowState**.

*Table D-11. **DataViewRowState** Enum Members*

Member Name	Description
Added	This includes **DataRows** that have been added to the **DataTable** or **DataView**.
CurrentRows	Current **DataRows** include added, modified, and unchanged rows in the **DataTable** or **DataView**.
Deleted	This includes **DataRows** that have been deleted from the **DataTable** or **DataView**.
ModifiedCurrent	This includes the current version of **DataRows** that have had the original data modified.
ModifiedOriginal	This includes the original version of **DataRows** that have had the original data modified.
None	No **DataRows**.
OriginalRows	This includes unchanged and deleted rows in the **DataTable** or **DataView**.
Unchanged	This includes **DataRows** that haven't changed since the **DataTable** or **DataView** was populated, or since the **AcceptChanges** method was called.

DataView Class

The **DataView** class has the properties shown in Table D-12 in alphabetical order. Please note that only the public, noninherited properties are shown. Table D-13 lists the noninherited and public methods of the **DataView** class in ascending order.

*Table D-12. **DataView** Class Properties*

Property Name	Description
AllowDelete	The **AllowDelete** property returns or sets a **Boolean** value that indicates if deletions in the **DataView**, or rather the underlying **DataTable**, are allowed.
AllowEdit	The **AllowEdit** property returns or sets a **Boolean** value that indicates if editing of the rows in the **DataView**, or rather the underlying **DataTable**, is allowed.
AllowNew	The **AllowNew** property returns or sets a **Boolean** value that indicates if you can add new rows to the **DataView**, or rather the underlying **DataTable**, with the **AddNew** method.
ApplyDefaultSort	This property returns or sets a **Boolean** value that indicates if the default sort order should be used. The default sort order is the primary key, but this property is ignored when the **Sort** property is an empty **String** or set to **Nothing**, or when there's no primary key in the **DataView**.
Count	This read-only property returns the number of visible rows in the view. By visible I mean rows that are not affected by the settings of the **RowFilter** and **RowStateFilter** properties.
DataViewManager	The **DataViewManager** property is read-only, and it returns the **DataViewManager** that is associated with this **DataView**, or rather the **DataView** manager that owns the **DataSet** and hence created this **DataView**. **Nothing** is returned if no **DataViewManager** exists.

*Table D-12. **DataView** Class Properties (Continued)*

Property Name	Description
RowFilter	The **RowFilter** property is a **String** property that retrieves or sets the expression that is used to filter which rows are visible in the **DataView**. See Listing 10-6 in Chapter 10 for an example of how to use this property. This property must hold a valid expression, formed as the **Expression** property of the **DataColumn** class.
RowStateFilter	This property retrieves or sets the row state filter that is used in the **DataView**. This means that you can filter the rows based on their row state, such as **Unchanged**, **Added**, or **Deleted**. The value must be a member of the **DataViewRowState** enum.
Sort	The **Sort** property retrieves or sets the sort column(s) and the sort order for the table. Some people refer to this as *alphabetizing*. The data type for the **Sort** property is **String**. You specify the columns separated by a comma and then followed by the sort direction, **ASC** (default) or **DESC** for ascending or descending, like this: dvwUser.Sort = "LastName DESC, FirstName ASC"
Table	This property returns or sets the source **DataTable**, meaning the **DataTable** that supplies the **DataView** with data. This property can be set only if the current value is **Nothing**, meaning you can't associate a different **DataTable** with your **DataView** once it's associated with a **DataTable**.

*Table D-13. **DataView** Class Methods*

Method Name	Description	Example
AddNew()	The **AddNew** method adds a new row to the **DataView**. The return value is of data type **DataRowView**. Please note that the **AllowNew** property must be set to **True**, or a **DataException** exception is thrown when you call this method.	`Dim drvNew As DataRowView = dvwUser.AddNew()`
Delete(ByVal intIndex As Integer)	This method deletes a row at the specified index, `intIndex`. If you regret deleting a row, you can undo it by calling the **RejectChanges** method on the **DataTable**. You can use the **Find** method to locate the index for a specific row. Please note that the **AllowDelete** property must be set to **True**, or a **DataException** exception is thrown when you call this method.	`dvwUser.Delete(5)`
Find()	This overloaded method is used for locating a row in the **DataView** by looking up one or more sort key values.	See the "Locating a Single Row" section in Chapter 10 for an example.
FindRows()	This overloaded method is used for returning an array of **DataRowView** objects from the **DataView**, where the sort key column values matches the values in the **Object** argument or array of **Object**'s argument.	See the "Finding Several Rows" section in Chapter 10 for an example.

DataRow Class

In Tables D-14 and D-15, you can see a description of all the noninherited, public properties and methods of the **DataRow** class, respectively.

*Table D-14. The **DataRow** Class Properties*

Property Name	Description
HasErrors	The **HasErrors** property returns a **Boolean** value that indicates if there are any errors in the row, or rather the columns collection. This property is read-only, but you can use it in conjunction with the **GetColumnsInError** method to detect and retrieve columns with errors.
Item	The **Item** property is the default property, meaning you don't really have to specify it. You can use this property to retrieve or set the data stored in the specified column of the **DataRow**. This property is overloaded, and you can use the name or the ordinal position of a column, or a **DataColumn** object as the first argument. You can also pass a member of the **DataRowVersion** enum as the second argument (see Table C-44 in Appendix C) if you want to retrieve a specific version of a value from a specific column.
ItemArray	The **ItemArray** property returns or sets the values for all the columns in this **DataRow** object using an array of **Object**s.
RowError	This property returns or sets a custom error description for a **DataRow**. You can use this property to indicate that an error in one or more columns applies to the whole of the row.
RowState	The **RowState** property, which is read-only, returns the current state of the **DataRow**. The returned value is one of the **DataRowState** enum values. The state of a row is used by the **GetChanges** and **HasChanges** methods, and you can change it manually by calling the **AcceptChanges** and **RejectChanges** methods.
Table	This read-only property returns the **DataTable** to which the row belongs, if any. If the **DataRow** hasn't been added to the **DataRowCollection** of a **DataTable**, this will be evident in the **RowState** property, which will return **DataRowState.Detached**.

Table D-15. **DataRow** *Class Methods*

Method Name	Description
AcceptChanges()	This method commits all changes made to the **DataRow** since the last time **AcceptChanges** was called or since the row was loaded. The **EndEdit** method is automatically called for any edits in progress.
BeginEdit()	The **BeginEdit** method starts an edit operation on the **DataRow**. When the row is in edit mode, all events are disabled. This means that you can make changes to the contents of the row without any events firing or validation rules triggering. Use this method in conjunction with the **EndEdit** method and/or the **CancelEdit** method.
CancelEdit()	This method cancels the current row editing. Use this method in conjunction with the **BeginEdit** method.
ClearErrors()	Use this method to clear all errors for the **DataRow**. This includes the **RowError** property and errors that has been set with the **SetColumnError** method.
Delete()	This method deletes the **DataRow**. Actually, this isn't entirely true. If the **RowState** of the row is **Added**, the row is deleted, but if not, the **RowState** is changed to **Deleted**. This means the row will not actually be deleted until you call the **AcceptChanges** method or the **Update** method on the **DataSet**. This also means that you can undo the deletion of the row by calling the **RejectChanges** method. If you try to delete a row that has already been marked **Deleted**, a **DeletedRowInaccessibleException** exception is thrown.
EndEdit()	This method ends the current editing of the row. Use this method in conjunction with the **BeginEdit** method.
GetChildRows()	This overloaded method is used for retrieving the child rows of the **DataRow**. This is done by passing a **DataRelation** object; the name of a **DataRelation** object; a **DataRelation** object and a **DataRowVersion** object (see Table C-44 in Appendix C); or the name of a **DataRelation** object and a **DataRowVersion** object. The return value is an array of **DataRow** objects.
GetColumnError()	This overloaded method returns the error description for the specified column using a **DataColumn** object, an **Integer** (column ordinal), or a **String** (column name).
GetColumnsInError()	The **GetColumnsInError** method returns an array of **DataColumn** objects in the **DataRow** that all have errors. You should use the **HasErrors** method of the **DataRow** object to determine if any errors exist in the row before calling this method.

Example

```
drwUser.AcceptChanges()
```

```
drwUser.BeginEdit()
```

```
drwUser.CancelEdit()
```

```
drwUser.ClearErrors()
```

```
drwUser.Delete()
```

```
drwUser.EndEdit()
```

```
Dim arrdrwChildRows() As DataRow = drwUser.GetChildRows(drlUser)
Dim arrdrwChildRows() As DataRow = drwUser.GetChildRows(strRelationName)
Dim arrdrwChildRows() As DataRow = drwUser.GetChildRows(drlUser, drvUser)
Dim arrdrwChildRows() As DataRow = drwUser.GetChildRows(strRelationName, drvUser)
```

```
Dim strError As String = drwUser.GetColumnError(dtcName)
Dim strError As String = drwUser.GetColumnError(intColumn)
Dim strError As String = drwUser.GetColumnError(strColumn)
```

```
Dim arrdtcError() As DataColumn = drwUser.GetColumnsInError()
```

*Table D-15. **DataRow** Class Methods (Continued)*

Method Name	Description
GetParentRow()	This overloaded method is used for retrieving the parent row of the **DataRow**. This is done by passing a **DataRelation** object; the name of a relation; a **DataRelation** object and a **DataRowVersion** object (see Table C-44 in Appendix C); or the name of a **DataRelation** object and a **DataRowVersion** object.
GetParentRows()	This overloaded method is used for retrieving the parent rows of the **DataRow**. This is done by passing a **DataRelation** object; the name of a relation; a **DataRelation** object and a **DataRowVersion** object (see Table C-44 in Appendix C); or the name of a **DataRelation** object and a **DataRowVersion** object.
HasVersion(ByVal drvVersion As DataRowVersion)	This method returns a **Boolean** value that indicates if the specified version (drvVersion) exists in the **DataRow**. The drvVersion argument must be one of the members of the **DataRowVersion** enum (see Table C-44 in Appendix C).
IsNull()	This overloaded method returns a **Boolean** value that indicates if the specified column contains a null value. This is done by passing a **DataColumn** object; the ordinal position of a column; the name of a column; or a **DataColumn** object and a **DataRowVersion** object (see Table C-44 in Appendix C).
RejectChanges()	Rejects all changes made to the row since **AcceptChanges** was last called or since the **DataRow** was loaded. If the row is still in edit mode, it's cancelled by calling the **CancelEdit** method.
SetColumnError()	The **SetColumnError** method, which is overloaded, sets the error description for the specified column. This is done by passing a **DataColumn** object and the error message; the ordinal position of a column and the error message; or the name of a column and the error message.
SetParentRow()	This overloaded method is used for setting the parent row of the **DataRow**. This is done using a **DataRow** object, or using a **DataRow** object and a **DataRelation** object.

Example

```
Dim drwParent As DataRow = drwUser.GetParentRow(drlUser)
Dim drwParent As DataRow = = drwUser.GetParentRow(strRelationName)
Dim drwParent As DataRow = drwUser.GetParentRow(drlUser, drvUser)
Dim drwParent As DataRow = drwUser.GetParentRow(strRelationName, drvUser)
```

```
Dim arrdrwParent() As DataRow = drwUser.GetParentRows(drlUser)
Dim arrdrwParent() As DataRow = drwUser.GetParentRows(strRelationName)
Dim arrdrwParent() As DataRow = drwUser.GetParentRows(drlUser, drvUser)
Dim arrdrwParent() As DataRow = drwUser.GetParentRows(strRelationName, drvUser)
```

```
Dim blnExist As Boolean = drwUser.HasVersion(DataRowVersion.Default)
```

```
Dim blnNull As Boolean = drwUser.IsNull(dtcNull)
Dim blnNull As Boolean = drwUser.IsNull(intColumn)
Dim blnNull As Boolean = drwUser.IsNull(strColumn)
Dim blnNull As Boolean = drwUser.IsNull(dtcNull, drwVersion)
```

```
drwUser.RejectChanges()
```

```
drwUser.SetColumnError(dtcError, strError)
drwUser.SetColumnError(intColumn, strError)
drwUser.SetColumnError(strColumn, strError)
```

```
drwUser.SetParentRow(drwParent)
drwUser.GetParentRow(drwParent, drlParent)
```

DataColumn Class

In Table D-16, you can see a description of all the noninherited, public properties of the **DataColumn** class. This table lists the various column properties that you need to set, depending on what type of column you're creating.

*Table D-16. The **DataColumn** Class Properties*

Property Name	Description
AllowDBNull	This property retrieves or sets a value that indicates if null values are allowed in the column. The data type for the property is **Boolean**, and the default value is **True**.
AutoIncrement	The **AutoIncrement** property retrieves or sets a value that indicates if the column automatically increments the value of the column when a new row is added to the table. The data type for the property is **Boolean**, and the default value is **False**. You should use this property with columns of integer data types. Setting this property to **True** for a column gives you the same functionality as the AutoNumber data type of a Microsoft Access database, the Identity data type of an IBM DB2 7.2 database, or the IDENTITY property of a Microsoft SQL Server database.
AutoIncrementSeed	The **AutoIncrementSeed** property retrieves or sets the starting value or seed for a column where the **AutoIncrement** property is set to **True**. The default value is 1.
AutoIncrementStep	The **AutoIncrementStep** property retrieves or sets the increment that is used by the column when the **AutoIncrement** property is set to **True**. This means the value that is added to the column value in the column of the row that was added to the table. Therefore, if the value of the column of the row that was last added is 5, and the increment is 1, then the value of the new column will be 6 (5 + 1).
Caption	This property sets or retrieves the caption for the column. This caption is used by controls that support the display of a column caption. One such control is the Windows DataGrid control (System.Windows.Forms.DataGrid). This means that instead of displaying the name of the column (**ColumnName**), the caption will be displayed instead. The default value of this property is that of the **ColumnName** property.
ColumnMapping	This property sets or retrieves the **MappingType** of the column. This property is for when the **DataSet** in which the column resides is saved in XML format, typically using the **WriteXml** method of the **DataSet** class. See Table D-17 for a list of members of the **MappingType** enum members.
ColumnName	The **ColumnName** property sets or retrieves the name of the column used in the **DataColumnCollection**. The default is an empty **String**, but once the column is added to a **DataColumnCollection**, the column is automatically assigned a name. This is obviously only true if you haven't already set this property. The name assigned depends on the location in the collection, meaning the first column is given the name "Column1" and the next column the name "Column2" and so on.

*Table D-16. The **DataColumn** Class Properties (Continued)*

Property Name	Description
DataType	This property is used for setting or retrieving the data type that can be stored in the column. The data type of the column is **Type** and it must be set to one of these .NET Frameworks base data types (native VB .NET data types in parentheses): **Boolean**, **Byte**, **Char**, **DateTime**, **Decimal**, **Double**, **Int16 (Short)**, **Int32 (Integer)**, **Int64 (Long)**, **SByte**, **Single**, **String**, **TimeSpan**, **UInt16**, **UInt32**, or **UInt64**. You can't set this property if the column is already storing data. One way of setting the property is using the **GetType** method of the **Type** class, like this: `dclUser.DataType = Type.GetType("System.String")`.
DefaultValue	The **DefaultValue** property is for setting or retrieving the default value for the column. This value is used when a new row is created, but you can't use this property when the **AutoIncrement** property is set to **True**.
Expression	This property is for retrieving or setting an expression that is used for filtering the rows, creating an aggregate column, or for calculating the values in the column. You must use the **ColumnName** property when referring to columns in the expression, but please remember that only columns from the **DataTable** in which the **DataColumn** resides can be used.
ExtendedProperties	Returns the collection of custom properties or custom user information. The returned data type is a **PropertyCollection** class. You can add information to the property collection by using the **Add** method of the collection as follows: `dclUser.ExtendedProperties.Add("New Property", "New Property Value")`. You should make sure that your extended properties are of data type **String**, because other data types won't be written when persisting to XML.
MaxLength	The **MaxLength** property is for setting or retrieving the maximum length of a text column, meaning the maximum number of characters allowed in the column. This property is ignored for columns that don't hold text values. The default value is -1, which is also the value of this property if there's no maximum length or if it's unknown.
Namespace	This read-write property holds the namespace for the column, and it's employed for scoping the XML elements and attributes in a **DataTable** that belongs to a **DataSet**. It's used when you read an XML document into the **DataSet** or when you write an XML document from the **DataSet**, using either of these methods: **ReadXml**, **ReadXmlSchema**, **WriteXml**, or **WriteXmlSchema**.
Ordinal	This property returns the position of the column in the **DataColumnCollection** collection. If the column isn't contained in a collection, -1 is returned.
Prefix	This read-write property holds the namespace prefix for the **DataSet**. The prefix is used in an XML document for identifying which elements belongs to the namespace of the **DataSet** object. The namespace is set with the **Namespace** property.

*Table D-16. The **DataColumn** Class Properties (Continued)*

Property Name	Description
ReadOnly	This property is used for indicating if the column is to allow changes to the column value, once the row which the column is part of has been added to the table. The data type for this property is **Boolean**, and the default value is **False**.
Table	This property returns the **DataTable** that the column is part of.
Unique	This property is used for indicating if the column values must be unique. This means that no two values in the columns of the rows that make up the table can be the same. The data type for this property is **Boolean**, and the default value is **False**. A unique constraint is created on the column when this property is set to **True**.

Table D-17 shows you the enum members for **MappingType**.

*Table D-17. **MappingType** Enum Members*

Member Name	Description
Attribute	The column maps to an XML attribute.
Element	This member specifies that the column maps to an XML element.
Hidden	The column maps to an internal structure.
SimpleContent	The column maps to an **XmlText** node.

DataRelation Class

Table D-18 shows you all the noninherited, public properties of the **DataRelation** class. Except for the **Nested** and **RelationName** properties, they're all read-only and can only be set indirectly, as when the **DataRelation** object is instantiated.

*Table D-18. The **DataRelation** Class Properties*

Property Name	Description
ChildColumns	The **ChildColumns** property, which is read-only, retrieves the child columns for the relationship. The child columns are returned as an array of **DataColumn** objects.
ChildKeyConstraint	This read-only property retrieves the foreign key constraints for the relationship. The return value is of data type **ForeignKeyConstraint**. The foreign key constraints help you set up rules for what happens when a row in a parent table, which has related data in the child table, is deleted. These constraints are part of the declarative referential integrity (DRI) you can specify. You can find more information about DRI in Chapter 2.
ChildTable	The read-only **ChildTable** property retrieves the relationships' child table. The child table is returned as an object of data type **DataTable**.
DataSet	This read-only property retrieves the **DataSet** that the relationship belongs to.
ExtendedProperties	The **ExtendedProperties** property, which is read-only, retrieves the customized properties. The customized properties are returned as a **PropertyCollection** object.
Nested	This property sets or retrieves a **Boolean** value that indicates if the data relation object is nested. Nesting can be in connection with hierarchical data, such as XML documents.
ParentColumns	The **ParentColumns** property, which is read-only, retrieves the parent columns for the relationship. The parent columns are returned as an array of **DataColumn** objects.
ParentKeyConstraint	This read-only property retrieves the unique constraint for the relationship. The return value is of data type **UniqueConstraint**.
ParentTable	The read-only **ParentTable** property retrieves the relationships' parent table. The parent table is returned as an object of data type **DataTable**.
RelationName	This property sets or retrieves the name of the relationship that is used for retrieving a **DataRelation** from the **DataRelationCollection** (see the **Relations** property of the **DataSet** class in Table D-1).

The properties for the **UniqueConstraint** and **ForeignKeyContstraint** classes are presented in TablesD-19 and D-20.

*Table D-19. The **UniqueConstraint** Class Properties*

Property Name	Description
Columns	This property returns an array of columns that is affected by the constraint.
ConstraintName	This property, which is inherited from the **Constraint** class, returns or sets a name of the constraint. This name must be unique (not case sensitive) in the **ConstraintCollection** for each **DataTable**.
ExtendedProperties	The **ExtendedProperties** property, which is inherited from the **Constraint** class, returns a collection of user -defined constraint properties.
IsPrimaryKey	This read-only property returns a **Boolean** value indicating if the constraint is set on the primary key. **True** is only returned if the unique constraint has been set on the whole of the primary key, meaning all of the columns that make up the primary key. This means that if you have a composite primary key made up of two columns, and the unique constraint is set on one of these columns, then the **IsPrimaryKey** property will return **False**.
Table	This read-only property returns the table to which the constraint belongs.

*Table D-20. The **ForeignKeyConstraint** Class Properties*

Property Name	Description
AcceptRejectRule	This property is used for specifying the action that takes place when the constraint is triggered by a call to the **AcceptChanges** method. You must set the property to a member of the **AcceptReject** enum (see Table D-21). **None** is the default value.
Columns	The read-only **Columns** property retrieves the child columns for the constraint as an array of **DataColumn** objects.
ConstraintName	The **ConstraintName** property, which is inherited from the **Constraint** class, is the name of the constraint in the **ConstraintCollection** class.
DeleteRule	The **DeleteRule** property retrieves or sets the action that is taken in the child table when a row is deleted in the parent table. You must set the property to a member of the **Rule** enum (see Table D-22). **Cascade** is the default value.
ExtendedProperties	This property, which is inherited from the **Constraint** class, retrieves the collection of user-defined constraint properties.

*Table D-20. The **ForeignKeyConstraint** Class Properties (Continued)*

Property Name	Description
RelatedColumns	This read-only property returns the parent columns for the constraint as an array of **DataColumn** objects.
RelatedTable	This property, which is read-only, returns the parent **DataTable** object f or the constraint.
Table	This property, which is read-only, returns the child **DataTable** object for the constraint.
UpdateRule	The **UpdateRule** property retrieves or sets the action that is taken in the child table when a row is updated in the parent table. You must set the property to a member of the **Rule** enum (see Table D-22). **Cascade** is the default value.

Tables D-21 and D-22 list the **AcceptReject** and **Rule** enum members.

*Table D-21. Members of the **AcceptReject** Enum*

Member Name	Description
Cascade	Changes are cascaded to both the parent and child table in the relationship.
None	This member specifies that no action should be taken.

*Table D-22. Members of the **Rule** Enum*

Member Name	Description
Cascade	Related rows in the child table are deleted or updated.
None	This member specifies that no action should be taken.
SetDefault	The **SetDefault** member specifies that values in related rows in the child table must be set to the default value, meaning the value of the **DefaultValue** property.
SetNull	The **SetNull** member specifies that values in related rows in the child table must be set to **DBNull**.

Summary

In this appendix, you saw the public, noninherited properties, methods, and events of **DataSet** class of the ADO.NET disconnected layer, and related classes and enums. The following classes and enums were shown:

- **DataSet**

- **DataRowState**

- **XmlReadMode and XmlWriteMode**

- **MissingSchemaAction**

- **DataTable**

- **DataViewRowState**

- **DataView**

- **DataRow**

- **DataColumn**

- **MappingType**

- **DataRelation**

- **UniqueConstraint**

- **ForeignKeyConstraint**

- **AcceptReject**

- **Rule**

Index

Q

Apress Titles

ISBN	PRICE	AUTHOR	TITLE
1-893115-73-9	$34.95	Abbott	Voice Enabling Web Applications: VoiceXML and Beyond
1-59059-061-9	$34.95	Allen	Bug Patterns in Java
1-893115-01-1	$39.95	Appleman	Dan Appleman's Win32 API Puzzle Book and Tutorial for Visual Basic Programmers
1-893115-23-2	$29.95	Appleman	How Computer Programming Works
1-893115-97-6	$39.95	Appleman	Moving to VB .NET: Strategies, Concepts, and Code
1-59059-023-6	$39.95	Baker	Adobe Acrobat 5: The Professional User's Guide
1-59059-039-2	$49.95	Barnaby	Distributed .NET Programming in C#
1-59059-068-6	$49.95	Barnaby	Distributed .NET Programming in VB .NET
1-893115-09-7	$29.95	Baum	Dave Baum's Definitive Guide to LEGO MINDSTORMS
1-893115-84-4	$29.95	Baum/Gasperi/Hempel/Villa	Extreme MINDSTORMS: An Advanced Guide to LEGO MINDSTORMS
1-893115-82-8	$59.95	Ben-Gan/Moreau	Advanced Transact-SQL for SQL Server 2000
1-893115-91-7	$39.95	Birmingham/Perry	Software Development on a Leash
1-893115-48-8	$29.95	Bischof	The .NET Languages: A Quick Translation Guide
1-59059-041-4	$49.95	Bock	CIL Programming: Under the Hood™ of .NET
1-59059-053-8	$44.95	Bock/Stromquist/Fischer/Smith	.NET Security
1-893115-67-4	$49.95	Borge	Managing Enterprise Systems with the Windows Script Host
1-59059-019-8	$49.95	Cagle	SVG Programming: The Graphical Web
1-893115-28-3	$44.95	Challa/Laksberg	Essential Guide to Managed Extensions for C++
1-893115-39-9	$44.95	Chand	A Programmer's Guide to ADO.NET in C#
1-59059-015-5	$39.95	Clark	An Introduction to Object Oriented Programming with Visual Basic .NET
1-893115-44-5	$29.95	Cook	Robot Building for Beginners
1-893115-99-2	$39.95	Cornell/Morrison	Programming VB .NET: A Guide for Experienced Programmers
1-893115-72-0	$39.95	Curtin	Developing Trust: Online Privacy and Security
1-59059-014-7	$44.95	Drol	Object-Oriented Macromedia Flash MX
1-59059-008-2	$29.95	Duncan	The Career Programmer: Guerilla Tactics for an Imperfect World
1-893115-71-2	$39.95	Ferguson	Mobile .NET
1-893115-90-9	$49.95	Finsel	The Handbook for Reluctant Database Administrators
1-893115-42-9	$44.95	Foo/Lee	XML Programming Using the Microsoft XML Parser
1-59059-024-4	$49.95	Fraser	Real World ASP.NET: Building a Content Management System
1-893115-55-0	$34.95	Frenz	Visual Basic and Visual Basic .NET for Scientists and Engineers
1-59059-038-4	$49.95	Gibbons	.NET Development for Java Programmers
1-893115-85-2	$34.95	Gilmore	A Programmer's Introduction to PHP 4.0
1-893115-36-4	$34.95	Goodwill	Apache Jakarta-Tomcat
1-893115-17-8	$59.95	Gross	A Programmer's Introduction to Windows DNA

ISBN	PRICE	AUTHOR	TITLE
1-893115-62-3	$39.95	Gunnerson	A Programmer's Introduction to C#, Second Edition
1-59059-030-9	$49.95	Habibi/Patterson/ Camerlengo	The Sun Certified Java Developer Exam with J2SE 1.4
1-893115-30-5	$49.95	Harkins/Reid	SQL: Access to SQL Server
1-59059-009-0	$49.95	Harris/Macdonald	Moving to ASP.NET: Web Development with VB .NET
1-59059-006-6	$39.95	Hetland	Practical Python
1-893115-10-0	$34.95	Holub	Taming Java Threads
1-893115-04-6	$34.95	Hyman/Vaddadi	Mike and Phani's Essential C++ Techniques
1-893115-96-8	$59.95	Jorelid	J2EE FrontEnd Technologies: A Programmer's Guide to Servlets, JavaServer Pages, and Enterprise JavaBeans
1-59059-029-5	$39.99	Kampa/Bell	Unix Storage Management
1-893115-49-6	$39.95	Kilburn	Palm Programming in Basic
1-893115-50-X	$34.95	Knudsen	Wireless Java: Developing with Java 2, Micro Edition
1-893115-79-8	$49.95	Kofler	Definitive Guide to Excel VBA
1-893115-57-7	$39.95	Kofler	MySQL
1-893115-87-9	$39.95	Kurata	Doing Web Development: Client-Side Techniques
1-893115-75-5	$44.95	Kurniawan	Internet Programming with Visual Basic
1-893115-38-0	$24.95	Lafler	Power AOL: A Survival Guide
1-59059-066-X	$39.95	Lafler	Power SAS: A Survival Guide
1-893115-46-1	$36.95	Lathrop	Linux in Small Business: A Practical User's Guide
1-59059-045-7	$49.95	MacDonald	User Interfaces in C#: Windows Forms and Custom Controls
1-893115-19-4	$49.95	Macdonald	Serious ADO: Universal Data Access with Visual Basic
1-59059-044-9	$49.95	MacDonald	User Interfaces in VB .NET: Windows Forms and Custom Controls
1-893115-06-2	$39.95	Marquis/Smith	A Visual Basic 6.0 Programmer's Toolkit
1-893115-22-4	$27.95	McCarter	David McCarter's VB Tips and Techniques
1-59059-040-6	$49.99	Mitchell/Allison	Real-World SQL-DMO for SQL Server
1-59059-021-X	$34.95	Moore	Karl Moore's Visual Basic .NET: The Tutorials
1-893115-27-5	$44.95	Morrill	Tuning and Customizing a Linux System
1-893115-76-3	$49.95	Morrison	C++ For VB Programmers
1-59059-003-1	$44.95	Nakhimovsky/Meyers	XML Programming: Web Applications and Web Services with JSP and ASP
1-893115-80-1	$39.95	Newmarch	A Programmer's Guide to Jini Technology
1-893115-58-5	$49.95	Oellermann	Architecting Web Services
1-59059-020-1	$44.95	Patzer	JSP Examples and Best Practices
1-893115-81-X	$39.95	Pike	SQL Server: Common Problems, Tested Solutions
1-59059-017-1	$34.95	Rainwater	Herding Cats: A Primer for Programmers Who Lead Programmers
1-59059-025-2	$49.95	Rammer	Advanced .NET Remoting (C# Edition)
1-59059-062-7	$49.95	Rammer	Advanced .NET Remoting in VB .NET
1-59059-028-7	$39.95	Rischpater	Wireless Web Development, Second Edition
1-893115-93-3	$34.95	Rischpater	Wireless Web Development with PHP and WAP
1-893115-89-5	$59.95	Shemitz	Kylix: The Professional Developer's Guide and Reference

ISBN	PRICE	AUTHOR	TITLE
1-893115-40-2	$39.95	Sill	The qmail Handbook
1-893115-24-0	$49.95	Sinclair	From Access to SQL Server
1-59059-026-0	$49.95	Smith	Writing Add-ins for Visual Studio .NET
1-893115-94-1	$29.95	Spolsky	User Interface Design for Programmers
1-893115-53-4	$44.95	Sweeney	Visual Basic for Testers
1-59059-035-X	$59.95	Symmonds	GDI+ Programming in C# and VB .NET
1-59059-002-3	$44.95	Symmonds	Internationalization and Localization Using Microsoft .NET
1-59059-010-4	$54.95	Thomsen	Database Programming with C#
1-59059-032-5	$59.95	Thomsen	Database Programming with Visual Basic .NET, Second Edition
1-893115-65-8	$39.95	Tiffany	Pocket PC Database Development with eMbedded Visual Basic
1-59059-027-9	$59.95	Torkelson/Petersen/ Torkelson	Programming the Web with Visual Basic .NET
1-59059-018-X	$34.95	Tregar	Writing Perl Modules for CPAN
1-893115-59-3	$59.95	Troelsen	C# and the .NET Platform
1-59059-011-2	$59.95	Troelsen	COM and .NET Interoperability
1-893115-26-7	$59.95	Troelsen	Visual Basic .NET and the .NET Platform: An Advanced Guide
1-893115-54-2	$49.95	Trueblood/Lovett	Data Mining and Statistical Analysis Using SQL
1-893115-68-2	$54.95	Vaughn	ADO.NET and ADO Examples and Best Practices for VB Programmers, Second Edition
1-59059-012-0	$49.95	Vaughn/Blackburn	ADO.NET Examples and Best Practices for C# Programmers
1-893115-83-6	$44.95	Wells	Code Centric: T-SQL Programming with Stored Procedures and Triggers
1-893115-95-X	$49.95	Welschenbach	Cryptography in C and C++
1-893115-05-4	$39.95	Williamson	Writing Cross-Browser Dynamic HTML
1-59059-060-0	$39.95	Wright	ADO.NET: From Novice to Pro, Visual Basic .NET Edition
1-893115-78-X	$49.95	Zukowski	Definitive Guide to Swing for Java 2, Second Edition
1-893115-92-5	$49.95	Zukowski	Java Collections
1-893115-98-4	$54.95	Zukowski	Learn Java with JBuilder 6

Available at bookstores nationwide or from Springer Verlag New York, Inc. at 1-800-777-4643; fax 1-212-533-3503. Contact us for more information at sales@apress.com.

books for professionals by professionals™

About Apress

Apress, located in Berkeley, CA, is a fast-growing, innovative publishing company devoted to meeting the needs of existing and potential programming professionals. Simply put, the "A" in Apress stands for *"The Author's Press*™*"* and its books have *"The Expert's Voice*™*"*. Apress' unique approach to publishing grew out of conversations between its founders Gary Cornell and Dan Appleman, authors of numerous best-selling, highly regarded books for programming professionals. In 1998 they set out to create a publishing company that emphasized quality above all else. Gary and Dan's vision has resulted in the publication of over 50 titles by leading software professionals, all of which have *The Expert's Voice*™.

Do You Have What It Takes to Write for Apress?

Apress is rapidly expanding its publishing program. If you can write and refuse to compromise on the quality of your work, if you believe in doing more than rehashing existing documentation, and if you're looking for opportunities and rewards that go far beyond those offered by traditional publishing houses, we want to hear from you!

Consider these innovations that we offer all of our authors:

- **Top royalties with *no* hidden switch statements**
  Authors typically only receive half of their normal royalty rate on foreign sales. In contrast, Apress' royalty rate remains the same for both foreign and domestic sales.

- **A mechanism for authors to obtain equity in Apress**
  Unlike the software industry, where stock options are essential to motivate and retain software professionals, the publishing industry has adhered to an outdated compensation model based on royalties alone. In the spirit of most software companies, Apress reserves a significant portion of its equity for authors.

- **Serious treatment of the technical review process**
  Each Apress book has a technical reviewing team whose remuneration depends in part on the success of the book since they too receive royalties.

Moreover, through a partnership with Springer-Verlag, New York, Inc., one of the world's major publishing houses, Apress has significant venture capital behind it. Thus, we have the resources to produce the highest quality books *and* market them aggressively.

If you fit the model of the Apress author who can write a book that gives the "professional what he or she needs to know™," then please contact one of our Editorial Directors, Dan Appleman (dan_appleman@apress.com), Gary Cornell (gary_cornell@apress.com), Jason Gilmore (jason_gilmore@apress.com), Simon Hayes (simon_hayes@apress.com), Karen Watterson (karen_watterson@apress.com), or John Zukowski (john_zukowski@apress.com) for more information.